海权论

(英汉双语)

[美]阿尔弗雷德·塞耶·马汉◎著　欧阳瑾◎译

THE INFLUENCE
OF
SEA POWER
UPON HISTORY
1660—1783

群言出版社
QUNYAN PRESS
·北京·

图书在版编目（CIP）数据

海权论 /（美）马汉著；欧阳瑾译. -- 北京：群言出版社，2015.11（2023.3 重印）
ISBN 978-7-80256-941-6

Ⅰ. ①海… Ⅱ. ①马… ②欧… Ⅲ. ①制海权 – 研究 Ⅳ. ① E815

中国版本图书馆 CIP 数据核字 (2015) 第 253551 号

责任编辑：	侯 莹　胡蔓青　张 程
封面设计：	同人阁文化·书装设计
出版发行：	群言出版社
地　　址：	北京市东城区东厂胡同北巷 1 号（100006）
网　　址：	www.qypublish.com（官网书城）
电子信箱：	qunyancbs@126.com
联系电话：	010-65267783　65263836
法律顾问：	北京法政安邦律师事务所
经　　销：	全国新华书店
印　　刷：	永清县晔盛亚胶印有限公司
版　　次：	2023 年 3 月第 2 版
印　　次：	2023 年 3 月第 1 次印刷
开　　本：	710mm×1000mm　　1/16
印　　张：	28.75
字　　数：	665 千字
书　　号：	ISBN 978-7-80256-941-6
定　　价：	98.00 元

【版权所有，侵权必究】

如有印装质量问题，请与本社发行部联系调换，电话：010-65263836

PREFACE

The definite object proposed in this work is an examination of the general history of Europe and America with particular reference to the effect of sea power upon the course of that history. Historians generally have been unfamiliar with the conditions of the sea, having as to it neither special interest nor special knowledge; and the profound determining influence of maritime strength upon great issues has consequently been overlooked. This is even more true of particular occasions than of the general tendency of sea power. It is easy to say in a general way, that the use and control of the sea is and has been a great factor in the history of the world; it is more troublesome to seek out and show its exact bearing at a particular juncture. Yet, unless this be done, the acknowledgment of general importance remains vague and unsubstantial; not resting, as it should, upon a collection of special instances in which the precise effect has been made clear, by an analysis of the conditions at the given moments.

A curious exemplification of this tendency to slight the bearing of maritime power upon events may be drawn from two writers of that English nation which more than any other has owed its greatness to the sea. "Twice," says Arnold in his History of Rome, "Has there been witnessed the struggle of the highest individual genius against the resources and institutions of a great nation, and in both cases the nation was victorious. For seventeen years Hannibal strove against Rome, for sixteen years Napoleon strove against England; the efforts of the first ended in Zama, those of the second in Waterloo." Sir Edward Creasy, quoting this, adds: "One point,

前　言

本书有着一个确切的目标，那就是具体地根据海权对历史进程的影响，来审视欧洲和美洲的概史。史学家们通常都不熟悉海洋的情况，他们对海洋既无特殊兴趣，也无专业知识；因此，海权对于一些重大问题所起的深刻而具有决定性的影响，往往就被他们忽略了。对于某些具体战例与海权总体的发展趋势而言，具体战例甚至更符合这种情况。泛泛而谈，说利用和控制海洋是而且一直是世界历史的一个重要因素，做到这一点并不难；但找出并说明它在某一具体时刻的准确影响，却要棘手得多。然而，不这样做的话，我们对海权整体重要性的认可，就是含糊而空洞的；因为我们本来应当是以一系列特定的、清晰地显示出海权准确影响的战例为基础，并且在分析了某一特定时刻的形势之后，才能进行此种认可的。

从英格兰民族的两位史家身上，即可以看出人们忽视海上力量影响历史事件的这种古怪倾向——英格兰民族之伟大，比其他任何民族都更可归因于海洋。阿诺德[1]在其《罗马史》中曾说："历史已经见证过，有两位最重要的个人天才，曾经与两个伟大国家的资源和制度进行斗争；而在这两次斗争中，最终都是国家获胜。汉尼拔与罗马斗争了17年，拿破仑与英国斗争了16年；前者付出了努力，却在扎马[2]折戟，而后者则在滑铁卢败北。"爱德华·克里西勋爵在引用了这种说法之后，又进一步说："然而，这

however, of the similitude between the two wars has scarcely been adequately dwelt on; that is, the remarkable parallel between the Roman general who finally defeated the great Carthaginian, and the English general who gave the last deadly overthrow to the French emperor. Scipio and Wellington both held for many years commands of high importance, but distant from the main theatres of warfare. The same country was the scene of the principal military career of each. It was in Spain that Scipio, like Wellington, successively encountered and overthrew nearly all the subordinate generals of the enemy before being opposed to the chief champion and conqueror himself. Both Scipio and Wellington restored their countrymen's confidence in arms when shaken by a series of reverses, and each of them closed a long and perilous war by a complete and overwhelming defeat of the chosen leader and the chosen veterans of the foe."

Neither of these Englishmen mentions the yet more striking coincidence, that in both cases the mastery of the sea rested with the victor. The Roman control of the water forced Hannibal to that long, perilous march through Gaul in which more than half his veteran troops wasted away; it enabled the elder Scipio, while sending his army from the Rhone on to Spain, to intercept Hannibal's communications, to return in person and face the invader at the Trebia. Throughout the war the legions passed by water, unmolested and unwearied, between Spain, which was Hannibal's base, and Italy, while the issue of the decisive battle of the Metaurus, hinging as it did upon the interior position of the Roman armies with reference to the forces of Hasdrubal and Hannibal, was ultimately due to the fact that the younger brother could not bring his succoring reinforcements by sea, but only by the land route through Gaul. Hence at the critical moment the two Carthaginian armies were separated by the length of Italy, and one was destroyed by the combined action of the Roman generals.

On the other hand, naval historians have troubled themselves little about the connection

两场战争相似性当中的一点，却并未得到充分的强调；那就是，最终击败了这位迦太基伟人的罗马将军，与最终给予法兰西皇帝以致命一击的那位英国将领之间，具有显著的相似性。西庇阿[3]与威灵顿[4]二人，虽说都曾身居高位数年，却都根本没有到过主战场。而二者主要的军事成就，也是在同一个国家取得的。西庇阿在西班牙时，跟威灵顿公爵一样，是在相继遭遇并且打败了敌人差不多所有的下级将领之后，才去面对敌军主帅或征服者本人的。西庇阿与威灵顿公爵二人，都在同胞遭遇了一系列挫折而产生动摇之后，重新让这些同胞恢复了对本国武装的信心，并且二者都是通过彻底而压倒性地击败了敌人的精兵强将，从而结束了一场旷日持久、危险可怕的战争。"

不过，这两位英国人都没有提及一种更为显著的一致性，那就是：获胜的一方控制了海洋。罗马人控制了水上，迫使汉尼拔不得不经由高卢进行遥远而危机四伏的行军，从而令其手下身经百战的部队损失过半；这也使得大西庇阿既能够让军队从罗纳河沿河而上前往西班牙，以切断汉尼拔的交通运输，同时还能亲自返回来，在特雷比亚面对入侵者。在整个战争期间，罗马军团都是经由水路，不受袭扰且毫不疲惫地往来于西班牙和意大利之间，可西班牙本来却是汉尼拔的大本营；而梅陶罗决战，则取决于罗马国内的军队对哈斯德鲁巴[5]与汉尼拔所率军队的态度，且最终原因还是在于汉尼拔的这位弟弟无法从海路带来援兵，只能经由高卢的陆路对其进行增援的事实。在如此关键的时刻，迦太基的两支军队却被长长的意大利分割开来，于是其中一支就被罗马将领们联合起来消灭了。

另一方面，研究海军的历史学家们，却又很少努力去了解普通历史与他们所研究专

between general history and their own particular topic, limiting themselves generally to the duty of simple chroniclers of naval occurrences. This is less true of the French than of the English; the genius and training of the former people leading them to more careful inquiry into the causes of particular results and the mutual relation of events.

There is not, however, within the knowledge of the author any work that professes the particular object here sought; namely, an estimate of the effect of sea power upon the course of history and the prosperity of nations. As other histories deal with the wars, politics, social and economical conditions of countries, touching upon maritime matters only incidentally and generally unsympathetically, so the present work aims at putting maritime interests in the foreground, without divorcing them, however, from their surroundings of cause and effect in general history, but seeking to show how they modified the latter, and were modified by them.

The period embraced is from 1660, when the sailing-ship era, with its distinctive features, had fairly begun, to 1783, the end of the American Revolution. While the thread of general history upon which the successive maritime events is strung is intentionally slight, the effort has been to present a clear as well as accurate outline. Writing as a naval officer in full sympathy with his profession, the author has not hesitated to digress freely on questions of naval policy, strategy, and tactics; but as technical language has been avoided, it is hoped that these matters, simply presented, will be found of interest to the unprofessional reader.

A. T. MAHAN
December, 1889.

题之间的联系，通常都只让自己成为海军历史事件的简单记录者。对于这一点，法国史学家的情况并不像英国的史学家那样绝对；因为法兰西民族的天赋和法国史学家所受的训练，使得他们能够更加细心地去探究特定事件的前因后果，以及各个事件之间的相互关系。

然而，据笔者所知，还没有哪一部著作阐述了此处我们所要探究的这个特殊目标；也就是说，评估海权对历史进程和各国繁荣的影响。由于其他历史科目在研究战争、政治以及各国的社会与经济状况时，对海洋事件都只会顺带涉及，并且通常都是淡然置之，所以本书之目标，便是将海洋利益推向前台，但又不将它们与普通历史的因果环境割裂开来，而是力图表明它们如何改变了普通历史的因果环境，以及它们是如何被普通历史的因果环境所改变的。

本书所选的时间段，是从具有显著特征的帆船时代已然开始的1660年，到美国革命结束时的1783年。虽说维系接连发生的那些海洋事件的普通历史线索都被人们有意地忽略掉了，但本书还是想努力为它们呈现出一个清晰而不失准确的轮廓来。作为一名对自己的职业深有感触的海军军官，笔者在写作本书时，会毫不犹豫、自由自在地去探究那些与海洋军事政策、战略以及战术相关的问题；不过，本书略去了一些太过专业的术语，寄望这些简单平实地呈现出来的事情，能够引起非专业读者的兴趣。

阿尔弗雷德·塞耶·马汉
1889年12月

译者注：

[1] 阿诺德（Thomas Arnold，1795~1842）。英国近代教育家，著有《罗马史》和其他一些布道作品，其子马修·阿诺德（Matthew Arnold）为著名诗人和评论家。

[2] Zama：扎马。北非古城，位于迦太基西南部。公元前202年，古罗马将领西庇阿在此击败迦太基将领汉尼拔，使之成为了结束第二次布匿战争（Bella punica，指古罗马与古迦太基之间的战争，共进行了3次）的古战场。

[3] 西庇阿（Publius Cornelius Scipio Africanus，公元前236~前184？），古罗马统帅和政治家，生于贵族家庭，公元前205年开始担任执政官，后因罪引退并死于流放途中。他因在扎马战役中打败了汉尼拔而获称"征服非洲的西庇阿"，或称"大西庇阿（Scipio the Elder）"，以区别于家族中的其他人。

[4] Wellington：威灵顿公爵（原名Arthur Wellesley，1769~1852，获封第一任威灵顿公爵）。英国政治家、军事家和外交家，拿破仑战争时期的英军将领，后为英国第21任首相，人称"铁公爵"。他也是历史上唯一一位获得7国（英国、法国、沙皇俄国、普鲁士、西班牙、葡萄牙、荷兰）元帅军衔的人。

[5] Hasdrubal：哈斯德鲁巴（公元前270~前221）。迦太基将领，汉尼拔的二弟。

目录 contents

INTRODUCTORY		1
导 论		1
CHAPTER I	Discussion of the Elements of Sea Power	29
第一章	海权诸要素之探讨	29
CHAPTER II	State of Europe in 1660	99
第二章	1660年之欧洲形势	99
CHAPTER III	English Revolution	152
第三章	英国革命	152
CHAPTER IV	War of the Spanish Succession, 1702–1713	181
第四章	1702–1713年间的西班牙王位继承战争	181
CHAPTER V	The Regency in France	214
第五章	法国摄政时期	214
CHAPTER VI	War between Great Britain and Spain, 1739	237
第六章	1739年的英西战争	237
CHAPTER VII	Seven Years' War, 1756–1763	266
第七章	1756–1763年的"七年战争"	266
CHAPTER VIII	Course of Events from the Peace of Paris to 1778	317
第八章	自《巴黎和约》到1778年间形势的发展	317

| CHAPTER IX | Maritime War in North America and West Indies, 1778-1781 ··· 347 |

第九章　1778-1781年间北美和西印度群岛的海上战争·················· 347

| CHAPTER X | Maritime War in Europe, 1779-1782································ 393 |

第十章　1779-1782年间的欧洲海战································· 393

| CHAPTER XI | Critical Discussion of the Maritime War of 1778 ················ 412 |

第十一章　批判性地讨论1778年海战································ 412

INTRODUCTORY

The history of Sea Power is largely, though by no means solely, a narrative of contests between nations, of mutual rivalries, of violence frequently culminating in war. The profound influence of sea commerce upon the wealth and strength of countries was clearly seen long before the true principles which governed its growth and prosperity were detected. To secure to one's own people a disproportionate share of such benefits, every effort was made to exclude others, either by the peaceful legislative methods of monopoly or prohibitory regulations, or, when these failed, by direct violence. The clash of interests, the angry feelings roused by conflicting attempts thus to appropriate the larger share, if not the whole, of the advantages of commerce, and of distant unsettled commercial regions, led to wars. On the other hand, wars arising from other causes have been greatly modified in their conduct and issue by the control of the sea. Therefore the history of sea power, while embracing in its broad sweep all that tends to make a people great upon the sea or by the sea, is largely a military history; and it is in this aspect that it will be mainly, though not exclusively, regarded in the following pages.

A study of the military history of the past, such as this, is enjoined by great military leaders as essential to correct ideas and to the skilful conduct of war in the future. Napoleon names among the campaigns to be studied by the aspiring soldier, those of Alexander, Hannibal, and Caesar, to whom gunpowder was unknown; and there is a substantial agreement among professional writers that, while many of the conditions of war vary from age to age with the

导 论

海权之历史，虽说并非全部，却也在很大程度上是一种对于国家间你争我斗、相互竞争以及以战争而告终之暴力的记述。在人们还没有揭示出控制海上贸易增长与繁荣的真正原则之前，海上贸易对于各国财富与实力所产生的深远影响，就早已清晰地显现出来。为了确保所属民族能够占有此种利益中超过其应得的份额，各国都会不遗余力地排斥其他国家，要么通过和平的立法途径，用垄断或者禁止性条例；要么便在立法途径失败之后，直接动用武力。利益冲突，即为了多占有贸易利益份额和远方那些归属未定的商业地区——即使不是为了全部占有——而发生冲突，这会激发冲突双方的愤怒之情，从而引发战争。另一方面，那些因为其他缘故而引发的战争，其进程与结果也受到了海洋控制权的极大影响。所以，海权的历史，既涵盖了某一民族试图在海洋上或者通过海洋来变得强大的所有行为，同时在很大程度上也是一种军事史；因此下文所涉及的，虽说并非全部，但主要还是军事这个方面的内容。

许多伟大的军事领袖都曾告诫我们，像本书这样来研究过去的军事史，对于在未来形成正确的军事思想，对于在未来熟练地进行战争，都至关重要。拿破仑曾与尚不知火药为何物的亚历山大大帝、汉尼拔和恺撒等人所进行的战争中，为手下那些有所抱负的士兵指定了一些必须加以研习的战役；而专业的史学家们实际上也一致认为，虽说随

progress of weapons, there are certain teachings in the school of history which remain constant, and being, therefore, of universal application, can be elevated to the rank of general principles. For the same reason the study of the sea history of the past will be found instructive, by its illustration of the general principles of maritime war, notwithstanding the great changes that have been brought about in naval weapons by the scientific advances of the past half century, and by the introduction of steam as the motive power.

It is doubly necessary thus to study critically the history and experience of naval warfare in the days of sailing-ships, because while these will be found to afford lessons of present application and value, steam navies have as yet made no history which can be quoted as decisive in its teaching. Of the one we have much experimental knowledge; of the other, practically none. Hence theories about the naval warfare of the future are almost wholly presumptive; and although the attempt has been made to give them a more solid basis by dwelling upon the resemblance between fleets of steamships and fleets of galleys moved by oars, which have a long and well-known history, it will be well not to be carried away by this analogy until it has been thoroughly tested. The resemblance is indeed far from superficial. The feature which the steamer and the galley have in common is the ability to move in any direction independent of the wind. Such a power makes a radical distinction between those classes of vessels and the sailing-ship; for the latter can follow only a limited number of courses when the wind blows, and must remain motionless when it fails. But while it is wise to observe things that are alike, it is also wise to look for things that differ; for when the imagination is carried away by the detection of points of resemblance, — one of the most pleasing of mental pursuits, — it is apt to be impatient of any divergence in its new-found parallels, and so may overlook or refuse to recognize such. Thus the galley and the steamship have in common, though unequally

着武器的发展，战争的许多情况每世纪都不相同，但历史这所学校中还是有着某些亘古不变的教训，它们得到了普遍的应用，因而能够被提升到一般原理的高度。我们也会发现，出于同样的原因，尽管在过去的半个世纪中，科技的进步和引入蒸汽动力已经使得海军的武器装备发生了巨变，但通过阐述海上战争的一般原则来研究过去的海权历史，还是很有教育意义的。

因此，批判性地研究帆船时期海上战争的历史与经验就更加必要了；尽管这些历史与经验为目前的海战提供了可以应用与颇有意义的教训，但汽船时代的海军，迄今为止还没有名垂史册，也没有什么具有决定性意义的战争经验可供引述。对于帆船时期的海战，我们有着许多的经验性知识；而对于汽船时代的海战，我们却几乎一无所知。因此，关于未来海战的诸多理论，差不多完全都是假定性的；尽管人们已经试着通过仔细研究汽船舰队与有着悠久历史且众所周知、以桨驱动的桨帆船队之间的相似之处，来给这些理论以更加坚实的基础，但我们最好还是不要陶醉于这种类推的方法，除非此种方法得到了彻底的验证。二者之间的这种相似性，实际上绝非只是表面上的。汽船与桨帆船的共同特征是，它们都能够不依赖于风向，能够转向自如地航行。这种能力，使得此类船舶与帆船有了根本性的区别；因为后者在有风的时候，只能沿着数量有限的一些航线航行，而若是无法沿着这些航线航行，它们就只能在原地打转了。不过，虽说观察相似之处很明智，但寻找相异的方面也是很可取的；因为当我们的想像力全都沉迷于探究事物的相似点——这是一种最令人愉快的精神追求——倘若新发现的相似物中出现不一致的地方，我们就极容易失去耐心，从而可能忽视或者不愿承认这种不一致。因

developed, the important characteristic mentioned, but in at least two points they differ; and in an appeal to the history of the galley for lessons as to fighting steamships, the differences as well as the likeness must be kept steadily in view, or false deductions may be made. The motive power of the galley when in use necessarily and rapidly declined, because human strength could not long maintain such exhausting efforts, and consequently tactical movements could continue but for a limited time [1]; and again, during the galley period offensive weapons were not only of short range, but were almost wholly confined to hand-to-hand encounter. These two conditions led almost necessarily to a rush upon each other, not, however, without some dexterous attempts to turn or double on the enemy, followed by a hand-to-hand mêlée. In such a rush and such a mêlée a great consensus of respectable, even eminent, naval opinion of the present day finds the necessary outcome of modern naval weapons, — a kind of Donnybrook Fair, in which, as the history of mêlées shows, it will be hard to know friend from foe. Whatever may prove to be the worth of this opinion, it cannot claim an historical basis in the sole fact that galley and steamship can move at any moment directly upon the enemy, and carry a beak upon their prow, regardless of the points in which galley and steamship differ. As yet this opinion is only a presumption, upon which final judgment may well be deferred until the trial of battle has given further light. Until that time there is room for the opposite view, — that a mêlée between numerically equal fleets, in which skill is reduced to a minimum, is not the best that can be done with the elaborate and mighty weapons of this age. The surer of himself an admiral is, the finer the tactical development of his fleet, the better his captains, the more reluctant must he necessarily be to enter into a mêlée with equal forces, in which all these advantages will be thrown away, chance reign supreme, and his fleet be placed on terms of equality with an assemblage of ships which have never before acted together. [2] History has lessons as to when

此，桨帆船与汽船虽说发展情况并不相同，但都有上述共同的特征；不过，它们之间至少也有两点不同，而在桨帆船的历史中寻求与汽船相似的作战教训过程中，我们必须始终记住其差异与相似点，否则我们可能会得出错误的推论。在航行的时候，桨帆船的动力会不可避免地迅速下降，因为这是一件相当繁重的工作，人力不可能长久坚持，所以桨帆船只能持续进行有限时间的战术运动[1]；另外，桨帆船时代所用的攻击性武器非但射程短，而且差不多完全属于短兵相接式的武器。这两个条件，几乎不可避免地导致了交战双方的相互袭击，但也不乏巧妙地攻击或夹击敌舰的方法，然后才是短兵相接的混战。就是在这种袭击和混战当中，人们对于目前海军那种可敬的、甚至是卓越的观点达成了一种重大的共识，从而发现了现代海军武器所导致的必然结果——即一种"唐尼布鲁克集市"[1]式的局面；正如混战历史所表明的那样，在此种局面中，我们是很难分清敌友。无论这种观点的最终价值如何，我们都不能仅凭桨帆船与汽船能够在任何时候直接进逼敌人、并且在船头装上金属撞角这一事实，而不顾桨帆船与汽船的差异，就说这种观点有了历史基础。到目前为止，这种观点还只是一种假设，我们不妨等到经过战斗验证、进行了进一步的阐述之后，再来做出最终的判断。在此之前，还是可以存在与之相对立的观点的——即对于数量相等的舰队来说，发生那种基本上无需战术的混战，并不是如今这个时代利用精巧而强大的武器所能取得的最佳结果。一位舰队司令越有把握，其舰队的战术发展得越完善，其手下的舰长们越称职，他就必然会越不愿意去与数量相等的敌军展开混战；因为这样一来，所有的这些优势便会付之东流，谁占上风全凭运气，而他手下的舰队就会跟那种以前从未集中作过战的乌合之众没什么两样了[2]。至于何时适

mêlées are, or are not, in order.

The galley, then, has one striking resemblance to the steamer, but differs in other important features which are not so immediately apparent and are therefore less accounted of. In the sailing-ship, on the contrary, the striking feature is the difference between it and the more modern vessel; the points of resemblance, though existing and easy to find, are not so obvious, and therefore are less heeded. This impression is enhanced by the sense of utter weakness in the sailing-ship as compared with the steamer, owing to its dependence upon the wind; forgetting that, as the former fought with its equals, the tactical lessons are valid. The galley was never reduced to impotence by a calm, and hence receives more respect in our day than the sailing-ship; yet the latter displaced it and remained supreme until the utilization of steam. The powers to injure an enemy from a great distance, to maneuver for an unlimited length of time without wearing out the men, to devote the greater part of the crew to the offensive weapons instead of to the oar, are common to the sailing vessel and the steamer, and are at least as important, tactically considered, as the power of the galley to move in a calm or against the wind.

In tracing resemblances there is a tendency not only to overlook points of difference, but to exaggerate points of likeness, — to be fanciful. It may be so considered to point out that as the sailing-ship had guns of long range, with comparatively great penetrative power, and carronades, which were of shorter range but great smashing effect, so the modern steamer has its batteries of long-range guns and of torpedoes, the latter being effective only within a limited distance and then injuring by smashing, while the gun, as of old, aims at penetration. Yet these are distinctly tactical considerations, which must affect the plans of admirals and captains; and the analogy is real, not forced. So also both the sailing-ship and the steamer contemplate direct

于混战或者不适于混战，历史上是有着许多教训的。

桨帆船与汽船虽说有着显著的相似之处，但在许多重要的特点上，它们却各具差异；由于这些重要特点并不是全都非常明显，因此我们都较少重视它们。相反，对于帆船而言，其显著特征却是它们与更为现代化的船舶之间的差异；虽说二者之间也存在相似之处，且这些相似之处也不难发现，但由于它们并不是很明显，因而我们同样也较少留意。这种印象，因帆船相比于汽船来说必须依赖风向而显示出全然不如汽船的这种感觉强化了；忘掉这一点，就像帆船在与其对手作战的时候那样，那么其中的战术教训就是正确的了。桨帆船从未在风平浪静的时候无法行动，因此才在我们这个时代受到了比帆船更多的敬重；不过，帆船还是取代了桨帆船，并且直至采用蒸汽动力之前，一直都保持着霸主的地位。能够从远距离击伤敌人，机动时间不受限制且不会让船员们累得筋疲力尽，大部分船员能够去控制攻击性武器而不是去划桨——这些本领，是帆船和汽船的共同特征；并且从战术上来考虑，它们起码也像桨帆船能够在无风情况下航行或者能够逆风行驶的本领一样重要。

在探究相似之处的过程中，我们都有一种倾向：不但会忽视有所差异的地方，还会夸大其相似之处——从而使得这种相似之处显得非常奇怪。我们可以这样来考虑：正如帆船装有射程较远、相对穿透力较大的火炮，以及虽说射程较短、却会产生巨大粉碎性效果的大口径火炮那样，现代汽船也装备了远程火炮组和鱼雷组——鱼雷仅在有限的距离内才能发挥作用，而火炮则跟原来的一样，旨在利用其穿透效果。不过，这些无疑都属于战术方面的问题，必然会影响到舰队司令与舰长们的作战计划；因而这种类推就是事

contact with an enemy's vessel, — the former to carry her by boarding, the latter to sink her by ramming; and to both this is the most difficult of their tasks, for to effect it the ship must be carried to a single point of the field of action, whereas projectile weapons may be used from many points of a wide area.

The relative positions of two sailing-ships, or fleets, with reference to the direction of the wind involved most important tactical questions, and were perhaps the chief care of the seamen of that age. To a superficial glance it may appear that since this has become a matter of such indifference to the steamer, no analogies to it are to be found in present conditions, and the lessons of history in this respect are valueless. A more careful consideration of the distinguishing characteristics of the lee and the weather "gage," [3] directed to their essential features and disregarding secondary details, will show that this is a mistake. The distinguishing feature of the weather-gage was that it conferred the power of giving or refusing battle at will, which in turn carries the usual advantage of an offensive attitude in the choice of the method of attack. This advantage was accompanied by certain drawbacks, such as irregularity introduced into the order, exposure to raking or enfilading cannonade, and the sacrifice of part or all of the artillery-fire of the assailant, — all which were incurred in approaching the enemy. The ship, or fleet, with the lee-gage could not attack; if it did not wish to retreat, its action was confined to the defensive, and to receiving battle on the enemy's terms. This disadvantage was compensated by the comparative ease of maintaining the order of battle undisturbed, and by a sustained artillery-fire to which the enemy for a time was unable to reply. Historically, these favorable and unfavorable characteristics have their counterpart and analogy in the offensive and defensive operations of all ages. The offence undertakes certain risks and disadvantages in order to reach and destroy the enemy; the defence, so long as it remains such, refuses the

实，而非牵强附会。所以，帆船与汽船也都会希望与敌舰短兵相接——前者通过强行登船攻占敌舰，而后者则通过猛撞来击沉敌舰；对于这两种船舶来说，此种任务都是极其艰巨的，因为要想完成这一任务，就得让自己的舰艇处于战场的某个位置上，可在这一位置上，敌方却可以在大范围内的多个位置上，使用投射武器来攻击我方。

两艘帆船或者两支舰队根据风向而定的相对位置，涉及到了绝大多数重要的战术问题，因此可能也是那个时代海军主要关注的问题。从表面上来看，似乎是由于这个方面对汽船来说变得无关紧要了，而这方面的历史教训也是毫无意义的，所以在目前的条件下不应当再进行什么类推。然而，倘若更加细致地考虑"下风"与"上风"[3]的一些显著特征，把注意力放在它们的基本特点上，而不去考虑那些次要细节的话，我们就会看出，这种想法是错误的。处于上风位置的显著特征是，能够想打就打、不想打就不打，并且反过来，还具有了在采取攻势时可以选择进攻方式的优势。当然，这种优势也伴随着某些弊端，诸如打乱战斗序列，会暴露在敌方斜向或纵向炮火的攻击之下，以及损失攻击用的部分或全部炮火等等——这一切，都会在逼近敌舰的过程中出现。而处于下风位置的船只或舰队则无法进击；倘若不想撤退，那么它的行动就只能是防御，只能是按照敌方的条件来被动作战。这种劣势，却会因保持战斗序列相对较易、可以进行持续炮击并令敌方一时无法还击的优势而得到弥补。从历史来看，这些有利或者不利的特点，在各个时代的进攻战和防御战中，都有着与之相对应和相类似的地方。进攻一方会冒着某些危险和劣势去接近并摧毁敌军；而防御的一方只要保持着防守态势，就不会贸然进击，就会保持着谨慎而有序的阵势，并且可以利用进攻者不得不暴露于我方炮火之

risks of advance, holds on to a careful, well-ordered position, and avails itself of the exposure to which the assailant submits himself. These radical differences between the weather and the lee gage were so clearly recognized, through the cloud of lesser details accompanying them, that the former was ordinarily chosen by the English, because their steady policy was to assail and destroy their enemy; whereas the French sought the lee-gage, because by so doing they were usually able to cripple the enemy as he approached, and thus evade decisive encounters and preserve their ships. The French, with rare exceptions, subordinated the action of the navy to other military considerations, grudged the money spent upon it, and therefore sought to economize their fleet by assuming a defensive position and limiting its efforts to the repelling of assaults. For this cause the lee-gage, skilfully used, was admirably adapted so long as an enemy displayed more courage than conduct; but when Rodney showed an intention to use the advantage of the wind, not merely to attack, but to make a formidable concentration on a part of the enemy's line, his wary opponent, De Guichen, changed his tactics. In the first of their three actions the Frenchman took the lee-gage; but after recognizing Rodney's purpose he manoeuvred for the advantage of the wind, not to attack, but to refuse action except on his own terms. The power to assume the offensive, or to refuse battle, rests no longer with the wind, but with the party which has the greater speed; which in a fleet will depend not only upon the speed of the individual ships, but also upon their tactical uniformity of action. Henceforth the ships which have the greatest speed will have the weather-gage.

It is not therefore a vain expectation, as many think, to look for useful lessons in the history of sailing-ships as well as in that of galleys. Both have their points of resemblance to the modern ship; both have also points of essential difference, which make it impossible to cite their experiences or modes of action as tactical precedents to be followed. But a precedent is

下的机会。人们已经透过种种较小的细节，非常清楚地认识到了上风位置与下风位置的这些根本差异，所以英国人才通常选择上风位置——英国人的一贯政策，便是进攻和消灭敌人；而法国人则喜欢下风位置，因为他们这样做，往往能够在敌人逼近的过程中削弱敌军实力，并且往往还能够让自己避开决战，从而保存好己方的舰艇实力。除了极少数例外情况，法国人一向都认为海军作战的重要性不如其他军种，一向都不愿意为海军多花军费，故他们更愿意通过采取守势，只愿意击退敌军的进攻，以便充分利用好自己的舰队。出于这一原因，只要敌方表现得有勇无谋，法国人就会令人佩服地加以调整，巧妙地利用下风位置；不过，当罗德尼[2]打算利用风向优势，非但要发动攻击，还想集中火力猛攻敌军防线一部的时候，其小心谨慎的对手基申伯爵却改变了战术。在双方3次作战行动的第一次中，法军处于下风位置；但意识到了罗德尼的目的之后，基申伯爵便利用风向优势，率领舰队进行了机动——不过其目的不是为了进攻，而是为了拒绝应战，为了只在能够按照自己意愿行事的情况下作战。所以，能够采取攻势或者能够拒绝应战，就不再取决于风向，而是取决于速度更快的那一方了；对于整支舰队而言，则不仅取决于每艘舰船的速度，还取决于它们在作战时的战术一致性。自此以后，那些速度最快的舰船就会占据上风位置了。

因此，既从帆船的历史、又从桨帆船的历史中寻求有益的教训，并不像很多人所认为的那样，只是一种徒劳无用的期望。这两种船只，与现代舰艇既有类似之处，也有根本性的差异，使得我们不可能将这些舰船的战斗经历或战斗模式，当成可以沿用的战术先例。不过，先例与基本原则并不相同，也不如基本原则那样有价值。前者可能原本就是有

different from and less valuable than a principle. The former may be originally faulty, or may cease to apply through change of circumstances; the latter has its root in the essential nature of things, and, however various its application as conditions change, remains a standard to which action must conform to attain success. War has such principles; their existence is detected by the study of the past, which reveals them in successes and in failures, the same from age to age. Conditions and weapons change; but to cope with the one or successfully wield the others, respect must be had to these constant teachings of history in the tactics of the battlefield, or in those wider operations of war which are comprised under the name of strategy.

It is however in these wider operations, which embrace a whole theatre of war, and in a maritime contest may cover a large portion of the globe, that the teachings of history have a more evident and permanent value, because the conditions remain more permanent. The theatre of war may be larger or smaller, its difficulties more or less pronounced, the contending armies more or less great, the necessary movements more or less easy, but these are simply differences of scale, of degree, not of kind. As a wilderness gives place to civilization, as means of communication multiply, as roads are opened, rivers bridged, food-resources increased, the operations of war become easier, more rapid, more extensive; but the principles to which they must be conformed remain the same. When the march on foot was replaced by carrying troops in coaches, when the latter in turn gave place to railroads, the scale of distances was increased, or, if you will, the scale of time diminished; but the principles which dictated the point at which the army should be concentrated, the direction in which it should move, the part of the enemy's position which it should assail, the protection of communications, were not altered. So, on the sea, the advance from the galley timidly creeping from port to port to the sailing-ship launching out boldly to the ends of the earth, and from the latter to the steamship of our

瑕疵的，或者可能在环境改变之后并不适用了；后者则植根于事物的本质当中，并且在应用的时候，无论因环境改变而有多么的变化无穷，它都会保持着某种标准，而我们在战斗中，则必须遵照这一标准才能获胜。战争中的确存在着这样一些基本原则；前人的研究已经揭示了它们的存在，无论获胜抑或失败，这些原则世世代代都是一样的。作战环境与作战武器都会变化；而为了应对作战环境，或者成功地运用好作战武器，我们就必须遵守那些大规模战争中属于临场战术或战略范畴的那些亘古不变的历史教训才行。

然而，正是在这些范围更广泛、涵盖在整个战场的战争中，也正是在可能覆盖了全球大部分区域的海战中，这些历史教训有着一种更为明显、也更为恒久的意义，因为它们的战争环境更为恒定。虽说战场范围可能或大或小，作战困难可能或显著或不显著，交战双方的军队可能强大或不强大，必要的战术运动可能容易不容易，但这些情况都只是范围或程度上的差异，而不是类别上有差异。虽然随着蛮荒被文明所取代，随着交通方式越来越多，随着道路开辟、河流架桥、粮食资源的增加，作战也变得更加容易、更加快捷、范围更加广泛了，但是作战时必须遵循的那些基本原则，却未曾改变。徒步行军被马车运送部队所取代，而马车运送又被铁路运送所取代之后，行军距离就大大增加了，或者，假如您愿意那样说的话，就是行军时间缩短了；但决定部队在哪里集结、部队向哪个方向运动、进袭敌人哪个部分和保护交通要道这些基本原则，却并未改变。所以，在海上，从桨帆船小心翼翼地在港口之间潜行，到帆船大胆出航至天涯海角，从帆船再到我们现在的蒸汽轮船，这种进步在增加了海军的作战范围和速度的同时，并没有绝对地改变了指导海军作战的那些基本原则；而之前我们引述过的2300多年前赫莫克

own time, has increased the scope and the rapidity of naval operations without necessarily changing the principles which should direct them; and the speech of Hermocrates twenty-three hundred years ago, before quoted, contained a correct strategic plan, which is as applicable in its principles now as it was then. Before hostile armies or fleets are brought into contact (a word which perhaps better than any other indicates the dividing line between tactics and strategy), there are a number of questions to be decided, covering the whole plan of operations throughout the theatre of war. Among these are the proper function of the navy in the war; its true objective; the point or points upon which it should be concentrated; the establishment of depots of coal and supplies; the maintenance of communications between these depots and the home base; the military value of commerce-destroying as a decisive or a secondary operation of war; the system upon which commerce-destroying can be most efficiently conducted, whether by scattered cruisers or by holding in force some vital centre through which commercial shipping must pass. All these are strategic questions, and upon all these history has a great deal to say. There has been of late a valuable discussion in English naval circles as to the comparative merits of the policies of two great English admirals, Lord Howe and Lord St. Vincent, in the disposition of the English navy when at war with France. The question is purely strategic, and is not of mere historical interest; it is of vital importance now, and the principles upon which its decision rests are the same now as then. St. Vincent's policy saved England from invasion, and in the hands of Nelson and his brother admirals led straight up to Trafalgar.

It is then particularly in the field of naval strategy that the teachings of the past have a value which is in no degree lessened. They are there useful not only as illustrative of principles, but also as precedents, owing to the comparative permanence of the conditions. This is less obviously true as to tactics, when the fleets come into collision at the point to which strategic

拉提斯[3]所说的话，也蕴含了一种正确的战略规划，其基本原则在如今与当时并无区别，仍然可加以应用。在与敌方部队或舰队发生接触之前（这样说，可能要比其他区分战术与战略的说法要更好），有许多问题需要进行决断，它们涉及到贯穿了整个战场的整体作战计划。其中包括：海军在战争中应当发挥的正确作用；海军的真正目标；海军应当集结的一处或多处地点；燃煤和军需补给站的建立；这些补给站与国内大本营之间交通补给线的维护；贸易破坏战作为一种决定性的或者辅助性的作战行动，具有什么样的军事意义；最有效地进行贸易破坏战的方法，是用分散的巡洋舰呢，还是有效地控制商船所必经的某一重要的航运中心……所有这些都属于战略问题；而关于这些问题，历史上也有着诸多的经验可循。近来，英国的海军界进行了一场很有意义的讨论，评价了豪勋爵[4]和圣文森特勋爵[5]这两位伟大的英国海军司令在英法战争中部署海军时各自所定政策的相对贡献。这个问题纯粹是战略性的，并非只有历史价值；如今这一问题则具有至关重要的意义，而决策所依赖的那些基本原则，在如今和当时都是相同的。圣文森特勋爵的政策使得英国免遭入侵，而在纳尔逊[6]及其同行海军将领的执行下，又直接导致了特拉法尔加海战那次大捷。

尤其是在当时的海军战略领域，过去的经验教训有着不可抹杀的意义。这些教训，非但具有示范基本原则的作用，还因为环境的相对稳定性而具有先例的作用。对于战术而言，当战略考量使得双方的舰队狭路相逢的时候，这一点却没有那样明显了。人类不安于现状，一直都在进步，使得武器不停地更新换代；随之而来的，则必然是作战方式的不断改变，即在战场上排兵布阵、部署舰船的方式在不断地发生着改变。这样一来，许

considerations have brought them. The unresting progress of mankind causes continual change in the weapons; and with that must come a continual change in the manner of fighting, — in the handling and disposition of troops or ships on the battlefield. Hence arises a tendency on the part of many connected with maritime matters to think that no advantage is to be gained from the study of former experiences; that time so used is wasted. This view, though natural, not only leaves wholly out of sight those broad strategic considerations which lead nations to put fleets afloat, which direct the sphere of their action, and so have modified and will continue to modify the history of the world, but is one-sided and narrow even as to tactics. The battles of the past succeeded or failed according as they were fought in conformity with the principles of war; and the seaman who carefully studies the causes of success or failure will not only detect and gradually assimilate these principles, but will also acquire increased aptitude in applying them to the tactical use of the ships and weapons of his own day. He will observe also that changes of tactics have not only taken place after changes in weapons, which necessarily is the case, but that the interval between such changes has been unduly long. This doubtless arises from the fact that an improvement of weapons is due to the energy of one or two men, while changes in tactics have to overcome the inertia of a conservative class; but it is a great evil. It can be remedied only by a candid recognition of each change, by careful study of the powers and limitations of the new ship or weapon, and by a consequent adaptation of the method of using it to the qualities it possesses, which will constitute its tactics. History shows that it is vain to hope that military men generally will be at the pains to do this, but that the one who does will go into battle with a great advantage, — a lesson in itself of no mean value.

We may therefore accept now the words of a French tactician, Morogues, who wrote a century and a quarter ago: "Naval tactics are based upon conditions the chief causes of which,

多研究海洋问题的人就产生了一种倾向，认为研究过去的经验教训带来不了什么益处，认为这样做是在浪费时间。虽说这种观点很正常，但它不仅全然忽视了那些显著的战略考量——正是这些战略上的考量，既使得各国都纷纷建造舰队、控制着各国的作战范围，也改变了、并且仍将继续改变世界的历史；而且，即便是从战术上来看，这也是一种片面而狭隘的观点。在作战时，过去是获胜还是失败，取决于是否遵照战争的基本原则去作战；而那些仔细研究获胜或失败原因的海军人士，则不仅会发现并逐渐吸收这些基本原则，还会提高自己的能力，使之能够在战术性地运用自己所处时代的舰船和武器的过程中，应用这些基本原则。这些人还会发现，战术不仅随着武器的改变而改变——此种情形是必然的——而且这些变化之间的时间跨度都很久。这种情况无疑是因为，武器的改良在于一两个人的力量，而战术上的改变则必须克服整个保守阶层的惰性才行；这种惰性，正是一种巨大的弊端。只有通过坦然地认识到每一种变革，通过仔细研究新舰艇、新武器的长处与局限，并且采取相应的办法，根据形成其战略的特性来对它们加以利用，才能纠正这一弊端。历史业已表明，虽说不要指望军人经常会不遗余力地来这样做，但那些这样做了的人，在战场上都会获得巨大的优势——这种教训，本身就具有极大的价值。

因此，如今我们可以接受法国战术家莫罗盖[7]的训导了。他曾在125年前这样写道："海军之战术，乃是以其主因——即武器装备——可能发生变化之前提为基础；此种主因，转而必然导致船舶结构、操作方法发生改变，并因而最终使得舰队之部署与调遣发生改变。"他还进一步指出，"此非一种以绝对不变原则为基础之科学"，但这一说法却更易招来人们的批评。更恰当一点的说法应当是，对海军战术基本原则的应用，

namely the arms, may change; which in turn causes necessarily a change in the construction of ships, in the manner of handling them, and so finally in the disposition and handling of fleets." His further statement, that "it is not a science founded upon principles absolutely invariable," is more open to criticism. It would be more correct to say that the application of its principles varies as the weapons change. The application of the principles doubtless varies also in strategy from time to time, but the variation is far less; and hence the recognition of the underlying principle is easier. This statement is of sufficient importance to our subject to receive some illustrations from historical events.

The battle of the Nile, in 1798, was not only an overwhelming victory for the English over the French fleet, but had also the decisive effect of destroying the communications between France and Napoleon's army in Egypt. In the battle itself the English admiral, Nelson, gave a most brilliant example of grand tactics, if that be, as has been defined, "the art of making good combinations preliminary to battles as well as during their progress." The particular tactical combination depended upon a condition now passed away, which was the inability of the lee ships of a fleet at anchor to come to the help of the weather ones before the latter were destroyed; but the principles which underlay the combination, namely, to choose that part of the enemy's order which can least easily be helped, and to attack it with superior forces, has not passed away. The action of Admiral Jervis at Cape St. Vincent, when with fifteen ships he won a victory over twenty-seven, was dictated by the same principle, though in this case the enemy was not at anchor, but under way. Yet men's minds are so constituted that they seem more impressed by the transiency of the conditions than by the undying principle which coped with them. In the strategic effect of Nelson's victory upon the course of the war, on the contrary, the principle involved is not only more easily recognized, but it is at once seen to be applicable

会随着武器装备的改变而不断改变。而应用这些基本原则时，在战术上无疑也是时常变化着的，只不过这种变化要小得多罢了，所以认识到这些基本原则也要容易得多。他的这一说法，对于我们论述的主题非常重要，从而让我们可以从历史事件中获得某些实例。

1798年的尼罗河河口之战[8]，不仅是英国海军对法国舰队一次压倒性的胜利，还对摧毁法国与位于埃及的拿破仑所率军队之间的交通补给产生了关键性的影响。此战中，英国海军司令纳尔逊为世人提供了一个极为杰出的"大战术"战例——假如可以这样说的话——正如"大战术"的定义所指出的那样："在战前与战中都充分组合的艺术。"特殊的战术组合，取决于如今已经不再存在的一种前提，即舰队中处于下风位置且已泊锚的船只，无法在处于上风位置的舰船被摧毁之前赶去救援；但是，此种战术组合的基本原则——即选择敌方战斗序列中最难施以援手的部分，用优势兵力加以攻击——却并未过时。海军司令杰维斯在圣文森特角之战中，以15艘舰船对阵敌方的27艘战舰并取得了胜利，遵循的正是相同的原则，只是在此役中，敌方的舰船并非停泊着，而是在航行中。然而，人们的思维却具有定式，他们对于环境无常的印象，似乎比对支配环境的基本原则更为深刻。与此相反，在纳尔逊获胜而对此次战争所产生的战略效果当中，涉及的基本原则却不但容易看出，还能让我们马上就明白，这一原则可以应用到我们所处的这个时代来。埃及战事中哪方获胜的问题，取决于能否让此处与法国之间的交通补给保持畅通。尼罗河河口大捷，摧毁了本可确保补给畅通的法国海军，从而决定了法国的最终失败；而我们马上也能看出，此次出击遵循的正是打击敌人交通补给线的原则，并且这一原则如今仍然有效。

to our own day. The issue of the enterprise in Egypt depended upon keeping open the communications with France. The victory of the Nile destroyed the naval force, by which alone the communications could be assured, and determined the final failure; and it is at once seen, not only that the blow was struck in accordance with the principle of striking at the enemy's line of communication, but also that the same principle is valid now, and would be equally so in the days of the galley as of the sailing-ship or steamer.

Nevertheless, a vague feeling of contempt for the past, supposed to be obsolete, combines with natural indolence to blind men even to those permanent strategic lessons which lie close to the surface of naval history. For instance, how many look upon the battle of Trafalgar, the crown of Nelson's glory and the seal of his genius, as other than an isolated event of exceptional grandeur? How many ask themselves the strategic question, "How did the ships come to be just there?" How many realize it to be the final act in a great strategic drama, extending over a year or more, in which two of the greatest leaders that ever lived, Napoleon and Nelson, were pitted against each other? At Trafalgar it was not Villeneuve that failed, but Napoleon that was vanquished; not Nelson that won, but England that was saved; and why? Because Napoleon's combinations failed, and Nelson's intuitions and activity kept the English fleet ever on the track of the enemy, and brought it up in time at the decisive moment. The tactics at Trafalgar, while open to criticism in detail, were in their main features conformable to the principles of war, and their audacity was justified as well by the urgency of the case as by the results; but the great lessons of efficiency in preparation, of activity and energy in execution, and of thought and insight on the part of the English leader during the previous months, are strategic lessons, and as such they still remain good.

In these two cases events were worked out to their natural and decisive end. A third may

尽管如此，人们还是怀有一种模糊的感觉，认为过去已被淘汰，从而轻视过去；再加上天生的惰性，所以即便是在海军历史上那些非常明显、具有永久意义的战略教训，他们也看不到。比如说，有多少人，不会将属于纳尔逊司令荣耀巅峰、标志着其天才的特拉法尔加海战，看成只是一件异常宏伟的孤立事件呢？有多少人，问过自己这样一个战略性的问题："那些舰船如何正好处于那里呢？"又有多少人认识到了，此次海战是为时一年或更久所上演的一部宏大战略戏剧的最后一幕，是拿破仑与纳尔逊这两位历史上最伟大的领袖在这幕大戏中相互对垒呢？在特拉法尔加海战中，并非是维尔纳夫[9]失利，而是拿破仑战败了；也并非是纳尔逊赢了，而是英格兰得救了。为什么呢？这是因为，拿破仑的战术组合失败了，而纳尔逊的洞察力与积极性却让英国舰队一直追击着敌人，从而让舰队在关键时刻及时抵达了战场。特拉法尔加海战所用的战术，虽说在细节上容易招致批评，但其主要特征还是符合战争原则的，而战术上的大胆创新，也因当时形势紧急以及结果取胜而变得合情合理了；不过，此战最大的教训，是备战富有效率、执行积极有力，以及英军统帅在战前数月间的深思熟虑和洞察入微。它们都是战略意义上的教训；就其本身而论，这些教训如今对我们来说仍然是很有裨益的。

在这两个战事中，战事都是以自然而具有决定意义的方式结束的。我们还可以看一看第三个战例：在这个战例中，由于没有出现如此明确的结果，所以对于该不该采用那样的战略战术，人们可能就会众说纷纭了。在美国革命战争中，法国和西班牙在1779年结成了同盟，共同对抗英国。法、西联合舰队曾3次进击英吉利海峡，前线作战舰船一度达到了66艘；由于英军舰船数量远不及对方，所以英国舰队只得回港避战。此时，西班牙的

be cited, in which, as no such definite end was reached, an opinion as to what should have been done may be open to dispute. In the war of the American Revolution, France and Spain became allies against England in 1779. The united fleets thrice appeared in the English Channel, once to the number of sixty-six sail of the line, driving the English fleet to seek refuge in its ports because far inferior in numbers. Now, the great aim of Spain was to recover Gibraltar and Jamaica; and to the former end immense efforts both by land and sea were put forth by the allies against that nearly impregnable fortress. They were fruitless. The question suggested — and it is purely one of naval strategy — is this: Would not Gibraltar have been more surely recovered by controlling the English Channel, attacking the British fleet even in its harbors, and threatening England with annihilation of commerce and invasion at home, than by far greater efforts directed against a distant and very strong outpost of her empire? The English people, from long immunity, were particularly sensitive to fears of invasion, and their great confidence in their fleets, if rudely shaken, would have left them proportionately disheartened. However decided, the question as a point of strategy is fair; and it is proposed in another form by a French officer of the period, who favored directing the great effort on a West India island which might be exchanged against Gibraltar. It is not, however, likely that England would have given up the key of the Mediterranean for any other foreign possession, though she might have yielded it to save her firesides and her capital. Napoleon once said that he would reconquer Pondicherry on the banks of the Vistula. Could he have controlled the English Channel, as the allied fleet did for a moment in 1779, can it be doubted that he would have conquered Gibraltar on the shores of England?

To impress more strongly the truth that history both suggests strategic study and illustrates the principles of war by the facts which it transmits, two more instances will be taken, which are more remote in time than the period specially considered in this work. How did it happen

最大目标就是夺回直布罗陀和牙买加；为了实现前一目标，对直布罗陀这个固若金汤的要塞，法、西同盟从海陆两个方面都尽了极大的努力。但这些努力，却全都无果而终。当时人们提出了一个问题——并且是一个纯粹的海军战略问题：如果控制英吉利海峡，进攻即便是泊在港口里的英军舰队，用摧毁其贸易、进攻其本土来威胁英国，比起费劲得多地去进攻英帝国这处偏远而坚固的前哨基地，是不是会更有把握来收复直布罗陀呢？由于长期未受战争困扰，英国民众尤其担心外敌入侵；并且，倘若有力地动摇他们对于英国舰队的极大信心，就会让他们变得同等程度地泄气了。无论从哪个方面来判断，作为一种战略，这个问题都是很有利的；但这个问题，却是当时一位法国军官用另一种方式提出来的，这名军官支持大力攻取西印度群岛中一处可以用来与直布罗陀进行交换的岛屿。然而，尽管可能会为了保护家园和首都而屈从，但英国是不太可能因为外国占领了该国别的领土而心甘情愿地放弃进出地中海的这处门户的。拿破仑曾经宣称，他会在维斯瓦河沿岸夺回庞迪切里。倘若他能像1779年法、西联合舰队暂时所做的那样，控制住英吉利海峡，那我们还能不能怀疑，他会在英国的海滩上夺回直布罗陀呢？

为了让大家对于历史既启发我们去进行战略研究、又通过史实阐明了战争原则这一道理的印象更加深刻，我们还可以举出另外两个战例来；它们发生的时间，比本书专门研究的这一时期更为久远。东西列强中，在地中海地区有两个敌对的大国，其中一个在已知世界所建立的那个帝国正危若累卵；双方舰队数次狭路相逢，彼此之间相距像阿克提姆与勒班陀[10]两地那样近——这种情况是怎样发生的呢？这是纯属巧合呢，还是由于出现

that, in two great contests between the powers of the East and of the West in the Mediterranean, in one of which the empire of the known world was at stake, the opposing fleets met on spots so near each other as Actium and Lepanto? Was this a mere coincidence, or was it due to conditions that recurred, and may recur again?[(4)] If the latter, it is worthwhile to study out the reason; for if there should again arise a great eastern power of the sea like that of Antony or of Turkey, the strategic questions would be similar. At present, indeed, it seems that the centre of sea power, resting mainly with England and France, is overwhelmingly in the West; but should any chance add to the control of the Black Sea basin, which Russia now has, the possession of the entrance to the Mediterranean, the existing strategic conditions affecting sea power would all be modified. Now, were the West arrayed against the East, England and France would go at once unopposed to the Levant, as they did in 1854, and as England alone went in 1878; in case of the change suggested, the East, as twice before, would meet the West half-way.

At a very conspicuous and momentous period of the world's history, Sea Power had a strategic bearing and weight which has received scant recognition. There cannot now be someone who had the full knowledge necessary for tracing in detail its influence upon the issue of the second Punic War; but the indications which remain are sufficient to warrant the assertion that it was a determining factor. An accurate judgment upon this point cannot be formed by mastering only such facts of the particular contest as have been clearly transmitted, for as usual the naval transactions have been slightly passed over; there is needed also familiarity with the details of general naval history in order to draw, from slight indications, correct inferences based upon a knowledge of what has been possible at periods whose history is well known. The control of the sea, however real, does not imply that an enemy's single ships or small squadrons cannot steal out of port, cannot cross more or less frequented tracts of ocean, make harassing

了相同的条件并且可能再次重现呢?[(4)]倘若属于后者,那么就值得研究,来找出其中的原因。因为,如果将来会重新崛起一个东方的海洋大国,就像安东尼或者土耳其帝国那样,那么所涉及的战略问题就是相似的了。的确,在如今看来,海上力量主要集中于英、法两国,它们似乎在西方占有绝对优势;但是,假如除了控制如今处于俄国手中的黑海盆地,有可能再占领地中海入口的话,那么影响制海权的现有战略条件,就会全盘改变了。如今,倘若西方能够联合起来,一致对抗东方,则英、法两国马上就会像它们在1854年、英国独自于1878年所干的那样,直取黎凡特[11],并且所向无敌;而一旦形势发生前面所提到的那种改变,那么东方国家就会像以前的那两次一样,向西方俯首称臣了。

在世界历史上一个值得注意的重要时期,制海权具有战略上的意义和重要性,但人们却并未充分认识到这种意义和重要性。如今,已经不可能再有人拥有全面而必要的知识,来详细地探究制海权对于第二次布匿战争[12]的结局所带来的影响了;不过,此次战争所遗留下来的迹象,仍然足以让我们断言:制海权是当时的一个决定性因素。要想对这一点形成一种准确的判断,仅仅掌握某次特定战争业已清晰地呈现出来的一些事实是不够的,因为在这些事实当中,海军事务照例已经被人们不经意间忽略掉了;所以,我们还需要熟悉海军通史的详细内容,以便根据一些细微的迹象,在了解那些众所周知的历史时期可能发生了什么的基础之上,做出正确的推断。不管有多千真万确,控制海洋都并不意味着,敌方的单艘舰船或者小型舰队就无法偷偷出港、就无法穿过那些或多或少有船只出没的海域、就无法对漫长海岸线上那些未设防的地方进行骚扰、就无法进

descents upon unprotected points of a long coast-line, enter blockaded harbors. On the contrary, history has shown that such evasions are always possible, to some extent, to the weaker party, however great the inequality of naval strength. It is not therefore inconsistent with the general control of the sea, or of a decisive part of it, by the Roman fleets, that the Carthaginian admiral Bomilcar in the fourth year of the war, after the stunning defeat of Cannae, landed four thousand men and a body of elephants in south Italy; nor that in the seventh year, flying from the Roman fleet off Syracuse, he again appeared at Tarentum, then in Hannibal's hands; nor that Hannibal sent despatch vessels to Carthage; nor even that, at last, he withdrew in safety to Africa with his wasted army. None of these things prove that the government in Carthage could, if it wished, have sent Hannibal the constant support which, as a matter of fact, he did not receive; but they do tend to create a natural impression that such help could have been given. Therefore the statement, that the Roman preponderance at sea had a decisive effect upon the course of the war, needs to be made good by an examination of ascertained facts. Thus the kind and degree of its influence may be fairly estimated.

At the beginning of the war, Mommsen says, Rome controlled the seas. To whatever cause, or combination of causes, it be attributed, this essentially non-maritime state had in the first Punic War established over its sea-faring rival a naval supremacy, which still lasted. In the second war there was no naval battle of importance, — a circumstance which in itself, and still more in connection with other well-ascertained facts, indicates a superiority analogous to that which at other epochs has been marked by the same feature.

As Hannibal left no memoirs, the motives are unknown which determined him to the perilous and almost ruinous march through Gaul and across the Alps. It is certain, however, that

入被封锁的海港了。恰恰相反，历史业已表明，在一定程度上，无论双方的海军实力悬殊相差多大，势弱的一方都总有可能实施这样的遁避之法。因此，在罗马舰队全面掌控了海洋或者控制了海上关键区域的情况下，迦太基的海军统帅波米尔卡在开战后的第四年中，即令人叹为观止的坎尼[13]大捷之后，还能率4000士兵和一队大象在意大利南部登陆，在第七年中，他避开了锡拉丘兹海岸边的罗马舰队，再次出现在当时为汉尼拔所控制的塔伦特姆，而汉尼拔能够派遣快船前往迦太基，与罗马控制了海洋并不矛盾；甚至最后汉尼拔率领手下的残兵败安全地撤往非洲，这些都与罗马控制了海洋并不矛盾。这些事件中，没有哪一件表明，迦太基的政府可能不断地为汉尼拔派遣了援军，而事实上，汉尼拔却从未得到过这样的支援；不过，这些东西的确会让人产生一种自然而然的印象，以为迦太基政府很可能对汉尼拔进行了这样的支援。因此，说罗马在海上所拥有的优势对于此次战争进程产生了决定性影响这句话，需要通过对业已确定的事实进行仔细研究，才能得到证实。因此，它产生了什么样的影响、影响的程度如何，就可以得到公正的评价了。

蒙森[14]曾经说过，在战争初期，罗马控制着海洋。无论是出于什么样的原因，还是由于种种原因的结合，在第一次布匿战争期间，本质上并不属于海洋国家的罗马，竟然胜过了习惯于航海的对手，掌握了制海权，并且后来还一直保持着这种状态。在第二次布匿战争中，并未发生过什么重大的海战——这种情况本身，连同人们已经确定了的、与这种情况相关的其他事实，都显示出了一种优势；而这一点，与其他时代以同一特征为标志的情况则是类似的。

由于汉尼拔并未留下回忆录，所以促使他下定决心经由高卢并翻越阿尔卑斯山，

his fleet on the coast of Spain was not strong enough to contend with that of Rome. Had it been, he might still have followed the road he actually did, for reasons that weighed with him; but had he gone by the sea, he would not have lost thirty-three thousand out of the sixty thousand veteran soldiers with whom he started.

While Hannibal was making this dangerous march, the Romans were sending to Spain, under the two elder Scipios, one part of their fleet, carrying a consular army. This made the voyage without serious loss, and the army established itself successfully north of the Ebro, on Hannibal's line of communications. At the same time another squadron, with an army commanded by the other consul, was sent to Sicily. The two together numbered two hundred and twenty ships. On its station each met and defeated a Carthaginian squadron with an ease which may be inferred from the slight mention made of the actions, and which indicates the actual superiority of the Roman fleet.

After the second year the war assumed the following shape: Hannibal, having entered Italy by the north, after a series of successes had passed southward around Rome and fixed himself in southern Italy, living off the country, — a condition which tended to alienate the people, and was especially precarious when in contact with the mighty political and military system of control which Rome had there established. It was therefore from the first urgently necessary that he should establish, between himself and some reliable base, that stream of supplies and reinforcements which in terms of modern war is called "communications." There were three friendly regions which might, each or all, serve as such a base, — Carthage itself, Macedonia, and Spain. With the first two, communication could be had only by sea. From Spain, where his firmest support was found, he could be reached by both land and sea, unless an enemy barred

从而踏上那条危机四伏、几近毁灭之途的动机，我们已经不得而知。然而，可以肯定的是，他部署在西班牙沿海的那支舰队并不强大，并不足以与罗马舰队相抗衡。就算这支舰队足够强大、能够与罗马舰队抗衡，他可能也会由于受到种种原因所左右，仍然踏上他实际所走的那条进军路线；但如果走的是海路，那么，他出发时所率的那60000名能征善战的士兵中，就不会损失掉33000人了。

就在汉尼拔开始这一危险进军之时，罗马人正派两位大西庇阿率罗马舰队一部，运送一支执政官集团军[15]前往西班牙。这支舰队在航行过程中并无重大损失，那支陆军则成功地在埃布罗河以北、汉尼拔的交通补给线上扎下了营寨。与此同时，另一支小型舰队与一支由另一名执政官所指挥的部队，则被派往了西西里。这两支舰队合并起来，舰船数量达到了220艘。它们在各自的战斗位置上，分别遭遇并击退了一支迦太基的小型舰队，且胜得轻而易举；这一点，可以从人们对战斗过程只是一笔带过的事实就可以推断出来，也显示出了罗马舰队的真正优势。

第二年过后，此次战争的形势是：从北部进入意大利、打了一系列胜仗的汉尼拔，已经绕过罗马向南进军，并在意大利南部驻扎下来，就地征取军粮——这种情况，往往会使民心背离，而在涉及到罗马帝国在该国所建立的那种强大的政治与军事制度时，则尤为危险。因此他的第一要务，就应当是在他自己与某个可靠基地之间，建立起畅通的补给与援兵线，用现代战争的话来说，就是应当建立起一条"交通补给线"。当时有3个友好地区，就是迦太基本土、马其顿和西班牙，它们各自或者合起来都可以形成这样的一个基地。对于前面两个地区而言，提供交通补给只能经由海上。而从最坚定地支持汉尼拔的西班牙，则既可以从陆上、也可以从海上获取补给，除非有敌军拦截；不过，

the passage; but the sea route was the shorter and easier.

In the first years of the war, Rome, by her sea power, controlled absolutely the basin between Italy, Sicily, and Spain, known as the Tyrrhenian and Sardinian Seas. The sea-coast from the Ebro to the Tiber was mostly friendly to her. In the fourth year, after the battle of Cannae, Syracuse forsook the Roman alliance, the revolt spread through Sicily, and Macedonia also entered into an offensive league with Hannibal. These changes extended the necessary operations of the Roman fleet, and taxed its strength. What disposition was made of it, and how did it thereafter influence the struggle?

The indications are clear that Rome at no time ceased to control the Tyrrhenian Sea, for her squadrons passed unmolested from Italy to Spain. On the Spanish coast also she had full sway till the younger Scipio saw fit to lay up the fleet. In the Adriatic, a squadron and naval station were established at Brindisi to check Macedonia, which performed their task so well that not a soldier of the phalanxes ever set foot in Italy. "The want of a war fleet," says Mommsen, "paralyzed Philip in all his movements." Here the effect of Sea Power is not even a matter of inference. In Sicily, the struggle centered about Syracuse. The fleets of Carthage and Rome met there, but the superiority evidently lay with the latter; for though the Carthaginians at times succeeded in throwing supplies into the city, they avoided meeting the Roman fleet in battle. With Lilybaeum, Palermo, and Messina in its hands, the latter was well based in the north coast of the island. Access by the south was left open to the Carthaginians, and they were thus able to maintain the insurrection.

Putting these facts together, it is a reasonable inference, and supported by the whole tenor of the history, that the Roman sea power controlled the sea north of a line drawn from Tarragona in Spain to Lilybaeum (the modern Marsala), at the west end of Sicily, thence round by the north

海路更近，也更容易。

在此次战争最初的那几年中，罗马通过其制海权完全掌控了位于意大利、西西里和西班牙之间的海域，即如今我们所知的第勒尼安海与撒丁尼亚海。从埃布罗河到台伯河的沿岸地区，多半都与罗马交好。在第四年的坎尼之战后，锡拉丘兹背弃了与罗马的同盟，整个西西里都发生了叛乱，而马其顿也与汉尼拔结成了攻守同盟。这些变化，使得罗马舰队的作战次数越来越多，因而削弱了舰队的实力。那么，罗马舰队做了什么样的部署，而此后罗马舰队又是如何影响到整个战争的呢？

种种迹象都很清楚地表明，罗马从未停止过对第勒尼安海的控制，因为该国的各分舰队一直都畅通无阻地往来于意大利和西班牙之间。而在西班牙沿海，直到小西庇阿认为可以让舰队退役之前，罗马也都完全掌握着控制权。在亚得里亚海，罗马则在布林迪西建立了一支小型舰队和一个军港，以遏制马其顿；这支舰队和军港的作用非常巨大，使得以方阵[16]著称的马其顿步兵从未踏上过意大利一步。"由于没有一支军舰舰队，"蒙森曾这样说，"所以腓力五世[17]在所有行动中都力不从心。"制海权在此处所产生的影响，就不再是一种推理了。在西西里，战争主要以锡拉丘兹为中心。迦太基与罗马双方的舰队在此遭遇，但优势显然在罗马舰队这一边；因为，尽管迦太基人多次把给养投入了城中，一直避免与罗马舰队直接交锋。由于掌控着利利俾、巴勒莫和墨西拿等地，所以罗马舰队一直牢牢地据守着西西里岛北部沿海。但迦太基人仍然可以从该岛南部进入，因此才能继续与罗马对抗。

把这些事实放在一起来看，我们便可推断出一个合理且被整个历史进程所支持的

side of the island through the straits of Messina down to Syracuse, and from there to Brindisi in the Adriatic. This control lasted, unshaken, throughout the war. It did not exclude maritime raids, large or small, such as have been spoken of; but it did forbid the sustained and secure communications of which Hannibal was in deadly need.

On the other hand, it seems equally plain that for the first ten years of the war the Roman fleet was not strong enough for sustained operations in the sea between Sicily and Carthage, nor indeed much to the south of the line indicated. When Hannibal started, he assigned such ships as he had to maintaining the communications between Spain and Africa, which the Romans did not then attempt to disturb.

The Roman sea power, therefore, threw Macedonia wholly out of the war. It did not keep Carthage from maintaining a useful and most harassing diversion in Sicily; but it did prevent her sending troops, when they would have been most useful, to her great general in Italy. How was it as to Spain?

Spain was the region upon which the father of Hannibal and Hannibal himself had based their intended invasion of Italy. For eighteen years before this began they had occupied the country, extending and consolidating their power, both political and military, with rare sagacity. They had raised, and trained in local wars, a large and now veteran army. Upon his own departure, Hannibal intrusted the government to his younger brother, Hasdrubal, who preserved toward him to the end a loyalty and devotion which he had no reason to hope from the faction-cursed mother-city in Africa.

At the time of his starting, the Carthaginian power in Spain was secured from Cadiz to the river Ebro. The region between this river and the Pyrenees was inhabited by tribes friendly to the Romans, but unable, in the absence of the latter, to oppose a successful resistance to

结论来：从西班牙的塔拉戈纳到西西里岛西端的利利俾（即如今的马尔萨拉），然后绕过该岛北侧，经由墨西拿海峡，向南至锡拉丘兹，再到亚得里亚海上的布林迪西，此线以北的海域，都由罗马海军控制着。并且，在整个战争期间，罗马都牢牢地保持着这种控制权。这并不是说，罗马并未受到过前面已经提及的、规模或大或小的海上袭扰；不过，它却确确实实地阻断了汉尼拔所急需的那种既不间断又很安全的交通补给。

另一方面，在此次战争的前10年间，罗马舰队仍然不够强大，无法在西西里与迦太基之间的海域持续作战，实际上也无法在前述那条线以南的许多海域持续作战，这一点似乎也同样非常明显。汉尼拔在出征之时，曾指派手下的一些船只在西班牙和非洲之间运送补给，而罗马人当时却并未试图去袭扰这些船只。

因此，虽然罗马的制海权将马其顿完全踢出了此次战局之外，但它并没有阻止迦太基在西西里维持其有效的、干扰性的牵制力量；不过，它的确让迦太基在最有利的时刻，无法向在意大利的汉尼拔这位伟大的将领派遣援军。至于西班牙，情况又如何呢？

汉尼拔之父与汉尼拔本人，都是因西班牙这一地区而产生了入侵意大利的企图。在入侵意大利的18年之前，他们就占领了西班牙，并以极为罕见的远见卓识，扩充并巩固了他们的政治和军事权力。在一场场局部战争中，他们招募并训练出了一支庞大、此时已身经百战的军队。汉尼拔出征之后，就将该国的行政委托给了其弟弟哈斯德鲁巴；后者至死都对汉尼拔忠心耿耿、毫无二心，而汉尼拔根本就不用指望从非洲那个派系林立、争斗不休的宗主国获得此种忠诚。

当他出征之时，迦太基在西班牙的势力范围，从加的斯到埃布罗河都很牢固。在埃布

Hannibal. He put them down, leaving eleven thousand soldiers under Hanno to keep military possession of the country, lest the Romans should establish themselves there, and thus disturb his communications with his base.

Cnaeus Scipio, however, arrived on the spot by sea the same year with twenty thousand men, defeated Hanno, and occupied both the coast and interior north of the Ebro. The Romans thus held ground by which they entirely closed the road between Hannibal and reinforcements from Hasdrubal, and whence they could attack the Carthaginian power in Spain; while their own communications with Italy, being by water, were secured by their naval supremacy. They made a naval base at Tarragona, confronting that of Hasdrubal at Cartagena, and then invaded the Carthaginian dominions. The war in Spain went on under the elder Scipios, seemingly a side issue, with varying fortune for seven years; at the end of which time Hasdrubal inflicted upon them a crushing defeat, the two brothers were killed, and the Carthaginians nearly succeeded in breaking through to the Pyrenees with reinforcements for Hannibal. The attempt, however, was checked for the moment; and before it could be renewed, the fall of Capua released twelve thousand veteran Romans, who were sent to Spain under Claudius Nero, a man of exceptional ability, to whom was due later the most decisive military movement made by any Roman general during the Second Punic War. This seasonable reinforcement, which again assured the shaken grip on Hasdrubal's line of march, came by sea, — a way which, though most rapid and easy, was closed to the Carthaginians by the Roman navy.

Two years later the younger Publius Scipio, celebrated afterward as Africanus, received the command in Spain, and captured Cartagena by a combined military and naval attack; after which he took the most extraordinary step of breaking up his fleet and transferring the seamen to the army. Not contented to act merely as the "containing" [5] force against Hasdrubal

罗河与比利牛斯山脉之间的地区，生活着与罗马人交好的一些部落；不过，倘若没有罗马人撑腰，这些部落是无法成功地抵抗汉尼拔的。汉尼拔镇压了这些部落，留下汉诺[18]率11000士卒武力镇守该国，以防罗马军队前来夺取并袭扰他与大本营之间的交通补给线。

然而，就在同一年间，格尼乌斯·西庇阿从海上率20000兵力也抵达了这一地区；他打败了汉诺，占领了沿海以及埃布罗河以北的内陆地区。这样一来，罗马人就站稳了脚跟，完全封锁了汉尼拔部与哈斯德鲁巴援军之间的道路，并由此可以去进攻西班牙的迦太基政权；而他们自己与意大利之间经由海上的交通补给，则因其海军优势而得以确保安全了。他们在塔拉戈纳建立了一个海军基地，以此来对抗位于卡塔赫纳的哈斯德鲁巴部的海军基地，然后侵入了迦太基的领土。西班牙之战是在两位大西庇阿的指挥之下进行的，尽管看上去似乎并不重要，但双方势力此消彼长，竟打了7年的拉锯战；最后，哈斯德鲁巴给了他们沉重一击，罗马军队一败涂地，大西庇阿兄弟战死，而迦太基人也差不多打通了通往比利牛斯山脉的道路，能够去支援汉尼拔部了。可是，当时这一尝试却遭到了罗马军队的拦截；而不待他们再一次试图支援，加普亚又被攻陷，腾出了12000名身经百战的罗马士兵，由克劳狄乌斯·尼禄率领，被派往西班牙。尼禄具有非凡的才能，后来在第二次布匿战争中，罗马将领最具决定意义的军事行动，都应归功于他。这支如及时之雨的援军是经由海路到达的，它重新控制了因哈斯德鲁巴部进军而本已岌岌可危的形势；海路虽说极为快捷和容易，但罗马海军却在海上已经完全阻断了迦太基人。

两年之后，更年轻的普布利乌斯·西庇阿——即后来声名显著的"非洲征服者"大西庇阿——接掌了西班牙之战的指挥权，并联合陆海两军攻取了卡塔赫纳；然后，他便

by closing the passes of the Pyrenees, Scipio pushed forward into southern Spain, and fought a severe but indecisive battle on the Guadalquivir; after which Hasdrubal slipped away from him, hurried north, crossed the Pyrenees at their extreme west, and pressed on to Italy, where Hannibal's position was daily growing weaker, the natural waste of his army not being replaced.

The war had lasted ten years, when Hasdrubal, having met little loss on the way, entered Italy at the north. The troops he brought, could they be safely united with those under the command of the unrivalled Hannibal, might give a decisive turn to the war, for Rome herself was nearly exhausted; the iron links which bound her own colonies and the allied States to her were strained to the utmost, and some had already snapped. But the military position of the two brothers was also perilous in the extreme. One being at the river Metaurus, the other in Apulia, two hundred miles apart, each was confronted by a superior enemy, and both these Roman armies were between their separated opponents. This false situation, as well as the long delay of Hasdrubal's coming, was due to the Roman control of the sea, which throughout the war limited the mutual support of the Carthaginian brothers to the route through Gaul. At the very time that Hasdrubal was making his long and dangerous circuit by land, Scipio had sent eleven thousand men from Spain by sea to reinforce the army opposed to him. The upshot was that messengers from Hasdrubal to Hannibal, having to pass over so wide a belt of hostile country, fell into the hands of Claudius Nero, commanding the southern Roman army, who thus learned the route which Hasdrubal intended to take. Nero correctly appreciated the situation, and, escaping the vigilance of Hannibal, made a rapid march with eight thousand of his best troops to join the forces in the north. The junction being effected, the two consuls fell upon Hasdrubal in overwhelming numbers and destroyed his army; the Carthaginian leader himself falling in

干出了一桩惊世之举：他解散了所率的舰队，并将水兵并入了陆军。由于并不满足于仅仅当一支"牵制"[5]力量，不满足于只是封锁比利牛斯山脉的各处关隘来对抗哈斯德鲁巴部，所以西庇阿率军推进到了西班牙南部，并在瓜达基维尔河上进行了一场具有决定意义的恶战；此战之后，哈斯德鲁巴部便弃战远遁，向北突入，越过比利牛斯山脉西端，奋力推进至意大利——其时，身处意大利的汉尼拔，由于所率军队的伤亡人员没有得到补充，所以处境岌岌可危。

当哈斯德鲁巴一路几乎没有什么损失的从北部突入意大利后，此时这场战争已经持续打了10年。他所率的军队，倘若能够与所向披靡的汉尼拔指挥的军队安全会师的话，可能会决定性地逆转整个战争，因为罗马当时本身已经被拖得筋疲力尽了；把各殖民地以及各盟国与罗马绑在一起的那种强大纽带，已经绷到了最大限度，有些地方还开始蠢蠢欲动了。不过，汉尼拔与哈斯德鲁巴两兄弟的形势，也已经危险到了极点。他们当中，一部位于梅陶罗河，另一部则位于阿普利亚，二者相距200英里，各自都面临着一支精锐敌军，而两支罗马军队也全都夹在这两兄弟所率部队之间。这种错误的阵势，以及哈斯德鲁巴久久未能前来支援汉尼拔部，都是由于罗马掌握了制海权；而整个战争期间，罗马的制海权都在阻碍着迦太基的这两兄弟在穿越高卢的进军路线上相互支援。就在哈斯德鲁巴正率军经由陆路，进行这种路途遥远而又危险重重的迂回之时，西庇阿却已从西班牙派遣了11000名士兵，经由海路前去支援与哈斯德鲁巴对抗的那支军队了。结果，哈斯德鲁巴派到汉尼拔那儿去的信使，由于不得不越过多个敌对国家，便落入了指挥南部罗马军队的克劳狄乌斯·尼禄手里，使得尼禄获悉了哈斯德鲁巴计划的行军路

the battle. Hannibal's first news of the disaster was by the head of his brother being thrown into his camp. He is said to have exclaimed that Rome would now be mistress of the world; and the battle of Metaurus is generally accepted as decisive of the struggle between the two States.

  The military situation which finally resulted in the battle of the Metaurus and the triumph of Rome may be summed up as follows: To overthrow Rome it was necessary to attack her in Italy at the heart of her power, and shatter the strongly linked confederacy of which she was the head. This was the objective. To reach it, the Carthaginians needed a solid base of operations and a secure line of communications. The former was established in Spain by the genius of the great Barca family; the latter was never achieved. There were two lines possible, — the one direct by sea, the other circuitous through Gaul. The first was blocked by the Roman sea power, the second imperiled and finally intercepted through the occupation of northern Spain by the Roman army. This occupation was made possible through the control of the sea, which the Carthaginians never endangered. With respect to Hannibal and his base, therefore, Rome occupied two central positions, Rome itself and northern Spain, joined by an easy interior line of communications, the sea; by which mutual support was continually given.

  Had the Mediterranean been a level desert of land, in which the Romans held strong mountain ranges in Corsica and Sardinia, fortified posts at Tarragona, Lilybaeum, and Messina, the Italian coast-line nearly to Genoa, and allied fortresses in Marseilles and other points; had they also possessed an armed force capable by its character of traversing that desert at will, but in which their opponents were very inferior and therefore compelled to a great circuit in order to concentrate their troops, the military situation would have been at once recognized, and no words would have been too strong to express the value and effect of that peculiar force. It would

线。尼禄正确地评估了此时的形势，在没有引起汉尼拔警觉的情况下，率领手下的8000精锐，飞速驰往北方参战。南北两军会师之后，这两位执政官便以压倒性的兵力开始进攻，击溃了哈斯德鲁巴部；这位迦太基将领本人也在战斗中阵亡了。直到敌军将他弟弟的头颅扔进军营，汉尼拔才得知这一噩耗。据说，当时他大叫大喊，说罗马此后就会是世界霸主了；而人们也一致公认，梅陶罗河一役是这两国之间的关键一战。

  最终导致梅陶罗河一役和罗马获胜的军事形势，可以归结如下：要想打倒罗马，就必须在属于其权力中心的意大利发起攻击，并且打破以其为首的强大同盟。这是目标。而要想实现这一目标，迦太基人需要有一个牢固的作战基地和一条安全的交通补给线。伟大的巴尔卡家族凭借他们的才能，已经在西班牙建立起了牢固的作战基地；但后者，却一直都未能实现。迦太基人有两条可能的进军路线——其一是直接从海上进击，而另一条则是穿过高卢，迂回进击。第一条被罗马的海上力量所阻，第二条则危险重重，并且最终也因罗马军队占领西班牙北部而被截断了。罗马军队通过制海权，是可以这样占领西班牙北部的，而迦太基人却一直都没有危及到罗马的制海权。因此，对于汉尼拔及其大本营来说，罗马就占据了两个中枢位置，即罗马本土和西班牙北部地区，它们之间通过毫不费力的内部交通补给线——即海路——相连；通过海路，两地的罗马军队都进行了持续的相互支援。

  假如地中海是一处平坦的陆上沙漠，罗马人掌控了科西嘉岛和撒丁岛上那些坚固的山脉，在靠近热那亚的意大利海岸线上的塔拉戈纳、利利俾和墨西拿等地筑有要塞，并且将马赛与其他各地的要塞都联合起来；假如他们还拥有一支武装力量，特点是能够随时越过这个沙漠，而敌人则没有这种能力，因而不得不绕上一大圈才能把军队集结起来；那

have been perceived, also, that the enemy's force of the same kind might, however inferior in strength, make an inroad, or raid, upon the territory thus held, might burn a village or waste a few miles of borderland, might even cut off a convoy at times, without, in a military sense, endangering the communications. Such predatory operations have been carried on in all ages by the weaker maritime belligerent, but they by no means warrant the inference irreconcilable with the known facts, "that neither Rome nor Carthage could be said to have undisputed mastery of the sea," because "Roman fleets sometimes visited the coasts of Africa, and Carthaginian fleets in the same way appeared off the coast of Italy." In the case under consideration, the navy played the part of such a force upon the supposed desert; but as it acts on an element strange to most writers, as its members have been from time immemorial a strange race apart, without prophets of their own, neither themselves nor their calling understood, its immense determining influence upon the history of that era, and consequently upon the history of the world, has been overlooked. If the preceding argument is sound, it is as defective to omit sea power from the list of principal factors in the result, as it would be absurd to claim for it an exclusive influence.

Instances such as have been cited, drawn from widely separated periods of time, both before and after that specially treated in this work, serve to illustrate the intrinsic interest of the subject, and the character of the lessons which history has to teach. As before observed, these come more often under the head of strategy than of tactics; they bear rather upon the conduct of campaigns than of battles, and hence are fraught with more lasting value. To quote a great authority in this connection, Jomini says: "Happening to be in Paris near the end of 1851, a distinguished person did me the honor to ask my opinion as to whether recent improvements in fire arms would cause any great modifications in the way of making war. I

么，我们马上就能看出此时的军事形势，并且无论怎样高度评价这支特殊军队的价值和作用，也不过分。我们或许还可以认识到，无论兵力多么弱小，同样的一支敌军也可能突袭或袭击罗马所占领土，可能让一个村庄变成焦土或者让其数英里的边陲变成不毛之地，甚至还可能时不时地切断一支护航舰队，但这些从军事意义来看，都并非威胁到了敌方的交通补给线。历朝历代，海上交战国中的弱势一方都曾经进行过这种掠夺性的军事行动，但我们却决不能仅凭这种军事行动，便做出与下述公认事实相矛盾的推断；这些事实就是："既不能说罗马无可争议地掌控着海上，也不能说迦太基无可争议地掌控着海上"，因为"罗马舰队有时会造访非洲沿岸，而迦太基的舰队也同样会出现在意大利沿海"。在前面假定的这种情形中，海军所起的作用，正是所设沙漠中这样一支部队的作用；不过，由于海军是在大多数史学家都不熟悉的环境中作战，由于海上军事人员从远古以来一直就是很奇特的一类人，没有他们自己的"先知书"，人们既不了解他们本身，也不了解他们所从事的这个行业，所以，海军对于那个时代的历史、并因此而对整个世界历史所产生的巨大而具有决定意义的影响，就被人们忽视了。假如前述论点站得住脚，那么，将制海权从结论的主要因素当中略去就是不全面的，跟宣称只有制海权产生了影响这种说法一样荒谬。

诸如本书中我们已经引用的这些例子，都是广泛地从各个时期中选取出来的，既有本书专门论述的这个时期之前的，也有之后的；它们都阐明了这一主题的内在价值，以及这些历史教训的特征。正如我们在前面已经说过的那样，这些战例常常都被归入了战略的范畴，而不是战术的范畴；由于它们针对的是战役的指挥，而不是战斗的指挥，因此具有更多的持久性价值。要引用这个方面的伟人名言的话，则有约米尼[19]，他曾说："1851

replied that they would probably have an influence upon the details of tactics, but that in great strategic operations and the grand combinations of battles, victory would, now as ever, result from the application of the principles which had led to the success of great generals in all ages; of Alexander and Caesar, as well as of Frederick and Napoleon." This study has become more than ever important now to navies, because of the great and steady power of movement possessed by the modern steamer. The best-planned schemes might fail through stress of weather in the days of the galley and the sailing-ship; but this difficulty has almost disappeared. The principles which should direct great naval combinations have been applicable to all ages, and are deducible from history; but the power to carry them out with little regard to the weather is a recent gain.

The definitions usually given of the word "strategy" confine it to military combinations embracing one or more fields of operations, either wholly distinct or mutually dependent, but always regarded as actual or immediate scenes of war. However this may be on shore, a recent French author is quite right in pointing out that such a definition is too narrow for naval strategy. "This," he says, "differs from military strategy in that it is as necessary in peace as in war. Indeed, in peace it may gain its most decisive victories by occupying in a country, either by purchase or treaty, excellent positions which would perhaps hardly be got by war. It learns to profit by all opportunities of settling on some chosen point of a coast, and to render definitive an occupation which at first was only transient." A generation that has seen England within ten years occupy successively Cyprus and Egypt, under terms and conditions on their face transient, but which have not yet led to the abandonment of the positions taken, can readily agree with this remark; which indeed receives constant illustration from the quiet persistency with which all the great sea powers are seeking position after position, less noted and less noteworthy

年末，有位杰出人士恰来巴黎，蒙其赏光问我道，近来火器之改良，会不会给战争方式带来什么巨大的变化。我回答道，此种改良很可能会对战术细节产生影响，但在大的战略行动和大的战役组合中，必须将那些让历代的伟大将领获得成功的基本原则加以应用，方能取胜；诸如亚历山大大帝和恺撒大帝的战争，以及腓特烈大帝和拿破仑的战争。"此种研究，如今由于汽船具有极大而稳定的机动能力而对海军变得越发重要了。在桨帆船和帆船时代，精心制定的作战方案，可能会因天气恶劣而流产；但如今，这个难题差不多已经不复存在了。指导海军进行大战略组合的那些基本原则，历代皆可通用，亦可从历史事实中推断出来；不过，几乎不用考虑天气状况就能应用这些基本原则，却是近来才做得到的。

人们给"战略"这个词所下的定义，通常都将其限制为包含一个或多个作战场所的军事组合；虽说这些战场或是完全独立，或是互为唇齿，但往往都被看作是实际的或直接的战争现场。无论对于陆上战争而言情况如何，近代一位法国作家的观点都是相当正确的；他曾指出，这一定义对于海军战略来说太过狭隘。他说："这与军事战略不同，因为无论是和平时期还是战时，军事战略都是必需的。事实上，在和平时期，可以运用战略，占领一国当中可能难以通过发动战争而获取的某些战略要地——或是通过出钱购买，或是通过缔结条约，来获取最具决定性的胜利。战略教导人们，应当利用好在沿岸某处选定之地安营扎寨的一切机会，并让起初只是暂时的占据状况变成确定无疑的占领状态。"看到了英国在10年之间，通过表面上属于暂据、迄今却仍未放弃这些所占之地的条款和条件，相继占领了塞浦路斯和埃及的那一代人，都是会欣然同意这种说法的；事实上，在不同的海域，凡是本国人民和本国舰船所到之处，所有的海洋大国都在不声不响、孜孜不倦地寻找

than Cyprus and Egypt, in the different seas to which their people and their ships penetrate.

"Naval strategy has indeed for its end to found, support, and increase, as well in peace as in war, the sea power of a country;" and therefore its study has an interest and value for all citizens of a free country, but especially for those who are charged with its foreign and military relations.

The general conditions that either are essential to or powerfully affect the greatness of a nation upon the sea will now be examined; after which a more particular consideration of the various maritime nations of Europe at the middle of the seventeenth century, where the historical survey begins, will serve at once to illustrate and give precision to the conclusions upon the general subject.

Note:

The brilliancy of Nelson's fame, dimming as it does that of all his contemporaries, and the implicit trust felt by England in him as the one man able to save her from the schemes of Napoleon, should not of course obscure the fact that only one portion of the field was, or could be, occupied by him. Napoleon's aim, in the campaign which ended at Trafalgar, was to unite in the West Indies the French fleets of Brest, Toulon, and Rochefort, together with a strong body of Spanish ships, thus forming an overwhelming force which he intended should return together to the English Channel and cover the crossing of the French army. He naturally expected that, with England's interests scattered all over the world, confusion and distraction would arise from ignorance of the destination of the French squadrons, and the English navy be drawn away from his objective point. The portion of the field committed to Nelson was the Mediterranean, where he watched the great arsenal of Toulon and the highways alike to the East and to the Atlantic.

着一个又一个战略要地——虽说它们都不如塞浦路斯和埃及那样知名和值得注意——就经常说明了这一点。"无论是和平时期还是战争时期，海军战略实际上都以确立、维持并扩大一国之制海权为最终目标"；因此，研究海军战略，对于一个自由国家的所有国民来说都是很有意义的；而对那些从事外交与军事关系的人来说，则尤为有价值。

下面，我们就来对那些要么属于必不可少的、要么会强有力地影响到一国制海权的一般性条件来进行研究；然后，再对17世纪中叶欧洲的各个海洋国家加以更为详尽的思考，从此处开始进行历史考察，马上就会正确地阐明我们根据总主题所得出的那些结论了。

注：

虽说纳尔逊的声望与其同时代的所有人一样正在日渐没落，但他的赫赫威名，以及英国人坚定不移地相信他才是能够将英国从拿破仑的阴谋中拯救出来的人，自然不应当掩盖这样一个事实：他只是，或者说只可能是各大作战区域中的一份子。在以特拉法尔加海战告终的那场战役中，拿破仑的目标，是将位于布雷斯特、土伦和罗什福尔的法国舰队与一群强大的西班牙舰船在西印度群岛联合起来，从而形成一支无人能敌的海军力量，并且打算让这支舰队返回英吉利海峡，去掩护法国陆军渡海。由于英国在世界各地都有殖民地，所以他自然希望，英国人会因为不知道法国舰队的目的地是哪儿而产生困惑，并将英国海军调离他所针对的目标。纳尔逊负责的是地中海地区，他在那里警戒着土伦这个大军港，以及通往东方与大西洋的各条交通要道。这件事情的重要性并不亚于其他行动，而由于确信拿破仑还会像以前那样企图攻取埃及，所以在纳尔逊看来，这

This was inferior in consequence to no other, and assumed additional importance in the eyes of Nelson from his conviction that the former attempts on Egypt would be renewed. Owing to this persuasion he took at first a false step, which delayed his pursuit of the Toulon fleet when it sailed under the command of Villeneuve; and the latter was further favored by a long continuance of fair winds, while the English had head winds. But while all this is true, while the failure of Napoleon's combinations must be attributed to the tenacious grip of the English blockade off Brest, as well as to Nelson's energetic pursuit of the Toulon fleet when it escaped to the West Indies and again on its hasty return to Europe, the latter is fairly entitled to the eminent distinction which history has accorded it, and which is asserted in the text. Nelson did not, indeed, fathom the intentions of Napoleon. This may have been owing, as some have said, to lack of insight; but it may be more simply laid to the usual disadvantage under which the defence lies before the blow has fallen, of ignorance as to the point threatened by the offence. It is insight enough to fasten on the key of a situation; and what this Nelson rightly saw was the fleet, not the station. Consequently, his action has afforded a striking instance of how tenacity of purpose and untiring energy in execution can repair a first mistake and baffle deeply laid plans. His Mediterranean command embraced many duties and cares; but amid and dominating them all, he saw clearly the Toulon fleet as the controlling factor there, and an important factor in any naval combination of the Emperor. Hence his attention was unwaveringly fixed upon it; so much so that he called it "his fleet," a phrase which has somewhat vexed the sensibilities of French critics. This simple and accurate view of the military situation strengthened him in taking the fearless resolution and bearing the immense responsibility of abandoning his station in order to follow "his fleet." Determined thus on a pursuit the undeniable wisdom of which should not obscure the greatness of mind that undertook it, he followed so vigorously as to

样做就更加重要了。因为有着这种信念，所以纳尔逊首先就走错了一步棋，拖延了他对由维尔纳夫所指挥的土伦舰队的追击；后者又因碰上长久持续的顺风、英军却需顶风航行而获得了更大的优势。不过，虽说拿破仑战术组合的失败必须归因于英军对于布雷斯特沿岸顽强有力的封锁，以及当土伦舰队遁往西印度群岛、之后又匆匆返回欧洲时，纳尔逊率军进行了积极有力的追击这两个因素，但历史所给予且在本书正文中得到维护的那种殊荣，纳尔逊还是当之无愧的。实际上，纳尔逊并未看穿拿破仑的意图。有人说，这或许是由于纳尔逊缺乏眼力所致；不过，将原因归结于常见的不利条件可能会更加简单：在这种不利条件下，由于不知道对方进攻的危险程度，所以都是先于攻击发起之前进行防守。能够抓住局势的关键，固然很具眼力；而这位纳尔逊，当时却只看到了舰队，而不是自己的战斗位置。因此，他的行动就给我们提供了一个突出的例子，表明不屈不挠地坚持目标且在执行过程中坚持不懈，是如何能够纠正最初所犯的错误，并且挫败对方经过深思熟虑而制定的计划的。他在地中海地区的指挥权，包括了许许多多的职责和操心事；但其中最主要的一项，却是他毫无疑问地认为土伦舰队是那里的控制性因素，也是法兰西帝国所有海军组合中的一个重要因素。因此，他才死死地盯着这支舰队；他如此关注，以至于将其称作是"他的舰队"，而这句话，曾经还让法国的评论家们感情上有点儿受不了呢。纳尔逊对军事形势所抱的这种简单而准确的见解，使得他既坚定又无畏地下定决心，承担起为追击"他的舰队"而放弃战斗岗位的巨大责任。由于决意这样去进行追击，从中体现出来的那种不可否认的智慧，并不会使承担此项任务的人蒙羞，所以他追赶得不遗余力；虽说由于虚假情报以及不确定敌军动向的原因，不可避免地耽搁了一些时

reach Cadiz on his return a week before Villeneuve entered Ferrol, despite unavoidable delays arising from false information and uncertainty as to the enemy's movements. The same untiring ardor enabled him to bring up his own ships from Cadiz to Brest in time to make the fleet there superior to Villeneuve's, had the latter persisted in his attempt to reach the neighborhood. The English, very inferior in aggregate number of vessels to the allied fleets, were by this seasonable reinforcement of eight veteran ships put into the best possible position strategically, as will be pointed out in dealing with similar conditions in the war of the American Revolution. Their forces were united in one great fleet in the Bay of Biscay, interposed between the two divisions of the enemy in Brest and Ferrol, superior in number to either singly, and with a strong probability of being able to deal with one before the other could come up. This was due to able action all round on the part of the English authorities; but above all other factors in the result stands Nelson's single-minded pursuit of "his fleet."

This interesting series of strategic movements ended on the 14th of August, when Villeneuve, in despair of reaching Brest, headed for Cadiz, where he anchored on the 20th. As soon as Napoleon heard of this, after an outburst of rage against the admiral, he at once dictated the series of movements which resulted in Ulm and Austerlitz, abandoning his purposes against England. The battle of Trafalgar, fought October 21, was therefore separated by a space of two months from the extensive movements of which it was nevertheless the outcome. Isolated from them in point of time, it was none the less the seal of Nelson's genius, affixed later to the record he had made in the near past. With equal truth it is said that England was saved at Trafalgar, though the Emperor had then given up his intended invasion; the destruction there emphasized and sealed the strategic triumph which had noiselessly foiled Napoleon's plans.

日,但在返回途中,他还是在维尔纳夫进入费罗尔之前一周便到达了加的斯。也正是这种相同的不懈动力,使得他能够及时将自己的舰队从加的斯调往布雷斯特,从而让那里的兵力超过了维尔纳夫,以防后者试图强行进击布雷斯特附近。那里的英军舰船在总数上本来大大劣于法、西联合舰队,但这一次却得到了8艘经验丰富的舰艇及时支援,并被部署到了最佳的战略位置上——后面在研究美国革命战争中与此相似的一些形势时,我们还会指出这一点。英军在比斯开湾汇合成了一支庞大的舰队,楔在了布雷斯特与费罗尔的两支敌军分舰队之间,不但舰船数量超过了其中的任何一支,而且很可能不待另一支前来支援就可以消灭掉其中的一支。这是由于英国当局处处都采取了出色的行动;不过,在导致这一结果的所有因素当中,最主要的还是纳尔逊一门心思地追击"他的舰队"。

这一系列有趣的战略运动在8月14日结束了;此时,由于前往布雷斯特无望,维尔纳夫便向加的斯进发,并于8月20日在加的斯泊锚了。拿破仑一听到这个消息,对这位海军司令大发了一通雷霆,之后马上就放弃了他对抗英国的那些目标,命令海军进行了一系列战略机动,结果引发了乌尔姆之战与奥斯特利茨之战。因此,10月21日进行的特拉法尔加海战,虽说同全面的军事行动之间有着两个月的间隙,却是这些军事机动所导致的结果。尽管时间上同这些军事机动并不相连,但此战仍然是纳尔逊天才的标志,后来又被添进他在不久前所立下的赫赫战功之中了。有人说,虽然拿破仑这位法兰西皇帝当时已经放弃了自己的入侵计划,但特拉法尔加海战还是拯救了英国,这种说法同样也是正确的;而此处对法军的毁灭性打击,则突出标志了那种无声无息地挫败拿破仑入侵计划的战略大捷。

FOOTNOTES:

[1] Thus Hermocrates of Syracuse, advocating the policy of thwarting the Athenian expedition against his city (B. C. 413) by going boldly to meet it, and keeping on the flank of its line of advance, said: "As their advance must be slow, we shall have a thousand opportunities to attack them; but if they clear their ships for action and in a body bear down expeditiously upon us, they must ply hard at their oars, and when spent with toil we can fall upon them."

[2] The writer must guard himself from appearing to advocate elaborate tactical movements issuing in barren demonstrations. He believes that a fleet seeking a decisive result must close with its enemy, but not until some advantage has been obtained for the collision, which will usually be gained by manoeuvring, and will fall to the best drilled and managed fleet. In truth, barren results have as often followed upon headlong, close encounters as upon the most timid tactical trifling.

[3] A ship was said to have the weather-gage, or "the advantage of the wind," or "to be to windward," when the wind allowed her to steer for her opponent, and did not let the latter head straight for her. The extreme case was when the wind blew direct from one to the other; but there was a large space on either side of this line to which the term "weather-gage" applied. If the lee ship be taken as the centre of a circle, there were nearly three eighths of its area in which the other might be and still keep the advantage of the wind to a greater or less degree. Lee is the opposite of weather.

[4] The battle of Navarino (1827) between Turkey and the Western Powers was fought in this neighborhood.

[5] A "containing" force is one to which, in a military combination, is assigned the duty of stopping, or delaying the advance of a portion of the enemy, while the main effort of the army or armies is being exerted in a different quarter.

原注：

（1）比如，锡拉丘兹的赫莫克拉提斯主张，采用大胆出击、阻遏进击其城邦的雅典远征军（公元前413年）并且坚守雅典远征军进军路线侧翼的政策；他曾说："由于他们的进军必定缓慢下来，所以我们就有无数的机会去进攻他们了；若是他们整理好船只来作战，准备全体出动、袭击我们的话，那他们就必须奋力划桨，而待他们筋疲力尽之时，我们就可以进攻了。"

（2）作者一定是想防止让自己显得似乎是在提倡进行复杂的、导致无益伴动的战术机动。他认为，虽说一支想获得决定性战果的舰队必须接近敌人，但并非一定要待获得某种优势来进行碰撞才罢休；这种优势，通常都会通过舰船的机动获得，并且属于训练最有素、指挥得最好的那支舰队。事实上，无效的伴动过后，往往就是仓促轻率的短兵相接，或者极为胆怯的战术拖延了。

（3）当风向允许一艘舰船驶向敌舰，而敌舰却无法径直驶向我方的时候，我们就说这艘舰船处于上风位置，或者"拥有风向优势"，或者说"顺风"。最极端的情形，便是海风从此舰径直吹向彼舰；不过，在这条线左右两边的广大范围之内，都可用"上风"这个术语。倘若将处于下风位置的舰船看作是一个圆的圆心，那么另一艘船可以在这个圆大约八分之三的面积范围内，或多或少地利用风向优势。"下风"即是"上风"的对立面。

（4）土耳其与西方列强之间的纳瓦里诺之战（1827年）就发生在此处附近。

（5）"牵制"部队是指，在一个联合军事单元中，在部队主力投入别的战场作战时，受命阻止或拖延敌军一部进击的队伍。

译者注：

[1] Donnybrook Fair：唐尼布鲁克集市。指1885年以前，曾经在爱尔兰都柏林东南郊唐尼布鲁克市所举办的、以酒色殴斗著称的一种一年一度的集市。

[2] 罗德尼（George Brydges Rodney，1719～1792）。英国军事家、海军上将，获封罗德尼男爵一世（1st Baron Rodney）。1780年4月7日，他率英国舰队与基申伯爵所率法国海军在马提尼克岛（南美加勒比海地区的一个法国殖民地）海域发生海战。基申伯爵（Comte De Guichen，1712～1790），法国军事家，海军上将。在马提尼克岛海战中，英法双方基本上不分胜负。

[3] Hermocrates：赫莫克拉提斯（公元前5世纪～公元前407年）。伯罗奔尼撒战争中雅典城邦发动西西里远征时期的一位将军，也是柏拉图晚期的对话集《蒂迈欧》（Timaeus）和《克里提亚斯》（Critias）中的人物。

[4] Lord Howe：豪勋爵（Richard Howe，1726～1799）。英国的军事家、舰队司令，曾任海军大臣，获封第一任豪伯爵。他既是一位才能卓异的海军指挥官，也是一位较有远见的政治家。

[5] Lord St. Vincent：圣文森特勋爵（原名John Jervis，1735～1823）。英国海军司令、国会议员，曾指挥舰队参加了"七年战争"、美国独立战争等多次战争。1797年，他在圣文森特角海战中取胜，从而声名大噪，并获封第一任圣文森特伯爵。

[6] 纳尔逊（Horatio Nelson，1758～1805）。英国海军指挥官、军事家，以杰出的领导才能与非常规战术著称，曾获数次海战大捷，1805年死于特拉法尔加海战。

[7] 莫罗盖（Sébastien-Francois Bigot, Vicomte de Morogues，1706～1781）。法国炮兵专家和海军战术家，著有《海军战术》（Tactique navale）一书。

[8] The Battle of the Nile：尼罗河口之战。英、法两国海军于1798年8月1日至2日在尼罗河河口附近发生的一次海战，以英军获胜告终。它是法国大革命战争中最重要的一次海战。由于战斗发生处为阿布基尔湾（Aboukir Bay），故此役又称"阿布基尔湾海战"。

[9] 维尔纳夫（Silvestre de Villeneuve，1763～1806）。法国贵族、海军将领，在1798年的尼罗河河口之战中，他为一艘主力舰的舰长。此役中拿破仑的埃及远征军舰队被纳尔逊歼灭，只有维尔纳夫的这艘舰艇和其他3艘得以逃脱。而在1805年的特拉法尔加海战中，他指挥无方，使得所率的法、西联合舰队再度惨败于纳尔逊之手，而他本人也成了英军的俘虏。

[10] Actium and Lepanto：阿克提姆和勒班陀。都是希腊地名，且都发生过历史上著名的海战。前者如今称为"圣尼古拉奥斯"，公元前31年古罗马帝国的屋大维与安东尼曾在此为争夺帝国的最高权力而爆发海战，以安东尼失败告终；后者如今在希腊语中称为"纳夫帕克托斯（Návpaktos）"，1571年欧洲列强曾在此击败了土耳其帝国。

[11] Levant：黎凡特。指地中海东部的西亚地区，包括埃及和希腊以东诸国和地区，故也译为"远东"或"东方"。

[12] Punic War：布匿战争。古罗马帝国与古迦太基之间为争夺地中海沿岸地区霸权而进行的3次战争，亦称迦太基战争。Punic一词，源于当时罗马人称迦太基为Punici。第一次布匿战争从公元前264年至公元前241年，第二次发生在公元前218年至公元前201年间，第三次则从公元前149年至公元前146年。其中，第二次布匿战争最为有名，当时迦太基一方的统帅即是汉尼拔。

[13] Cannae：坎尼。古城名，在今意大利东南部巴列塔的奥凡托河注入亚得里亚海附近。公元216年，古罗马和迦太基进行的第二次布匿战争期间，迦太基统帅汉尼拔率军和古罗马决战于此，并获大捷。

[14] 蒙森（Christian Matthias Theodor Mommsen，1817～1903）。德国古典学者、法学家、历史学家、记者、政治家、考古学家和作家，1902年诺贝尔文学奖的获得者，著有《罗马史》等作品。

[15] Consular army：执政官（所率）集团军。古罗马最常见的一种部队单元和战斗序列，一般包括两个罗马军团和两支兵力相等的同盟部队，总兵力达2万人。

[16] Phalanx：（马其顿）方阵。一种早期步兵作战时所用的战术。在荷马时代以前，步兵打起仗来像一窝蜂似的，杂乱无章，所以，具有严格阵法的马其顿方阵能够轻易地打败数量上占优势但较混乱的敌人，这在当时可以说是战术上的创新。

[17] 腓力五世（Philip V，公元前238年~前179年），马其顿国王。他在第二次布匿战争中与迦太基结盟，对罗马宣战，从而开始了马其顿战争。

[18] Hanno：汉诺。迦太基将领中有多人均叫此名，但此处的"汉诺"应指汉尼拔的另一个弟弟。

[19] 约米尼（Antoine-Henri Jomini，1779~1869）。法国将领、军事家和作家，曾在瑞士、法国和俄国军队中服役，被誉为"现代战略之父"。

CHAPTER I　Discussion of the Elements of Sea Power

The first and most obvious light in which the sea presents itself from the political and social point of view is that of a great highway; or better, perhaps, of a wide common, over which men may pass in all directions, but on which some well-worn paths show that controlling reasons have led them to choose certain lines of travel rather than others. These lines of travel are called trade routes; and the reasons which have determined them are to be sought in the history of the world.

Notwithstanding all the familiar and unfamiliar dangers of the sea, both travel and traffic by water have always been easier and cheaper than by land. The commercial greatness of Holland was due not only to her shipping at sea, but also to the numerous tranquil water-ways which gave such cheap and easy access to her own interior and to that of Germany. This advantage of carriage by water over that by land was yet more marked in a period when roads were few and very bad, wars frequent and society unsettled, as was the case two hundred years ago. Sea traffic then went in peril of robbers, but was nevertheless safer and quicker than that by land. A Dutch writer of that time, estimating the chances of his country in a war with England, notices among other things that the water-ways of England failed to penetrate the country sufficiently; therefore, the roads being bad, goods from one part of the kingdom to the other must go by sea, and be exposed to capture by the way. As regards purely internal trade, this danger has generally disappeared at the present day. In most civilized countries, now, the destruction or

第一章　海权诸要素之探讨

从政治和社会的观点来看，海洋首先并且最为明显地呈现给人们的就是，它是一条广袤的通途；或者更准确一点来说，是一条宽广的公用通道，人们可以在这条通道上向四面八方通行。但其中存在着一些交通繁忙的线路，这表明还是有着一些控制性的原因，才使得人们选择了这些交通路线而不是其他的。这些交通路线被称作"商路"；而决定它们成为商路的原因，则应从世界历史中去探寻。

虽说海洋上有着人类所熟知与否的种种危险，但经由水路旅行或者说水上交通，一向都比陆路更容易，花费也更少。荷兰的贸易业之所以获得了伟大的成就，不仅是由于其海上航运，也是由于它有着无数风平浪静的水道，使得人们可以经由费用不高而快捷的通道进入荷兰以及德国内地。水路运输相对于陆路运输的这一优势，在陆路数量很少、路况又不佳、战乱频繁、社会不安定的历史时期，则显得更为突出，就像200年前的情况那样。虽说那时的海上交通有遭遇海盗的危险，但还是比陆上交通更加安全和快捷。当时的一位荷兰史学家在评估荷兰与英国开战的可能性时，从中注意到了一个事实，那就是英国的水道并未充分深入到该国内陆；由于陆路状况糟糕，故要将货物从英国的一地运往另一地，就必须经由海路，所以在途中就有可能被敌军夺取。至于纯粹的内陆贸易，如今通常都已不再存在这种危险了。目前，在大多数文明国家，即便沿海贸

disappearance of the coasting trade would only be an inconvenience, although water transit is still the cheaper. Nevertheless, as late as the wars of the French Republic and the First Empire, those who are familiar with the history of the period, and the light naval literature that has grown up around it, know how constant is the mention of convoys stealing from point to point along the French coast, although the sea swarmed with English cruisers and there were good inland roads.

Under modern conditions, however, home trade is but a part of the business of a country bordering on the sea. Foreign necessaries or luxuries must be brought to its ports, either in its own or in foreign ships, which will return, bearing in exchange the products of the country, whether they be the fruits of the earth or the works of men's hands; and it is the wish of every nation that this shipping business should be done by its own vessels. The ships that thus sail to and fro must have secure ports to which to return, and must, as far as possible, be followed by the protection of their country throughout the voyage.

This protection in time of war must be extended by armed shipping. The necessity of a navy, in the restricted sense of the word, springs, therefore, from the existence of a peaceful shipping, and disappears with it, except in the case of a nation which has aggressive tendencies, and keeps up a navy merely as a branch of the military establishment. As the United States has at present no aggressive purposes, and as its merchant service has disappeared, the dwindling of the armed fleet and general lack of interest in it are strictly logical consequences. When for any reason sea trade is again found to pay, a large enough shipping interest will reappear to compel the revival of the war fleet. It is possible that when a canal route through the Central-American Isthmus is seen to be a near certainty, the aggressive impulse may be strong enough to lead to the same result. This is doubtful, however, because a peaceful, gain-loving nation is not far-sighted, and far-sightedness is needed for adequate military preparation, especially in

易遭到破坏或者没有沿海贸易，也只是会让人觉得不方便罢了；但是，水上交通依然是费用较低的一种运输方式。虽说如此，晚至法兰西共和国与法兰西第一帝国的战争期间，那些熟悉这一时期历史的人都知道，而从发展于这一时期的一些消遣性海军文学作品当中也可看出，人们经常提及沿着法国海岸线到处劫掠的私掠船队，尽管此时海上到处都是英国的巡逻舰船，而英国国内也有着良好的内陆道路。

然而，在现代环境下，国内贸易只是沿海国家商业的一部分。外国出产的生活必需品和奢侈品，都得用本国船只或外国船只运送到本国的港口来；然后，这些船只又会载上该国的产品返航，或是农产品，或是手工艺品；而每一个国家，都希望这种海上运输由本国的船只来进行。如此往来航行的船只，必须拥有安全的返航港口，并且在整个航行过程中，必须充分得到本国的保护才行。

在战争时期，就必须由武装运送来实施此种护卫了。因此，从严格意义上来说，之所以需要海军，原因即在于存在和平海运这一事实；并且，海军会随着和平海运的消失而消失，除非是一个国家有着侵略野心，纯粹将它作为军事编制中的一个分支。由于美国目前并无侵略目标，由于其海上贸易已经消失，所以其武装舰船数量减少、民众对海军兴趣渐失，完全是一种合乎逻辑的结果。但无论出于何种原因，只要人们再次发现海上贸易有利可图，就会重新出现一种规模巨大的海运事业，迫使军事舰队重新发展起来。有可能，当穿过中美地峡的运河开通之后，那种侵略的欲望可能会很强大，从而导致出现相同的结果。然而，这一点还是未知之数，因为一个太平而趋利的国家是不会眼光远大的；而要做好充分的军事准备，则需要远大的眼光，尤其是在如今这个时代。

these days.

As a nation, with its unarmed and armed shipping, launches forth from its own shores, the need is soon felt of points upon which the ships can rely for peaceful trading, for refuge and supplies. In the present day friendly, though foreign, ports are to be found all over the world; and their shelter is enough while peace prevails. It was not always so, nor does peace always endure, though the United States have been favored by so long a continuance of it. In earlier times the merchant seaman, seeking for trade in new and unexplored regions, made his gains at risk of life and liberty from suspicious or hostile nations, and was under great delays in collecting a full and profitable freight. He therefore intuitively sought at the far end of his trade route one or more stations, to be given to him by force or favor, where he could fix himself or his agents in reasonable security, where his ships could lie in safety, and where the merchantable products of the land could be continually collecting, awaiting the arrival of the home fleet, which should carry them to the mother-country. As there was immense gain, as well as much risk, in these early voyages, such establishments naturally multiplied and grew until they became colonies; whose ultimate development and success depended upon the genius and policy of the nation from which they sprang, and form a very great part of the history, and particularly of the sea history, of the world. All colonies had not the simple and natural birth and growth above described. Many were more formal, and purely political, in their conception and founding, the act of the rulers of the people rather than of private individuals; but the trading-station with its after expansion, the work simply of the adventurer seeking gain, was in its reasons and essence the same as the elaborately organized and chartered colony. In both cases the mother-country had won a foothold in a foreign land, seeking a new outlet for what it had to sell, a new sphere for its shipping, more employment for its people, more comfort and wealth for itself.

一旦一个国家的非武装舰船或者武装舰船从本国海岸起航，人们很快就会感受到船只赖以进行和平贸易、避难和补给的种种需要了。如今，世界各地都可找到虽说陌生、态度却很友好的港口；当和平是世界主流的时候，有这些港口的庇护就足够了。不过，虽说美国已经得天独厚，享受了长久的和平形势，但情况不会总是如此，而和平也并非总能永远持续下去。在早期，那些希望同新的、未开发的地区进行贸易的海上商务人士，是冒着自己的生命危险，在猜忌或者怀有敌意的国度上岸；并且，要想采集到能够装满船只、有利可赚的货物，往往耗时甚久。因此，他们会本能地在商路的尽头寻找一个或者多个驻地，无论是通过武力取得还是通过好感获取，以便让自己或代办们在该地拥有合理的安全保障，让自己的船只能够安全地泊锚，并且能够持续采集该地的适销商品，然后等着本国舰队到来，带领他们回国。由于利润巨大，风险也高，所在这些早期的航海活动中，这样的驻地自然就越来越多，最后变成了各个殖民地；这些殖民地的最终发展和成功，则取决于其所属国家当中的天才人物和政策，而其发展与成功又构成了世界历史，尤其是世界海洋史的一大组成部分。殖民地的出现和发展，并非都像上面所描述的那样简单而自然。许多殖民地在其计划与成立之时，都是统治者的行动而非个人行为，所以更多的是一种形式，纯属政治考量；不过，贸易站点及其日后的扩张和探险者唯求谋利的行为，它们的出发点与本质，都与经过深思熟虑的组织并特许建立起来的殖民地是一样的。在这两种情况下，母国都是在国外获得了据点，找到了出售本国商品的新途径和一种新的海运领域，使本国人民有了新的就业机会，并使本国获得了支援和财富。

The needs of commerce, however, were not all provided for when safety had been secured at the far end of the road. The voyages were long and dangerous, the seas often beset with enemies. In the most active days of colonizing there prevailed on the sea a lawlessness the very memory of which is now almost lost, and the days of settled peace between maritime nations were few and far between. Thus arose the demand for stations along the road, like the Cape of Good Hope, St. Helena, and Mauritius, not primarily for trade, but for defence and war; the demand for the possession of posts like Gibraltar, Malta, Louisburg, at the entrance of the Gulf of St. Lawrence, — posts whose value was chiefly strategic, though not necessarily wholly so. Colonies and colonial posts were sometimes commercial, sometimes military in their character; and it was exceptional that the same position was equally important in both points of view, as New York was.

In these three things — production, with the necessity of exchanging products, shipping, whereby the exchange is carried on, and colonies, which facilitate and enlarge the operations of shipping and tend to protect it by multiplying points of safety — is to be found the key to much of the history, as well as of the policy, of nations bordering upon the sea. The policy has varied both with the spirit of the age and with the character and clear-sightedness of the rulers; but the history of the seaboard nations has been less determined by the shrewdness and foresight of governments than by conditions of position, extent, configuration, number and character of their people, — by what are called, in a word, natural conditions. It must however be admitted, and will be seen, that the wise or unwise action of individual men has at certain periods had a great modifying influence upon the growth of sea power in the broad sense, which includes not only the military strength afloat, that rules the sea or any part of it by force of arms, but also the peaceful commerce and shipping from which alone a military fleet naturally and healthfully

然而，当商路另一端的安全得到了保障之后，所有的贸易需求并非全都就此得到了满足。航程既遥远又危险，而海上经常到处都是敌人。在各国纷纷进行殖民的那些年代，海洋基本上处于一种无管理的状况，可如今的人几乎都已完全忘记了；当时的海洋国家之间通过和平解决争端的情况，是极为罕见的。这样一来，就需要在商路沿线设立驻地了，比如好望角、圣海伦那以及毛里求斯，其主要目的原本并非是为了贸易，而是为了防卫和作战；这样一来，也就需要占据诸如直布罗陀、马耳他和圣劳伦斯湾入口的路易斯堡等要塞了——占领这些要塞的意义，主要是战略性的，虽说情况并非一概如此。从特征上来看，殖民地和殖民据点有的时候是商业性的，有的时候又是军事性的；同一个地方从两个方面来看都同等重要，比如纽约，则属于例外情况。

在这三个方面——产品与商品贸易的必要性，实施商品贸易的海运，促进和扩大海运规模并且通过增加安全地点而有助于保护海运的殖民地——当中，我们可以看到大部分历史、政策以及临海国家的关键线索。政策既会随着时代精神的不同而改变，也会随着历任统治者的性格与眼光不同而改变；但沿海国家的历史，却较少由政府的英明与远见所决定，更多的是取决于其地理位置、国土范围、资源配置、人口数量以及民族性格——总而言之，即是由我们所称的自然条件所决定。然而，我们非但必须承认，而将来也会看到，个人在某些特定时期的英明之举或不明智的行为，对于广义上的海权发展会产生一种极大的修正性影响；这种影响，不但包括利用武力统治海洋或其一部分的海上军事力量，还包括了和平贸易，以及使得军事性舰队自然而健全地出现并且是确保军事性舰队安全之基础的海运。

springs, and on which it securely rests.

The principal conditions affecting the sea power of nations may be enumerated as follows: I. Geographical Position. II. Physical Conformation, including, as connected therewith, natural productions and climate. III. Extent of Territory. IV. Number of Population. V. Character of the People. VI. Character of the Government, including therein the national institutions.

I. Geographical Position. — It may be pointed out, in the first place, that if a nation be so situated that it is neither forced to defend itself by land nor induced to seek extension of its territory by way of the land, it has, by the very unity of its aim directed upon the sea, an advantage as compared with a people one of whose boundaries is continental. This has been a great advantage to England over both France and Holland as a sea power. The strength of the latter was early exhausted by the necessity of keeping up a large army and carrying on expensive wars to preserve her independence; while the policy of France was constantly diverted, sometimes wisely and sometimes most foolishly, from the sea to projects of continental extension. These military efforts expended wealth; whereas a wiser and consistent use of her geographical position would have added to it.

The geographical position may be such as of itself to promote a concentration, or to necessitate a dispersion, of the naval forces. Here again the British Islands have an advantage over France. The position of the latter, touching the Mediterranean as well as the ocean, while it has its advantages, is on the whole a source of military weakness at sea. The eastern and western French fleets have only been able to unite after passing through the Straits of Gibraltar, in attempting which they have often risked and sometimes suffered loss. The position of the United States upon the two oceans would be either a source of great weakness or a cause of enormous expense, had it a large sea commerce on both coasts.

影响到各国制海权的主要条件，可以列举如下：（一）地理位置。（二）自然结构，包括与之相关的自然物产与气候。（三）领土范围。（四）人口数量。（五）民族性格。（六）政府的特征，包括其国家机构的特征。

（一）**地理位置**——首先不妨指出，倘若一个国家的地理位置，使得它既无需在陆地上捍卫自身，也不会受到诱惑，经由陆路去试图扩张自己的领土范围，那么，由于其目标一致针对的是海洋，所以它跟那些边境之一为陆地的民族相比，就具有了一种优势。作为一个海洋大国，英国胜过法国和荷兰的一大优势一直就是这一点。荷兰的力量，早就因为必须维持一支庞大的陆军、必须进行代价巨大的战争来保护本国的独立而消耗殆尽了；而法国的政策有的时候非常英明，有的时候又极为愚蠢，目标一直都在从海上扩张向陆上扩张偏移。这些军事活动都会消耗国家的财力；而更聪明地坚持利用本国的地理位置，却是会增加国家财力的。

地理位置本身既可以促进海军进行集结，又可以迫使海军解散。在这个方面，不列颠群岛又一次具备了胜过法兰西的一种优势。后者的位置既临地中海，又临大西洋，尽管也有着自己的优势，但总体上却是使得法国海上力量薄弱的一个原因。分处东、西两面的法国舰队，只有穿过直布罗陀海峡之后才能汇合起来；法国舰队经常冒着这样的危险，有时还损失惨重。地处两大洋之间的美国，倘若东西沿海都有着大规模的海上贸易，那么它的地理位置要么会成为其海上力量极为薄弱的一个原因，要么就会让它付出高昂的代价。

由于拥有一个庞大的殖民帝国，所以英国已经失去了这种优势的许多方面，无法将

England, by her immense colonial empire, has sacrificed much of this advantage of concentration of force around her own shores; but the sacrifice was wisely made, for the gain was greater than the loss, as the event proved. With the growth of her colonial system her war fleets also grew, but her merchant shipping and wealth grew yet faster. Still, in the wars of the American Revolution, and of the French Republic and Empire, to use the strong expression of a French author, "England, despite the immense development of her navy, seemed ever, in the midst of riches, to feel all the embarrassment of poverty." The might of England was sufficient to keep alive the heart and the members; whereas the equally extensive colonial empire of Spain, through her maritime weakness, but offered so many points for insult and injury.

The geographical position of a country may not only favor the concentration of its forces, but give the further strategic advantage of a central position and a good base for hostile operations against its probable enemies. This again is the case with England; on the one hand she faces Holland and the northern powers, on the other France and the Atlantic. When threatened with a coalition between France and the naval powers of the North Sea and the Baltic, as she at times was, her fleets in the Downs and in the Channel, and even that off Brest, occupied interior positions, and thus were readily able to interpose their united force against either one of the enemies which should seek to pass through the Channel to effect a junction with its ally. On either side, also, Nature gave her better ports and a safer coast to approach. Formerly this was a very serious element in the passage through the Channel; but of late, steam and the improvement of her harbors have lessened the disadvantage under which France once labored. In the days of sailing-ships, the English fleet operated against Brest making its base at Torbay and Plymouth. The plan was simply this: in easterly or moderate weather the blockading fleet kept its position without difficulty; but in westerly gales, when too severe, they bore up

兵力集中到自己的沿海地区；不过，做出这种牺牲是很英明的，因为历史最终证明，它获得的利益要比失去的东西多得多。随着殖民体系的成长，其作战舰队也发展起来，因而英国的商船运输和国家财力增长得甚至更快了。尽管如此，但在美国革命战争期间，在法兰西共和国和法兰西帝国战争期间，用一位法国作家措辞强烈的话语来说，就是："虽说海军得到了巨大的发展，但英国身处各个富裕国家当中时，似乎永远都觉得自己穷得要命。"当时，英国的实力已经足以维持本国和各个殖民地的生存了；而西班牙这个同样广袤的殖民帝国，却因其海上力量薄弱，受到了他国的侮辱和侵害。

一个国家的地理位置，不仅会有利于其兵力集结，还可以带来进一步的战略优势，使之具有核心的阵地和优良的基地，以防可能的敌人发动敌对行动。这种优势，又是英国所拥有的；它一面朝着荷兰和北欧各个列强，另一面则朝着法兰西和大西洋。有的时候，倘若法国与北海、波罗的海各个海上强国联合起来威胁到英国，那么位于唐斯锚地和英吉利海峡的英国舰队，甚至是位于布雷斯特沿海的英国舰队，都可以回到国内严阵以待，从而能够轻而易举地将这些舰队的兵力联合起来，集中打击试图穿过英吉利海峡、去与其盟国汇合的敌人。在其两侧，大自然也将一些更加优良的港口和能更安全靠近的海岸赐予给了英国。在以前，这是通过英吉利海峡的一个重要因素；但近来，蒸汽动力的出现以及这些海港条件的改善，已经弱化了法国曾经所苦的那种劣势。在帆船时代，英国舰队进击布雷斯特时，曾将基地设在托贝港和普利茅斯。这种部署的目的很简单：在刮东风或者天气平稳的时候，负责封锁的舰队可以毫不费力地守住自己的作战位置；而在刮起猛烈的西风时，舰队便可顺风驶向英国的港口，因为英军知道，法国舰队在风向改变之前是没法出击

for English ports, knowing that the French fleet could not get out till the wind shifted, which equally served to bring them back to their station.

The advantage of geographical nearness to an enemy, or to the object of attack, is nowhere more apparent than in that form of warfare which has lately received the name of commerce-destroying, which the French call guerre de course. This operation of war, being directed against peaceful merchant vessels which are usually defenceless, calls for ships of small military force. Such ships, having little power to defend themselves, need a refuge or point of support near at hand; which will be found either in certain parts of the sea controlled by the fighting ships of their country, or in friendly harbors. The latter give the strongest support, because they are always in the same place, and the approaches to them are more familiar to the commerce-destroyer than to his enemy. The nearness of France to England has thus greatly facilitated her guerre de course directed against the latter. Having ports on the North Sea, on the Channel, and on the Atlantic, her cruisers started from points near the focus of English trade, both coming and going. The distance of these ports from each other, disadvantageous for regular military combinations, is an advantage for this irregular secondary operation; for the essence of the one is concentration of effort, whereas for commerce-destroying diffusion of effort is the rule. Commerce-destroyers scatter, that they may see and seize more prey. These truths receive illustration from the history of the great French privateers, whose bases and scenes of action were largely on the Channel and North Sea, or else were found in distant colonial regions, where islands like Guadaloupe and Martinique afforded similar near refuge. The necessity of renewing coal makes the cruiser of the present day even more dependent than of old on his port. Public opinion in the United States has great faith in war directed against an enemy's commerce; but it must be remembered that the Republic has no ports very near the great centers of trade abroad.

的，而风向一旦改变，又会将英国舰队重新带回到自己的作战位置上去。

地理位置上靠近敌人或攻击目标的这一优势，在哪里也没有在最近才得名的"贸易破坏战"这一战争形式中体现得更加明显；法国人称之为"游击战"。这种作战行动，由于通常针对的是没有自卫能力的普通商船，因此只需配备了小支军队的舰船来实施。这种舰船基本上也没有什么自卫能力，所以需要就近有隐蔽之处或者补给点；这种地方，要么是本国军舰所控制的某些海域，要么就是与本国交好的外邦海港。后者对这种舰船的支援力度最大，因为港口总是在同一个地方，所以贸易破坏舰前往这种港口时，要比敌舰前往此种港口更为轻车熟路。法国与英国相距甚近，因此极大地助长了法国针对英国而进行的"游击战"。由于在北海、英吉利海峡和大西洋沿岸都有港口，所以法国巡洋舰的出发之地，离英国进行贸易的中心地带很近。这些港口之间的距离，虽说不利于进行常规的军事联合部署，但对于这种非常规的、辅助性的作战行动来说，却是一种优势；因为对于前者来说，最重要的特点就是集中兵力，而对于贸易破坏战来说，其原则却是扩散兵力。贸易破坏舰会散布于各处，从而可以发现并捕获更多的商船。那些了不起的法国私掠船的历史，就说明了这种事实；这些私掠船的据点与作战场所，主要都是在英吉利海峡和北海上，不然就是在一些遥远的殖民地区，比如瓜达鲁佩岛与马提尼克岛，它们为私掠船提供了相似的、距离不远的隐蔽点。由于需要加煤，所以如今的巡洋舰比过去的巡洋舰更加依赖于港口了。美国人都极为认同这种针对敌国贸易所进行的战争；但我们必须记住，美国并没有与大型海外贸易中心相距极近的港口。因此，美国的地理位置非常不利于成功地进行此种贸易破坏战，除非它能够在盟国的一些港口中建立自己的据点。

Her geographical position is therefore singularly disadvantageous for carrying on successful commerce-destroying, unless she find bases in the ports of an ally.

If, in addition to facility for offence, Nature has so placed a country that it has easy access to the high sea itself, while at the same time it controls one of the great thoroughfares of the world's traffic, it is evident that the strategic value of its position is very high. Such again is, and to a greater degree was, the position of England. The trade of Holland, Sweden, Russia, Denmark, and that which went up the great rivers to the interior of Germany, had to pass through the Channel close by her doors; for sailing-ships hugged the English coast. This northern trade had, moreover, a peculiar bearing upon sea power; for naval stores, as they are commonly called, were mainly drawn from the Baltic countries.

But for the loss of Gibraltar, the position of Spain would have been closely analogous to that of England. Looking at once upon the Atlantic and the Mediterranean, with Cadiz on the one side and Cartagena on the other, the trade to the Levant must have passed under her hands, and that round the Cape of Good Hope not far from her doors. But Gibraltar not only deprived her of the control of the Straits, it also imposed an obstacle to the easy junction of the two divisions of her fleet.

At the present day, looking only at the geographical position of Italy, and not at the other conditions affecting her sea power, it would seem that with her extensive sea-coast and good ports she is very well placed for exerting a decisive influence on the trade route to the Levant and by the Isthmus of Suez. This is true in a degree, and would be much more so did Italy now hold all the islands naturally Italian; but with Malta in the hands of England, and Corsica in those of France, the advantages of her geographical position are largely neutralized. From race affinities and situation those two islands are as legitimately objects of desire to Italy as Gibraltar

倘若除了赋予一国以进攻的条件，大自然还让该国位于一处既能够毫不费力地前往公海，同时还控制了世界交通要道之一的位置，那么很显然，该国地理位置所具有的战略意义就是很重大的了。英国的位置，在很大程度上又是这样。荷兰、瑞典、俄罗斯、丹麦等国的贸易，以及沿一些大河而上、直达德国内陆地区的贸易，都得经由靠近英国国门的英吉利海峡；因为帆船都是沿着英国海岸航行的。此外，这种北方贸易对制海权还存在着一种独特的影响；因为通常所称的海军军需，主要都是从波罗的海沿岸各国获取的。

如果没有失去直布罗陀，西班牙的位置跟英国的位置本来是极为相似的。由于直接濒临大西洋和地中海，并且朝大西洋一侧是加的斯，朝地中海一侧是卡塔赫纳，所以欧洲通往黎凡特的商路，就必须经过西班牙掌控的地区，即使是绕道好望角的贸易线路，也离西班牙的国门不远。不过，直布罗陀非但使西班牙失去了对直布罗陀海峡的控制权，还构成了一处障碍，使得它原本容易汇合的两支舰队，如今无法轻易会师了。

在如今，倘若只看地理位置，而不考虑影响到制海权的其他条件的话，那么，由于有着漫长的海岸线和诸多优良的港口，意大利的地理位置似乎就非常不错，可以对通往黎凡特或经由苏伊士地峡的贸易线路施加决定性的影响。在某种程度上来说，的确是这样；而要是意大利如今还拥有原属于它的所有岛屿的话，就更是如此了。不过，由于马耳他由英国控制，而科西嘉则在法国手里，所以意大利在地理位置上的优势，就大打折扣了。从种族亲疏和位置来说，这两个岛都是意大利希望拥有的合理目标，就像直布罗陀与西班牙的关系那样。倘若亚德里亚海是一条巨大的贸易通途，那么意大利的位置也会有影响力得多。地理完整性当中的这些瑕疵，加上不利于形成制海权的一些其他原因，使得意大利是

is to Spain. If the Adriatic were a great highway of commerce, Italy's position would be still more influential. These defects in her geographical completeness, combined with other causes injurious to a full and secure development of sea power, make it more than doubtful whether Italy can for some time be in the front rank among the sea nations.

As the aim here is not an exhaustive discussion, but merely an attempt to show, by illustration, how vitally the situation of a country may affect its career upon the sea, this division of the subject may be dismissed for the present; the more so as instances which will further bring out its importance will continually recur in the historical treatment. Two remarks, however, are here appropriate.

Circumstances have caused the Mediterranean Sea to play a greater part in the history of the world, both in a commercial and a military point of view, than any other sheet of water of the same size. Nation after nation has striven to control it, and the strife still goes on. Therefore a study of the conditions upon which preponderance in its waters has rested, and now rests, and of the relative military values of different points upon its coasts, will be more instructive than the same amount of effort expended in another field. Furthermore, it has at the present time a very marked analogy in many respects to the Caribbean Sea, — an analogy which will be still closer if a Panama canal-route ever be completed. A study of the strategic conditions of the Mediterranean, which have received ample illustration, will be an excellent prelude to a similar study of the Caribbean, which has comparatively little history.

The second remark bears upon the geographical position of the United States relatively to a Central-American canal. If one be made, and fulfill the hopes of its builders, the Caribbean will be changed from a terminus, and place of local traffic, or at best a broken and imperfect line of travel, as it now is, into one of the great highways of the world. Along this path a great commerce

不是能够在一段时间内跻身于一流海洋大国这个问题变得令人怀疑。

由于此处的目的并非是进行无休无止的讨论，而只是想通过实例说明，一国的位置会如何严重地影响到其海洋事业的发展，所以我们不妨暂时把这部分内容先放一放；后面的历史论述中，还会经常出现更多深入揭示其重要性的实例。不过，下面这两种说法还是恰如其分的。

从贸易和军事角度来看，环境已使得地中海对世界历史所起的作用，比其他任何同等面积的水域对世界历史所起的作用都要大。无数国家，一个接一个地都想控制地中海，并且这种努力如今仍在继续着。因此，对地中海这一海域的优势条件，以及沿岸相对军事意义进行研究，就会比对其他领域进行相同的研究更为有益。此外，如今的地中海，在许多方面都与加勒比海有着显著的相似之处——假如经由马拿马运河的贸易线路建成了的话，那二者就更为类似了。因此，研究已有大量例证的地中海地区战略条件，就会成为一种极佳的前奏，从而开启对历史相对较短的加勒比海地区进行相似研究的过程。

第二种说法，关系到美国相对于中美运河的地理位置。如果开凿一条运河，并且能够达成开凿者的希望，那么加勒比海就会从如今的商路终点和一个局部的交通中心，或者充其量是一条断断续续而不完整的交通线，变成世界的大型交通要道之一。沿着这条线路，会形成规模巨大的商业贸易，会将其他大国的利益、欧洲各国的利益，前所未有地带到我们的沿海地区。这样一来，我们就不会再像以前那样容易置身于国际纠纷之外了。美国相对于这条商路的位置，与英国相对于英吉利海峡的位置，与地中海沿岸各国

will travel, bringing the interests of the other great nations, the European nations, close along our shores, as they have never been before. With this it will not be so easy as heretofore to stand aloof from international complications. The position of the United States with reference to this route will resemble that of England to the Channel, and of the Mediterranean countries to the Suez route. As regards influence and control over it, depending upon geographical position, it is of course plain that the centre of the national power, the permanent base, [1] is much nearer than that of other great nations. The positions now or hereafter occupied by them on island or mainland, however strong, will be but outposts of their power; while in all the raw materials of military strength no nation is superior to the United States. She is, however, weak in a confessed unpreparedness for war; and her geographical nearness to the point of contention loses some of its value by the character of the Gulf coast, which is deficient in ports combining security from an enemy with facility for repairing war-ships of the first class, without which ships no country can pretend to control any part of the sea. In case of a contest for supremacy in the Caribbean, it seems evident from the depth of the South Pass of the Mississippi, the nearness of New Orleans, and the advantages of the Mississippi Valley for water transit, that the main effort of the country must pour down that valley, and its permanent base of operations be found there. The defence of the entrance to the Mississippi, however, presents peculiar difficulties; while the only two rival ports, Key West and Pensacola, have too little depth of water, and are much less advantageously placed with reference to the resources of the country. To get the full benefit of superior geographical position, these defects must be overcome. Furthermore, as her distance from the Isthmus, though relatively less, is still considerable, the United States will have to obtain in the Caribbean stations fit for contingent, or secondary, bases of operations; which by their natural advantages, susceptibility of defence, and nearness to the central strategic issue, will enable her

相对于经由苏伊士运河的那条商路的位置，都很相似。至于影响和控制这条商路取决于地理位置这个方面，很显然的是，美国的国家权力中心这个永久性的基地[1]，跟其他大国的权力中心相比，距其相应的商路要近得多。这些国家目前或日后在岛屿或者大陆上所占的位置，无论多么强大，都将只是各国势力的边远基地罢了；而在支撑军事实力的全部原生因素方面，也没有哪一个国家胜过了美国。不过，美国在尽人皆知的备战方面很不行；而其地理位置虽说靠近各国纷争之地，这一优势却因墨西哥湾沿岸的特点而少了许多价值——因为在墨西哥湾沿岸，没有足够多拥有能维修先进战舰的设备并能防御敌人进攻的港口；而没有这样的港口，任何国家的军舰都是无法伪称自己控制了哪处海洋的。倘若出现各国争夺加勒比海地区霸权的情况，那么，从密西西比河"南方通道"的水深、新奥尔良的近便以及密西西比河流域的水运优势来看，美国的主要精力似乎必须放在这一流域才行，而美国永久性的作战基地也应当建在此处。然而，防守密西西比河河口却有着重重特殊的困难；仅有的基韦斯特与彭萨科拉这两处可与对手相匹敌的港口却又太浅，并且从获取该国资源来看，它们在位置上也没有什么优势。要想获得地理位置所带来的全部好处，就必须克服这些不利之处。更何况，美国与中美地峡之间的距离虽说相对较短，但仍属遥远，所以在加勒比海上，美国必须拥有适于建立临时的或辅助性作战基地的据点才行；凭借其自然优势、易守难攻以及靠近核心战略争端之地的特点，这些据点就能够让美国的舰队跟敌人的舰队一样地靠近战场了。充分保护好密西西比河的出入口，手中又拥有这样的前沿基地，并且保障好这些基地与大本营之间的交通联系之后——一言以蔽之，就是利用该国所拥有的一切必要手段，做好充分的军事

fleets to remain as near the scene as any opponent. With ingress and egress from the Mississippi sufficiently protected, with such outposts in her hands, and with the communications between them and the home base secured, in short, with proper military preparation, for which she has all necessary means, the preponderance of the United States on this field follows, from her geographical position and her power, with mathematical certainty.

II. Physical Conformation. — The peculiar features of the Gulf coast, just alluded to, come properly under the head of Physical Conformation of a country, which is placed second for discussion among the conditions which affect the development of sea power.

The seaboard of a country is one of its frontiers; and the easier the access offered by the frontier to the region beyond, in this case the sea, the greater will be the tendency of a people toward intercourse with the rest of the world by it. If a country be imagined having a long seaboard, but entirely without a harbor, such a country can have no sea trade of its own, no shipping, no navy. This was practically the case with Belgium when it was a Spanish and an Austrian province. The Dutch, in 1648, as a condition of peace after a successful war, exacted that the Scheldt should be closed to sea commerce. This closed the harbor of Antwerp and transferred the sea trade of Belgium to Holland. The Spanish Netherlands ceased to be a sea power.

Numerous and deep harbors are a source of strength and wealth, and doubly so if they are the outlets of navigable streams, which facilitate the concentration in them of a country's internal trade; but by their very accessibility they become a source of weakness in war, if not properly defended. The Dutch in 1667 found little difficulty in ascending the Thames and burning a large fraction of the English navy within sight of London; whereas a few years later the combined fleets of England and France, when attempting a landing in Holland, were foiled by

准备之后，美国在这个方面便会因为地理位置而带来优势，而它在这一地区取得霸权地位，也是确定无疑的了。

（二）自然结构——我们刚才已经提到，墨西哥湾沿岸具有独特的特征，它完全适合于归入一个国家的"自然结构"当中，是我们在影响制海权发展的条件中进行讨论的第二个问题。

海岸线是一个国家的边境之一；而由边境通往异域（在此种情形下，异域即是海洋）的途径越便捷，一个民族经由此种途径与世界其他民族进行交流的意向就会越强烈。想像一下，假如一个国家具有漫长的海岸线，却根本没有海港，那么这种国家就不可能有自己的海上贸易，不可能拥有自己的海上运输，也不可能拥有自己的海军。比利时在它还是西班牙和奥地利一个行省的时候，差不多正是这种情况。1648年，在成功地打赢了一场战争之后的和平状态下，荷兰人坚持要求不得将斯凯尔特河向海上贸易开放。这种做法使得安特卫普港关闭了，并将比利时的海上贸易转移到了荷兰。这样一来，西属尼德兰便不再是一个海上强国了。

数量众多的深水海港，是一国的国力与财富之源；而倘若它们同时还是可通航河流的入海口，那就更加如此了——这些可通航的河流，会使得该国的国内贸易都集中于这些河流上；但是，也正因为它们容易到达，所以在战争中，若是防守不当的话，这些河流就会变成其薄弱之处。1667年，荷兰人不费吹灰之力便沿泰晤士河而上，在距伦敦不远的地方焚毁了英国海军的大部；而数年之后，英、法两国的联合舰队试图在荷兰登陆时，却遭到了荷兰舰队的顽强抵抗，还被荷兰沿海的重重困难所阻，因此不得不无功

the difficulties of the coast as much as by the valor of the Dutch fleet. In 1778 the harbor of New York, and with it undisputed control of the Hudson River, would have been lost to the English, who were caught at disadvantage, but for the hesitancy of the French admiral. With that control, New England would have been restored to close and safe communication with New York, New Jersey, and Pennsylvania; and this blow, following so closely on Burgoyne's disaster of the year before, would probably have led the English to make an earlier peace. The Mississippi is a mighty source of wealth and strength to the United States; but the feeble defences of its mouth and the number of its subsidiary streams penetrating the country made it a weakness and source of disaster to the Southern Confederacy. And lastly, in 1814, the occupation of the Chesapeake and the destruction of Washington gave a sharp lesson of the dangers incurred through the noblest water-ways, if their approaches be undefended; a lesson recent enough to be easily recalled, but which, from the present appearance of the coast defences, seems to be yet more easily forgotten. Nor should it be thought that conditions have changed; circumstances and details of offence and defence have been modified, in these days as before, but the great conditions remain the same.

Before and during the great Napoleonic wars, France had no port for ships-of-the-line east of Brest. How great the advantage to England, which in the same stretch has two great arsenals, at Plymouth and at Portsmouth, besides other harbors of refuge and supply. This defect of conformation has since been remedied by the works at Cherbourg.

Besides the contour of the coast, involving easy access to the sea, there are other physical conditions which lead people to the sea or turn them from it. Although France was deficient in military ports on the Channel, she had both there and on the ocean, as well as in the Mediterranean, excellent harbors, favorably situated for trade abroad, and at the outlet of large

而返。1778年，要不是法国的海军司令犹豫不决的话，纽约港以及它对哈德逊河无可辩驳的控制权本来是会易手，不再由处于劣势的英军所掌控的。有了这种控制权，新英格兰本可以与纽约、新泽西以及宾夕法尼亚诸地，重新恢复那种密切而安全的交通补给关系；而这次重击，又是紧随着前一年伯格因[1]的惨败而来，本来也是很有可能让英国人更早地签署和约的。密西西比河是美国一处强大有力的财富与国力之源；但其河口处防守薄弱，而此河深入美国内陆的支流数量又众多，从而使得它成了南部邦联的一处软肋和祸端。最后，到了1814年，切萨皮克湾被占、华盛顿遭毁，给了美国人一个惨痛的教训，使之明白了倘若一路上不加防卫，这些最宽阔的水道也能带来危险；虽说这个教训在时间上距今如此之近，我们很容易就能回想起来，但从目前海岸防御的表象来看，人们却似乎更容易将其忘记。我们也不应当认为，如今形势已经发生了变化；因为虽说环境与攻守的具体情况古今都在发生着变化，但大前提还是一样的。

在伟大的拿破仑战争之前和该次战争期间，法兰西在布雷斯特以东并没有适于泊驻轻型战列舰的港口。而英国却有着多么巨大的优势啊；它在这一地区的普利茅斯和朴茨茅斯有两座大型的军舰修造厂，此外还拥有诸多其他的避风港和补给点。不过，法国这种结构上的弱点，此后已由在瑟堡修筑的工事得以弥补过来了。

除了涉及到能否便捷出海的海岸线轮廓，还有其他的自然条件，使得人们或是跨洋过海，或是避开海洋。尽管法兰西在英吉利海峡上的军港数量不足，但该国在英吉利海峡、大西洋和地中海上都有良港，这些良港的位置都很有利于进行海外贸易；而在一些可以促进法国国内交通条件的大河入海口，该国也有着一些优质的海港。不过，当黎

rivers, which would foster internal traffic. But when Richelieu had put an end to civil war, Frenchmen did not take to the sea with the eagerness and success of the English and Dutch. A principal reason for this has been plausibly found in the physical conditions which have made France a pleasant land, with a delightful climate, producing within itself more than its people needed. England, on the other hand, received from Nature but little, and, until her manufactures were developed, had little to export. Their many wants, combined with their restless activity and other conditions that favored maritime enterprise, led her people abroad; and they there found lands more pleasant and richer than their own. Their needs and genius made them merchants and colonists, then manufacturers and producers; and between products and colonies shipping is the inevitable link. So their sea power grew. But if England was drawn to the sea, Holland was driven to it; without the sea England languished, but Holland died. In the height of her greatness, when she was one of the chief factors in European politics, a competent native authority estimated that the soil of Holland could not support more than one eighth of her inhabitants. The manufactures of the country were then numerous and important, but they had been much later in their growth than the shipping interest. The poverty of the soil and the exposed nature of the coast drove the Dutch first to fishing. Then the discovery of the process of curing the fish gave them material for export as well as home consumption, and so laid the corner-stone of their wealth. Thus they had become traders at the time that the Italian republics, under the pressure of Turkish power and the discovery of the passage round the Cape of Good Hope, were beginning to decline, and they fell heirs to the great Italian trade of the Levant. Further favored by their geographical position, intermediate between the Baltic, France, and the Mediterranean, and at the mouth of the German rivers, they quickly absorbed nearly all the carrying-trade of Europe. The wheat and naval stores of the Baltic, the trade

塞留结束了内战之后，法国人却并未像英国人和荷兰人那样，急于并且成功地向海上进军。其主要原因，似乎可以从法国的自然条件中找到；正是这些自然条件，使得法国成了一个宜居之地，拥有令人愉快的气候，丰富的物产，而人民的生活也很富足。另一方面，大自然赐予英国的东西却很少，直到制造业发展起来之前，英国都没有什么东西可供出口。英国人的诸多需求，连同他们那种不安于现状的活动，以及有利于航海事业的其他条件，都使得英国人能够漂洋海外；而在国外，英国人则发现了许多比本国气候更为宜人、物产更为富饶的地方。他们的需求与本领，使得他们成了商人和殖民者，然后又成了制造者和出产者；而海运，就是产品与殖民地之间不可或缺的一环。于是，他们的海上力量便发展起来了。不过，要说英国是被吸引到海上的，那么荷兰便是被逼到海上的；因为倘若没有海洋，英国只会衰落，而荷兰却会灭亡。在荷兰到达其辉煌的巅峰、尚是欧洲政治中的一个主角之时，该国一位称职的权威人士就曾预计，荷兰的国土是无法养活八分之一的荷兰人的。当时荷兰的制造企业虽说数量众多且举足轻重，但其增长一直要远远滞后于海运业的增长，土地的贫瘠以及沿岸地区光突少树的情况，先是迫使荷兰人出海捕鱼，然后，他们发现了腌制鱼类的加工方法，有了可供出口和供本国消费的商品，从而为财富的积累奠定了基础。这样一来，在发现绕道好望角的航线之后，当仍处于土耳其当局压迫之下的意大利各共和国开始没落之时，荷兰人便成了商人，接过了意大利在黎凡特地区的大规模贸易。由于荷兰地处波罗的海、法兰西和地中海之间，并且位于德国诸河的入海口，具有更多的优势，所以荷兰诸省很快就吞并了欧洲差不多所有的海运业务。在200多年前，波罗的海地区的小麦与海军军需物资、西班牙与新世界的

of Spain with her colonies in the New World, the wines of France, and the French coasting-trade were, little more than two hundred years ago, transported in Dutch shipping. Much of the carrying-trade of England, even, was then done in Dutch bottoms. It will not be pretended that all this prosperity proceeded only from the poverty of Holland's natural resources. Something does not grow from nothing. What is true, is, that by the necessitous condition of her people they were driven to the sea, and were, from their mastery of the shipping business and the size of their fleets, in a position to profit by the sudden expansion of commerce and the spirit of exploration which followed on the discovery of America and of the passage round the Cape. Other causes concurred, but their whole prosperity stood on the sea power to which their poverty gave birth. Their food, their clothing, the raw material for their manufactures, the very timber and hemp with which they built and rigged their ships (and they built nearly as many as all Europe besides), were imported; and when a disastrous war with England in 1653 and 1654 had lasted eighteen months, and their shipping business was stopped, it is said "the sources of revenue which had always maintained the riches of the State, such as fisheries and commerce, were almost dry. Workshops were closed, work was suspended. The Zuyder Zee became a forest of masts; the country was full of beggars; grass grew in the streets, and in Amsterdam fifteen hundred houses were untenanted." A humiliating peace alone saved them from ruin.

This sorrowful result shows the weakness of a country depending wholly upon sources external to itself for the part it is playing in the world. With large deductions, owing to differences of conditions which need not here be spoken of, the case of Holland then has strong points of resemblance to that of Great Britain now; and there are true prophets, though they seem to be having small honor in their own country, who warn her that the continuance

西属殖民地之间所进行的贸易、法国的葡萄酒及其沿海贸易，都是由荷兰船舶来进行运输的，甚至于英国沿海贸易的一大部分，当时也是由荷兰货船来完成的。但我们并不能因此而妄称，这种繁荣全都只是由于荷兰自然资源匮乏所致的。因为有些东西，根本就没法无中生有。事实是，荷兰人民因贫困而被迫出海，之后由于掌控了海运业务、舰队庞大，故在发现美洲、发现绕道好望角的航线之后，他们便能够抓住突如其来的那种贸易扩张和探险大潮的机会来获利。虽说与此同时还有其他的原因，但他们的繁荣整体上依赖的是制海权，而这种制海权又是他们的贫困所造成的。他们的食品、衣物、制造企业所用的原材料、建造和装配船只所用的木材和麻绳（他们建造的船只，差不多相当于其他欧洲国家所建造船只的总数），都是进口得来的；所以，当1653年至1654年间荷兰同英国爆发了一场长达18个月的恶战，使得该国的海运业务中止之后，据说"曾经一向支撑着国家富裕阶层的税收资源，比如渔业和贸易，差不多都已枯竭。工厂关门，工人失业。须德海[2]成了一片船桅之林；国内到处都是乞丐；街上杂草丛生，而阿姆斯特丹则有1500座房子无人租住。"最终靠一份屈辱的和约，才让这些房子免于变成了一堆废墟。

这种凄惨的结局，说明了一个全靠外部资源来支撑自己在世界上发挥作用的国家，是多么的脆弱。除了大范围的方面，还有一些不同的情况，使得当时荷兰的情形同如今英国的情形有许多相似之处，但此处对这些情况我们无需加以说明；如今英国有一些真正的先知，虽说在国内似乎不太受人敬重，但他们却都提醒说，英国国内的持续繁荣，主要取决于保持英国在海外的势力。没有政治上的特权，人们或许会感到不满；但倘若没有面包，那他们就会紧张得多了。注意到下述这一点，对美国人来说则更具益处：对

of her prosperity at home depends primarily upon maintaining her power abroad. Men may be discontented at the lack of political privilege; they will be yet more uneasy if they come to lack bread. It is of more interest to Americans to note that the result to France, regarded as a power of the sea, caused by the extent, delightfulness, and richness of the land, has been reproduced in the United States. In the beginning, their forefathers held a narrow strip of land upon the sea, fertile in parts though little developed, abounding in harbors and near rich fishing-grounds. These physical conditions combined with an inborn love of the sea, the pulse of that English blood which still beat in their veins, to keep alive all those tendencies and pursuits upon which a healthy sea power depends. Almost every one of the original colonies was on the sea or on one of its great tributaries. All export and import tended toward one coast. Interest in the sea and an intelligent appreciation of the part it played in the public welfare were easily and widely spread; and a motive more influential than care for the public interest was also active, for the abundance of ship-building materials and a relative fewness of other investments made shipping a profitable private interest. How changed the present condition is, all know. The centre of power is no longer on the seaboard. Books and newspapers vie with one another in describing the wonderful growth, and the still undeveloped riches, of the interior. Capital there finds its best investments, labor its largest opportunities. The frontiers are neglected and politically weak; the Gulf and Pacific coasts actually so, the Atlantic coast relatively to the central Mississippi Valley. When the day comes that shipping again pays, when the three sea frontiers find that they are not only militarily weak, but poorer for lack of national shipping, their united efforts may avail to lay again the foundations of our sea power. Till then, those who follow the limitations which lack of sea power placed upon the career of France may mourn that their own country is being led, by a like redundancy of home wealth, into the same neglect of that great

于被视为一个海上强国的法兰西而言，由该国国土面积、气候宜人与富饶所导致的这一结果，已经在美国重现了。起初，美国人的先辈只拥有沿海一片狭长的土地，虽说没怎么开发出来，但许多地方都很肥沃，港口良多，离一些富产的渔场也很近。这些自然条件，同美国人那种天生的爱海情节结合起来；因为美国人的血管中仍然奔涌着英国人的血液，使得他们想要将一种健全的制海权所依赖的那些倾向与追求保持下去。在最初的那13个殖民地里，差不多所有人都沿海而居，或是居于大河的沿岸。所有的出口与进口货物，常常都指向同一个沿海地区。对海洋的兴趣、了解并认识到海洋在社会福利方面所起的作用，都很容易、很广泛地扩散开来了；而一种比关注公共利益更有势力的动机也很盛行：因为造船材料丰富，其他方面的投资相对较少，所以海运便成了一种有利可图的私人利益。我们大家都明白，如今情况已经发生了多大的变化。现在，权力中心已不再集中于沿海地区了。图书和报纸都在竞相描述内陆地区不可思议的发展，以及那些尚未开发的财富。资本在内陆地区找到了最佳的投资渠道，而劳动力则在内陆地区找到了最大的就业机会。边远地区被人们视而不见，而它们在政治上也毫无影响力；事实上，墨西哥湾和太平洋沿岸地区就是这样，而大西洋沿岸相对于处在中心地带的密西西比河流域来说，也是这样。当海运再一次变得有利可图的时候，当那3个沿海的边远地区发现它们不仅在军事上处于弱势，还因为没有国内航运而更加贫困的时候，它们的共同努力或许就会有利于再次为我们的制海权打下基础了。到了那时，那些密切关注法国由于没有制海权而在国家事业上受到了种种牵制的人，可能就会痛惜祖国被一种国家财富貌似过剩的情况所引领，进入一种相同的、被那种强大工具所忽视的状况了。

instrument.

Among modifying physical conditions may be noted a form like that of Italy, — a long peninsula, with a central range of mountains dividing it into two narrow strips, along which the roads connecting the different ports necessarily run. Only an absolute control of the sea can wholly secure such communications, since it is impossible to know at what point an enemy coming from beyond the visible horizon may strike; but still, with an adequate naval force centrally posted, there will be good hope of attacking his fleet, which is at once his base and line of communications, before serious damage has been done. The long, narrow peninsula of Florida, with Key West at its extremity, though flat and thinly populated, presents at first sight conditions like those of Italy. The resemblance may be only superficial, but it seems probable that if the chief scene of a naval war were the Gulf of Mexico, the communications by land to the end of the peninsula might be a matter of consequence, and open to attack.

When the sea not only borders, or surrounds, but also separates a country into two or more parts, the control of it becomes not only desirable, but vitally necessary. Such a physical condition either gives birth and strength to sea power, or makes the country powerless. Such is the condition of the present kingdom of Italy, with its islands of Sardinia and Sicily; and hence in its youth and still existing financial weakness it is seen to put forth such vigorous and intelligent efforts to create a military navy. It has even been argued that, with a navy decidedly superior to her enemy's, Italy could better base her power upon her islands than upon her mainland; for the insecurity of the lines of communication in the peninsula, already pointed out, would most seriously embarrass an invading army surrounded by a hostile people and threatened from the sea.

The Irish Sea, separating the British Islands, rather resembles an estuary than an actual

在不断改变的那些自然条件当中，可能有一种形式的条件值得注意，就像意大利的情形那样——意大利是一个长长的半岛，其间有一条中央山脉，将该国分成了两个狭长的区域，而连接不同港口的道路，则必然沿着这两个区域延伸。只有绝对控制住海上，才能完全保护这些交通要道，因为我们不可能知道，从远处冒出来的敌人会进攻哪个地方；但是，倘若在中心位置驻有一支合适的海军，那么在我方遭受重大损失之前，去攻击同样属于对方基地与交通补给线的敌方舰队，还是大有希望的。狭长的佛罗里达半岛一端是基韦斯特，虽说地势平坦、人烟稀少，但一眼看去，与意大利的自然条件还是很相似的。这种相似性可能只是表面上的，但十有八九，倘若一场海战的主战场就在墨西哥湾，那么，经由陆路前往半岛末端的交通补给线可能就是一个重要问题，就会很容易遭到敌人攻击了。

倘若海洋不仅濒临或包围着一个国家，还将这个国家分成了两个或者多个部分，那么控制海洋就不仅有利，而且是一种极为必要的举措了。这样一种自然条件，要么会导致并加强该国的制海权，要么就会让该国变得软弱无能。这就是如今的意大利王国、连同撒丁和西西里二岛的情形；因此，我们可以看到，在早期以及如今仍然存在的金融劣势中，意大利早已开始了这种轰轰烈烈而明智的努力，来创建一支海军。人们甚至还认为，有了一支明显优于敌人的海军之后，意大利就能以其岛屿为实力基础，效果可能会比以其本土为实力基础更好；因为我们在前面已经指出，意大利半岛上的交通补给线很不安全，会让一支入侵的敌军在被敌意重重的意大利人所包围并受到来自海上的威胁之后，陷入一种严重的不利之境。

虽说爱尔兰海把不列颠群岛分割开来了，但它更像是一个港湾，而这种分割也并不

division; but history has shown the danger from it to the United Kingdom. In the days of Louis XIV., when the French navy nearly equalled the combined English and Dutch, the gravest complications existed in Ireland, which passed almost wholly under the control of the natives and the French. Nevertheless, the Irish Sea was rather a danger to the English — a weak point in their communications — than an advantage to the French. The latter did not venture their ships-of-the-line in its narrow waters, and expeditions intending to land were directed upon the ocean ports in the south and west. At the supreme moment the great French fleet was sent upon the south coast of England, where it decisively defeated the allies, and at the same time twenty-five frigates were sent to St. George's Channel, against the English communications. In the midst of a hostile people, the English army in Ireland was seriously imperiled, but was saved by the battle of the Boyne and the flight of James II. This movement against the enemy's communications was strictly strategic, and would be just as dangerous to England now as in 1690.

Spain, in the same century, afforded an impressive lesson of the weakness caused by such separation when the parts are not knit together by a strong sea power. She then still retained, as remnants of her past greatness, the Netherlands (now Belgium), Sicily, and other Italian possessions, not to speak of her vast colonies in the New World. Yet so low had the Spanish sea power fallen, that a well-informed and sober-minded Hollander of the day could claim that "in Spain all the coast is navigated by a few Dutch ships; and since the peace of 1648 their ships and seamen are so few that they have publicly begun to hire our ships to sail to the Indies, whereas they were formerly careful to exclude all foreigners from there. ... It is manifest," he goes on, "that the West Indies, being as the stomach to Spain (for from it nearly all the revenue is drawn), must be joined to the Spanish head by a sea force; and that Naples and

是真正的割裂；不过历史业已表明，它给联合王国带来了危险。在路易十四统治时期，当时的法国海军堪与英、荷两国的联合海军相匹敌；因为存在严重的内乱，所以爱尔兰政府差不多全部为当地人和法国人所掌控了。尽管如此，爱尔兰海仍是英国人的一大危险——即他们交通补给方面的一处薄弱环节，也并不是法国人的一大优势。法国并不敢派遣轻型战列舰进入这片狭窄的水域，而该国旨在登陆的远征军，攻击的也是爱尔兰南部或者西部的海港。在决战之时，伟大的法国舰队被派往英格兰南部沿海，并在那儿击溃了英、荷联军，同时派了25艘护卫舰前往圣乔治海峡，以阻击英军的交通补给线。在爱尔兰的英军虽然身处一个充满敌意的民族当中，处境极其危险，但因博因河之战以及詹姆士二世逃跑而脱离了险境。这种针对敌军交通补给线的作战行动，完全是战略性的；所以对于目前的英国来说，形势就跟1690年时一样危险。

在同一个世纪中，西班牙也给我们提供了一个令人印象深刻的教训，表明这种领土分割倘若未由一种强大的制海权联结起来，便会带来极大的劣势。此时，西班牙凭借昔日辉煌的余势，仍然保有尼德兰（即如今的比利时）、西西里以及其他本属意大利的领地，而且还在新世界里有着数量众多的殖民地。然而，西班牙的海上力量已经衰落到无以复加的地步，所以当时一位见多识广、头脑冷静的荷兰人都可以这样说："西班牙所有的沿海地区，都有一些荷兰船只在航行；自1648年和约签订以来，该国的船只和水手数量都在急剧减少，所以他们开始公开招募我国船只前往印度群岛，而在以前，他们却非常谨慎，从不让外国人去那儿……"他接着说："很显然，作为西班牙之'胃'的西印度群岛（因为西班牙差不多所有的税收都来自于此处），必须由一支海军来将它与

the Netherlands, being like two arms, they cannot lay out their strength for Spain, nor receive anything thence but by shipping, — all which may easily be done by our shipping in peace, and by it obstructed in war." Half a century before, Sully, the great minister of Henry IV., had characterized Spain "as one of those States whose legs and arms are strong and powerful, but the heart infinitely weak and feeble." Since his day the Spanish navy had suffered not only disaster, but annihilation; not only humiliation, but degradation. The consequences briefly were that shipping was destroyed; manufactures perished with it. The government depended for its support, not upon a wide-spread healthy commerce and industry that could survive many a staggering blow, but upon a narrow stream of silver trickling through a few treasure-ships from America, easily and frequently intercepted by an enemy's cruisers. The loss of half a dozen galleons more than once paralyzed its movements for a year. While the war in the Netherlands lasted, the Dutch control of the sea forced Spain to send her troops by a long and costly journey overland instead of by sea; and the same cause reduced her to such straits for necessaries that, by a mutual arrangement which seems very odd to modern ideas, her wants were supplied by Dutch ships, which thus maintained the enemies of their country, but received in return specie which was welcome in the Amsterdam exchange. In America, the Spanish protected themselves as best they might behind masonry, unaided from home; while in the Mediterranean they escaped insult and injury mainly through the indifference of the Dutch, for the French and English had not yet begun to contend for mastery there. In the course of history the Netherlands, Naples, Sicily, Minorca, Havana, Manila, and Jamaica were wrenched away, at one time or another, from this empire without a shipping. In short, while Spain's maritime impotence may have been primarily a symptom of her general decay, it became a marked factor in precipitating her into the abyss from which she has not yet wholly emerged.

西班牙的'头'联结起来才行；那不勒斯与尼德兰虽说就像两只胳膊，但它们无法为西班牙出力，并且除了海运，也无法从西班牙那里获得什么利益——在和平时期，我们的运输船只都可以做到这些；而在战时，则可用船只来进行阻挠。"半个世纪之前，亨利四世的一位大臣萨利曾经归纳了西班牙的特点，说它属于"那种双腿与两只胳膊都强大有力，可内心却软弱无比的国家之一。"自此以后，西班牙海军所遭遇的就不仅是损失惨重，还被完全摧毁了；它不仅受到了羞辱，还完全落魄了。简而言之，结果就是西班牙的海运毁于一旦，并且制造业也随之衰落了。西班牙政府不是凭借一种广泛而健全、本可以使之经受起多次重大打击的贸易业和工业，而是依赖于一条小小的资金流，通过不多的宝船从美洲将银子运回；这些船只，很容易并且经常被敌人的巡逻船所截获。损失6条大帆船，就会让西班牙政府一年都无法行动，而出现这种情况，却早已不止一次了。就在尼德兰的战争持续进行之时，荷兰便控制了海上，迫使西班牙不得不经由漫长、代价巨大的陆路运送部队，而无法经由海上来运送。同一原因，也使得西班牙只剩下为数不多的海峡可以运送生活必需品了；但西、荷双方却一致商定，由荷兰船只来运送西班牙所需的补给品——在现代人看来，这种做法是非常怪异的。荷兰船只虽说以这种方式支持了本国的敌人，但作为回报，它们却获得了当时很受阿姆斯特丹交易所欢迎的银币。在美洲，西班牙人得不到本国的支援，躲在砖石结构的建筑里，尽可能地明哲保身；与此同时，地中海地区的西班牙人，则主要是利用荷兰人的毫不在乎而躲过了一劫，因为法国人和英国人那时还没有开始争夺此处的主导权。随着历史的发展，尼德兰、那不勒斯、西西里、米诺卡、哈瓦那、马尼拉和牙买加等地，或早或晚，都一一被从这个没有航运业的国家手中夺走了。总之，虽

Except Alaska, the United States has no outlying possession, — no foot of ground inaccessible by land. Its contour is such as to present few points specially weak from their saliency, and all important parts of the frontiers can be readily attained, — cheaply by water, rapidly by rail. The weakest frontier, the Pacific, is far removed from the most dangerous of possible enemies. The internal resources are boundless as compared with present needs; we can live off ourselves indefinitely in "our little corner," to use the expression of a French officer to the author. Yet should that little corner be invaded by a new commercial route through the Isthmus, the United States in her turn may have the rude awakening of those who have abandoned their share in the common birthright of all people, the sea.

III. Extent of Territory. — The last of the conditions affecting the development of a nation as a sea power, and touching the country itself as distinguished from the people who dwell there, is Extent of Territory. This may be dismissed with comparatively few words.

As regards the development of sea power, it is not the total number of square miles which a country contains, but the length of its coast-line and the character of its harbors that are to be considered. As to these it is to be said that, the geographical and physical conditions being the same, extent of sea-coast is a source of strength or weakness according as the population is large or small. A country is in this like a fortress; the garrison must be proportioned to the enceinte. A recent familiar instance is found in the American War of Secession. Had the South had a people as numerous as it was warlike, and a navy commensurate to its other resources as a sea power, the great extent of its sea-coast and its numerous inlets would have been elements of great strength. The people of the United States and the Government of that day justly prided themselves on the effectiveness of the blockade of the whole Southern coast. It was a great feat, a very great feat; but it would have been an impossible feat had the Southerners been more

然西班牙海上力量的软弱可能是其全面衰落的一种征兆，但它也成为了让该国陷入无底深渊的一个显著因素，而迄今为止，西班牙也还没有完全跳出这个深渊。

除了阿拉斯加，美国并没有海外领土——即没有什么领土是无法从陆上到达的。它的外形轮廓，使得该国没有什么特别薄弱的特点，而其边境上的所有重要区域，也都能够轻易到达——水路很便宜，铁路又很快捷。最为薄弱的边境就是太平洋沿岸，但此处离那些最危险的敌人都很远。与该国目前所需相比，美国的国内资源可谓无穷无尽；用一位法国官员对作者所说的话来说，就是我们可以在"我们的这个小角落里"靠自己世世代代地永远生活下去。然而，倘若一条经由中美地峡的新商路侵入了这个"小角落"，那么，美国可能就会像那些已经放弃了海洋——各个民族与生俱来即对海洋拥有权力——的人一样，猛然觉醒了。

（三）领土范围——影响到一个海洋大国的发展，并且涉及到该民族区别于居住在该国之人的最后一个条件，便是领土范围。对于这一点，用较少的内容就能加以说明。

从制海权的发展来说，领土范围并不是指一个国家的总面积，而是指其海岸线的长度，以及所要考虑之海港的特征。关于这些方面，我们要说的是，如果地理和自然条件相同，那么海岸线的长度，根据人口多寡的比例来看，就是一国国力强大或者衰弱的根源了。在这个方面，一个国家就像是一座要塞；卫戍部队的兵力，必须与要塞城郭的长度成正比才行。最近有一个人们都很熟悉的例子，这便是美国内战。倘若南方人口数量众多且英勇无畏，还有一支与这个海上强国其他资源相称的海军，那么其漫长的海岸线以及数不胜数的小港，就会是使得南部邦联具有强大实力的基本要素了。合众国人民以及

numerous, and a nation of seamen. What was there shown was not, as has been said, how such a blockade can be maintained, but that such a blockade is possible in the face of a population not only unused to the sea, but also scanty in numbers. Those who recall how the blockade was maintained, and the class of ships that blockaded during great part of the war, know that the plan, correct under the circumstances, could not have been carried out in the face of a real navy. Scattered unsupported along the coast, the United States ships kept their places, singly or in small detachments, in face of an extensive network of inland water communications which favored secret concentration of the enemy. Behind the first line of water communications were long estuaries, and here and there strong fortresses, upon either of which the enemy's ships could always fall back to elude pursuit or to receive protection. Had there been a Southern navy to profit by such advantages, or by the scattered condition of the United States ships, the latter could not have been distributed as they were; and being forced to concentrate for mutual support, many small but useful approaches would have been left open to commerce. But as the Southern coast, from its extent and many inlets, might have been a source of strength, so, from those very characteristics, it became a fruitful source of injury. The great story of the opening of the Mississippi is but the most striking illustration of an action that was going on incessantly all over the South. At every breach of the sea frontier, war-ships were entering. The streams that had carried the wealth and supported the trade of the seceding States turned against them, and admitted their enemies to their hearts. Dismay, insecurity, paralysis, prevailed in regions that might, under happier auspices, have kept a nation alive through the most exhausting war. Never did sea power play a greater or a more decisive part than in the contest which determined that the course of the world's history would be modified by the existence of one great nation, instead of several rival States, in the North American continent. But while just pride is felt in the well-

当时的合众国政府都很有理由自豪，因为他们极为有效地封锁了南方的整个沿海地区。这是一件了不起的壮举，一件极其了不起的壮举；不过，倘若南方人口很多、全民皆水兵的话，那么这就会是一种不可能实现的壮举了。此例所表明的，并不是如何才能维持这样一种封锁，就像之前已经说过的那样，而是在面对一帮非但不习惯于海战、而且数量稀少的南方人时，是有可能进行这种封锁的。那些能够回想起这种封锁是如何维持下去的人都明白，这个封锁计划虽说在当时的情况下是正确的，但在面对一支真正的海军时，却根本不可能实现。合众国的舰船散布在沿海地区，无人支援，单独或以小支舰队为单位驻守自己的阵地，而面对的却是一张有利于敌人进行秘密集结的、巨大的内河交通网。第一道内河交通线的背后，是长长的港湾和星罗棋布的坚固要塞，敌舰以前一向都是可以撤退到这两个地方，来躲避追击或者受到掩护的。倘若有一支南方海军能够利用这些优势，或者能够利用合众国舰船散布各处、不集中的情况进击，那么合众国的舰船就不可能再像以前那样分散了；而由于合众国的舰船不得不集结起来彼此支援，所以就会留下许多虽小却很有用的通路，南方就可以进行贸易了。不过，就像南方沿海地区因为面积广阔、港湾众多而本可以成为一种实力之源那样，也正是这些特点，使得它成为了让南方不断受到攻击的一大原因。打开密西西比河的伟大经历，只不过是南方各地正在不断进行的作战行动中，一个最为引人注目的例子罢了。每攻破一处海疆，都会有战舰驶入内陆。那些曾经运送财富、支撑脱联各州贸易的河流，如今开始不利于它们，让敌人能够深入各州腹地了。许多地区都开始惊慌沮丧、心神不安、政务瘫痪起来；假如保护得更恰当一点儿的话，这些地区本来是可以让一个国家保持生机，度过这场极为费神的战争的。在北美大陆，制海权还从未

earned glory of those days, and the greatness of the results due to naval preponderance is admitted, Americans who understand the facts should never fail to remind the over-confidence of their countrymen that the South not only had no navy, not only was not a seafaring people, but that also its population was not proportioned to the extent of the sea-coast which it had to defend.

IV. Number of Population. — After the consideration of the natural conditions of a country should follow an examination of the characteristics of its population as affecting the development of sea power; and first among these will be taken, because of its relations to the extent of the territory, which has just been discussed, the number of the people who live in it. It has been said that in respect of dimensions it is not merely the number of square miles, but the extent and character of the sea-coast that is to be considered with reference to sea power; and so, in point of population, it is not only the grand total, but the number following the sea, or at least readily available for employment on ship-board and for the creation of naval material, that must be counted.

For example, formerly and up to the end of the great wars following the French Revolution, the population of France was much greater than that of England; but in respect of sea power in general, peaceful commerce as well as military efficiency, France was much inferior to England. In the matter of military efficiency this fact is the more remarkable because at times, in point of military preparation at the outbreak of war, France had the advantage; but she was not able to keep it. Thus in 1778, when war broke out, France, through her maritime inscription, was able to man at once fifty ships-of-the-line. England, on the contrary, by reason of the dispersal over the globe of that very shipping on which her naval strength so securely rested, had much trouble in manning forty at home; but in 1782 she had one hundred and twenty in commission or ready

比在这场战争中那样，发挥过更加巨大或者更具决定性的作用；这场战争，决定了世界历史进程将由一个大国而非数个相互竞争之国家所改写。不过，虽说人们为那个年代所获得的辉煌成就而感到自豪，也承认那些赫赫战果应当归功于海军所占的优势，但了解事实的美国人决不应该忘记提醒自己的同胞不要过分自信，因为当时的南方诸州非但没有海军，南方人非但不是一个从事航海业的民族，而且南方的人口数量也与它必须防御的漫长海岸线不成正比。

（四）人口数量——探讨过一个国家的自然条件之后，接下来我们就应当来审视一下影响到一国制海权发展的人口特点了；而首先应当加以研究的，便是居于该国之中的总人口，原因就在于前面我们刚刚讨论过的、一国总人口与其领土范围的关系。我们已经说过，领土范围并非仅仅是指一国有多少平方英里，它还包括与制海权相关的、需要加以考虑的海岸线的长度与特点；因此，说到人口数量，它也并非仅仅是指一国的总人口，还应当包括该国的海员人数，或者起码来说，也应当算上那些可以上船工作、能够创造海军用品的人才行。

比如说，从前以及直到法国大革命之后历次大战结束的时候，法国人口都大大超过了英国；不过，就总体的制海权、和平的商业贸易以及军事效率而言，法国却大不如英国。在军事效率方面，这一事实则更为显著；因为有的时候，虽说法国在战争爆发之初的军事准备方面具有优势，但该国却无力保持住这种优势。因此，在1778年战争爆发的时候，法国由于海员在册人数众多，所以能够一次性装备50艘轻型战列舰。与此相反，英国却由于自己的海运船只散布于世界各地——其海军实力也因此而得到了保存——所以，在本国装

for commission, while France had never been able to exceed seventy-one. Again, as late as 1840, when the two nations were on the verge of war in the Levant, a most accomplished French officer of the day, while extolling the high state of efficiency of the French fleet and the eminent qualities of its admiral, and expressing confidence in the results of an encounter with an equal enemy, goes on to say: "Behind the squadron of twenty-one ships-of-the-line which we could then assemble, there was no reserve; not another ship could have been commissioned within six months." And this was due not only to lack of ships and of proper equipments, though both were wanting. "Our maritime inscription," he continues, "was so exhausted by what we had done [in manning twenty-one ships], that the permanent levy established in all quarters did not supply reliefs for the men, who were already more than three years on cruise."

A contrast such as this shows a difference in what is called staying power, or reserve force, which is even greater than appears on the surface; for a great shipping afloat necessarily employs, besides the crews, a large number of people engaged in the various handicrafts which facilitate the making and repairing of naval material, or following other callings more or less closely connected with the water and with craft of all kinds. Such kindred callings give an undoubted aptitude for the sea from the outset. There is an anecdote showing curious insight into this matter on the part of one of England's distinguished seamen, Sir Edward Pellew. When the war broke out in 1793, the usual scarceness of seamen was met. Eager to get to sea and unable to fill his complement otherwise than with landsmen, he instructed his officers to seek for Cornish miners; reasoning from the conditions and dangers of their calling, of which he had personal knowledge, that they would quickly fit into the demands of sea life. The result showed his sagacity, for, thus escaping an otherwise unavoidable delay, he was fortunate enough to capture the first frigate taken in the war in single combat; and what is especially instructive

备40艘战船都难以做到；但到了1782年，英国却有了120艘现役和预备役战列舰，而法国的战列舰总数却一直都没有超过71艘。此外，晚至1840年，当英法两国在黎凡特剑拔弩张、战事一触即发的时候，当时一位极为博学的法国军官，在赞扬法国舰队的高效以及法国海军司令的诸多杰出品质，并且表达出遭遇同等规模的敌军时法国能打胜仗的信心之后，接着说："我们除了当时所能集结的、由21艘战列舰所组成的这支小型舰队之外，并无预备舰船；而在6个月内，也不可能再有另外一艘舰船来服役。"出现这种状况，并不仅仅是因为没有舰船和合适的装备，尽管这二者法军都很匮乏。"我们的海军兵源，"这名法国军官接着说，"因为我们所做的工作（即装备了21艘船只）已经消耗殆尽了，所以各地制定的永久性征兵政策，并没有让那些已经在军舰上服役了3年多的海员得以轮换。"

这样一种对比，表明了在所谓的"持久力"或者"后备力量"方面的差异，且此种差异比表面看起来的更加巨大；因为一支大型的海上舰队，除了船员，必然还会招募一大批其他人员，来从事能够促进生产和维修海军用品的体力工作，或者完成与海洋、与各种船只多少密切相关的其他工作。这种工作任务，从一开始就具有确定的海上性质。有一件趣闻，表现了属于英国最杰出水兵之一的爱德华·佩鲁爵士对这个问题具有一种古怪的见解。1793年战争爆发之时，照常出现了海员不足的问题。由于渴望出海作战，而除了没有出过海的人，他又补不满全员，于是他便命令手下的军官去找康沃尔郡的矿工；对于他们所要执行任务的环境与种种危险，他自己都非常了解，故推断出这些人会很快适应海上的生活。结果证明了爱德华的睿智与远见，因为这样一来，他就丝毫也没有耽误时间，而他的运气也很好，俘虏了此次战争中单场战斗所缴获的第一艘护卫舰；尤具启发性的是，尽

is, that although but a few weeks in commission, while his opponent had been over a year, the losses, heavy on both sides, were nearly equal.

It may be urged that such reserve strength has now nearly lost the importance it once had, because modern ships and weapons take so long to make, and because modern States aim at developing the whole power of their armed force, on the outbreak of war, with such rapidity as to strike a disabling blow before the enemy can organize an equal effort. To use a familiar phrase, there will not be time for the whole resistance of the national fabric to come into play; the blow will fall on the organized military fleet, and if that yield, the solidity of the rest of the structure will avail nothing. To a certain extent this is true; but then it has always been true, though to a less extent formerly than now. Granted the meeting of two fleets which represent practically the whole present strength of their two nations, if one of them be destroyed, while the other remains fit for action, there will be much less hope now than formerly that the vanquished can restore his navy for that war; and the result will be disastrous just in proportion to the dependence of the nation upon her sea power. A Trafalgar would have been a much more fatal blow to England than it was to France, had the English fleet then represented, as the allied fleet did, the bulk of the nation's power. Trafalgar in such a case would have been to England what Austerlitz was to Austria, and Jena to Prussia; an empire would have been laid prostrate by the destruction or disorganization of its military forces, which, it is said, were the favorite objective of Napoleon.

But does the consideration of such exceptional disasters in the past justify the putting a low value upon that reserve strength, based upon the number of inhabitants fitted for a certain kind of military life, which is here being considered? The blows just mentioned were dealt by men of exceptional genius, at the head of armed bodies of exceptional training, esprit-de-corps, and

管他的手下才服役数周，敌军服役却已一年多了，但双方的损失都差不多，都很惨重。

或许有人会坚持说，这样的后备力量，如今不像以前那样重要了，因为现代舰船和现代武器制造起来耗时颇久，还因为现代各国的目标都是加强武装部队的整体力量，以便一旦开战，便能在敌人发起同样的进攻之前，以迅雷不及掩耳之势，对敌人进行毁灭性的打击。用大家都很熟悉的话来说，就是不会有时间来让国家结构所组织的全面性抵抗发挥作用；这种打击针对的是已经组建起来的作战舰队，倘若作战舰队都投降了，那么国家结构中的其余部分哪怕再坚实，也会无济于事。在某种程度上，言之有理；不过在当时，情况却一向如此，只是过去的程度比如今稍轻而已。假定有两支事实上代表了两国目前整体力量的舰队遭遇了，要是其中一支被击溃，而另一支仍能正常作战的话，那么战败的一方能够重建海军、继续这场战争的希望，如今就会比以前要小得多了；而战争结果所造成的损失，也会与该国对海军的依赖程度成正比。倘若当时的英国舰队跟法、西班牙联合舰队一样，代表了该国的整体力量，那么，一场特拉法尔加这样的海战，就会给英国带来致命一击，并且程度要比它给法国带来的打击沉重得多。对于英国来说，特拉法尔加海战的后果，本来会像奥斯特利茨之战对奥地利、耶拿[3]战役对俄罗斯的后果一样；一个庞大的帝国，会因军事力量被摧毁或因军队瓦解而不得不向敌人俯首称臣——据说，这就是拿破仑最为钟爱的作战目标。

但是，考虑到过去这些特殊的惨败，是不是就让我们有了理由，来轻视此处所研究的、以适合于服某种兵役的人口数量为基础的那种后备力量呢？前面所提到的军事打击，都是由一些非凡的天才人物所进行的，他们指挥着经过特殊训练、有着集体荣誉感

prestige, and were, besides, inflicted upon opponents more or less demoralized by conscious inferiority and previous defeat. Austerlitz had been closely preceded by Ulm, where thirty thousand Austrians laid down their arms without a battle; and the history of the previous years had been one long record of Austrian reverse and French success. Trafalgar followed closely upon a cruise, justly called a campaign, of almost constant failure; and farther back, but still recent, were the memories of St. Vincent for the Spaniards, and of the Nile for the French, in the allied fleet. Except the case of Jena, these crushing overthrows were not single disasters, but final blows; and in the Jena campaign there was a disparity in numbers, equipment, and general preparation for war, which makes it less applicable in considering what may result from a single victory.

England is at the present time the greatest maritime nation in the world; in steam and iron she has kept the superiority she had in the days of sail and wood. France and England are the two powers that have the largest military navies; and it is so far an open question which of the two is the more powerful, that they may be regarded as practically of equal strength in material for a sea war. In the case of a collision can there be assumed such a difference of personnel, or of preparation, as to make it probable that a decisive inequality will result from one battle or one campaign? If not, the reserve strength will begin to tell; organized reserve first, then reserve of seafaring population, reserve of mechanical skill, reserve of wealth. It seems to have been somewhat forgotten that England's leadership in mechanical arts gives her a reserve of mechanics, who can easily familiarize themselves with the appliances of modern iron-clads; and as her commerce and industries feel the burden of the war, the surplus of seamen and mechanics will go to the armed shipping.

The whole question of the value of a reserve, developed or undeveloped, amounts now to

且威名远播的军队，给予那些因为知道自己不如对方、或者因为以前的失败而多少有点儿士气低落的敌人以沉重打击。奥斯特利茨战役之前不久，刚刚发生了乌尔姆之战，此战中有35000名奥地利士兵不发一枪便放下了武器；而在此前的许多年间，一直都是奥地利失败、法国取胜。特拉法尔加海战，也是紧随一次节节失利的巡航（或者完全可以称之为一场战役）之后发生的；再往前看，不过仍属于近来发生的战斗，就是西班牙人记忆中的圣文森特角战役、法国人记忆中的尼罗河河口之战，两次都是这两国的联合舰队在作战。除了耶拿之战，这些决定性的失败都并非是单次战斗的惨败，而都是最后一击；在耶拿战役中，由于双方兵力、武器装备和整体备战等方面悬殊都很大，所以不太适合据此来研究某一次获胜可能会带来什么样的结果。

英国是目前世界上最大的海洋国家；凭借铁甲汽船，它继续保持着木制帆船时代的那种优势。法、英是两大列强，拥有规模最大的海军，而对于两国之间究竟谁更强大这个问题，迄今尚无定论；或许我们可以认为，它们在进行海战时，兵力和装备等方面实际上是不分伯仲的。假如爆发战争的话，那我们能不能认为，有这样一种兵力或者准备上的差异，使得仅凭一场战斗或者一次战役，就很可能带来一种具有决定意义的力量悬殊呢？倘若没有的话，那么后备力量就是差异了；首先是有组织的后备力量，然后就是航海人口的储备、机械技术和财力的储备了。人们似乎有点儿忘记了，英国在机械工艺方面的领先地位，使得它储备了大量的技师，这些技师能够轻而易举地熟悉现代铁甲船的种种设备；而随着人们感到了战争给商贸与工业所带来的重负，这些富余的水手与技师就会投身到军舰上去。

this: Have modern conditions of warfare made it probable that, of two nearly equal adversaries, one will be so prostrated in a single campaign that a decisive result will be reached in that time? Sea warfare has given no answer. The crushing successes of Prussia against Austria, and of Germany against France, appear to have been those of a stronger over a much weaker nation, whether the weakness were due to natural causes, or to official incompetency. How would a delay like that of Plevna have affected the fortune of war, had Turkey had any reserve of national power upon which to call?

If there be, as is everywhere admitted, a supreme factor in war, it behooves countries whose genius is essentially not military, whose people, like all free people, object to pay for large military establishments, to see to it that they are at least strong enough to gain the time necessary to turn the spirit and capacity of their subjects into the new activities which war calls for. If the existing force by land or sea is strong enough so to hold out, even though at a disadvantage, the country may rely upon its natural resources and strength coming into play for whatever they are worth, — its numbers, its wealth, its capacities of every kind. If, on the other hand, what force it has can be overthrown and crushed quickly, the most magnificent possibilities of natural power will not save it from humiliating conditions, nor, if its foe be wise, from guarantees which will postpone revenge to a distant future. The story is constantly repeated on the smaller fields of war: "If so-and-so can hold out a little longer, this can be saved or that can be done;" as in sickness it is often said: "If the patient can only hold out so long, the strength of his constitution may pull him through."

England to some extent is now such a country. Holland was such a country; she would not pay, and if she escaped, it was but by the skin of her teeth. "Never in time of peace and from fear of a rupture," wrote their great statesman, De Witt, "will they take resolutions strong

  无论后备力量发达与否，我们讨论的问题实质就是，现代战争的条件，会不会很可能导致出现这样一种情形：两个势均力敌的国家，其中的一国在某一次战役中被打得落花流水，从而一蹶不振。海上战争并未给出这一问题的答案。普鲁士对奥地利、德意志对法国的压倒性胜利，似乎都是势力悬殊的强国对弱国的胜利，无论这种弱势是因为自然原因还是政府的无能所导致的。倘若土耳其拥有能够征召的全国性后备力量，那么，像普列文[4]之战中那样的贻误战机，又怎么会影响到战争的命运呢？

  假如像世界各国都公认的那样，战争中有一种至高无上的主导因素，那么，国内的人才并非军事性的、民众也像所有崇尚自由的民族一样反对为庞大的军事机构买单的那些国家，就理应确保自己至少具有赢得必要的时间、将国民的精神和力量转向战争所要求的种种新行动中去的能力。倘若现存的陆军或者海军足够强大，即便处于劣势也能坚持抵抗的话，那么，该国就可以依赖其自然资源与自然力量——即人口、财力以及其他种种生产能力，而不论这些自然资源和自然力量价值如何——来发挥作用了。另一方面，倘若该国拥有的这些资源能被敌人很快地摧毁并碾碎，那么就算自然之力鬼斧神工，也是不会让其免于蒙羞的；并且，假如敌人够聪明，还不会让它有在遥远的将来进行复仇的机会。这种情况，在那些规模较小的战场不停地重现。"倘若如此能够再坚持一会儿，就能挽救这个或完成那个了"；这就像是在生病的时候，人们常说的那样："就算病人只能坚持这么久，病人的体力也可以让其恢复健康的。"

  从某种程度上来说，英国如今就是这样的一个国家。荷兰也是这样；它是不会有什么好结果的，而倘若它逃过一劫的话，那也不过是虎口余生罢了。伟大的政治家德·威

enough to lead them to pecuniary sacrifices beforehand. The character of the Dutch is such that, unless danger stares them in the face, they are indisposed to lay out money for their own defence. I have to do with a people who, liberal to profusion where they ought to economize, are often sparing to avarice where they ought to spend."

That our own country is open to the same reproach, is patent to all the world. The United States has not that shield of defensive power behind which time can be gained to develop its reserve of strength. As for a seafaring population adequate to her possible needs, where is it? Such a resource, proportionate to her coast-line and population, is to be found only in a national merchant shipping and its related industries, which at present scarcely exist. It will matter little whether the crews of such ships are native or foreign born, provided they are attached to the flag, and her power at sea is sufficient to enable the most of them to get back in case of war. When foreigners by thousands are admitted to the ballot, it is of little moment that they are given fighting-room on board ship.

Though the treatment of the subject has been somewhat discursive, it may be admitted that a great population following callings related to the sea is, now as formerly, a great element of sea power; that the United States is deficient in that element; and that its foundations can be laid only in a large commerce under her own flag.

V. National Character. — The effect of national character and aptitudes upon the development of sea power will next be considered.

If sea power be really based upon a peaceful and extensive commerce, aptitude for commercial pursuits must be a distinguishing feature of the nations that have at one time or another been great upon the sea. History almost without exception affirms that this is true. Save the Romans, there is no marked instance to the contrary.

特曾这样写道:"在和平时期,由于害怕关系破裂,他们绝不会预先就下定会导致国家财力受损的决心。荷兰人的性格就是这样,除非危险到了眼前,否则他们是不愿意留出资金来进行防御的。我是在同一个这样的民族打交道,他们在应当节省的地方慷慨得很,而在应当花钱的时候往往却又省得抠门、贪得无厌。"

我国也容易遭到这样的指摘,全世界都知道这一点。美国并没有那种可以让它赢得时间来发展后备力量的防御和保护力量。至于能够满足它可能的发展所需的海上从业人口,又在哪儿呢?这样一种与海岸线与总人口成正比的资源,只存在于全国性的商船运输业及其相关产业里,而目前美国这样的相关产业却极少。这种船只上的船员是本国人还是外国人并不重要,只要他们忠于美国就行;而万一爆发战争,美国的海上力量只要足以让他们中的大多数人活着回来就行。倘若允许成千上万的外国人服兵役,那么他们上船之后,给予他们应有的作战空间就并不重要了。

虽说在讨论这一主题时有些不着边际,但毫无疑问,有大量人口从事与海洋相关的工作,是制海权的一大要素,这一点古今并无不同;美国在这一要素上无疑是有着缺陷的;只有当美国有了自己的大规模贸易之后,才能为确立其制海权奠定基础。

(五)民族性格——接下来,我们就来讨论一下民族性格与民族习性对于发展制海权的影响。

假如制海权确实是以一种和平而广泛的商业贸易为基础的,那么从事商业活动的习性,便必定是曾经在海洋上取得过伟大成就的所有民族一个显著的特征。历史几乎证明了这一点,除了罗马人,我们找不到与此相反的其他显著例子。

All men seek gain and, more or less, love money; but the way in which gain is sought will have a marked effect upon the commercial fortunes and the history of the people inhabiting a country.

If history may be believed, the way in which the Spaniards and their kindred nation, the Portuguese, sought wealth, not only brought a blot upon the national character, but was also fatal to the growth of a healthy commerce; and so to the industries upon which commerce lives, and ultimately to that national wealth which was sought by mistaken paths. The desire for gain rose in them to fierce avarice; so they sought in the new-found worlds which gave such an impetus to the commercial and maritime development of the countries of Europe, not new fields of industry, not even the healthy excitement of exploration and adventure, but gold and silver. They had many great qualities; they were bold, enterprising, temperate, patient of suffering, enthusiastic, and gifted with intense national feeling. When to these qualities are added the advantages of Spain's position and well-situated ports, the fact that she was first to occupy large and rich portions of the new worlds and long remained without a competitor, and that for a hundred years after the discovery of America she was the leading State in Europe, she might have been expected to take the foremost place among the sea powers. Exactly the contrary was the result, as all know. Since the battle of Lepanto in 1571, though engaged in many wars, no sea victory of any consequence shines on the pages of Spanish history; and the decay of her commerce sufficiently accounts for the painful and sometimes ludicrous inaptness shown on the decks of her ships of war. Doubtless such a result is not to be attributed to one cause only. Doubtless the government of Spain was in many ways such as to cramp and blight a free and healthy development of private enterprise; but the character of a great people breaks through or shapes the character of its government, and it can hardly be doubted that had the bent of

所有的人都图谋利益，并且或多或少都喜欢钱财；不过，谋求利益的方式，却会对居于一国之中的某个民族的商业命运以及历史产生明显的影响。

倘若历史可信的话，西班牙人以及与之同源的葡萄牙人追求财富的方式，就不仅给其民族性格带来了污点，还危及到了其商业贸易的健康成长；同样，这也给商业贸易所赖以生存的一些产业带来了危害，并最终危及到了那些通过错误方法所获得的国家财富。对于利润的渴求，在他们心中变成了一种强烈的贪婪；因此，在给欧洲各国商业贸易和海洋事业发展带来了如此巨大动力的新世界，他们寻求的不是新的产业领域，甚至也不是探索和探险带来的那种健康的兴奋之感，而是金子和银子。他们有着种种了不起的品质：大胆、有进取心、温和、任劳任怨、充满热情，并且天生具有强烈的民族感情。当这些品质加上位置优势和有诸多良港的优势，以及它率先在新世界占领了广大的富庶之地并在很长时间内没有敌手，而且在发现美洲之后的100年间它一直是欧洲首屈一指的国家等事实后，西班牙本来是有望在海洋大国中占据最为重要的位置的。可众所周知，结果却恰好相反。自1571年的勒班陀之战后，尽管参加过多次战争，但在西班牙历史上，却从未在海战中获得过什么具有重大意义的胜利；而其商业贸易的衰退，则充分说明了该国战舰表现出来的那种可悲的、有时甚至是很荒谬的不当行为的原因。毫无疑问，我们并不能将这种结果仅仅归结于一个原因。西班牙政府无疑也用尽了种种办法，来限制和破坏私有企业，使之无法自由而健康地发展；不过，一个伟大的民族是会突破政府的限制，或者塑造政府的品格的，而倘若民众嗜好贸易，则其政府也会被吸引到这种趋势当中来，这一点也是无可置疑的。并且，西班牙诸殖民地的广袤土地，都远

the people been toward trade, the action of government would have been drawn into the same current. The great field of the colonies, also, was remote from the centre of that despotism which blighted the growth of old Spain. As it was, thousands of Spaniards, of the working as well as the upper classes, left Spain; and the occupations in which they engaged abroad sent home little but specie, or merchandise of small bulk, requiring but small tonnage. The mother-country herself produced little but wool, fruit, and iron; her manufactures were naught; her industries suffered; her population steadily decreased. Both she and her colonies depended upon the Dutch for so many of the necessaries of life, that the products of their scanty industries could not suffice to pay for them. "So that Holland merchants," writes a contemporary, "who carry money to most parts of the world to buy commodities, must out of this single country of Europe carry home money, which they receive in payment of their goods." Thus their eagerly sought emblem of wealth passed quickly from their hands. It has already been pointed out how weak, from a military point of view, Spain was from this decay of her shipping. Her wealth being in small bulk on a few ships, following more or less regular routes, was easily seized by an enemy, and the sinews of war paralyzed; whereas the wealth of England and Holland, scattered over thousands of ships in all parts of the world, received many bitter blows in many exhausting wars, without checking a growth which, though painful, was steady. The fortunes of Portugal, united to Spain during a most critical period of her history, followed the same downward path: although foremost in the beginning of the race for development by sea, she fell utterly behind.

"The mines of Brazil were the ruin of Portugal, as those of Mexico and Peru had been of Spain; all manufactures fell into insane contempt; ere long the English supplied the Portuguese not only with clothes, but with all merchandise, all commodities, even to salt-fish and grain. After their gold, the Portuguese abandoned their very soil; the vineyards of Oporto were finally

离该国专制政治的中心；而正是这种专制政治，束缚了旧西班牙的发展。结果就是，成千上万的西班牙人，其中既有工人阶层，也有上流人士，都离开了西班牙；但他们在国外所从事的工作，却并没有给祖国带回来什么东西；他们带回的只有银币，或者只需小吨位船舶即可运送的小宗商品。西班牙国内的物产极少，只有羊毛、水果和铁器；该国完全没有制造企业；工业企业经营状况惨淡；人口数量也一直在减少。西班牙及其各个殖民地，都严重依赖于荷兰人为其提供大量的生活必需品，以至于该国仅有的那些工业企业所生产的商品，还不够用于购买这些生活必需品。"因此，"当时有人这样写道，"那些带着钱到世界各地购买商品的荷兰商人，必定会把货物卖给欧洲这一个国家，然后再把所收到的货款带回家。"这样，西班牙人热衷于寻求的这种财富象征，很快又从他们的手中流走了。前面我们已经指出，从军事角度来看，西班牙因其海运业的这种衰退，已经变得极为脆弱了。该国的财源，全都一小批一小批地集中于为数不多的船只上，而这些船只几乎一直都沿着惯常的航线航行，所以很容易被敌人截获，从而切断该国用于支撑战争的财力资源；但英国和荷兰的财富，则归功于两国在世界各地散布着成千上万条船只，所以虽说在多次旷日持久的战争中也受到过许多沉重的打击，却并未阻碍到两国财力的增长；而且，这种增长尽管费劲得很，却一直都很平稳。葡萄牙由于在历史上一个极为关键的时期与西班牙搅和在一起，所以它的国力也同样日益衰弱了：尽管在海权发展的初期，它名列各国前茅，但如今却完全落后了。"巴西的矿山是葡萄牙的没落之源，就像墨西哥和秘鲁的矿山是西班牙的没落之源那样；所有的制造企业全都陷入了受人鄙视的荒唐处境，而不久之后，非但是衣物，连所有的商品，甚至是咸鱼和

bought by the English with Brazilian gold, which had only passed through Portugal to be spread throughout England." We are assured that in fifty years, five hundred millions of dollars were extracted from "the mines of Brazil, and that at the end of the time Portugal had but twenty-five millions in specie," — a striking example of the difference between real and fictitious wealth.

The English and Dutch were no less desirous of gain than the southern nations. Each in turn has been called "a nation of shopkeepers;" but the jeer, in so far as it is just, is to the credit of their wisdom and uprightness. They were no less bold, no less enterprising, no less patient. Indeed, they were more patient, in that they sought riches not by the sword but by labor, which is the reproach meant to be implied by the epithet; for thus they took the longest, instead of what seemed the shortest, road to wealth. But these two peoples, radically of the same race, had other qualities, no less important than those just named, which combined with their surroundings to favor their development by sea. They were by nature business-men, traders, producers, negotiators. Therefore both in their native country and abroad, whether settled in the ports of civilized nations, or of barbarous eastern rulers, or in colonies of their own foundation, they everywhere strove to draw out all the resources of the land, to develop and increase them. The quick instinct of the born trader, shopkeeper if you will, sought continually new articles to exchange; and this search, combined with the industrious character evolved through generations of labor, made them necessarily producers. At home they became great as manufacturers; abroad, where they controlled, the land grew richer continually, products multiplied, and the necessary exchange between home and the settlements called for more ships. Their shipping therefore increased with these demands of trade, and nations with less aptitude for maritime enterprise, even France herself, great as she has been, called for their products and for the

粮食，葡萄牙也都要由英国来供应了。为了淘金，葡萄牙人放弃了自己的土地；而波尔图的葡萄园，最终也被英国人用源自巴西的黄金买走了——这些黄金，只是在葡萄牙人手中过了一遍，就流入到英国各地去了。"我们可以确定，在50年间，"从巴西的矿山中"榨取的财富高达5亿美元，"而最终，葡萄牙却只剩下2500万美元的金币"——这可是关于真实财富与虚假财富之间差异的一个突出的例子。

英国人与荷兰人的逐利之心，并不亚于欧洲南方的各个民族。这两个民族，每一个都曾经被世人称作"小店主民族"[5]，不过这种讥讽要是公正的话，就说明他们的聪明与公正名不虚传。他们一样大胆，一样有事业心，一样能够吃苦耐劳。事实上，他们更加任劳任怨，因为他们并不是凭借刀枪来掠夺财富，而是通过劳动来逐利的，这也是前述绰号隐含了那种指摘之意的原因；因为这样一来，他们走的就是一条最远的、而非看上去最近的致富之路。但是，这两个民族从根本上来说属于同一种族，还有着与上述特点同样重要的其他品质；这些品质与他们所处的环境结合起来，便极大地有利于其海洋事业的发展了。他们天生就是实业家、商人、生产者和航海家。因此，在本国或者国外，无论是在文明国家的港口，还是处于野蛮残暴的东方君主统治之下，或者是在自己建立的各个殖民地中，他们都见缝插针，努力地利用并开发所有的土地资源。这种天生的商人，或者"小店主"——要是您愿意这样称呼他们的话——有着机敏的本能，使得他们孜孜不倦地去寻找可用于交换的新商品；而这种求索精神，与因世代辛劳而进化出来的那种勤奋性格结合起来，就让他们必然地变成了生产者。在本国，他们与制造者一样伟大；在国外，他们所辖之地的土地日益富庶，物产也日益倍增，而要在国内与这些殖

service of their ships. Thus in many ways they advanced to power at sea. This natural tendency and growth were indeed modified and seriously checked at times by the interference of other governments, jealous of a prosperity which their own people could invade only by the aid of artificial support, — a support which will be considered under the head of governmental action as affecting sea power.

  The tendency to trade, involving of necessity the production of something to trade with, is the national characteristic most important to the development of sea power. Granting it and a good seaboard, it is not likely that the dangers of the sea, or any aversion to it, will deter a people from seeking wealth by the paths of ocean commerce. Where wealth is sought by other means, it may be found; but it will not necessarily lead to sea power. Take France. France has a fine country, an industrious people, an admirable position. The French navy has known periods of great glory, and in its lowest estate has never dishonored the military reputation so dear to the nation. Yet as a maritime State, securely resting upon a broad basis of sea commerce, France, as compared with other historical sea-peoples, has never held more than a respectable position. The chief reason for this, so far as national character goes, is the way in which wealth is sought. As Spain and Portugal sought it by digging gold out of the ground, the temper of the French people leads them to seek it by thrift, economy, hoarding. It is said to be harder to keep than to make a fortune. Possibly; but the adventurous temper, which risks what it has to gain more, has much in common with the adventurous spirit that conquers worlds for commerce. The tendency to save and put aside, to venture timidly and on a small scale, may lead to a general diffusion of wealth on a like small scale, but not to the risks and development of external trade and shipping interests. To illustrate, — and the incident is given only for what it is worth, —

民地之间进行必要的商品交换，就得有更多的船舶。因此，他们的运输业便随着这些贸易需求节节增长了，而那些发展海洋事业的能力较弱的民族，即便是一向伟大的法兰西，也需要英国人和荷兰人的产品，也需要英、荷两国的船舶来为他们效力了。这样，他们便通过种种途径，开始取得海洋的控制权。这种自然而然的趋势和发展，实际上曾不时因别国政府的干预而被改变，并且受到了严重的制约；那些国家妒忌英、荷两国的繁荣兴旺，但那些国家的人民只有在得到人为的撑腰时才能干扰这种繁荣和兴旺——所以，这种撑腰就可以看作是政府为影响制海权而采取的行动。

  对于贸易的这种爱好，必然还会导致他们生产出某种东西来进行贸易；而对于制海权的发展来说，这就是最重要的一种民族特质。有了这种特质和条件优异的沿海地区之后，来自海上的危险或者不愿意出海的心态，就不太可能会阻碍一个民族通过海上贸易去追逐财富了。在用其他方式追求财富的国度，可能也存在着这种特质；但是，它并非一定就会使某个民族获得制海权。以法国为例。法国是一个美好的国家，有着勤劳的民族，地理位置也很不错。法国海军曾经有过一段极为辉煌、威名远扬的时期；而哪怕是处于最底层的官兵，也从未让整个民族所珍视的法国军队的声誉受过损害。然而，作为一个海洋国家，虽然拥有安全而广泛的海上贸易基础，但法兰西跟历史上其他从事海洋事业的民族相比，却从未维持过一种受人敬重的地位。其主要原因，就民族性格这方面来看，即在于他们追逐财富所用的方式。正如西班牙和葡萄牙两国从地下挖掘金矿来追求财富那样，法兰西民族的性格，决定了他们是通过节约、省俭和聚积来追逐财富的。据说，守财比生财更难。可能是这样吧；不过，喜欢冒险、为了获取更多而甘愿冒险的性格，与那种为了商业贸易而征服世界的冒险精神，是有诸多共同之处的。喜欢节约、喜欢积蓄、进行谨慎而小规模

a French officer, speaking to the author about the Panama Canal, said: "I have two shares in it. In France we don't do as you, where a few people take a great many shares each. With us a large number of people take one share or a very few. When these were in the market my wife said to me, 'You take two shares, one for you and one for me.'" As regards the stability of a man's personal fortunes this kind of prudence is doubtless wise; but when excessive prudence or financial timidity becomes a national trait, it must tend to hamper the expansion of commerce and of the nation's shipping. The same caution in money matters, appearing in another relation of life, has checked the production of children, and keeps the population of France nearly stationary.

The noble classes of Europe inherited from the Middle Ages a supercilious contempt for peaceful trade, which has exercised a modifying influence upon its growth, according to the national character of different countries. The pride of the Spaniards fell easily in with this spirit of contempt, and co-operated with that disastrous unwillingness to work and wait for wealth which turned them away from commerce. In France, the vanity which is conceded even by Frenchmen to be a national trait led in the same direction. The numbers and brilliancy of the nobility, and the consideration enjoyed by them, set a seal of inferiority upon an occupation which they despised. Rich merchants and manufacturers sighed for the honors of nobility, and upon obtaining them, abandoned their lucrative professions. Therefore, while the industry of the people and the fruitfulness of the soil saved commerce from total decay, it was pursued under a sense of humiliation which caused its best representatives to escape from it as soon as they could. Louis XIV., under the influence of Colbert, put forth an ordinance "authorizing all noblemen to take an interest in merchant ships, goods and merchandise, without being

投机的脾性，虽说可能会使财富以小规模进行扩散，不会有风险，但也不会让对外贸易和航运业务得以发展起来。举例来说——举此例子，只是因为它具有积极的一面———位法国军官在跟作者谈到巴拿马运河时，是这样说的："我在其中入了两股。在法国，我们不会像你们那样由少数人持股，每个人的股份都很多。我们是由许多人持股，每个人都只持一股或者几股。巴拿马运河的股票上市时，我的妻子这样跟我说：'你去买两股吧，一股给你，另一股给我。'"就个人财产的稳定性而论，这种谨慎无疑是很明智的；不过，倘若过分谨慎或者让金融上的胆小变成了一种民族特征，就必然会阻碍到商业贸易和该国运输业的扩张了。而他们在另一种生活关系中，表现出来的那种对于金钱问题的小心谨慎，已经妨碍到了人们的生儿育女，使得法国的人口增长几乎一直都停滞不前了。

欧洲的贵族阶层，从中世纪起就有目空一切地轻视商业贸易的传统；这种态度，依不同国家的民族特性而定，已经对和平贸易的发展产生了根本性的影响。西班牙人的自负，与这种蔑视精神一拍即合，还与那种不愿工作、不愿等待的糟糕态度结合起来了。在法国，连法国人自己都承认是民族特性的那种虚荣心，也是朝着这个方向发展的。贵族阶层的人数和显赫地位，以及他们受到的敬重，都给他们所鄙视的贸易这一职业贴上了"低人一等"的标签。富有的商人和工厂主都渴望得到贵族封号，而一旦他们获得贵族头衔，便都不再从事那些生财有道的职业了。因此，虽说人民的勤劳和土地的多产并未让该国的商业贸易完全衰退下去，但人们都是带着一种羞耻感来从事贸易的，使得那些最有商业贸易才能的人一旦有可能，便纷纷离开了这一行业。在柯尔贝尔[6]的影响下，路易十四颁布了一项法令，"授权所有贵族都可参股商船、货物和商品并获利，只要他们不参与零售，就不会被认为有损贵族声誉"；而采取这一行动的原因则是，"它关系到我国臣民的切身利

considered as having derogated from nobility, provided they did not sell at retail;" and the reason given for this action was, "that it imports the good of our subjects and our own satisfaction, to efface the relic of a public opinion, universally prevalent, that maritime commerce is incompatible with nobility." But a prejudice involving conscious and open superiority is not readily effaced by ordinances, especially when vanity is a conspicuous trait in national character; and many years later Montesquieu taught that it is contrary to the spirit of monarchy that the nobility should engage in trade.

In Holland there was a nobility; but the State was republican in name, allowed large scope to personal freedom and enterprise, and the centres of power were in the great cities. The foundation of the national greatness was money — or rather wealth. Wealth, as a source of civic distinction, carried with it also power in the State; and with power there went social position and consideration. In England the same result obtained. The nobility were proud; but in a representative government the power of wealth could be neither put down nor overshadowed. It was patent to the eyes of all; it was honored by all; and in England, as well as Holland, the occupations which were the source of wealth shared in the honor given to wealth itself. Thus, in all the countries named, social sentiment, the outcome of national characteristics, had a marked influence upon the national attitude toward trade.

In yet another way does the national genius affect the growth of sea power in its broadest sense; and that is in so far as it possesses the capacity for planting healthy colonies. Of colonization, as of all other growths, it is true that it is most healthy when it is most natural. Therefore colonies that spring from the felt wants and natural impulses of a whole people will have the most solid foundations; and their subsequent growth will be surest when they are least trammelled from home, if the people have the genius for independent action. Men of the past

益和我们自身的满意度，会消除大众关于贵族阶层不适于从事海洋贸易的普遍观念。"但是，一种涉及有意的、公开的优越感的偏见，是不会轻易地被法令消除的，尤其是当虚荣心变成了民族性格中一种明显的特征之后；何况多年之后，孟德斯鸠又告诫人们说，贵族从事贸易，是与君主制度的精神背道而驰的。

在荷兰，也存在着一个贵族阶层；不过，该国名义上却属于共和政体，容许存在广泛的个人自由和自主性，而国家的权力中心也都位于大城市里。国家强盛伟大的基础，便是金钱——或者说财富。作为一种使公民之间产生差异的原因，财富在国家当中同时也伴随着权力；有了权力之后，便有了社会地位和荣誉。在英国，也出现了同样的结果。贵族阶层十分自负；但在一个代议制政府里，既没法遏制有钱人的力量，也无法让财富的势力显得不重要。大家都知道这一点，大家也都尊重这一点；英国与荷兰一样，那些能够带来财富的职业，共同分享着财富本身所赋予的那种尊荣。因此，在上述两国，民族性格所导致的社会舆情，显著地影响到了整个民族对待贸易的态度。

然而，民族精神的确还以另外一种方式，影响着最为广义的制海权发展；这一点，就是迄今为止制海权能够让诸多兴旺发达的殖民地建立起来的原因。殖民事业的发展，就像其他方面的发展那样，在最自然的时候的确是最兴旺的。因此，整个民族因感受到种种需求和自然冲动而建立起来的殖民地，就会拥有最为坚实的基础；而要是该国人民还拥有独立自主的精神，那么当这些殖民地受到本国束缚最少的时候，它们随后的发展就会最有保障。过去三个世纪，人们已经深切地感受到了殖民地作为本国产品的销售市场，作为哺育商业和海运业的温床，对于母国的重要性了；但在殖民事业上所做的努

three centuries have keenly felt the value to the mother-country of colonies as outlets for the home products and as a nursery for commerce and shipping; but efforts at colonization have not had the same general origin, nor have different systems all had the same success. The efforts of statesmen, however far-seeing and careful, have not been able to supply the lack of strong natural impulse; nor can the most minute regulation from home produce as good results as a happier neglect, when the germ of self-development is found in the national character. There has been no greater display of wisdom in the national administration of successful colonies than in that of unsuccessful. Perhaps there has been even less. If elaborate system and supervision, careful adaptation of means to ends, diligent nursing, could avail for colonial growth, the genius of England has less of this systematizing faculty than the genius of France; but England, not France, has been the great colonizer of the world. Successful colonization, with its consequent effect upon commerce and sea power, depends essentially upon national character; because colonies grow best when they grow of themselves, naturally. The character of the colonist, not the care of the home government, is the principle of the colony's growth.

This truth stands out the clearer because the general attitude of all the home governments toward their colonies was entirely selfish. However founded, as soon as it was recognized to be of consequence, the colony became to the home country a cow to be milked; to be cared for, of course, but chiefly as a piece of property valued for the returns it gave. Legislation was directed toward a monopoly of its external trade; the places in its government afforded posts of value for occupants from the mother-country; and the colony was looked upon, as the sea still so often is, as a fit place for those who were ungovernable or useless at home. The military administration, however, so long as it remains a colony, is the proper and necessary attribute of the home government.

力，却并非出于同一种原因，而不同的殖民制度，也并非全都一样地获得了成功。政治家们的努力，无论是多么的深谋远虑和小心谨慎，都无法替代那种强烈的自然冲动；倘若在民族性格中开始出现自我发展的萌芽，那么就算本国最缜密的法规，也不如一种巧妙的忽视，能够让它带来好的结果。在国家对那些成功兴旺的殖民地的管辖中，跟对那些不成功的殖民地进行管辖相比，并没有表现出什么更伟大的智慧来。也许，前者所表现出来的智慧，甚至还不如后者呢。假如精心设计的制度和监管、切实改变实现目标的手段和勤勉的呵护，能够有益于殖民地发展的话，那么英格兰民族精神中的这种系统化能力，就不如法兰西的民族精神；可是，世界上最大的殖民者却是英国，而不是法国。成功的殖民事业，连同它随后对商业贸易和制海权所产生的影响，都主要取决于民族性格；因为各个殖民地都是在自我成长、自然发展的时候，发展得最好。殖民地发展的源泉，是殖民者的性格，而不是母国政府对殖民地的监管。

这一事实，因为所有本国政府对待殖民地的态度通常都是完全自私的，而显得更为清晰。无论殖民地是怎样建立的，一旦人们看到了它的重要性，对于祖国来说，该殖民地就成了一头能够挤奶的奶牛；当然，殖民地也需要照管，但其祖国政府主要是把它当成一种财产，重视它所能带来的回报，才去照管的。制定法律法规，目的是垄断殖民地的对外贸易；殖民地政府中的各个职位，为母国派遣的人员提供了重要的岗位；而且人们都认为，殖民地是一个安置本国难以管束或毫无用处者的合适之所，就像如今人们仍然经常那样看待海洋一样。然而，只要殖民地存在一天，军事管治就是母国政府正当而且必要的统治手段。

The fact of England's unique and wonderful success as a great colonizing nation is too evident to be dwelt upon; and the reason for it appears to lie chiefly in two traits of the national character. The English colonist naturally and readily settles down in his new country, identifies his interest with it, and though keeping an affectionate remembrance of the home from which he came, has no restless eagerness to return. In the second place, the Englishman at once and instinctively seeks to develop the resources of the new country in the broadest sense. In the former particular he differs from the French, who were ever longingly looking back to the delights of their pleasant land; in the latter, from the Spaniards, whose range of interest and ambition was too narrow for the full evolution of the possibilities of a new country.

The character and the necessities of the Dutch led them naturally to plant colonies; and by the year 1650 they had in the East Indies, in Africa, and in America a large number, only to name which would be tedious. They were then far ahead of England in this matter. But though the origin of these colonies, purely commercial in its character, was natural, there seems to have been lacking to them a principle of growth. "In planting them they never sought an extension of empire, but merely an acquisition of trade and commerce. They attempted conquest only when forced by the pressure of circumstances. Generally they were content to trade under the protection of the sovereign of the country." This placid satisfaction with gain alone, unaccompanied by political ambition, tended, like the despotism of France and Spain, to keep the colonies mere commercial dependencies upon the mother-country, and so killed the natural principle of growth.

Before quitting this head of the inquiry, it is well to ask how far the national character of Americans is fitted to develop a great sea power, should other circumstances become favorable.

It seems scarcely necessary, however, to do more than appeal to a not very distant past to

英国作为一个伟大的殖民国家,其独一无二且精彩非凡的成功也极其明显,故无需我们再来详述;而该国成功的原因,似乎主要在于其民族性格中的两种特质。英国的殖民者很自然、也很乐意生活在自己新开辟的国土之上,把新国家的利益当成自己的利益;并且,他们尽管保持着对祖国充满深情的回忆,但并没有急于返回祖国的这种不安分想法。其次,英国人会马不停蹄地去开发新国家中最为广义的种种资源。在前一种特质上,英国人与法国人完全不同,因为法国人始终都热切地回想着生活在美丽祖国时的种种乐事;而在后一种特质上,英国人则有别于西班牙人,因为对于一个有着种种可能、会全面发展起来的新国家而言,西班牙人的兴趣范围太过狭窄了。

荷兰人的性格和需求,使得他们自然而然地开始建立殖民地;到了1650年,他们已经在东印度群岛、非洲和美洲拥有了数不胜数的殖民地了。当时,在建立殖民地这个方面,荷兰要领先于英国许多。不过,在性质上纯属商业逐利的这些殖民地似乎一直缺乏一种令它们发展繁荣起来的源泉。"在建立这些殖民地的过程中,他们从未想过帝国扩张的问题,只是想着通过商业贸易来获利。他们只是在为环境压力所迫时,才会想要去进行征服。通常来说,能够在本国君主的保护之下进行贸易,他们就心满意足了。"这种没有政治野心、只想获利的温和的满足感,常常就像法国和西班牙的独裁统治一样,使得诸殖民地只是一种依赖于母国的商业属地,从而切断了其自然发展与繁荣的源泉。

在不再进行这方面的探究之前,我们不妨还问上一问,假如其他条件有利的话,美国人的民族性格,在多大程度上适合于建立起一种伟大的制海权。

不过,我们无需费神,只需看一看不久之前的历史就能证明,要是没有法律上的

prove that, if legislative hindrances be removed, and more remunerative fields of enterprise filled up, the sea power will not long delay its appearance. The instinct for commerce, bold enterprise in the pursuit of gain, and a keen scent for the trails that lead to it, all exist; and if there be in the future any fields calling for colonization, it cannot be doubted that Americans will carry to them all their inherited aptitude for self-government and independent growth.

VI. Character of the Government. — In discussing the effects upon the development of a nation's sea power exerted by its government and institutions, it will be necessary to avoid a tendency to over-philosophizing, to confine attention to obvious and immediate causes and their plain results, without prying too far beneath the surface for remote and ultimate influences.

Nevertheless, it must be noted that particular forms of government with their accompanying institutions, and the character of rulers at one time or another, have exercised a very marked influence upon the development of sea power. The various traits of a country and its people which have so far been considered constitute the natural characteristics with which a nation, like a man, begins its career; the conduct of the government in turn corresponds to the exercise of the intelligent will-power, which, according as it is wise, energetic and persevering, or the reverse, causes success or failure in a man's life or a nation's history.

It would seem probable that a government in full accord with the natural bias of its people would most successfully advance its growth in every respect; and, in the matter of sea power, the most brilliant successes have followed where there has been intelligent direction by a government fully imbued with the spirit of the people and conscious of its true general bent. Such a government is most certainly secured when the will of the people, or of their best natural exponents, has some large share in making it; but such free governments have sometimes fallen short, while on the other hand despotic power, wielded with judgment and consistency, has

障碍，要是在开拓进取中有更多划算的领域得到了充实，那么，确立制海权就要不了多久。喜欢从事商业贸易的天性，在逐利过程中的大胆精神，以及对于通往财富之路的敏锐嗅觉，美国人全都具备；所以，将来倘若有什么值得进行殖民的领域，那么毫无疑问，美国人就会带着传承下来的那种民主自治和独立发展的天资，进入这些领域。

（六）政府的特征——在讨论一个国家的政府和制度对于其制海权所产生的影响时，必须避免那种过度哲学化的倾向，不能将注意力只限于那些明显而直接的原因，以及它们清晰的结果上，而不去深入探究表面之下那些深远而终极的影响。

尽管如此，我们还是必须认识到，不同的政府形式、与之相应的政治制度以及统治者的性格，都曾对制海权的发展产生过极其重大的影响。我们已经详细探讨过，一个国家与该国国民的不同特点，构成了一个民族的自然特征，就像一个人在开始其事业时所带有的那些自然特征一样；而政府的行为，反过来又与明智地发挥其自制力相对应：倘若发挥得明智、有力而坚忍不拔，就会让一个人在人生中、一个国家在历史上获得成功；倘若与此相反，自然就会导致失败。

一个完全顺应民众嗜好的政府，似乎在各个方面都很可能极为成功地促进其自身的发展；并且，在制海权这个问题上，史上最为辉煌的成就，都是在一个完全充满了民众的精神、很清楚民众真正普遍爱好的政府英明领导之下取得的。倘若人民的意愿，或者说自然拥戴政府的精英们的意愿，在创建政府的过程中发挥了重要的参与作用，那么，这样的政府才是最为稳固的。不过，这种自由民主的政府并不多，一方面，明智而不懈地运用专制权力，有的时候也会很直接地建立起规模庞大的海洋贸易和一支杰出的海军，而自

created at times a great sea commerce and a brilliant navy with greater directness than can be reached by the slower processes of a free people. The difficulty in the latter case is to insure perseverance after the death of a particular despot.

England having undoubtedly reached the greatest height of sea power of any modern nation, the action of her government first claims attention. In general direction this action has been consistent, though often far from praiseworthy. It has aimed steadily at the control of the sea. One of its most arrogant expressions dates back as far as the reign of James I., when she had scarce any possessions outside her own islands; before Virginia or Massachusetts was settled. Here is Richelieu's account of it: ——

"The Duke of Sully, minister of Henry IV. [one of the most chivalrous princes that ever lived], having embarked at Calais in a French ship wearing the French flag at the main, was no sooner in the Channel than, meeting an English despatch-boat which was there to receive him, the commander of the latter ordered the French ship to lower her flag. The Duke, considering that his quality freed him from such an affront, boldly refused; but this refusal was followed by three cannon-shot, which, piercing his ship, pierced the heart likewise of all good Frenchmen. Might forced him to yield what right forbade, and for all the complaints he made he could get no better reply from the English captain than this: 'That just as his duty obliged him to honor the ambassador's rank, it also obliged him to exact the honor due to the flag of his master as sovereign of the sea.' If the words of King James himself were more polite, they nevertheless had no other effect than to compel the Duke to take counsel of his prudence, feigning to be satisfied, while his wound was all the time smarting and incurable. Henry the Great had to practise moderation on this occasion; but with the resolve another time to sustain the rights of his crown by the force that, with the aid of time, he should be able to put upon the sea."

由民族则由于进展比较缓慢，所以这一点是难以企及的。另一方面的难处在于，在某位专制君主去世之后，如何才能确保继续坚定不移地将其政策执行下去。

英国无疑是现代所有国家中达到了海权巅峰的一个国家，所以英国政府的作为，值得我们首先来加以注意。这种作为，虽说常常不值得称颂，但在总体方针上却是连贯一致的。它的目标，一直都是控制海洋。英国人最自负地表达这一点的一个例子，可以远溯到詹姆士一世统治时期；当时，英国除了本国的各个岛屿，几乎还没有占领过别的地方，而弗吉尼亚或马萨诸塞等地也还没有开始拓殖。下面就是黎塞留对这种情况的报告：

"身为亨利四世（历史上最具骑士风度的亲王之一）重臣的苏利公爵[7]，在加来港乘坐一艘主桅悬挂法国国旗的法国船只出发，一抵达英吉利海峡，便碰上了一艘守候在那里多时了的英国通信船；英国通信船上的舰长命令这艘法国船只落旗投降。苏利公爵认为自己有能力免受此种屈辱，便鲁莽地拒绝投降；但他拒绝之后，便挨了三炮，炮弹击穿了他的座舰，击中了船体中心，也击穿了所有优秀法国人的心。武力使他不得不在道义所禁止的东西面前屈服了，而他提出的所有控诉，都只换来了英王这样的回答：'正如职责令他必须尊重您这位大使的官衔一样，他的职责，也让他为了行使他的主人作为海洋领袖的权力。'就算英王詹姆士这话说得更有礼貌一点儿，其效果无非也是使苏利公爵在假装满意的同时，不得不去深思自己应该谨慎这个问题；而他所受的创伤，却是痛苦而永久的了。亨利大帝这一次不得不采取温和稳健的措施了；不过，由于他决心下次一定要通过武力来维护自己的王权，因此在时间的帮助之下，他应当是有能力威胁到海洋的。"

This act of unpardonable insolence, according to modern ideas, was not so much out of accord with the spirit of nations in that day. It is chiefly noteworthy as the most striking, as well as one of the earliest indications of the purpose of England to assert herself at all risks upon the sea; and the insult was offered under one of her most timid kings to an ambassador immediately representing the bravest and ablest of French sovereigns. This empty honor of the flag, a claim insignificant except as the outward manifestation of the purpose of a government, was as rigidly exacted under Cromwell as under the kings. It was one of the conditions of peace yielded by the Dutch after their disastrous war of 1654. Cromwell, a despot in everything but name, was keenly alive to all that concerned England's honor and strength, and did not stop at barren salutes to promote them. Hardly yet possessed of power, the English navy sprang rapidly into a new life and vigor under his stern rule. England's rights, or reparation for her wrongs, were demanded by her fleets throughout the world, — in the Baltic, in the Mediterranean, against the Barbary States, in the West Indies; and under him the conquest of Jamaica began that extension of her empire, by force of arms, which has gone on to our own days. Nor were equally strong peaceful measures for the growth of English trade and shipping forgotten. Cromwell's celebrated Navigation Act declared that all imports into England or her colonies must be conveyed exclusively in vessels belonging to England herself, or to the country in which the products carried were grown or manufactured. This decree, aimed specially at the Dutch, the common carriers of Europe, was resented throughout the commercial world; but the benefit to England, in those days of national strife and animosity, was so apparent that it lasted long under the monarchy. A century and a quarter later we find Nelson, before his famous career had begun, showing his zeal for the welfare of England's shipping by enforcing this same act in the West Indies against American merchant-ships. When Cromwell was dead, and Charles II. sat on the

从现代的观点来看，此种不可饶恕的傲慢行径，是最为明显、也是最早表明了英国不惜一切代价都要维持其海上霸权的标志；而这次事件，竟然是由英国最为胆小谨慎的一位国王所为。这种空洞的国家荣誉，除了向外界表明了一国政府的目标之外，其实是一种无足轻重的权利；但在克伦威尔治下，跟在历任英王统治下那样，英国却一直生硬地坚持着这种权利。这是荷兰人在经历了1645年那场损失惨重的战争之后，所放弃的和平条件之一。除了名义上，克伦威尔其实是一个彻头彻尾的暴君，他对于英国荣誉和力量相关的所有事情都很积极，并不会因为别国表现出了空泛的敬意，就停止提升英国威望和势力的脚步。虽说此时还并不强大，但英国海军却在他的严酷统治之下，迅速地获得了新生和活力。散布于世界各地的英国舰队——在波罗的海和地中海地区对抗巴巴里诸国[8]，以及在西印度群岛——都需要拥有英国的种种权利，或者说都需要弥补它们曾经犯下的失误；在他的统治之下，征服牙买加就是开始了通过武力扩张大英帝国的步伐，而这种扩张，一直持续到了如今我们所处的这个时代。人们也并没有忘记，使得英国商业贸易和海上运输发展壮大起来的那些同样强大有力的和平措施。克伦威尔那部赫赫有名的《航海法案》，规定英国及其各殖民地进口的所有货物，都必须由英国本国的船只来运输，或是由商品出产国的船只来运输。这一法令虽是专门针对号称"欧洲公共承运者"的荷兰人的，却招来了整个商贸世界的不满；不过，在那个充斥着民族冲突和民族仇恨的时代，这样做对英国人的好处却是非常明显的，所以这一法令在英国的君主统治之下持续实行了很久的时间。125年之后，我们还能看到，纳尔逊曾在西印度群岛实行此法案来对抗美国商船，表现出了他维护英国航运利益的拳拳之心；而此时的纳

throne of his father, this king, false to the English people, was yet true to England's greatness and to the traditional policy of her government on the sea. In his treacherous intrigues with Louis XIV., by which he aimed to make himself independent of Parliament and people, he wrote to Louis: "There are two impediments to a perfect union. The first is the great care France is now taking to create a commerce and to be an imposing maritime power. This is so great a cause of suspicion with us, who can possess importance only by our commerce and our naval force, that every step which France takes in this direction will perpetuate the jealousy between the two nations." In the midst of the negotiations which preceded the detestable attack of the two kings upon the Dutch republic, a warm dispute arose as to who should command the united fleets of France and England. Charles was inflexible on this point. "It is the custom of the English," said he, "to command at sea;" and he told the French ambassador plainly that, were he to yield, his subjects would not obey him. In the projected partition of the United Provinces he reserved for England the maritime plunder in positions that controlled the mouths of the rivers Scheldt and Meuse. The navy under Charles preserved for some time the spirit and discipline impressed on it by Cromwell's iron rule; though later it shared in the general decay of morale which marked this evil reign. Monk, having by a great strategic blunder sent off a fourth of his fleet, found himself in 1666 in presence of a greatly superior Dutch force. Disregarding the odds, he attacked without hesitation, and for three days maintained the fight with honor, though with loss. Such conduct is not war; but in the single eye that looked to England's naval prestige and dictated his action, common as it was to England's people as well as to her government, has lain the secret of final success following many blunders through the centuries. Charles's successor, James II., was himself a seaman, and had commanded in two great sea-fights. When William III. came to the throne, the governments of England and Holland were under one hand,

尔逊，还没开始从事他那份声名远扬的职业呢。克伦威尔去世之后，查理二世坐上了父亲的王位；这位国王，虽说对英国人民毫无诚信可言，但也还是一心维护和信守着英国政府对于海洋的传统政策。在他阴险地与路易十四暗中勾结，企图就此不受议会和人民约束的时候，他给路易十四写信说："要形成一种完美无缺的联盟，还有两大障碍。第一，是目前法国正不遗余力地想要开辟商业贸易，想要成为一个真正的海上强国。对于我们来说，这一目标能否实现，却极为值得怀疑；我们只有通过自己的商业贸易和海军，才拥有了如今的重要地位，所以法国在这个方面采取的每一项措施，都会让两国之间的相互猜忌长久地无法得以消除。"在这两位国王联手对荷兰共和国发动可恶进攻之前的谈判过程中，对于该由哪国来指挥英、法联合舰队的问题，双方发生了激烈的争执。在这个问题上，查理二世毫不退让。他称："在海上发号施令，英国人已经习惯了；"他还明明白白地告诉法国大使，假如屈从于法国的话，他的臣民是不会服从其命令的。在分割"联合省"[9]的计划中，他为英国保留了在控制斯凯尔特河与默兹河两个河口的一些位置上进行海上劫掠的权利。查理二世治下的海军，将打上了克伦威尔苛政烙印的那种精神和风纪保持了一段时间；但后来，海军也有了那种标志着查理二世罪恶统治的士气普遍衰落之象了。1666年，蒙克[10]犯了一个极大的战略错误，派出了所率舰队的四分之一，却发现自己要面对兵力大大超过了英军的荷兰军队。他没去考虑有多大胜算，便毫不迟疑地发动了进攻，并且尽管伤亡惨重，却与荷兰人英勇奋战了3天。这种做法还算不上是战争；但从渴望英国海军树立威望并支配其行动的专一目标来看，这种做法却说明了数个世纪中英国屡败屡战并最终获得胜利的奥秘——这正是英国

and continued united in one purpose against Louis XIV. until the Peace of Utrecht in 1713; that is, for a quarter of a century. The English government more and more steadily, and with conscious purpose, pushed on the extension of her sea dominion and fostered the growth of her sea power. While as an open enemy she struck at France upon the sea, so as an artful friend, many at least believed, she sapped the power of Holland afloat. The treaty between the two countries provided that of the sea forces Holland should furnish three eighths, England five eighths, or nearly double. Such a provision, coupled with a further one which made Holland keep up an army of 102,000 against England's 40,000, virtually threw the land war on one and the sea war on the other. The tendency, whether designed or not, is evident; and at the peace, while Holland received compensation by land, England obtained, besides commercial privileges in France, Spain, and the Spanish West Indies, the important maritime concessions of Gibraltar and Port Mahon in the Mediterranean; of Newfoundland, Nova Scotia, and Hudson's Bay in North America. The naval power of France and Spain had disappeared; that of Holland thenceforth steadily declined. Posted thus in America, the West Indies, and the Mediterranean, the English government thenceforth moved firmly forward on the path which made of the English kingdom the British Empire. For the twenty-five years following the Peace of Utrecht, peace was the chief aim of the ministers who directed the policy of the two great seaboard nations, France and England; but amid all the fluctuations of continental politics in a most unsettled period, abounding in petty wars and shifty treaties, the eye of England was steadily fixed on the maintenance of her sea power. In the Baltic, her fleets checked the attempts of Peter the Great upon Sweden, and so maintained a balance of power in that sea, from which she drew not only a great trade but the chief part of her naval stores, and which the Czar aimed to make a Russian lake. Denmark endeavored to establish an East India company aided by foreign

人民与政府的共同看法。查理二世的继任者詹姆士二世，本身就曾是一名水兵，并指挥进行过两次大规模的海战。威廉三世登基后，英、荷两国政府便为一人所掌控，并且为了对抗路易十四这个相同的目标而联合起来，直到1713年签订《乌特勒支和约》；也就是说，两国结盟长达25年。有着清晰目标的英国政府，便日益平稳地推进其海洋霸权，从而促进了该国制海权的发展。尽管它是法国公开的敌人，在海上打击法国，但许多人认为，它至少也是个狡诈的友邦，也削弱了荷兰的海洋实力。两国签订的条约规定，荷兰应当装备联合海军的八分之三，英国装备八分之五，几乎是荷兰的两倍。这一条款，加上让荷兰维持102000陆军、而英国只维持40000陆军的另一条款，实际上就是规定了一国负责陆上战争，而另一国负责海上战争。不管是不是有意为之，这种倾向性都是很明显的；而根据和约，虽说荷兰获得了土地补偿，但英国除了在法国、西班牙和西属西印度群岛拥有了商贸特权，还攫取了地中海地区的直布罗陀和马翁港这两处要地，以及北美的纽芬兰、新斯科舍和哈德逊湾。法国和西班牙的海洋实力，此时已经荡然无存；而荷兰的海洋实力，此后也日益衰落下去了。在美洲、西印度群岛和地中海地区这样扎稳脚跟之后，英国政府便开始坚定地走上了一条让英王国变成大不列颠帝国的道路。《乌特勒支和约》签订之后的25年间，各国制定对英、对法政策的大臣们，首要的目标都是与这两个沿海大国和平相处；但在社会极为动荡不安、欧洲大陆政治形势风云变幻、小规模战争不断和各种狡猾的条约层出不穷的那个时期，英国的注意力却一直牢牢地放在保持其制海权上。在波罗的海，英国舰队挫败了彼得大帝对瑞典的袭击，从而维持了波罗的海地区海上势力的均衡；从这一地区，英国不仅获取了大规模的贸易利润，

capital; England and Holland not only forbade their subjects to join it, but threatened Denmark, and thus stopped an enterprise they thought adverse to their sea interests. In the Netherlands, which by the Utrecht Treaty had passed to Austria, a similar East India company, having Ostend for its port, was formed, with the emperor's sanction. This step, meant to restore to the Low Countries the trade lost to them through their natural outlet of the Scheldt, was opposed by the sea powers England and Holland; and their greediness for the monopoly of trade, helped in this instance by France, stifled this company also after a few years of struggling life. In the Mediterranean, the Utrecht settlement was disturbed by the emperor of Austria, England's natural ally in the then existing state of European politics. Backed by England, he, having already Naples, claimed also Sicily in exchange for Sardinia. Spain resisted; and her navy, just beginning to revive under a vigorous minister, Alberoni, was crushed and annihilated by the English fleet off Cape Passaro in 1718; while the following year a French army, at the bidding of England, crossed the Pyrenees and completed the work by destroying the Spanish dockyards. Thus England, in addition to Gibraltar and Mahon in her own hands, saw Naples and Sicily in those of a friend, while an enemy was struck down. In Spanish America, the limited privileges to English trade, wrung from the necessities of Spain, were abused by an extensive and scarcely disguised smuggling system; and when the exasperated Spanish government gave way to excesses in the mode of suppression, both the minister who counselled peace and the opposition which urged war defended their opinions by alleging the effects of either upon England's sea power and honor. While England's policy thus steadily aimed at widening and strengthening the bases of her sway upon the ocean, the other governments of Europe seemed blind to the dangers to be feared from her sea growth. The miseries resulting from the overweening power of Spain in days long gone by seemed to be forgotten; forgotten also the more

而且其主要的海军军需品也都来自这里，可沙皇却想把这里变成俄国的一个内湖。丹麦努力想要借助外国资金，建立起一个东印度公司；可英国和荷兰非但禁止两国臣民加入，还威胁丹麦，从而阻止了该公司的成立，因为英、荷都认为这个公司不利于两国的海洋利益。在尼德兰——《乌特勒支和约》已规定将这一地区割让给了奥地利——奥地利皇帝批准成立了一个类似于东印度公司、以奥斯坦德为口岸的公司。这一做法，旨在通过斯凯尔特河的天然入海口，恢复低地国家[11]已经输给英、荷两国的贸易业，却遭到了这两个海上强国的反对；两国都贪得无厌，想垄断贸易，在这件事情中又得到了法国相助，所以该公司在步履维艰地坚持了数年之后，也被两国扼杀了。在地中海地区，奥地利皇帝破坏了《乌特勒支和约》；但在当时的欧洲政治格局中，奥地利皇帝却是英国的天然盟友。在英国的支持下，已经攫取了那不勒斯的奥地利皇帝，又要求用西西里交换撒丁岛。西班牙拒绝了这一要求；于是，由阿尔韦罗尼[12]这位精力充沛的大臣统领、刚刚开始复兴的西班牙海军，1718年便在帕萨罗角海岸被英国舰队击溃和消灭了。而在第二年，一支法国陆军在英国的要求下越过比利牛斯山脉，又摧毁了西班牙的造船厂，从而结束了这次战争。如此一来，英国除了将直布罗陀和马翁港掌控在自己手中之外，还让那不勒斯和西西里掌控在盟友手中，从而打垮了自己的一大敌人。在西属美洲，英国虽说从西班牙生活必需品中榨取到了有限的贸易特权，却深受一种覆盖面广且差不多属于明目张胆的走私制度之害；而当恼羞成怒的西班牙政府开始大肆进行压制之后，那位建议和谈的大臣与力挺开战的反对派，便都用和谈或开战对英国制海权和声誉的影响，来捍卫自己的观点。虽说英国的政策一向如此，旨在扩大和加强它统治海

recent lesson of the bloody and costly wars provoked by the ambition and exaggerated power of Louis XIV. Under the eyes of the statesmen of Europe there was steadily and visibly being built up a third overwhelming power, destined to be used as selfishly, as aggressively, though not as cruelly, and much more successfully than any that had preceded it. This was the power of the sea, whose workings, because more silent than the clash of arms, are less often noted, though lying clearly enough on the surface. It can scarcely be denied that England's uncontrolled dominion of the seas, during almost the whole period chosen for our subject, was by long odds the chief among the military factors that determined the final issue. [2] So far, however, was this influence from being foreseen after Utrecht, that France for twelve years, moved by personal exigencies of her rulers, sided with England against Spain; and when Fleuri came into power in 1726, though this policy was reversed, the navy of France received no attention, and the only blow at England was the establishment of a Bourbon prince, a natural enemy to her, upon the throne of the two Sicilies in 1736. When war broke out with Spain in 1739, the navy of England was in numbers more than equal to the combined navies of Spain and France; and during the quarter of a century of nearly uninterrupted war that followed, this numerical disproportion increased. In these wars England, at first instinctively, afterward with conscious purpose under a government that recognized her opportunity and the possibilities of her great sea power, rapidly built up that mighty colonial empire whose foundations were already securely laid in the characteristics of her colonists and the strength of her fleets. In strictly European affairs her wealth, the outcome of her sea power, made her play a conspicuous part during the same period. The system of subsidies, which began half a century before in the wars of Marlborough and received its most extensive development half a century later in the Napoleonic wars, maintained the efforts of her allies, which would have been crippled, if not paralyzed, without them. Who

洋的各种基础，但欧洲其他各国政府似乎都看不到这一危险，都毫不担心英国在海洋上的发展壮大。西班牙这个大国因为过去那种盲目自大的势力而导致的可悲境遇，似乎都被人们忘记了；而最近因路易十四的野心和言过其实的实力所激起的那一场场血腥、代价巨大的战争所带来的教训，也都被人们遗忘了。在欧洲的政治家们看来，欧洲正在平稳而明显地崛起第三种不可抗拒的力量；这种力量注定要被人们自私地加以利用，虽说并不像以前那样残酷，却会强有力地加以利用，并且会比以前的所有力量利用得更加成功。这便是海洋的力量；由于不像短兵相接那样喧嚣，所以它的影响尽管非常明显地摆在人们面前，人们往往却很少注意到它。不可否认，在我们为这一主题所选择的、差不多整个这一段时间内，英国那种势不可挡的海洋霸权，无疑都是决定最终结果的军事因素中最主要的一个。[2]然而，在《乌特勒支和约》签订之后，一直都无人预见到这种影响，以至于在长达12年的时间里，法国都在其君主个人经历的驱使之下，站在英国一边对抗西班牙；1726年弗勒里[13]掌权之后，虽说这一政策已经取消，但法国海军仍然无人重视，而该国对英国的唯一打击，便是在1736年扶持英国的天敌、波旁王朝的一位亲王登上了两西西里王国[14]的王位。1739年与西班牙开战的时候，英国海军在兵力上比法、西两国海军加起来还要多；而在随后几乎战火不断的25年间，这种兵力差距变得越来越巨大了。在这些战争中，英国迅速建立起了一个强大的殖民帝国——起初是凭直觉，后来则是因为英国政府看到了机会，看到了英国拥有强大制海权的可能性，从而具有了明确的目的；而英国殖民者的性格和英国舰队的力量，则为这一殖民帝国打下了坚实的基础。在纯粹的欧洲事务中，因为拥有制海权而攫取的财富，使得英国在同一时期发挥了极为显著的作用。始于半个世

can deny that the government which with one hand strengthened its fainting allies on the continent with the life-blood of money, and with the other drove its own enemies off the sea and out of their chief possessions, Canada, Martinique, Guadeloupe, Havana, Manila, gave to its country the foremost role in European politics; and who can fail to see that the power which dwelt in that government, with a land narrow in extent and poor in resources, sprang directly from the sea? The policy in which the English government carried on the war is shown by a speech of Pitt, the master-spirit during its course, though he lost office before bringing it to an end. Condemning the Peace of 1763, made by his political opponent, he said: "France is chiefly, if not exclusively, formidable to us as a maritime and commercial power. What we gain in this respect is valuable to us, above all, through the injury to her which results from it. You have left to France the possibility of reviving her navy." Yet England's gains were enormous; her rule in India was assured, and all North America east of the Mississippi in her hands. By this time the onward path of her government was clearly marked out, had assumed the force of a tradition, and was consistently followed. The war of the American Revolution was, it is true, a great mistake, looked at from the point of view of sea power; but the government was led into it insensibly by a series of natural blunders. Putting aside political and constitutional considerations, and looking at the question as purely military or naval, the case was this: The American colonies were large and growing communities at a great distance from England. So long as they remained attached to the mother-country, as they then were enthusiastically, they formed a solid base for her sea power in that part of the world; but their extent and population were too great, when coupled with the distance from England, to afford any hope of holding them by force, if any powerful nations were willing to help them. This "if," however, involved a notorious probability; the humiliation of France and Spain was so bitter and so recent that

纪之前的马尔伯勒[15]征战中，并在半个世纪后的拿破仑战争中得到最充分发展的拨款津贴制度，使得英国的盟国一直能够为其出力；倘若没有这些友邦，英国就算不是完全任人宰割，其势力也会大大削弱的。谁也无法否认，一个政府倘若左手握着金钱命脉，巩固欧洲大陆上那些虚弱不堪的盟国，右手又将自己的敌人赶下海去并将它们逐出加拿大、马提尼克、瓜达鲁佩、哈瓦那、马尼拉等主要的殖民地，就会让本国在欧洲政治中扮演最重要的角色；又有谁看不到，因为国土面积狭窄、资源匮乏，所以该国政府的力量都是直接来自于海洋呢？皮特[16]的一次演说，表明了英国政府在战争中所坚持的政策；他是英国在战争过程中涌现出来的一位杰出人物，尽管不待战争结束他便丢了官。在谴责政敌所订的《1763年和约》时，他说："法国就算不是只针对我国，也是我国海上力量和贸易力量的主要威胁。我们在这方面所取得的成就，尤其是通过损害法国利益而让我国获益这一点，弥足珍贵。可你们却给了法国复兴该国海军的机会。"不过，英国的收获是巨大的；它对印度的统治得到了巩固，而北美密西西比河以东的所有地区，也都为它一手所掌控了。到了此时，英国政府已经明确地规划出了自己的前进道路，并且已经采取了一种传统的力量，一直遵循着这条道路前进。的确，从制海权的角度来看，美国革命战争是它犯下的一个巨大失误；不过，英国政府是被一系列的非人为错误所误导，不知不觉地参与进去的。倘若不考虑政治和宪法这两个方面，而将这个问题看作是纯粹的军事问题或海军问题的话，那么，情况就是这样的：美洲的殖民地数量众多，并且当时正在距英国极为遥远的地方发展成为一个一个的社会。只要它们继续隶属于祖国——当时，诸殖民地对于这一点极为狂热——那么，它们就会成为英国在这一地区确立制海权的牢固基地；不过，它们面积

they were sure to seek revenge, and it was well known that France in particular had been carefully and rapidly building up her navy. Had the colonies been thirteen islands, the sea power of England would quickly have settled the question; but instead of such a physical barrier they were separated only by local jealousies which a common danger sufficiently overcame. To enter deliberately on such a contest, to try to hold by force so extensive a territory, with a large hostile population, so far from home, was to renew the Seven Years' War with France and Spain, and with the Americans, against, instead of for, England. The Seven Years' War had been so heavy a burden that a wise government would have known that the added weight could not be borne, and have seen it was necessary to conciliate the colonists. The government of the day was not wise, and a large element of England's sea power was sacrificed; but by mistake, not wilfully; through arrogance, not through weakness.

This steady keeping to a general line of policy was doubtless made specially easy for successive English governments by the clear indications of the country's conditions. Singleness of purpose was to some extent imposed. The firm maintenance of her sea power, the haughty determination to make it felt, the wise state of preparation in which its military element was kept, were yet more due to that feature of her political institutions which practically gave the government, during the period in question, into the hands of a class, — a landed aristocracy. Such a class, whatever its defects otherwise, readily takes up and carries on a sound political tradition, is naturally proud of its country's glory, and comparatively insensible to the sufferings of the community by which that glory is maintained. It readily lays on the pecuniary burden necessary for preparation and for endurance of war. Being as a body rich, it feels those burdens less. Not being commercial, the sources of its own wealth are not so immediately endangered, and it does not share that political timidity which characterizes those whose property is

太大、人口太多，加之与英国相距遥远，所以，倘若其他强国愿意为它们撑腰，那就不要指望能够用武力去控制它们。然而，这个"倘若"也包括了一种众所周知的可能性：法国和西班牙所受的屈辱是如此的刻骨铭心，其受辱的时间又如此之近，所以它们一定会寻找报仇雪恨的机会；特别是法国，它一直都在认真而快速地建立自己的海军，这一点世人皆知。倘若这些殖民地是13个岛屿，那么英国凭借制海权，就会迅速解决掉这一问题；可它们并没有这样的自然屏障，只能通过内讧才能把它们分开来，而某种共同的危险即足以消除这种内讧。刻意地介入这场战争、试图用武力控制面积如此广袤、民众如此敌视、距本国如此遥远的一片地区，就是与法、西两国重新开始一场"七年战争"，而此次，美洲人民并非支持英国，而是反抗英国了。"七年战争"曾经给英国带来极为沉重的负担，所以一个明智的政府本该明白，哪怕再重一点点，自己都是承受不起的，因而也会明白，对殖民者必须加以安抚才行。当时的政府并不明智，所以英国就失去了大部分制海权。不过，这是失误而非存心；这是因为骄傲自大，而非由于软弱才失去的。

对于英国后来的历任政府来说，通过种种明确迹象表明，来平稳地执行一条总的政策路线，无疑都是极其容易的。而目标专一，从某种程度上来说是被迫的。坚定不移地维护制海权、傲慢自大地要别国感受到这种制海权、明智地筹划制海权在军事中所占的分量，都更多地应当归因于英国政治制度的特点；这种政治制度，使得英国政府在我们所讨论的这一时期内，落入了土地贵族阶层的手中。这样一个阶层，无论它在别的方面有什么样的缺陷，都很容易采取并且坚持一种良好的政治传统，也自然会以祖国的荣誉为傲，而对保持此种荣誉的社会疾苦相对却比较麻木。这个阶层常常会将备战和打持久

exposed and business threatened, — the proverbial timidity of capital. Yet in England this class was not insensible to anything that touched her trade for good or ill. Both houses of Parliament vied in careful watchfulness over its extension and protection, and to the frequency of their inquiries a naval historian attributes the increased efficiency of the executive power in its management of the navy. Such a class also naturally imbibes and keeps up a spirit of military honor, which is of the first importance in ages when military institutions have not yet provided the sufficient substitute in what is called esprit-de-corps. But although full of class feeling and class prejudice, which made themselves felt in the navy as well as elsewhere, their practical sense left open the way of promotion to its highest honors to the more humbly born; and every age saw admirals who had sprung from the lowest of the people. In this the temper of the English upper class differed markedly from that of the French. As late as 1789, at the outbreak of the Revolution, the French Navy List still bore the name of an official whose duty was to verify the proofs of noble birth on the part of those intending to enter the naval school.

Since 1815, and especially in our own day, the government of England has passed very much more into the hands of the people at large. Whether her sea power will suffer therefrom remains to be seen. Its broad basis still remains in a great trade, large mechanical industries, and an extensive colonial system. Whether a democratic government will have the foresight, the keen sensitiveness to national position and credit, the willingness to insure its prosperity by adequate outpouring of money in times of peace, all which are necessary for military preparation, is yet an open question. Popular governments are not generally favorable to military expenditure, however necessary, and there are signs that England tends to drop behind.

战所必需的经济负担，轻描淡写地强加于人民身上。作为一个富有阶层，他们并不觉得那些负担很沉重。由于不从事商业贸易，这一阶层本身的财富并不会直接受到威胁；所以在政治上，他们不像那些财产毫无保障、生意受到威胁的人一样胆小谨慎——这就是人所共知的"资本的胆小"。不过在英国，这一阶层对于触及到英国贸易的事情，无论是有利还是不利，也并非一概都是麻木不仁的。国会上下两院都竞相小心地照管着英国贸易的发展并对其加以保护，所以一位海军历史学家曾把控制海军过程中行政权力效率的增加，归因于上下两院对海军情况的经常质询。这个阶层，还自然而然地接受并保持了一种军事荣誉精神；在军事制度尚未提供某种足以取代所谓"集体荣誉感"的时代，这种荣誉精神是极为重要的。不过，虽说充满了阶级感情和阶级成见，使得别人在海军和其他领域都能感受到他们的存在，但他们的实用主义，却让他们允许地位较卑贱的人获得晋升并得到最高的荣誉；因为每个时代，都有出身于最底层的海军司令。在这一点上，英国上流阶层的脾性与法国有着天壤之别。近至1789年法国革命爆发的时候，法国海军名册上仍保留着这样一位军官的名字：这位军官的职责，就是核实那些有意加入海军的人所提供的贵族血统证明。

自1815年以来，尤其是在如今的这个时代，英国政府已经将很多权利移交给了普通民众。英国的制海权是否会因此而受到损害，仍有待观察。英国制海权的广泛基础，仍然存在于该国规模巨大的贸易、大型的机械工业以及全面的殖民体系当中。英国政府是否具有远见，对国家地位和信誉是否具有锐利的敏感性，是否愿意在和平时期出钱来确保国家的繁荣——这些方面都是做好军事准备所必需的——也仍是一个存有争议的问题。平民政府通常都并不赞成军费支出的，无论这些军费支出有多么必要，故有迹象表

It has already been seen that the Dutch Republic, even more than the English nation, drew its prosperity and its very life from the sea. The character and policy of its government were far less favorable to a consistent support of sea power. Composed of seven provinces, with the political name of the United Provinces, the actual distribution of power may be roughly described to Americans as an exaggerated example of States Rights. Each of the maritime provinces had its own fleet and its own admiralty, with consequent jealousies. This disorganizing tendency was partly counteracted by the great preponderance of the Province of Holland, which alone contributed five sixths of the fleet and fifty-eight per cent of the taxes, and consequently had a proportionate share in directing the national policy. Although intensely patriotic, and capable of making the last sacrifices for freedom, the commercial spirit of the people penetrated the government, which indeed might be called a commercial aristocracy, and made it averse to war, and to the expenditures which are necessary in preparing for war. As has before been said, it was not until danger stared them in the face that the burgomasters were willing to pay for their defences. While the republican government lasted, however, this economy was practised least of all upon the fleet; and until the death of John De Witt, in 1672, and the peace with England in 1674, the Dutch navy was in point of numbers and equipment able to make a fair show against the combined navies of England and France. Its efficiency at this time undoubtedly saved the country from the destruction planned by the two kings. With De Witt's death the republic passed away, and was followed by the practically monarchical government of William of Orange. The life-long policy of this prince, then only eighteen, was resistance to Louis XIV. and to the extension of French power. This resistance took shape upon the land rather than the sea, — a tendency promoted by England's withdrawal from the

明，英国已经有了落后的趋势。

人们已经看到，荷兰共和国的繁荣与荷兰人民的生活，甚至比英格兰这个民族还要更得益于海洋。荷兰政府的特点和政策，根本谈不上有利于始终如一地支持该国拥有制海权。荷兰共和国由7个省份所组成，政治上号称"联合省"；在美国人看来，该国实际的权力分配情况，大体上可以说成是一种夸大了的"州权"的例子。每一个沿海省份都有自己的舰队和海军本部，因此互有猜忌。这种混乱不堪的瓦解趋势，因为荷兰省具有极大的优势而部分地得到了遏制；这一个省就占了全国舰队的六分之五；税收则占全国的85%，因此在制定国家政策时，相应的权力也很大。尽管有着强烈的爱国之情，也能够为了自由而做出最后的牺牲，但民众从事商业贸易的精神还是渗入到了该国政府——它实际上可以称为一个商业贵族政府——当中，并使得它反对战争，反对把钱花在备战所必需的军费上。正如前面已经说过的那样，只有到了危险迫在眉睫的时候，各地长官才愿意花钱来进行防御。然而，在荷兰共和国政府存续期间，这种节省的做法却一点儿也没用在舰队上；直到1672年约翰·德·威特去世、1674年与英国签订和约时，荷兰海军的数量和装备都足以在英、法两国的联合海军面前趾高气扬。此时荷兰海军的实力无疑挽救了该国，使之没有被英、法两国国王密谋消灭掉。随着德·威特去世，共和政体也一去不返，继之而来的，实际上是奥兰治的威廉君主政府了。这位亲王彼时年方18岁，其终生的政策便是对抗路易十四、对抗法国势力的扩张。此种对抗，体现在陆地上而不是在海洋上——这种变化趋势，是由英国退出战争所促成的。早在1676年，舰队司令德·鲁伊特[17]就发现，他的兵力根本应付不了法国海军这一方。由于政府的注意力一直都集中于陆上边疆，所以荷兰海军迅速衰落下去了。1688年，当奥兰治亲王威

war. As early as 1676, Admiral De Ruyter found the force given him unequal to cope with the French alone. With the eyes of the government fixed on the land frontier, the navy rapidly declined. In 1688, when William of Orange needed a fleet to convoy him to England, the burgomasters of Amsterdam objected that the navy was incalculably decreased in strength, as well as deprived of its ablest commanders. When king of England, William still kept his position as stadtholder, and with it his general European policy, he found in England the sea power he needed, and used the resources of Holland for the land war. This Dutch prince consented that in the allied fleets, in councils of war, the Dutch admirals should sit below the junior English captain; and Dutch interests at sea were sacrificed as readily as Dutch pride to the demands of England. When William died, his policy was still followed by the government which succeeded him. Its aims were wholly centred upon the land, and at the Peace of Utrecht, which closed a series of wars extending over forty years, Holland, having established no sea claim, gained nothing in the way of sea resources, of colonial extension, or of commerce.

Of the last of these wars an English historian says: "The economy of the Dutch greatly hurt their reputation and their trade. Their men-of-war in the Mediterranean were always victualled short, and their convoys were so weak and ill-provided that for one ship that we lost, they lost five, which begat a general notion that we were the safer carriers, which certainly had a good effect. Hence it was that our trade rather increased than diminished in this war."

From that time Holland ceased to have a great sea power, and rapidly lost the leading position among the nations which that power had built up. It is only just to say that no policy could have saved from decline this small, though determined, nation, in face of the persistent

廉需要一支舰队护送他前往英国的时候，阿姆斯特丹的官员们都极力反对，说海军的力量已经不可估量地削弱了，又缺少有才干的指挥官。当上了英国国王之后，威廉仍然兼任荷兰执政，并且在荷兰继续执行其全面的欧洲政策；此时他发现，英国正好拥有自己所需要的那种制海权，所以便开始利用荷兰的资源来进行陆上战争。这位荷兰亲王同意，在联合舰队中、在军事会议上，荷兰各舰队司令都应当坐在那些资历较低的英军舰长的下首；而荷兰的海洋利益，就像荷兰人的自负那样，轻而易举地为了满足英国的需要而牺牲掉了。威廉死后，下一届政府仍然继续执行着他的政策。这届政府的目标，全都集中在陆地上；而在结束了一系列长达40多年战争的《乌特勒支和约》中，由于没有任何海洋权利诉求，因此在海洋资源、殖民扩张或商业贸易等方面，荷兰都一无所获。

对于其中的最后一次战争，有位英国历史学家曾经如此说道："荷兰人的节俭，极大地损害了他们的名声和贸易。他们在地中海的作战人员总是军粮短缺，而他们的护航队兵力既弱，装备又落后，所以我们每损失1艘船，他们就会损失5艘，使得大家都认为，我们才是更安全的承运人，这当然产生了很好的效果。在这场战争中，我国的贸易是增长而不是削弱了，原因即在于此。"

自那时起，荷兰就不再拥有一种强大的制海权了，因而在确立了制海权的国家中，它很快就丧失了领先地位。公平地来说，是没有什么政策，可以在路易十四那种固执持久的敌意面前，挽救这个虽说意志坚定却很小的国家，使它不致衰落下去的。与法国的友好关系，确保了该国陆地边疆的和平，本来也是可以让它坚持得更久一点，来与英国

enmity of Louis XIV. The friendship of France, insuring peace on her landward frontier, would have enabled her, at least for a longer time, to dispute with England the dominion of the seas; and as allies the navies of the two continental States might have checked the growth of the enormous sea power which has just been considered. Sea peace between England and Holland was only possible by the virtual subjection of one or the other, for both aimed at the same object. Between France and Holland it was otherwise; and the fall of Holland proceeded, not necessarily from her inferior size and numbers, but from faulty policy on the part of the two governments. It does not concern us to decide which was the more to blame.

France, admirably situated for the possession of sea power, received a definite policy for the guidance of her government from two great rulers, Henry IV. and Richelieu. With certain well-defined projects of extension eastward upon the land were combined a steady resistance to the House of Austria, which then ruled in both Austria and Spain, and an equal purpose of resistance to England upon the sea. To further this latter end, as well as for other reasons, Holland was to be courted as an ally. Commerce and fisheries as the basis of sea power were to be encouraged, and a military navy was to be built up. Richelieu left what he called his political will, in which he pointed out the opportunities of France for achieving sea power, based upon her position and resources; and French writers consider him the virtual founder of the navy, not merely because he equipped ships, but from the breadth of his views and his measures to insure sound institutions and steady growth. After his death, Mazarin inherited his views and general policy, but not his lofty and martial spirit, and during his rule the newly formed navy disappeared. When Louis XIV. took the government into his own hands, in 1661, there were but thirty ships of war, of which only three had as many as sixty guns. Then began a

争夺海洋统治权的；而作为盟友，这两个大陆国家的海军本来也是可以遏制前述这种庞大的制海权，使其无法发展扩大起来的。英、荷两国之间在海洋上的和平，只有在一国事实上臣服于另一国的前提下，才有可能实现；这是因为，两国所致力的都是同一个目标。而法、荷之间则不一样；荷兰的衰落，并不一定是因为其国土面积和人口数量不如别国，而是因为两国政府的错误政策。至于评判哪国政府应负更大的责任，则无需我们去关心了。

法国非但位置十分有利于拥有制海权，还从亨利四世和黎塞留这两位伟大的统治者那里，获得了一种引导其政府行政的明确政策。除了在陆地上向东扩张的某些明确计划，它还一直在对抗奥地利的哈布斯堡王朝——当时，哈布斯堡王朝统治着奥地利和西班牙两国——并出于相同的目的，而在海洋上与英国抗衡。为了推动后一个目标，以及出于其他诸多原因，使得法国必须设法让荷兰成为其盟国。它必须鼓励民众从事商业贸易和渔业，因为二者是获得制海权的基础；还必须建立一支能够打仗的海军。黎塞留留下了一份他自己所称的"政治遗嘱"，指出了法国在其位置和资源的基础上成就制海权的诸多机会；法国史学家们都认为他是法国海军真正的创始人，并不仅仅是因为他装备了许多舰船，而是因为他的眼界之宽广，以及他为确保制度合理和平稳发展而采取的诸多措施。他去世之后，马萨林继承了他的观点和所有的政策，却没有继承他那种崇高而尚武的精神，所以在马萨林统治法国期间，刚刚建立起来的海军又逐渐没落了。1661年路易十四掌控政府之时，法国只有30艘战舰，其中仅有3艘战舰上拥有60门火炮。接下来，就开始出现了一种极为惊人的文治武功；这种文治武功，只有一个巧妙而系统地加

most astonishing manifestation of the work which can be done by absolute government ably and systematically wielded. That part of the administration which dealt with trade, manufactures, shipping, and colonies, was given to a man of great practical genius, Colbert, who had served with Richelieu and had drunk in fully his ideas and policy. He pursued his aims in a spirit thoroughly French. Everything was to be organized, the spring of everything was in the minister's cabinet. "To organize producers and merchants as a powerful army, subjected to an active and intelligent guidance, so as to secure an industrial victory for France by order and unity of efforts, and to obtain the best products by imposing on all workmen the processes recognized as best by competent men. ... To organize seamen and distant commerce in large bodies like the manufactures and internal commerce, and to give as a support to the commercial power of France a navy established on a firm basis and of dimensions hitherto unknown," — such, we are told, were the aims of Colbert as regards two of the three links in the chain of sea power. For the third, the colonies at the far end of the line, the same governmental direction and organization were evidently purposed; for the government began by buying back Canada, Newfoundland, Nova Scotia, and the French West India Islands from the parties who then owned them. Here, then, is seen pure, absolute, uncontrolled power gathering up into its hands all the reins for the guidance of a nation's course, and proposing so to direct it as to make, among other things, a great sea power.

To enter into the details of Colbert's action is beyond our purpose. It is enough to note the chief part played by the government in building up the sea power of the State, and that this very great man looked not to any one of the bases on which it rests to the exclusion of the others, but embraced them all in his wise and provident administration. Agriculture, which increases the products of the earth, and manufactures, which multiply the products of man's industry;

以控制的专制政府，才能得以实现。对贸易、制造业、运输业和殖民地事务进行管理的政府部门，交给了柯尔贝尔这个具有极大实干天赋的人；他曾经与黎塞留共过事，并且充分汲取了黎塞留的观点和政策。他以一种彻底的法国精神，追求着自己的目标。一切都必须有条有理，一切政令均出自这位首相的内阁。"要将生产者和商人组织起来，变成一支强大的军队，使之受到积极而睿智的指导，从而通过有秩序的、一致的努力，确保法国在实业上的胜利，并且要通过强制所有工人接受有识之士所公认的加工流程，来获得品质最佳的产品……要像制造业和国内贸易那样，将水手和远洋贸易组织成大型实体企业，并且让一支建立在牢固基础之上、规模之大前所未有的海军，成为支撑法国贸易实力的后盾，"——我们得知，这些就是柯尔贝尔的目标，它们都与制海权链条上三大环节中的两环相关。至于第三环，即位于最远端的殖民地，柯尔贝尔显然也打算采取相同的施政方针和组织方式；因为法国政府首先就从当时的所有者手中，将加拿大、纽芬兰、新斯科舍和法属西印度群岛重新赎了回来。因此，我们从中便可看出，这种纯粹、绝对而不加约束的权力，将指引一国发展之路的支配权集于一身，其目的就是通过这样做，使得国家除了在其他方面发展起来之外，还能确立起一种伟大的制海权。

详细了解柯尔贝尔的施政行为，并不是我们的目的。我们注意到下述两点就足够了：一是法国政府在确立该国制海权的过程中发挥了主导作用；二是这位伟人所关注的，并非仅仅是为确立制海权打下某个方面的基础，而是在其睿智而颇具远见卓识的行政任期之内，为确立该国制海权打下所有的基础。农业生产能增加土地的产品，各类制造业能够让人类的工业产品倍增；国内设立的贸易线路和制定的法律法规，使得产品销

internal trade routes and regulations, by which the exchange of products from the interior to the exterior is made easier; shipping and customs regulations tending to throw the carrying-trade into French hands, and so to encourage the building of French shipping, by which the home and colonial products should be carried back and forth; colonial administration and development, by which a far-off market might be continually growing up to be monopolized by the home trade; treaties with foreign States favoring French trade, and imposts on foreign ships and products tending to break down that of rival nations, — all these means, embracing countless details, were employed to build up for France (1) Production; (2) Shipping; (3) Colonies and Markets, — in a word, sea power. The study of such a work is simpler and easier when thus done by one man, sketched out by a kind of logical process, than when slowly wrought by conflicting interests in a more complex government. In the few years of Colbert's administration is seen the whole theory of sea power put into practice in the systematic, centralizing French way; while the illustration of the same theory in English and Dutch history is spread over generations. Such growth, however, was forced, and depended upon the endurance of the absolute power which watched over it; and as Colbert was not king, his control lasted only till he lost the king's favor. It is, however, most interesting to note the results of his labors in the proper field for governmental action — in the navy. It has been said that in 1661, when he took office, there were but thirty armed ships, of which three only had over sixty guns. In 1666 there were seventy, of which fifty were ships of the line and twenty were fire-ships; in 1671, from seventy the number had increased to one hundred and ninety-six. In 1683 there were one hundred and seven ships of from twenty-four to one hundred and twenty guns, twelve of which carried over seventy-six guns, besides many smaller vessels. The order and system introduced into the dock-yards made them vastly more efficient than the English. An English captain,

往国外更加容易；海运业和海关方面的法律法规，往往会让法国不费吹灰之力便可揽得海外运输业务，从而促进了法国的造船业，使得国内与诸殖民地之间的商品可以畅通地往来；通过殖民制度以及殖民地的发展，一个遥远的市场可以持续成长起来，并为国内贸易所垄断；与外国签订的各个条约都有利于法国贸易业的发展，而对外国船只的商品课税，往往则会削弱竞争国的贸易——所有这些手段，还包括无数的具体措施，都被用于加强法国的：（1）生产能力；（2）运输业；（3）殖民地和市场；总之，就是加强法国的制海权。倘若这一切都是由一个人物实施的，并且大致上是一种合乎逻辑的过程，那么我们对这一成就的研究，就要比这一切由一个较复杂的政府中有着利益冲突的各方缓慢地完成的情形更简单，也更轻松。柯尔贝尔在任的那数年中，法国人以自己那种有条有理的、集中的方式，实施着整套制海权理论；而同一理论的阐述，在英国和荷兰历史上，却经历了数代才得以完成。不过，法国的这种发展却是被动的，并且取决于监管此种发展的绝对权力能够持续多久；由于柯尔贝尔并非国王，所以一旦在国王那里失宠，他就失去了掌控权。不过，注意到他的辛劳在政府行为特有的一个领域——即海军领域——里所取得的成绩，是很有意思的。前面已经说过，1661年他走马上任时，法国只有30艘军舰，其中又只有3艘军舰上的火炮达到了60门。1666年，法国有了70艘军舰，其中50艘是战列舰，20艘是火攻船；1671年，该国的军舰数量已从70艘激增到了196艘。到了1683年，除了许多较小的舰船之外，法国已有107艘所载火炮从24门到120门的军舰，其中还有12艘携带的火炮数量超过了76门。海军的造船厂都井然有序、制度分明，使得其生产效率远远高于英国人。在柯尔贝尔的政策影响继续在他儿子手中得以

a prisoner in France while the effect of Colbert's work still lasted in the hands of his son, writes: —

"When I was first brought prisoner thither, I lay four months in a hospital at Brest for care of my wounds. While there I was astonished at the expedition used in manning and fitting out their ships, which till then I thought could be done nowhere sooner than in England, where we have ten times the shipping, and consequently ten times the seamen, they have in France; but there I saw twenty sail of ships, of about sixty guns each, got ready in twenty days' time; they were brought in and the men were discharged; and upon an order from Paris they were careened, keeled up, rigged, victualled, manned, and out again in the said time with the greatest ease imaginable. I likewise saw a ship of one hundred guns that had all her guns taken out in four or five hours' time; which I never saw done in England in twenty-four hours, and this with the greatest ease and less hazard than at home. This I saw under my hospital window."

A French naval historian cites certain performances which are simply incredible, such as that the keel of a galley was laid at four o'clock and that at nine she left port, fully armed. These traditions may be accepted as pointing, with the more serious statements of the English officer, to a remarkable degree of system and order, and abundant facilities for work.

Yet all this wonderful growth, forced by the action of the government, withered away like Jonah's gourd when the government's favor was withdrawn. Time was not allowed for its roots to strike down deep into the life of the nation. Colbert's work was in the direct line of Richelieu's policy, and for a time it seemed there would continue the course of action which would make France great upon the sea as well as predominant upon the land. For reasons which it is not yet necessary to give, Louis came to have feelings of bitter enmity against Holland;

发挥的那个时期，一位被俘的英军上校，曾经如此写道：

"我被那边俘虏之后，首先便在布雷斯特的医院里躺了4个月疗伤。在那里，他们配置和装备军舰的速度让我感到极为震惊；当时，我还以为没有别的国家能够快过英国呢，因为我国的舰船数量10倍于法国，所以水兵数量也10倍于法国。但我在那里却看到，20艘军舰，每艘约有60门火炮，20天之后便装备好了；这些舰船先是被拖进港来，解散了船员；然后巴黎一声令下，这些船只便开始倾侧检修、龙骨朝上、装上船帆、配备食品和人员，然后便在规定的时间重新出海了———一切都进行得极为轻松，简直令人无法想像。同样，我还看到过一艘军舰，它配有的100门火炮，在四五个小时内就全部卸下来了；在英国，我还从未见过哪儿能在24个小时内卸下这么多的火炮呢。可在这里，法国人却干得如此轻而易举，危险情况出现得也比我国要少得多。"

有位法国的海军历史学家，还引述了一些简直是不可思议的做法，比如在4点钟给桨帆船装上龙骨，而9点钟这艘船就全副武装，离港而去了。用那位英国军官更具严肃性的话语来说，我们可以承认，这些传说表明了法国人有着极为卓越的制度与秩序，以及丰富的设备和设施。

不过，这种了不起的发展全都是政府的行为强制促成的，所以一旦政府失道，它就像约拿的葫芦藤[18]一样，渐渐消亡了。它并没有充足的时间来深深扎根于法兰西民族的生活中。柯尔贝尔的做法，与黎塞留的政策是一脉相承的，所以柯尔贝尔政府一度似乎会继续保持这种施政方针，会让法国既在海洋上变得强大起来，也会在陆地上逐渐掌握主导权。由于此处无需列举的种种原因，路易十四开始变得极其憎恨荷兰；因为查

and as these feelings were shared by Charles II., the two kings determined on the destruction of the United Provinces. This war, which broke out in 1672, though more contrary to natural feeling on the part of England, was less of a political mistake for her than for France, and especially as regards sea power. France was helping to destroy a probable, and certainly an indispensable, ally; England was assisting in the ruin of her greatest rival on the sea, at this time, indeed, still her commercial superior. France, staggering under debt and utter confusion in her finances when Louis mounted the throne, was just seeing her way clear in 1672, under Colbert's reforms and their happy results. The war, lasting six years, undid the greater part of his work. The agricultural classes, manufactures, commerce, and the colonies, all were smitten by it; the establishments of Colbert languished, and the order he had established in the finances was overthrown. Thus the action of Louis — and he alone was the directing government of France — struck at the roots of her sea power, and alienated her best sea ally. The territory and the military power of France were increased, but the springs of commerce and of a peaceful shipping had been exhausted in the process; and although the military navy was for some years kept up with splendor and efficiency, it soon began to dwindle, and by the end of the reign had practically disappeared. The same false policy, as regards the sea, marked the rest of this reign of fifty-four years. Louis steadily turned his back upon the sea interests of France, except the fighting-ships, and either could not or would not see that the latter were of little use and uncertain life, if the peaceful shipping and the industries, by which they were supported, perished. His policy, aiming at supreme power in Europe by military strength and territorial extension, forced England and Holland into an alliance, which, as has before been said, directly drove France off the sea, and indirectly swamped Holland's power thereon. Colbert's navy perished, and for the last ten years of Louis' life no great French fleet put to sea, though there

理二世也憎恨荷兰，所以两国国王便决定，要联手消灭这个"联合省"。此次战争爆发于1672年；尽管它与英国人民的自然感情更加背道而驰，但对英国而言，此战却不像它对法国而言那样，不是一个政治上的错误，尤其是从制海权方面来看。在此次战争中，法国是在协助消灭一个可能的、当然也是不可或缺的盟国；而英国则是在协助摧毁本国在海洋上最大的、此时事实上在贸易上也胜过英国的竞争对手。路易十四登基时的法国正债务缠身、金融紊乱，原本是到了1672年才在柯尔贝尔的改革措施及其所带来的成就之下，看清了自己的道路。可这场持续了6年的战争，却让柯尔贝尔的努力大多付之东流了。农业生产、制造业、商业和殖民地，全都深受其害；柯尔贝尔所确立的制度、法规，全都荒废了，而他在金融领域所确立下来的秩序，也被颠覆了。这样一来，路易十四的统治——此时，他独揽法国政府大权——就损害了法国海上力量的根基，并且疏远了法国在海上的最佳盟友。虽说法国的领土扩张了，军事力量也增强了，但在此过程中，进行商业贸易的种种源泉业已枯竭，一种和平的海洋运输已经不复存在了；并且，尽管在此后数年间，法国海军仍称得上是势力显赫和富有效率，但它很快就衰落下去，而到了最后，法国海军的主导优势实际上完全丧失殆尽了。对于海洋的这种相同的错误政策，就成了法国占据了长达54年的主导地位之后的标志。除了建造军舰，路易十四一直都对法国的海洋利益无动于衷；他要么是看不到，要么就是不愿意看到这一点：倘若支撑海军的商船运输业和工业被毁，军舰就会毫无用处、命运难料了。他所制定的政策，目的本在于通过军事实力和领土扩张，让法国获得欧洲霸权，可结果却迫使英国和荷兰结成了同盟；这种结果，正如前面已经说过的那样，不但直接从海上击败了法国，自此以后还间接削弱了荷兰的势

was constant war. The simplicity of form in an absolute monarchy thus brought out strongly how great the influence of government can be upon both the growth and the decay of sea power.

The latter part of Louis' life thus witnessed that power failing by the weakening of its foundations, of commerce, and of the wealth that commerce brings. The government that followed, likewise absolute, of set purpose and at the demand of England, gave up all pretence of maintaining an effective navy. The reason for this was that the new king was a minor; and the regent, being bitterly at enmity with the king of Spain, to injure him and preserve his own power, entered into alliance with England. He aided her to establish Austria, the hereditary enemy of France, in Naples and Sicily to the detriment of Spain, and in union with her destroyed the Spanish navy and dock-yards. Here again is found a personal ruler disregarding the sea interests of France, ruining a natural ally, and directly aiding, as Louis XIV. indirectly and unintentionally aided, the growth of a mistress of the seas. This transient phase of policy passed away with the death of the regent in 1726; but from that time until 1760 the government of France continued to disregard her maritime interests. It is said, indeed, that owing to some wise modifications of her fiscal regulations, mainly in the direction of free trade (and due to Law, a minister of Scotch birth), commerce with the East and West Indies wonderfully increased, and that the islands of Guadeloupe and Martinique became very rich and thriving; but both commerce and colonies lay at the mercy of England when war came, for the navy fell into decay. In 1756, when things were no longer at their worst, France had but forty-five ships-of-the-line, England nearly one hundred and thirty; and when the forty-five were to be armed and equipped, there was found to be neither material nor rigging nor supplies; not even enough artillery. Nor was this all.

力。由于柯尔贝尔建立的海军就此消失了，故在路易十四执政的最后10年间，尽管战火不断，法国在海上却并没有什么大规模的舰队。因此，君主专制政体形式的单一性，就清楚地表明了一国政府对于制海权的发展与衰落会产生多么巨大的影响。

这样，路易十四的后半生，也就见证了法国的制海权因其基础、商贸以及商贸所带来的财富被削弱而导致的衰落。他死后的那一届政府同样专制、有着自己既定的目标，并在英国的要求之下，完全不再坚持维持一支强大的海军了。个中原因，便在于新任国王年纪尚幼；而摄政王因为极其痛恨西班牙国王，为了不利于西班牙国王且保住自己的权力，便同英国结成了联盟。在那不勒斯和西西里，他协助英国扶植了奥地利的势力，以此来打击西班牙，还联手摧毁了西班牙的海军和造船厂，可奥地利本来却是法国的宿敌。在这儿，我们又看到了这样一个例子：一个统治者置法国的海洋利益于不顾，既毁掉了一个天生的盟友，又直接帮助了英国这个海洋霸主[19]发展壮大起来，就像路易十四间接和无意地帮助了英国那样。这一政策实施的时间并不长，随着1726年那位摄政王的辞世而结束了；但从那时起，直到1760年，法国政府却仍然无视自己的海洋利益。实际上，据说由于财政法规做了一些很明智的修正，主要是自由贸易方面的（这应当归功于那位出生于苏格兰的大臣洛），所以法国同东、西印度群岛的商业贸易有了大幅增长，而瓜达鲁佩和马提尼克诸岛也开始富裕、兴旺起来了；不过，一旦开战，法国的贸易业和各个殖民地便都只能任由英国宰割，因为法国海军已经完全没落不堪了。1756年，形势有所好转之后，法国仍然只有45艘战列舰，英国却有近130艘；而要装备这45艘舰船的时候，法国却发现既无材料、帆索，又无补给，甚至连火炮也不足。反正是什么都没有。

"Lack of system in the government," says a French writer, "brought about indifference, and opened the door to disorder and lack of discipline. Never had unjust promotions been so frequent; so also never had more universal discontent been seen. Money and intrigue took the place of all else, and brought in their train commands and power. Nobles and upstarts, with influence at the capital and self-sufficiency in the seaports, thought themselves dispensed with merit. Waste of the revenues of the State and of the dock-yards knew no bounds. Honor and modesty were turned into ridicule. As if the evils were not thus great enough, the ministry took pains to efface the heroic traditions of the past which had escaped the general wreck. To the energetic fights of the great reign succeeded, by order of the court, 'affairs of circumspection.' To preserve to the wasted material a few armed ships, increased opportunity was given to the enemy. From this unhappy principle we were bound to a defensive as advantageous to the enemy as it was foreign to the genius of our people. This circumspection before the enemy, laid down for us by orders, betrayed in the long run the national temper; and the abuse of the system led to acts of indiscipline and defection under fire, of which a single instance would vainly be sought in the previous century."

A false policy of continental extension swallowed up the resources of the country, and was doubly injurious because, by leaving defenceless its colonies and commerce, it exposed the greatest source of wealth to be cut off, as in fact happened. The small squadrons that got to sea were destroyed by vastly superior force; the merchant shipping was swept away, and the colonies, Canada, Martinique, Guadeloupe, India, fell into England's hands. If it did not take too much space, interesting extracts might be made, showing the woful misery of France, the country that had abandoned the sea, and the growing wealth of England amid all her sacrifices and exertions. A contemporary writer has thus expressed his view of the policy of France at this

"政府的行政无方，"一位法国史学家说，"会让官员们麻木不仁，并为不法行为与纪律涣散打开方便之门。以前从未有过如此之多不公正的擢升现象；因此，以前也从未有过如此普遍的不满情绪。金钱和阴谋取代了其他的一切，并且带来了与金钱和诡计伴生的种种权力。那些能够影响到各个海港的资金和自给自足的贵族和暴发户，认为他们无需荣誉。国家税收和海军造船厂的浪费，就像无底洞一样。荣誉感和谦虚变成了笑柄。而政府却仿佛觉得这些弊端不够厉害似的，还不遗余力地想要将过去那些幸免于破坏殆尽的英雄主义传统消灭干净。至于继任的这位伟大国王的强大斗志，宫廷曾经下令，'须事事小心'才行。倘若将浪费的材料留下来用于武装舰船，那就是给敌人增加了获胜的机会。由于这种不恰当的政策，我们就必然处于一种守势，而敌人则占有优势；这种情形，正是我国人民的传统精神所不愿见到的。我们按照命令行事，在敌人面前畏首畏尾，从长远来看，是有悖于我们的民族性格的；而对制度的不当运用，则导致了毫无纪律和在战斗中变节的行为，可在前一个世纪中，我们根本就不曾看到过这种行为。"

在欧洲大陆上扩张领土的错误政策，耗尽了法国的各种资源，并且还带来了双重害处；因为它让各个殖民地和商业贸易处于一种毫无防备的状态，使得最大的一种财富来源很容易被敌人切断，而实际上也的确发生过这种事情。在海上航行的小型舰队，被占有巨大兵力优势的敌军一支支地摧毁了；商船被掳掠一空，而加拿大、马提尼克、瓜达鲁佩和印度等殖民地，也统统落入了英国之手。要不是所占篇幅太大，我们本来可以摘选出一些有趣的材料，来说明法国这个放弃了海洋的国度所遭受的可悲苦难，以及在法国做出了所有牺牲和努力的过程中，英国的财力却日益强大起来的情况。有位当代的作

period: —

"France, by engaging so heartily as she has done in the German war, has drawn away so much of her attention and her revenue from her navy that it enabled us to give such a blow to her maritime strength as possibly she may never be able to recover. Her engagement in the German war has likewise drawn her from the defence of her colonies, by which means we have conquered some of the most considerable she possessed. It has withdrawn her from the protection of her trade, by which it is entirely destroyed, while that of England has never, in the profoundest peace, been in so flourishing a condition. So that, by embarking in this German war, France has suffered herself to be undone, so far as regards her particular and immediate quarrel with England."

In the Seven Years' War France lost thirty-seven ships-of-the-line and fifty-six frigates, — a force three times as numerous as the whole navy of the United States at any time in the days of sailing-ships. "For the first time since the Middle Ages," says a French historian, speaking of the same war, "England had conquered France single-handed, almost without allies, France having powerful auxiliaries. She had conquered solely by the superiority of her government." Yes; but it was by the superiority of her government using the tremendous weapon of her sea power, — the reward of a consistent policy perseveringly directed to one aim.

The profound humiliation of France, which reached its depths between 1760 and 1763, at which latter date she made peace, has an instructive lesson for the United States in this our period of commercial and naval decadence. We have been spared her humiliation; let us hope to profit by her subsequent example. Between the same years (1760 and 1763) the French people rose, as afterward in 1793, and declared they would have a navy. "Popular feeling, skilfully directed by the government, took up the cry from one end of France to the other, 'The

家，曾经如此表达了他对法国在这一时期所采取政策的看法：

"由于法国像以前一样全身心地投入了普法战争，将大部分精力和财力都不再放在海军上了，所以我们才可以对其海上力量进行如此沉重的打击，使得它可能永远都无法恢复元气。参与普法战争，同样也使得法国无暇防守各个殖民地，所以我们便趁机征服了其中一些最重要的法属殖民地。战争也让法国无法保护本国的贸易，使得法国的贸易完全被摧毁了；而英国的贸易，却在一种最彻底的和平状态下，前所未有地兴旺起来了。所以，发动此次普法战争，使得法国在与英国发生具体而直接的对抗时，便只能承受落败的结局了。"

在"七年战争"中，法国损失了37艘战列舰和56艘护卫舰——这支兵力，数量上相当于美国在帆船时代任何一个时期内整个海军的3倍。有位法国历史学家在谈及此次战争时，曾经说道："自中世纪以来，英国第一次在几乎没有盟国支持、而法国却有着强大外援的情况下，独自打败了法国。英国完全是通过政府所具有的优势，才战胜了法国的。"的确是这样；不过，英国是通过该国政府利用制海权这种巨型武器的优势，才战胜了法国的——这就是坚定不移地执行针对一个目标的政策所带来的回报。

法国所受的深切耻辱，在1760年至1763年间达到了极致，于是它便在1763年同英国媾和了；在我们这个商业贸易衰退、海军没落的时代，这种耻辱对于美国而言，是很有教育意义的。我们并未遭受过法国那样的耻辱；所以，就让我们寄望，美国可以从法国后来的这个例子中获益吧。在这几年间（1760年到1763年），法国人民揭竿而起，就像后来的1793年起义一样，并且宣称他们会建立一支海军。"政府巧妙地引导着民意，将下述呼声

navy must be restored.' Gifts of ships were made by cities, by corporations, and by private subscriptions. A prodigious activity sprang up in the lately silent ports; everywhere ships were building or repairing." This activity was sustained; the arsenals were replenished, the material of every kind was put on a satisfactory footing, the artillery reorganized, and ten thousand trained gunners drilled and maintained.

The tone and action of the naval officers of the day instantly felt the popular impulse, for which indeed some loftier spirits among them had been not only waiting but working. At no time was greater mental and professional activity found among French naval officers than just then, when their ships had been suffered to rot away by governmental inaction. Thus a prominent French officer of our own day writes: —

"The sad condition of the navy in the reign of Louis XV., by closing to officers the brilliant career of bold enterprises and successful battles, forced them to fall back upon themselves. They drew from study the knowledge they were to put to the proof some years later, thus putting into practice that fine saying of Montesquieu, 'Adversity is our mother, Prosperity our step-mother.' ... By the year 1769 was seen in all its splendor that brilliant galaxy of officers whose activity stretched to the ends of the earth, and who embraced in their works and in their investigations all the branches of human knowledge. The Académie de Marine, founded in 1752, was reorganized."

The Académie's first director, a post-captain named Bigot de Morogues, wrote an elaborate treatise on naval tactics, the first original work on the subject since Paul Hoste's, which it was designed to supersede. Morogues must have been studying and formulating his problems in tactics in days when France had no fleet, and was unable so much as to raise her head at sea under the blows of her enemy. At the same time England had no similar book;

传遍了法国南北：'必须重建海军。'各个城市、公司纷纷制作舰船礼品，而个人也纷纷展开了募捐。不久前还默默无闻的一些港口，开始大张旗鼓地干起来；到处都在建造或者修理舰船。"这种做法一直持续着；军械库里补充了武器，各种材料都各归其位，放置得井井有条，而炮兵也得到了重组，经常操练并保持了10000名经过训练的炮手。

当时，海军官兵们马上就感受到了民意的沸腾；事实上，他们心中的一些高尚情操不仅在等待释放，而且也在起着作用。法国海军官兵们那种心理上和职业上的活动，没有什么时候要比当时更强烈；因为当时的法国海军，已经因为政府的碌碌无为而日益衰弱下去了。因此，法国一位杰出的当代军官曾这样写道：

"路易十五统治时期，海军的可悲状况使得官兵们无法在勇敢进取、战争获胜中体现出职业的辉煌，迫使他们只能靠自己的努力来争取。他们从学习中汲取了知识，并在数年之后对这些知识进行了检验，比如践行孟德斯鸠的那句名言：'逆境者，吾人得生；成功者，吾人得养。'……而到了1769年，海军便变得光彩夺目了，无数优秀官兵的足迹遍及世界各地，他们的著作与调查研究涵盖了人类知识的方方面面。1752年成立的海军学院，又重新整顿起来了。"

海军学院的首任院长是一位退役舰长，名叫比戈·德·莫罗古斯，他写了一部关于海军战术的专著，内容详尽；这是自保罗·何斯德[20]以来，首部关于海军战术、并且旨在代替何斯德专著的原创著作。莫罗古斯一定是在法国还没有舰队、并且在敌人的打击之下根本无法在海洋上抬头的那个时期，研究并系统地阐述其战术思想的。在同一时期，英国并未出现类似的著作；1762年，一名英国中尉也只是翻译了何斯德著作的一部

and an English lieutenant, in 1762, was just translating a part of Hoste's great work, omitting by far the larger part. It was not until nearly twenty years later that Clerk, a Scotch private gentleman, published an ingenious study of naval tactics, in which he pointed out to English admirals the system by which the French had thwarted their thoughtless and ill-combined attacks.[3] "The researches of the Académie de Marine, and the energetic impulse which it gave to the labors of officers, were not, as we hope to show later, without influence upon the relatively prosperous condition in which the navy was at the beginning of the American war."

It has already been pointed out that the American War of Independence involved a departure from England's traditional and true policy, by committing her to a distant land war, while powerful enemies were waiting for an opportunity to attack her at sea. Like France in the then recent German wars, like Napoleon later in the Spanish war, England, through undue self-confidence, was about to turn a friend into an enemy, and so expose the real basis of her power to a rude proof. The French government, on the other hand, avoided the snare into which it had so often fallen. Turning her back on the European continent, having the probability of neutrality there, and the certainty of alliance with Spain by her side, France advanced to the contest with a fine navy and a brilliant, though perhaps relatively inexperienced, body of officers. On the other side of the Atlantic she had the support of a friendly people, and of her own or allied ports, both in the West Indies and on the continent. The wisdom of this policy, the happy influence of this action of the government upon her sea power, is evident; but the details of the war do not belong to this part of the subject. To Americans, the chief interest of that war is found upon the land; but to naval officers upon the sea, for it was essentially a sea war. The intelligent and systematic efforts of twenty years bore their due fruit; for though the warfare afloat ended

分，而略去了其中的大部分内容。直到差不多20年后，克拉克这位苏格兰的低调绅士，才将他对海军战术所进行的独创性研究发表出来；在他的著作中，他为英国的舰队司令们指出了法国是如何挫败他们那种轻率而联合不善的攻击的。[3] "海军学院的研究，以及海军学院为官兵们注入的那种强大的精神动力，正如我们过后打算说明的那样，对法国海军在美洲战争之初那种相对发达的状况而言，并不是没有产生影响。"

我们已经指出，美国独立战争背离了英国传统的、正确的政策，让该国在一处遥远的大陆上参战，而强大的敌人则伺机在海上攻击它。与距当时不久的普法战争中的法国，以及后来在西班牙战争中的拿破仑一样，英国因为过分自信而让一个盟友变成了敌人，从而使得其实力的真正基础遭受到了严峻的考验。另一方面，法国政府却没有陷入到那种它经常陷入的麻烦中去。由于法国将注意力不再放在欧洲大陆上，在那儿它可以采取中立，并且确定无疑地与西班牙结了盟，让西班牙站在自己这一边，所以凭借一支精良的海军，以及一群虽说经验相对较少却很杰出的海军官兵，法国开始到海上与他国一较雌雄了。在大西洋另一侧的西印度群岛和美洲大陆上，法国得到了一个友好民族的支持，也获得了法属港口或盟国港口的支援。这一政策的明智，以及此种政府行为对法国制海权所产生的良好影响，都是很明显的；不过，此次战争的详情，并不属于本书主题这一部分的内容。对于美国人来说，陆上才是此次战争最主要的利益所在；但在海军官兵看来，最主要的利益却是在海上，因为此次战争本质上就是一场海上战争。法国20年来明智而系统的努力，终于结出了预期的硕果；虽说海上战争以损失惨重而告结束，但法、西两国舰队通力合作，无疑压制住了英国的势力，并且从英国手中夺得了许多殖

with a great disaster, the combined efforts of the French and Spanish fleets undoubtedly bore down England's strength and robbed her of her colonies. In the various naval undertakings and battles the honor of France was upon the whole maintained; though it is difficult, upon consideration of the general subject, to avoid the conclusion that the inexperience of French seamen as compared with English, the narrow spirit of jealousy shown by the noble corps of officers toward those of different antecedents, and above all, the miserable traditions of three quarters of a century already alluded to, the miserable policy of a government which taught them first to save their ships, to economize the material, prevented French admirals from reaping, not the mere glory, but the positive advantages that more than once were within their grasp. When Monk said the nation that would rule upon the sea must always attack, he set the keynote to England's naval policy; and had the instructions of the French government consistently breathed the same spirit, the war of 1778 might have ended sooner and better than it did. It seems ungracious to criticise the conduct of a service to which, under God, our nation owes that its birth was not a miscarriage; but writers of its own country abundantly reflect the spirit of the remark. A French officer who served afloat during this war, in a work of calm and judicial tone, says: —

"What must the young officers have thought who were at Sandy Hook with D'Estaing, at St. Christopher with De Grasse, even those who arrived at Rhode Island with De Ternay, when they saw that these officers were not tried at their return?"

Again, another French officer, of much later date, justifies the opinion expressed, when speaking of the war of the American Revolution in the following terms: —

"It was necessary to get rid of the unhappy prejudices of the days of the regency and of Louis XV.; but the mishaps of which they were full were too recent to be forgotten by our

民地。在海军各种各样的任务与战斗中，法国的荣誉整体上得到了维护；但从一般主题这方面来看，我们很难不得出这样的结论：跟英国海军相比，法国水兵缺少经验，而贵族军官对出身不同的其他官兵也表现出了一种狭隘的猜忌之心；并且首要的是，前面已经提及的那种长达75年的可悲传统，以及政府教导他们首先是保住船只以节省材料的可悲政策，都阻碍着法国的海军将领们，使他们非但无法获得荣耀，还无法发挥出他们数次胜券在握的大好优势。蒙克说过，一个国家想要统治海洋，就必须不停出击，这就为英国的海军政策奠定了基调；而倘若法国政府的命令也始终如一地表现出一种同样的精神的话，那么1778年战争可能就会更早结束，结果也会比实际情况更好。对一种我们国家在神的庇佑之下应当感激的奉献行为加以批评，说这种行为的出现就是一种灾难，似乎有点儿失敬；不过，法国作家们却充分地反省了此话所表达的那种思想。一位曾经在此次战争中出海服役的法国军官，在一部作品中用冷静而公正的语气，如此说道：

"看到德斯坦[21]在桑迪岬之战中的手下，德·格拉斯[22]在圣克里斯托弗所率的军队，甚至是随德·泰尔奈[23]抵达罗德岛的官兵，回来之后并没有受到审判，那些年轻的官兵们又会怎么想呢？"

而很久之后的另一位法国军官，在谈到美国独立战争时，也用下面的话语也证明了上述观点的正确性：

"必须消除摄政时期与路易十五统治时期种种不恰当的成见；不过，这两个时期所充斥的这些悲剧距今都太近，我国的大臣们都没法忘记。由于一种不幸的犹豫态度，我国业已充分激起英国之警惕的舰队数量，才降低到了正常的比例。政府为了固守一种虚

ministers. Thanks to a wretched hesitation, fleets, which had rightly alarmed England, became reduced to ordinary proportions. Intrenching themselves in a false economy, the ministry claimed that, by reason of the excessive expenses necessary to maintain the fleet, the admirals must be ordered to maintain the 'greatest circumspection,' as though in war half measures have not always led to disasters. So, too, the orders given to our squadron chiefs were to keep the sea as long as possible, without engaging in actions which might cause the loss of vessels difficult to replace; so that more than once complete victories, which would have crowned the skill of our admirals and the courage of our captains, were changed into successes of little importance. A system which laid down as a principle that an admiral should not use the force in his hands, which sent him against the enemy with the foreordained purpose of receiving rather than making the attack, a system which sapped moral power to save material resources, must have unhappy results. ... It is certain that this deplorable system was one of the causes of the lack of discipline and startling defections which marked the periods of Louis XVI., of the [first] Republic, and of the [first] Empire."

Within ten years of the peace of 1783 came the French Revolution; but that great upheaval which shook the foundations of States, loosed the ties of social order, and drove out of the navy nearly all the trained officers of the monarchy who were attached to the old state of things, did not free the French navy from a false system. It was easier to overturn the form of government than to uproot a deep-seated tradition. Here again a third French officer, of the highest rank and literary accomplishments, speaking of the inaction of Villeneuve, the admiral who commanded the French rear at the battle of the Nile, and who did not leave his anchors while the head of the column was being destroyed: —

"A day was to come [Trafalgar] in which Villeneuve in his turn, like De Grasse before

假的节约，宣称由于维护舰队需要庞大的军费支出，所以必须命令海军将领们保持'最大限度的慎重'，好像这种措施在战争中向来都没有导致过惨败似的。因此，下达给我们各分舰队指挥官的命令，就是尽可能久地在海上航行，而不要参与任何可能导致难以补替之舰船损失的作战行动；于是，本来可以为我国海军将领的军事才能和舰长们的勇气带来莫大荣誉的多次大捷，都变成了无关紧要的小胜。一种制度，倘若规定一位将领不应当运用手中的力量，即让将领怀着被动挨打而非主动出击的预定目标去迎敌，倘若为了节省物质资源而消耗道德力量，就必定会导致不幸的结果……这种可叹的政策，当然就是路易十六统治时期、（第一）共和国时期以及（第一）帝国时期海军纪律涣散、官兵变节情况惊人的原因之一。"

1783年和约签订10年后，爆发了法国革命；不过，这次伟大的剧变尽管动摇了各国的基础，松散了社会各阶层之间的联系，并且将君主制度下那些训练有素而食古不化的将领差不多全都赶出了海军，却并未将法国海军从一种错误的制度下解放出来。推翻一种政府形式，要比彻底消除一种根深蒂固的传统更容易。对于这一点，又有一名职位极高、文学成就也很大的法国将领，谈到了维尔纳夫[24]的不作为——在尼罗河河口之战中，维尔纳夫指挥着法国的后卫舰队，但在其纵列舰队前锋受到重创时，他却按兵不动，没有前去支援：

"终有一天（即特拉法尔加海战），会轮到维尔纳夫抱怨说他被自己的舰队抛弃了，就像他之前的德·格拉斯和杜歇拉一样。我们已经慢慢开始怀疑，这种致命的巧合可能会存在着某种隐秘的原因。在这么多可敬之人当中，经常有海军将领和官兵遭受这样

him, and like Duchayla, would complain of being abandoned by part of his fleet. We have come to suspect some secret reason for this fatal coincidence. It is not natural that among so many honorable men there should so often be found admirals and captains incurring such a reproach. If the name of some of them is to this very day sadly associated with the memory of our disasters, we may be sure the fault is not wholly their own. We must rather blame the nature of the operations in which they were engaged, and that system of defensive war prescribed by the French government, which Pitt, in the English Parliament, proclaimed to be the forerunner of certain ruin. That system, when we wished to renounce it, had already penetrated our habits; it had, so to say, weakened our arms and paralyzed our self-reliance. Too often did our squadrons leave port with a special mission to fulfill, and with the intention of avoiding the enemy; to fall in with him was at once a piece of bad luck. It was thus that our ships went into action; they submitted to it instead of forcing it. ... Fortune would have hesitated longer between the two fleets, and not have borne in the end so heavily against ours, if Brueys, meeting Nelson half way, could have gone out to fight him. This fettered and timid war, which Villaret and Martin had carried on, had lasted long, thanks to the circumspection of some English admirals and the traditions of the old tactics. It was with these traditions that the battle of the Nile had broken; the hour for decisive action had come."

Some years later came Trafalgar, and again the government of France took up a new policy with the navy. The author last quoted speaks again: —

"The emperor, whose eagle glance traced plans of campaign for his fleets as for his armies, was wearied by these unexpected reverses. He turned his eyes from the one field of battle in which fortune was faithless to him, and decided to pursue England elsewhere than upon the seas; he undertook to rebuild his navy, but without giving it any part in the struggle

的耻辱，是很不正常的。倘若如今我们还遗憾地将他们当中某个人的名字，与我国的各种灾难联系起来的话，那么我们就可以确定，这并不全是他们的错。我们必须将责任归咎于他们所进行的那种作战行动的性质，以及法国政府规定他们只能进行防御作战的制度——皮特曾在英国国会宣称，这种制度，就是灭亡的前兆。到了我们不愿承认的时候，那种制度早已渗入到了我们的习惯当中；可以这么说，它已经让我们的双臂变得衰弱，并且让我们丧失了自立精神。我国的小型舰队离港去完成某项特定任务时，常常首先就抱有避开敌人的想法；要是遭遇了敌人，那就是运气不好。我们的舰队就是这样卷入战斗的；它们都是被动地接受战斗，而不是主动地迫使敌人进行战斗……其实，双方舰队的运气本来可能差不多，倘若途中遭遇纳尔逊的布律埃斯[25]能够勇敢出击的话，结局并非一定就会对我们如此不利了。维拉雷[26]和马丁曾经参与了的那场缩手缩脚、胆小谨慎的战争，只是由于一些英国将领的谨慎小心，以及原有战术上的种种传统，才持续了很久。正是因为这些传统，尼罗河河口之战中法军才失败了；所以，采取关键行动的时刻已经到来。"

数年之后，便爆发了特拉法尔加海战，法国政府再一次对海军采取了一种新的政策。上面这位作者又说：

"法国皇帝虽然有着鹰隼般犀利的眼光，制定了法国舰队和陆军的作战计划，但这些意想不到的失利，却让他倍感厌烦了。于是，他的目光不再盯着这个运气并不眷顾他的战场，决定在别的地方而不是在海上与英国继续纠缠下去；他开始重组法国海军，却不让海军在这场变得愈加激烈的战争中发挥作用……尽管如此，我国各个海军造船厂的生产却并未松懈下来，而是再次增加了。年年都建造新的战列舰，或者年年都有新的战

which became more furious than ever. ... Nevertheless, far from slackening, the activity of our dock-yards redoubled. Every year ships-of-the-line were either laid down or added to the fleet. Venice and Genoa, under his control, saw their old splendors rise again, and from the shores of the Elbe to the head of the Adriatic all the ports of the continent emulously seconded the creative thought of the emperor. Numerous squadrons were assembled in the Scheldt, in Brest Roads, and in Toulon. ... But to the end the emperor refused to give this navy, full of ardor and self-reliance, an opportunity to measure its strength with the enemy. ... Cast down by constant reverses, he had kept up our armed ships only to oblige our enemies to blockades whose enormous cost must end by exhausting their finances."

When the empire fell, France had one hundred and three ships-of-the-line and fifty-five frigates.

To turn now from the particular lessons drawn from the history of the past to the general question of the influence of government upon the sea career of its people, it is seen that that influence can work in two distinct but closely related ways.

First, in peace: The government by its policy can favor the natural growth of a people's industries and its tendencies to seek adventure and gain by way of the sea; or it can try to develop such industries and such sea-going bent, when they do not naturally exist; or, on the other hand, the government may by mistaken action check and fetter the progress which the people left to themselves would make. In any one of these ways the influence of the government will be felt, making or marring the sea power of the country in the matter of peaceful commerce; upon which alone, it cannot be too often insisted, a thoroughly strong navy can be based.

Secondly, for war: The influence of the government will be felt in its most legitimate manner in maintaining an armed navy, of a size commensurate with the growth of its shipping

列舰加入舰队。法国控制下的威尼斯和热那亚，又看到了过去种种辉煌的再次崛起，而自易北河河岸直到亚得里亚海顶端，欧洲大陆上的所有港口也都在热切地支持法国皇帝这种颇具创造性的想法。斯凯尔特河、布雷斯特、都灵……到处都集结着众多的小型舰队。可最终，皇帝却不愿给予这支热情满怀、自信非凡的海军一个与敌人一较高下的机会……不断的失败已让他极感沮丧，所以他坚持只让我们的军舰起到这样的作用：迫使敌人进行封锁，因为封锁要付出巨大的代价，最终必然会耗尽敌人的财力。"

法兰西帝国倒台的时候，法国仍有103艘战列舰和55艘护卫舰。

现在，让我们把目光从过去具体的历史教训，转到政府对一国人民的海洋事业所产生的影响这个一般性问题上来；看得出来，此种影响可以从两个相互独立却又紧密相关的方面产生作用。

首先是在和平时期：政府通过它所制定的政策，可以促进一个民族的工业发展，可以促进该民族通过海洋来寻求冒险和收获的癖好；或者，在它们并非自然存在的情况下，政府也可以尽量开发这样的产业，并且培养人民的航海爱好。而从另一方面来说，政府也可能通过错误的行为，遏制和束缚人民在没有政府管理的情况下自发获得的进步。在这些方面，政府要么会成就、要么会毁掉该国赖以进行和平贸易的制海权；以此种制海权为基础，是可以建立起一支十分强大的海军的，这一点我们怎么坚持也不过分。

其次是在战争时期：政府的影响体现在用最合理的方式维持一支海军，海军的规模应与该国海洋运输业的发展及其相关利益的重要性相适应。比海军规模更为重要的，就

and the importance of the interests connected with it. More important even than the size of the navy is the question of its institutions, favoring a healthful spirit and activity, and providing for rapid development in time of war by an adequate reserve of men and of ships and by measures for drawing out that general reserve power which has before been pointed to, when considering the character and pursuits of the people. Undoubtedly under this second head of warlike preparation must come the maintenance of suitable naval stations, in those distant parts of the world to which the armed shipping must follow the peaceful vessels of commerce. The protection of such stations must depend either upon direct military force, as do Gibraltar and Malta, or upon a surrounding friendly population, such as the American colonists once were to England, and, it may be presumed, the Australian colonists now are. Such friendly surroundings and backing, joined to a reasonable military provision, are the best of defences, and when combined with decided preponderance at sea, make a scattered and extensive empire, like that of England, secure; for while it is true that an unexpected attack may cause disaster in some one quarter, the actual superiority of naval power prevents such disaster from being general or irremediable. History has sufficiently proved this. England's naval bases have been in all parts of the world; and her fleets have at once protected them, kept open the communications between them, and relied upon them for shelter.

Colonies attached to the mother-country afford, therefore, the surest means of supporting abroad the sea power of a country. In peace, the influence of the government should be felt in promoting by all means a warmth of attachment and a unity of interest which will make the welfare of one the welfare of all, and the quarrel of one the quarrel of all; and in war, or rather for war, by inducing such measures of organization and defence as shall be felt by all to be a fair distribution of a burden of which each reaps the benefit.

Such colonies the United States has not and is not likely to have. As regards purely

是海军制度的问题；它们应当有利于形成一种健康的精神与活力，并且考虑到本民族的性格与爱好，通过储备适当的人员和舰船，通过各种措施来发挥出前面已经指出的那种全面性备用力量的作用，来为战时的迅速发展做好准备。毫无疑问，在上述第二种军事准备中，还得包括在偏远的、须有军舰保护商船的地方，拥有一些合适的军港。保护这些军港，要么必须依赖于直接的武装力量，就像保护直布罗陀和马耳他那样；要么必须依赖于军港周边的友好民族，比如曾经属于英国的美洲各殖民地那样，并且可想而知，如今的英属澳洲各殖民地也是这样。此种友好的环境与支持，加上合理的军事准备，就是最佳的防御之法；倘若再加上一种明显的海上优势，就足以确保一个像英国这样分散而广袤的帝国无虞了，因为虽说出其不意的攻击的确可能给某个地区带来灭顶之灾，但制海权方面实实在在的优势，自然会阻止这种败局蔓延，从而不致造成不可收拾的局面。历史已经充分证明了这一点。英国的海军基地遍布世界各地；英国舰队也曾一度保护过这些基地，使它们之间的交通补给畅通无阻，并且倚赖这些基地，把它们当成避难所。

因此，附属于母国的殖民地，便为一个国家提供了支撑其制海权的最安全的途径。在和平时期，政府的作用应当是千方百计地促进这些殖民地与母国之间保持一种温暖人心的附属关系，在利益上保持团结，使得一地的福祉即是整个帝国的福祉，一处之纠纷即是整个帝国之纠纷；而在战时，或者更准确一点说，在备战时，则应采取恰当的组织与防御措施，根据各地所获得的利益，公平地分配每个地方应当承担的义务。

美国没有这样的殖民地，日后也不太可能拥有。对于纯粹的海军军港，100年前一

military naval stations, the feeling of her people was probably accurately expressed by an historian of the English navy a hundred years ago, speaking then of Gibraltar and Port Mahon. "Military governments," said he, "agree so little with the industry of a trading people, and are in themselves so repugnant to the genius of the British people, that I do not wonder that men of good sense and of all parties have inclined to give up these, as Tangiers was given up." Having therefore no foreign establishments, either colonial or military, the ships of war of the United States, in war, will be like land birds, unable to fly far from their own shores. To provide resting-places for them, where they can coal and repair, would be one of the first duties of a government proposing to itself the development of the power of the nation at sea.

As the practical object of this inquiry is to draw from the lessons of history inferences applicable to one's own country and service, it is proper now to ask how far the conditions of the United States involve serious danger, and call for action on the part of the government, in order to build again her sea power. It will not be too much to say that the action of the government since the Civil War, and up to this day, has been effectively directed solely to what has been called the first link in the chain which makes sea power. Internal development, great production, with the accompanying aim and boast of self-sufficingness, such has been the object, such to some extent the result. In this the government has faithfully reflected the bent of the controlling elements of the country, though it is not always easy to feel that such controlling elements are truly representative, even in a free country. However that may be, there is no doubt that, besides having no colonies, the intermediate link of a peaceful shipping, and the interests involved in it, are now likewise lacking. In short, the United States has only one link of the three.

The circumstances of naval war have changed so much within the last hundred years, that

位英国海军史学家在谈到当时的直布罗陀和马翁港时，很可能就已经准确地表达出了美国人民的感受。"军事政府，"他说，"一般极少认可一个贸易民族的勤勉，而这种政府的内部，也对英国人民的才干充满厌恶之情；因此，我并不怀疑，那些明智人士以及属于各个党派的人一直都倾向于放弃这些军港，就像抛弃丹吉尔军港一样。"美国并没有海外机构，既无殖民地，又无军港，故战争时期的美国军舰就会像陆地上的鸟儿一样，无法远离本国海岸。因此，为军舰提供泊锚之处，使之能够在这些地方添煤、维修，对于一个打算发展制海权的政府来说，就是它的首要职责了。

我们这种探究的实际目标，是从历史教训中得出适用于我国行政事业的结论；所以，现在我们不妨来问一问，美国的现状在多大程度上会使它陷入严重的危险当中，在多大程度上会为了重新确立美国的制海权而要求政府采取行动。很难说自美国内战以来至今，美国政府的行动都有效地把精力集中在所谓制海权因素链中的第一环这个唯一的目标上。国内的发展、大规模生产以及相应的自给自足之目的，连同自给自足所带来的自豪感，这些一直都是美国政府的目标；从某种程度上来说，这些也是美国政府行动的结果。在这个方面，政府如实地反映了该国统治阶层的喜好；尽管我们很难说，即便是在一个民主自由的国度里，这些统治阶层也具有真正的代表性。但无论情形怎样，可以确定的是，除了没有殖民地之外，商船运输这个中间环节以及它所带来的利益，如今的美国也同样没有。总之，在制海权这一链条上，美国只拥有其中的一环。

在过去的100年间，海洋战争的环境已经发生了巨大的变化，使得人们可能会怀

it may be doubted whether such disastrous effects on the one hand, or such brilliant prosperity on the other, as were seen in the wars between England and France, could now recur. In her secure and haughty sway of the seas England imposed a yoke on neutrals which will never again be borne; and the principle that the flag covers the goods is forever secured. The commerce of a belligerent can therefore now be safely carried on in neutral ships, except when contraband of war or to blockaded ports; and as regards the latter, it is also certain that there will be no more paper blockades. Putting aside therefore the question of defending her seaports from capture or contribution, as to which there is practical unanimity in theory and entire indifference in practice, what need has the United States of sea power? Her commerce is even now carried on by others; why should her people desire that which, if possessed, must be defended at great cost? So far as this question is economical, it is outside the scope of this work; but conditions which may entail suffering and loss on the country by war are directly pertinent to it. Granting therefore that the foreign trade of the United States, going and coming, is on board ships which an enemy cannot touch except when bound to a blockaded port, what will constitute an efficient blockade? The present definition is, that it is such as to constitute a manifest danger to a vessel seeking to enter or leave the port. This is evidently very elastic. Many can remember that during the Civil War, after a night attack on the United States fleet off Charleston, the Confederates next morning sent out a steamer with some foreign consuls on board, who so far satisfied themselves that no blockading vessel was in sight that they issued a declaration to that effect. On the strength of this declaration some Southern authorities claimed that the blockade was technically broken, and could not be technically re-established without a new notification. Is it necessary, to constitute a real danger to blockade-runners, that the blockading fleet should be in sight? Half a dozen fast steamers, cruising twenty miles off-shore between the New Jersey and Long Island coast, would be a very real danger to ships seeking to go in or out by the

疑，一边是海洋战争这种灾难性的后果、另一边则是如此了不起的繁荣——就像我们在英法战争中所看到的那样——这种情形如今是不是还有可能发生。英国凭借其稳妥而神气的海洋霸主地位，让各中立国唯命是从的情形，今后这些中立国再也不会容忍了；而国旗涵盖了该国财产的原则，也已永久地确立下来了。因此，交战国的物资，除了战时禁运品和运往被封锁港口的那些物资，如今都可以安全地由中立国船只进行运输了；至于封锁港口，我们也可以确定，今后不会再有什么纸上封锁[27]了。所以，撇开为了不让本国海港被敌人攻陷或者被迫向敌人纳贡而进行防御这个问题不谈——因为对于这个问题，各国在理论上完全一致，可实际运用起来却截然不同——美国在制海权方面又有什么样的需求呢？即便是现在，美国的贸易也是由别国来进行的；那么，美国人民又怎么会渴望那种在获得之后需要付出巨大代价才能守住的制海权呢？这个问题属于经济问题，由此来看，它超出了本书论述的范围；不过，一些可能导致交战国蒙受损失和伤亡的情况，却与这个问题有着直接的联系。因此，假定美国的对外贸易往来都是由外国船只进行的，除了驶往被封锁港口的情形之外，敌方都无法对付这些船只，那么，什么才是一种有效的封锁呢？目前对于"有效封锁"的定义，是指对试图进出港口的船只构成明显的威胁。显然，这一定义非常灵活。许多人都还记得，美国内战中，在对查尔斯顿沿海的合众国舰队进行了一次夜袭之后，第二天早上，南部邦联便派一艘汽船，载着一些外国领事出海了；这些外国领事没有看到封锁船只，都很高兴，便发表了一份大意是没有封锁船只的声明。南方当局又以这份声明为依据，宣称已经依规打破了北方的封

principal entrance to New York; and similar positions might effectively blockade Boston, the Delaware, and the Chesapeake. The main body of the blockading fleet, prepared not only to capture merchant-ships but to resist military attempts to break the blockade, need not be within sight, nor in a position known to the shore. The bulk of Nelson's fleet was fifty miles from Cadiz two days before Trafalgar, with a small detachment watching close to the harbor. The allied fleet began to get under way at 7 A.M., and Nelson, even under the conditions of those days, knew it by 9.30. The English fleet at that distance was a very real danger to its enemy. It seems possible, in these days of submarine telegraphs, that the blockading forces in-shore and off-shore, and from one port to another, might be in telegraphic communication with one another along the whole coast of the United States, readily giving mutual support; and if, by some fortunate military combination, one detachment were attacked in force, it could warn the others and retreat upon them. Granting that such a blockade off one port were broken on one day, by fairly driving away the ships maintaining it, the notification of its being re-established could be cabled all over the world the next. To avoid such blockades there must be a military force afloat that will at all times so endanger a blockading fleet that it can by no means keep its place. Then neutral ships, except those laden with contraband of war, can come and go freely, and maintain the commercial relations of the country with the world outside.

It may be urged that, with the extensive sea-coast of the United States, a blockade of the whole line cannot be effectively kept up. No one will more readily concede this than officers who remember how the blockade of the Southern coast alone was maintained. But in the present condition of the navy, and, it may be added, with any additions not exceeding those so far proposed by the government,[4] the attempt to blockade Boston, New York, the Delaware, the

锁，而北方则必须重新发表一份通告，才能依照规则再次实行封锁。是不是非得看见执行封锁任务的舰队，才能说是对突破封锁的船只构成了真正的威胁呢？在新泽西和长岛之间离岸20英里之处进行巡逻的6艘快艇，对于试图通过主要入口进出纽约的船只来说，就会构成一种真正巨大的威胁；而在相似的地点进行巡逻，也可以有效地封锁波士顿、特拉华河和切萨皮克湾。执行封锁任务的舰队主力，非但有着俘获商船的准备，也作好了抵御军事突破封锁的准备，并不需要别人看得见，也不需要待在岸上人所熟知的某个地方。特拉法尔加海战爆发的前两天，纳尔逊舰队的主力位于距加的斯港50英里的地方，并有一个小分队严密监视着该港。法、西联合舰队在早上7点开始出港，而即便是在那时的条件下，纳尔逊也在9点就得知了这一消息。英国舰队虽说相距如此遥远，但对敌人来说，却是一种真正巨大的威胁。从已有越洋电报的如今看来，在近海与远海、从此港到彼港执行封锁任务的舰队，可以沿着整个美国海岸线用电报相互联络，从而轻松地支援彼此，这一点是有可能做到的；并且，倘若有着某种有利的军事联合机制，一支小分队遭受猛烈进攻时，就可以警告其他分队，并且向其他分队方向撤退。假设对一个港口的这种远海封锁有一天被突破，那些执行封锁的舰船被彻底赶跑了，那么，第二天就可以把重新进行封锁的通告，用电报发往世界各地。要想避免这样的封锁，就必须有一支海上部队，始终威胁到敌方执行封锁任务的舰队，使之根本无法待在自己的战位上。这样，除了那些装有战时禁运物品的，中立船只便可来去自如，维持该国与外界之间的通商贸易了。

有人或许会说，美国的沿海地区广袤得很，是不可能有效地封锁整个海岸线的。那些还记得在内战中是如何维持对南部沿海进行封锁的军官，最容易承认这一观点。不

Chesapeake, and the Mississippi, in other words, the great centres of export and import, would not entail upon one of the large maritime nations efforts greater than have been made before. England has at the same time blockaded Brest, the Biscay coast, Toulon, and Cadiz, when there were powerful squadrons lying within the harbors. It is true that commerce in neutral ships can then enter other ports of the United States than those named; but what a dislocation of the carrying traffic of the country, what failure of supplies at times, what inadequate means of transport by rail or water, of dockage, of lighterage, of warehousing, will be involved in such an enforced change of the ports of entry! Will there be no money loss, no suffering, consequent upon this? And when with much pain and expense these evils have been partially remedied, the enemy may be led to stop the new inlets as he did the old. The people of the United States will certainly not starve, but they may suffer grievously. As for supplies which are contraband of war, is there not reason to fear that the United States is not now able to go alone if an emergency should arise?

The question is eminently one in which the influence of the government should make itself felt, to build up for the nation a navy which, if not capable of reaching distant countries, shall at least be able to keep clear the chief approaches to its own. The eyes of the country have for a quarter of a century been turned from the sea; the results of such a policy and of its opposite will be shown in the instance of France and of England. Without asserting a narrow parallelism between the case of the United States and either of these, it may safely be said that it is essential to the welfare of the whole country that the conditions of trade and commerce should remain, as far as possible, unaffected by an external war. In order to do this, the enemy must be kept not only out of our ports, but far away from our coasts.[5]

Can this navy be had without restoring the merchant shipping? It is doubtful. History has

过,从美国海军目前的情况来看,倘若再加上美国政府提出的增补力量,[4]封锁波士顿、纽约、特拉华河、切萨皮克湾和密西西比河——换句话说,就是封锁那些大型的贸易进出口中心——并不会让一个海洋大国要费比过去更大的劲儿。英国曾经同时封锁过布雷斯特、比斯开湾沿岸、土伦和加的斯,当时这些海港中都驻扎有一些兵力强大的小型舰队。那时,中立国的商船确实能够进入美国的其他港口,而无法进入上述地区;但是,进口贸易所倚赖的港口被迫发生此种改变,会给该国的贸易运输业带来多大的混乱,会使得补给时不时发生多么严重的中断,又会导致铁路和水路交通的方式、船坞使用方式、驳船运输的方式以及仓储方式变得多么的不足啊!该国难道不会因此而蒙受金钱上的损失,不会因此而承受苦难么?而当费尽力气和巨大代价,部分地改善了这些弊端之后,敌人可能又会像对付原来那些港口一样,去封锁新的港口了。美国人民当然不会挨饿,但他们可能会极为难受。至于属于战时禁运品的那些补给物资,我们难道没有理由担心,一旦出现紧急情况,美国如今已无法独自承受了吗?

这是一个突出的问题,政府在这个问题上的作用,应当是为美国建立起一支海军;就算这支海军无法前往那些遥远的国家,起码也应当能够保持通往本国的交通要道畅通无阻才行。我国不再关注海洋已达25年之久;这样一种政策的结果,以及与之相对的政策的结果,从法、英两国的例子中就可以看得出来。我们不用在美国的情形与这两国中任何一国的情形之间进行狭隘的类比,而是可以肯定地说,通过外部战争尽量让商业贸易环境不受影响,这一点对于整个国家的福祉来说是至关重要的。为了做到这一点,我们不但必须将敌人拒之于我国诸港之外,还得使敌人远离我们的沿海地区才行。[5]

这样的一支海军,是否不用恢复商船运输业就能建立起来呢?值得怀疑。历史已经

proved that such a purely military sea power can be built up by a despot, as was done by Louis XIV.; but though so fair seeming, experience showed that his navy was like a growth which having no root soon withers away. But in a representative government any military expenditure must have a strongly represented interest behind it, convinced of its necessity. Such an interest in sea power does not exist, cannot exist here without action by the government. How such a merchant shipping should be built up, whether by subsidies or by free trade, by constant administration of tonics or by free movement in the open air, is not a military but an economical question. Even had the United States a great national shipping, it may be doubted whether a sufficient navy would follow; the distance which separates her from other great powers, in one way a protection, is also a snare. The motive, if any there be, which will give the United States a navy, is probably now quickening in the Central American Isthmus. Let us hope it will not come to the birth too late.

Here concludes the general discussion of the principal elements which affect, favorably or unfavorably, the growth of sea power in nations. The aim has been, first to consider those elements in their natural tendency for or against, and then to illustrate by particular examples and by the experience of the past. Such discussions, while undoubtedly embracing a wider field, yet fall mainly within the province of strategy, as distinguished from tactics. The considerations and principles which enter into them belong to the unchangeable, or unchanging, order of things, remaining the same, in cause and effect, from age to age. They belong, as it were, to the Order of Nature, of whose stability so much is heard in our day; whereas tactics, using as its instruments the weapons made by man, shares in the change and progress of the race from generation to generation. From time to time the superstructure of tactics has to be altered or wholly torn down; but the old foundations of strategy so far remain, as though laid upon a

证明，一位专制君主也能建立起这样一种纯粹的军事制海权，比如路易十四；但尽管看上去如此公平，经验却已表明，他的海军就像是无根之木，很快就凋落了。不过，在一个代议制政府里，任何军费支出都必须有力地代表着某种利益，并且确定有必要支出才行。在制海权中，这样的一种利益并不存在，没有政府参与的话，海上行动也不可能存在。此种商船运输业如何才能建立起来，无论是通过补贴还是通过自由贸易，也无论是通过持续刺激其发展还是让其自由发展，都属于经济问题，而非军事问题。即便是拥有了一种大规模的国家航运业，美国能否因此而建立起一支强大的海军，这一点也仍是值得怀疑的；美国与其他列强格格不入，从某种意义上来看就是一种保护主义，也是一种陷阱。促使美国建立海军的动因——倘若存在这种动因的话——如今很可能正在中美地峡有如胎动般地蓬勃兴起。让我们翘首期待这个"胎儿"不要降生得太迟吧。

对于影响到各国制海权发展——无论有利还是不利——的主要因素的一般性讨论，我们就到此为止。进行讨论的目的，首先是考虑这些因素的自然属性是有利于制海权的发展，还是不利于制海权的发展，然后再用具体事例或者过去的经验教训，对此加以说明。这样的讨论，虽说无疑涉及到了更为广泛的范围，但主要还是属于不同于"战术"的"战略"范畴。讨论中所涉及到的问题与原则，都是不可改变的、或者说永恒不变的自然法则，其因果关系世世代代都是始终如一的。可以说，这些问题与原则都属于自然规律，并且我们如今也已熟知，自然规律都是极其稳固的；而战术呢，因为它以人类所造之武器为工具，所以与人类一样，会一代又一代地变化和进步的。战术的上层建筑，时常必须加以改变，或者彻底推倒重构才行；但迄今为止，战略原有的那些基础却仍然

rock. There will next be examined the general history of Europe and America, with particular reference to the effect exercised upon that history, and upon the welfare of the people, by sea power in its broad sense. From time to time, as occasion offers, the aim will be to recall and reinforce the general teaching, already elicited, by particular illustrations. The general tenor of the study will therefore be strategical, in that broad definition of naval strategy which has before been quoted and accepted: "Naval strategy has for its end to found, support, and increase, as well in peace as in war, the sea power of a country." In the matter of particular battles, while freely admitting that the change of details has made obsolete much of their teaching, the attempt will be made to point out where the application or neglect of true general principles has produced decisive effects; and, other things being equal, those actions will be preferred which, from their association with the names of the most distinguished officers, may be presumed to show how far just tactical ideas obtained in a particular age or a particular service. It will also be desirable, where analogies between ancient and modern weapons appear on the surface, to derive such probable lessons as they offer, without laying undue stress upon the points of resemblance. Finally, it must be remembered that, among all changes, the nature of man remains much the same; the personal equation, though uncertain in quantity and quality in the particular instance, is sure always to be found.

FOOTNOTES:

(1) By a base of permanent operations "is understood a country whence come all the resources, where are united the great lines of communication by land and water, where are the arsenals and armed posts."

(2) An interesting proof of the weight attributed to the naval power of Great Britain by a great military authority will be found in the opening chapter of Jomini's "History of the Wars of the French Revolution."

存在，并且坚若磐石。后文中，我们会具体地根据最广义的制海权对这段历史以及对两洲人民福祉所产生的影响，来研究欧美两洲的一般性历史。如有机会，我们还会时不时地通过具体的例证，回忆并强化我们已经得出的一般性结论。因此，这种研究的总体思路就是战略性的，依据的是前面已经引述过、业已得到公认的那种最广义的海军战略之定义："海军战略之目标，旨在和平时期与战争时期建立、支撑并扩大一国之制海权。"至于具体的战事，虽然可以坦承因为具体情况不同，所以根据这些战事总结出来的许多理论业已过时，但我们仍会尽量指出，哪些战事因为应用或者忽视了真正的普遍原则而产生了决定性的结果；并且在其他条件相同的情况下，我们还会介绍一些特定的战事——因为它们都与一些极为杰出的将领紧密相关，所以我们相信，这些战事可以说明，在某一特定年代或者某一特定的军事职责当中，能够获得多么正确的战术思想。在古、今武器装备表面上很相似的一些战事中，我们也值得去推断其中所提供的、那些有充分根据的教训，而不必过分强调这些战事在武器装备上的相似之处。最后，我们必须记住，尽管世间事物千变万化，人的本性却一如既往；虽说在具体事例上表现的程度不一，但仁者见仁、智者见智这一点，我们却会时时见到。

原注：

（1）通过永久性的作战基地，"可以了解一个国家的所有资源来自何处，水陆交通干线在何处交汇，以及该国的军械库与武装要塞位于何处。"

（2）从约米尼的《法国革命战争史》一书的第一章，我们可以看到一位伟大的军事权威极其

He lays down, as a fundamental principle of European policy, that an unlimited expansion of naval force should not be permitted to any nation which cannot be approached by land, — a description which can apply only to Great Britain.

(3) Whatever may be thought of Clerk's claim to originality in constructing a system of naval tactics, and it has been seriously impugned, there can be no doubt that his criticisms on the past were sound. So far as the author knows, he in this respect deserves credit for an originality remarkable in one who had the training neither of a seaman nor of a military man.

(4) Since the above was written, the secretary of the navy, in his report for 1889, has recommended a fleet which would make such a blockade as here suggested very hazardous.

(5) The word "defence" in war involves two ideas, which for the sake of precision in thought should be kept separated in the mind. There is defence pure and simple, which strengthens itself and awaits attack. This may be called passive defence. On the other hand, there is a view of defence which asserts that safety for one's self, the real object of defensive preparation, is best secured by attacking the enemy. In the matter of sea-coast defence, the former method is exemplified by stationary fortifications, submarine mines, and generally all immobile works destined simply to stop an enemy if he tries to enter. The second method comprises all those means and weapons which do not wait for attack, but go to meet the enemy's fleet, whether it be but for a few miles, or whether to his own shores. Such a defence may seem to be really offensive war, but it is not; it becomes offensive only when its object of attack is changed from the enemy's fleet to the enemy's country. England defended her own coasts and colonies by stationing her fleets off the French ports, to fight the French fleet if it came out. The United States in the Civil War stationed her fleets off the Southern ports, not because she feared for her own, but to break down the Confederacy by isolation from the rest of the world, and ultimately by attacking the ports. The methods were the same; but the purpose in one case was defensive, in the other offensive.

重视英国制海权的一个很有意思的证据。他为欧洲政策制定了一项基本原则，即不允许任何无法经由陆路到达的国家不加限制地扩张海军——这种办法，其实只适用于英国。

（3）对于克拉克的说法，不管人们认为它在建立一个海军战术体系方面具有什么样的新颖性，也无论它受到了人们何种严厉的抨击，他对于过去的批判无疑都是正确的。正如作者所认为的那样，作为一个既未接受过海员训练、又未接受过军事训练的人，他已经很值得大家称颂了。

（4）写下上述文字之后，海军部长在其1889年的报告中，已经提议建立一支能够完成这种封锁任务、但此处却已表明相当危险的舰队。

（5）在战争时期，"防御"一词有两种意思；为严谨起见，我们在心中必须将它们区分开来才行。纯粹的防御是指加强自身的力量，以待敌人攻击。这种防御可称之为"被动防御"。而另一方面，有一种防御观念却认为，主动进攻敌人可以最好的保护好自身的安全，并且达到进行防御准备的真正目标。对于沿海防御而言，沿岸固定的防御工事、鱼雷，以及所有无法移动、只是为了阻止敌军进入沿海地区而建立起来的普通工事，都是前一种方式的例证。第二种方式则包括了并非守株待兔、而是出海迎击敌方舰队的所有手段，不论出击距离只有数英里远，还是直达敌国沿海。这样一种防御，虽说看上去可能是一种真正的进攻战，但实际上却不是；只有当攻击目标从敌方舰队变成了敌方国土，才会变成攻击战。英国曾将自己的舰队部署在法国沿海诸港外，如果法国舰队出海的话，就进行攻击，以此来保卫英国的海岸线和殖民地。合众国在内战中也曾将舰队部署在南方诸港沿海，并非是因为合众国担心自身的安全，而是为了通过隔绝南部邦联与外界的联系，并最终进攻这些南方港口，从而打垮南部邦联。两国所采用的，都是相同的方式；但英国的目的是为了防御，而美国的目的则是为了进攻。

混淆这两种概念，会使我们对于陆军和海军在沿海防卫方面的恰当作用产生许多不必要的争

The confusion of the two ideas leads to much unnecessary wrangling as to the proper sphere of army and navy in coast-defence. Passive defences belong to the army; everything that moves in the water to the navy, which has the prerogative of the offensive defence. If seamen are used to garrison forts, they become part of the land forces, as surely as troops, when embarked as part of the complement, become part of the sea forces.

论。被动防御属于陆军；凡是在水上运动的装备与方式，则都属于海军，它们都有执行进攻性防御的特点。倘若水兵经常驻守要塞，那他们就变成了陆军的一份子，这跟陆军部队登上舰船补充海军兵力之后，无疑就变成了海军的一部分是一样的。

译者注：

〔1〕伯格因（John Burgoyne，1722～1792）。美国独立战争时期的英军将领之一，也是一位剧作家。1777年秋，他在萨拉托加第二战役中惨败，并向北美殖民地军队投降。

〔2〕Zuyder Zee：须德海。欧洲北海的一个海湾，在荷兰西北部。它是13世纪时海水冲进内陆，同原有的湖沼汇合而成，英国称之为"南海"（Southern Sea）。亦拼作Zuider Zee。

〔3〕Jena：耶拿。德国西南部的一个城市。1806年发生的耶拿战役，是拿破仑指挥的法军与第四次反法同盟进行的一场著名战役，以法军获胜而告结束，并集中体现了拿破仑杰出的军事指挥才能。

〔4〕Plevna：普列文。欧洲地名，现属保加利亚。1877～1878年俄土战争期间，俄国与罗马尼亚联军凭借兵力优势，在此击败土耳其。

〔5〕a nation of shopkeepers：小店主民族，小店主之国。这是拿破仑对英国人的蔑称，源于英国的贸易业发达，指英国人会做生意。

〔6〕柯尔贝尔（Jean-Baptiste Colbert，1619～1683）。法国政治家和国务活动家，曾长期担任财政大臣和海军国务大臣，是路易十四时期最著名的政治人物之一。

〔7〕Duke of Sully：苏利公爵（Maximilien de Béthune，1560～1641）。法国政治家，法国国王亨利四世的重臣。1603年，任驻英王詹姆斯一世宫廷的特命大使（后面引文中所称的"大使"即是指他），后获封苏利公爵一世。

〔8〕Barbary States：巴巴里诸国。指16世纪至19世纪间埃及以西信奉伊斯兰教的北非各国，如摩洛哥、阿尔及利亚、突尼斯和利比亚等，故亦称"北非诸国"。

〔9〕United Provinces：联合省。即荷兰共和国。荷兰资产阶级革命时期，北方7省和南方部分城市于1579年1月23日缔结乌特勒支同盟，为共和国的成立奠定了基础。1581年，由北方各省组成的三级会议宣布废黜西班牙国王腓力二世，并正式成立"联合省共和国"。由于荷兰省在"联合省"中的经济和政治地位最重要，因此亦称荷兰共和国。

〔10〕蒙克（George Monk，1608～1670）。英国内战时期在爱尔兰和苏格兰作战的国会派将领、苏格兰总督，亦为第一次英荷战争和第二次英荷战争时英军的舰队司令。他是促成查理二世王政复辟的关键人物。亦拼成George Monck。

〔11〕Low Countries：低地国家。指欧洲大陆西北沿海地区，广义上包括如今的荷兰、比利时、卢森堡，以及法国北部和德国西部，狭义上则仅指荷、比、卢三国。

〔12〕阿尔韦罗尼（Giulio Alberoni，1664～1752）。意大利教士、政治家和军事家，1715年至1719年间任西班牙首相和主教，在西班牙王位继承战中起到了重要作用。他曾试图废除《乌特勒支和约》，进而掌控奥地利在意大利的财产，但此举遭到英、法、德、荷四国的反对，导致爆发了四国同盟战争。

〔13〕弗勒里（Cardinal André-Hercule de Fleury, Bishop of Fréjus，1653～1743）。法国的枢机主教，路易十五时代的首席大臣。

〔14〕The Two Sicilies：两西西里王国。1282年，西西里王国分裂，从而出现了"两西西里"这一名称，其范围包括意大利南部和西西里岛。在拿破仑入侵以前，南意大利和西西里岛虽均由波

旁王朝统治，但两地统治者不同。1734年，西班牙国王查理七世（当时还未继位）夺取了西西里和那不勒斯王位，使得两西西里回到了西班牙手中。1816年，斐迪南一世将西西里和那不勒斯统一成两西西里王国，首都在那不勒斯。

　　[15] Marlborough：马尔伯勒（John Churchill，1650～1722）。英国历史上最伟大的军事统帅之一，1672至1673年间随英国远征军参加英荷战争，立有战功，获封马尔伯勒公爵（Duke of Marlborough）。

　　[16] 皮特（William Pitt，1708～1778）。英国政治家，第9任首相，"七年战争"中英国的实际领导人，获封查塔姆伯爵一世（1st Earl of Chatham）。其儿子与他同名，为英国历史上最年轻的首相（小皮特任首相时，才24岁）。两人都擅长演说，皆被认为是英国历史上最伟大的首相之一。

　　[17] 德·鲁伊特（Michiel de Ruyter，1607～1676）。荷兰历史上最著名的海军司令之一，以其在英荷战争中的表现而闻名。他率军多次同英、法两国海军交战并获胜，还在1667年突袭麦德威一役中重挫英国，从而结束了第二次英荷战争。后在1676年死于海战。

　　[18] Jonah's gourd：约拿的葫芦藤。源于《圣经》故事。约拿是《旧约》中的一个先知，因认为神不公正而坐在城外生气。神让一根葫芦藤生长起来，为约拿遮阴，约拿很高兴；但第二天，神又让虫子啃食葫芦藤根部，使得葫芦藤迅速枯萎了。约拿很难过，神便借此开导他。后人多用"约拿的葫芦藤"比喻"来得快去得也快的东西"，或者"朝生暮死"等意思。

　　[19] Mistress of the seas：海洋霸主。英国昔日因海洋力量强大而获得的绰号。

　　[20] 保罗·何斯德（Paul Hoste，1652～1700）。法国耶稣会教士、海军战术家，出版了世界首部关于海军战术的重要著作。

　　[21] 德斯坦（Charles Hector, Comte D'Estaing，1729～1794）。法国军事家和海军上将，在美国独立战争期间曾率第一支法国舰队支援美国。

　　[22] 德·格拉斯（Fran?ois-Joseph Paul, marquis De Grasse Tilly, Comte De Grasse，1722～1788）。法国海军将领。在美国独立战争中，他指挥法国海军参与了切萨皮克湾海战，并直接导致英军在约克镇投降。但他在次年的桑迪海峡战役中，被罗德尼击败并被俘。他也因在这次战役中的表现而广受批判。回国后他希望受到军事法庭审判，但最终被判无罪。

　　[23] 德·泰尔奈（Charles-Henri-Louis D'Arsac, Chevalier De Ternay，1723～1780）。法国海军将领。他在"七年战争"和美国独立战争中最为活跃，曾于1762年率远征军攻取了纽芬兰，又于1780年被任命为皇家海军司令，率军开赴美洲。

　　[24] 维尔纳夫（Silvestre De Villeneuve，1763～1806）。法国贵族、海军将领。1798年拿破仑埃及远征军的舰队在尼罗河河口之战中，被英国的纳尔逊舰队歼灭，但维尔纳夫侥幸逃脱，后在特拉法尔加海战中投降英国。

　　[25] 布律埃斯（Fran?ois-Paul Brueys D'Aigalliers, Comte De Brueys，1753～1798）。法国海军副司令，1798年在尼罗河河口之战中的阿布基尔被纳尔逊打败并阵亡。

　　[26] 维拉雷（Louis-Thomas Villaret De Joyeuse，1747～1812）。法国海军将领，曾任法属马提尼克和圣卢西亚岛总督。

　　[27] paper blockade：纸上封锁。军事封锁的一种，亦称"拟制封锁"、"宽松封锁"等，指虽然宣告某地已成为本国封锁的禁地，但并不真正派遣海军前去实行的封锁，实际上属于一种外交宣示。17～19世纪的封锁多属此类，但此种封锁对交战国和中立国均会造成困扰，1805年的特拉法尔加海战便是其中著名例子之一。

CHAPTER II   State of Europe in 1660

Second Anglo-Dutch War, 1665-1667.
Sea Battles of Lowestoft and of the Four Days.

The period at which our historical survey is to begin has been loosely stated as the middle of the seventeenth century. The year 1660 will now be taken as the definite date at which to open. In May of that year Charles II. was restored to the English throne amid the general rejoicing of the people. In March of the following year, upon the death of Cardinal Mazarin, Louis XIV. assembled his ministers and said to them: "I have summoned you to tell you that it has pleased me hitherto to permit my affairs to be governed by the late cardinal; I shall in future be my own prime minister. I direct that no decree be sealed except by my orders, and I order the secretaries of State and the superintendent of the finances to sign nothing without my command." The personal government thus assumed was maintained, in fact as well as in name, for over half a century.

Within one twelvemonth then are seen, setting forward upon a new stage of national life, after a period of confusion more or less prolonged, the two States which, amid whatever inequalities, have had the first places in the sea history of modern Europe and America, indeed, of the world at large. Sea history, however, is but one factor in that general advance and decay of nations which is called their history; and if sight be lost of the other factors to which it is so

第二章   1660年之欧洲形势

1665—1667年间的第二次英荷战争；
洛斯托夫特海战与"四日海战"

我们进行此种历史研究的起始时期，人们一直广泛地称之为17世纪中叶。现在，我们把1660年作为开始研究的准确时间。在那一年的五月，查理二世在人民普遍的欢欣鼓舞中，重新登上了英国王位。第二年三月，当马萨林主教去世之后，路易十四也将自己的大臣召集拢来，对他们说："我召你们来，是为了告诉你们，至今我都很满意，能够将我的事情托付给已故的大主教掌管；但从今以后，我会亲自来总理国家事务。我规定，除非有我的命令，否则任何法令都不能批准，并且我还命令各位国务大臣和财务大臣，没有我的命令，就不能签署任何文件。"如此夺得权力的这个专制政府，名义上和实际上都持续存在了半个多世纪。

前述的这一年间，在经历了一个有点儿旷日持久的混乱时期、国家生活开始朝着一个新的阶段前进之后，尽管彼此有着诸多差异，但英、法这两个国家开始在欧洲和美洲的海洋历史上，事实上是在整个世界的海洋史上，位列前茅了。然而海洋的历史，不过是国家兴衰的一个因素罢了，各国都把这种兴衰称之为本国的历史；倘若忽视了与历史紧密相关

closely related, a distorted view, either exaggerated or the reverse, of its importance will be formed. It is with the belief that that importance is vastly underrated, if not practically lost sight of, by people unconnected with the sea, and particularly by the people of the United States in our own day, that this study has been undertaken.

The date taken, 1660, followed closely another which marked a great settlement of European affairs, setting the seal of treaty upon the results of a general war, known to history as the Thirty Years' War. This other date was that of the Treaty of Westphalia, or Munster, in 1648. In this the independence of the Dutch United Provinces, long before practically assured, was formally acknowledged by Spain; and it being followed in 1659 by the Treaty of the Pyrenees between France and Spain, the two gave to Europe a state of general external peace, destined soon to be followed by a series of almost universal wars, which lasted as long as Louis XIV. lived, — wars which were to induce profound changes in the map of Europe; during which new States were to arise, others to decay, and all to undergo large modifications, either in extent of dominion or in political power. In these results maritime power, directly or indirectly, had a great share.

We must first look at the general condition of European States at the time from which the narrative starts. In the struggles, extending over nearly a century, whose end is marked by the Peace of Westphalia, the royal family known as the House of Austria had been the great overwhelming power which all others feared. During the long reign of the Emperor Charles V., who abdicated a century before, the head of that house had united in his own person the two crowns of Austria and Spain, which carried with them, among other possessions, the countries we now know as Holland and Belgium, together with a preponderating influence in Italy. After his abdication the two great monarchies of Austria and Spain were separated; but though ruled

的其他因素，对于海洋历史的重要性，我们就会形成一种扭曲的观念，不是言过其实，便是轻蔑待之。正是由于我们觉得，那些与海洋无关的人，尤其是如今的美国人，就算并非全然无视，也是极大地低估了此种重要性，所以我们才来进行此种研究。

我们所选的1660年这个时间点，紧跟着另一时间点；后者标志着根据一场全面战争——即史称的"三十年战争"——的结果而达成的条约生效，欧洲形势极大地稳定下来了。这另一个时间点，便是签署《威斯特伐利亚条约》或《明斯特和约》的1648年。在这份条约中，西班牙正式承认荷兰联合省王国独立——实际上，这种独立早就存在了；1659年，法、西两国继而签署了《比利牛斯条约》，虽说这使得欧洲拥有了一种全面的外部和平形势，但注定很快就会爆发出一系列几乎席卷全球、持续时间与路易十四在世时间一样久的战争——它们将会给欧洲版图带来深刻的变化；在这些战争中，一些新的国家将会崛起，而其他一些国家则会衰落，并且所有国家都会经历种种巨变，这些变化不是领土范围上的，就是政治权力上的。对于这些结果的出现，制海权都直接或间接地发挥了巨大的作用。

我们首先必须来看一看，在研究开始的那个时间，欧洲各国的一般形势。在长达一个世纪左右、并以《威斯特伐利亚条约》为标志而结束的一系列战争中，史称"哈布斯堡王朝"的英国皇室一直都是他国所畏惧的一个无敌大国。在英王查理五世漫长的统治时期——他在一个世纪前就退位了——这个王朝的首脑将奥地利和西班牙两顶王冠集于自己一身，而随着这两顶王冠而来的，除了其他财产之外，还有如今我们所知的荷兰与比利时两国国土，以及在意大利国内一种压倒性的影响力。查理五世退位之后，奥

by different persons, they were still in the same family, and tended toward that unity of aim and sympathy which marked dynastic connections in that and the following century. To this bond of union was added that of a common religion. During the century before the Peace of Westphalia, the extension of family power, and the extension of the religion professed, were the two strongest motives of political action. This was the period of the great religious wars which arrayed nation against nation, principality against principality, and often, in the same nation, faction against faction. Religious persecution caused the revolt of the Protestant Dutch Provinces against Spain, which issued, after eighty years of more or less constant war, in the recognition of their independence. Religious discord, amounting to civil war at times, distracted France during the greater part of the same period, profoundly affecting not only her internal but her external policy. These were the days of St. Bartholomew, of the religious murder of Henry IV., of the siege of La Rochelle, of constant intriguing between Roman Catholic Spain and Roman Catholic Frenchmen. As the religious motive, acting in a sphere to which it did not naturally belong, and in which it had no rightful place, died away, the political necessities and interests of States began to have juster weight; not that they had been wholly lost sight of in the mean time, but the religious animosities had either blinded the eyes, or fettered the action, of statesmen. It was natural that in France, one of the greatest sufferers from religious passions, owing to the number and character of the Protestant minority, this reaction should first and most markedly be seen. Placed between Spain and the German States, among which Austria stood foremost without a rival, internal union and checks upon the power of the House of Austria were necessities of political existence. Happily, Providence raised up to her in close succession two great rulers, Henry IV. and Richelieu, — men in whom religion fell short of bigotry, and who, when forced to recognize it in the sphere of politics, did so as masters and not as slaves. Under

地利和西班牙的两位伟大君主便都脱离了哈布斯堡王朝；不过，尽管由不同的君主所统治，它们却仍属于同一家族，并且往往有着一种标志着当时那个世纪以及下一个世纪中王朝之间关系的统一目标和一致行动。在这种紧密的家族关系之上，还有共同的宗教信仰这一纽带。在《威斯特伐利亚条约》签订前的那一个世纪里，皇室权力和宗教势力的扩张，就是政治行动最有力的两大动因。这一时期，大规模的宗教战争频发，使得国家反目、诸侯成仇，而在一国内部，则常常导致派系争雄。宗教迫害曾经导致了信奉新教的荷兰共和国发生反抗西班牙的起义，在经历了80年的持续战争之后，最终才以西班牙承认荷兰独立而告结束。不时演变为内战的宗教纷争，在同一时期的大部分时间里也分散了法国的注意力，不但深刻地影响到了该国的内政，还深刻地影响到了该国的对外政策。这就是圣巴塞洛缪的时代，是亨利四世因宗教而被谋杀的时代，是围攻拉罗谢尔[1]的时代，也是信奉罗马天主教的西班牙与同样信奉天主教的法国人之间不断密谋勾结的时代。由于宗教动因在一个本来并不属于它的领域内起作用，并且它也在此领域内因为没有正当的地位而逐渐衰弱下去，所以各国的政治需要与利益开始具有更加正当的重要性了；不是说各国在此期间完全没有看到这种重要性，而是因为宗教仇恨或是遮蔽了政治家们的双眼，或是束缚了政治家们的行动。由于新教少数派的人数与性格方面的原因，法国成为了最大的宗教狂热受害国之一；所以，我们在法国首先且最为明显地看到这种反应，就是自然而然的了。法国位于西班牙和日耳曼各国之间，而奥地利又傲立其中，无可匹敌，所以内部的团结以及遏制哈布斯堡王朝的势力，就是法国在政治上得以生存的必备条件。幸亏，老天相继为法国培养了两位伟大的统治者，即亨利四世和黎塞

them French statesmanship received a guidance, which Richelieu formulated as a tradition, and which moved on the following general lines, — (1) Internal union of the kingdom, appeasing or putting down religious strife and centralizing authority in the king; (2) Resistance to the power of the House of Austria, which actually and necessarily carried with it alliance with Protestant German States and with Holland; (3) Extension of the boundaries of France to the eastward, at the expense mainly of Spain, which then possessed not only the present Belgium, but other provinces long since incorporated with France; and (4) The creation and development of a great sea power, adding to the wealth of the kingdom, and intended specially to make head against France's hereditary enemy, England; for which end again the alliance with Holland was to be kept in view. Such were the broad outlines of policy laid down by statesmen in the front rank of genius for the guidance of that country whose people have, not without cause, claimed to be the most complete exponent of European civilization, foremost in the march of progress, combining political advance with individual development. This tradition, carried on by Mazarin, was received from him by Louis XIV.; it will be seen how far he was faithful to it, and what were the results to France of his action. Meanwhile it may be noted that of these four elements necessary to the greatness of France, sea power was one; and as the second and third were practically one in the means employed, it may be said that sea power was one of the two great means by which France's external greatness was to be maintained. England on the sea, Austria on the land, indicated the direction that French effort was to take.

As regards the condition of France in 1660, and her readiness to move onward in the road marked by Richelieu, it may be said that internal peace was secured, the power of the nobles wholly broken, religious discords at rest; the tolerant edict of Nantes was still in force, while the remaining Protestant discontent had been put down by the armed hand. All power

留——这两位统治者心中的宗教信仰,并未达到偏执的程度;而当他们被迫在政治领域认可宗教信仰的时候,他们也做得像是宗教的主人,而非宗教的奴隶。在他们治下,法国的政治家们得到了指引;这种指引,被黎塞留系统地阐述为一种传统,并且按照下述总的路线发展着:(1)安抚或者镇压宗教纷争,并将权力集中到国王手中,保持王国内部的统一;(2)抵制哈布斯堡王朝的势力,这实际上伴随着、也必然会导致法国与信奉新教的各日耳曼国家以及荷兰结成联盟;(3)向东扩张法国国土,主要是会损及西班牙的利益,当时的西班牙不仅拥有如今的比利时,还占领着长久以来就并入了法国的许多其他省份;(4)在王国财力的基础之上,创建并发展一种强大的制海权,旨在专门抵制法国的宿敌英国;为达成这一目标,同样也必须不忘与荷兰结盟。这些,就是该国一流的政治家为指导国家发展而制定的政策的大致内容;法国人民完全有理由宣称自己是欧洲文明最彻底的典型,并声称自己走在政治进步与个人发展之路的前列。马萨林所坚持的这种传统,被路易十四从他那儿继承下来了;我们将会看到,路易十四是多么忠实地践行着这种传统,而他的做法又给法国带来了什么样的后果。与此同时,我们还应注意到,在指引法国走向伟大的这4个必要因素当中,制海权就是其中之一;从采用的手段上来看,第二点和第三点其实属于同一个因素,因此我们可以说,制海权是法国维持其外在伟大性的两大手段之一。海洋上的英国和大陆上的奥地利,都表明了法国日后努力的方向。

至于1660年法国的形势,以及法国是否准备好沿着黎塞留所标明的道路前进,我们可以这样说:该国内部已经实现和平,贵族阶层的势力已经彻底瓦解,宗教纷争已经平息;规定信仰自由的《南特敕令》[2]仍然有效,而新教徒其他的不满也已通过武力

was absolutely centred in the throne. In other respects, though the kingdom was at peace, the condition was less satisfactory. There was practically no navy; commerce, internal and external, was not prosperous; the finances were in disorder; the army small.

Spain, the nation before which all others had trembled less than a century before, was now long in decay and scarcely formidable; the central weakness had spread to all parts of the administration. In extent of territory, however, she was still great. The Spanish Netherlands still belonged to her; she held Naples, Sicily, and Sardinia; Gibraltar had not yet fallen into English hands; her vast possessions in America — with the exception of Jamaica, conquered by England a few years before — were still untouched. The condition of her sea power, both for peace and war, has been already alluded to. Many years before, Richelieu had contracted a temporary alliance with Spain, by virtue of which she placed forty ships at his disposal; but the bad condition of the vessels, for the most part ill armed and ill commanded, compelled their withdrawal. The navy of Spain was then in full decay, and its weakness did not escape the piercing eye of the cardinal. An encounter which took place between the Spanish and Dutch fleets in 1639 shows most plainly the state of degradation into which this once proud navy had fallen.

"Her navy at this time," says the narrative quoted, "met one of those shocks, a succession of which during this war degraded her from her high station of mistress of the seas in both hemispheres, to a contemptible rank among maritime powers. The king was fitting out a powerful fleet to carry the war to the coasts of Sweden, and for its equipment had commanded a reinforcement of men and provisions to be sent from Dunkirk. A fleet accordingly set sail, but were attacked by Von Tromp, some captured, the remainder forced to retire within the harbor again. Soon after, Tromp seized three English [neutral] ships carrying 1070 Spanish soldiers

手段得以压制。国家的所有权力，全都集中到了国王手中。不过，尽管整个王国一片太平，其他方面的形势却并不那么令人满意。当时该国几乎没有海军；国内和对外商业贸易并不兴旺；国家财政混乱不堪；陆军规模也很小。

不到一个世纪之前，其他各国在面对它时还都惶恐不安的西班牙，如今早已没落下去，并不令人敬畏了；该国中央政府的软弱无能，已经蔓延到了政府的各个部门。然而，从国土面积来看，西班牙却依然强大得很。在继续占有西属尼德兰的同时，该国还占领了那不勒斯、西西里和撒丁岛；直布罗陀此时还没有落入英国手中；西班牙在美洲的广袤殖民地——除了牙买加，因为数年前此处就已经被英国攻占了——也仍然原封未动。该国和平时期与战时的海上力量情况，前面都已经提及。多年以前，黎塞留曾与西班牙订立条约并与之暂时结盟，借此将西班牙的40艘舰船置于自己的掌控之下；不过，这些船只的状况都极差，因为大部分都没什么武器装备，指挥水平又低劣，所以法国不得不又将它们退回了西班牙。当时，西班牙海军正在全面没落下去，而其软弱并未逃过马萨林大主教的火眼金睛。1639年，西班牙舰队与荷兰舰队之间爆发的一场遭遇战，就极为明显地表现出了这支昔日自负得很的海军所陷入的那种落魄境地。

"此时，该国的海军，"引述的历史记载中称，"遭遇到了多次沉重打击中的一次；在此次战争中，一连串这样的打击，使得该国从全球海洋霸主的高位，一下子跌至了令人鄙视的地位。西班牙国王正在装备一支强有力的舰队，准备打到瑞典沿海去；而为了装备这支舰队，他下令从敦克尔克调派支援部队和给养。于是，一支舰队奉命从敦克尔克起航，却遭到了范·特龙普[3]的袭击，一些人被俘，剩下的人只得再次退回敦

from Cadiz to Dunkirk; he took the troops out, but let the ships go free. Leaving seventeen vessels to blockade Dunkirk, Tromp with the remaining twelve advanced to meet the enemy's fleet on its arrival. It was soon seen entering the Straits of Dover to the number of sixty-seven sail, and having two thousand troops. Being joined by De Witt with four more ships, Tromp with his small force made a resolute attack upon the enemy. The fight lasted till four P.M., when the Spanish admiral took refuge in the Downs. Tromp determined to engage if they should come out; but Oquendo with his powerful fleet, many of which carried from sixty to a hundred guns, suffered himself to be blockaded; and the English admiral told Tromp he was ordered to join the Spaniards if hostilities began. Tromp sent home for instructions, and the action of England only served to call out the vast maritime powers of the Dutch. Tromp was rapidly reinforced to ninety-six sail and twelve fire-ships, and ordered to attack. Leaving a detached squadron to observe the English, and to attack them if they helped the Spaniards, he began the fight embarrassed by a thick fog, under cover of which the Spaniards cut their cables to escape. Many running too close to shore went aground, and most of the remainder attempting to retreat were sunk, captured, or driven on the French coast. Never was victory more complete."

When a navy submits to such a line of action, all tone and pride must have departed; but the navy only shared in the general decline which made Spain henceforward have an ever lessening weight in the policy of Europe.

"In the midst of the splendors of her court and language," says Guizot, "the Spanish government felt itself weak, and sought to hide its weakness under its immobility. Philip IV. and his ministers, weary of striving only to be conquered, looked but for the security of peace, and only sought to put aside all questions which would call for efforts of which they felt themselves

克尔克港内。不久之后，范·特龙普俘获了3条英国的（中立）船只，船上载有1070名从加的斯前往敦克尔克的西班牙士兵；他俘虏了这支部队，但释放了那3艘船只。特龙普留下17艘舰船封锁敦克尔克，自己则率其余的12艘军舰，动身前去迎击到来的敌方舰队。很快，他就看到敌方舰队进入了多佛海峡，舰船数量达67艘，兵力则有2000名。待德·威特率另外4艘船与他会合之后，特龙普便指挥自己这支小型分舰队，坚定地向敌人发起了进攻。战斗持续到了下午4点，之后西班牙的舰队司令便率军躲进了唐斯锚地。特龙普决定，倘若敌军出来，他还会继续战斗；但在西班牙这一方，奥肯多和他那支强大的舰队，其中许多军舰携带的火炮数量都在60门至100门之间，却甘愿被荷军封锁；而英国的舰队司令又通告特龙普说，如果再开战，英军便会奉命加入西班牙一方。特龙普便派人回国寻求指示，所以英国的这一做法仅仅是引出了荷兰数量庞大的海军力量。特龙普的舰队很快得到了支援，舰船数量达到了96艘，外加12艘火攻船，于是他便下令进攻。他留下一支小分队监视英国人——假如英国人支援西班牙的话，那就进攻英军——之后便开始在大雾中强行作战；西班牙人在大雾的掩护之下，割断缆绳逃跑了。由于逃跑时离岸太近，许多舰船都搁了浅，而其余绝大部分试图撤退的船只要么被击沉，要么被俘虏，要么被驱赶到了法国沿海。历史上还从未有过如此完美的大捷呢。"

一支海军在承受了这样的一次战斗之后，其所有的力量与自负必定都会烟消云散；不过，这支海军还只是西班牙全面衰落的一个方面，而这种全面衰落，使得西班牙在欧洲政治舞台上的作用，自此以后便日益削弱下去了。

"就在西班牙宫廷和语言都显赫非凡的时候，"基佐[4]曾说，"西班牙政府却感

incapable. Divided and enervated, the house of Austria had even less ambition than power, and except when absolutely forced, a pompous inertia became the policy of the successors of Charles V."

Such was the Spain of that day. That part of the Spanish dominions which was then known as the Low Countries, or the Roman Catholic Netherlands (our modern Belgium), was about to be a fruitful source of variance between France and her natural ally, the Dutch Republic. This State, whose political name was the United Provinces, had now reached the summit of its influence and power, — a power based, as has already been explained, wholly upon the sea, and upon the use of that element made by the great maritime and commercial genius of the Dutch people. A recent French author thus describes the commercial and colonial conditions, at the accession of Louis XIV., of this people, which beyond any other in modern times, save only England, has shown how the harvest of the sea can lift up to wealth and power a country intrinsically weak and without resources: —

"Holland had become the Phoenicia of modern times. Mistresses of the Scheldt, the United Provinces closed the outlets of Antwerp to the sea, and inherited the commercial power of that rich city, which an ambassador of Venice in the fifteenth century had compared to Venice herself. They received besides in their principal cities the workingmen of the Low Countries who fled from Spanish tyranny of conscience. The manufactures of clothes, linen stuffs, etc., which employed six hundred thousand souls, opened new sources of gain to a people previously content with the trade in cheese and fish. Fisheries alone had already enriched them. The herring fishery supported nearly one fifth of the population of Holland, producing three hundred thousand tons of salt-fish, and bringing in more than eight million francs annually.

觉到了自己所处的劣势，并且试图通过按兵不动来掩盖这种劣势。腓力四世和手下的大臣们，都对那种虽然努力但最终却被别国征服的事情感到厌倦了，所以只想确保天下太平，只想将那些耗不起精力的问题抛到一边。由于已经四分五裂、衰弱无力，哈布斯堡王朝的野心甚至比其业已拥有的权力更少，所以除了在完全被迫的情况下，查理五世之后历任继承者的政策，便都变成了一种盲目自大、不思进取的政策。"

那个时代的西班牙就是这样的。时称"低地国家"或者"信奉罗马天主教的尼德兰"（即如今的比利时）这一部分西班牙领土，不久就会让法国与其天然盟友荷兰共和国因为此处而产生出无尽的纷争来。荷兰共和国的政治名称本为"联合省"，此时已经到达了其影响力与势力的巅峰——正如前面已经说明的那样，这种势力完全是以海洋为基础，是完全建立在利用荷兰人民那种伟大的海洋与商业天赋所创造的环境这一基础之上的。近代的一位法国作家，是如此描述路易十四退位之时，这个民族所处的商业贸易和殖民环境的——在现代，除了英国，还没有哪个国家像荷兰那样，表明海洋上的收获是如何能够让一个本质衰弱、缺乏资源的国家，上升到财力与实力的顶峰的：

"荷兰已经成为了现代的腓尼基。联合省是斯凯尔特河上的霸主，它封锁了安特卫普通往海洋的诸条水路，还继承了这个富庶之市的商业实力；15世纪时，一位威尼斯的大使曾认为，该市堪与威尼斯相媲美。除此之外，他们的主要城市还接收了'低地国家'中从西班牙道德暴政下逃离出来的大量工人。服装、亚麻制品等制造业吸纳了60万人就业，为这个以前只满足于奶酪与鱼类贸易的民族开辟了新的获利来源。渔业一项，本就已经让他们富裕起来了。鲱鱼产业养活了荷兰差不多1/5的人口，该国每年能够生

"The naval and commercial power of the republic developed rapidly. The merchant fleet of Holland alone numbered 10,000 sail, 168,000 seamen, and supported 260,000 inhabitants. She had taken possession of the greater part of the European carrying-trade, and had added thereto, since the peace, all the carriage of merchandise between America and Spain, did the same service for the French ports, and maintained an importation traffic of thirty-six million francs. The north countries, Brandenburg, Denmark, Sweden, Muscovy, Poland, access to which was opened by the Baltic to the Provinces, were for them an inexhaustible market of exchange. They fed it by the produce they sold there, and by purchase of the products of the North, — wheat, timber, copper, hemp, and furs. The total value of merchandise yearly shipped in Dutch bottoms, in all seas, exceeded a thousand million francs. The Dutch had made themselves, to use a contemporary phrase, the wagoners of all seas."

It was through its colonies that the republic had been able thus to develop its sea trade. It had the monopoly of all the products of the East. Produce and spices from Asia were by her brought to Europe of a yearly value of sixteen million francs. The powerful East India Company, founded in 1602, had built up in Asia an empire, with possessions taken from the Portuguese. Mistress in 1650 of the Cape of Good Hope, which guaranteed it a stopping-place for its ships, it reigned as a sovereign in Ceylon, and upon the coasts of Malabar and Coromandel. It had made Batavia its seat of government, and extended its traffic to China and Japan. Meanwhile the West India Company, of more rapid rise, but less durable, had manned eight hundred ships of war and trade. It had used them to seize the remnants of Portuguese power upon the shores of Guinea, as well as in Brazil.

The United Provinces had thus become the warehouse wherein were collected the products of all nations.

产30万吨咸鱼，并且带来800多万法郎的收入。

"这个共和国的海军实力与商业实力得到了飞速的发展。单是荷兰的商船队，就有10000艘船只、168000名水手，养活了26万居民。它已经获取了欧洲的大部分海外贸易，而自和约签订以后，它不但垄断了美洲和西班牙之间所有往来的商品运输，还为法国诸港口提供相同的运输业务，并且保持了高达3600万法郎的进口贸易。由于联合省可以从波罗的海前往勃兰登堡、丹麦、瑞典、莫斯科大公国、波兰等北方诸国，所以这些地方就成了联合省一个广袤无边的商品交换市场。联合省将商品售卖给这些国家，然后再购买北方诸国的产品，比如小麦、木材、铜、大麻和皮草，从而滋养着这个市场。荷兰商船在所有海域运送的商品总价值，每年都超过了10亿法郎。用当代的话来说，荷兰人已经让自己成为了'全球海洋的搬运工'。"

正是通过自己的殖民地，荷兰共和国才能如此发展其海上贸易。它垄断了东方的所有商品。它将亚洲的农产品和香料运往欧洲，年均价值达到了1600万法郎。成立于1602年的东印度公司非常强大，已经通过夺取葡萄牙的领地与利益，在亚洲建立起了一个商业帝国。1650年时，荷兰已经称霸好望角，使得该国的船只有了一个停靠之所；而且，它还像君主一样统治着锡兰，还有马拉巴尔和科罗曼德尔海岸。它将巴达维亚定为行政中心，然后将贸易扩张到了中国和日本。与此同时，崛起速度更快、但存续时间较短的西印度公司，则装备好了800艘战舰与商船，利用这些舰船，该国消灭了葡萄牙在几内亚以及巴西沿海的残余势力。

就这样，荷兰共和国便成了一个汇集各国商品的大货栈。

The colonies of the Dutch at this time were scattered throughout the eastern seas, in India, in Malacca, in Java, the Moluccas, and various parts of the vast archipelago lying to the northward of Australia. They had possessions on the west coast of Africa, and as yet the colony of New Amsterdam remained in their hands. In South America the Dutch West India Company had owned nearly three hundred leagues of coast from Bahia in Brazil northward; but much had recently escaped from their hands.

The United Provinces owed their consideration and power to their wealth and their fleets. The sea, which beats like an inveterate enemy against their shores, had been subdued and made a useful servant; the land was to prove their destruction. A long and fierce strife had been maintained with an enemy more cruel than the sea, — the Spanish kingdom; the successful ending, with its delusive promise of rest and peace, but sounded the knell of the Dutch Republic. So long as the power of Spain remained unimpaired, or at least great enough to keep up the terror that she had long inspired, it was to the interest of England and of France, both sufferers from Spanish menace and intrigue, that the United Provinces should be strong and independent. When Spain fell, — and repeated humiliations showed that her weakness was real and not seeming, — other motives took the place of fear. England coveted Holland's trade and sea dominion; France desired the Spanish Netherlands. The United Provinces had reason to oppose the latter as well as the former.

Under the combined assaults of the two rival nations, the intrinsic weakness of the United Provinces was soon to be felt and seen. Open to attack by the land, few in numbers, and with a government ill adapted to put forth the united strength of a people, above all unfitted to keep up adequate preparation for war, the decline of the republic and the nation was to be more striking and rapid than the rise. As yet, however, in 1660, no indications of the coming fall

此时荷兰的众多殖民地散布在东方的各个海域，有印度、马六甲、爪哇、摩鹿加群岛，以及澳大利亚北方众多群岛中的许多地区。该国在非洲西海岸也有殖民地，并且到那时为止，新阿姆斯特丹这个殖民地也还掌控在荷兰手中。在南美洲，荷属西印度公司本已拥有从巴西的巴伊亚一直向北、长约300里格[5]的沿海地区；不过，近来很多地方都摆脱了该公司的掌控。

荷兰共和国认为，一个国家所获得的尊重与实力，都应归功于该国的财力和舰队。所以荷兰征服了大海，使之变成了一个用处颇大的仆人；但陆地却会见证该国的没落。荷兰人民与另一个比海洋更加残暴的敌人，一直进行着持久而激烈的斗争，这个敌人就是西班牙王国；斗争的结果虽说很成功，让西班牙王国虚假地承诺止戈息争，却敲响了荷兰共和国的丧钟。只要西班牙的实力未遭到削弱，或者西班牙的实力至少足以维持其早已造成的恐怖气氛，那么荷兰王国应当强大、应当独立这一点，便是符合英、法两国利益的，因为这两个国家都曾深受西班牙的威胁和阴谋诡计之苦。而当西班牙垮台之后——该国一而再、再而三地遭受到的屈辱，表明它的弱点是实实在在而非表面上的——两国便不再担忧，而是有了其他的心思。英国觊觎着荷兰的贸易和海洋霸权；法国则想攫取西属尼德兰。在这两个方面，荷兰共和国都完全有理由去反抗英、法两国。

在这两个敌国的联合攻击之下，荷兰共和国固有的弱点很快就暴露无遗了。该国陆军兵力极少，陆地上很容易遭到攻击，而政府又不擅协调，没有发挥民族团结的力量，尤其是备战很不充分；所以，荷兰共和国和荷兰这个民族的衰落的速度，就必定会比其崛起的速度更快。然而，到当时的1660年为止，人们却并未注意到即将到来的衰落所

were remarked. The republic was still in the front rank of the great powers of Europe. If, in 1654, the war with England had shown a state of unreadiness wonderful in a navy that had so long humbled the pride of Spain on the seas, on the other hand the Provinces, in 1657, had effectually put a stop to the insults of France directed against her commerce; and a year later, "by their interference in the Baltic between Denmark and Sweden, they had hindered Sweden from establishing in the North a preponderance disastrous to them. They forced her to leave open the entrance to the Baltic, of which they remained masters, no other navy being able to dispute its control with them. The superiority of their fleet, the valor of their troops, the skill and firmness of their diplomacy, had caused the prestige of their government to be recognized. Weakened and humiliated by the last English war, they had replaced themselves in the rank of great powers. At this moment Charles II. was restored."

The general character of the government has been before mentioned, and need here only be recalled. It was a loosely knit confederacy, administered by what may not inaccurately be called a commercial aristocracy, with all the political timidity of that class, which has so much to risk in war. The effect of these two factors, sectional jealousy and commercial spirit, upon the military navy was disastrous. It was not kept up properly in peace, there were necessarily rivalries in a fleet which was rather a maritime coalition than a united navy, and there was too little of a true military spirit among the officers. A more heroic people than the Dutch never existed; the annals of Dutch sea-fights give instances of desperate enterprise and endurance certainly not excelled, perhaps never equalled, elsewhere; but they also exhibit instances of defection and misconduct which show a lack of military spirit, due evidently to lack of professional pride and training. This professional training scarcely existed in any navy of that

表现出的种种迹象。荷兰共和国仍然在欧洲列强中首屈一指。虽说在1654年的英荷战争中，这支在海洋上一直长久打压着西班牙自尊的海军，不可思议地表现得毫无准备，但另一方面，1657年荷兰共和国却又成功地阻止了法国针对其商业贸易而进行的侵犯；而且一年之后，"通过介入位于丹麦与瑞典之间的波罗的海，该国又阻止了瑞典，使之无法在北方确立一种会给诸联合省带来灾难性后果的优势。该国迫使瑞典敞开了波罗的海入口，并且仍然主宰着此处，因为没有别国的海军能够与之争夺此处的控制权。荷兰舰队所具有的优势，荷兰军队的勇猛以及荷兰外交手段的娴熟与坚定，都使得荷兰共和国政府赢得了各国公认的威望。但由于在最后一次英荷战争中实力被削弱并蒙受了耻辱，该国便不再站在强国之列里了。就在此时，查理二世重新登上了王位。"

荷兰共和国政府的总体特点，前文已经提到过；所以，此处我们只需回想一下就行了。这是一个关系松散的联邦制政府，由一个或许可以并不准确地称之为"商业贵族"的阶层所统治；这个阶层在政治上很谨慎，使得政府在战争时期要冒极大的风险。部门之间的相互猜忌和从事商业贸易的精神这两个因素，给属于军事领域的海军带来了灾难性的影响。在和平时期，海军并未妥善地保持着良好的状态；同一支舰队里，也必然存在着种种竞争行为。所以，与其说这支舰队是一支统一的海军，还不如说它是一种海上联合体；并且，荷兰海军官兵当中也没有一种真正的尚武精神。虽说还没有哪一个民族比荷兰人民更为英勇，而关于荷兰人海战的历史记载，也为我们提供了他们孤注一掷、破釜沉舟以及持久坚韧的实例——在别的地方，还没有人超过了他们的这种精神，或许甚至永远也无法与之相媲美——不过，其中也有变节和行为不端的例子，这说明他们缺乏尚武精神，显然也是由于他们缺少职业荣誉感和专业训练所致。当时，各国海军几乎都没有这样的专业训

day, but its place was largely supplied in monarchical countries by the feeling of a military caste. It remains to be noted that the government, weak enough from the causes named, was yet weaker from the division of the people into two great factions bitterly hating each other. The one, which was the party of the merchants (burgomasters), and now in power, favored the confederate republic as described; the other desired a monarchical government under the House of Orange. The Republican party wished for a French alliance, if possible, and a strong navy; the Orange party favored England, to whose royal house the Prince of Orange was closely related, and a powerful army. Under these conditions of government, and weak in numbers, the United Provinces in 1660, with their vast wealth and external activities, resembled a man kept up by stimulants. Factitious strength cannot endure indefinitely; but it is wonderful to see this small State, weaker by far in numbers than either England or France, endure the onslaught of either singly, and for two years of both in alliance, not only without being destroyed, but without losing her place in Europe. She owed this astonishing result partly to the skill of one or two men, but mainly to her sea power.

The conditions of England, with reference to her fitness to enter upon the impending strife, differed from those of both Holland and France. Although monarchical in government, and with much real power in the king's hands, the latter was not able to direct the policy of the kingdom wholly at his will. He had to reckon, as Louis had not, with the temper and wishes of his people. What Louis gained for France, he gained for himself; the glory of France was his glory. Charles aimed first at his own advantage, then at that of England; but, with the memory of the past ever before him, he was determined above all not to incur his father's fate nor a repetition of his own exile. Therefore, when danger became imminent, he gave way before the feeling of the

练；但在君主制国家里，军人阶层的社会地位感在很大程度上弥补了专业训练的缺失。我们还须注意，由于前述种种原因而变得相当软弱的荷兰共和国政府，又因整个民族分裂成了两个相互极为仇视的派别而更加软弱了。第一派是商贾（即各市镇长官），此时正掌大权，他们拥护前面所说的那种联邦制共和政体；另一派则想要一种由奥兰治王室统治之下的君主政体。共和派希望与法国结盟，如果可能的话，还希望拥有一支强大的海军；奥兰治派则更想与英国结盟，因为奥兰治亲王与英国王室关系密切，他们还想拥有一支强大的陆军。由于处在这样的政权形势之下，人口数量又不如别国多，所以财力雄厚、海外活动频繁的荷兰共和国在1660年时，就像是一个靠兴奋剂支撑着的人那样。这种人为的力量，是不可能无限期地支撑下去的；不过令人惊奇的是，这个人口数量远远逊于英、法两国的小国，既经受住了这两个国家单独的进攻，还在两国的联合进击之下坚持了两年，并且不但没有被两国消灭，还没有失去自己在欧洲所处的地位。虽说该国把这一令人称奇的结果部分地归功于一两个人物的本领，但主要还是应当归功于它所拥有的制海权。

英国的形势，就其是否适合加入这一即将发生的纷争来看，与荷兰和法国都不相同。尽管属于君主政体，国王手中也有很多实实在在的权力，但英国国王并不能完全随意地左右整个王国的政策。他必须考虑手下臣民的脾性与意愿，而路易十四却没有这么做。路易十四为法国获取了什么，他也为自己获取了什么；法国的荣耀，也就是他的荣耀。英王查理二世的目标，首先却是自己的利益，然后才是英国的利益；不过，因为还记得过去的教训，所以他首先就下定了决心，既不能重蹈父亲的覆辙，自己也不能再次被流放。因此，当危险迫近之时，他还是在英国人民的感受面前让了步。查理二世本人很不喜欢荷兰；他憎恨这是一个共和国；他憎恨该国当时的政府，因为这个政府在内部

English nation. Charles himself hated Holland; he hated it as a republic; he hated the existing government because opposed in internal affairs to his connections, the House of Orange; and he hated it yet more because in the days of his exile, the republic, as one of the conditions of peace with Cromwell, had driven him from her borders. He was drawn to France by the political sympathy of a would-be absolute ruler, possibly by his Roman Catholic bias, and very largely by the money paid him by Louis, which partially freed him from the control of Parliament. In following these tendencies of his own, Charles had to take account of certain decided wishes of his people. The English, of the same race as the Dutch, and with similar conditions of situation, were declared rivals for the control of the sea and of commerce; and as the Dutch were now leading in the race, the English were the more eager and bitter. A special cause of grievance was found in the action of the Dutch East India Company, "which claimed the monopoly of trade in the East, and had obliged distant princes with whom it treated to close their States to foreign nations, who were thus excluded, not only from the Dutch colonies, but from all the territory of the Indies." Conscious of greater strength, the English also wished to control the action of Dutch politics, and in the days of the English Republic had even sought to impose a union of the two governments. At the first, therefore, popular rivalry and enmity seconded the king's wishes; the more so as France had not for some years been formidable on the continent. As soon, however, as the aggressive policy of Louis XIV. was generally recognized, the English people, both nobles and commons, felt the great danger to be there, as a century before it had been in Spain. The transfer of the Spanish Netherlands (Belgium) to France would tend toward the subjection of Europe, and especially would be a blow to the sea power both of the Dutch and English; for it was not to be supposed that Louis would allow the Scheldt and port of Antwerp to remain closed, as they then were, under a treaty wrung by the Dutch from the weakness of

事务上总与他的亲戚即奥兰治王室作对；而且，因为在他流亡期间，荷兰共和国曾将他逐出国境，以此作为该国与克伦威尔达成和约的条件之一，所以他更憎恨这个共和国了。他倒向了法国这一边的原因，是被可以成为一个绝对统治者的这种政治同感所吸引，可能还是被自己所奉罗马天主教的偏见所吸引，并且更主要的，是被路易十四给他的大笔资金所吸引——这些资金，使他部分地摆脱了英国议会的控制。由于自己的这些脾性，所以查理二世不得不顾及到臣民们某些坚定的意愿。英国人与荷兰人属于同一种族，而所处形势也相类似，但在争夺海洋和贸易控制权上，却是公开的对手；由于荷兰人此时在争夺中领先，所以英国人就更加急不可耐、痛苦万分了。荷属东印度公司的做法，也是引起英国人不满的一个特殊原因："东印度公司要求垄断东方的贸易，并且迫使一些与该公司进行贸易的、偏远地区的统治者答应，这些国家都不接纳异族，从而使得这些民族非但被排除在荷属诸殖民地之外，也被排除在印度群岛的所有殖民地之外了。"认识到自己的实力增强了之后，英国人还想控制荷兰的政治行为；而在英国的共和时代，英国人甚至还试图迫使两国政府合并起来呢。因此从一开始，民众的争斗与敌意就有利于达成英王的心愿；而后来，由于法国在欧洲大陆已经多年不再称霸，就更是这样了。然而，一旦路易十四那种穷兵黩武的政策变得路人皆知，不论是贵族还是平民，英国人民便都觉得这是一种巨大的威胁，跟一个世纪之前西班牙所带来的威胁一样了。将西属尼德兰（比利时）让给法国，可能会让整个欧洲都臣服于法国脚下，尤其是可能会给荷、英两国的制海权带来沉重的打击；因为我们不可能指望，路易十四会允许荷兰继续像当时那样不开放斯凯尔特河与安特卫普港——这种封锁，是荷兰人抓住西班牙的痛处，迫使后者签署

Spain. The reopening to commerce of that great city would be a blow alike to Amsterdam and to London. With the revival of inherited opposition to France the ties of kindred began to tell; the memory of past alliance against the tyranny of Spain was recalled; and similarity of religious faith, still a powerful motive, drew the two together. At the same time the great and systematic efforts of Colbert to build up the commerce and the navy of France excited the jealousy of both the sea powers; rivals themselves, they instinctively turned against a third party intruding upon their domain. Charles was unable to resist the pressure of his people under all these motives; wars between England and Holland ceased, and were followed, after Charles's death, by close alliance.

Although her commerce was less extensive, the navy of England in 1660 was superior to that of Holland, particularly in organization and efficiency. The stern, enthusiastic religious government of Cromwell, grounded on military strength, had made its mark both on the fleet and army. The names of several of the superior officers under the Protector, among which that of Monk stands foremost, appear in the narrative of the first of the Dutch wars under Charles. This superiority in tone and discipline gradually disappeared under the corrupting influence of court favor in a licentious government; and Holland, which upon the whole was worsted by England alone upon the sea in 1665, successfully resisted the combined navies of England and France in 1672. As regards the material of the three fleets, we are told that the French ships had greater displacement than the English relatively to the weight of artillery and stores; hence they could keep, when fully loaded, a greater height of battery. Their hulls also had better lines. These advantages would naturally follow from the thoughtful and systematic way in which the French navy at that time was restored from a state of decay, and has a lesson of hope for us in the present analogous condition of our own navy. The Dutch ships, from the character of their

了一份条约，并按照该条约规定实施的。让安特卫普这座大城市重新打开商业贸易的大门，对阿姆斯特丹和伦敦来说，同样都是一种打击。随着民众那种传承下来的、反对法国的态度日益复兴起来，两国之间的种族纽带又开始发挥作用了：人们想起了以前两国联手对抗西班牙暴政的经历；而宗教信仰方面的相似性，此时也仍然是一种强大的动力，从而使得两国能够团结起来。与此同时，柯尔贝尔付出了巨大而系统的努力，想要逐步增强法国的商业贸易和海军的实力，这一做法却激起了英、荷两个海洋大国的猜忌；尽管两国本身也是对手，但它们还是本能地联合起来，转而开始对付一个侵害两国势力范围的第三国了。子民们在这些动力驱使之下对他施加的压力，查理二世是无法抗拒的；由于此时英、荷两国之间的战火也早已平息，所以查理二世死后，两国又成为关系密切的盟国了。

尽管英国的商业贸易规模相对较小，但1660年英国的海军却已胜过了荷兰海军，尤其是在海军的编制和作战效率方面。克伦威尔时期的英国政府，是一个法令严酷、宗教狂热的政府，以军事实力为基础，给英国的舰队和陆军都打上了深深的烙印。摄政时期几位最高将领的名字——其中蒙克的威望最高——也出现在查理二世统治时期的第一次英荷战争史中。在一个放纵荒淫、专事宫廷争宠的政府治下，这种士气与风纪上的优势，因受到腐蚀而日渐消失殆尽了；而荷兰呢，虽说在1665年的海战中被英国这一个国家基本上击溃了，却仍然成功地抵挡住了1672年英、法两国海军的联合进攻。至于这三支舰队的装备情况，我们得知，相对于火炮与补给的重量来说，法国舰船的排水量都比英国舰船大；所以在满载的情况下，法国舰船的炮台位置也更高。法国舰队的船体轮廓设计得也更好。这些优势，自然是当时法国海军正深思熟虑、有条不紊地从一种没落状态恢复过来的结果，而

coast, were flatter-bottomed and of less draught, and thus were able, when pressed, to find a refuge among the shoals; but they were in consequence less weatherly and generally of lighter scantling than those of either of the other nations.

Thus as briefly as possible have been sketched the conditions, degree of power, and aims which shaped and controlled the policy of the four principal seaboard States of the day, — Spain, France, England, and Holland. From the point of view of this history, these will come most prominently and most often into notice; but as other States exercised a powerful influence upon the course of events, and our aim is not merely naval history but an appreciation of the effect of naval and commercial power upon the course of general history, it is necessary to state shortly the condition of the rest of Europe. America had not yet begun to play a prominent part in the pages of history or in the policies of cabinets.

Germany was then divided into many small governments, with the one great empire of Austria. The policy of the smaller States shifted, and it was the aim of France to combine as many of them as possible under her influence, in pursuance of her traditional opposition to Austria. With France thus working against her on the one side, Austria was in imminent peril on the other from the constant assaults of the Turkish Empire, still vigorous though decaying. The policy of France had long inclined to friendly relations with Turkey, not only as a check upon Austria, but also from her wish to engross the trade with the Levant. Colbert, in his extreme eagerness for the sea power of France, favored this alliance. It will be remembered that Greece and Egypt were then parts of the Turkish Empire.

Prussia as now known did not exist. The foundations of the future kingdom were then being prepared by the Elector of Brandenburg, a powerful minor State, which was not yet able to stand quite alone, but carefully avoided a formally dependent position. The kingdom of Poland still

对于目前正处于相似形势之下的我国海军来说，也是一种很值得我们期待的教训。由于沿海地区的特点，荷兰舰船的底部更为平坦，吃水也更浅，因而在被敌军追击时能够躲进浅水区；不过，它们的抢风航行能力也因此而比较弱，船体通常也比其余两国的舰船要小。

上面我们尽量简要地概括了决定并控制当时西班牙、法国、英国和荷兰这4个主要沿海国家政策走向的形势、实力强弱和目标。从这段历史的角度来看，上述三个方面最为突出，也最经常被人们注意到；不过，因为其他国家对历史进程也产生了巨大的影响，而我们的目的也并非仅仅是海军历史，而是理解海军与贸易实力对普通历史进程所产生的共同影响，所以还得简短地来说明一下欧洲其余国家的情况。此时，在史册中或者在内阁政策方面，美国还谈不上发挥出了什么重要的作用。

当时的德国分裂成了多个小型政权，还有一个庞大的奥地利帝国。那些较小国家的政策多变，因此，法国的目标就是尽可能多地将这些国家联合起来，置于自己的羽翼之下，以共同进行其一贯抵抗奥地利的行动。奥地利呢，因为法国在其一侧对其如此不利，而在另一侧，土耳其帝国又不断袭击它，使得此时虽已开始没落却仍然强大有力的奥地利觉得如剑悬顶。长久以来，法国的政策一直都倾向于与土耳其帝国搞好关系，这是因为法国不仅想让土耳其遏制奥地利，还希望垄断与黎凡特之间的贸易。柯尔贝尔因急于确立法国的制海权，所以支持这种同盟关系。我们都不会忘记，希腊和埃及当时还是土耳其帝国的一部分。

如今我们所知的普鲁士，当时还没有出现。这个未来王国的基础，是勃兰登堡选帝侯[6]这个强有力的小国打下的；其时，虽说勃兰登堡尚无能力独立，它却小心谨慎地

existed, a most disturbing and important factor in European politics, because of its weak and unsettled government, which kept every other State anxious lest some unforeseen turn of events there should tend to the advantage of a rival. It was the traditional policy of France to keep Poland upright and strong. Russia was still below the horizon; coming, but not yet come, within the circle of European States and their living interests. She and the other powers bordering upon the Baltic were naturally rivals for preponderance in that sea, in which the other States, and above all the maritime States, had a particular interest as the source from which naval stores of every kind were chiefly drawn. Sweden and Denmark were at this time in a state of constant enmity, and were to be found on opposite sides in the quarrels that prevailed. For many years past, and during the early wars of Louis XIV., Sweden was for the most part in alliance with France; her bias was that way.

The general state of Europe being as described, the spring that was to set the various wheels in motion was in the hands of Louis XIV. The weakness of his immediate neighbors, the great resources of his kingdom, only waiting for development, the unity of direction resulting from his absolute power, his own practical talent and untiring industry, aided during the first half of his reign by a combination of ministers of singular ability, all united to make every government in Europe hang more or less upon his action, and be determined by, if not follow, his lead. The greatness of France was his object, and he had the choice of advancing it by either of two roads, — by the land or by the sea; not that the one wholly forbade the other, but that France, overwhelmingly strong as she then was, had not power to move with equal steps on both paths.

Louis chose extension by land. He had married the eldest daughter of Philip IV., the then reigning king of Spain; and though by the treaty of marriage she had renounced all claim to

没有让自己变成一个正式的附属国。波兰王国当时也还存在，由于该国政府软弱无能、动荡不安，所以它是欧洲政治中一个极为令人不安和重要的因素，使得其他各国都焦虑不已，严防出现什么有利于对手的、不可预见的形势逆转。法国长久以来的政策，便是让波兰不致垮台并保持强大。俄国此时尚默默无闻；虽说已经出现，却仍未进入欧洲国家之列，也未进入各国现存利益之列，它与波罗的海沿岸其他列强之间是天生的对头，相互争夺在这一海域的优势地位；而在这一点上，其他国家，尤其是所有的海洋国家，都有着特殊的兴趣，因为它们的各种海军补给品主要都来自于波罗的海地区。此时的瑞典和丹麦一直保持敌对状态，因而在当时的各种纷争中，两国支持的都是对立的各方。在过去的许多年间，以及在路易十四早期发动的战争当中，瑞典多半都是法国的盟国；由此即可看出该国的成见来。

由于欧洲的整体形势如上所述，所以开动各国战争机器的发条，就掌握在路易十四的手中。法国的近邻都软弱无能，法国又拥有丰富的资源，只待开发，路易十四大权在握使得法国有着统一的方针政策，路易十四本人又有着实干才能，并且勤奋不懈，在其统治法国的前半期，又有许多能力非凡的大臣协助——这一切结合起来，便使得欧洲各国政府或多或少都唯他的马首是瞻，即便不能说是全听他指挥，起码也是对他亦步亦趋。让法国走向伟大和辉煌，就是他的目标；而他有两条道路可供选择，来推进这一进程——要么是经由陆地，要么便是经由海洋。这并不是因为选择其中之一，便必须完全排除另一条，而是因为法国当时尽管极为强大，却仍然不具备在两条道路上同时推进的实力。

路易十四选择了从陆地上进行扩张。他已经迎娶了当时西班牙国王腓力四世的大

her father's inheritance, it was not difficult to find reasons for disregarding this stipulation. Technical grounds were found for setting it aside as regarded certain portions of the Netherlands and Franche Comté, and negotiations were entered into with the court of Spain to annul it altogether. The matter was the more important because the male heir to the throne was so feeble that it was evident that the Austrian line of Spanish kings would end in him. The desire to put a French prince on the Spanish throne — either himself, thus uniting the two crowns, or else one of his family, thus putting the House of Bourbon in authority on both sides of the Pyrenees — was the false light which led Louis astray during the rest of his reign, to the final destruction of the sea power of France and the impoverishment and misery of his people. Louis failed to understand that he had to reckon with all Europe. The direct project on the Spanish throne had to wait for a vacancy; but he got ready at once to move upon the Spanish possessions to the east of France.

In order to do this more effectually, he cut off from Spain every possible ally by skilful diplomatic intrigues, the study of which would give a useful illustration of strategy in the realm of politics, but he made two serious mistakes to the injury of the sea power of France. Portugal had until twenty years before been united to the crown of Spain, and the claim to it had not been surrendered. Louis considered that were Spain to regain that kingdom she would be too strong for him easily to carry out his aims. Among other means of prevention he promoted a marriage between Charles II. and the Infanta of Portugal, in consequence of which Portugal ceded to England, Bombay in India, and Tangiers in the Straits of Gibraltar, which was reputed an excellent port. We see here a French king, in his eagerness for extension by land, inviting England to the Mediterranean, and forwarding her alliance with Portugal. The latter was the more curious, as Louis already foresaw the failure of the Spanish royal house, and should rather

姐；尽管缔结婚约时她已经宣布放弃了父亲的所有遗产，但要找个借口无视这一约定却并不困难。他们找出了一些合乎法律的理由，撤销了这一约定对尼德兰和弗朗什孔泰某些地区的约束力，并进而与西班牙王室进行谈判，完全废除了这一约定。对路易十四来说，这个问题更为重要，因为当时西班牙的男性王储极为懦弱，该国的哈布斯堡血统显然会在这位王储手中断送掉。路易十四很想扶植一位法国亲王登上西班牙的王位——要么是他自己，从而将两个王权政府合并归一；要么是他的家人之一，从而使得波旁王室在比利牛斯山两侧都掌权——但这是一种虚假的浮光，使得路易十四在余下的统治时期误入了歧途，并最终导致了法国制海权的覆灭，以及法国人民的贫困与苦难。路易十四没有明白，自己必须去应对欧洲各国。直接觊觎西班牙的王位，那也必须等到无人继承大统的时候；可他却急不可耐，准备马上向法国东面的西班牙领土进逼了。

为了更加有效地实现这一目标，他通过种种巧妙的外交阴谋，离间了西班牙每一个可能的盟国——研究这些外交阴谋，可以很好地说明政治领域的战略；不过，他犯下了两个严重的错误，从而极大地损害了法国的制海权。直到20年前，葡萄牙才并入西班牙王国治下，但此时尚未放弃自己的主权声索要求。路易十四认为，倘若这个王国重新回到西班牙手中，那么西班牙就会变得极其强大，他就没那么容易实现自己的目的了。于是，他用尽了种种手段进行阻挠，还促成了查理二世与葡萄牙公主的婚事，使得葡萄牙因此而将印度的孟买以及位于直布罗陀海峡、久负盛名的良港丹吉尔割让给了英国。从中我们即可看出，这位法国国王因为急于扩张领土，从而怂恿英国进入地中海地区，并且促成了英、葡之间的联盟。后面这个结果更为奇怪，因为路易十四既已预见到了西班

have wished the union of the peninsular kingdoms. As a matter of fact, Portugal became a dependent and outpost of England, by which she readily landed in the Peninsula down to the days of Napoleon. Indeed, if independent of Spain, she is too weak not to be under the control of the power that rules the sea and so has readiest access to her. Louis continued to support her against Spain, and secured her independence. He also interfered with the Dutch, and compelled them to restore Brazil, which they had taken from the Portuguese.

On the other hand, Louis obtained from Charles II. the cession of Dunkirk on the Channel, which had been seized and used by Cromwell. This surrender was made for money, and was inexcusable from the maritime point of view. Dunkirk was for the English a bridge-head into France. To France it became a haven for privateers, the bane of England's commerce in the Channel and the North Sea. As the French sea power waned, England in treaty after treaty exacted the dismantling of the works of Dunkirk, which it may be said in passing was the home port of the celebrated Jean Bart and other great French privateersmen.

Meanwhile the greatest and wisest of Louis' ministers, Colbert, was diligently building up that system of administration, which, by increasing and solidly basing the wealth of the State, should bring a surer greatness and prosperity than the king's more showy enterprises. With those details that concern the internal development of the kingdom this history has no concern, beyond the incidental mention that production, both agricultural and manufacturing, received his careful attention; but upon the sea a policy of skilful aggression upon the shipping and commerce of the Dutch and English quickly began, and was instantly resented. Great trading companies were formed, directing French enterprise to the Baltic, to the Levant, to the East and West Indies; customs regulations were amended to encourage French manufactures, and to allow goods to be stored in bond in the great ports, by which means it was hoped to make

牙王室的衰败，就更应当希望将伊比利亚半岛上的这两个王国统一起来才是。事实上，葡萄牙变成了英国的附属国与前哨基地，使得英国晚至拿破仑时代，都可以轻而易举地登陆伊比利亚半岛了。的确，倘若不倚赖西班牙，葡萄牙也会因为实力太弱而受到英国这个海洋大国的控制，从而使得英国不费吹灰之力便可侵入该国。可路易十四却一直支持该国反抗西班牙，最终使得葡萄牙独立了。他还对荷兰人进行了干涉，迫使他们把从葡萄牙人手中夺取的巴西归还给了葡萄牙。

另一方面，路易十四从查理二世手中获得了位于英吉利海峡上、由克伦威尔攻取并一直加以利用的敦克尔克。查理二世割让此处虽是为了钱，但从制海权的角度来看，这种做法却是不可宽恕的。敦克尔克是英国进入法国的桥头堡，而对于法国来说，这儿却是私掠者们的天堂，是祸害英国在英吉利海峡和北海地区商业贸易的灾星。由于法国的海上实力日渐衰落，英国便通过一个又一个条约，迫使法国拆除了敦克尔克的防御工事——顺便说一句，敦克尔克正是赫赫有名的让·巴尔[7]以及法国其他主要私掠者的母港。

与此同时，柯尔贝尔这位路易十四手下最伟大、最睿智的大臣，正在孜孜不倦地建立起一套行政制度；通过增加国家财力并夯实国家财力的基础，比起国王那些华而不实的做法来说，这一制度应该更有可能让法国变得伟大而繁荣起来。这一时期，与柯尔贝尔对法国国内发展的那些具体政策并无关系，他只是慎重地关注了偶尔提及到的农业生产和工业生产；但在海上，法国却很快开始实施一种巧妙地侵袭荷、英两国海运与贸易的政策，并随即招来了这两个国家的不满。法国成立了许多大型的贸易公司，使得法国的商业贸易扩张到了波罗的海、黎凡特以及东、西印度群岛；海关法规进行了修订，目

France take Holland's place as the great warehouse for Europe, a function for which her geographical position eminently fitted her; while tonnage duties on foreign shipping, direct premiums on home-built ships, and careful, rigorous colonial decrees giving French vessels the monopoly of trade to and from the colonies, combined to encourage the growth of her mercantile marine. England retaliated at once; the Dutch, more seriously threatened because their carrying-trade was greater and their home resources smaller, only remonstrated for a time; but after three years they also made reprisals. Colbert, relying on the great superiority of France as an actual, and still more as a possible producer, feared not to move steadily on the grasping path marked out; which, in building up a great merchant shipping, would lay the broad base for the military shipping, which was being yet more rapidly forced on by the measures of the State. Prosperity grew apace. At the end of twelve years everything was flourishing, everything rich in the State, which was in utter confusion when he took charge of the finances and marine.

"Under him," says a French historian, "France grew by peace as she had grown by war. ... The warfare of tariffs and premiums skilfully conducted by him tended to reduce within just limits the exorbitant growth of commercial and maritime power which Holland had arrogated at the expense of other nations; and to restrain England, which was burning to wrest this supremacy from Holland in order to use it in a manner much more dangerous to Europe. The interest of France seemed to be peace in Europe and America; a mysterious voice, at once the voice of the past and of the future, called for her warlike activity on other shores."

This voice found expression through the mouth of Leibnitz, one of the world's great men, who pointed out to Louis that to turn the arms of France against Egypt would give her, in the dominion of the Mediterranean and the control of Eastern trade, a victory over Holland greater

的是刺激法国的制造业，并允许货物存储在大型港口的保税仓库里——法国希望通过这些措施，让本国取代荷兰而成为"欧洲大货栈"，因为法国的地理位置极适合于让它成为这样的角色；而对外国船只征收吨位税、对国内建造的船只进行直接补贴，以及制定细致而严厉的殖民法令，让法国船只垄断与各殖民地之间的贸易往来，这些措施结合起来，都刺激了法国商业贸易的发展和壮大。英国马上就进行了报复；荷兰人受到的威胁更为严重，因为他们的海外贸易规模较大，国内资源也较少，可他们却只是抗议了一阵子；不过，3年之后他们也采取了报复行动。柯尔贝尔坚信，法国成为一个真正的生产国之后，就会具有极大的优势，即便是成为一个潜在的生产国也是如此，所以他毫不担心，继续平稳地沿着业已制定的贪婪道路走下去；一旦建立起规模庞大的商船运输业，就会为军事航运奠定广泛的基础——事实上，该国采取的措施此时正迫使军事航运以更快的速度发展着。法国迅速繁荣起来了。12年之后，法国的各行各业便都欣欣向荣了；而在柯尔贝尔刚刚接管财政和海洋事务之初，各行各业却还是乱成一团呢。

"在他的治下，"一位法国历史学家如是说道，"法国和平地发展起来，就像过去通过战争壮大起来一样……他老练地挑起的关税和补贴冲突，既有助于将荷兰曾经用牺牲他国利益的办法而僭取的贸易和海洋实力上的过度增长，降低到合理的限度内；也有助于遏制英国，因为英国当时正急于从荷兰手中，用一种严重威胁整个欧洲的方式来夺取海上霸权。在欧洲和美洲保持和平状态，似乎符合法国的利益；但一种神秘的召唤，即过去与未来合二为一的召唤，却要求法国在别的沿海地区采取军事行动。"

这种召唤，从位列世界伟人之一的莱布尼茨[8]口中表达了出来；他向路易十四指

than the most successful campaign on land; and while insuring a much needed peace within his kingdom, would build up a power on the sea that would insure preponderance in Europe. This memorial called Louis from the pursuit of glory on the land to seek the durable grandeur of France in the possession of a great sea power, the elements of which, thanks to the genius of Colbert, he had in his hands. A century later a greater man than Louis sought to exalt himself and France by the path pointed out by Leibnitz; but Napoleon did not have, as Louis had, a navy equal to the task proposed. This project of Leibnitz will be more fully referred to when the narrative reaches the momentous date at which it was broached; when Louis, with his kingdom and navy in the highest pitch of efficiency, stood at the point where the roads parted, and then took the one which settled that France should not be the power of the sea. This decision, which killed Colbert and ruined the prosperity of France, was felt in its consequences from generation to generation afterward, as the great navy of England, in war after war, swept the seas, insured the growing wealth of the island kingdom through exhausting strifes, while drying up the external resources of French trade and inflicting consequent misery. The false line of policy that began with Louis XIV. also turned France away from a promising career in India, in the days of his successor.

Meanwhile the two maritime States, England and Holland, though eying France distrustfully, had greater and growing grudges against each other, which under the fostering care of Charles II. led to war. The true cause was doubtless commercial jealousy, and the conflict sprang immediately from collisions between the trading companies. Hostilities began on the west coast of Africa; and an English squadron, in 1664, after subduing several Dutch stations there, sailed to New Amsterdam (now New York), and seized it. All these affairs took place before the formal declaration of war in February, 1665. This war was undoubtedly popular in England;

出，将法国的兵力转而针对埃及，会让法国在称霸地中海地区、掌控东方贸易两个方面击败荷兰，并且效果会比最成功的陆上大捷都好；而在保持好国内迫切需要之和平局势的同时，这也会为法国建立起制海权，从而确保法国在欧洲的优势。这次请愿，要求路易十四不再在欧洲大陆上追求荣耀，转而在拥有制海权这个方面去寻求法国更为持久的辉煌；多亏了柯尔贝尔的才干，此时建立制海权的各种要素，都已握在了路易十四的手中。100年过后，拿破仑这位比路易十四更加伟大的人，又试图让法国按照莱布尼茨所指出的那条道路走下去；可他却不像路易十四，并没有一支可以担当上述重任的海军。当本书所述之历史到达莱布尼茨提出这一建议的重大时刻时，我们会更加完整地说明这一建议的内容；此时，路易十四治下的法国和法国海军都处于效率的巅峰，他正站在一个分岔口上，之后便选择了一条让法国不会成为海洋大国的道路。导致柯尔贝尔去世并且摧毁了法国繁荣之势的这一决定，影响到了后来一代又一代的法国人；因为英国庞大的海军通过一场又一场战争横扫了各个海域，通过种种倾尽全力的争夺，保证了这个岛国财力的持续增长，同时榨干了法国贸易业的外部资源，并使法国人民遭受了相应的不幸。开始于路易十四时期的这种错误方针，还使得在下一任国王统治的时期，法国在印度群岛的殖民贸易事业开始变得前途黯淡起来。

在此期间，虽说英国和荷兰这两个海洋国家都认为法国靠不住，但它们之间的积怨却也越来越深、越来越多；这种积怨在查理二世的大力推动下，最终导致了战争。两国积怨的真正原因，在于商业贸易上的猜忌；而这种矛盾，又直接源于两国贸易公司之间的摩擦。两国的敌对行动，开始于非洲西海岸；1664年，一支英国舰队在当地攻下了荷

the instinct of the people found an expression by the lips of Monk, who is reported to have said, "What matters this or that reason? What we want is more of the trade which the Dutch now have." There is also little room to doubt that, despite the pretensions of the trading companies, the government of the United Provinces would gladly have avoided the war; the able man who was at their head saw too clearly the delicate position in which they stood between England and France. They claimed, however, the support of the latter in virtue of a defensive treaty made in 1662. Louis allowed the claim, but unwillingly; and the still young navy of France gave practically no help.

The war between the two sea States was wholly maritime, and had the general characteristics of all such wars. Three great battles were fought, — the first off Lowestoft, on the Norfolk coast, June 13, 1665; the second, known as the Four Days' Battle in the Straits of Dover, often spoken of by French writers as that of the Pas de Calais, lasting from the 11th to the 14th of June, 1666; and the third, off the North Foreland, August 4 of the same year. In the first and last of these the English had a decided success; in the second the advantage remained with the Dutch. This one only will be described at length, because of it alone has been found such a full, coherent account as will allow a clear and accurate tactical narrative to be given. There are in these fights points of interest more generally applicable to the present day than are the details of somewhat obsolete tactical movements.

In the first battle off Lowestoft, it appears that the Dutch commander, Opdam, who was not a seaman but a cavalry officer, had very positive orders to fight; the discretion proper to a commander-in-chief on the spot was not intrusted to him. To interfere thus with the commander in the field or afloat is one of the most common temptations to the government in the cabinet, and is generally disastrous. Tourville, the greatest of Louis XIV.'s admirals, was forced thus to

兰的数个军事驻地之后，开始驶向新阿姆斯特丹（即如今的纽约），并且攻占了该地。这些战事都发生在1665年2月两国正式宣战之前。这次战争，在英国国内无疑是尽人皆知的；而英国民众的反应，则从蒙克的话可以看出来——据闻，蒙克曾经这样说道："这个原因也好，那个原因也好，又有什么关系呢？我们想要的，就是荷兰现在所拥有的、更多的贸易。" 我们也没有什么理由来怀疑，尽管诸贸易公司有着种种要求，但荷兰共和国政府应当是巴不得免去这场战争的；当时该国政府的首脑是个能力出众的人，很清醒地认识到了他们夹在英、法两国之间的那种微妙形势。然而，他们却根据1662年签订的一份防御条约，要求法国支援。路易十四虽说批准进行支援，却是极不情愿的；而实际上，当时仍然羽翼未丰的法国海军也没有起到什么作用。

英、荷两个海洋国家之间的这场战争，完全是在海上进行的，并且具备所有此种海战的共同特征。两国间进行了3次大规模的海战——第一次是1665年6月13日发生在诺福克海岸的洛斯托夫特海战；第二次是史称多佛海峡的"四日海战"，而法国史学家则常常称之为加来海峡的"四日海战"，从1666年6月11日一直持续到了14日；第三次则是同年8月4日在北福兰海域发生的海战。在其中的第一次和第三次海战中，英军都大获全胜；而在第二次海战中，优势却在荷兰这一方。我们只会详细地描述这一场战斗，因为只有此次海战才有全面、连贯的记述，才能够清楚、准确地说明其战术。跟那些有点儿老式的战术运动的详细情况相比，这几次海战具有一些值得关注的地方，更能普遍地适用于如今的形势。

在洛斯托夫特海域进行的第一场战斗中，原非水兵而是骑兵将领的荷兰海军司令奥普丹，似乎有着明确的作战命令；可他却没有被授予一个作战总指挥所应有的那种自由

risk the whole French navy against his own judgment; and a century later a great French fleet escaped from the English admiral Keith, through his obedience to imperative orders from his immediate superior, who was sick in port.

In the Lowestoft fight the Dutch van gave way; and a little later one of the junior admirals of the centre, Opdam's own squadron, being killed, the crew was seized with a panic, took the command of the ship from her officers, and carried her out of action. This movement was followed by twelve or thirteen other ships, leaving a great gap in the Dutch line. The occurrence shows, what has before been pointed out, that the discipline of the Dutch fleet and the tone of the officers were not high, despite the fine fighting qualities of the nation, and although it is probably true that there were more good seamen among the Dutch than among the English captains. The natural steadfastness and heroism of the Hollanders could not wholly supply that professional pride and sense of military honor which it is the object of sound military institutions to encourage. Popular feeling in the United States is pretty much at sea in this matter; there is with it no intermediate step between personal courage with a gun in its hand and entire military efficiency.

Opdam, seeing the battle going against him, seems to have yielded to a feeling approaching despair. He sought to grapple the English commander-in-chief, who on this day was the Duke of York, the king's brother. He failed in this, and in the desperate struggle which followed, his ship blew up. Shortly after, three, or as one account says four, Dutch ships ran foul of one another, and this group was burned by one fire-ship; three or four others singly met the same fate a little later. The Dutch fleet was now in disorder, and retreated under cover of the squadron of Van Tromp, son of the famous old admiral who in the days of the Commonwealth sailed through the Channel with a broom at his masthead.

裁量权。如此牵制战场或海上指挥官的做法，是内阁政府中最为常见的恶行之一，通常都会带来灾难性的后果。图维尔是路易十四手下最杰出的一位舰队司令，就是因为政府掣肘，才不得不违背自己的判断，拿整个法国海军去冒险；而100年之后，一支大型的法国舰队也因为英国舰队司令基斯服从其直接上司的紧急命令而逃过了一劫——当时，基斯的直接上级因病而留在港内，没有出海。

在洛斯托夫特海战中，荷兰的先头部队被击退了；不久之后，在奥普丹亲率的中锋舰队中，有位资历较浅的将领牺牲了，全舰水兵便都惊慌失措，从军官们手中夺取了该舰的指挥权，并率该舰退出了战斗。接着，又有12艘或13艘舰船随之撤离了，在荷军的战线上留下了一个大大的缺口。这一事件表明，正如之前已经指出的那样，荷兰舰队的纪律和官兵的士气都不高；尽管荷兰这个民族有着良好的战斗素质，并且尽管荷兰舰队中的优秀水兵人数很可能多过英国海军官兵，但这些都于事无补。荷兰人天生的毅力和英雄气概，并不能完整地带来职业自豪感和军事荣誉感，而这种职业自豪感和军事荣誉感，则正是那些健全的军事制度所要鼓励实现的目标。在这个问题上，如今美国的民心几乎全都是茫然一片；而在手中有枪的个人勇气与全面的军事效率之间，却并没有什么中间阶段。

奥普丹看到战斗不利于自己之后，似乎也开始感到绝望了。他试图抓住英军的总司令；此日的英军总司令，正是英王的弟弟约克公爵。奥普丹非但没能抓住约克公爵，而且在接下来孤注一掷的殊死战斗中，他的座舰又被炸坏了。旋即，3艘荷兰军舰——据另一份记录称，是4艘荷兰军舰——彼此相撞，然后就被一艘火攻船给烧毁了；不久后，又有3或4艘落了单的军舰遭遇了与此相同的命运。此时，荷兰舰队已经乱成一团，

Fire-ships are seen here to have played a very conspicuous part, more so certainly than in the war of 1653, though at both periods they formed an appendage to the fleet. There is on the surface an evident resemblance between the role of the fire-ship and the part assigned in modern warfare to the torpedo-cruiser. The terrible character of the attack, the comparative smallness of the vessel making it, and the large demands upon the nerve of the assailant, are the chief points of resemblance; the great points of difference are the comparative certainty with which the modern vessel can be handled, which is partly met by the same advantage in the iron-clad over the old ship-of-the-line, and the instantaneousness of the injury by torpedo, whose attack fails or succeeds at once, whereas that of the fire-ship required time for effecting the object, which in both cases is total destruction of the hostile ship, instead of crippling or otherwise reducing it. An appreciation of the character of fire-ships, of the circumstances under which they attained their greatest usefulness, and of the causes which led to their disappearance, may perhaps help in the decision to which nations must come as to whether the torpedo-cruiser, pure and simple, is a type of weapon destined to survive in fleets.

A French officer, who has been examining the records of the French navy, states that the fire-ship first appears, incorporated as an arm of the fleet, in 1636.

"Whether specially built for the purpose, or whether altered from other purposes to be fitted for their particular end, they received a special equipment. The command was given to officers not noble, with the grade of captain of fire-ship. Five subordinate officers and twenty-five seamen made up the crew. Easily known by grappling-irons which were always fitted to their yards, the fire-ship saw its role growing less in the early years of the eighteenth century. It was finally to disappear from the fleets whose speed it delayed and whose evolutions were

只得在范·特龙普的掩护下撤退——这个范·特龙普，正是荷兰共和国时期曾率领舰队通过英吉利海峡，并在桅顶悬挂金雀花的那位有名的原海军将领的儿子。

在此役中我们可以看到，火攻船发挥了极为显著的作用，比在1653年那场战争中发挥的作用更为明显，尽管在这两个时期，火攻船都只是整个舰队的附属武器。从表面来看，火攻船的作用与现代战争中鱼雷巡洋舰的作用有着明显的相似之处。它们在攻击时都具有令人觉得可怖的特点，在建造时船体尺寸都相对较小，并且进攻时都极大地考验着攻击者的神经，这些就是两者主要的相似之处；而它们的重大差异，一是现代的鱼雷巡洋舰操纵起来相对更有把握——这一点，在一定程度上来说，足以媲美铁甲舰船具有胜过原来的战列舰的那种相同的优势；二是鱼雷的瞬间杀伤力，因为鱼雷发射之后，要么击不中，要么便是一击而中，而火攻船则需要时间才能实现目标——但在这两种情形下，开火的目标都是彻底摧毁敌舰，而不是仅仅使之受损或者用其他的方式将其削弱。充分认识到火攻船的特点，认识到它们在什么样的环境下威力最大，并且认识到导致它们销声匿迹的原因，可能会有助于各国进行决策，以便判断纯粹的鱼雷巡洋舰是不是一种注定会在舰队中存续下去的武器。

一位曾经研究过法国海军历史记载的法国军官称，火攻船是在1636年作为武器编入舰队而首次出现的。

"无论是为火攻而特意建造的，还是用别的船只改造成符合其特定用途的，它们都会安装一种特殊的设备。命令则会按照火攻船舰长的级别，下达给并非贵族的那些军官。一艘火攻船上，有5名下级军官和25名水兵。由于其帆桁上总是安放着多爪锚，敌人很容易辨认出来，所以在18世纪早期，人们认为火攻船的用处越来越少了。火攻船最

by it complicated. As the ships-of-war grew larger, their action in concert with fire-ships became daily more difficult. On the other hand, there had already been abandoned the idea of combining them with the fighting-ships to form a few groups, each provided with all the means of attack and defence. The formation of the close-hauled line-of-battle, by assigning the fire-ships a place in a second line placed half a league on the side farthest from the enemy, made them more and more unfitted to fulfill their office. The official plan of the battle of Malaga (1704), drawn up immediately after the battle, shows the fire-ship in this position as laid down by Paul Hoste. Finally the use of shells, enabling ships to be set on fire more surely and quickly, and introduced on board at the period of which we are now treating, though the general use did not obtain until much later, was the last blow to the fire-ship."

Those who are familiar with the theories and discussions of our own day on the subject of fleet tactics and weapons, will recognize in this short notice of a long obsolete type certain ideas which are not obsolete. The fire-ship disappeared from fleets "whose speed it delayed." In heavy weather small bulk must always mean comparatively small speed. In a moderate sea, we are now told, the speed of the torpedo-boat falls from twenty knots to fifteen or less, and the seventeen to nineteen knot cruiser can either run away from the pursuing boats, or else hold them at a distance under fire of machine and heavy guns. These boats are sea-going, "and it is thought can keep the sea in all weathers; but to be on board a 110-foot torpedo-boat, when the sea is lively, is said to be far from agreeable. The heat, noise, and rapid vibrations of the engines are intense. Cooking seems to be out of the question, and it is said that if food were well cooked few would be able to appreciate it. To obtain necessary rest under these conditions, added to the rapid motions of the boat, is most difficult." Larger boats are to be built; but the factor of

终消失的原因，一方面，在于它们既拖累了整个舰队的速度，也是因为它们使得舰队的战术机动变得很复杂，由于军舰建造得越来越大，所以它们与火攻船的协同作战也变得日益困难了。另一方面，人们也已放弃了用火攻船与军舰联合起来形成数个战斗群、每个群都配备全部攻防武器的那种观念。迎风展开战斗队形，将火攻船置于离敌舰最远那一侧达半里格的第二防线，这样的阵形使得火攻船越发不适合于发挥它们的作用了。1704年马拉加海战之后立即起草的官方作战计划，表明是保罗·何斯德规定将火攻船部署于此处的。最终，由于炮弹能让敌舰更有可能、也更快速地燃烧起来，并在我们所论述的这一时期被运用到了军舰上，从而给了火攻船最后一击；尽管直到过后很久，各国才开始在军舰上普遍使用炮弹。"

熟悉我们这个时代与舰队战术和武器装备相关的那些理论和论述的人，从这一段关于早已过时的火攻船的简短介绍中，便可以看出一些并不过时的观点来。火攻船从舰队中消失，是因为"它拖累了舰队的速度"。在恶劣的天气条件下，船体小就必定意味着航行速度也相对较小。如今我们知道，海上风平浪静的时候，鱼雷艇的速度会从20节下降到15节，甚至更低，而速度在17节至19节的巡洋舰要么可以摆脱其他船只的追击，要么就可以远距离用机关枪和大炮的火力压制住它们。这些舰船都是海轮，"人们以为这种舰船在所有天气情况下都能在海上来去自如；不过据说，在大海波涛汹涌的时候登上一艘110英尺长的鱼雷艇，那可不是闹着玩的。热浪、嘈杂、发动机的快速转动，都会令人喘不过气来。做饭烧菜似乎根本就不可能，并且据说，就算饭菜做得再可口，也没有几个人能够吃好。在这样的条件之下，船只又在快速航行，所以要想得到必要的休息，是难如登天的。"因此，人们就必须建造出体积更大的舰船才行；不过，除非将鱼雷巡洋舰的船体加

loss of speed in rough weather will remain, unless the size of the torpedo-cruiser is increased to a point that will certainly lead to fitting them with something more than torpedoes. Like fire-ships, small torpedo-cruisers will delay the speed and complicate the evolutions of the fleet with which they are associated. [1] The disappearance of the fire-ship was also hastened, we are told, by the introduction of shell firing, or incendiary projectiles; and it is not improbable that for deep-sea fighting the transfer of the torpedo to a class of larger ships will put an end to the mere torpedo-cruiser. The fire-ship continued to be used against fleets at anchor down to the days of the American Civil War; and the torpedo-boat will always be useful within an easy distance of its port.

A third phase of naval practice two hundred years ago, mentioned in the extract quoted, involves an idea very familiar to modern discussions; namely, the group formation. "The idea of combining fire-ships with the fighting-ships to form a few groups, each provided with all the means of attack and defence," was for a time embraced; for we are told that it was later on abandoned. The combining of the ships of a fleet into groups of two, three, or four meant to act specially together is now largely favored in England; less so in France, where it meets strong opposition. No question of this sort, ably advocated on either side, is to be settled by one man's judgment, nor until time and experience have applied their infallible tests. It may be remarked, however, that in a well-organized fleet there are two degrees of command which are in themselves both natural and necessary, that can be neither done away nor ignored; these are the command of the whole fleet as one unit, and the command of each ship as a unit in itself. When a fleet becomes too large to be handled by one man, it must be subdivided, and in the heat of action become practically two fleets acting to one common end; as Nelson, in his noble order at Trafalgar, said, "The second in command will, after my intentions are made known to him"

大到某种程度，使之完全能够配备其他武器装备，而不仅仅只是鱼雷，否则的话，在恶劣天气中速度降低这个因素就会依然存在。与火攻船一样，小型鱼雷巡洋舰也会拖累所属舰队的速度，也会让舰队的战术机动变得复杂起来。[1] 我们知道，采用炮弹或燃烧弹发射的技术，加速了火攻船的绝迹；所以对于深海作战来说，将鱼雷艇变成一种更大型的舰船会终结单纯的鱼雷巡洋舰，这也不是不可能的。晚至美国内战时期，火攻船一直都被继续用于攻击停泊着的舰队；而鱼雷艇在距其不远的范围内，也总是能发挥出威力。

前述摘录中提及了200年前海军实践的第三个阶段，它涉及到现代论述中很常见的一种观念，即群组编队。人们曾经在一段时间里，接受了"将火攻船与军舰联合起来形成数个战斗群、每个群都配备全部攻防武器的观念"；因为我们得知，后来这种观念被人们舍弃了。但在如今的英国，人们却大多支持将舰队中的舰船编组成2、3或4个舰群，并专门让这些舰群一起作战的做法；在法国则不然，很多人都强烈地反对这样做。此种情况，由于双方提倡得都很巧妙，所以是不可能通过一个人的意见就能解决得了的，也只有当时间和经验已经可靠地检验过了之后，这个问题才能尘埃落定。不过我们可以说，在一支井然有序的舰队里，有两种层次的指挥权，它们本身都是正常而且必要的，既不能废止，也不能无视；这就是整支舰队的指挥权，以及每艘舰船本身的指挥权。当一支舰队过于庞大，一个人指挥不了的时候，这支舰队就得再进行拆分，而在激烈的战斗中，这支舰队实际上就变成了两支协同作战以达到同一目标的舰队了；正因为如此，纳尔逊在特拉法尔加海战中才下了一道庄严的命令，说："在我的作战意图传达给他之后，副司令"（注意"之后"这个词的实质，它有效地保护了总司令和副司令各自的职权）"对其所率部队具

(mark the force of the "after," which so well protects the functions both of the commander-in-chief and the second), "have the entire direction of his line, to make the attack upon the enemy, and to follow up the blow until they are captured or destroyed."

The size and cost of the individual iron-clad of the present day makes it unlikely that fleets will be so numerous as to require subdivision; but whether they are or not does not affect the decision of the group question. Looking simply to the principle underlying the theory, and disregarding the seeming tactical clumsiness of the special groups proposed, the question is: Shall there be introduced between the natural commands of the admiral and of the captains of individual ships a third artificial contrivance, which on the one hand will in effect partly supersede the supreme authority, and on the other will partly fetter the discretion of commanders of ships? A further difficulty springing from the narrow principle of support specially due to particular ships, on which the group system rests, is this: that when signals can no longer be seen, the duty of the captain to his own ship and to the fleet at large will be complicated by his duty to observe certain relations to particular ships; which particular ships must in time come to have undue prominence in his views. The group formation had its day of trial in old times, and disappeared before the test of experience; whether in its restored form it will survive, time will show. It may be said, before quitting the subject, that as an order of sailing, corresponding to the route-step of an army in march, a loose group formation has some advantages; maintaining some order without requiring that rigid exactness of position, to observe which by day and night must be a severe strain on captain and deck-officers. Such a route-order should not, however, be permitted until a fleet has reached high tactical precision.

To return to the question of fire-ships and torpedo-boats, the role of the latter, it is often

有完全的指挥权，可以对敌发动攻击，可以继续追击，直至俘虏或摧毁敌军。"

如今铁甲舰船的大小和造价，使得舰队的数量不太可能多到需要再进行拆分的程度了；不过，无论舰队是多是少，都不会影响到对群组编队问题的决策。只要看一看这种理论中的基本原则，不去考虑前面提到的、从战术角度来看特定编队并不灵活的方面，那么这个问题就成了：在海军司令的正常指挥权和各个舰长的正常指挥权之间，应不应该增加第三种人工机制，使之一方面能够部分地代行最高指挥权，另一方面又能部分地约束各舰指挥官的自由裁量权呢？而进行支援时尤其应当倚赖特殊舰船的这种狭隘原则，又带来了另一个难题，那就是：在无法再看见信号的时候，一名舰长对于自己所率舰船的职责，以及对于整支舰队所负的职责，会因他执行对特殊舰船所负有的某些职责而变得复杂起来；这些特殊舰船，必须能够及时让他想起、并且让他觉得必须极其重视才行。群组编队阵法在过去有幸得到了实验，但还未经过实践检验就销声匿迹了；这种阵法是否会以其复兴之后的形式继续存在下去，时间会给出答案的。在放弃这个话题之前，我们可以这么说，作为一种航行次序，松散的群组编队相当于陆军在行军时的便步行军，还是具有某些优势的；因为这样既可以保持某种次序，又无需严格、准确地坚守自己的位置——夜以继日地保持好自己的位置，对舰长和驾驶人员来说，都必定是一种极大的压力。然而，只有一支舰队达到了高超的战术精度之后，才能允许它保持此种航行秩序。

再回到火攻船和鱼雷艇的问题上来。人们常说，后者的作用从双方舰队的混战中可以看出来，因为这种混战，往往会在两支舰队当中猛然地撕开数个缺口。而在战火纷飞、乱成一团的这个时刻，鱼雷艇的机会便来了。这种说法听起来自然貌似很有道理，

said, is to be found in that mêlée which is always to succeed a couple of headlong passes between the opposing fleets. In the smoke and confusion of that hour is the opportunity of the torpedo-boat. This certainly sounds plausible, and the torpedo vessel certainly has a power of movement not possessed by the fire-ship. A mêlée of the two fleets, however, was not the condition most favorable for the fire-ship. I shall quote here from another French officer, whose discussion of these Anglo-Dutch sea-fights, in a late periodical, is singularly clear and suggestive. He says:

"Far from impeding the direct action of the fire-ship, which was naught or nearly so during the confused battles of the war of 1652, the regularity and ensemble newly attained in the movements of squadrons seem rather to favor it. The fire-ships played a very important part at the battles of Lowestoft, Pas de Calais, and the North Foreland. Thanks to the good order preserved by the ships-of-the-line, these incendiary ships can indeed be better protected by the artillery; much more efficiently directed than before toward a distinct and determined end."

In the midst of the confused mêlées of 1652 the fire-ship "acted, so to speak, alone, seeking by chance an enemy to grapple, running the risk of a mistake, without protection against the guns of the enemy, nearly sure to be sunk by him or else burned uselessly. All now, in 1665, has become different. Its prey is clearly pointed out; it knows it, follows it easily into the relatively fixed position had by it in the enemy's line. On the other hand, the ships of his own division do not lose sight of the fire-ship. They accompany it as far as possible, cover it with their artillery to the end of its course, and disengage it before burning, if the fruitlessness of the attempt is seen soon enough. Evidently under such conditions its action, always uncertain (it cannot be otherwise), nevertheless acquires greater chances of success." These instructive comments need perhaps the qualifying, or additional, remark that confusion in the enemy's

并且鱼雷艇自然也有着火攻船所不具备的机动能力。然而，两支舰队的混战，并非最有利于火攻船的条件。在此，我将引述另一位法国将领的话，他在前不久的一份杂志上论述了英、荷两国之间的那些海战。他说：

"1652年战争期间的多次混战当中，火攻船都没有直接参战，或者参战次数几近于零；而分舰队机动中刚刚实现的整齐划一，却似乎并未妨碍火攻船的直接作战，反而是对其有利的。在加来海峡的洛斯托夫特海战以及北福兰海战中，火攻船都发挥了极其重要的作用。多亏了那些战列舰保持着良好的秩序，这些火攻船事实上才能得到火炮更好的掩护，才能比以前得到更加有效的指挥，从而实现其明确而坚定的目的。"

在1652年的这场混战当中，火攻船却"可以说是单独作战，随机地寻找敌舰来进行攻击，冒着犯下错误的危险，毫无掩护地暴露在敌舰炮火之下，被敌舰击沉或者烧毁几成定局。如今，在1665年，一切却都迥然不同了。火攻船的目标，已经明确地指出来了；火攻船知道自己的目标是哪艘敌舰，可以轻而易举地尾随目标，进入它在敌方阵线相对固定的战位。另一方面，火攻船这一方的舰船，都不会看不到它。它们会尽量地伴随在其左右，用自己的火炮掩护它，直到它到达自己的目标位置，并且一旦认识到火攻无果，就会在它遭到攻击和着火之前，让它撤出战斗。显然，在这些条件之下，火攻船的行动虽说一向都没有什么把握（不可能有别的指望），却获得了更多成功的机会。"这些颇具启发性的话语，或许还需恰当地补充一点，那就是当敌舰乱成一团而己方秩序井然的时候，也是开始绝地反击的最佳时机。接下来，作者继续探索火攻船销声匿迹的原因：

"在此我们看到，火攻船的重要性达到了顶峰。这种重要性是会下降的，而在下述情

order at the time that your own remains good gives the best opening for a desperate attack. The writer goes on to trace the disappearance of the fire-ship: —

"Here then we see the fire-ship at the point of its highest importance. That importance will decrease, the fire-ship itself will end by disappearing from engagements in the open sea, when naval artillery becoming more perfect shall have greater range, be more accurate and more rapid; [2] when ships receiving better forms, greater steering power, more extensive and better balanced sail power, shall be able, thanks to quicker speed and handling, to avoid almost certainly the fire-ships sent against them; when, finally, fleets led on principles of tactics as skilful as they were timid, a tactics which will predominate a century later during the whole war of American Independence, when these fleets, in order not to jeopardize the perfect regularity of their order of battle, will avoid coming to close quarters, and will leave to the cannon alone to decide the fate of an action."

In this discussion the writer has in view the leading feature which, while aiding the action of the fire-ship, also gives this war of 1665 its peculiar interest in the history of naval tactics. In it is found for the first time the close-hauled line-of-battle undeniably adopted as the fighting order of the fleets. It is plain enough that when those fleets numbered, as they often did, from eighty to a hundred ships, such lines would be very imperfectly formed in every essential, both of line and interval; but the general aim is evident, amid whatever imperfections of execution. The credit for this development is generally given to the Duke of York, afterward James II.; but the question to whom the improvement is due is of little importance to sea-officers of the present day when compared with the instructive fact that so long a time elapsed between the appearance of the large sailing-ship, with its broadside battery, and the systematic adoption of the order which was best adapted to develop the full power of the fleet for mutual

况下，火攻船本身就不会再出海参战，从而退出历史舞台了：待海军的火炮更加完善，使得火炮射程更远、射击更精确、速度更快了之后[2]；当外形更加完美、更易操纵、具有更多更平稳动力的那些帆船因为速度更快、机动性更好，因而应当差不多有十足把握避开敌方火攻船的时候；最后，当舰船由一种战术的基本原则所引领，既灵巧又谨慎，而这种战术在100年后的整个美国独立战争期间都大行其道，当这些舰队为了不危及到其战斗序列那种完美的整齐划一而避免扎成一堆，并让大炮独自来决定战斗结局的时候。"

　　在这段论述中，作者考虑到了一个主要的特点；这个主要特点，在协助火攻船实施作战行动的同时，也让1665年的这场战争在海军战术史上具有了独特的重要性。在这场战争中，我们首次看到了迎风展开的战线，这种阵法无疑就是舰队所采用的作战序列。很显然，当舰队的舰船数量达到80艘至100艘之后——当时的舰队规模常常如此——这样的战线，从舰船队列和间隔这两个要点来看，编队都是极不完善的；不过，无论在实施过程中有着什么样的缺陷，其总体目标都是很明确的。开发出这种战阵的功劳，人们通常都认为应当归于詹姆士二世之后的约克公爵；不过，这种进步应当归因于何人，对如今的海军将领来说，跟拥有侧舷排炮的大型帆船问世之后过了很久，人们才开始系统地采用最能发挥出整个舰队威力、以便相互支援的战斗序列这一问题相比，根本就不重要了。由于掌握了这个问题的基本要素，又有最终实现的结果，所以对于我们而言，这一结果似乎就相当简单，差不多是不言而喻的了。那么，为什么当时那些能人花了那么久的时间，才得出了这一结果呢？个中原因——其中也含有如今的海军将领可以汲取的教训——与使得此时的作战序列如此没有把握的原因，无疑是相同的；也就是说，在荷兰人最终遭遇英国人、两者在海洋上

support. To us, having the elements of the problem in our hands, together with the result finally reached, that result seems simple enough, almost self-evident. Why did it take so long for the capable men of that day to reach it? The reason — and herein lies the lesson for the officer of to-day — was doubtless the same that leaves the order of battle so uncertain now; namely, that the necessity of war did not force men to make up their minds, until the Dutch at last met in the English their equals on the sea. The sequence of ideas which resulted in the line-of-battle is clear and logical. Though familiar enough to seamen, it will be here stated in the words of the writer last quoted, because they have a neatness and precision entirely French: —

"With the increase of power of the ship-of-war, and with the perfecting of its sea and warlike qualities, there has come an equal progress in the art of utilizing them. ... As naval evolutions become more skilful, their importance grows from day to day. To these evolutions there is needed a base, a point from which they depart and to which they return. A fleet of war-ships must be always ready to meet an enemy; logically, therefore, this point of departure for naval evolutions must be the order of battle. Now, since the disappearance of galleys, almost all the artillery is found upon the sides of a ship of war. Hence it is the beam that must necessarily and always be turned toward the enemy. On the other hand, it is necessary that the sight of the latter must never be interrupted by a friendly ship. Only one formation allows the ships of the same fleet to satisfy fully these conditions. That formation is the line ahead [column]. This line, therefore, is imposed as the only order of battle, and consequently as the basis of all fleet tactics. In order that this order of battle, this long thin line of guns, may not be injured or broken at some point weaker than the rest, there is at the same time felt the necessity of putting in it only ships which, if not of equal force, have at least equally strong sides. Logically it follows, at the same moment in which the line ahead became definitively the order for battle, there was

棋逢对手之前，战争的必要性都并没有迫使人们下定决心。导致出现作战队形的那种理念脉络，既清晰，又合乎逻辑。尽管水兵都相当熟悉这一点，但此处我们还是要用上面那位作者的话加以说明，因为这位作者的阐述，具有一种纯属法国式的简洁性与准确性：

"随着军舰作战力量的提升，随着军舰进行航海与作战的能力日趋完善起来，人们利用军舰来作战的技术也有了同样的进步……由于海军的战术机动变得越来越巧妙，所以海军的重要性也日益增加了。为了实施这些战术机动，海军就必须拥有一个基地，使得它可以从此处出发，之后再返回此处。一支军事舰队，必须时刻准备着遭遇敌人；因此，从逻辑上来看，进行海军战术机动的这种舰队的出发之地，就必定是战斗编队。如今，自从桨帆船消失之后，几乎所有的火炮都是安放在战舰的两侧。因此，必须并且一向都是将船体一侧转向敌人。另一方面，敌舰必须时时能够看到，决不能被友舰所遮挡才行。只有一种编队，能够让同一支舰队的所有舰船都充分地满足这些条件。此种编队，就是纵列排阵（即排成纵队）。因此，这种纵队就不得不成了唯一的战斗序列，并成为了所有舰队战术的基础。要想让这种战斗序列、让这种窄长的纵列炮阵不至于在某个薄弱之处受损或断裂，那么我们同时必须确保，舰队中所有船只的兵力就算不是完全相等，至少其两侧的兵力要同样强大才行。因此，合乎逻辑的结论就是，一旦纵列排阵最终变成了战斗序列，那么就已表明了'纵列当中'那些船只——它们注定要编入其中——与派作其他用场的轻型舰船之间的差异。"

倘若在这些原因之外，再加上那些使得把迎风展开的队形当成战斗队列的理由，那

established the distinction between the ships 'of the line,' alone destined for a place therein, and the lighter ships meant for other uses."

If to these we add the considerations which led to making the line-of-battle a close-hauled line, we have the problem fully worked out. But the chain of reasoning was as clear two hundred and fifty years ago as it is now; why then was it so long in being worked out? Partly, no doubt, because old traditions — in those days traditions of galley-fighting — had hold of and confused men's minds; chiefly because men are too indolent to seek out the foundation truths of the situation in their day, and develop the true theory of action from its base up. As a rare instance of clear-sightedness, recognizing such a fundamental change in conditions and predicting results, words of Admiral Labrousse of the French navy, written in 1840, are most instructive. "Thanks to steam," he wrote, "ships will be able to move in any direction with such speed that the effects of collision may, and indeed must, as they formerly did, take the place of projectile weapons and annul the calculations of the skilful manoeuvrer. The ram will be favorable to speed, without destroying the nautical qualities of a ship. As soon as one power shall have adopted this terrible weapon, all others must accept it, under pain of evident inferiority, and thus combats will become combats of ram against ram." While forbearing the unconditional adhesion to the ram as the controlling weapon of the day, which the French navy has yielded, the above brief argument may well be taken as an instance of the way in which researches into the order of battle of the future should be worked out. A French writer, commenting on Labrousse's paper, says: —

"Twenty-seven years were scarce enough for our fathers, counting from 1638, the date of building the 'Couronne,' to 1665, to pass from the tactical order of the line abreast, the order for galleys, to that of the line ahead. We ourselves needed twenty-nine years from 1830, when the first steamship was brought into our fleet, to 1859, when the application of the principle

我们就算充分弄懂这个问题了。不过，此种推理过程在250年前和现在一样清晰，当时的人怎么花了那么久才弄明白呢？毫无疑问，原因部分在于，以前的种种传统——在那个时代，就是用桨帆船作战的传统——禁锢并搅混了人们的思维；而主要原因，则是人们太过懒惰，以至于无法找出当时形势的基本事实，并且无法以这些事实为基础，往上形成正确的作战理论。法国海军司令拉布鲁斯在1840年写下的话语，是一个不可多得的、敏锐地认识到形势发生了根本变化并且预计到了结果的例子，故极具启发意义。"由于有了蒸汽动力，"他写道，"舰船便能以很快的速度向各个方向移动；因此，人们可能、事实上也必然会像以前那样，用碰撞来取代抛射武器，并且打消掉进行巧妙机动的念头。撞角既有利于提高速度，同时又不会毁掉一艘船的航海功用。一旦某个大国采用了这种可怕的武器，其他国家便只能接受这种做法，忍受技不如人之痛了；这样一来，海战便会变成撞角对撞角的战斗。"尽管容忍毫无限制地使用法国海军所发明的撞角，把撞角当作当时最厉害的武器，但我们不妨把上面这段简短的论述，当成是对未来的战斗序列进行研究时应当加以解决的方式的一个例子。一位法国作家在评论拉布鲁斯的文章时称：

"从1638年建造'皇冠'号之日起，到1665年这短短的27年，并不足以让我们的先辈从适用于桨帆船的战术横阵过渡到战术纵阵。我们自己都花了29年，从第一艘汽轮进入我国海军服役的1830年始，到通过建造'索尔费里诺'号和'马真塔'号而确定应用撞角战术的1859年，才在相反的方向实现了一次彻底的变革；因此，真理确实是不会轻易地被人们理解的……这种转变之所以并不是突然之间发生的，原因不但在于新的舰船

of ram-fighting was affirmed by laying down the 'Solferino' and the 'Magenta' to work a revolution in the contrary direction; so true it is that truth is always slow in getting to the light. ... This transformation was not sudden, not only because the new material required time to be built and armed, but above all, it is sad to say, because the necessary consequences of the new motive power escaped most minds."

We come now to the justly celebrated Four Days' Battle of June, 1666, which claims special notice, not only on account of the great number of ships engaged on either side, nor yet only for the extraordinary physical endurance of the men who kept up a hot naval action for so many successive days, but also because the commanders-in-chief on either side, Monk and De Ruyter, were the most distinguished seamen, or rather sea-commanders, brought forth by their respective countries in the seventeenth century. Monk was possibly inferior to Blake in the annals of the English navy; but there is a general agreement that De Ruyter is the foremost figure, not only in the Dutch service, but among all the naval officers of that age. The account about to be given is mainly taken from a recent number of the "Revue Maritime et Coloniale," and is there published as a letter, recently discovered, from a Dutch gentleman serving as volunteer on board De Ruyter's ship, to a friend in France. The narrative is delightfully clear and probable, — qualities not generally found in the description of those long-ago fights; and the satisfaction it gave was increased by finding in the Memoirs of the Count de Guiche, who also served as volunteer in the fleet, and was taken to De Ruyter after his own vessel had been destroyed by a fire-ship, an account confirming the former in its principal details. This additional pleasure was unhappily marred by recognizing certain phrases as common to both stories; and a comparison showed that the two could not be accepted as independent narratives. There are, however, points of internal difference which make it possible that the two accounts are by different eye-witnesses, who compared and corrected their versions before sending them

需要时间才能建造和装备起来，而且说来可悲，最主要的原因还是这种新的驱动力所能带来的必然结果并未引起大多数的人注意。"

现在，我们再来看一看1666年6月那场名不虚传的"四日海战"；我们对于此战之所以需要特别注意，原因不仅在于双方投入作战的舰船数量众多，也不仅仅在于参战官兵具有非凡的耐力，使得一场白热化的海战持续进行了这么多天，还在于参战双方的海军总司令——蒙克和德·鲁伊特——都是两国在17世纪分别培养出来的最杰出的水兵，或者更准确一点来说，都是最杰出的海上指挥官。在英国海军史册上，蒙克的地位可能稍逊于布雷克；但世人却公认，德·鲁伊特不但是当时荷兰海军中最重要的人物，也是那个时代所有海军将领中的佼佼者。下面将要说明的内容，主要选自近一期《海洋和殖民杂志》中所发表的一封信件；这是一位曾在德·鲁伊特座舰上当志愿兵的荷兰绅士写给一位法国朋友的信，最近才被发现。此信赏心悦目，叙述清晰、可信——在记载很久以前那些战斗的史料中，通常是看不到如此上乘的材料的；而我们在《基申伯爵回忆录》中看到的内容，也证实了前者所述的主要细节，从而大大增加了此信的可信度——基申伯爵当时也是该舰队中的一名志愿兵，在他所属的那艘军舰被一艘火攻船摧毁之后，他被派到了德·鲁伊特的船上。遗憾的是，这两份材料中都使用了一些共同的说法，从而有损于这种额外的快感；将它们进行比较之后，结果表明我们不能认为这两份材料是彼此独立的。然而，二者还是存在着一些内在的不同点，使得这两种记述有可能是由不同的目击者记录下来的；可能是他们对各自的说法进行了比较和订正之后，才邮寄给朋友或者写在日记上的。

out to their friends or writing them in their journals.

The numbers of the two fleets were: English about eighty ships, the Dutch about one hundred; but the inequality in numbers was largely compensated by the greater size of many of the English. A great strategic blunder by the government in London immediately preceded the fight. The king was informed that a French squadron was on its way from the Atlantic to join the Dutch. He at once divided his fleet, sending twenty ships under Prince Rupert to the westward to meet the French, while the remainder under Monk were to go east and oppose the Dutch.

A position like that of the English fleet, threatened with an attack from two quarters, presents one of the subtlest temptations to a commander. The impulse is very strong to meet both by dividing his own numbers as Charles did; but unless in possession of overwhelming force it is an error, exposing both divisions to be beaten separately, which, as we are about to see, actually happened in this case. The result of the first two days was disastrous to the larger English division under Monk, which was then obliged to retreat toward Rupert; and probably the opportune return of the latter alone saved the English fleet from a very serious loss, or at the least from being shut up in their own ports. A hundred and forty years later, in the exciting game of strategy that was played in the Bay of Biscay before Trafalgar, the English admiral Cornwallis made precisely the same blunder, dividing his fleet into two equal parts out of supporting distance, which Napoleon at the time characterized as a glaring piece of stupidity. The lesson is the same in all ages.

The Dutch had sailed for the English coast with a fair easterly wind, but it changed later to southwest with thick weather, and freshened, so that De Ruyter, to avoid being driven too far, came to anchor between Dunkirk and the Downs. The fleet then rode with its head to the southwest and the van on the right; while Tromp, who commanded the rear division

两支舰队的舰船数量分别是：英国大约有80艘，荷兰大约有100艘；不过，英国的许多舰船船体都比较大，在很大程度上弥补了兵力不平等所带来的劣势。战斗马上就要打响的时候，伦敦的英国政府却犯下了一个重大的战略错误。英王得知，一支小型的法国舰队正从大西洋上赶来，准备加入荷兰一方作战。他马上将舰队一分为二，由鲁珀特王子率20艘舰船向西迎击法军，余下的军舰则由蒙克统率，向东进击荷兰海军。

英国舰队当时有可能受到两面夹击，这种局面会对指挥官产生一种最为微妙的诱惑。像英王查理二世所做的那样，将自己的兵力一分为二来应对两方之敌，这种冲动往往是很强烈的；不过，除非自己拥有压倒性的优势兵力，否则这种做法就是错误的，会让两支兵力分别被敌人打败，正如我们将要看到的那样，在此战中确实出现了这样的结果。最初两天的战斗，给蒙克所率的那支兵力较强的舰队带来了灾难性的后果，所以他不得不撤向鲁珀特王子所率舰队；很有可能，是后者适时回师，才使得英军舰队免遭重大损失，或者说，至少没有让敌人将英国舰队堵在自己的港口里。140年后，在特拉法尔加海战爆发之前的比斯开湾海战这场激动人心的战略豪赌中，英国海军司令康华里又犯了与此一模一样的错误，将所率舰队分成了兵力对等的两支舰队，使它们之间相距遥远，无法彼此支援；当时，拿破仑把康华里的做法归结为一种显而易见的愚蠢。所以，这种教训世世代代都是相同的。

荷兰人本已借着顺向的东风，驶向了英国海岸，但后来风向却转为西南，天色阴暗下来，风力也增强了；于是，德·鲁伊特为了不让舰队被风吹得太远，就在敦克尔克和唐斯锚地之间泊了锚。接着，荷兰舰队便头朝西南泊在海面上，右翼为先锋；而按照正

in the natural order, was on the left. For some cause this left was most to windward, the centre squadron under Ruyter being to leeward, and the right, or van, to leeward again of the centre. This was the position of the Dutch fleet at daylight of June 11, 1666; and although not expressly so stated, it is likely, from the whole tenor of the narratives, that it was not in good order.

The same morning Monk, who was also at anchor, made out the Dutch fleet to leeward, and although so inferior in numbers determined to attack at once, hoping that by keeping the advantage of the wind he would be able to commit himself only so far as might seem best. He therefore stood along the Dutch line on the starboard tack, leaving the right and centre out of cannon-shot, until he came abreast of the left, Tromp's squadron. Monk then had thirty-five ships well in hand; but the rear had opened and was straggling, as is apt to be the case with long columns. With the thirty-five he then put his helm up and ran down for Tromp, whose squadron cut their cables and made sail on the same tack; the two engaged lines thus standing over toward the French coast, and the breeze heeling the ships so that the English could not use their lower-deck guns. The Dutch centre and rear also cut, and followed the movement, but being so far to leeward, could not for some time come into action. It was during this time that a large Dutch ship, becoming separated from her own fleet, was set on fire and burned, doubtless the ship in which was Count de Guiche.

As they drew near Dunkirk the English went about, probably all together; for in the return to the northward and westward the proper English van fell in with and was roughly handled by the Dutch centre under Ruyter himself. This fate would be more likely to befall the rear, and indicates that a simultaneous movement had reversed the order. The engaged ships had naturally lost to leeward, thus enabling Ruyter to fetch up with them. Two English flag-

常顺序指挥着后卫舰队的特龙普一部，则位于左翼。由于某种原因，这支左翼舰队大部分都处于上风向，鲁伊特所率的中央舰队则处于下风向，而右翼或者说前锋舰队又处在中央舰队的下风向。这就是荷兰舰队在1666年6月11日白天的阵势；尽管没有明确说出来，但从史料记载的大意来看，当时荷兰舰队的秩序可能保持得并不好。

这天上午，同样处于泊锚状态的蒙克，看出了荷兰舰队处于下风向；尽管兵力数量远不如敌军，但他还是决定立即发起攻击，希望通过保持风向优势，自己能够尽力一搏，取得迄今为止的最佳战绩。因此，他沿着荷兰舰队阵线，右舷抢风摆阵，将右翼和中央舰队置于大炮射程之外，直至他横过来与左翼的特龙普舰队并排。当时，蒙克能够完全掌控的战舰有35艘；不过，其后翼却已散开，掉了队——纵列过长时，是经常会出现这种情况的。接下来，他便率领这35艘战舰，迎风满舵，朝特龙普舰队冲去——此时，特龙普的舰队已经砍断缆绳，沿同一方向张帆起航了；这样一来，交战的这两支舰队便都是朝着法国海岸，而海风则是侧着刮，使得英国人无法使用下层甲板上的火炮。荷兰人的后翼也脱离了中央舰队，虽说也随之进行了机动，但因处于下风位置如此遥远的地方，一时半会儿根本就无法投入战斗。就是在这段时间里，一艘大型的荷兰军舰因为脱离了自己所属的舰队而被敌军点着了火，烧了起来；这艘战舰，无疑就是基申伯爵服役的那条船。

随着向敦克尔克靠近，英国舰队散了开来，很可能全都散开了；因为在向北和向西返回的途中，英军原本的前锋舰队遇上了鲁伊特亲自指挥的荷兰中央舰队，并遭到了后者的痛击。这种噩运，本来是更有可能由后翼来承受的；它还表明，同时机动让整个舰队的摆阵顺序调转过来了；因此，参战舰船自然被落在了下风位置，从而使得鲁伊特能

ships were here disabled and cut off; one, the "Swiftsure," hauled down her colors after the admiral, a young man of only twenty-seven, was killed. "Highly to be admired," says a contemporary writer, "was the resolution of Vice-Admiral Berkeley, who, though cut off from the line, surrounded by enemies, great numbers of his men killed, his ship disabled and boarded on all sides, yet continued fighting almost alone, killed several with his own hand, and would accept no quarter; till at length, being shot in the throat with a musket-ball, he retired into the captain's cabin, where he was found dead, extended at his full length upon a table, and almost covered with his own blood." Quite as heroic, but more fortunate in its issue, was the conduct of the other English admiral thus cut off; and the incidents of his struggle, though not specially instructive otherwise, are worth quoting, as giving a lively picture of the scenes which passed in the heat of the contests of those days, and afford coloring to otherwise dry details.

"Being in a short time completely disabled, one of the enemy's fire-ships grappled him on the starboard quarter; he was, however, freed by the almost incredible exertions of his lieutenant, who, having in the midst of the flames loosed the grappling-irons, swung back on board his own ship unhurt. The Dutch, bent on the destruction of this unfortunate ship, sent a second which grappled her on the larboard side, and with greater success than the former; for the sails instantly taking fire, the crew were so terrified that nearly fifty of them jumped overboard. The admiral, Sir John Harman, seeing this confusion, ran with his sword drawn among those who remained, and threatened with instant death the first man who should attempt to quit the ship, or should not exert himself to quench the flames. The crew then returned to their duty and got the fire under; but the rigging being a good deal burned, one of the topsail yards fell and broke Sir John's leg. In the midst of this accumulated distress, a third fire-ship

够追上它们。两艘英军旗舰在此失去了作战能力，遭到了重创；另一艘叫"敏捷"号的军舰，则在其年仅27岁的舰长牺牲之后，降下旗帜投降了。"值得高度赞赏的，"一位当代史学家曾如此说道，"是海军中将伯克利的殊死决心；尽管他脱离了舰队纵列，为敌舰所包围，无数手下都已牺牲，他的舰船动弹不得，敌人也从两侧纷纷登船，可他却继续孤身奋战，亲手杀死了数名敌人，并且拒绝投降；直到最后，他的咽喉被一颗子弹击中，他才退回船长室——后来，人们发现他死在船长室里，躺在一张桌子上，全身上下都被自己的鲜血染红了。"尽管这样做极具英雄气概，但结局更为幸运的，却是同样被拦截的另一位英军舰长；这位舰长的作战经历，虽说没有什么特别的启发意义，却值得我们引述，来生动地描述当时的场景——这些场景，在那个时代的激烈战斗中很快就被人们忘记了——也能给枯燥无味的战斗叙述过程，增添一丝丝情调。

"由于很快就完全失去了作战能力，所以敌军的一艘火攻船用锚钩住了它的右舷后部；然而，在该船副将那几乎令人难以置信的努力下，它竟然摆脱了——这位副将在火海中解开了敌舰的多爪锚，然后又毫发无损地回到了自己的船上。荷兰人一心想要置这艘运气不好的军舰于死地，便再次掷锚，钩住了它的左舷，并且比上一次钩得要牢固得多；船帆马上就着火了，船上的官兵都惊恐万分，其中差不多有50人跳下了海。舰长约翰·哈曼勋爵看到了这种混乱情况，便拔出剑来，跑到留在船上的人中间，威胁说谁敢带头弃船，谁敢不尽力灭火，便立即处死。这样一来，船员们便纷纷回到自己的岗位上，控制住了火势；但是，由于船上的缆索已经烧了好久，所以一根上桅横桁掉了下来，把约翰勋爵的一条腿砸断了。在危险变得越来越严重的过程中，敌军的第三艘火攻

prepared to grapple him, but was sunk by the guns before she could effect her purpose. The Dutch vice-admiral, Evertzen, now bore down to him and offered quarter; but Sir John replied, 'No, no, it is not come to that yet,' and giving him a broadside, killed the Dutch commander; after which the other enemies sheered off."

It is therefore not surprising that the account we have been following reported two English flag-ships lost, one by a fire-ship. "The English chief still continued on the port tack, and," says the writer, "as night fell we could see him proudly leading his line past the squadron of North Holland and Zealand [the actual rear, but proper van], which from noon up to that time had not been able to reach the enemy from their leewardly position." The merit of Monk's attack as a piece of grand tactics is evident, and bears a strong resemblance to that of Nelson at the Nile. Discerning quickly the weakness of the Dutch order, he had attacked a vastly superior force in such a way that only part of it could come into action; and though the English actually lost more heavily, they carried off a brilliant prestige and must have left considerable depression and heart-burning among the Dutch. The eye-witness goes on: "The affair continued until ten P.M., friends and foes mixed together and as likely to receive injury from one as from the other. It will be remarked that the success of the day and the misfortunes of the English came from their being too much scattered, too extended in their line; but for which we could never have cut off a corner of them, as we did. The mistake of Monk was in not keeping his ships better together;" that is, closed up. The remark is just, the criticism scarcely so; the opening out of the line was almost unavoidable in so long a column of sailing-ships, and was one of the chances taken by Monk when he offered battle.

The English stood off on the port tack to the west or west-northwest, and next day returned to the fight. The Dutch were now on the port tack in natural order, the right leading, and were

船又准备钩住这艘船，不过还没等它钩住，就被炮火击沉了。此时，荷兰的海军中将埃弗顿率军逼近，提出让该船投降；可约翰勋爵回答道：'不，不，还没有到那一步，'然后就舷炮齐射，结果了这位荷兰指挥官，于是别的敌舰便纷纷转向逃走了。"

因此，我们一直关注的这种记述称，英国损失了两艘旗舰，其中有一艘是被火攻船烧毁的，这一说法就是合情合理的了。"英军的主舰继续左舷抢风航行，并且，"这位作者又说，"随着夜幕降临，我们看到，它自豪地带领着纵列舰队驶过了北荷兰和西兰两支小型舰队（实际上是后卫舰队，而原本应是前锋），这两支小型舰队由于都处在下风位置，所以从当天中午直到此时，一直都未能赶上敌人。"作为一种大战术，蒙克冒险进攻的意义是很明显的，并且与纳尔逊在尼罗河河口之战中采取的战术极为相似。他敏锐地捕捉到了荷兰战阵的弱点，然后如此这般地对一支兵力大大优于己方的敌军发起攻击，使得敌军中只有一部分能够参与作战；尽管英军的实际损失比敌方更为严重，但他们却获得了辉煌的声誉，从而必定在荷兰人心中留下了沉重的沮丧和怨恨之情。这位目击者继续描述道："战事持续到了晚上10点钟，此时双方混战在一起，敌我难分，既有可能受到敌方的攻击，也有可能受到己方的攻击。有人会说，我方白天的胜利和英军的不幸，源于英国舰队过于分散，阵线拉得过长；倘若不是这样的话，我们绝不可能像此战中已经做到的那样，抄近路赶上它们。蒙克的失误，在于没有让所率舰船更好地抱成一团，"也就是说，让它们靠得更拢。这种说法是很公正的，但对蒙克的批评却是不公正的；如此之长的一列帆船，纵列中间出现缺口是在所难免的，而这也是蒙克主动出击时抓住的机会之一。

英军左舷抢风，迎着西风或西北风在岸边泊锚，第二天又返回继续战斗。此时，荷

to windward; but the enemy, being more weatherly and better disciplined, soon gained the advantage of the wind. The English this day had forty-four ships in action, the Dutch about eighty; many of the English, as before said, larger. The two fleets passed on opposite tacks, the English to windward; but Tromp, in the rear, seeing that the Dutch order of battle was badly formed, the ships in two or three lines, overlapping and so masking each other's fire, went about and gained to windward of the enemy's van; which he was able to do from the length of the line, and because the English, running parallel to the Dutch order, were off the wind. "At this moment two flag-officers of the Dutch van kept broad off, presenting their sterns to the English. Ruyter, greatly astonished, tried to stop them, but in vain, and therefore felt obliged to imitate the manoeuvre in order to keep his squadron together; but he did so with some order, keeping some ships around him, and was joined by one of the van ships, disgusted with the conduct of his immediate superior. Tromp was now in great danger, separated [by his own act first and then by the conduct of the van] from his own fleet by the English, and would have been destroyed but for Ruyter, who, seeing the urgency of the case, hauled up for him," the van and centre thus standing back for the rear on the opposite tack to that on which they entered action. This prevented the English from keeping up the attack on Tromp, lest Ruyter should gain the wind of them, which they could not afford to yield because of their very inferior numbers. Both the action of Tromp and that of the junior flag-officers in the van, though showing very different degrees of warlike ardor, bring out strongly the lack of subordination and of military feeling which has been charged against the Dutch officers as a body; no signs of which appear among the English at this time.

How keenly Ruyter felt the conduct of his lieutenants was manifested when "Tromp, immediately after this partial action, went on board his flagship. The seamen cheered him; but

兰舰队已经排成正常序列左舷抢风、右翼领头，并且占了上风；而敌军则由于抢风航行能力较强、纪律也较严明，所以很快便夺得了风向上的优势。此日，英军投入了44艘舰船作战，荷兰则投入了大约80艘；正如前面已经说过的那样，许多英国舰船的船体都比较大。两支舰队相互对舷驶过，英军向风；但位于后翼的特龙普看到荷兰舰队的战阵摆得不成样子，其中的舰船排成了两、三列，互有重叠，从而挡住了彼此的火力，便指挥后翼舰队散开来，夺得了敌军前锋的上风；他之所以能够这样做，是因为舰队纵列拉得很长，还因为与荷兰舰阵平行的英军舰队是顺风航行。"就在此时，荷兰前锋舰队的两位海军将领拉开了彼此之间的距离，将自己的后卫暴露在英军面前。鲁伊特大吃一惊，试图阻止他们，却徒劳无用，所以觉得必须进行与之相同的机动，才能让他所率的舰队靠拢；不过，他在机动时保持了一定的秩序，让一些船只围在自己四周，之后，前锋舰队中便有一艘厌恶其顶头上司做法的军舰，加入了鲁伊特所率舰队。这样一来，特龙普便陷入了极大的危险之中，被英国人将他与他所率的舰队隔开来了（当然，首先是被他自己的行动，然后才是被前锋舰队的做法隔离开来的）；要不是鲁伊特看到形势紧急，迎风驶来支援，他就会被英军消灭了，"这样一来，前锋和中央舰队为了支援后翼而抢风回撤，加入了战斗。这让英军没法继续进攻特龙普了，否则就会被鲁伊特抢占上风；他们因为兵力大大不如对方，所以不能放弃上风。特龙普和先头部队中那几位下级将领的行为，虽说都表现出了不同程度的战斗精神，但都显示出荷兰的所有将领整体上缺乏服从命令的精神和军人的职业素质；而当时的英军，却并未出现此种迹象。

鲁伊特极其敏锐地感受到了其副将们的行为所暴露出来的问题，当"特龙普在这次

Ruyter said, 'This is no time for rejoicing, but rather for tears.' Indeed, our position was bad, each squadron acting differently, in no line, and all the ships huddled together like a flock of sheep, so packed that the English might have surrounded all of them with their forty ships. The English were in admirable order, but did not push their advantage as they should, whatever the reason." The reason no doubt was the same that often prevented sailing-ships from pressing an advantage, — disability from crippled spars and rigging, added to the inexpediency of such inferior numbers risking a decisive action.

Ruyter was thus able to draw his fleet out into line again, although much maltreated by the English, and the two fleets passed again on opposite tacks, the Dutch to leeward, and Ruyter's ship the last in his column. As he passed the English rear, he lost his maintopmast and mainyard. After another partial encounter the English drew away to the northwest toward their own shores, the Dutch following them; the wind being still from southwest, but light. The English were now fairly in retreat, and the pursuit continued all night, Ruyter's own ship dropping out of sight in the rear from her crippled state.

The third day Monk continued retreating to the westward. He burned, by the English accounts, three disabled ships, sent ahead those that were most crippled, and himself brought up the rear with those that were in fighting condition, which are variously stated, again by the English, at twenty-eight and sixteen in number. One of the largest and finest of the English fleet, the "Royal Prince," of ninety guns, ran aground on the Galloper Shoal and was taken by Tromp; but Monk's retreat was so steady and orderly that he was otherwise unmolested. This shows that the Dutch had suffered very severely. Toward evening Rupert's squadron was seen; and all the ships of the English fleet, except those crippled in action, were at last united.

局部行动之后，随即登上了他的旗舰。水兵们都向特龙普欢呼；可鲁伊特却说：'现在可不是庆功的时候，而应当是悲痛的时候。'事实上，我们这一方的形势很不利，每支分舰队都是自行作战，毫无阵法可言，所有舰船都像羊群一样挤成一团，密得英军用40艘军舰就可以将他们完全包围起来。英军的秩序虽然极为井然，但不知何故，却没有充分利用这一优势。"至于其中的原因，无疑与经常阻碍帆船利用某种优势的原因是相同的——因为桅桁和索具受损而动弹不得，再说英军兵力太少，也不适于冒着风险果断行动。

这样一来，尽管不断受到英军的猛击，鲁伊特还是让其舰队重整了队形、排成了阵势；敌我两支舰队便再一次相向对舷而行，荷军处于下风位置，纵列末端便是鲁伊特的座舰。在经过英国舰队后翼的时候，他的座舰损失了主桅和主帆。一场局部交战过后，英军向西北方向的英国海岸避去，荷军则尾随追击；风向虽说仍是西南风，但风力却变小了。英军此时简直就是在撤退，而荷兰海军则追击了一整夜；鲁伊特的座舰因为受损严重而远远地落到了舰队后面，看都看不到了。

第三天，蒙克继续向西撤退。据英国史料记载，他焚毁了3艘失去了作战能力的舰船，提前遣走了那些受损极为严重的军舰，自己则率领那些虽说状况不同、却仍能作战的舰船断后；又据英国史料称，前者为28艘，后者为16艘。装备了90门火炮、属于英国舰队中船体最大、装备最精良军舰之一的"皇家王子"号，在戈勒普滩搁了浅，被特龙普俘虏了；但蒙克的撤退组织得相当稳当、相当有序，所以在其他方面并没有出现什么麻烦。这表明，荷兰军队的实力已经受损严重。傍晚时分，鲁珀特王子的舰队出现了；除了那些在战斗中受损的，英军舰队的所有舰船终于集结起来了。

The next day the wind came out again very fresh from the southwest, giving the Dutch the weather-gage. The English, instead of attempting to pass upon opposite tacks, came up from astern relying upon the speed and handiness of their ships. So doing, the battle engaged all along the line on the port tack, the English to leeward. The Dutch fire-ships were badly handled and did no harm, whereas the English burned two of their enemies. The two fleets ran on thus, exchanging broadsides for two hours, at the end of which time the bulk of the English fleet had passed through the Dutch line. [3] All regularity of order was henceforward lost. "At this moment," says the eye-witness, "the lookout was extraordinary, for all were separated, the English as well as we. But luck would have it that the largest of our fractions surrounding the admiral remained to windward, and the largest fraction of the English, also with their admiral, remained to leeward. This was the cause of our victory and their ruin. Our admiral had with him thirty-five or forty ships of his own and of other squadrons, for the squadrons were scattered and order much lost. The rest of the Dutch ships had left him. The leader of the van, Van Ness, had gone off with fourteen ships in chase of three or four English ships, which under a press of sail had gained to windward of the Dutch van. Van Tromp with the rear squadron had fallen to leeward, and so had to keep on [to leeward of Ruyter and the English main body] after Van Ness, in order to rejoin the admiral by passing round the English centre." De Ruyter and the English main body kept up a sharp action, beating to windward all the time. Tromp, having carried sail, overtook Van Ness, and returned bringing the van back with him; but owing to the constant plying to windward of the English main body he came up to leeward of it and could not rejoin Ruyter, who was to windward. Ruyter, seeing this, made signal to the ships around him, and the main body of the Dutch kept away before the wind, which was then very strong. "Thus in less than no time we found ourselves in the midst of the English; who, being attacked on both

接下来的第二天，海上又刮起了强劲的西南风，使得荷兰人占领了上风位置。英军此次并没有试图与敌军相向对舷航行，而是凭借其军舰的速度和灵巧，倒着驶向敌军。这样一来，参战船只全都是左舷抢风的那一纵列，英军则处于逆风位置。荷军火攻船的指挥非常糟糕，丝毫没有损伤英舰，而英军却烧毁了两艘敌舰。两支舰队就这样继续交火，轮流用舷炮猛攻对方，鏖战了两个小时，最后，英军舰队的大部分军舰都穿过了荷军的阵线。[3] 此后，双方队形便都如一盘散沙了。"此时，"那位目击者说，"整个战场的景象令人称奇，因为无论是英军一方还是我方，所有军舰都是单独作战。但幸运的是，我方围在海军司令四周的那最大一部分舰船仍然是顺风，而同样追随其司令的英军最大一部分舰队则仍然处于逆风位置。这就是我方获胜而英军惨败的原因。我方海军司令率领着自己手下以及其他分舰队的35或40艘军舰，因为这些分舰队当时都七零八落，毫无队形可言。其余的荷兰舰船，则都不在他身边。前锋舰队的指挥官是范·内斯，他领着14艘舰船追击3或4艘英国军舰去了，这几艘英国军舰在满帆状态下，夺得了荷兰前锋舰队的上风位置。范·特龙普所率后翼分队则落入了下风，所以不得不一直跟在范·内斯后面（处于鲁伊特与英军主力的下风向），以便绕过英军的中央主力，重新与海军司令汇合。"德·鲁伊特与英军主力舰队进行了激烈的交锋，并且始终都是顺风攻击。特龙普率舰张起船帆，反超了范·内斯，然后再率领前锋舰队折回来；但由于之前一直都在折向英军主力的上风面，此时他已处于英军主力的下风向，所以无法再与处于上风向的鲁伊特汇合了。鲁伊特见此情景，便向周围的舰船发出信号，荷兰主力舰队便趁着当时风大，转成了顺风。"这样，一眨眼的工夫，我们就陷入了英军的包围之

sides, were thrown into confusion and saw their whole order destroyed, as well by dint of the action, as by the strong wind that was then blowing. This was the hottest of the fight. We saw the high admiral of England separated from his fleet, followed only by one fire-ship. With that he gained to windward, and passing through the North Holland squadron, placed himself again at the head of fifteen or twenty ships that rallied to him."

Thus ended this great sea-fight, the most remarkable, in some of its aspects, that has ever been fought upon the ocean. Amid conflicting reports it is not possible to do more than estimate the results. A fairly impartial account says: "The States lost in these actions three vice-admirals, two thousand men, and four ships. The loss of the English was five thousand killed and three thousand prisoners; and they lost besides seventeen ships, of which nine remained in the hands of the victors." There is no doubt that the English had much the worst of it, and that this was owing wholly to the original blunder of weakening the fleet by a great detachment sent in another direction. Great detachments are sometimes necessary evils, but in this case no necessity existed. Granting the approach of the French, the proper course for the English was to fall with their whole fleet upon the Dutch before their allies could come up. This lesson is as applicable to-day as it ever was. A second lesson, likewise of present application, is the necessity of sound military institutions for implanting correct military feeling, pride, and discipline. Great as was the first blunder of the English, and serious as was the disaster, there can be no doubt that the consequences would have been much worse but for the high spirit and skill with which the plans of Monk were carried out by his subordinates, and the lack of similar support to Ruyter on the part of the Dutch subalterns. In the movements of the English, we hear nothing of two juniors turning tail at a critical moment, nor of a third, with misdirected ardor, getting on the wrong side of the enemy's fleet. Their drill also, their tactical precision,

中；由于受到两面夹击，英军惊慌失措，眼睁睁地看着他们的整个阵形被战斗、被当时刮得正猛的大风打得七零八落。这是战斗最为激烈的时刻。我们看到，英军主帅的座舰落了单，脱离了他所率的舰队，只有一艘火攻船跟着。接着，他抢占了上风位置，穿过了北荷兰舰队，再次回到了向他集结过来的那15或20艘舰船的前头。"

这场伟大的海战就此结束了；从此战的某些方面来看，它也是有史以来在海上进行的最非凡的一场战斗。由于各种记载相互冲突，所以我们只能大致估计一下此战的结果。有一份相当公正的记载，称："此战中，荷兰共和国折损了3名海军中将、2000名水兵和4艘战舰。英军的损失是，5000名水兵丧生、3000人被俘；此外，他们还损失了17艘军舰，其中有9艘是被胜利的荷兰一方俘虏了。"毫无疑问，英军的损失最为惨重；而出现这种惨败，无疑完全是由于最初的失误，不该将大量舰船派往另一个方向，以致削弱了整支舰队的力量。在有的时候，虽说是祸，也不得不派遣大型分队；但在此战中，却并不是非得如此。就算法国海军会前来支援，英国海军的正确做法，也应当是趁其盟军未到，而集中整支舰队的力量，给荷军以重击。这个教训，对于如今来说，跟过去一样适用。第二个教训，同样也适用于现在；这就是，必须建立起各种健全的军事制度，来向官兵灌输正确的军人情感、职业自豪感和纪律。英国人最初犯下的错误如此巨大，遭受的损失如此惨重，倘若不是蒙克的下属们斗志昂扬、技巧娴熟地执行他所制定的计划，倘若不是荷兰军队中鲁伊特的手下没有同样地支持他的话，那么，对于英军来说，后果无疑会严重得多。在英军进行机动的过程中，我们没有听说过有两位下属在关键时刻掉头逃跑的事情，也没听说过还有下属按捺不住、鲁莽地跑到敌方舰队另一侧

was remarked even then. The Frenchman De Guiche, after witnessing this Four Days' Fight, wrote: —

"Nothing equals the beautiful order of the English at sea. Never was a line drawn straighter than that formed by their ships; thus they bring all their fire to bear upon those who draw near them.... They fight like a line of cavalry which is handled according to rule, and applies itself solely to force back those who oppose; whereas the Dutch advance like cavalry whose squadrons leave their ranks and come separately to the charge."

The Dutch government, averse to expense, unmilitary in its tone, and incautious from long and easy victory over the degenerate navy of Spain, had allowed its fleet to sink into a mere assembly of armed merchantmen. Things were at their worst in the days of Cromwell. Taught by the severe lessons of that war, the United Provinces, under an able ruler, had done much to mend matters, but full efficiency had not yet been gained.

"In 1666 as in 1653," says a French naval writer, "the fortune of war seemed to lean to the side of the English. Of the three great battles fought two were decided victories; and the third, though adverse, had but increased the glory of her seamen. This was due to the intelligent boldness of Monk and Rupert, the talents of part of the admirals and captains, and the skill of the seamen and soldiers under them. The wise and vigorous efforts made by the government of the United Provinces, and the undeniable superiority of Ruyter in experience and genius over any one of his opponents, could not compensate for the weakness or incapacity of part of the Dutch officers, and the manifest inferiority of the men under their orders."

England, as has been said before, still felt the impress of Cromwell's iron hand upon her military institutions; but that impress was growing weaker. Before the next Dutch war Monk was dead, and was poorly replaced by the cavalier Rupert. Court extravagance cut down the

这样的事情。他们的训练有素、他们的精密战术，在那时就已引起世人的注意了。法国的基申伯爵在目睹了这次"四日海战"之后，如此写道：

"英军在海战中的阵法之美，简直无与伦比。从来没有哪个纵队，有英国舰船所组成的纵列那样笔直；所以，他们能将所有的火炮都对准那些靠近的敌舰……他们就像是一列完全按照规则行动的铁骑，唯一的目标便是击退那些来犯之敌；而荷兰舰队在进军时，却像是一队争先恐后地离开队伍、并且各自单打独斗的散兵游勇。"

荷兰政府反对军费支出，没有尚武风气，并且长久以来因西班牙海军的衰落而轻易获得了多次胜利，所以任由该国的舰队堕落成为了一支仅仅是由武装商人所组成的乌合之众。在克伦威尔执政时期，该国海军形势达到了最严峻的地步。汲取了此次海战的教训之后，荷兰共和国虽说在一位明君的治下实施了许多改善之举，但还是没有取得全面的效果。

"在1666年，就像在1653年一样，"一位法国海军作家说，"战争的好运似乎一直都偏向于英国这一方。在两国所进行的三次大型海战中，英国获得了两次决定性的胜利；而第三次虽说是荷兰战胜，但结果也只是增加了英国海军的荣耀。这应归功于蒙克和鲁珀特的胆大心细、部分将领和舰长的才能以及他们手下海员和官兵的本领。荷兰共和国政府明智而坚定的努力，以及鲁伊特在经验和才能上都不可否认地拥有胜过所有敌手的优势，都无法弥补荷兰海军中部分将领的软弱或无能，也无法弥补他们的手下明显技不如人的劣势。"

正如之前所述，英国此时仍然留有克伦威尔铁腕治军、制度严明的痕迹；不过，这种影响正在日益弱化下去。第二次英荷战争爆发前，蒙克去世了，由皇室出身的鲁珀特

equipment of the navy as did the burgomaster's parsimony, and court corruption undermined discipline as surely as commercial indifference. The effect was evident when the fleets of the two countries met again, six years later.

There was one well-known feature of all the military navies of that day which calls for a passing comment; for its correct bearing and value is not always, perhaps not generally, seen. The command of fleets and of single vessels was often given to soldiers, to military men unaccustomed to the sea, and ignorant how to handle the ship, that duty being intrusted to another class of officer. Looking closely into the facts, it is seen that this made a clean division between the direction of the fighting and of the motive power of the ship. This is the essence of the matter; and the principle is the same whatever the motive power may be. The inconvenience and inefficiency of such a system was obvious then as it is now, and the logic of facts gradually threw the two functions into the hands of one corps of officers, the result being the modern naval officer, as that term is generally understood. [4] Unfortunately, in this process of blending, the less important function was allowed to get the upper hand; the naval officer came to feel more proud of his dexterity in managing the motive power of his ship than of his skill in developing her military efficiency. The bad effects of this lack of interest in military science became most evident when the point of handling fleets was reached, because for that military skill told most, and previous study was most necessary; but it was felt in the single ship as well. Hence it came to pass, and especially in the English navy, that the pride of the seaman took the place of the pride of the military man. The English naval officer thought more of that which likened him to the merchant captain than of that which made him akin to the soldier. In the French navy this result was less general, owing probably to the more military spirit of the government, and especially of the nobility, to whom the rank of officer was reserved. It was not possible that

很不恰当地代替了他的职位。宫廷的奢侈浪费，跟荷兰人的节俭一样，使得海军装备被削减了，而宫廷的腐败也像商人的漠不关心一样，使得海军丧失了纪律。6年之后，当两国舰队再度仇人相见的时候，这种影响就变得很明显了。

当时，各国海军都有一个众所周知的特点，需要顺带说一说，因为人们一向或者说通常都看不到这种特点的意义和价值。各支舰队和各艘军舰，通常都是交由陆军官兵、交由不熟悉海洋的军人来指挥，他们对如何操纵船只一无所知，所以驾驶舰船的职责，又是由另一类军官来负责。仔细分析这些事实便可看出，这种做法使得作战指令与舰船机动指令之间明显地割裂开来了。这才是问题的实质；无论舰船以何种动力驱动，其基本原理都是一样的。此种制度既不方便又无效率，这在当时和如今都是显而易见的，所以这些事实的逻辑性便逐渐将这两种职能集中到了一类官兵身上，结果便成了人们通常都理解的现代"海军将领"。[4]可惜的是，在这种融合的过程中，人们却让一些重要性较低的职能占据了优势；于是，海军将领便开始对自己能够灵巧驾驭舰船的能力更感自豪，而不是以自己能够提升舰船的军事效率为傲了。这种对兵法不感兴趣的恶果，在上升到操纵舰队的高度——因为军事技巧在这方面的内容最多，而过去也最需要对这方面进行研究——之后，便变得极为明显了；不过，在单艘舰船的操纵上也是看得到此种恶果的。所以，尤其是在英国海军中，就出现了海员比军人更加自豪的现象。英国的海军将领考虑得更多的，是那种让他们更像是商船船长的方面，而不是那些让他们更像一个军人的方面。在法国海军中，这种恶果没有那么普遍，很可能是因为法国政府，尤其是专门担任军官职务的贵族阶层，更具尚武精神所致。那些交往的全都是军人、所有朋

men whose whole association was military, all of whose friends looked upon arms as the one career for a gentleman, could think more of the sails and rigging than of the guns or the fleet. The English corps of officers was of different origin. There was more than the writer thought in Macaulay's well-known saying: "There were seamen and there were gentlemen in the navy of Charles II.; but the seamen were not gentlemen, and the gentlemen were not seamen." The trouble was not in the absence or presence of gentlemen as such, but in the fact that under the conditions of that day the gentleman was pre-eminently the military element of society; and that the seaman, after the Dutch wars, gradually edged the gentleman, and with him the military tone and spirit as distinguished from simple courage, out of the service. Even "such men of family as Herbert and Russell, William III.'s admirals," says the biographer of Lord Hawke, "were sailors indeed, but only able to hold their own by adopting the boisterous manners of the hardy tarpaulin." The same national traits which made the French inferior as seamen made them superior as military men; not in courage, but in skill. To this day the same tendency obtains; the direction of the motive power has no such consideration as the military functions in the navies of the Latin nations. The studious and systematic side of the French character also inclined the French officer, when not a trifler, to consider and develop tactical questions in a logical manner; to prepare himself to handle fleets, not merely as a seaman but as a military man. The result showed, in the American Revolutionary War, that despite a mournful history of governmental neglect, men who were first of all military men, inferior though they were in opportunities as seamen to their enemies, could meet them on more than equal terms as to tactical skill, and were practically their superiors in handling fleets. The false theory has already been pointed out, which directed the action of the French fleet not to crushing its enemy, but to some ulterior aim; but this does not affect the fact that in tactical skill the military men were superior to the mere

友都把军职视为绅士唯一之终生职业的人，对于船帆、索具的考虑，是不可能超过他们对于枪炮或者舰队的关注的。而英国的军官阶层，出身却并不一样。情况比麦考利[9]在他的一句名言中所说的更加复杂："查理二世治下之海军中，既有水兵也有绅士；但水兵并非绅士，绅士亦非水兵。"问题并非是海军中有还是没有这样的绅士，而是在当时的环境下，绅士是整个社会中杰出的军事中坚这一事实；英荷战争之后，普通水兵便带着那种不同于淳朴勇猛的军人风气和精神，逐渐开始将绅士挤出了军队。甚至是"威廉三世时的海军司令赫伯特和拉塞尔这样的名门子弟，"霍克勋爵的传记作者说，"实际上也都出身于普通水兵，而他们也只有采取吃苦耐劳的水兵那种粗暴的方式，才能坚持下去。"让法国人作为水兵低人一等的这种相同的民族性格，却让英国水兵变成了优秀的军人；不是在英勇方面，而是在本领方面。直到今天，仍然存在着这种相同的趋势；在拉丁国家的海军中，人们对于舰船机动能力的指挥并不如对其作战能力那么关注。法国人性格中勤奋好学和有条有理的一面，往往也使得法国的将领，去用合乎逻辑的方式思考和阐述战术上的一些问题，以便让自己做好准备，让自己并非仅仅像一个普通水兵，而是像一个真正的军人那样来指挥舰队。美国革命战争的结果表明，尽管有一段被政府忽视的可叹历史，但起初便是军人的那些人，虽然机遇方面跟普通水兵一样，但在战术技能方面却要高他们一筹，并且实际上在指挥舰队时也比他们更优秀。前面我们已经指出了那种错误的理论，它使得法国舰队不是去粉碎敌军，而是去实现某种间接目标；但这并不会影响到军人在战术技能方面比普通水兵优秀的事实，只不过他们的战术技能，是被用于去实现错误的战略目标罢了。荷兰所募海军官兵的主要来源，并不是

seamen, though their tactical skill was applied to mistaken strategic ends. The source whence the Dutch mainly drew their officers does not certainly appear; for while the English naval historian in 1666 says that most of the captains of their fleet were sons of rich burgomasters, placed there for political reasons by the Grand Pensionary, and without experience, Duquesne, the ablest French admiral of the day, comments in 1676 on the precision and skill of the Dutch captains in terms very disparaging to his own. It is likely, from many indications, that they were generally merchant seamen, with little original military feeling; but the severity with which the delinquents were punished both by the State and by popular frenzy, seems to have driven these officers, who were far from lacking the highest personal courage, into a sense of what military loyalty and subordination required. They made a very different record in 1672 from that of 1666.

Before finally leaving the Four Days' Fight, the conclusions of another writer may well be quoted: —

"Such was that bloody Battle of the Four Days, or Straits of Calais, the most memorable sea-fight of modern days; not, indeed, by its results, but by the aspect of its different phases; by the fury of the combatants; by the boldness and skill of the leaders; and by the new character which it gave to sea warfare. More than any other this fight marks clearly the passage from former methods to the tactics of the end of the seventeenth century. For the first time we can follow, as though traced upon a plan, the principal movements of the contending fleets. It seems quite clear that to the Dutch as well as to the British have been given a tactical book and a code of signals; or, at the least, written instructions, extensive and precise, to serve instead of such a code. We feel that each admiral now has his squadron in hand, and that even the commander-in-chief disposes at his will, during the fight, of the various subdivisions of his fleet. Compare

必然存在的；因为，尽管一位英国海军历史学者在1666年称，荷兰舰队中的绝大部分舰长都是富裕的市镇官员之子，让他们服役是出于共和执政时期的种种政治原因，所以他们都毫无经验可言，但当时法国最卓越的海军司令杜肯在1676年评价荷兰舰长们的严谨与能力时，却对他们大加赞扬，而很瞧不起法国的舰长。从多种迹象来看，原因可能是：这些舰长通常都是商船上的海员，并没有什么原始的尚武精神；但国家和民众的狂热使得他们对玩忽职守者的惩处极为严厉，似乎迫使这些并不缺乏最大之个人勇气的将领，使之具有了军人的忠诚与服从命令所必需的素质。他们在1672年的记录，已与1666年的情况大为不同了。

在最终结束讨论"四日海战"之前，我们不妨再来引述一下另一位史学家所下的结论：

"这场血腥的'四日海战'或者'加来海峡之战'就是这样，它是现代最令人难以忘怀的一场海战；事实上，它之所以值得纪念，并不是因为此战的结局，而是因为此战不同阶段的形势，是因为双方参战人员交火时的猛烈，是因为战争领袖们的胆识与本领，也是因为它给海战赋予了新的特征。跟其他任何一场海战相比，此战都更加清晰地标志着我们从以前的作战方式发展到17世纪末期的战术作战这一过程。我们第一次可以像在一张平面图上进行描绘那样，看清交战双方实施的主要运动。荷兰海军与英国海军似乎都获得了一本战术教材和一整套旗语；或者说，起码也各有一套全面而准确的书面指令，来取代这一套旗语。我们认为，每位海军将领如今都可以完全指挥其手下的小型分舰队；即便是海军总司令，在战斗中也可以任意指挥舰队中不同的下属部门了。将此战与1652年发生的那一场场战斗相比，一个浅显的事实就会明明白白地呈现在您的面

this action with those of 1652, and one plain fact stares you in the face, — that between the two dates naval tactics have undergone a revolution.

"Such were the changes that distinguish the war of 1665 from that of 1652. As in the latter epoch, the admiral still thinks the weather-gage an advantage for his fleet; but it is no longer, from the tactical point of view, the principal, we might almost say the sole, preoccupation. Now he wishes above all to keep his fleet in good order and compact as long as possible, so as to keep the power of combining, during the action, the movements of the different squadrons. Look at Ruyter, at the end of the Four Days' Fight; with great difficulty he has kept to windward of the English fleet, yet he does not hesitate to sacrifice this advantage in order to unite the two parts of his fleet, which are separated by the enemy. If at the later fight off the North Foreland great intervals exist between the Dutch squadrons, if the rear afterward continues to withdraw from the centre, Ruyter deplores such a fault as the chief cause of his defeat. He so deplores it in his official report; he even accuses Tromp [who was his personal enemy] of treason or cowardice, — an unjust accusation, but which none the less shows the enormous importance thenceforth attached, during action, to the reunion of the fleet into a whole strictly and regularly maintained."

This commentary is justified in so far as it points out general aims and tendencies; but the results were not as complete as might be inferred from it.

The English, notwithstanding their heavy loss in the Four Days' Battle, were at sea again within two months, much to the surprise of the Dutch; and on the 4th of August another severe fight was fought off the North Foreland, ending in the complete defeat of the latter, who retired to their own coasts. The English followed, and effected an entrance into one of the Dutch harbors, where they destroyed a large fleet of merchantmen as well as a town of some

前：在此期间，海军战术已经发生了一场革命。

这些，就是让1665年海战不同于1652年战争的一些变化。在1665年这个时代，海军将领仍然认为顺风是所率舰队的一大优势；但从战术角度来看，顺风不再是舰队的第一要务，我们也可以说，它不再是舰队唯一的大事了。如今，一位海军将领首先是希望尽可能长久地让舰队保持良好而紧凑的阵形，以便在战斗中能够协同不同分舰队的机动。看看鲁伊特，在'四日海战'的最后，他克服了巨大的困难才抢占了英军舰队的上风位置，可为了让己方舰队被敌军分隔开来的那两个部分汇合到一处，他便毫不犹豫地牺牲了这一优势。在后来的北福兰海战中，荷兰各支分舰队间存在巨大的缺口，而后翼也一直在拉大它与中央舰队的距离，因此鲁伊特才会痛惜犯下了此种失误，将这种失误归结为自己战败的主要原因。他在自己的正式报告中正是这样痛惜的，甚至还指控特龙普（他是鲁伊特的仇人）叛国或临阵脱逃——这种指控并不公正，但它仍然表明，从那以后，把散开的船只重新集结成一支阵形完整、整齐划一的舰队，在战斗中就具有极其重要的意义了。"

这一评论指出了海军的总体目标和趋向，从这个方面来说还是很中肯的；不过，从中得出的结论，却并不全面。

尽管在"四日海战"中受到重创，但两个月后，英国海军却又出现在海上，让荷兰人惊愕不已；于是，8月4日，两军在北福兰海域又进行了一场激烈的海战，最终使得荷兰海军惨败，并退回了该国沿海地区。英军尾随追击，并且攻进了荷兰的一处港口，摧毁了一支庞大的商船队和一个比较重要的城镇。到了1666年末，双方都不想再战，因为战争

importance. Toward the end of 1666 both sides were tired of the war, which was doing great harm to trade, and weakening both navies to the advantage of the growing sea power of France. Negotiations looking toward peace were opened; but Charles II., ill disposed to the United Provinces, confident that the growing pretensions of Louis XIV. to the Spanish Netherlands would break up the existing alliance between Holland and France, and relying also upon the severe reverses suffered at sea by the Dutch, was exacting and haughty in his demands. To justify and maintain this line of conduct he should have kept up his fleet, the prestige of which had been so advanced by its victories. Instead of that, poverty, the result of extravagance and of his home policy, led him to permit it to decline; ships in large numbers were laid up; and he readily adopted an opinion which chimed in with his penury, and which, as it has had advocates at all periods of sea history, should be noted and condemned here. This opinion, warmly opposed by Monk, was: —

"That as the Dutch were chiefly supported by trade, as the supply of their navy depended upon trade, and, as experience showed, nothing provoked the people so much as injuring their trade, his Majesty should therefore apply himself to this, which would effectually humble them, at the same time that it would less exhaust the English than fitting out such mighty fleets as had hitherto kept the sea every summer.... Upon these motives the king took a fatal resolution of laying up his great ships and keeping only a few frigates on the cruise."

In consequence of this economical theory of carrying on a war, the Grand Pensionary of Holland, De Witt, who had the year before caused soundings of the Thames to be made, sent into the river, under De Ruyter, a force of sixty or seventy ships-of-the-line, which on the 14th of June, 1667, went up as high as Gravesend, destroying ships at Chatham and in the Medway, and taking possession of Sheerness. The light of the fires could be seen from London, and

极大地损害了两国的贸易、削弱了两国海军的实力，会让法国的海上实力趁机日益强大起来。两国开始议和；可查理二世因为对荷兰共和国不怀好意，确信路易十四日益想要攫取西属尼德兰的野心会打破现存的荷、法同盟，还倚仗着荷兰在海上遭受了重重失败，因而目空一切地提出了苛刻的要求。为了支撑并维护这种做法，他本来应当保持好英国舰队因为获胜而大大得以提升了的威望才是；可他却没有这样做，因为国内政策和宫廷奢侈浪费所导致的贫困，使得查理二世任由海军衰落下去了；大量舰船退了役；并且，他还欣然采纳了一种与其吝啬相应的意见——这种意见，由于在海军历史上的各个时期都有人提倡，所以在此我们应当加以注意和声讨才行。这种观点，蒙克曾经强烈反对过，那就是：

"由于荷兰海军的军需补给全都倚赖于贸易，所以破坏其贸易最能激怒荷兰人，故国王陛下应当致力于此事；如此一来，既可有效地让荷兰人威风扫地，同时跟迄今为止每年夏季都必须装备如此强大之舰队的做法相比，也会降低英国实力的消耗……出于这些原因，英王做出了一项致命的决定，让大多数军舰退役，而只留下少量护卫舰进行巡逻。"

由于英国有着此种节俭战争的理论，所以前一年间曾力促测试了泰晤士河水深的荷兰省大议长德·威特，便派德·鲁伊特率领一支由60或70艘战列舰组成的舰队驶入了该河；1667年6月14日，这支舰队深入到了格雷夫森德，击毁了查塔姆和梅德威河中的船只，并且占领了希尔内斯港。从伦敦都可看到熊熊燃起的火光，而荷兰舰队直至月底都一直占领着泰晤士河河口。在这次紧跟着大瘟疫和伦敦大火[10]而来、雪上加霜式的打击之下，查理二世同意并于1667年7月31日与荷兰签订了和约，史称《布雷达和约》。

the Dutch fleet remained in possession of the mouth of the river until the end of the month. Under this blow, following as it did upon the great plague and the great fire of London, Charles consented to peace, which was signed July 31, 1667, and is known as the Peace of Breda. The most lasting result of the war was the transfer of New York and New Jersey to England, thus joining her northern and southern colonies in North America.

Before going on again with the general course of the history of the times, it will be well to consider for a moment the theory which worked so disastrously for England in 1667; that, namely, of maintaining a sea-war mainly by preying upon the enemy's commerce. This plan, which involves only the maintenance of a few swift cruisers and can be backed by the spirit of greed in a nation, fitting out privateers without direct expense to the State, possesses the specious attractions which economy always presents. The great injury done to the wealth and prosperity of the enemy is also undeniable; and although to some extent his merchant-ships can shelter themselves ignobly under a foreign flag while the war lasts, this guerre de course, as the French call it, this commerce-destroying, to use our own phrase, must, if in itself successful, greatly embarrass the foreign government and distress its people. Such a war, however, cannot stand alone; it must be supported, to use the military phrase; unsubstantial and evanescent in itself, it cannot reach far from its base. That base must be either home ports, or else some solid outpost of the national power, on the shore or the sea; a distant dependency or a powerful fleet. Failing such support, the cruiser can only dash out hurriedly a short distance from home, and its blows, though painful, cannot be fatal. It was not the policy of 1667, but Cromwell's powerful fleets of ships-of-the-line in 1652, that shut the Dutch merchantmen in their ports and caused the grass to grow in the streets of Amsterdam. When, instructed by the suffering of that time, the Dutch kept large fleets afloat through two exhausting wars, though their commerce

此次战争影响最为深远的结果，便是荷兰将纽约和新泽西割让给了英国，从而使得英国在北美洲南北两方的各个殖民地都连成了一片。

在沿着当时历史的总进程继续往下论述之前，我们不妨再来思考一下导致英国在1667年遭受如此惨败的那种理论；也就是说，维持海上战争主要是为了掠夺敌人商业贸易的理论。这种只是保持少量快速巡洋舰，认为民族的贪婪之心可以支撑并配备私掠船，而无需直接损耗国家财力的办法，有着节俭经常能够表现出来的种种虚假的吸引力。不可否认，这种方法也给敌国的财力和繁荣带来了巨大的损害；并且从某种程度上来说，尽管敌国的商船在战争期间可以不光彩地悬挂他国旗帜来进行自保，但法国人所称的这种"游击战"——用我们自己的话来说，就是这种破坏贸易的行为——就算本身很成功，也必定会让别国政府感到极其难堪，并且会让该国民众感到担忧的。然而，这样的战争是不能单独进行的，用军事术语来说，就是必须得到支援才行；由于本身很脆弱、很短暂，所以是不可能远离大本营去作战的。这种大本营要么必须是本国海港，要么就必须是本国势力所及的某处牢固的前沿基地，无论是在岸上还是在海上，无论是一个遥远的属国，还是一支强大的舰队。倘若没有这样的支援，巡洋舰只能匆匆离开母港一点点远的距离，并且其打击力度虽说令人伤脑筋，但不可能是致命性的。将荷兰商船封锁在港内，并让阿姆斯特丹的大街小巷长满杂草的，并不是1667年的这种政策，而是1652年克伦威尔那支强大的战列舰舰队。由于牢记着当时的遭遇，所以荷兰维持了大量的舰队，熬过了两次旷日持久的战争；尽管商业贸易损失巨大，但他们还是打起精神，承受住了英、法两国的联合攻击。40年后，路易十四因为无计可施，也不得不转向查理二世所采取过的那种政

suffered greatly, they bore up the burden of the strife against England and France united. Forty years later, Louis XIV. was driven, by exhaustion, to the policy adopted by Charles II. through parsimony. Then were the days of the great French privateers, Jean Bart, Forbin, Duguay-Trouin, Du Casse, and others. The regular fleets of the French navy were practically withdrawn from the ocean during the great War of the Spanish Succession (1702-1712). The French naval historian says: —

"Unable to renew the naval armaments, Louis XIV. increased the number of cruisers upon the more frequented seas, especially the Channel and the German Ocean [not far from home, it will be noticed]. In these different spots the cruisers were always in a position to intercept or hinder the movements of transports laden with troops, and of the numerous convoys carrying supplies of all kinds. In these seas, in the centre of the commercial and political world, there is always work for cruisers. Notwithstanding the difficulties they met, owing to the absence of large friendly fleets, they served advantageously the cause of the two peoples [French and Spanish]. These cruisers, in the face of the Anglo-Dutch power, needed good luck, boldness, and skill. These three conditions were not lacking to our seamen; but then, what chiefs and what captains they had!"

The English historian, on the other hand, while admitting how severely the people and commerce of England suffered from the cruisers, bitterly reflecting at times upon the administration, yet refers over and over again to the increasing prosperity of the whole country, and especially of its commercial part. In the preceding war, on the contrary, from 1689 to 1697, when France sent great fleets to sea and disputed the supremacy of the ocean, how different the result! The same English writer says of that time: —

"With respect to our trade it is certain that we suffered infinitely more, not merely than the French, for that was to be expected from the greater number of our merchant-ships, but than

策，通过节俭来进行应对。那时，正是让·巴尔、福尔班、迪盖–特鲁安、杜·卡斯以及其他著名法国私掠者横行的时代。法国海军中的常规舰队，在伟大的"西班牙王位继承战"（1702～1712年）中，差不多都从海上撤了回来。那位法国海军史学家曾称：

"由于无力更新海军的武器装备，路易十四便增加了交通比较繁忙的海域，尤其是英吉利海峡和日尔曼海（我们会注意到，这两处海域都离法国本土不远）上巡洋舰的数量。在这些地方，巡洋舰往往能够拦截或者阻挠运送兵力的舰船，以及无数运送各种补给装备的护卫舰。在属于世界贸易和政治中心地带的这些海域，巡洋舰总是有事可做的。尽管由于没有大型友舰伴随护卫，它们遇到过种种困难，但它们给（法国和西班牙）两国人民的事业都带来了好处。这些巡洋舰在面对英、荷这两个列强时，须有好的运气、胆大以及本领才行。我国的水兵并不缺少这三个条件；可在当时，他们的上司和舰长都是些什么人哪！"

而另一方面，英国的史学家尽管承认英国人民和英国贸易受到了这些巡洋舰的重创，还时不时苦涩地反思当时的行政情况，却一再提起国家整体上日益繁荣兴旺的情况，尤其是该国商业贸易日益繁荣起来的事实。相反，在上一次发生于1689年至1697年间的战争中，当法国派出大量舰队与英国争夺海洋霸权的时候，结果是多么的截然不同啊！这位英国史学家在谈到那个时代的时候，如此说道：

"至于我国的商业贸易，可以确定的是，我们的损失非但要比法国大得多——因为我国的商船数量也多得多，所以这一点可想而知——而且也要比我们在以前任何一次战

we ever did in any former war. ... This proceeded in great measure from the vigilance of the French, who carried on the war in a piratical way. It is out of all doubt that, taking all together, our traffic suffered excessively; our merchants were many of them ruined."

Macaulay says of this period: "During many months of 1693 the English trade with the Mediterranean had been interrupted almost entirely. There was no chance that a merchantman from London or Amsterdam would, if unprotected, reach the Pillars of Hercules without being boarded by a French privateer; and the protection of armed vessels was not easily obtained." Why? Because the vessels of England's navy were occupied watching the French navy, and this diversion of them from the cruisers and privateers constituted the support which a commerce-destroying war must have. A French historian, speaking of the same period in England (1696), says: "The state of the finances was deplorable; money was scarce, maritime insurance thirty per cent, the Navigation Act was virtually suspended, and the English shipping reduced to the necessity of sailing under the Swedish and Danish flags." Half a century later the French government was again reduced, by long neglect of the navy, to a cruising warfare. With what results? First, the French historian says: "From June, 1756, to June, 1760, French privateers captured from the English more than twenty-five hundred merchantmen. In 1761, though France had not, so to speak, a single ship-of-the-line at sea, and though the English had taken two hundred and forty of our privateers, their comrades still took eight hundred and twelve vessels. But," he goes on to say, "the prodigious growth of the English shipping explains the number of these prizes." In other words, the suffering involved to England in such numerous captures, which must have caused great individual injury and discontent, did not really prevent the growing prosperity of the State and of the community at large. The English naval historian, speaking of the same period, says: "While the commerce of France was nearly destroyed, the trading-fleet of England covered the seas. Every year her commerce was increasing; the money

争中遭受的损失大得多……这在很大程度上源于法国人的警惕性，他们是用海盗的方式来进行战争的。毫无疑问，总的来说，我国的贸易业受创极其严重，因为我国的许多商家都破产了。"

对于这一时期，麦考利是这样说的："在1693年的数月间，英国与地中海地区的贸易几乎完全中断了。一艘从伦敦或阿姆斯特丹出发的商船，要是不加保护，是不可能逃过法国私掠者的登船洗劫，安全抵达海格力斯之柱[11]的；而用军舰进行护卫，也没法轻易做到。"为什么呢？因为英国海军的舰船都正忙于监视法国海军，而分散它们对付巡洋舰和私掠船的力量，正是贸易破坏战所必需的支援。一位法国历史学家在谈到同一时期（1696年）的英国时，说："金融形势糟糕透顶；资金紧缺，海损保险只有30%，《航海法案》几近废止，而英国商船也堕落到了必须悬挂瑞典和丹麦国旗才能航行的地步。"半个世纪过后，由于长期忽视了海军，法国政府便再一次被迫用巡洋舰来进行战争。结局呢？首先，那位法国历史学家称："自1756年6月至1760年6月，法国私掠者从英国手中俘虏了超过2500艘商船。在1761年，尽管法国可以说没有一条战舰在海上，尽管英国俘虏了我国240艘私掠船，但其他私掠船还是俘获了812艘商船。不过，"他接着说，"英国商船运输业的巨大增长，解释了他们能俘获如此之多战利品的原因。"换句话说，虽说被俘船只数不胜数，并且这种形势必定导致巨大的个人损失，引发民众广泛的不满情绪，但英国所遭受的这些损失，并未真正阻碍到该国以及整个社会的日益繁荣。那位英国史学家在谈到同一时期的时候，说："当法国贸易几乎完蛋的时候，英国

which the war carried out was returned by the produce of her industry. Eight thousand merchant vessels were employed by the English merchants." And again, summing up the results of the war, after stating the immense amount of specie brought into the kingdom by foreign conquests, he says: "The trade of England increased gradually every year, and such a scene of national prosperity, while waging a long, bloody, and costly war, was never before shown by any people in the world." On the other hand, the historian of the French navy, speaking of an earlier phase of the same wars, says: "The English fleets, having nothing to resist them, swept the seas. Our privateers and single cruisers, having no fleet to keep down the abundance of their enemies, ran short careers. Twenty thousand French seamen lay in English prisons." When, on the other hand, in the War of the American Revolution France resumed the policy of Colbert and of the early reign of Louis XIV., and kept large battle-fleets afloat, the same result again followed as in the days of Tourville. "For the first time," says the Annual Register, forgetting or ignorant of the experience of 1693, and remembering only the glories of the later wars, "English merchant-ships were driven to take refuge under foreign flags." Finally, in quitting this part of the subject, it may be remarked that in the island of Martinique the French had a powerful distant dependency upon which to base a cruising warfare; and during the Seven Years' War, as afterward during the First Empire, it, with Guadeloupe, was the refuge of numerous privateers. "The records of the English admiralty raise the losses of the English in the West Indies during the first years of the Seven Years' War to fourteen hundred merchantmen taken or destroyed." The English fleet was therefore directed against the islands, both of which fell, involving a loss to the trade of France greater than all the depredations of her cruisers on the English commerce, besides breaking up the system; but in the war of 1778 the great fleets protected the islands,

的商船队却遍布了整个世界。该国的贸易，年年都在增长；战争所耗费的资金，因为该国的工业生产而赚了回来。英国商人总共拥有8000艘商船。"此外，在说明通过对外征服而将巨额金币掳入了这个王国的情况，随后总结战争所带来的结果时，他又称："英国的贸易逐年增长；而在进行一场旷日持久、血腥非凡而代价高昂的战争的同时，还能出现这样一种全国繁荣的景象，世界上其他任何一个民族都未曾有过。"另一方面，那位法国海军历史学家在谈到这些战争的早期阶段时，也称："英国的舰队所向无敌，在各个海域都通行无阻。我国的私掠船和单打独斗的巡洋舰，由于没有舰队护航来压制层出不穷的敌军，所以并没有蹦跶多久。有20000名法国水手被俘，投入了英国的监狱。"但是，尽管在美国革命战争中，法国重新采取了柯尔贝尔的政策以及路易十四早期的政策，在海上保持了数量庞大的作战舰队，可后来的结果，却再一次跟图维尔所处的那个时代没什么两样。然而，《年鉴》[12]或是忘记了、或是并不知道1693年的情况，而只记得后来历次战争中的辉煌，却称："英国商船第一次不得不悬挂他国旗帜来自保了。"最后，在结束这一部分讨论的时候，我们可以这样说：法国拥有了马提尼克岛这样一个强大而遥远的属国，能够以此为基地来用巡洋舰作战了；而在"七年战争"中，以及后来的法兰西第一帝国期间，这儿和瓜达鲁佩则是无数私掠者的避难所。"英国海军部的记载中，提高了'七年战争'最初那几年中英国在西印度群岛的损失，称有1400艘商船被俘或被毁。"于是，英国舰队开始进击并攻陷了这两个岛；这给法国贸易所造成的损失，比法国巡洋舰给英国贸易所造成的损失更加巨大，还粉碎了法国整个巡航作战的体系；但在1778年战争中，因为有数量庞大的舰队防守着这两个岛，所以它们一直都没有受到威胁。

which were not even threatened at any time.

So far we have been viewing the effect of a purely cruising warfare, not based upon powerful squadrons, only upon that particular part of the enemy's strength against which it is theoretically directed, — upon his commerce and general wealth; upon the sinews of war. The evidence seems to show that even for its own special ends such a mode of war is inconclusive, worrying but not deadly; it might almost be said that it causes needless suffering. What, however, is the effect of this policy upon the general ends of the war, to which it is one of the means, and to which it is subsidiary? How, again, does it react upon the people that practise it? As the historical evidences will come up in detail from time to time, it need here only be summarized. The result to England in the days of Charles II. has been seen, — her coast insulted, her shipping burned almost within sight of her capital. In the War of the Spanish Succession, when the control of Spain was the military object, while the French depended upon a cruising war against commerce, the navies of England and Holland, unopposed, guarded the coasts of the peninsula, blocked the port of Toulon, forced the French succors to cross the Pyrenees, and by keeping open the sea highway, neutralized the geographical nearness of France to the seat of war. Their fleets seized Gibraltar, Barcelona, and Minorca, and cooperating with the Austrian army failed by little of reducing Toulon. In the Seven Years' War the English fleets seized, or aided in seizing, all the most valuable colonies of France and Spain, and made frequent descents on the French coast. The War of the American Revolution affords no lesson, the fleets being nearly equal. The next most striking instance to Americans is the War of 1812. Everybody knows how our privateers swarmed over the seas, and that from the smallness of our navy the war was essentially, indeed solely, a cruising war. Except upon the

前面我们一直都在研究一种纯粹的巡航作战的效果，以及进行战争的主要资源；这种战争并不倚赖于强大的舰队，只是倚赖于此种战争理论上所针对的、敌国在某一具体方面的力量——即敌国的贸易和整体财力。证据似乎表明，即便是对于其自身的特定目标而言，此种战争模式也是结果不定、令人担忧的，不过并不是致命的；可以说，这种战争模式只是导致了不必要的苦难。然而，这一政策对于整个战争总体目标的影响——政策是达到这些总体目标的手段之一，亦是这一总体目标的附属品——是什么呢？再者，这种政策对实行此种政策的民众又会产生什么样的影响呢？由于历史证据会时时详尽地呈现于我们面前，所以此处只需概括性地说一说即可。在查理二世统治时期，这种政策对英国的影响我们已经看到了——沿海地区遭敌侵犯，商船几乎就在首都的眼皮子底下被烧毁。在西班牙王位继承战中，由于英国的军事目标是控制西班牙，而法国则是采取巡航作战的办法来破坏其贸易，所以无人可敌的英、荷舰队防守着伊比利亚半岛沿岸地区，封锁了土伦港，不但迫使法国援军翻越比利牛斯山脉，还通过打通海上的交通干线，抵消了法国在地理上距战场很近的这一优势。两国舰队攻陷了直布罗陀、巴塞罗那和米诺卡岛，并且与奥地利陆军合作，一点一点地攻陷了土伦。在"七年战争"中，英国舰队攻陷——或者说是协助攻陷——了法国和西班牙所有最重要的殖民地，并且经常袭扰法国的沿海地区。美国革命战争没给我们提供什么教训，因为双方舰队差不多是势均力敌的。让美国人印象最为深刻的下一个例子，便是1812年战争。大家都知道，我国的私掠船遍布于各个海域，并且由于我国海军规模很小，因此这场战争基本上、并且事实上也只是一场巡航战争。除了在五大湖区，我国在其他时候还有没有过两艘军舰协同作战的情况，都是值得怀疑的。此次，一个相距遥远、一直被人轻视的敌人出其不意

lakes, it is doubtful if more than two of our ships at any time acted together. The injury done to English commerce, thus unexpectedly attacked by a distant foe which had been undervalued, may be fully conceded; but on the one hand, the American cruisers were powerfully supported by the French fleet, which being assembled in larger or smaller bodies in the many ports under the emperor's control from Antwerp to Venice, tied the fleets of England to blockade duty; and on the other hand, when the fall of the emperor released them, our coasts were insulted in every direction, the Chesapeake entered and controlled, its shores wasted, the Potomac ascended, and Washington burned. The Northern frontier was kept in a state of alarm, though there squadrons, absolutely weak but relatively strong, sustained the general defence; while in the South the Mississippi was entered unopposed, and New Orleans barely saved. When negotiations for peace were opened, the bearing of the English toward the American envoys was not that of men who felt their country to be threatened with an unbearable evil. The late Civil War, with the cruises of the "Alabama" and "Sumter" and their consorts, revived the tradition of commerce-destroying. In so far as this is one means to a general end, and is based upon a navy otherwise powerful, it is well; but we need not expect to see the feats of those ships repeated in the face of a great sea power. In the first place, those cruises were powerfully supported by the determination of the United States to blockade, not only the chief centres of Southern trade, but every inlet of the coast, thus leaving few ships available for pursuit; in the second place, had there been ten of those cruisers where there was one, they would not have stopped the incursion in Southern waters of the Union fleet, which penetrated to every point accessible from the sea; and in the third place, the undeniable injury, direct and indirect, inflicted upon individuals and upon one branch of the nation's industry (and how high that shipping industry stands in the writer's estimation need not be repeated), did not in the least influence or retard the event

地出击，给英国贸易造成了重创，或许英国已经完全承认了；而另一方面，美国的巡逻舰得到了法国舰队的强大支援，因为法国的舰队规模或大或小，都遍布于从安特卫普到威尼斯等法兰西帝国所掌控的诸多港口，牵制着英国舰队，使它们不得不留在那些地方进行封锁；但是，待法兰西帝国一垮台，英国舰队能够腾出手来之后，我国的沿海地区便处处受侵了——切萨皮克湾被英军入侵并控制，两岸都受到了蹂躏；英军还沿波托马克河而上，并在华盛顿烧杀掳掠。尽管有一些小型舰队在进行着全面的防御，但北部边境一直都处在一种惶惶不安的形势之下；这些小型舰队虽说绝对力量很弱，但相对来说还是比较强大的。而在南方，英军沿密西西比河长驱直入，新奥尔良也是好不容易才得以保住的。和谈开始后，英国人对于美国使节的态度，也并不是那种觉得自己祖国受到了无法容忍之魔鬼所威胁的人的态度。而在近来的美国内战中，像"阿拉巴马"号与"萨姆特"号这样的巡洋舰及其僚舰，却又恢复了破坏贸易的传统做法。从这是一种实现总体目标的方式，并且是建立在有一支其他方面都很强大的海军的基础之上来看，此种做法是很恰当的；但我们不要指望，这些舰船在面对一个海洋大国的时候，会再次立下赫赫战功。首先，这些巡航得到了美国一种强大决心的支持，它决意不但要封锁南方各个主要的贸易中心，还要封锁沿海的每一处港口，从而只留下少量舰船需要进行追击；其次，就算有10艘那样的巡洋舰来对付1艘南方舰船，它们也不可能阻挡住邦联舰队在南方海域突破封锁，因为邦联舰队可以从海上深入到南部的每一个地方；第三，战争给个人和国家的各行各业所带来的直接或间接的、无可否认的损害（至于在作者看来，航运行业有多么重要，这一点就无需赘述了），一点儿也没有影响或者妨碍到战

of the war. Such injuries, unaccompanied by others, are more irritating than weakening. On the other hand, will any refuse to admit that the work of the great Union fleets powerfully modified and hastened an end which was probably inevitable in any case? As a sea power the South then occupied the place of France in the wars we have been considering, while the situation of the North resembled that of England; and, as in France, the sufferers in the Confederacy were not a class, but the government and the nation at large. It is not the taking of individual ships or convoys, be they few or many, that strikes down the money power of a nation; it is the possession of that overbearing power on the sea which drives the enemy's flag from it, or allows it to appear only as a fugitive; and which, by controlling the great common, closes the highways by which commerce moves to and from the enemy's shores. This overbearing power can only be exercised by great navies, and by them (on the broad sea) less efficiently now than in the days when the neutral flag had not its present immunity. It is not unlikely that, in the event of a war between maritime nations, an attempt may be made by the one having a great sea power and wishing to break down its enemy's commerce, to interpret the phrase "effective blockade" in the manner that best suits its interests at the time; to assert that the speed and disposal of its ships make the blockade effective at much greater distances and with fewer ships than formerly. The determination of such a question will depend, not upon the weaker belligerent, but upon neutral powers; it will raise the issue between belligerent and neutral rights; and if the belligerent have a vastly overpowering navy he may carry his point, just as England, when possessing the mastery of the seas, long refused to admit the doctrine of the neutral flag covering the goods.

事。这些损害，倘若不加上其他的损害，更多的只是令人恼火，而非削弱了其实力。另一方面，就算不承认规模庞大的南方邦联舰队的作用，这样做难道就会强有力地改变或者加速出现那种无论如何都是必然的下场吗？作为一个海洋大国，当时的南方取代了法国在我们前面所研究的那些战争中原有的地位，而北方联邦的形势则与那时的英国相似；并且，与在法国一样，南部邦联中受苦的并不是哪一个阶层，而是政府和整个国家。并不是俘虏一些舰船或者护航队——无论是多是少——就能打垮一个国家的财力；只有掌握了海上霸权，迫使敌人无法在海上立足或是让敌人在海上有如丧家之犬，或者通过控制大部分公共海域，封锁敌人沿海地区进行贸易往来的交通要道，才能打垮它。这种霸权，只能在拥有强大的海军之后才能实现，但因为中立国的国旗如今具有强大的豁免权，所以海军（在广阔的大海上）已经不再像过去那样有力量了。两个海洋国家之间发生战争的时候，其中拥有强大制海权、希望摧毁敌国贸易的那个国家，是不太可能试图将"有效封锁"这个词按照当时最适合其利益的方式来阐述的；它也是不太可能声称自己舰船的速度和部署可以从很远的地方、用比以前更少的舰船来实施有效封锁的。这样一个问题，并非取决于交战双方势力较弱的那一国，而是取决于中立国；它会引发交战国与中立国权利的争端；倘若交战国拥有一支无可匹敌的海军，那么它可能就会像英国一样，让别的国家承认它的观点，并且在它掌控制海权的时候，一直拒绝承认中立国所运物资受到保护的那条原则。

FOOTNOTES:

(1) Since the above was written, the experience of the English autumn manoeuvres of 1888 has verified this statement; not indeed that any such experiment was needed to establish a self-evident fact.

(2) The recent development of rapid-firing and machine guns, with the great increase of their calibre and consequent range and penetration, reproduces this same step in the cycle of progress.

(3) This result was probably due simply to the greater weatherliness of the English ships. It would perhaps be more accurate to say that the Dutch had sagged to leeward so that they drifted through the English line.

(4) The true significance of this change has often been misunderstood, and hence erroneous inferences as to the future have been drawn. It was not a case of the new displacing the old, but of the military element in a military organization asserting its necessary and inevitable control over all other functions.

原注：

（1）写下上述内容以后，英国在1888年秋季的机动过程，已经证实了这种说法的正确性；事实上，并非任何一种这样的实验，都必须去证实一种不言自喻的事实。

（2）近来速射火炮和机关枪的发展，以及枪炮口径、射程和穿透力方面的发展，再现了进步周期中相同的这个阶段。

（3）这一结果，很可能仅仅是由于英国舰船具有较强的抗风能力。或许，说荷兰舰船漂到了下风位置并因而漂离了英军战线，可能更准确一点。

（4）人们经常误解了这种变化真正的重要性，因而得出了许多关于未来的错误结论。这种情况并不是新旧交替，而是一个军事组织中的某个军事要素，坚持它对于其他所有职能都拥有必要而且必然的掌控权力。

译者注：

［1］La Rochelle：拉罗谢尔。法国西南部海港，1627～1628年间法王路易十三率军与胡格诺派教徒在此发生战争，标志着法国天主教与新教之间的矛盾达到了顶峰，结果是法王路易十三和天主教徒大获全胜。

［2］Edict of Nantes：《南特敕令》。1598年法王亨利四世颁布的一道敕令，赋予胡格诺派教徒一定的政治权利，以保护法国新教。敕令承认了法国国内胡格诺教徒的信仰自由，并在法律上享有和公民同等的权利。它也是世界上第一份有关宗教信仰自由的敕令。亦译《南特法令》、《南特诏令》等。

［3］范·特龙普（Cornelis Martinus Von Tromp，1629～1691）。荷兰军事家。第一次英荷战争期间，他因抗击英军表现出色，被晋升为海军少将。1665年第二次英荷战争爆发后，他任海军中将，不久又任荷兰海军总司令。1676年，他任丹麦荷兰联合舰队总司令，同瑞典人作战取得成功。1691年任荷兰共和国军队总司令，同年病死。

［4］基佐（Francois Pierre Guillaume Guizot，1787～1874）。法国政治家和该国第22任首相（1847～1848年在任）。

［5］league：里格。长度单位，1里格相当于大约3英里或3海里。在美国英语中亦可指"平方里格"，1平方里格相当于约4400英亩。

［6］Elector of Brandenburg：勃兰登堡选帝侯。选帝侯是德意志历史上的一种特殊现象，指那些拥有选举罗马国王和神圣罗马帝国皇帝权利的诸侯。这一制度由1356年的卢森堡王朝建立，当时确定了7个选帝侯，勃兰登堡即为其中之一。1806年，拿破仑解散了神圣罗马帝国，这种削弱王权的选侯权便失去了意义。

［7］让·巴尔（Jean Bart，1650～1702）。著名的私掠船船长，被称为"爱国海盗"。后加入法国海军，在路易十四时期的许多战争中都立有战功，以机智勇敢而著称，官至海军少将。

［8］莱布尼茨（G. W. Leibnitz，1646~1716）。德国数学家、哲学家和逻辑学家。1672年他被派到巴黎进行游说，以动摇路易十四对入侵荷兰及其他邻国的兴趣，并使之将精力转向埃及，但并未成功。他还与牛顿一起，被世人认为是微积分的奠基者。

［9］麦考利（Thomas Babington Macaulay，1800~1859）。英国政治家、历史学家，曾担任英国战争大臣一职，著有《论英国历史》等论著，获封麦考利男爵一世。

［10］Great Fire of London：伦敦大火。1666年9月2日至5日伦敦发生的一场火灾，是英国历史上最严重的一次火灾，烧毁了许多建筑，其中包括著名的圣保罗大教堂。但此次大火，也结束了伦敦自1665以来的鼠疫疫情（即前文所称的"大瘟疫"）。

［11］Pillars of Hercules：海格力斯之柱，指直布罗陀。海格力斯是古希腊神话中宙斯与阿尔克墨涅所生之子，他力大无比，因完成天后赫拉所要求的12项任务而获得永生。这些任务中，有一项便是到西方牵回巨人革律翁的牛群；这是海格力斯往西出行最远的一次，其终点即是所称的"海格力斯之柱"。直布罗陀海峡两侧对峙的两座峭壁，被古人认为正是海格力斯此次西行的终点，故后人就用此名指代直布罗陀。

［12］The Annual Register：《年鉴》。一份历史悠久的年度出版物，创刊于1758年，起初主要是记录和分析每一年世界发生的一些重大事件、发展情况和趋势，如今内容更加翔实，前半部分主要是记录和分析世界各国、各地区的情况，后半部分多为综合性的文章，涉及到国际机构和组织、经济、环境、科学等各个方面。

CHAPTER III   English Revolution

War of the League of Augsburg, 1688–1697. —
Sea Battles of Beachy Head and La Hougue.

The Peace of Nimeguen was followed by a period of ten years in which no extensive war broke out. They were, however, far from being years of political quiet. Louis XIV. was as intent upon pushing on his frontiers to the eastward in peace as in war, and grasped in quick succession fragments of territory which had not been given him by the peace. Claiming this and that in virtue of ancient feudal ties; this and that other as implicitly surrendered by the treaty, because dependent upon something else that had been explicitly surrendered; purchasing at one time, using bare force in other cases, and backing up all the so-called peaceful methods of obtaining his asserted rights by the presence of armed power, he carried on this process of extension between 1679 and 1682. The aggression most startling to Europe, and above all to the German Empire, was the seizure of the then imperial city of Strasburg on the 30th of September, 1681; and on the same day Casale, in Italy, was sold to him by the Duke of Mantua, showing that his ambitions were directed that way as well as to the north and east. Both of these were positions of great strategic importance, threatening, the one Germany, the other Italy, in case of war.

The excitement throughout Europe was very great; in every direction Louis, serenely

第三章[1]   英国革命

1688-1697年间的奥格斯堡同盟[2]战争；
比奇角海战与拉和岬海战

《奈梅亨和约》[3]签订之后的10年间，是一段没有发生过大规模战争的时期。然而，这并不是一个政治上非常安定的时期。路易十四无论是在和平时期还是在战争时期，都决意向东扩张法国领土，所以不久就接二连三地攫取了和约并未给予他的许多小片领土。他根据古时的领地关系，一会儿声索这里，一会儿又声索那里；他依据和约中隐含了别的让与内容，便声称和约中也隐含着将此处和彼处让与法国的内容；他有时通过购买，其他情况下则动用赤裸裸的武力，并且摆出自己的军事实力，来为得到他所声称的那些权利而采取的一切所谓的和平方式撑腰，并在1679年至1682年间一直进行着此种扩张进程。而让欧洲各国，尤其是德意志帝国极其震惊的挑衅，则是1681年9月30日法国攻占了当时尚属德意志帝国的城市斯特拉斯堡；并且就在同一天，迈图阿公爵也将意大利的卡萨莱卖给了他，表明他除了向北和向东扩张，还野心勃勃地想向意大利那边扩张。这两个地方在战略上都极其重要，一旦发生战争，就会对德国和意大利分别构成威胁。

这种做法在欧洲搅起了轩然大波，因为路易十四冷静地凭借着自己的实力，正在

trusting to his power, was making new enemies and alienating former friends. The king of Sweden, directly insulted, and injured in his duchy of Deux-Ponts, turned against him, as did the Italian States; and the Pope himself sided with the enemies of a king who was already showing his zeal for the conversion of the Protestants, and was preparing for the revocation of the Edict of Nantes. But the discontent, though deep and general, had to be organized and directed; the spirit necessary to give it form and final effective expression was found again in Holland, in William of Orange. Time, however, was needed to mature the work. "No one yet armed himself; but everyone talked, wrote, agitated, from Stockholm to Madrid. ... The war of the pen preceded by many years the war of the sword; incessant appeals were made to European opinion by indefatigable publicists; under all forms was diffused the terror of the New Universal Monarchy," which was seeking to take the place once filled by the House of Austria. It was known that Louis sought to make himself or his son emperor of Germany. But complications of different kinds, private interests, lack of money, all combined to delay action. The United Provinces, despite William's wishes, were yet unwilling to act again as banker for a coalition, and the emperor was so threatened on his eastern frontier by the rebel Hungarians and the Turks that he dared not risk a western war.

Meanwhile the armed navy of France was daily growing in strength and efficiency under Colbert's care, and acquiring the habit of war by attacks upon the Barbary pirates and their ports. During the same years the navies both of England and of Holland were declining in numbers and efficiency. It has already been said that in 1688, when William needed Dutch ships for his expedition to England, it was objected that the navy was in a far different condition from 1672, "being incalculably decreased in strength and deprived of its most able commanders." In England, the decline of discipline had been followed by an economical

四面树新敌、八方疏旧友。直接受到侵犯并因其双桥大公国受到了侵害的瑞典国王，就像意大利诸邦那样，开始反抗路易十四；可教皇本人却站在这个敌国国王一边，因为这位国王已经表明有心皈依新教，并且正在准备废除《南特敕令》。不过，欧洲各国的这种不满情绪尽管强烈而普遍，但必须有人来加以组织和指导才行；而能够让这种不满得以成形并最终有效地表达出来的气魄，则再一次在于荷兰，在于奥兰治的威廉身上。然而，这种事情是需要时间才能完善起来的。"此时尚无人武装起来；但从斯德哥尔摩到马德里，人人都在谈论、撰写文章、进行激烈的辩论……在真正的战争爆发之前，这种口诛笔伐就已进行了多年；不屈不挠的政论家们一直在向欧洲各国的民众进行呼吁；所有这些形式之下，都弥漫着对于这个'新的世界帝国'的恐惧，"这个"世界帝国"正在试图取代哈布斯堡王朝曾经的位置。人们都知道，路易十四试图想让自己或他的儿子成为德国皇帝。但各种各样节外生枝的事情、私利以及没有资金等情况结合起来阻碍了他，使得他没有采取行动。尽管威廉有心，但荷兰共和国还是不愿意再次牵头进行联合，而法国皇帝因为东面偏远地区受到匈牙利人和土耳其人起义的威胁，故还不敢冒险在西部发动战争。

与此同时，法国海军在柯尔贝尔的悉心经营之下，实力与效率都在日益增强，并且通过进攻巴巴里地区的海盗及其港口，逐渐习惯了战争。而在这些年间，英国和荷兰舰队的数量都日益减少，效率也都日益下降了。前文已经说过，在1688年，当威廉需要荷兰舰队护送他远征英国的时候，大臣们都反对说，海军的状况已经远不如1672年了，"海军实力已经大大下降，并且没有了那些最能干的指挥官。"在英国，海军非但纪律

policy as to material, gradually lessening the numbers and injuring the condition of the fleet; and after the little flare-up and expected war with France in 1678, the king gave the care of the navy to a new body of men, concerning whom an English naval historian says: "This new administration lasted five years, and if it had continued five years longer would in all probability have remedied even the numerous and mighty evils it had introduced, by wearing out the whole royal navy, and so leaving no room for future mistakes. However, a just sense of this induced the king, in 1684, to resume the management of the fleet into his own hands, restoring most of the old officers; but before any great progress in the work of restoration could be made, his Majesty died," — in 1685. The change of sovereigns was of vast importance, not merely to the English navy, but from the ultimate effect it was to have upon the designs of Louis XIV. and the fortune of the general war which his aggressions were preparing. James II. was peculiarly interested in the navy, being himself a seaman, and having commanded in chief at Lowestoft and Southwold Bay. He knew its actual depressed condition; and the measures he at once took to restore it, both in numbers and efficiency, were thoughtful and thorough. In the three years of his reign very much indeed was done to prepare a weapon which was first proved against himself and his best friend.

The accession of James II., which promised fairly for Louis, precipitated the action of Europe against him. The House of Stuart, closely allied to the King of France, and sympathizing with his absolutist rule, had used the still great power of the sovereign to check the political and religious enmity of the English nation to France. James II. added to the same political sympathies a strength of Roman Catholic fervor which led him into acts peculiarly fitted to revolt the feeling of the English people, with the final result of driving him from the throne, and calling to it, by the voice of Parliament, his daughter Mary, whose husband was William of

日渐涣散，随后英国政府又制定了一项节省材料的政策，从而逐渐减少了舰船数量，损害了舰队的状况；而在1678年与法国发生了一场小小的冲突，进行了一场意料之中的战争之后，英王又将监管海军的任务交给了另一拨人；关于这一群人，有位英国海军历史学家曾称："这个新的部门存在了5年，倘若它再存在5年的话，就十有八九会通过折腾整个皇家海军，从而纠正该部门所导致的无数巨大弊端，使得将来再也不会有犯错的空间。然而，正是这种合理的感觉，却让英王在1684年将舰队的管理权收回了自己手中，重新启用了原来的大部分军官；可不等这种恢复工作有什么起色，陛下便归了天，"——此时正值1685年。改朝换代，不仅对英国海军具有非常重大的意义，而且从它对路易十四的图谋以及他正野心勃勃地准备进行的这场全面战争之命运的最终影响来看，也是极其重要的。詹姆士二世对海军尤为感兴趣，因为他原本就是一名水兵，并且曾在洛斯托夫特和索思沃尔德湾海战中担任过总司令一职。他很清楚英国海军此时的低迷处境，于是他立即开始采取措施来重建海军；这些涉及到海军兵力数量和作战效率的措施，既经过了深思熟虑，又很全面。在位的那3年间，他实际上做了很多工作来准备海军这种武器，可结果呢，海军却被首先用于对付他和他最好的朋友。

詹姆士二世登基，对路易十四非常有利，却引发了欧洲各国的群起反对。斯图亚特皇室本是法国国王的亲密盟友，又支持路易十四那种专制统治，因此利用了当时仍然势力强大的英王，来遏制英国国内反对法国的政治和宗教敌对势力。詹姆士二世除了具有这种相同的政治同感之外，还对罗马天主教极为狂热，使得他对英国人民的情绪尤为反感；而最终的结果，便是他被赶下了王位，国会则呼吁由他的女儿玛丽——其丈夫即是

Orange.

In the same year that James became king, a vast diplomatic combination against France began. This movement had two sides, religious and political. The Protestant States were enraged at the increasing persecutions of the French Protestants, and their feelings became stronger as the policy of James of England showed itself more and more bent toward Rome. The Protestant northern States, Holland, Sweden, and Brandenburg, drew together in alliances; and they counted for support upon the Emperor of Austria and Germany, upon Spain and other Roman Catholic States whose motives were political apprehension and anger. The emperor had latterly been successful against the Turks, thus freeing his hands for a move against France. July 9, 1686, there was signed at Augsburg a secret agreement between the emperor, the kings of Spain and Sweden, and a number of German princes. Its object was at first defensive only against France, but it could readily be turned into an offensive alliance. This compact took the name of the League of Augsburg, and from it the general war which followed two years later was called the War of the League of Augsburg.

The next year, 1687, saw yet greater successes of the Empire over the Turks and Hungarians. It was evident that France could expect no more from diversions in that quarter. At the same time the discontent of the English and the ambitions of the Prince of Orange, who hoped from his accession to the throne of England no ordinary personal aggrandizement, but the fulfilment of his strongest political wish and conviction, in curbing forever the power of Louis XIV., became more and more plain. But for his expedition into England, William needed ships, money, and men from the United Provinces; and they hung back, knowing that the result would be war with the French king, who proclaimed James his ally. Their action was at last decided by the course of Louis, who chose this moment to revoke concessions made at Nimeguen to

奥兰治亲王威廉——来继承王位。

就在詹姆士登基的那一年，欧洲各国开始逐渐联合，形成了一种在外交上反对法国的强大势力。这一运动有两个方面，一是在宗教上，二是在政治上。那些信奉新教的国家，因为法国国内的新教徒所受迫害日盛而义愤填膺，又因为英王詹姆士的政策表明该国越来越偏向了罗马天主教，所以他们的这种义愤也就变得越来越强烈了。信奉新教的北方诸国、荷兰、瑞典和勃兰登堡团结起来，结成了同盟；这些国家，都指望着获得神圣罗马帝国皇帝的支持，指望着西班牙和其他一些信奉罗马天主教的国家的支持，而后者这样做的动机，即在于政治上的顾虑和愤怒。神圣罗马帝国皇帝最近刚刚成功地对付了土耳其，故他可以腾出手来对付法国了。1686年7月9日，神圣罗马帝国皇帝与西班牙、瑞典两国的国王，连同许多德意志诸侯，在奥格斯堡签署了一份秘密条约。该条约的目标，起初只是为了防御法国，但很容易转变成为一种进攻性的同盟条约。这份条约史称《奥格斯堡同盟条约》，而两年之后因此而发生的那场全面战争，便被称作"奥格斯堡同盟战争"。

第二年，即1687年，神圣罗马帝国在对付土耳其人和匈牙利人的过程中，取得了更大的胜利。很显然，法国在这一地区分心，是不可能指望获得更多好处的。与此同时，英国国内的不满情绪以及奥兰治亲王的野心也变得日益明显起来；这位奥兰治亲王登上英国王位之后，期待的可不是什么普通的个人财富、威望或者权力，而是希望在不懈地遏制路易十四势力的过程中，实现其最大的政治抱负与信念。不过，为了远征英国，他就需要荷兰共和国为他提供舰船、资金和人员；而各联合省对此却犹豫不决，因为大家都明白，这样做的结果将是与宣称詹姆士二世是其盟友的法国国王开战。可路易十四的行为，最终却决

Dutch trade. The serious injury thus done to Holland's material interests turned the wavering scale. "This violation of the conventions of Nimeguen," says a French historian, "by giving a severe blow to Dutch commerce, reducing her European trade more than one fourth, removed the obstacle that religious passions still encountered in material interests, and put all Holland at the disposition of William, none having reason longer to conciliate France." This was in November, 1687. In the summer of the following year the birth of an heir to the English throne brought things to an issue. English loyalty might have put up with the reign of the father, now advanced in years, but could not endure the prospect of a continued Roman Catholic royalty.

Matters had at last reached the crisis to which they had been tending for years. Louis and William of Orange, long-standing enemies, and at the moment the two chief figures in European politics, alike from their own strong personalities and the cause which either represented, stood on the brink of great actions, whose effects were to be felt through many generations. William, despotic in temper himself, stood on the shores of Holland looking hopefully toward free England, from which he was separated by the narrow belt of water that was the defence of the island kingdom, and might yet be an impassable barrier to his own high aims; for the French king at that moment could control the sea if he would. Louis, holding all the power of France in his single grasp, facing eastward as before, saw the continent gathering against him; while on his flank was England heartily hostile, longing to enter on the strife against him, but as yet without a leader. It still remained with him to decide whether he would leave the road open for the head to join the waiting body, and to bring Holland and England, the two sea powers, under one rule. If he attacked Holland by land, and sent his superior navy into the Channel, he might well keep William in his own country; the more so as the English navy, beloved and petted by the king, was likely to have more than the usual loyalty of seamen to their chief. Faithful to

定了荷兰共和国的抉择；因为他选择在这个时候，撤销了他在《奈梅亨和约》中对荷兰贸易所做的种种让步。这样一来，荷兰共和国因为在物质利益上受到了严重损害，从而扭转了左右不定的局面。有位法国历史学家曾经说："违反奈梅亨所签诸协议的这种做法，给了荷兰的商业贸易以重重一击，使之在欧洲的贸易额减少了四分之一强，从而消除了在物质利益中依然存有宗教狂热的这一障碍，将整个荷兰都交到了威廉的手中，而荷兰人也没有理由再对法国怀有好感了。"此时，正值1687年的11月份。第二年夏天，英国王位继承人降生，从而导致该国出现了一个问题。英国人的忠诚，使得他们可以容忍威廉这位父亲的统治，但他们却无法容忍将来继续由一个信奉罗马天主教的王室来统治英国。

经过多年的磕绊之后，形势终于发展到了紧要关头。路易十四和奥兰治的威廉既是宿敌，当时也是欧洲政坛中的两大主要人物，二人都有着同样刚强的个性以及各自所代表的奋斗目标；而此时，二人正站在爆发一场后果将会波及数代人的大战边缘。威廉本性专横暴虐，他站在荷兰的海岸边，充满期待地眺望着自由的英格兰；眼前窄窄的一片水域，既是英国这个岛上王国的屏障，将他与自由的英格兰隔了开来，还可能是一道让他无法实现自己远大目标的、不可逾越的鸿沟；因为只要愿意，当时的法国国王便可控制住英吉利海峡。在法国大权独揽、像以前一样盯着东方的路易十四，看到整个欧洲大陆都团结起来反对他了；而在他的一侧，英国又极为敌视，渴望着正式跟他宣战，只是直到那时还没有一个领头人罢了。此时，是否应当让开道路，让威廉这个领头人加入正在等待着的英国，从而让荷兰与英国这两个海洋大国并入一人治下，此种决定权仍然掌握在他的手中。假如他在陆上进攻荷兰，并将手下那支无人能敌的海军派往英吉利海峡，或许就可以将威廉堵

the bias of his life, perhaps unable to free himself from it, he turned toward the continent, and September 24, 1688, declared war against Germany and moved his armies toward the Rhine. William, overjoyed, saw removed the last obstacle to his ambition. Delayed for some weeks by contrary winds, he finally set sail from Holland on the 30th of October. More than five hundred transports, with fifteen thousand troops, escorted by fifty men-of-war, formed the expedition; and it is typical of its mingled political and religious character, that the larger part of the army officers were French Protestants who had been driven from France since the last war, the commander-in-chief under William being the Huguenot Schomberg, late a marshal of France. The first start was foiled by a violent storm; but sailing again on the 10th of November, a fresh, fair breeze carried the ships through the Straits and the Channel, and William landed on the 15th at Torbay. Before the end of the year, James had fled from his kingdom. On the 21st of the following April, William and Mary were proclaimed sovereigns of Great Britain, and England and Holland were united for the war, which Louis had declared against the United Provinces as soon as he heard of William's invasion. During all the weeks that the expedition was preparing and delayed, the French ambassador at the Hague and the minister of the navy were praying the king to stop it with his great sea power, — a power so great that the French fleet in the first years of the war outnumbered those of England and Holland combined; but Louis would not. Blindness seems to have struck the kings of England and France alike; for James, amid all his apprehensions, steadily refused any assistance from the French fleet, trusting to the fidelity of the English seamen to his person, although his attempts to have Mass celebrated on board the ships had occasioned an uproar and mutiny which nearly ended in the crews throwing the priests overboard.

France thus entered the War of the League of Augsburg without a single ally. "What her

在荷兰；但由于英国海军深受英王宠爱，所以他越是这样做的话，可能英国海军官兵就越会对其领袖怀有非比寻常的忠心。因为坚持着自己的成见，或许也是因为无法摆脱这种成见，所以路易十四转向了欧洲大陆，并于1688年9月24日向德意志宣战，然后让部队开往了莱茵河地区。威廉欣喜若狂，明白阻碍实现自己野心的最后一道障碍终于可以被清除了。由于风向不利，他耽搁了数周，最后才在10月30日率领舰队从荷兰起航。他的远征队包括500多艘运输船和15000名士兵，由15艘军舰护送；这支远征队兼具政治与宗教两方面的特点，因为部队中的大多数军官都是法国清教徒，都是自上一次战争以来被逐出法国的人，而威廉手下的总司令，则是曾任法国元帅的胡格诺派教徒绍姆贝格。他们第一次出发时，曾为疾风暴雨所阻；但11月10日再次起航后，强劲而利于航行的海风将舰船一路吹过了诸道峡湾和英吉利海峡，而威廉便于15日在托贝港上了岸。是年年底前，詹姆士二世逃出了自己的王国。第二年的4月21日，威廉和玛丽宣布登基，成为了大不列颠的君主，而英、荷两国也联合起来，开始同法国作战；因为路易十四一听说威廉入侵英国，便对荷兰共和国宣了战。在威廉准备远征军、后来出发又一再耽搁的这段时间里，身处海牙的法国大使和法国的海军大臣，都曾恳请法国国王利用本国强大的海军实力，阻止威廉成行——当时该国海军的实力极其强大，所以在此次战争最初的那几年中，法国舰队在兵力上甚至超过了英、荷两国舰队合起来之后的兵力；可路易十四却没有听从这一建议。英、法两国国王似乎都同样丧失了判断力；因为詹姆士二世忧惧交加，一直拒绝接受法国舰队的支援，只依靠英国海军官兵对他个人的忠心，但他规定在军舰上做弥撒，而这种做法却时不时地引起官兵们的骚乱和哗变，并且几乎每次都是以船员们将牧师扔出船外而告终。

policy had most feared, what she had long averted, was come to pass. England and Holland were not only allied, but united under the same chief; and England entered the coalition with all the eagerness of passions long restrained by the Stuart policy." As regards the sea war, the different battles have much less tactical value than those of De Ruyter. The chief points of strategic interest are the failure of Louis, having a decided superiority at sea, properly to support James II. in Ireland, which remained faithful to him, and the gradual disappearance from the ocean of the great French fleets, which Louis XIV. could no longer maintain, owing to the expense of that continental policy which he had chosen for himself. A third point of rather minor interest is the peculiar character and large proportions taken on by the commerce-destroying and privateering warfare of the French, as their large fleets were disappearing. This, and the great effect produced by it, will appear at first to contradict what has been said as to the general inadequacy of such a warfare when not supported by fleets; but an examination of the conditions, which will be made later on, will show that the contradiction is rather apparent than real.

Taught by the experience of the last conflict, the chief effort of the French king, in the general war he had brought upon himself, should have been directed against the sea powers, — against William of Orange and the Anglo-Dutch alliance. The weakest point in William's position was Ireland; though in England itself not only were there many partisans of the exiled king, but even those who had called in William fenced his kingship about with jealous restrictions. His power was not secure so long as Ireland was not subdued. James, having fled from England in January, 1689, landed in Ireland in the following March, accompanied by French troops and a French squadron, and was enthusiastically welcomed everywhere but in the Protestant North. He made Dublin his capital, and remained in the country until July of

　　法国就这样孤家寡人般地开始了奥格斯堡同盟战争。"该国政策最害怕的事情，以及该国长久以来一直避免的局面，终于要出现了。英、荷两国不但结成了同盟，还合并到了一个君主的统治之下；并且，英国是带着长久以来一直被斯图亚特王朝政策所束缚的渴望与激情与荷兰结盟的。"至于海战方面，此次战争中的历次战斗，与德·鲁伊特所进行的海战相比，战术上的意义都要小得多。战略上最值得我们注意的，就是路易十四的失败——他在海上本来占有决定性的优势，是完全可以支持身处爱尔兰、此时仍对他忠心耿耿的那位詹姆士二世的；还有自此以后，原本强大的法国舰队便逐渐从海洋上销声匿迹了——由于路易十四所选的那种欧洲大陆政策耗资巨大，所以他无法再将海军维持下去。第三点，也是很次要的一点，便是随着法国大型舰队的消失，法国所采用的贸易破坏战与私掠战的罕见性质与巨大规模。这种做法，以及这种做法所产生的巨大影响，首先看上去就与我们已经说过的那种原则相矛盾：要是没有舰队支援，通常就不适合进行这种战争；不过，仔细研究一下当时的形势（稍后我们会进行此种探究）就会看出，此种矛盾更多的是表面上的，而非真实存在的。

　　由于有了上一次战争的教训，所以法国国王在给自己招来的这场全面战争中，主要精力本该针对两个海洋大国——即针对奥兰治的威廉和英荷同盟才是。威廉所处形势最薄弱的地方，便是爱尔兰；而在英国本土，非但那位被流放的前任国王有着众多党羽，而且，甚至是那些邀请威廉来到英国的人，也采用了各种戒心重重的限制措施，约束着他的王权。只要爱尔兰未被征服，威廉的权力就不会稳固。詹姆士二世是在1689年1月逃离英国的，1690年3月，他在法国军队和一支法国舰队的护送之下，抵达了爱尔兰；

the next year. During these fifteen months the French were much superior at sea; they landed troops in Ireland on more than one occasion; and the English, attempting to prevent this, were defeated in the naval battle of Bantry Bay. But although James was so well established, and it was of the utmost importance to sustain him; although it was equally important to keep William from getting a foothold till James was further strengthened and Londonderry, then passing through its famous siege, reduced; and although the French were superior to the united English and Dutch on the seas in 1689 and 1690; nevertheless, the English admiral Rooke was able, unmolested, to throw succors and troops into Londonderry, and afterward landed Marshal Schomberg, with a small army, near Carrickfergus. Rooke stopped intercourse between Ireland and Scotland, where were many Stuart partisans, and then with his small squadron passed along the east coast of Ireland, attempted to burn the shipping in Dublin harbor, failing only through lack of wind, and finally came off Cork, then occupied by James, took possession of an island in the harbor, and returned in safety to the Downs in October. These services, which raised the siege of Londonderry and kept open the communications between England and Ireland, extended throughout the summer months; nor was any attempt made by the French to stop them. There can be little doubt that an effective co-operation of the French fleet in the summer of 1689 would have broken down all opposition to James in Ireland, by isolating that country from England, with corresponding injury to William's power.

The following year the same strategic and political mistake was made. It is the nature of an enterprise such as James's, dependent upon a weaker people and foreign help, to lose strength if it does not progress; but the chances were still in his favor, provided France cooperated heartily, and above all, with her fleet. It is equally the nature of a merely military navy like that of France to be strongest at the beginning of hostilities; whereas that of the allied sea

除了信奉新教的北方地区，他所到之处，爱尔兰民众全都夹道相迎。他将都柏林定为首都，并在该国一直待到了第二年的7月。在这15个月里，法国在海上都很有优势，不止一次将部队运送到了爱尔兰；英国人曾经试图加以阻止，却在班特里湾海战中战败了。不过，尽管詹姆士二世根基甚深，支持他也极其重要；尽管在詹姆士二世的实力进一步加强之前，在当时刚刚经历了那次有名的围城战的伦敦德里[4]被攻陷之前，不让威廉有立足之地也同样重要；并且，尽管在1689年和1690年，法国海军比英、荷联军要强大；但是，英国的海军司令鲁克却能够毫无困难地将补给物资和援军送往伦敦德里，后来还派绍姆贝格元帅率一小支陆军，在卡里克弗格斯附近登陆了。鲁克封锁了爱尔兰与有着众多斯图亚特王朝党羽的苏格兰之间的交通联络，之后便率领自己的那支小型舰队，绕过爱尔兰东部海岸，试图去烧毁停泊在都柏林港里的船只，只是因为风向不对才作了罢；最后，他到达了当时为詹姆士二世所据的科克港，在港口里攻占了一个小岛，然后又在10月份安全地回到了唐斯锚地。这些导致了伦敦德里之围以及保持英格兰与爱尔兰之间交通联络的作战行动，持续了一整个夏天；可法国海军并没有试图去加以阻止。毫无疑问，倘若法国舰队在1689年夏天能够有效地协同作战，本来是可以通过隔绝爱尔兰与英格兰之间的联系并相应打击威廉的实力，从而将爱尔兰国内反对詹姆士二世的所有势力统统瓦解掉的。

第二年，法国在战略和政治上又犯了同样的错误。詹姆士二世这种倚赖于一个不够强大的民族和外国援助来进行的事业，本来就是不进则退的；不过，只要法国真心合作，尤其是利用法国的舰队，那么此时的詹姆士二世还是有机会成功的。同样，一支像法国那样纯军事性质的海军，在战争初期本来就是最强大的；而两个海洋强国的海军联

powers grew daily stronger, drawing upon the vast resources of their merchant shipping and their wealth. The disparity of force was still in favor of France in 1690, but it was not as great as the year before. The all-important question was where to direct it. There were two principal courses, involving two views of naval strategy. The one was to act against the allied fleet, whose defeat, if sufficiently severe, might involve the fall of William's throne in England; the other was to make the fleet subsidiary to the Irish campaign. The French king decided upon the former, which was undoubtedly the proper course; but there was no reason for neglecting, as he did, the important duty of cutting off the communications between the two islands. As early as March he had sent a large fleet with six thousand troops and supplies of war, which were landed without any trouble in the southern ports of Ireland; but after performing that service, the ships employed returned to Brest, and there remained inactive during May and June while the grand fleet under the Comte de Tourville was assembling. During those two months the English were gathering an army on their west coast, and on the 21st of June, William embarked his forces at Chester on board two hundred and eighty-eight transports, escorted by only six men-of-war. On the 24th he landed in Carrickfergus, and the ships-of-war were dismissed to join the English grand fleet, which, however, they were not able to do; Tourville's ships having in the mean time got to sea and occupied the channel to the eastward. There is nothing more striking than the carelessness shown by both the contending parties, during the time that Ireland was in dispute, as to the communications of their opponents with the island; but this was especially strange in the French, as they had the larger forces, and must have received pretty accurate information of what was going on from disaffected persons in England. It appears that a squadron of twenty-five frigates, to be supported by ships-of-the-line, were told off for duty in St. George's Channel; but they never reached their station, and only ten of the frigates had got as far as Kinsale by the

合起来，却会凭借两国巨大的贸易资源和财力而变得日益强大起来。虽说1690年在兵力对比上，法国仍然是具有优势的，但此种优势的程度，却不如前一年那样强大了。而重中之重的问题，便是将这种兵力优势放在哪儿。当时，法国有两条行动路线，涉及到两种不同的海军战略观点。一条是对英国的大型舰队作战，倘若打败这支联合舰队，使之受到重创，可能就会让威廉在英国垮台；另一条则是派法国舰队前去协助爱尔兰的战事。法国国王经过考虑后，选取了前者，这无疑也是一条正确的道路；不过，他却无缘无故地忽略了切断爱尔兰与英格兰两岛之间交通联系的这一重要任务。早在3月份，他就派遣了一支庞大的舰队，运送6000名士兵和给养，毫无困难地在爱尔兰南部诸港登陆了；可在完成这一任务之后，舰队却返回了布雷斯特，并且在5月和6月间一直都闲着，而此时图维尔伯爵所率的大型舰队却正在集结。这两个月里，英国正在其西海岸集结一支陆军部队；到了6月21日，威廉便令部队在切斯特登上了288艘舰船，只由6艘战舰护航。24日，他在卡里克弗格斯登陆，并令那6艘战舰加入英国的大型舰队，但它们没能做到这一点；与此同时，图维尔的大舰队也出海起航，占领了向东去的水路。在爱尔兰国内正争论着敌人与该岛之间交通运输问题的这段时间里，交战双方所表现出来的那种粗心大意，都是极其罕见的；尤为奇怪的是法国，因为该国非但兵力较强，还必定从一些心怀不满的英国人那里获得了相当准确的情报。法国似乎派出了一支由25艘护卫舰组成的小型舰队，在一些战列舰的支援下，前往圣乔治海峡去作战；可其中没有一艘到达了作战位置，并且直到詹姆士二世在博因河之战中彻底溃败了之后，才有10艘护卫舰抵达了金塞尔。所以，英军的交通补给压根儿就没有受到威胁。

time James had lost all at the battle of the Boyne. The English communications were not even threatened for an hour.

Tourville's fleet, complete in numbers, having seventy-eight ships, of which seventy were in the line-of-battle, with twenty-two fire-ships, got to sea June 22, the day after William embarked. On the 30th the French were off the Lizard, to the dismay of the English admiral, who was lying off the Isle of Wight in such an unprepared attitude that he had not even lookout ships to the westward. He got under way, standing off-shore to the southeast, and was joined from time to time, during the next ten days, by other English and Dutch ships. The two fleets continued moving to the eastward, sighting each other from time to time.

The political situation in England was critical. The Jacobites were growing more and more open in their demonstrations, Ireland had been in successful revolt for over a year, and William was now there, leaving only the queen in London. The urgency of the case was such that the council decided the French fleet must be fought, and orders to that effect were sent to the English admiral, Herbert. In obedience to his instructions he went out, and on the 10th of July, being to windward, with the wind at northeast, formed his line-of-battle, and then stood down to attack the French, who waited for him, with their foretopsails aback on the starboard tack, heading to the northward and westward.

The fight that followed is known as the battle of Beachy Head. The ships engaged were, French seventy, English and Dutch according to their own account fifty-six, according to the French sixty. In the allied line of battle the Dutch were in the van; the English, commanded in person by Herbert, in the centre; and the rear was made up partly of English and partly of Dutch ships. The stages of the battle were as follows: —

1. The allies, being to windward, bore down together in line abreast. As usual, this

图维尔所率舰队编制完整，共有78艘舰船，其中的70艘是战列舰，还有22艘火攻船；这支舰队是在6月22日，即威廉登船的第二天起航出海的。到了30日，法军出现在利扎尔海域，使得这位英军司令大惊失色，因为当时他的舰队正停泊在怀特岛海域，完全没有作战准备，以至于舰队西边连一艘警戒船都没有。于是他便拔锚起航，一直沿着海岸向东南而去；在接下来的10天中，则时不时地有其他的英国舰船和荷兰舰船加入到了这支舰队当中。之后，这两支舰队便继续向东航行，彼此经常还能看得到。

英国国内的政治形势已经到了紧要关头。詹姆士二世党人的游行示威活动越来越明目张胆，爱尔兰爆发的革命也已成功了一年多；此时威廉又身处爱尔兰，伦敦只留下了女王一人，孤身独撑大局。形势如此危急，因此议会决定，必须与法国舰队决一死战，并将这一命令下达给了英国的海军司令赫伯特。于是，赫伯特便服从命令率军出海，并在7月10日占据了上风向之后，趁着此时正刮的东北风摆开阵形，向法军冲了过去；而法国舰队此时则严阵以待，其前主帆向后、右舷抢风，朝北、朝西航行。

接下来的战斗，就是世人所知的"比奇角海战"。交战双方的舰船数量，法国是70艘，英、荷联军据他们自己的说法是56艘，据法国的说法是60艘。在联军阵列中，荷兰舰队是前锋；英军由赫伯特亲自指挥，坐镇中央；后卫一部分是英国舰船、一部分是荷兰战船。此次战斗的三个阶段如下：

1. 英、荷联军由于顺风，因此阵形一字摆开，压向敌军。跟往常一样，这种机动实施得很糟糕，并且也像一般情况下那样，前锋先于中军和后卫部队而受到了敌人的火力攻击，承受了主要的伤亡。

manoeuvre was ill performed, and as also generally happens, the van came under fire before the centre and rear, and bore the brunt of the injury.

2. Admiral Herbert, though commander-in-chief, failed to attack vigorously with the centre, keeping it at long range. The allied van and rear came to close action. Paul Hoste's account of this manoeuvre of the allies is that the admiral intended to fall mainly on the French rear. To that end he closed the centre to the rear and kept it to windward at long cannon-shot (refused it), so as to prevent the French from tacking and doubling on the rear. If that were his purpose, his plan, though tolerably conceived in the main, was faulty in detail, for this manoeuvre of the centre left a great gap between it and the van. He should rather have attacked, as Ruyter did at the Texel, as many of the rear ships as he thought he could deal with, and refused his van, assigning to it the part of checking the French van. It may be conceded that an admiral who, from inferior numbers, cannot spread as long and close a line as his enemy, should not let the latter overlap the extremities of his fleet; but he should attain his end not, as Herbert did, by leaving a great opening in the centre, but by increasing each interval between the ships refused. The allied fleet was thus exposed to be doubled on at two points, both van and centre; and both points were attacked.

3. The commander of the French van, seeing the Dutch close to his line and more disabled than himself, pressed six of his leading ships ahead, where they went about, and so put the Dutch between two fires.

At the same time Tourville, finding himself without adversaries in the centre, having beaten off the leading division of the enemy's centre, pushed forward his own leading ships, which Herbert's dispositions had left without opponents; and these fresh ships strengthened the attack upon the Dutch in the van.

2. 赫伯特上将尽管是总司令，却没有率领中军进行有力的攻击，一直都在隔岸观火。于是，联军前锋与后卫开始靠近，协同作战。保罗·何斯德对于此次机动的描述是，赫伯特司令是想主攻法国舰队的后翼。为了实现这一目标，他才让自己的中军靠近法军后翼，并保持在炮弹射程之外很远的上风向（以免受到炮击），从而阻止法国舰队抢风并夹击其后翼。如果他的目的是那样，那么，虽然他的作战计划总的来说构思很巧妙，但细节上却是有败笔的，因为中军的这种机动，使得它与前锋之间留下了一个巨大的缺口。他本来是更应当发动进攻的，就像鲁伊特在特塞尔海战中那样，去进攻法军后翼中尽可能多的舰船，并且应当避开其前锋，而指定己方前锋负责压制法国舰队的前锋。当然，我们可以承认，由于兵力较少而无法像敌军那样展开长长的阵形且闭合阵线的一位海军司令，是不应该让敌军舰队的首尾重叠起来的；但尽管如此，为了实现目标，他也不应当像赫伯特那样让中军留下一个巨大的缺口，而应当增大所拒舰船之间的每一处间隙。这样一来，联合舰队的前锋和中军这两处便有遭受两面夹击的危险了；而事实上，这两处也受到了敌人的攻击。

3. 法军前锋的指挥官看到荷兰舰队向其阵线靠拢，并且比他自己还没有战斗力，便催促己方的6艘前导舰船先行，然后再抢风转向，从而将荷兰舰队置于两面夹击的境地。

与此同时，图维尔发现自己在中军位置毫无敌手，便在击退了敌方中军的先头分队之后，率领手下的前导舰船向前推进，因为赫伯特的部署使得图维尔所率的这些舰船无敌可击；于是，这些新加入的舰船便加强了对处于前锋位置的荷兰舰队的攻击。

This brought about a mêlée at the head of the lines, in which the Dutch, being inferior, suffered heavily. Luckily for the allies the wind fell calm; and while Tourville himself and other French ships got out their boats to tow into action again, the allies were shrewd enough to drop anchor with all sail set, and before Tourville took in the situation the ebb-tide, setting southwest, had carried his fleet out of action. He finally anchored a league from his enemy.

At nine P.M., when the tide changed, the allies weighed and stood to the eastward. So badly had many of them been mauled, that, by English accounts, it was decided rather to destroy the disabled ships than to risk a general engagement to preserve them.

Tourville pursued; but instead of ordering a general chase, he kept the line-of-battle, reducing the speed of the fleet to that of the slower ships. The occasion was precisely one of those in which a mêlée is permissible, indeed, obligatory. An enemy beaten and in flight should be pursued with ardor, and with only so much regard to order as will prevent the chasing vessels from losing mutual support, — a condition which by no means implies such relative bearings and distances as are required in the beginning or middle of a well-contested action. The failure to order such general pursuit indicates the side on which Tourville's military character lacked completeness; and the failure showed itself, as is apt to be the case, at the supreme moment of his career. He never had such another opportunity as in this, the first great general action in which he commanded in chief, and which Hoste, who was on board the flag-ship, calls the most complete naval victory ever gained. It was so indeed at that time, — the most complete, but not the most decisive, as it perhaps might have been. The French, according to Hoste, lost not even a boat, much less a ship, which, if true, makes yet more culpable the sluggishness of the pursuit; while the allies fled, casting sixteen of their ships ashore and burning them in

这使得阵线前部发生了一场混战，荷军由于兵力不如敌人，所以损失惨重。对于联军来说，幸好此时风停了；而当图维尔与其他法国舰船放出小艇，拖曳着准备再次作战的时候，由于联军狡猾得很，都是张着所有船帆泊锚的，所以还没等图维尔明白是怎么回事，往西南方向而去的落潮便将他手下的舰队带离了战场。最后，他在离敌军1里格之外的地方才泊下了锚。

到了晚上9点，潮汐转向，联军便拔锚向东驶去。其中的许多舰船都遭到了重创；据英国人的记载，联军当时就已经做出决定，宁可毁掉那些失去了作战能力的船只，也不能再冒着全面交战的危险而将它们留下来。

图维尔进行了追击；可他并没有组织全线追击，而是保持着战斗队形，使得整支舰队的速度都慢了下来。此种情形，正是那种允许进行混战、事实上也只能进行混战的情形之一。一个敌人被打败了，逃跑了，就应当劲头十足地去追击；至于秩序，只要能够不让追击的船只彼此之间无法支援，就只能考虑那么多了——这种情况，决不会像一场旗鼓相当的战斗的初期或者中期那样，需要考虑舰船的相对方位与距离。没有组织起这样一种全面的追击，表明图维尔的军人性格在这方面并不完美；而这种欠缺，正好在其军事生涯的关键时刻表现了出来，这也是人之常情。他以前从未碰到过像此次海战那样的机会；此次海战，也是他出任总司令后的第一场大规模全面作战，而当时待在旗舰上的何斯德，却称此战是有史以来最为完美的一次海军大捷。在当时来看，确实如此——是最完美的一次，而非最具决定意义的一次，虽说或许它本来是可以成为最具决定意义的一次大捷的。据何斯德称，法军连一艘小艇都没有损失，更不用说损失什么舰

sight of the enemy, who pursued as far as the Downs. The English indeed give the allied loss as only eight ships, — an estimate probably full as much out one way as the French the other. Herbert took his fleet to the Thames, and baffled the enemy's further pursuit by removing the buoys.[1]

  Tourville's is the only great historical name among the seamen of this war, if we except the renowned privateersmen at whose head was Jean Bart. Among the English, extraordinary merit cannot be claimed for any one of the gallant and enterprising men who commanded squadrons. Tourville, who by this time had served afloat for nearly thirty years, was at once a seaman and a military man. With superb courage, of which he had given dazzling examples in his youth, he had seen service wherever the French fleets had fought, — in the Anglo-Dutch war, in the Mediterranean, and against the Barbary pirates. Reaching the rank of admiral, he commanded in person all the largest fleets sent out during the earlier years of this war, and he brought to the command a scientific knowledge of tactics, based upon both theory and experience, joined to that practical acquaintance with the seaman's business which is necessary in order to apply tactical principles upon the ocean to the best advantage. But with all these high qualities he seems to have failed, where so many warriors fail, in the ability to assume a great responsibility.[2] The caution in his pursuit of the allies after Beachy Head, though so different in appearance, came from the same trait which impelled him two years later to lead his fleet into almost certain destruction at La Hougue, because he had the king's order in his pocket. He was brave enough to do anything, but not strong enough to bear the heaviest burdens. Tourville was in fact the forerunner of the careful and skilful tacticians of the coming era, but with the savor still of the impetuous hard-fighting which characterized the sea commanders of the seventeenth century. He doubtless felt, after Beachy Head, that he had done very well and

船了——倘若果真如此，那么，法军的追击不力就更值得指责了；联军在逃跑的时候，让16艘舰船随浪搁岸，并在尾随追击至唐斯锚地的敌人视线之内，烧毁了这些船只。英国实际上认为联军只损失了8艘舰船——对于这种估算，很可能英国用的是一种方式，法国用的又是另一种方式，并且理由都一样充分。最后，赫伯特率领舰队避入了泰晤士河，并且撤除了河上的航标，使得敌方无法继续追击了。[1]

  倘若我们把以让·巴尔为首的那些著名的私掠者排除在外，那么图维尔就是此战中唯一的一位历史伟人了。在英国人当中，我们说不出那些英勇而大胆的舰队指挥官当中，有哪一个取得了什么非凡的功绩。而此时的图维尔已在海军中服役了近30年；他既是一位海员，也是一名军人。他英勇过人，年轻时就有过诸多壮举，并且无论法国舰队在何处作战——在英荷战争中，在地中海地区，以及在对巴巴里海盗的作战中——都可以看到他的身影。晋升为海军上将之后，他在此次战争的头几年中，都是亲自率领规模最大的所有舰队出征，并且结合自己对于海员这一职业的实践知识，将以理论和经验为基础的战术科学知识带到了指挥当中；而要想在海洋上最出色地应用各种战术原则，就必须具有海员这一职业的实践知识。不过，虽说有着如此种种的高尚品质，但他似乎还是像许多勇士那样，在承担伟大责任的能力这方面有所欠缺。[2]比奇角海战之后，他在追击英荷联军过程中所表现出来的那种谨慎，虽说从表面上来看并不相同，但跟两年之后的拉和岬海战中，由于随身携带着国王的谕令，所以他不得不将舰队带入了一种几乎确定无疑的毁灭处境的那种性格，实际上是一脉相承的。他虽说很勇猛，无所不能，但还不够坚强，无法担当大任。确切地说，图维尔是即将到来的这个时代中那种谨慎而娴熟的战术家的先驱，不过他

could be satisfied; but he could not have acted as he did had he felt, to use Nelson's words, that "if we had taken ten ships out of the enemy's eleven, and let the eleventh escape, being able to take her, I could never call such a good day."

The day after the sea fight off Beachy Head, with its great but still partial results, the cause of James II. was lost ashore in Ireland. The army which William had been allowed to transport there unmolested was superior in number and quality to that of James, as William himself was superior as a leader to the ex-king. The counsel of Louis XIV. was that James should avoid decisive action, retiring if necessary to the Shannon, in the midst of a country wholly devoted to him. It was, however, a good deal to ask, this abandonment of the capital after more than a year's occupancy, with all the consequent moral effect; it would have been much more to the purpose to stop William's landing. James undertook to cover Dublin, taking up the line of the river Boyne, and there on the 11th of July the two armies met, with the result that James was wholly defeated. The king himself fled to Kinsale, where he found ten of those frigates that had been meant to control St. George's Channel. He embarked, and again took refuge in France, begging Louis to improve the victory at Beachy Head by landing him with another French army in England itself. Louis angrily refused, and directed that the troops still remaining in Ireland should be at once withdrawn.

The chances of a rising in favor of James, at least upon the shores of the Channel, if they existed at all, were greatly exaggerated by his own imagination. After the safe retreat of the allied fleet to the Thames, Tourville, in accordance with his instructions, made several demonstrations in the south of England; but they were wholly fruitless in drawing out any show of attachment to the Stuart cause.

In Ireland it was different. The Irish army with its French contingent fell back, after the

的身上仍然带有属于十七世纪海军指挥官特点的那种鲁莽拼搏之精神。比奇角海战之后，他无疑是认为自己干得很不错，可以满意了；不过，要是他感受到了下面这一点，就不会那样想了：用纳尔逊的话来说，就是"假如在11艘敌舰中我们攻取了10艘，却在本来也能够攻取的情况下让第11艘逃跑了，那我是绝不可能说自己这一天干得很漂亮的。"

比奇角海战虽说战果辉煌，却仍然只能说是一种局部胜利；此战的第二天，詹姆士二世的目标便在爱尔兰海岸折翼了。威廉批准运送到那儿的陆军非但丝毫没有受到阻拦，而在兵力和作战素质上也优于詹姆士二世所率的军队，因为威廉本身就是一个比这位前国王要优秀的领导者。路易十四劝告詹姆士二世，说他应当避免进行决战，并且在必要的时候可以撤至香农[5]，那儿的民众都是全心全意地忠于詹姆士二世的。然而，这样做会带来很多的问题，占领了一年多之后再这样放弃首都，也会在道义上产生出许多负面效应；本来阻止威廉登陆爱尔兰才是上上之策。于是，詹姆士二世开始防守都柏林，并且整饬了博因河这道防线；7月11日，两军在此遭遇，结果却是詹姆士二世被彻底打败了。詹姆士二世本人逃往了金塞尔；在这儿，他找到了原本受命控制圣乔治海峡的那支舰队中的10艘护卫舰。他登上了船，再一次前往法国避难，请求路易十四趁着比奇角海战的胜利势头，派另一支法国军队随他登陆英国本土。路易十四一气之下，却拒绝了他的要求，并且下令立即撤回此时仍然留守在爱尔兰的法国军队。

就算确实存在的话，英国国内或者至少是在英吉利海峡沿岸地区爆发起义支持詹姆士二世的这种可能性，也是在詹姆士二世的想像中被严重地夸大了。英、荷联合舰队安全撤入泰晤士河之后，图维尔曾下令在英格兰南部发动了几次游行示威活动；可这些游

battle of the Boyne, to the Shannon, and there again made a stand; while Louis, receding from his first angry impulse, continued to send reinforcements and supplies. But the increasing urgency of the continental war kept him from affording enough support, and the war in Ireland came to a close a little over a year later, by the defeat at Aghrim and capitulation of Limerick. The battle of the Boyne, which from its peculiar religious coloring has obtained a somewhat factitious celebrity, may be taken as the date at which the English crown was firmly fixed on William's head. Yet it would be more accurate to say that the success of William, and with it the success of Europe against Louis XIV. in the War of the League of Augsburg, was due to the mistakes and failure of the French naval campaign in 1690; though in that campaign was won the most conspicuous single success the French have ever gained at sea over the English. As regards the more striking military operations, it is curious to remark that Tourville sailed the day after William left Chester, and won Beachy Head the day before the battle of the Boyne; but the real failure lay in permitting William to transport that solid body of men without hindrance. It might have been favorable to French policy to let him get into Ireland, but not with such a force at his back. The result of the Irish campaign was to settle William safely on the English throne and establish the Anglo-Dutch alliance; and the union of the two sea peoples under one crown was the pledge, through their commercial and maritime ability, and the wealth they drew from the sea, of the successful prosecution of the war by their allies on the continent.

The year 1691 was distinguished by only one great maritime event. This was ever afterward known in France as Tourville's "deep-sea" or "off-shore" cruise; and the memory of it as a brilliant strategic and tactical display remains to this day in the French navy. That staying power, which has already been spoken of as distinctive of nations whose sea power is not a mere

行都徒劳无功，根本就没有诱使民众表现出对斯图亚特王朝还有什么留恋之心。

在爱尔兰，情况则不同。博因河之战过后，爱尔兰军队和法军撤到了香农，并在那儿继续负隅顽抗；而待最初的怒气平息下来之后，路易十四也还是继续向这儿派遣了援军，运送了给养。但是，欧洲大陆上的战事日益吃紧，使得他无法提供充足的支援，所以爱尔兰的战事在一年多之后，便以奥赫里姆惨败和利默里克投降[6]而告终。博因河之战，虽说因为有着独特的宗教色彩而获得了不实之名，但我们可以将其视为让威廉在英国的王位牢固地确立起来的日子。不过，更准确一点儿说，威廉获胜以及欧洲各国在奥格斯堡同盟战争中战胜路易十四，原因都在于1690年法国海军在战争中所犯的错误和失败；尽管在那段时间的战斗中，法国获得了在海上对抗英国以来最为显著的单次胜利。至于那些更加突出的军事行动，其中耐人寻味的是，图维尔在威廉离开切斯特的第二天起航，并在博因河之战的前一天赢得了比奇角海战；不过，他真正的失职，仍在于让威廉毫无阻碍地运送充足的英军。让威廉进入爱尔兰，虽说可能对法国的政策有利，但也不应当让他有这样一支部队为自己撑腰才是。爱尔兰战争的结果，便是让威廉安然坐稳了英国的王位，并且确立了英、荷之间的同盟关系；而这两个海上民族统一起来，由同一位君主统治，便成了他们凭借自己的贸易才能、航海才能以及通过海洋获取的财富，在欧洲大陆上联合起来成功地发动战争的保证了。

1691这一年，因为唯——一桩伟大的海洋事件而著称。这就是后来法国人所知的图维尔的"深海"或"离岸"巡航；直至今日，法国海军仍然将其作为一次杰出的战略和战术展示而铭记着。我们业已谈到，此种持久的实力，就是那些制海权并非仅仅是一种军

military institution, but based upon the character and pursuits of the people, had now come into play with the allies. Notwithstanding the defeat and loss of Beachy Head, the united fleets took the sea in 1691 with one hundred ships-of-the-line under the command of Admiral Russell. Tourville could only gather seventy-two, the same number as the year before. "With these he left Brest June 25. As the enemy had not yet appeared upon the coasts of the Channel, he took up his cruising ground at the entrance, sending lookout ships in all directions. Informed that the allies had stationed themselves near the Scilly Islands to cover the passage of a convoy expected from the Levant, Tourville did not hesitate to steer for the English coasts, where the approaching arrival of another merchant fleet from Jamaica was equally expected. Deceiving the English cruisers by false courses, he reached the latter fleet, took from it several ships, and dispersed it before Russell could come up to fight him. When at last Tourville was in presence of the allied fleet, he manoeuvred so skilfully, always keeping the weather-gage, that the enemy, drawn far out into the ocean, lost fifty days without finding an opportunity to engage. During this time French privateers, scattered throughout the Channel, harassed the enemy's commerce and protected convoys sent into Ireland. Worn out by fruitless efforts, Russell steered for the Irish coast. Tourville, after having protected the return of the French convoys, anchored again in Brest Roads."

The actual captures made by Tourville's own fleet were insignificant, but its service to the commerce-destroying warfare of the French, by occupying the allies, is obvious; nevertheless, the loss of English commerce was not as great this year as the next. The chief losses of the allies seem to have been in the Dutch North Sea trade.

The two wars, continental and maritime, that were being waged, though simultaneous, were as yet independent of each other. It is unnecessary in connection with our subject to mention the

事机制、而是以民族性格与追求为基础的民族之特征；如今，此种特征开始对英、荷联军产生影响了。尽管在比奇角海战中战败且损失惨重，但联合舰队在1691年又出海了，当时它有100艘战列舰，由海军上将拉塞尔指挥。图维尔只能集结起72艘，这个数量与前一年是一样的。"他在6月25日率领这支舰队离开了布雷斯特。由于敌人还未在英吉利海峡沿海现身，所以他便占领了海峡入口处的航行区，向各个方向都派出了警戒船。英、荷联合舰队为了保护一队即将从黎凡特而来的商船通过，因而驻扎在离西西里群岛不远的地方；得知这一消息之后，图维尔便毫不犹豫地转向了英国海岸，而另一支从牙买加而来的商船队也将抵达那里。他用假的航向骗过了英国的巡逻舰，赶上了这支商船队，夺取了其中的数艘船只，并且不待拉塞尔赶来与他作战，便将这支船队驱赶得七零八落了。当图维尔最终与联合舰队遭遇之后，他又娴熟地指挥着舰队进行机动，总是占领着有利的上风位置，使得被诱入大洋中的敌军在海上浪费了50天，愣是没有找到交战的机会。而在此期间，散布在整个英吉利海峡上的法国私掠船，则不断袭扰敌人的商船，并且保护着派往爱尔兰的护航队。徒劳无功且筋疲力尽的拉塞尔，便率军前往爱尔兰沿海去了。而图维尔在保护法国护航队返回之后，再一次驻扎回了布雷斯特锚地。"

虽说图维尔所率舰队的实际战利品微不足道，但它通过拖住英、荷联合舰队而对法国进行的贸易破坏战所做的贡献，却是显而易见的；不过这一年中，英国贸易业所遭受的损失，并不像第二年那样严重。英、荷联军主要遭受的，似乎都是荷兰在北海地区的贸易损失。

此时正如火如荼的陆上战争与海上战争虽说是同时进行的，但迄今为止，二者还是相

operations of the former. In 1692 there occurred the great disaster to the French fleet which is known as the battle of La Hougue. In itself, considered tactically, it possesses little importance, and the actual results have been much exaggerated; but popular report has made it one of the famous sea battles of the world, and therefore it cannot be wholly passed by.

Misled by reports from England, and still more by the representations of James, who fondly nursed his belief that the attachment of many English naval officers to his person was greater than their love of country or faithfulness to their trust, Louis XIV. determined to attempt an invasion of the south coast of England, led by James in person. As a first step thereto, Tourville, at the head of between fifty and sixty ships-of-the-line, thirteen of which were to come from Toulon, was to engage the English fleet; from which so many desertions were expected as would, with the consequent demoralization, yield the French an easy and total victory. The first hitch was in the failure of the Toulon fleet, delayed by contrary winds, to join; and Tourville went to sea with only forty-four ships, but with a peremptory order from the king to fight when he fell in with the enemy, were they few or many, and come what might.

On the 29th of May, Tourville saw the allies to the northward and eastward; they numbered ninety-nine sail-of-the-line. The wind being southwest, he had the choice of engaging, but first summoned all the flag-officers on board his own ship, and put the question to them whether he ought to fight. They all said not, and he then handed them the order of the king.[3] No one dared dispute that; though, had they known it, light vessels with contrary orders were even then searching for the fleet. The other officers then returned to their ships, and the whole fleet kept away together for the allies, who waited for them, on the starboard tack, heading south-southeast, the Dutch occupying the van, the English the centre and rear. When they were within easy range, the French hauled their wind on the same tack, keeping the weather-gage.

互独立的。因为与论述的主题无关，所以我们没有必要提及陆上战争中的历次作战行动。1692年，发生了一场给法国舰队带来巨大灾难的海战，史称"拉和岬海战"。假如从战术角度来看，此战本身并不重要，人们对于此战的结果也是言过其实了；不过，由于铺天盖地的报道业已让它成为了世界著名的海战之一，所以我们也无法全然忽视这场海战。

由于被来自英国的那些报告所误导，尤其是被詹姆士二世的话语所误导，路易十四决定派詹姆士二世亲率法军入侵英格兰南部沿海地区；詹姆士二世曾经天真地认为，许多英国海军官兵对他本人的忠心，既超过了他们的爱国之心，也超过了他们对于自己职责的忠诚。作为第一步，图维尔将率领50艘至60艘战列舰——其中有13艘将由土伦调来——打头阵，去与英国舰队交战；法军以为，英国舰队中临阵脱逃者众多，并且士气会因此而低落，所以会让法军轻而易举地打个大胜仗的。但出师后的第一个不利，便是土伦那支舰队由于风向不对而耽搁了，没能与图维尔所率舰队会合；所以，图维尔只带了44艘军舰便出征了。而当他遭遇敌军后，法国国王却又断然下令：不管敌军多寡，无论发生什么情况，他都必须战斗。

5月29日，图维尔看到英、荷联合舰队在北面和东面现身了；联军有99艘战舰。风向为西南，交战与否的选择权掌握在他的手里；但他首先是将所有的将领都召集到自己的船上，问他们该不该交战。将领们都说不行，然后他就把国王的谕令给他们看。[3] 没有人敢再提出异议了；不过，他们并不知道，当时一些轻型舰船正携带着与此相反的命令在搜寻他们这支舰队。其他将领纷纷回到各自的舰船上，整支舰队便散了开来，一齐向联军驶去。联军等待着他们，右舷抢风，航向为东南偏南；荷兰舰队为前锋，英国舰船为中军

Tourville, being so inferior in numbers, could not wholly avoid the enemy's line extending to the rear of his own, which was also necessarily weak from its extreme length; but he avoided Herbert's error at Beachy Head, keeping his van refused with long intervals between the ships, to check the enemy's van, and engaging closely with his centre and rear. It is not necessary to follow the phases of this unequal fight; the extraordinary result was that when the firing ceased at night, in consequence of a thick fog and calm, not a single French ship had struck her colors nor been sunk. No higher proof of military spirit and efficiency could be given by any navy, and Tourville's seamanship and tactical ability contributed largely to the result, which it must also be confessed was not creditable to the allies. The two fleets anchored at nightfall, a body of English ships remaining to the southward and westward of the French Later on, these cut their cables and allowed themselves to drift through the French line in order to rejoin their main body; in doing which they were roughly handled.

  Having amply vindicated the honor of his fleet, and shown the uselessness of further fighting, Tourville now thought of retreat, which was begun at midnight with a light northeast wind and continued all the next day. The allies pursued, the movements of the French being much embarrassed by the crippled condition of the flag-ship "Royal Sun," the finest ship in the French navy, which the admiral could not make up his mind to destroy. The direction of the main retreat was toward the Channel Islands, thirty-five ships being with the admiral; of them twenty passed with the tidal current through the dangerous passage known as the Race of Alderney, between the island of that name and the mainland, and got safe to St. Malo. Before the remaining fifteen could follow, the tide changed; and the anchors which had been dropped dragging, these ships were carried to the eastward and to leeward of the enemy. Three sought refuge in Cherbourg, which had then neither breakwater nor port, the remaining twelve at Cape

和后翼。接近敌军之后，法国人同样右舷抢风，并占据着上风位置。因为兵力大大不如敌军，图维尔根本就无法阻止敌军阵线延伸到自己的后翼去；而由于阵线拉得太长，图维尔后翼的兵力也势必薄弱得很。不过，他避免了赫伯特在比奇角海战中所犯的错误，不让前锋各舰船之间相距太远，以便遏制敌军前锋，并且让中军与后翼紧密结合在一起作战。我们没有必要再来详述这场兵力不对等的战斗的不同阶段了；而结局则令人称奇：到了晚上，因海上起了大雾且风平浪静而停火之后，法国舰船中竟然没有一艘降旗投降，也没有一艘被敌军击沉。可能没有哪一支海军，具有比法国海军更高的军事精神和作战效率了；图维尔的航海技能与战术才能为战斗胜利做出了主要的贡献，而我们也必须承认，英、荷联军在这个方面并不值得称颂。两支舰队都在日落时分都息战泊锚了；但此时仍有一部分英国舰船留在法国舰队的南边和西边。后来，这些舰船为了重新与联军主力会合，便断缆起航，想随波漂流并通过法军阵线；在这一过程中，它们又遭到了法国舰队的猛烈攻击。

  在充分证明了法国舰队的荣耀，并且表明再战无益之后，图维尔便开始考虑撤退，并在正轻轻刮着东北风的午夜开始实行了，而且第二天又继续撤退了一整天。英、荷联军进行了追击，而法军的行动却因旗舰"皇家太阳"号遭到了重创而受阻严重；这艘旗舰是法国海军中最精锐的一艘战船，所以海军上将图维尔下不了决心去毁掉它。法军主力的撤退方向是朝着海峡群岛[7]，图维尔手下当时有35艘舰船跟着；其中有20艘随着潮汐洋流穿过了位于奥尔德尼岛与法国大陆之间的"奥尔德尼湍流"这处有名的危险水道，从而安全地抵达了圣马洛。不待余下的那15艘舰船跟上，洋流便转了向；尽管有锚拽着，这些舰船还是被洋流带着往东并向敌人的下风向漂去。其中有3艘避进了瑟堡，

La Hougue; and they were all burned either by their own crews or by the allies. The French thus lost fifteen of the finest ships in their navy, the least of which carried sixty guns; but this was little more than the loss of the allies at Beachy Head. The impression made upon the public mind, accustomed to the glories and successes of Louis XIV., was out of all proportion to the results, and blotted out the memory of the splendid self-devotion of Tourville and his followers. La Hougue was also the last general action fought by the French fleet, which did rapidly dwindle away in the following years, so that this disaster seemed to be its death-blow. As a matter of fact, however, Tourville went to sea the next year with seventy ships, and the losses were at the time repaired. The decay of the French navy was not due to any one defeat, but to the exhaustion of France and the great cost of the continental war; and this war was mainly sustained by the two sea peoples whose union was secured by the success of William in the Irish campaign. Without asserting that the result would have been different had the naval operations of France been otherwise directed in 1690, it may safely be said that their misdirection was the immediate cause of things turning out as they did, and the first cause of the decay of the French navy.

The five remaining years of the War of the League of Augsburg, in which all Europe was in arms against France, are marked by no great sea battles, nor any single maritime event of the first importance. To appreciate the effect of the sea power of the allies, it is necessary to sum up and condense an account of the quiet, steady pressure which it brought to bear and maintained in all quarters against France. It is thus indeed that sea power usually acts, and just because so quiet in its working, it is the more likely to be unnoticed and must be somewhat carefully pointed out.

The head of the opposition to Louis XIV. was William III., and his tastes being military

当时的瑟堡既无防波堤，又无港口，而剩下的那12艘则避往了拉和岬角；这些舰船，或是被己方的船员，或是被英、荷联军烧毁了。这样一来，法国海军就损失了15艘最为精良的战舰，其中每艘战舰上至少都携带了60门火炮；但是，这种损失不过是比联军在比奇角海战中的损失稍重一点儿罢了。法国民众由于习惯了路易十四的种种荣耀与成功，所以此种损失给他们的印象，完全与此战的结果不相称，使得他们完全不记得图维尔及其手下所做出的杰出牺牲了。拉和岬海战也是法国舰队所进行的最后一场全面作战行动，因为法国舰队在接下来的数年中迅速淡出了人们的记忆，以至于此次惨败似乎就是对法国海军的致命一击。然而，实际上在第二年，图维尔还曾经率领70艘战舰出海，当时拉和岬海战中遭受的损失已经恢复过来了。法国海军的没落，并非是任何一次战败所导致的，而是因法国上下都已经疲惫不堪，以及该国在欧洲大陆上所进行的战争付出了巨大的代价所致；这场战争，主要都是英、荷两国人民在承受，而威廉在爱尔兰战事中所取得的胜利，又确保了这两个海上民族的团结。虽然我们无需断言，说倘若1690年法国海军的作战行动是以其他方式进行指挥的话，可能就会是另一种结果；但我们完全可以说，这些作战行动中的指挥失误，就是出现此种实际结局的直接原因，也是导致法国海军没落下去的首要原因。

在奥格斯堡同盟战争剩下的那5年间，欧洲各国全都武装起来反对法国了；这个时期的特点是，没有发生大规模海战，也没有发生什么重大的海洋事件。为了理解英、荷联军制海权的影响，对于这种影响给所有对抗法国的地区带来并保持的那种无声而稳定的压力，我们必须加以总结和简要说明才行。制海权的影响，通常的确就是这样的；并且，正是因为其作用是如此的悄无声息，所以才更容易为人们所忽视，我们才必须仔细将其指出来。

反对路易十四的领头人是威廉三世，他感兴趣的是陆军而非海军，这一点与路易

rather than naval combined with the direction of Louis' policy to make the active war continental rather than maritime; while the gradual withdrawal of the great French fleets, by leaving the allied navies without enemies on the sea, worked in the same way. Furthermore, the efficiency of the English navy, which was double in numbers that of the Dutch, was at this time at a low pitch; the demoralizing effects of the reign of Charles II. could not be wholly overcome during the three years of his brother's rule, and there was a yet more serious cause of trouble growing out of the political state of England. It has been said that James believed the naval officers and seamen to be attached to his person; and, whether justly or unjustly, this thought was also in the minds of the present rulers, causing doubts of the loyalty and trustworthiness of many officers, and tending to bring confusion into the naval administration. We are told that "the complaints made by the merchants were extremely well supported, and showed the folly of preferring unqualified men to that board which directed the naval power of England; and yet the mischief could not be amended, because the more experienced people who had been long in the service were thought disaffected, and it appeared the remedy might have proved worse than the disease." Suspicion reigned in the cabinet and the city, factions and irresolution among the officers; and a man who was unfortunate or incapable in action knew that the yet more serious charge of treason might follow his misadventure.

After La Hougue, the direct military action of the allied navies was exerted in three principal ways, the first being in attacks upon the French ports, especially those in the Channel and near Brest. These had rarely in view more than local injury and the destruction of shipping, particularly in the ports whence the French privateers issued; and although on some occasions the number of troops embarked was large, William proposed to himself little more than the

十四的政策方向结合起来，便使得双方之间的战争主要都发生在大陆上，而不是发生在海洋上；而法国舰队逐渐没落，使得英、荷两国的联合海军在海上没有了敌手，所起的作用也与此相同。此外，英国海军虽说兵力两倍于荷兰海军，但其作战效率此时正处于低谷之中；查理二世在位时所造成的那种令人沮丧的影响，是不可能在其兄弟的3年统治期里得以彻底消除的，并且，英格兰的政治形势还产生了一个更加严重、导致麻烦的问题。前面已经说过，詹姆士二世认为海军官兵和海员都对他本人都很有感情；而不管有没有理由，英国现任的这位君主心里也有着此种想法，从而导致他对许多将领的忠诚度与可靠性产生了疑忌，常常给海军的行政管理带来困惑。我们得知，"商务人士所发的牢骚极为有理，表明让无法胜任的人去指挥英国的海上力量是非常荒唐的；可这种危害却没法改正，因为那些在海军中服役很久、较有经验的人，都被认为有不忠思想，所以纠正措施似乎比弊病本身更加糟糕。"内阁和城市里猜忌之风盛行，官兵当中派系和骑墙者林立；在战斗中运气不好或者无能胜任的人，都明白在战斗中不幸地遭遇失败之后，自己可能还会遭到更加严重的叛国指控。

在拉和岬海战后，英、荷两国联合海军直接的军事行动，是通过三种主要的方式来实施的。首先是攻击法国的各个港口，尤其是那些位于英吉利海峡沿岸和布雷斯特附近的海港。这些行动，一般只会造成局部损失和舰船损毁，尤其是让派出私掠船的那些法国海港遭受局部损失，而罕有其他效果；尽管在某些情况下投入的部队数量众多，但威廉也只会进行此种威胁所导致的佯动，迫使路易十四从战场回师进行海岸防御。可以说，在拉和岬海战和后来的历次战争中，针对法国海岸而实施的所有作战计划，普遍都没有什么效果；即便是作为一种佯动，也并未在多大程度上削弱法国陆军的实力。假如

diversion which such threats caused, by forcing Louis to take troops from the field for coast defence. It may be said generally of all these enterprises against the French coast, in this and later wars, that they effected little, and even as a diversion did not weaken the French armies to any great extent. If the French ports had been less well defended, or French water-ways open into the heart of the country, like our own Chesapeake and Delaware bays and the Southern sounds, the result might have been different.

In the second place, the allied navies were of great direct military value, though they fought no battles, when Louis XIV. decided in 1694 to make his war against Spain offensive. Spain, though so weak in herself, was yet troublesome from her position in the rear of France; and Louis finally concluded to force her to peace by carrying the war into Catalonia, on the northeast coast. The movement of his armies was seconded by his fleet under Tourville; and the reduction of that difficult province went on rapidly until the approach of the allied navies in largely superior force caused Tourville to retire to Toulon. This saved Barcelona; and from that time until the two sea nations had determined to make peace, they kept their fleets on the Spanish coast and arrested the French advance. When, in 1697, William had become disposed to peace and Spain refused it, Louis again invaded, the allied fleet did not appear, and Barcelona fell. At the same time a French naval expedition was successfully directed against Cartagena in South America, and under the two blows, both of which depended upon the control of the sea, Spain yielded.

The third military function of the allied navies was the protection of their sea commerce; and herein, if history may be trusted, they greatly failed. At no time has war against commerce been conducted on a larger scale and with greater results than during this period; and its operations were widest and most devastating at the very time that the great French fleets were

法国诸港防守得不是那么好，或者假如法国的河流直通该国腹地，就像我国的切萨皮克湾、特拉华湾以及南方诸峡湾一样，那么就会是一种不同的结局了。

其次，英、荷联合海军具有极大而直接的军事意义，尽管自1694年路易十四决定进攻西班牙以来，两国联合海军并未真正作过战。西班牙本身实力非常薄弱，但由于它身处法国后方，所以还是让法国觉得很麻烦；因此路易十四最终决定，通过将战火烧至其东北沿海的加泰罗尼亚，来迫使西班牙签署和约。法国陆军的作战运动，由图维尔所率的舰队进行支援；于是，加泰罗尼亚这个困难重重的行省迅速被法军蚕食，直至英、荷联合海军率大批优势兵力赶来，才使图维尔撤回了土伦。这样，巴塞罗那就幸免于陷入法军之手了；自那时起，直到英、法这两个海洋国家决定议和为止，英、荷联合舰队一直都游弋于西班牙沿海地区，以阻止法军继续进击。1697年，当威廉有意言和而西班牙却拒绝议和之后，路易十四便再次入侵了西班牙；这一次，联合舰队没有赶来，于是巴塞罗那就被法军攻陷了。与此同时，一支法国海军远征军成功地对南美洲的卡塔赫纳发起了攻击；在这双重打击下——两种打击所依赖的都是制海权——西班牙便投降了。

联合海军的第三种军事功能，便是保护两国的海上贸易；而在这一点上，倘若历史记载可信的话，那么它们在很大程度上并未做到。跟这一时期相比，历史上还没有哪个时代，有哪个国家针对贸易发动过规模更大、结果也更重要的战争；而这些军事行动范围最广、最具毁灭性的时候，也正是伟大的法国舰队在拉和岬海战之后数年间日益销声匿迹的时候，因此，这种情况显然与"此种战争必须以强大的舰队或以附近强大的海港为基础"的论断相矛盾。对此，我们应当加以详细讨论，因为私掠船给商业贸易所带来的灾难，是

disappearing, in the years immediately after La Hougue, apparently contradicting the assertion that such a warfare must be based on powerful fleets or neighboring seaports. A somewhat full discussion is due, inasmuch as the distress to commerce wrought by the privateers was a large factor in bringing the sea nations to wish for peace; just as the subsidies, which their commerce enabled them to pay the continental armies, besides keeping up their own, were the chief means by which the war was prolonged and France brought to terms. The attack and defence of commerce is still a living question.

In the first place it is to be observed that the decay of the French fleet was gradual, and that the moral effect of its appearance in the Channel, its victory at Beachy Head, and gallant conduct at La Hougue remained for some time impressed on the minds of the allies. This impression caused their ships to be kept together in fleets, instead of scattering in pursuit of the enemy's cruisers, and so brought to the latter a support almost equal to an active warfare on the seas. Again, the efficiency of the English navy, as has been said, was low, and its administration perhaps worse; while treason in England gave the French the advantage of better information. Thus in the year following La Hougue, the French, having received accurate information of a great convoy sailing for Smyrna, sent out Tourville in May, getting him to sea before the allies were ready to blockade him in Brest, as they had intended. This delay was due to bad administration, as was also the further misfortune that the English government did not learn of Tourville's departure until after its own fleet had sailed with the trade. Tourville surprised the convoy near the Straits, destroyed or captured one hundred out of four hundred ships, and scattered the rest. This is not a case of simple cruising warfare, for Tourville's fleet was of seventy-one ships; but it shows the incompetency of the English administration. In truth, it was immediately after La Hougue that the depredations of cruisers became most ruinous; and the

导致海洋国家希望和平的一个重要因素；正如财政补贴是它们拖延战争并迫使法国接受条件的主要方式一样——这些国家的商业贸易，使得它们既能够维持各自的陆军，还能对大陆军团进行财政补贴。所以，贸易上的攻防这个问题，直到如今也依然存在。

首先我们必须注意到，法国舰队的没落是一个渐进的过程，而法国舰队出现在英吉利海峡、在比奇角海战中获胜以及在拉和岬海战中的英勇行为所产生的心理效果，都在联合海军官兵们的心里长久地留下了深刻的印象。此种印象，使得两国的船只在舰队中都抱成一团，不再在追击敌军巡洋舰的过程中有如一盘散沙并各自为战，不再让敌军的巡洋舰有了喘息之机，从而不让敌军几乎获得了进行一场有力之海战的勇气。此外，我们已经说过，英国海军的作战效率低下，而其指挥管理或许更加糟糕；而英格兰的叛国者又让法国人具有了获得更准确情报的优势。所以，在拉和岬海战之后的第二年，法国人才获得了准确的情报，得知有一支大型的商船队准备前往士麦那[8]；由于英、荷联军打算将图维尔封锁在布雷斯特，法国人便在5月份派图维尔赶在联军准备好封锁之前出了海。联军之所以耽搁了封锁，完全是由于管理不善；而更糟糕的是，英国政府直到本国舰队跟着商船队起航之后，才得知图维尔出发的消息。图维尔在直布罗陀海峡附近突然出现，吓了护航队一大跳，然后便击毁和俘虏了这支护航队总计400艘舰船中的100艘，并将其余舰船打得七零八落。这并不是一次单纯的巡航战，因为图维尔所率的舰队有71艘战舰；不过，这也表明了英国政府的无能。的确，正是在拉和岬海战之后不久，巡逻舰的劫掠才开始变得极具破坏性；而导致这一结果的原因有两个：首先，联合舰队在斯皮特海德集结了两个多月，准备集结军队登上欧洲大陆，这才使得法国的巡洋舰在海上畅通无阻；其次，法国由于当

reason was twofold: first, the allied fleet was kept together at Spithead for two months and more, gathering troops for a landing on the continent, thus leaving the cruisers unmolested; and in the second place, the French, not being able to send their fleet out again that summer, permitted the seamen to take service in private ships, thus largely increasing the numbers of the latter. The two causes working together gave an impunity and extension to commerce-destroying which caused a tremendous outcry in England. "It must be confessed," says the English naval chronicler, "that our commerce suffered far less the year before, when the French were masters at sea, than in this, when their grand fleet was blocked up in port." But the reason was that the French having little commerce and a comparatively large number of seamen, mainly employed in the fleet, were able, when this lay by, to release them to cruisers. As the pressure of the war became greater, and Louis continued to reduce the number of his ships in commission, another increase was given to the commerce-destroyers. "The ships and officers of the royal navy were loaned, under certain conditions, to private firms, or to companies who wished to undertake privateering enterprises, in which even the cabinet ministers did not disdain to take shares;" indeed, they were urged to do so to please the king. The conditions generally provided that a certain proportion of the profits should go to the king, in return for the use of the ships. Such employment would be demoralizing to any military service, but not necessarily all at once; and the conditions imparted for the time a tone and energy to privateering that it cannot always have. In truth, the public treasury, not being able to maintain the navy, associated with itself private capital, risking only material otherwise useless, and looking for returns to robbing the enemy. The commerce-destroying of this war, also, was no mere business of single cruisers; squadrons of three or four up to half a dozen ships acted together under one man, and it is only just to say that under seamen like Jean Bart, Forbin, and Duguay-Trouin, they were even

年夏天无法再派遣舰队出海，便允许水兵去私人舰船上服役，从而极大地增加了私掠船的数量。这两个原因结合起来，便使得这种贸易破坏活动既安全，波及范围又很广，从而在英国国内引发了巨大的抗议之声。"必须承认，"那位英国海军编年史作家说，"在法国人称霸海上的去年，我国贸易所遭受的损失，要比法国的大型舰队被封锁在港内的今年低得多。"不过，此种情况的原因，却在于法国贸易规模小、海员人数却相对较多，这些海员主要都是在舰队里服役，所以当舰队不出海的时候，就能将他们转到巡洋舰上去。由于战争的压力变得越来越大，路易十四不断地削减现役军舰的数量，所以贸易破坏船的数量就增加了。"皇家海军的舰船和官兵，在一定条件下被租借给一些私营公司或者其他一些希望进行武装私掠的公司；就算是那些内阁大臣们，也都不会对自己在这一行业里所占的份额嗤之以鼻。"事实上，他们是为了取悦国王，才去这样做的。这种条件通常会规定，私掠所得的一部分收益应归于国王，以此作为使用舰船的回报。此种工作，对于任何兵役制度来说，都会导致士气低落的问题，但其后果却并不一定马上会显现出来；这些条件传递出了当时进行私掠的风气与干劲，而这种风气与干劲是不可能一直存在的。事实上，公共财政由于无法维持海军的支出，便与私人资本结合起来，这样它就只要承担放在别处并无所用的物质上的损失，并且寄望通过掠夺敌人而获取回报就行了。此战中的贸易破坏活动，也并非仅仅是单艘巡洋舰的事情；法国的贸易破坏活动，往往是由三四艘，甚至是由多至6艘舰船组成一支小型舰队，在某一个人的指挥之下协同进行的；并且公正地来说，在让·巴尔、福尔班和杜瓦-特鲁安之流的水兵领导下，这些小型舰队是更乐意去与敌作战，而不愿去劫掠财物的。其中最大的一支，并且是唯一一支远离法国沿海的私人远征

more ready to fight than to pillage. The largest of these private expeditions, and the only one that went far from the French shores, was directed in 1697 against Cartagena, on the Spanish Main. It numbered seven ships-of-the-line and six frigates, besides smaller vessels, and carried twenty-eight hundred troops. The chief object was to lay a contribution on the city of Cartagena; but its effect on the policy of Spain was marked, and led to peace. Such a temper and concert of action went far to supply the place of supporting fleets, but could not wholly do so; and although the allies continued to keep their large fleets together, still, as the war went on and efficiency of administration improved, commerce-destroying was brought within bounds. At the same time, as an evidence of how much the unsupported cruisers suffered, even under these favorable conditions, it may be mentioned that the English report fifty-nine ships-of-war captured against eighteen admitted by the French during the war, — a difference which a French naval historian attributes, with much probability, to the English failing to distinguish between ships-of-war properly so called, and those loaned to private firms. Captures of actual privateers do not appear in the list quoted from. "The commerce-destroying of this war, therefore, was marked by the particular characteristics of cruisers acting together in squadron, not far from their base, while the enemy thought best to keep his fleet concentrated elsewhere; notwithstanding which, and the bad administration of the English navy, the cruisers were more and more controlled as the great French fleets disappeared." The results of the war of 1689-1697 do not therefore vitiate the general conclusion that "a cruising, commerce-destroying warfare, to be destructive, must be seconded by a squadron warfare, and by divisions of ships-of-the-line; which, forcing the enemy to unite his forces, permit the cruisers to make fortunate attempts upon his trade. Without such backing the result will be simply the capture of the cruisers." Toward the end of this war the real tendency was becoming manifest, and was still more plainly seen in the next,

队，在1697年对拉丁美洲北部的卡塔赫纳发动了袭击。远征队有7艘战列舰和6艘护卫舰，还有一些小型舰船以及2800名士兵。此战的首要目标，便是向卡塔赫纳市征收捐税；但此战对西班牙政策的影响也是很显著的，于是两国便议和了。这种性质的一致行动，虽说极大地有助于为舰队支援提供场所，但并不能统统这样干；并且，尽管联军继续将大量舰队汇集一处，但由于战争还在进行，行政效率也已改善，所以贸易破坏活动还是保持在允许的范围之内。与此同时，我们还可以提一提此战中英国人的一份报告——这份报告称，他们俘虏了59艘战舰，而法国人却只承认被俘了18艘——以此作为那些没有支援力量的巡洋舰即便是在如此有利的条件下也损失惨重的证据。一位法国的海军历史学家曾经十分肯定地将这种分歧，归因于英国人没有区分那些可以称作真正的战舰的船只与那些租借给私人公司的船只。在所引述的名单中，并没有实际上属于私掠船的舰船被俘记录。"因此，这场战争中贸易破坏活动的标志，便是以巡洋舰组成小型舰队、待敌人认为最好将其舰队集结于别处时，在离基地不远的海域协同行动这些独特的特点；尽管如此，也尽管英国海军的管理糟糕得很，但随着伟大的法国舰队销声匿迹，这些巡洋舰的行动便日益捉襟见肘起来。"所以，1689年至1697年间这场战争的结果，与下述一般性结论并不矛盾："一种巡航贸易破坏战要想给敌人以毁灭性的打击，就必须得到作战舰队和战舰小分队的支援；这样就会迫使敌人将兵力集中起来，从而使得巡洋舰可以顺利地去攻击敌人的贸易船队。倘若没有这样的支援，结果就只是让那些巡洋舰白白地去送死。"到此次战争结束的时候，这种趋势正日益变得明显起来；而在下一次战争中，当法国海军已经陷入到一种更加羸弱的状态时，这种趋势也就更加显而易见了。

when the French navy had sunk to a yet lower state of weakness.

Notwithstanding their losses, the sea nations made good their cause. The war, which began with the French taking the offensive, ended by reducing them everywhere to the defensive, and forced Louis to do violence at once to his strongest prejudices and his most reasonable political wishes, by recognizing as king of England him whom he looked upon as a usurper as well as his own inveterate enemy. On its surface, and taken as a whole, this war will appear almost wholly a land struggle, extending from the Spanish Netherlands down the line of the Rhine, to Savoy in Italy and Catalonia in Spain. The sea fights in the Channel, the Irish struggle receding in the distance, look like mere episodes; while the underlying action of trade and commerce is wholly disregarded, or noticed only as their outcries tell of their sufferings. Yet trade and shipping not only bore the burden of suffering, but in the main paid the armies that were fighting the French; and this turning of the stream of wealth from both sea nations into the coffers of their allies was perhaps determined, certainly hastened, by the misdirection of that naval supremacy with which France began the war. It was then possible, as it will usually be possible, for a really fine military navy of superior force to strike an overwhelming blow at a less ready rival; but the opportunity was allowed to slip, and the essentially stronger, better founded sea power of the allies had time to assert itself.

The peace signed at Ryswick in 1697 was most disadvantageous to France; she lost all that had been gained since the Peace of Nimeguen, nineteen years before, with the single important exception of Strasburg. All that Louis XIV. had gained by trick or force during the years of peace was given up. Immense restitutions were made to Germany and to Spain. In so far as the latter were made in the Netherlands, they were to the immediate advantage of the United

尽管损失颇大，但英、荷两个海洋国家却都蒸蒸日上地发展起来了。此次战争，以法国发动进攻开始，又以压制住法国、使得法国处处被动防御而告结束，还迫使路易十四违背他自己那种最根深蒂固的成见，违背他那些最合理的政治抱负，不得不承认威廉这个他视为篡位者且与他势不两立的仇敌是英国国王。从表面上和整体上来看，这场战争似乎差不多完全是一场陆上战争，从西属尼德兰始，沿莱茵河而下，直至意大利的萨伏伊和西班牙的加泰罗尼亚。英吉利海峡中的数次作战与渐渐消弭的爱尔兰战事，看起来不过都是一些小小的插曲罢了；而在贸易和商业领域内所进行的隐形战争，却全然被人们忽视了，或者只是在商人们抗议自己遭受了损失的时候，才被人们注意到。然而，贸易和海运业非但承受了损失，还基本上提供了支撑陆军与法国作战的军费开支；而财富从这两个海洋国家转而流向其联合舰队的小金库，则可能是由法国发动战争凭借的那种制海权的误导所决定的，并且自然也因此种误导而加快了速度。因此，一支拥有优势兵力、真正精良的海军，是有可能、并且通常都可以对一个准备没有那么充分的敌人发动势不可挡的打击的；但由于法国错失了机会，所以联合舰队那种本来就更强大、基础也更牢固的制海权，还是有时间来维护其实力的。

1697年于里斯维克签署的那份和约，对法国来说是极为不利的；该国失去了自19年前签署《奈梅亨和约》以来获得的全部领土，只有一个重要的例外，那就是没有失去斯特拉斯堡。路易十四在和平时期通过阴谋诡计或者通过武力所获取的一切，都不得不放弃了。该国还向德国和西班牙支付了巨额赔偿。由于赔偿西班牙是在尼德兰进行的，所以此种赔偿直接有利于荷兰共和国，并且事实上也给整个欧洲和西班牙带来了直接的好处。这份条约为英、荷两个海洋国家带来了商业利益，从而有利于两国的制海权，还相

Provinces, and indeed of all Europe as well as of Spain. To the two sea nations the terms of the treaty gave commercial benefits, which tended to the increase of their own sea power and to the consequent injury of that of France.

France had made a gigantic struggle; to stand alone as she did then, and as she has since done more than once, against all Europe is a great feat. Yet it may be said that as the United Provinces taught the lesson that a nation, however active and enterprising, cannot rest upon external resources alone, if intrinsically weak in numbers and territory, so France in its measure shows that a nation cannot subsist indefinitely off itself, however powerful in numbers and strong in internal resources.

It is said that a friend once found Colbert looking dreamily from his windows, and on questioning him as to the subject of his meditations, received this reply: "In contemplating the fertile fields before my eyes, I recall those which I have seen elsewhere; what a rich country is France!" This conviction supported him amid the many discouragements of his official life, when struggling to meet the financial difficulties arising from the extravagance and wars of the king; and it has been justified by the whole course of the nation's history since his days. France is rich in natural resources as well as in the industry and thrift of her people. But neither individual nations nor men can thrive when severed from natural intercourse with their kind; whatever the native vigor of constitution, it requires healthful surroundings, and freedom to draw to itself from near and from far all that is conducive to its growth and strength and general welfare. Not only must the internal organism work satisfactorily, the processes of decay and renewal, of movement and circulation, go on easily, but, from sources external to themselves, both mind and body must receive healthful and varied nourishment. With all

应地削弱了法国的制海权。

法国已经做出了巨大的努力；像当时这样，像它已经不止一次地孤身对抗整个欧洲那样，都算得上是一种伟大的壮举。不过我们可以说，由于荷兰共和国已经给了我们教训，说一个国家无论是多么的积极进取，倘若其人口数量和领土面积根本不大的话，就决不能只倚赖于外部资源，所以衡量一下法国我们就明白，一个国家无论人口数量如何庞大、内部资源如何丰富，也都绝不可能无限制地倚赖自身而存在下去。

据说，有位朋友曾经发现柯尔贝尔出神地望着窗外，便问他在沉思些什么，柯尔贝尔回答道："看着眼前这些肥田沃土，我想起了在别处所看到的那些土地；法国是多么富饶的一个国度啊！"此种信念，支撑着他在自己的仕途生涯中度过了诸多的挫折，努力解决了因国王的奢侈浪费和穷兵黩武而导致的种种财政难题；而该国历史自他那个时代以来的总体进程，也已证明他的这种信念是正确的。法国的自然资源丰富，工业生产发达，人口增长也很兴旺，但无论是国家还是个人，倘若割断了与他国或他人之间的自然交往，便都是不可能兴旺发达起来的；无论其体制或者体格天生具有什么样的活力，国家或个人都需要有一个健全的环境，都需要有自由，以便将远近各处凡是有益于其成长、有益于其实力、有益于其公共福利的一切，全都吸引到身边来。非但是内部机体必须运行良好，去腐存新的过程和运动、循环的过程必须顺畅进行，而且身心两方面也都必须从外部资源中获得健康而多样的滋养才行。尽管有着丰富的自然资源，法国却日渐没落下去，原因即在于它本身各个部位之间缺乏那种充满活力的相互交流，而法兰西与别的民族也缺少一贯的交往——这种交流和交往，即是我们所知的商业贸易，亦即国内贸易和国外贸易。说战争是导致出现这些缺陷的原因，至少是指出了部分事实；不过，

her natural gifts France wasted away because of the want of that lively intercourse between the different parts of her own body and constant exchange with other people, which is known as commerce, internal or external. To say that war was the cause of these defects is to state at least a partial truth; but it does not exhaust the matter. War, with its many acknowledged sufferings, is above all harmful when it cuts a nation off from others and throws it back upon itself. There may indeed be periods when such rude shocks have a bracing effect, but they are exceptional, and of short duration, and they do not invalidate the general statement. Such isolation was the lot of France during the later wars of Louis XIV., and it well-nigh destroyed her; whereas to save her from the possibility of such stagnation was the great aim of Colbert's life.

War alone could not entail it, if only war could be postponed until the processes of circulation within and without the kingdom were established and in vigorous operation. They did not exist when he took office; they had to be both created and firmly rooted in order to withstand the blast of war. Time was not given to accomplish this great work, nor did Louis XIV. support the schemes of his minister by turning the budding energies of his docile and devoted subjects into paths favorable to it. So when the great strain came upon the powers of the nation, instead of drawing strength from every quarter and through many channels, and laying the whole outside world under contribution by the energy of its merchants and seamen, as England has done in like straits, it was thrown back upon itself, cut off from the world by the navies of England and Holland, and the girdle of enemies which surrounded it upon the continent. The only escape from this process of gradual starvation was by an effectual control of the sea; the creation of a strong sea power which should insure free play for the wealth of the land and the industry of the people. For this, too, France had great natural advantages in her three seaboards,

此种说法并没有彻底地说明这个问题。世人公认会带来诸多苦难的战争，一旦将一个国家与别的国家割裂开来并迫使它不得不完全依赖自身，首先就是有害的。的确，可能也有此种猛烈打击产生了鼓舞人心之效果的时期，不过，这属于例外情况，其存在时间不会长久，而且这种情况与我们所得的普遍结论也并不相左。在路易十四后来进行的历次战争中，法国正是处于这样的一种孤立状态，也正是这种孤立，差不多毁灭了整个法国；而柯尔贝尔一生的伟大目标，就是将法国从此种毫无希望的可能性中挽救出来。

仅凭战争，是不可能挽救法国的；只有当战争能够推迟，直至法国国内与国外的诸多循环过程已经稳定下来，并且发挥强大作用的时候，才能做到这一点。柯尔贝尔上任的时候，这种情况并不存在；它们既需开创，也需牢固地扎下根来，才能承受住战争的考验。他没有时间来完成这一伟业，而路易十四也并不支持这位大臣的计划，并不赞同将本国顺从而忠心的臣民那种崭露头角的精力，转到有利于这一伟业的道路上去。所以，等到巨大的压力降临到国家权力头上之后，法国并未像英国处在相似困境中所做的那样，没有从各个地区、通过多种途径汲取力量，也没有通过本国商人和海员的力量而让整个外部世界为本国做出贡献，而是被迫完全倚赖于自己，在海上被英、荷两国海军、在大陆上则被其他敌人重重包围，从而割断了该国与世界的联系。从这种逐渐被饿死的过程中逃脱出来的唯一之法，便是有效地控制海洋；便是开创一种可以确保国家财富与人民的勤劳得到自由发挥的强大制海权。对于这一点，法国也拥有巨大的自然优势，因为它拥有三大沿海地区，即英吉利海峡沿海、大西洋沿海和地中海沿岸；而在政治上，它也有过很好的机会，能够与荷兰结成友好同盟，从而将荷兰的海上力量与本国的

on the Channel, the Atlantic, and the Mediterranean; and politically she had had the fair opportunity of joining to her own maritime power that of the Dutch in friendly alliance, hostile or at least wary toward England. In the pride of his strength, conscious of absolute control in his kingdom, Louis cast away this strong reinforcement to his power, and proceeded to rouse Europe against him by repeated aggressions. In the period which we have just considered, France justified his confidence by a magnificent, and upon the whole successful, maintenance of his attitude against all Europe; she did not advance, but neither did she greatly recede. But this display of power was exhausting; it ate away the life of the nation, because it drew wholly upon itself and not upon the outside world, with which it could have been kept in contact by the sea. In the war that next followed, the same energy is seen, but not the same vitality; and France was everywhere beaten back and brought to the verge of ruin. The lesson of both is the same; nations, like men, however strong, decay when cut off from the external activities and resources which at once draw out and support their internal powers. A nation, as we have already shown, cannot live indefinitely off itself, and the easiest way by which it can communicate with other peoples and renew its own strength is the sea.

FOOTNOTES:
(1) Ledyard says the order to remove the buoys was not carried out (Naval History, vol. ii. p. 636).
(2) Seignelay, the French minister of marine of the day, called him "poltron de tête, mais pas de coeur."
(3) The author has followed in the text the traditional and generally accepted account of Tourville's orders and the motives of his action. A French writer, M. de Crisenoy, in a very interesting paper upon the secret history preceding and accompanying the event, traverses many of these traditional statements. According to him, Louis XIV. was not under any illusion as to the loyalty of the English officers to their flag; and the instructions

海上力量结合起来，与英国为敌，或者起码也会让英国不敢轻举妄动。由于对自己的实力过于自负，并且知道自己绝对掌控着法国，所以路易十四抛弃了这种本来可以有力地加强其权力的势力，并且通过反复的挑衅，开始激起英国对自己的敌意。在我们刚刚讨论过的那个时期，法国出色、全面而成功地维护了他反对整个欧洲的态度，从而使得他的自信有了充分的理由；虽说该国并未向前发展，但也没有什么重大的倒退。不过，此种权力展示是消耗性的；它侵蚀掉了该国的活力，因为它汲取的全然是本国的资源，而不是外部世界的资源，何况该国本来是可以通过海洋与外部世界保持联系的。在接下来发生的这场战争中，我们虽然看到了同样的力量，但这种力量却没有了同样的生命力；因而法国到处都被打得节节败退，已经到了亡国的边缘。这两次教训都是相同的；国家跟个人一样，无论有多么强大，一旦将其与曾经导致并且支撑其内部权力的外部活动和资源割裂开来，便会衰落下去。正如我们业已表明的那样，一个国家是不可能永远倚赖自身存在下去的，而它可以与其他民族进行交流并复兴自己实力最容易的一条途径，便是海洋。

原注：
（1）莱迪亚德称，移除浮标的命令并未执行（《海军历史》，第二卷，第636页）。
（2）当时法国的海军大臣塞格莱称他为"谨慎，但缺乏信心"。
（3）在本文中，作者是遵循传统的、世人所公认的方式，来描述图维尔的命令及其行为动机的。法国史学家M·德·克里斯诺伊在一篇论述这一事件之前和事件当时秘史的论文中，否定了这些传统表述中的许多说法，很有意思。根据他的观点，对于英国海军官兵的爱国之心，路易十四根

given to Tourville, while peremptory under certain conditions, did not compel him to fight in the situation of the French fleet on the day of the battle. The tone of the instructions, however, implied dissatisfaction with the admiral's action in previous cruises, probably in the pursuit after Beachy Head, and a consequent doubt of his vigor in the campaign then beginning. Mortification therefore impelled him to the desperate attack on the allied fleet; and, according to M. de Crisenoy, the council of war in the admiral's cabin, and the dramatic production of the king's orders, had no existence in fact.

本就没有抱任何幻想；而他给图维尔所下的命令，虽说在某些情形下具有强制性，但并没有在战斗打响当天法国舰队所处的那种形势下强令他去作战。不过，这道命令的语气，却隐含着路易十四对这位海军将领在以前巡航作战中的行动感到不满，很可能是对他在比奇角海战后的追击过程中的做法不满，以及因此而对他在刚刚开始的这场战役中的精神有所疑虑。因此，是羞愧感迫使图维尔孤注一掷地对英、荷联合舰队发动了进攻；并且，根据M·德·克里斯诺伊的说法，在这位海军上将座舱里召开的作战会议，以及他戏剧性地出示国王命令的情节，事实上根本就不存在。

译者注：

[1] 本章为原文中第四章。第三章"1672-1674年间的英、法联合对荷战争"（War of England and France in Alliance against the United Provinces, 1672-1674）由于涉及的是具体的战争经过，故略去未译。后续各章序号也照此类推。

[2] League of Augsburg：奥格斯堡同盟。反对法王路易十四的欧洲诸国于1686年7月在德国奥格斯堡成立的一个同盟，1689年后改称"大同盟"。参与国有奥地利、荷兰、葡萄牙、西班牙和巴伐利亚等。

[3] Peace of Nimeguen：《奈梅亨和约》。1678年8月法、荷两国在如今荷兰与德国交界处的奈梅亨所签署的一份和约，标志着法、荷战争结束。

[4] Londonderry：伦敦德里。爱尔兰西北角的一个城市，伦敦德里郡的首府。1689年冬季，詹姆士二世与法、爱联军将爱尔兰残余的英军围困于此，史称"围困伦敦德里"。由于在此次围城中，伦敦德里的城墙从未被炮弹击穿过，故此处获得了"处女城（Maiden City）"的绰号。

[5] Shannon：香农河。今爱尔兰共和国中西部的一条河流，也是爱尔兰最长的河流。

[6] Limerick：利默里克。爱尔兰著名港市，位于香农河畔。1691年支持詹姆士二世的爱尔兰军队和法军在此向威廉投降。前面的Aghrim（奥赫里姆）是香农河畔的一个村庄。

[7] the Channel Islands：海峡群岛。位于法国科唐坦半岛西北、圣马洛湾入口处的英吉利海峡中，由泽西岛、根西岛、奥尔德尼岛和萨克岛等组成，属于英王领地。在法语中被称作"诺曼底群岛"。

[8] Smyrna：士麦那。土耳其西部的港口城市，现称伊兹密尔。

CHAPTER IV War of the Spanish Succession, 1702-1713

Sea Battle of Malaga.

During the last thirty years of the seventeenth century, amid all the strifes of arms and diplomacy, there had been clearly foreseen the coming of an event which would raise new and great issues. This was the failure of the direct royal line in that branch of the House of Austria which was then on the Spanish throne; and the issues to be determined when the present king, infirm both in body and mind, should die, were whether the new monarch was to be taken from the House of Bourbon or from the Austrian family in Germany; and whether, in either event, the sovereign thus raised to the throne should succeed to the entire inheritance, the Empire of Spain, or some partition of that vast inheritance be made in the interests of the balance of European power. But this balance of power was no longer understood in the narrow sense of continental possessions; the effect of the new arrangements upon commerce, shipping, and the control both of the ocean and the Mediterranean, was closely looked to. The influence of the two sea powers and the nature of their interests were becoming more evident.

It is necessary to recall the various countries that were ruled by Spain at that time in order to understand the strategic questions, as they may fairly be called, now to be settled. These were, in Europe, the Netherlands (now Belgium); Naples and the south of Italy; Milan and other provinces in the north; and, in the Mediterranean, Sicily, Sardinia, and the Balearic

第四章　1702-1713年间的西班牙王位继承战争

马拉加海战

在17世纪最后的30年里，人们从种种武装冲突与外交纷争当中已经清楚地预见到，即将发生一桩会引发诸多新的重大问题的事件。这就是，当时仍然据有西班牙王位的这一支哈布斯堡皇室没有后嗣，皇家直系血统断裂了；要是体弱多病、意志也很不坚定的现任国王一死，那么就需要决断下述问题：新主是应当从波旁王室中选取呢，还是应当从德国的哈布斯堡皇族中选取；并且，无论是哪种情况，新登基的君主是应当完全继承王室的遗产，即整个西班牙帝国呢，还是应当将这笔巨大遗产中的一部分用来平衡欧洲各国的势力。不过，人们已经不再狭隘地将这种力量平衡，理解为各国在欧洲大陆上所占领土的多少了；人们也密切关注着此种新的局面对于商业贸易、海洋运输以及对大西洋与地中海的控制权会产生什么样的影响。此时，两个海洋大国以及它们利益的性质，已经变得日益明显起来了。

为了理解此时应当解决的那些战略问题——这些问题完全可以称作是战略问题——我们必须回想一下当时西班牙帝国所统治的那些国家。在欧洲有尼德兰（即如今的比利时）；那不勒斯和意大利南部；米兰和其他北部行省；在地中海地区有西西里、撒丁和

Isles. Corsica at that time belonged to Genoa. In the western hemisphere, besides Cuba and Porto Rico, Spain then held all that part of the continent now divided among the Spanish American States, a region whose vast commercial possibilities were coming to be understood; and in the Asian archipelago there were large possessions that entered less into the present dispute. The excessive weakness of this empire, owing to the decay of the central kingdom, had hitherto caused other nations, occupied as they were with more immediate interests, to regard with indifference its enormous extent. This indifference could not last when there was a prospect of a stronger administration, backed possibly by alliances with one of the great powers of Europe.

It would be foreign to our subject to enter into the details of diplomatic arrangement, which, by shifting about peoples and territories from one ruler to another, sought to reach a political balance peacefully. The cardinal points of each nation's policy may be shortly stated. The Spanish cabinet and people objected to any solution which dismembered the empire. The English and the Dutch objected to any extension of France in the Spanish Netherlands, and to the monopoly by the French of the trade with Spanish America, both which they feared as the results of placing a Bourbon on the Spanish throne. Louis XIV. wanted Naples and Sicily for one of his sons, in case of any partition; thus giving France a strong Mediterranean position, but one which would be at the mercy of the sea powers, — a fact which induced William III. to acquiesce in this demand. The Emperor of Austria particularly objected to these Mediterranean positions going away from his family, and refused to come into any of the partition treaties. Before any arrangement was perfected, the actual king of Spain died, but before his death was induced by his ministers to sign a will, bequeathing all his States to the grandson of Louis XIV., then Duke of Anjou, known afterward as Philip V. of Spain. By this step it was hoped to

巴利阿里群岛。科西嘉那时尚属于热那亚。在西半球，除了古巴和波多黎各，西班牙当时还据有如今分属拉美诸国的整个中美大陆，人们很快也会认识到这一地区巨大的贸易潜力；而在亚洲列岛，西班牙也有着大片的领地，还没怎么成为目前争论的内容。这个帝国，由于其中央王国的衰落而变得极其脆弱，迄今已使得其他国家对这个帝国广袤的领土范围毫不在意了；这些国家，都是因为具有更多直接利益而被西班牙占领的。倘若有可能出现一个更加强大的政府，可能与欧洲列强之一结盟而得到支持，那么这种漠视态度就不可能继续存在下去了。

详细分析当时的外交政策，与我们所论述的主题无关；当时，这些外交政策都是通过将民众与领土从一个君主手中转到另一个君主，试图和平地达到一种政治上的平衡。不过，我们可以简单地说明一下每个国家所定政策的要点。西班牙内阁和西班牙人民都反对将这个帝国进行分割的任何解决办法。英国和荷兰反对法国在西属尼德兰有任何的领土扩张，反对法国垄断与拉丁美洲之间的贸易；两国都担心，倘若让波旁王室的人登上西班牙王位，就会出现这两种结果。路易十四想要把那不勒斯和西西里给自己的一个儿子，假如分割西班牙帝国的话；这样，法国在地中海地区就拥有了一个强大的战略要地，但这是一个任由海洋强国宰割的战略要地——正是这一事实，才使得威廉三世勉强同意了法国的这个要求。奥国皇帝尤其反对将地中海地区的这些地方拱手送出，反对让这些地方不再受哈布斯堡王族统治，并且拒绝参与签署分割西班牙帝国的任何条约。还不待他们做好安排，西班牙的现任国王就一命呜呼了；不过，在临死前，大臣们说服他签署了一份遗嘱，将帝国所辖各国全都遗赠给了路易十四的孙子，即当时的安茹公爵，

preserve the whole, by enlisting in its defence the nearest and one of the most powerful States in Europe, — nearest, if are excepted the powers ruling the sea, which are always near any country whose ports are open to their ships.

Louis XIV. accepted the bequest, and in so doing felt bound in honor to resist all attempts at partition. The union of the two kingdoms under one family promised important advantages to France, henceforth delivered from that old enemy in the rear, which had balked so many of her efforts to extend her frontiers eastward. As a matter of fact, from that time, with rare breaks, there existed between the two kingdoms an alliance, the result of family ties, which only the weakness of Spain kept from being dangerous to the rest of Europe. The other countries at once realized the situation, and nothing could have saved war but some backward step on the part of the French king. The statesmen of England and Holland, the two powers on whose wealth the threatened war must depend, proposed that the Italian States should be given to the son of the Austrian emperor, Belgium be occupied by themselves, and that the new king of Spain should grant no commercial privileges in the Indies to France above other nations. To the credit of their wisdom it must be said that this compromise was the one which after ten years of war was found, on the whole, best; and in it is seen the growing sense of the value of extension by sea. Louis, however, would not yield; on the contrary, he occupied, by connivance of the Spanish governors, towns in the Netherlands which had been held by Dutch troops under treaties with Spain. Soon after, in February, 1701, the English Parliament met, and denounced any treaty which promised France the dominion of the Mediterranean. Holland began to arm, and the Emperor of Austria pushed his troops into northern Italy, where a campaign followed, greatly to the disadvantage of Louis.

In September of the same year, 1701, the two sea powers and the Emperor of Austria

亦即后来史称的西班牙菲利普五世。通过这步棋，那些大臣们希望得到法国的保护，因为法国离西班牙最近，且属于欧洲最强大的国家之一，从而可以保持西班牙帝国的完整性；倘若除去称霸海洋、离任何国家都很近便且各个港口也向西班牙敞开的那些大国，法国就是离西班牙帝国最近的一国了。

路易十四接受了这种遗赠，并因此而感到自己在道义上有责任抵制瓜分西班牙帝国的任何企图。这两个王国团结在一个家族的统治之下，将会给法国带来极其重要的优势，能够使法国自此以后摆脱掉身后那个宿敌的威胁；这个宿敌，已经极大地阻碍到了法国向东扩张领土的进程。事实上，从那时起，这两个王国之间便因为皇族血统而结成了同盟，中间几乎没怎么间断过，只是因为西班牙的软弱，才没给欧洲其他国家带来威胁。其他国家马上看清了当时的形势；此时，除非法国国王做出某种让步，否则就只有开战了。即将爆发的这场战争，取决于英、荷两个大国的财力，所以两国的政治家便提出，意大利诸国应当交给奥地利皇帝之子，比利时应由英、荷两国自己占领，而在印度群岛地区，西班牙新任国王授予给法国的商业贸易特权，也不应当超过其他国家。我们不得不说，这是10多年战乱之后整体上最佳的一个妥协方案，应当归功于这些政治家们的智慧；并且，从中我们可以看出，他们开始越来越重视在海洋上的势力扩张了。然而，路易十四不肯让步；相反，他在西班牙统治者的默许之下，还占领了尼德兰的一些城镇——这些城镇，本来都是荷兰根据与西班牙达成的条约而派兵驻守着的。不久之后，在1701年的2月份，英国国会召开会议，废除了承诺将地中海地区某些领地让与法国的所有条约。荷兰开始武装起来，奥地利皇帝则派兵进入了意大利北部，紧接着便在

signed a secret treaty, which laid down the chief lines of the coming war, with the exception of that waged in the Spanish peninsula itself. By it the allies undertook to conquer the Spanish Netherlands in order to place a barrier between France and the United Provinces; to conquer Milan as a security for the emperor's other provinces; and to conquer Naples and Sicily for the same security, and also for the security of the navigation and commerce of the subjects of his Britannic Majesty and of the United Provinces. The sea powers should have the right to conquer, for the utility of the said navigation and commerce, the countries and towns of the Spanish Indies; and all that they should be able to take there should be for them and remain theirs. The war begun, none of the allies could treat without the others, nor without having taken just measures — first, to prevent the kingdoms of France and Spain from ever being united under the same king; second, to prevent the French from ever making themselves masters of the Spanish Indies, or from sending ships thither to engage, directly or indirectly, in commerce; third, to secure to the subjects of his Britannic Majesty and of the United Provinces the commercial privileges which they enjoyed in all the Spanish States under the late king.

It will be noticed that in these conditions there is no suggestion of any intention to resist the accession of the Bourbon king, who was called to the throne by the Spanish government and at first acknowledged by England and Holland; but, on the other hand, the Emperor of Austria does not withdraw the Austrian claim, which centred in his own person. The voice of the sea powers was paramount in the coalition, as the terms of the treaty safeguarding their commercial interests show, though, as they were about to use German armies for the land war, German claims also had to be considered. As a French historian points out: —

"This was really a new treaty of partition. ... William III., who had conducted all, had taken care not to exhaust England and Holland, in order to restore the Spanish monarchy,

此处发起了一场对路易十四极为不利的战役。

1701年9月，英、荷两个海洋大国与奥地利皇帝签署了一份密约，为即将爆发的这场大战确定了主要方针，但不包括在西班牙半岛本土上进行的战争。根据这份密约，联军开始攻取西属尼德兰，以便在法国和荷兰共和国之间设置一道屏障；还开始攻取米兰，以保障奥地利的其他省份；并且开始攻取那不勒斯和西西里，目的既是保障奥地利的其他省份，也是为了保护英王陛下之臣民以及荷兰共和国人民的航海和贸易安全。这些海洋大国，为了上述的航海和贸易安全，应当有权在西属印度群岛攻城掠地；而各国在此夺取的一切，都应当属于它们，并且一直留在它们手中。战争开始了，三个盟国只有相互支援才能应对，也只有采取下述措施才能应对——首先，让法国和西班牙这两个王国永远都无法团结起来，无法由一位国王所统治；第二，让法国永远都无法在西属印度群岛地区称霸，也永远无法派遣船只去那儿直接或者间接地从事商业贸易；第三，保护英王陛下之臣民与荷兰共和国人民在已故西班牙国王治下所享受的那些商贸特权。

我们会注意到，这些条件中并未提出抵制那位波旁皇族的国王登基的什么想法，因为那位国王是受西班牙政府邀请前来担任该国国王的，并且首先得到了英国和荷兰两国的认可；但另一方面，奥地利皇帝并未收回以他本人为中心的、对哈布斯堡皇族王位继承权的声索。英、荷两个海洋大国在联盟中的话语权最大，从密约中保护两国贸易利益的条款即可看出这一点；不过，由于它们打算利用德意志的军队来进行陆上战争，所以德意志的要求也必须加以考虑才行。正如一位法国历史学家所指出的那样：

"这实际上是一份新的瓜分条约……一直不遗余力的威廉三世小心行事，避免让英国

intact, to the emperor; his final condition was to reduce the new king, Philip V., to Spain proper, and to secure to England and Holland at once the commercial use of all the regions that had been under the Spanish monarchy, together with important military and maritime positions against France."

But though war was imminent, the countries about to engage hesitated. Holland would not move without England, and despite the strong feeling of the latter country against France, the manufacturers and merchants still remembered the terrible sufferings of the last war. Just then, as the scales were wavering, James II. died. Louis, yielding to a sentiment of sympathy and urged by his nearest intimates, formally recognized the son of James as king of England; and the English people, enraged at what they looked on as a threat and an insult, threw aside all merely prudential considerations. The House of Lords declared that "there could be no security till the usurper of the Spanish monarchy was brought to reason;" and the House of Commons voted fifty thousand soldiers and thirty-five thousand seamen, besides subsidies for German and Danish auxiliaries. William III. died soon after, in March, 1702; but Queen Anne took up his policy, which had become that of the English and Dutch peoples.

Louis XIV. tried to break part of the on-coming storm by forming a league of neutrals among the other German States; but the emperor adroitly made use of the German feeling, and won to his side the Elector of Brandenburg by acknowledging him as king of Prussia, thus creating a North-German Protestant royal house, around which the other Protestant States naturally gathered, and which was in the future to prove a formidable rival to Austria. The immediate result was that France and Spain, whose cause was thenceforth known as that of the two crowns, went into the war without any ally save Bavaria. War was declared in May by Holland against the kings of France and Spain; by England against France and

和荷兰为了将西班牙王国原封不动地交给奥地利皇帝而变得国穷财尽；他的最后一个条件，便是将新任国王菲利普五世的权力限制在西班牙本土，以及确保英国和荷兰能够利用原为西班牙王国所统治地区的贸易，连同那些重要的军事据点和海洋基地，共同来对抗法国。"

不过，虽说战争一触即发，但准备参战的这些国家却又犹豫起来。英国不动，荷兰也就不会动，而尽管英国有着强烈的反法情绪，但该国的制造商和商人，却仍然忘不了上一次战争中他们所遭受的惨痛损失。就在此时，正当战争之势左右不定的时候，詹姆士二世归天了。路易十四心有戚戚，便在詹姆士二世最亲密至交的要求下，正式承认詹姆士二世之子为英国国王；英国民众则把这种做法看成是一种威吓和侮辱，都极为愤慨，从而抛弃了所有的谨慎考虑。上议院宣布，"在西班牙王国的篡位者恢复理智之前，是不可能安全的；"下议院则表决通过了议案，除了拨款给德国和丹麦并向两国雇用援军之外，还派出了50000陆军和35000海军。不久，威廉三世便于1702年3月去世了；但安妮女王继承了他的政策，使之成为了英、荷两国人民共同的政策。

路易十四试图通过在其他日耳曼国家中组织起一个中立同盟，来消弭这种即将到来的暴风骤雨；但奥地利皇帝巧妙地利用了德国人民的情感，通过承认勃兰登堡选帝侯为普鲁士国王而将他争取到了自己这一边，从而建立了一个北德新教王室，而其他信奉新教的邦国便自然而然地在这个王室周围团结起来，最后变成了奥地利帝国最有力的竞争对手。这样做的直接结果，便是法国和西班牙两国在开战之后，除了巴伐利亚，就没有任何盟国了——从那以后，法、西两国的共同目标即被称为"二皇目标"。5月，荷兰宣布对法、西两国国王开战；英国也对法、西两国开战了，安妮女王甚至不承认菲利普

Spain, Anne refusing to recognize Philip V. even in declaring war, because he had recognized James III. as king of England; while the emperor was still more outspoken, declaring against the King of France and the Duke of Anjou. Thus began the great War of the Spanish Succession.

It is far from easy, in dealing with a war of such proportions, lasting for more than ten years, to disentangle from the general narrative that part which particularly touches our subject, without at the same time losing sight of the relation of the one part to the whole. Such a loss, however, is fatal to the end in view, which is not a mere chronicle of naval events, nor even a tactical or strategic discussion of certain naval problems divorced from their surroundings of cause and effect in general history, but an appreciation of the effect of sea power upon the general result of the war and upon the prosperity of nations. It will conduce to clearness, however, to point out again that the aim of William III. was not to dispute the claim of Philip V. to the throne, — a matter of comparative indifference to the sea powers, — but to seize, to the benefit of their commerce and colonial empire, such portions of the Spanish American possessions as he could, and at the same time to impose such conditions upon the new monarchy as would at least prevent any loss, to English and Dutch commerce, of the privileges they had had under the Austrian line. Such a policy would not direct the main effort of the sea nations upon the Spanish peninsula, but upon America; and the allied fleets might not have entered the Straits. Sicily and Naples were to go, not to England, but to Austria. Subsequent causes led to an entire change in this general plan. A new candidate, a son of the Emperor of Germany, was set up in 1703 by the coalition under the name of Carlos III., and the peninsula became the scene of a doubtful and bloody war, keeping the Anglo-Dutch fleets hovering round the coasts; with the result, as regards the sea powers, that nothing of decisive importance

五世的宣战，因为他曾承认詹姆士三世为英国国王；奥地利皇帝则更为坦率，直言对法国国王和安茹公爵宣战。这样，伟大的西班牙王位继承战便开始了。

在论述一场规模如此之大、持续时间长达10多年的战争时，要想从一般性的叙述中疏理出与我们论述主题相关的内容，同时又不忽略掉这部分内容与整个战争的关系，是非常不容易做到的。然而，这样一种忽略，对于我们最终目标而言，关系却极为重大；我们的最终目标，并非仅仅是记录下海军历史上的诸多事件，甚至也不是对普通历史上海军领域里某些脱离了其因果环境的问题进行战术或者战略上的讨论，而是理解制海权对战争一般结果所产生的影响，以及它给各国繁荣带来的影响。不过，再一次指出下述这一点，还是有助于我们去清楚地对其加以理解的：威廉三世的目的，并非是阻止菲利普五世登上西班牙王位——对那几个海洋大国来说，这个问题相对而言并不重要——而是为了其商业贸易和殖民帝国的利益，尽量夺取西属美洲殖民地中的某些地区，并且在此同时，将某些起码不致让英、荷两国失去它们在哈布斯堡王朝时代所得到的那些商贸特权的条件，强加给这个新的王国。这样一种政策，使得这几个海洋大国的主要精力不会放在西班牙半岛上，而是会放在美洲；英、荷联合舰队本来也可以不进入直布罗陀海峡。西西里和那不勒斯不会归英国，而是会给奥地利。可随后的一些原因，却使得这一总体计划发生了根本性的变化。1703年，联盟以卡洛斯三世的名义，扶持德意志皇帝的一个儿子为王储，西班牙半岛便变成了一场难以预料的血腥战争的战场，使得英、荷联合舰队不得不一直在该国沿海游弋；结果，就制海权而言，盟国在西属美洲并未取得什么重大成果，只是让英国在此战中得到了直布罗陀和马翁港，并且此后即成了地中海地区的霸主。与此同时，英国

was done in Spanish America, but that England issued from the strife with Gibraltar and Port Mahon in her hands, to be thenceforth a Mediterranean power. At the same time that Carlos III. was proclaimed, a treaty was negotiated with Portugal, known as the Methuen Treaty, which gave England the practical monopoly of Portuguese trade, and sent the gold of Brazil by way of Lisbon to London, — an advantage so great that it aided materially in keeping up the war on the continent as well as in maintaining the navy. At the same time the efficiency of the latter so increased that the losses by French cruisers, though still heavy, were at no time unendurable.

When the war broke out, in pursuance of the original policy, Sir George Rooke, with a fleet of fifty ships-of-the-line and transports carrying fourteen thousand troops, was sent against Cadiz, which was the great European centre of the Spanish-American trade; there came the specie and products of the West, and thence they were dispersed through Europe. It had been the purpose of William III. also to seize Cartagena, one of the principal centres of the same trade in the other hemisphere; and to that end, six months before his death, in September, 1701, he had despatched there a squadron under that traditional seaman of the olden time, Benbow. Benbow fell in with a French squadron sent to supply and strengthen the place, and brought it to action north of Cartagena; but though superior in force, the treason of several of his captains, who kept out of action, defeated his purpose, and after fighting till his ship was helpless and he himself had received a mortal wound, the French escaped and Cartagena was saved. Before his death Benbow received a letter from the French commodore to this effect: "Yesterday morning I had no hope but I should have supped in your cabin. As for those cowardly captains of yours, hang them up, for, by God! they deserve it." And hanged two of them were. Rooke's expedition against Cadiz also failed, as it was nearly certain to do; for his instructions were so to

正式宣布卡洛斯三世为西班牙国王,并与葡萄牙通过谈判达成了一项条约,史称《梅休因条约》;这份条约,使得英国实际上垄断了葡萄牙的贸易,并且通过里斯本将葡萄牙从巴西得来的黄金输送给了伦敦——英国从中获利颇丰,既极大地有助于它继续在欧洲大陆作战,同时又让它能够维持住自己的海军。与此同时,由于英国海军的作战效率大幅提高了,所以法国巡逻舰给英国带来的损失虽说仍然巨大,但不再是无法承受的了。

战争爆发之后,根据原有政策,英国派遣乔治·鲁克勋爵率领一支由50艘战舰和运输船所组成的舰队,运送14000兵力前去攻打加的斯;此处是欧洲与西属拉丁美洲之间最大的贸易中心,西方的金币与商品都汇聚于此,然后再从此处散布到欧洲各国。威廉三世本来还想攻取卡塔赫纳,该地位于地球的另一边,是西属拉丁美洲最主要的贸易中心之一;为了实现这一目标,他在自己去世之前6个月,即1701年9月,就已派本鲍这个属于过去传统上的海军将领,率领一支小型舰队前往该地。本鲍遇上了一支被派去给该地运送给养和增援的法国舰队,便在卡塔赫纳以北与之交上了火;可是,虽说兵力超过敌人,但他手下的数名舰长通敌,没有参加战斗,使得他的目标落了空。他坚持战斗着,直到自己的座舰孤立无援,而他本人也受了重伤之后,法国人便避而不战了,而卡塔赫纳也没有攻下来。临死之前,本鲍收到了那支法国舰队的司令写给他的一封信,大意是:"昨天上午,在下只有一个希望,那就是在阁下的座舱里享受晚餐。至于您手下那些胆小如鼠的舰长,请以上帝之名,通通都绞死吧,因为他们活该!"本鲍绞死了其中的两名舰长。鲁克远征攻打加的斯也没有成功,这种结果本来差不多是可想而知的;因为给他的命令似乎是要他去安抚西班牙人,使西班牙人不再甘愿追随那位波旁皇室的国王。这种模棱两可的命令缚住

act as to conciliate the Spanish people and disincline them to the Bourbon king. Such doubtful orders tied his hands; but after failing there, he learned that the galleons from the West Indies, loaded with silver and merchandise, had put into Vigo Bay under escort of French ships-of-war. He went there at once, and found the enemy in a harbor whose entrance was but three quarters of a mile wide, defended by fortifications and a heavy boom; but a passage was forced through the boom under a hot fire, the place seized, and all the shipping, with much of the specie, either taken or sunk. This affair, which is known in history as that of the Vigo galleons, was a brilliant and interesting feat of arms, but has no military features calling for mention, except the blow it gave to the finances and prestige of the two crowns.

The affair at Vigo had, however, important political results, and helped to that change in the general plan of the sea powers which has been mentioned. The King of Portugal, moved by fear of the French, had acknowledged Philip V.; but his heart was against him, for he dreaded French influence and power brought so near his little and isolated kingdom. It had been a part of Rooke's mission to detach him from the alliance of the two crowns; and the affair of Vigo, happening so near his own frontiers, impressed him with a sense of the power of the allied navies. In truth, Portugal is nearer to the sea than to Spain, and must fall naturally under the influence of the power controlling the sea. Inducements were offered, — by the Emperor of Austria a cession of Spanish territory, by the sea powers a subsidy; but the king was not willing to declare himself until the Austrian claimant should have landed at Lisbon, fairly committing the coalition to a peninsular as well as a continental war. The emperor transferred his claims to his second son, Charles; and the latter, after being proclaimed in Vienna and acknowledged by England and Holland, was taken by the allied fleets to Lisbon, where he landed in March, 1704. This necessitated the important change in the plans of the sea powers. Pledged to the support

了他的手脚；但在此处失利之后，他得到情报，说满载着金银财宝和商品的一支西班牙船队，已经在法国军舰的护送之下，驶入了维哥湾。他马上率军赶往维哥湾，发现敌人正停泊在一处海港内，海港入口处只有四分之三英里宽，两边都筑有防御工事，还有一道重型挡栅；不过，鲁克勋爵下令用烈火焚烧挡栅，硬生生从中打开了一条通道，然后攻下了这个港口，而所有的商船，连同许多的金币，不是被鲁克缴获，便是沉到了水下。这一事件史称"维哥湾西班牙商船事件"，虽说是一种杰出而有意思的赫赫战绩，但在军事上并无值得我们关注的特色，只是打击了法、西两国的金融和名誉罢了。

然而，维哥湾海战在政治上却带来了重要的影响，促使上述海洋大国的总体计划发生了改变。葡萄牙国王因对法国人的担忧深有同感，便承认了菲利普五世的西班牙国王身份；但是，他的内心却是反对菲利普五世的，因为他担心法国的影响和势力会就此蔓延到他这个小而孤立的王国附近来。鲁克所接受的任务中，有一项便是离间葡萄牙国王与法、西同盟之间的关系；而维哥湾海战离葡萄牙边境如此之近，使得葡萄牙国王印象深刻地感受到了英、荷联合海军的强大实力。事实上，葡萄牙距海洋比距西班牙更近，所以必定会受到制海权的影响。盟国对他进行了利诱——奥地利皇帝提出割让西班牙的一处领土，而英、荷两个海洋大国则提出拨款给葡萄牙；可在奥地利的使节到达里斯本、并且公平合理地让盟国承诺在欧洲大陆进行战争的同时确保半岛安全之前，葡萄牙国王并不愿意表明自己的态度。奥地利皇帝把自己的权利转给了二儿子查理；而查理在越南发表了通告，得到英、荷两国的认可之后，便率联合舰队前往里斯本，并于1704年3月抵达了那里。这就使得英、荷两个海洋大国的政策，必须做出重大改变才行了。

of Carlos, their fleets were thenceforth tied to the shores of the peninsula and the protection of commerce; while the war in the West Indies, becoming a side issue on a small scale, led to no results. From this time on, Portugal was the faithful ally of England, whose sea power during this war gained its vast preponderance over all rivals. Her ports were the refuge and support of English fleets, and on Portugal was based in later days the Peninsular war with Napoleon. In and through all, Portugal, for a hundred years, had more to gain and more to fear from England than from any other power.

Great as were the effects of the maritime supremacy of the two sea powers upon the general result of the war, and especially upon that undisputed empire of the seas which England held for a century after, the contest is marked by no one naval action of military interest. Once only did great fleets meet, and then with results that were indecisive; after which the French gave up the struggle at sea, confining themselves wholly to a commerce-destroying warfare. This feature of the War of the Spanish Succession characterizes nearly the whole of the eighteenth century, with the exception of the American Revolutionary struggle. The noiseless, steady, exhausting pressure with which sea power acts, cutting off the resources of the enemy while maintaining its own, supporting war in scenes where it does not appear itself, or appears only in the background, and striking open blows at rare intervals, though lost to most, is emphasized to the careful reader by the events of this war and of the half-century that followed. The overwhelming sea power of England was the determining factor in European history during the period mentioned, maintaining war abroad while keeping its own people in prosperity at home, and building up the great empire which is now seen; but from its very greatness its action, by escaping opposition, escapes attention. On the few occasions in which it is called to fight, its superiority is so marked that the affairs can scarcely be called battles; with the possible

由于承诺支持卡洛斯国王，所以两国舰队此后都不得不游弋于半岛沿海地区，以保护该地区的商业贸易；而在西印度群岛所进行的战争，由于规模小而变成了一个次要问题，也没有分出什么胜负来。从这时起，葡萄牙就成了英国的一个忠实盟友，而英国的制海权也在此次战争中获得了无可匹敌的优势。葡萄牙的港口，成了英国舰队的避难所和获取补给和支援之地，而后来，英国也是以葡萄牙为基地，展开了与拿破仑之间的半岛战争。总而言之，葡萄牙在这100年间，从英国得到的利益比从其他任何一个海洋大国得到的都要多，而它对英国的畏惧，也比对其他任何一个海洋大国都要厉害。

尽管英、荷两个海洋大国的制海权对此次战争一般性结果的影响非常巨大，尤其是给后来英国又保持了100年之久的那种毫无争议的海上帝国地位带来了巨大的影响，但此次战争的特点，却是没有发生过一场具有军事价值的海战。双方的大型舰队确实曾经遭遇过一回，可结果却并不具有决定意义；之后，法国便放弃了与盟国在海上争雄，而是一心一意地进行贸易破坏战了。西班牙王位继承战的这种特征，差不多是整个18世纪的特点，只是不包括美国革命战争。此次战争和接下来半个世纪中的诸多事件，都向细心的读者强调了制海权所带来的那种无声无息、持久稳定而又令人筋疲力尽的压力，能够切断敌方的资源而维持好己方的各种资源，能在海军不用到场或者只是处于幕后的情况下为战争提供支援，并且会极为偶尔地进行大多数人都没有注意到的公开打击等方面的特点。英国那种势不可挡的制海权，就是欧洲这一时期历史上的一个决定性因素；这种制海权既让该国能够在国外发动战争，同时又能让本国民众繁荣兴旺起来，并且建立起了如今我们所见的这个庞大帝国；也正是因为它庞大，行动起来所向无敌，所以才不为世人所注意。在少

exceptions of Byng's action at Minorca and Hawke's at Quiberon, the latter one of the most brilliant pages in naval history, no decisive encounter between equal forces, possessing military interest, occurs between 1700 and 1778.

Owing to this characteristic, the War of the Spanish Succession, from the point of view of our subject, has to be blocked out in general outline, avoiding narrative and indicating general bearings, especially of the actions of the fleets. With the war in Flanders, in Germany, and in Italy the navies had naturally no concern; when they had so protected the commerce of the allies that there was no serious check to that flow of subsidies upon which the land war depended, their part toward it was done. In the Spanish peninsula it was different. Immediately after landing Carlos III. at Lisbon, Sir George Rooke sailed for Barcelona, which it was understood would be handed over when the fleets appeared; but the governor was faithful to his king and kept down the Austrian party. Rooke then sailed for Toulon, where a French fleet was at anchor. On his way he sighted another French fleet coming from Brest, which he chased but was unable to overtake; so that both the enemy's squadrons were united in the port. It is worthwhile to note here that the English navy did not as yet attempt to blockade the French ports in winter, as they did at a later date. At this period fleets, like armies, went into winter quarters. Another English admiral, Sir Cloudesley Shovel, had been sent in the spring to blockade Brest; but arriving too late, he found his bird flown, and at once kept on to the Mediterranean. Rooke, not thinking himself strong enough to resist the combined French squadrons, fell back toward the Straits; for at this time England had no ports, no base, in the Mediterranean, no useful ally; Lisbon was the nearest refuge. Rooke and Shovel met off Lagos, and there held a council of war, in which the former, who was senior, declared that his instructions forbade his

数几次可称之为搏斗的情况下，因为英军的优势过于明显，以至于其中发生的事件都很少被称作是战斗；所以，自1700年至1778年间，可能除了拜恩在米诺卡岛、霍克在基伯龙湾这两次作战行动，根本就没有出现过敌我兵力平等、具有决定性意义和军事价值的会战。

因为有着这一特点，所以从我们论述的主题角度来看，西班牙王位继承战就必须排除在论述主题大纲之外，既无需叙述，也应避免表明它具有什么普遍意义，尤其是舰队的那些作战行动。各国海军自然与在佛兰德斯[1]、在德国和意大利发生的战事无关；它们只需如此这般地保护好盟国的商业贸易往来，使得陆上战争所倚赖的财政支援不会受到什么严重的制约，就算是起到了自己的作用。但在西班牙半岛上，情况则有所不同。卡洛斯三世在里斯本登陆之后不久，乔治·鲁克勋爵便率军驶往巴塞罗那，并且以为他的舰队一抵达，巴塞罗那就会移交给他；可该省省长却忠于西班牙国王，压制住了哈布斯堡王朝党人。于是，鲁克便驶往土伦，那里停泊着一支法国舰队。在途中，他看到了从布雷斯特而来的另一支法国舰队，便进行了追赶，但没有赶上；这样，敌方的两支舰队便在土伦港会师了。在这里，我们应当注意，英国海军此时尚未像后来那样，试图在冬季封锁法国的港口。在这一时期，舰队跟陆军一样，也会进入冬季船坞进行休整。另一名英国海军上将，即克劳兹利·沙吾尔勋爵，春季的时候就已被派去封锁布雷斯特；可由于到得太晚，他发现到手的鸭子飞了，于是马上继续率军驶往地中海。鲁克因为没有考虑到己方足够强大，可以抵御那两支法国舰队的联合进攻，便向直布罗陀海峡撤退；因为此时英国在地中海地区尚无港口、基地，也没有盟军可用；最近的一处避敌之地也在里斯本。鲁克与沙吾尔两部在拉各斯海岸会合后，就在此处召开了一次军事会议；在会议上，级别较高的鲁克称，他接受的命令是，倘若没有得到西班牙和葡萄牙两国

undertaking anything without the consent of the kings of Spain and Portugal. This was indeed tying the hands of the sea powers; but Rooke at last, chafing at the humiliating inaction, and ashamed to go home without doing something, decided to attack Gibraltar for three reasons: because he heard it was insufficiently garrisoned, because it was of infinite importance as a port for the present war, and because its capture would reflect credit on the queen's arms. The place was attacked, bombarded, and then carried by an assault in boats. The English possession of Gibraltar dates from August 4, 1704, and the deed rightly keeps alive the name of Rooke, to whose judgment and fearlessness of responsibility England owes the key of the Mediterranean.

The Bourbon king of Spain at once undertook to retake the place, and called upon the French fleet in Toulon to support his attack. Tourville had died in 1701, and the fleet was commanded by the Count of Toulouse, — a natural son of Louis XIV., only twenty-six years old. Rooke also sailed eastward, and the two fleets met on the 24th of August off Velez Malaga. The allies were to windward with a northeast wind, both fleets on the port tack heading to the southward and eastward. There is some uncertainty as to the numbers; the French had fifty-two ships-of-the-line, their enemy probably half a dozen more. The allies kept away together, each ship for its opposite; there was apparently no attempt on Rooke's part at any tactical combination. The battle of Malaga possesses indeed no military interest, except that it is the first in which we find fully developed that wholly unscientific method of attack by the English which Clerk criticised, and which prevailed throughout the century. It is instructive to notice that the result in it was the same as in all others fought on the same principle. The van opened out from the centre, leaving quite an interval; and the attempt made to penetrate this gap and isolate the van

国王首肯，就不得鲁莽行事。这实际上是缚住了两支海军的手脚；不过，由于气恼无所作为所带来的耻辱，也不好意思什么都没做就回师国内，所以鲁克最终还是基于下述三个理由，决定攻打直布罗陀：一是因为他听说此处防守力量不足，二是因为此处对于当时正在进行的战争来说是一个极其重要的港口，三是因为攻陷此处会给女王陛下的军队增光。英军便对该港发动进攻，狂轰滥炸一通之后便用小艇进行突袭，从而攻克了此地。英军对直布罗陀的占领自1704年8月4日始，而这一行动也使得鲁克之名流芳千古了；英国拥有了这个通往地中海地区的门户，完全应当归功于鲁克的判断力和无畏的责任感才是。

西班牙的那位波旁国王，马上开始重新攻取此处，并要求驻土伦的法国舰队在他进攻时提供支援。图维尔已于1701年辞世，此时的法国舰队由图卢兹伯爵指挥——他是路易十四的亲生儿子，当时才26岁。鲁克也向东驶去，于是8月24日双方舰队在维勒斯马拉加海域遭遇了。此时正刮东北风，英、荷联军处于上风位置，两支舰队都是左舷抢风，朝东、朝南航行。双方兵力数量不太确定；法军有52艘战舰，而其敌人很可能只有60来艘战舰。联军并未靠在一起，而是每艘舰船各自为战；所以，鲁克这一方显然并未想要编成什么战术组合。事实上，马拉加海战并没有什么军事价值，只是我们发现，英军在此战中充分发挥了那种完全不科学的进攻方法；这种进攻方法曾饱受克拉克诟病，也是整个十八世纪最常用的一种进攻方法。注意到此战之结果与根据同一原则进行的其他战斗之结果相同，对于我们来说是很有教益的。前锋脱离了中军，留下了一处大大的缺口；而试图插入这一缺口、以便将敌方的前锋孤立起来，则是法军所进行的唯一一次战术机动。在马拉加海战中，我们并未看到有什么谨慎而娴熟的战术痕迹，而克拉克则很正确地认为，人们在此后才开始认识到这种战术的价值。由蒙克、鲁伊特和图维尔这些将领曾经

was the only tactical move of the French. We find in them at Malaga no trace of the cautious, skilful tactics which Clerk rightly thought to recognize at a later day. The degeneracy from the able combinations of Monk, Ruyter, and Tourville to the epoch of mere seamanship is clearly marked by the battle of Malaga, and gives it its only historical importance. In it was realized that primitive mode of fighting which Macaulay has sung, and which remained for many years the ideal of the English navy: —

"Then on both sides the leaders
Gave signal for the charge;
And on both sides the footmen
Strode forth with lance and targe;
And on both sides the horsemen
Struck their spurs deep in gore,
And front to front the armies
Met with a mighty roar."

Human movement is not always advance; and there are traces of a somewhat similar ideal in the naval periodical literature of our own day. The fight was severe, lasting from ten in the morning till five in the afternoon, but was entirely indecisive. The next day the wind shifted, giving the weather-gage to the French, but they did not use the opportunity to attack; for which they were much to blame, if their claim of the advantage the day before is well founded. Rooke could not have fought; nearly half his fleet, twenty-five ships, it is said, had used up all their ammunition. Even during the battle itself several of the allied ships were towed out of line, because they had not powder and ball for a single broadside. This was doubtless due to the attack upon Gibraltar, in which fifteen thousand shot were expended, and to the lack of any

实施过的那些出色的战术组合，堕落到一个仅仅倚赖航海技术去作战的时代——马拉加海战清晰地标志了这一过程，也使得此战仅仅具有这方面的一点儿历史意义。我们从中可以看到麦考利所吟唱过、属于英国海军多年来的理想模式的那种原始作战模式：

"然后，双方领袖
发出进攻信号；
敌我步兵
大步向前，手执盾与矛；
两方骑兵
猛蹬马刺，鲜血迸流；
两军狭路逢
天地尽怒吼。"

人类的活动，并非总是向前进步的；我们如今的海军期刊文献中，也有着此种类似的理想之痕迹。虽说战斗极其惨烈，从上午10点持续进行到了下午5点，但完全没有决定性的意义。第二天，风向变了，使得法军占据了上风位置，可他们却没有利用这个机会展开攻击；倘若他们理直气壮地宣称前一天是因为自己没有这种优势的话，那么在这一点上，他们自己就应当承担很大的责任。鲁克本来无力再战；其所率舰队中差不多半数舰船——据说是25艘——的弹药都已经打光了。甚至还在战斗过程中，联合舰队中就有好几艘舰船被拖出了阵列，因为它们连进行一次舷炮齐射的火药和炮弹都没有了。无疑，这是因为它们曾经用了15000发炮弹攻打过直布罗陀，又没有哪个港口可以为它们进行补给所致——

port serving as a base of supplies, — a deficiency which the new possession would hereafter remove. Rooke, in seizing Gibraltar, had the same object in view that prompted the United States to seize Port Royal at the beginning of the Civil War, and which made the Duke of Parma urge upon his king, before sending the Spanish Great Armada, to seize Flushing on the coast of Holland, — advice which, had it been followed, would have made unnecessary that dreary and disastrous voyage to the north of England. The same reasons would doubtless lead any nation intending serious operations against our seaboard, to seize points remote from the great centres and susceptible of defence, like Gardiner's Bay or Port Royal, which in an inefficient condition of our navy they might hold with and for their fleets.

Rooke retired in peace to Lisbon, bestowing by the way on Gibraltar all the victuals and ammunition that could be spared from the fleet. Toulouse, instead of following up his victory, if it was one, went back to Toulon, sending only ten ships-of-the-line to support the attack on Gibraltar. All the attempts of the French against the place were carried on in a futile manner; the investing squadron was finally destroyed and the land attack converted into a blockade. "With this reverse," says a French naval officer, "began in the French people a regrettable reaction against the navy. The wonders to which it had given birth, its immense services, were forgotten. Its value was no longer believed. The army, more directly in contact with the nation, had all its favor, all its sympathy. The prevailing error, that the greatness or decay of France depended upon some Rhenish positions, could not but favor these ideas adverse to the sea service, which have made England's strength and our weakness."

During this year, 1704, the battle of Blenheim was fought, in which the French and Bavarian troops were wholly overthrown by the English and German under Marlborough and Prince Eugene. The result of this battle was that Bavaria forsook the French alliance, and

但占领了直布罗陀之后，这种缺陷就不再存在了。鲁克在攻克了直布罗陀之后，还抱有一个目标；这个目标，与促使合众国在内战初期占领皇家港[2]的目标是相同的，而这也是曾经使得帕尔马公爵[3]敦促国王在派出西班牙无敌舰队之前，先攻克荷兰沿海的弗拉辛的原因——倘若西班牙国王听从了这一建议，那么西班牙就根本没有必要沉闷枯燥而又损失惨重地去远征英国北部[4]了。一个想要严重打击我国沿海地区的国家，无疑也会出于相同的原因，而去攻取那些远离大的中心城市、因而防守力量薄弱的地点，比如贾迪纳湾或者皇家港；由于我国海军作战效率低下，所以别国的舰队有可能攻下并守住这些地方。

鲁克全身而退，回到了里斯本，途中还在直布罗陀卸下了舰队余下的给养和弹药。图卢兹伯爵没有乘胜追击——假如能说他取胜了的话——而是返回了土伦，只派了10艘战舰前去支援攻打直布罗陀。法军对此处发动的攻击，一次次都是徒劳无果；担任围攻任务的那支小型舰队最终被击溃，而陆上进攻则变转成了封锁。"由于此次失败，"一位法国海军将领曾说，"法国民众便都开始反对海军，真是十分可悲。海军曾经创造过的种种奇迹，曾经起到过的巨大作用，都被人们遗忘了。人们认为海军不再重要了。与整个民族关系更加直接的陆军，则获得了人们原本给予海军的那种青睐和支持。当时普遍的错误思想，是认为法国的兴衰取决于莱茵河上的数个战略要地；它们只是助长了不利于海军作用的这些观念，而这些观念又导致了英国的强大和我国的弱小。"

在1704年这一年间，还发生了布伦海姆之战，其间法国和巴伐利亚的军队被马尔伯勒[5]和欧根亲王[6]所率的英德联军彻底击溃了。此战的结果，便是巴伐利亚放弃了与法国的同盟关系，而德国则成了大战的第二战场；自此以后，这场大战主要就是在尼德

Germany became a secondary theatre of the general war, which was waged thereafter mainly in the Netherlands, Italy, and the Peninsula.

The following year, 1705, the allies moved against Philip V. by two roads, — from Lisbon upon Madrid, and by way of Barcelona. The former attack, though based upon the sea, was mainly by land, and resultless; the Spanish people in that quarter showed unmistakably that they would not welcome the king set up by foreign powers. It was different in Catalonia. Carlos III. went there in person with the allied fleet. The French navy, inferior in numbers, kept in port. The French army also did not appear. The allied troops invested the town, aided by three thousand seamen and supported by supplies landed from the fleet, which was to them both base of supplies and line of communications. Barcelona surrendered on the 9th of October; all Catalonia welcomed Carlos, and the movement spread to Aragon and Valencia, the capital of the latter province declaring for Carlos.

The following year, 1706, the French took the offensive in Spain on the borders of Catalonia, while defending the passes of the mountains toward Portugal. In the absence of the allied fleet, and of the succors which it brought and maintained, the resistance was weak, and Barcelona was again besieged, this time by the French party supported by a French fleet of thirty sails-of-the-line and numerous transports with supplies from the neighboring port of Toulon. The siege, begun April 5, was going on hopefully; the Austrian claimant himself was within the walls, the prize of success; but on the 10th of May the allied fleet appeared, the French ships retired, and the siege was raised in disorder. The Bourbon claimant dared not retreat into Aragon, and so passed by Roussillon into France, leaving his rival in possession. At the same time there moved forward from Portugal — that other base which the sea power of the English and Dutch at once controlled and utilized — another army maintained by the

兰、意大利和西班牙半岛进行了。

第二年，即1705年，联军兵分两路，向菲利普五世发动了进攻———一路是从里斯本向马德里进击，另一路则是经由巴塞罗那进击。前一种进击虽说以海洋为基础，但主要还是经由陆路，而最后则无果而终；那一地区的西班牙民众清清楚楚地表明，他们不会欢迎那位由外国势力扶植起来的国王。但在加泰罗尼亚，情形则大不一样。卡洛斯三世亲随联合舰队前往该地。由于兵力弱于敌人，所以法国海军都缩在港内，按兵不动。法国陆军也未现身。盟国陆军便在3000名水兵的协助下开始攻打该市，舰队则在军需补给方面进行支援；对盟国陆军而言，联合舰队既是其给养基地，也是其交通补给线。10月9日，巴塞罗那投降了，加泰罗尼亚全境都对卡洛斯夹道相迎，盟军也继续向阿拉贡和巴伦西亚推进；巴伦西亚省的首府，则宣布支持卡洛斯三世。

第二年，即1706年，法国开始在西班牙境内进攻加泰罗尼亚省的边境地区，同时还防守着通往葡萄牙的诸座山口。由于没有了联合舰队，也没有联合舰队所运送和维持的那些援军，所以此处的抵抗软弱无力，巴塞罗那便再次被围了，只不过这一次它是被法军所围；有一支由30艘战船所组成的法国舰队，以及从附近的土伦港运送给养的无数船只对法军进行支援。此次围困自4月5日开始，进行得很顺利；奥地利王子查理本人正在城中，攻陷此处之后，他也会成为法军的战利品；不过，5月10日联合舰队赶来了，法国舰船纷纷撤退，在一片混乱之中，围困便解除了。波旁皇室的那位继承人不敢撤进阿拉贡省，便经由鲁西隆地区进入了法国，任由对手占领了该地。与此同时，另一支由海上贸易所赚取的援助金而得以维持的陆军，则从葡萄牙开始向前推进——葡萄牙正是

subsidies earned from the ocean. This time the western attack was more successful; many cities in Estremadura and Leon fell, and as soon as the allied generals learned the raising of the siege of Barcelona, they pressed on by way of Salamanca to Madrid. Philip V., after escaping into France, had returned to Spain by the western Pyrenees; but on the approach of the allies he had again to fly, leaving to them his capital. The Portuguese and allied troops entered Madrid, June 26, 1706. The allied fleet, after the fall of Barcelona, seized Alicante and Cartagena.

So far success had gone; but the inclinations of the Spanish people had been mistaken, and the strength of their purpose and pride, supported by the natural features of their country, was not yet understood. The national hatred to the Portuguese was aroused, as well as the religious dislike to heretics, the English general himself being a Huguenot refugee. Madrid and the surrounding country were disaffected, and the south sent the Bourbon king assurance of its fidelity. The allies were not able to remain in the hostile capital, particularly as the region around was empty of supplies and full of guerillas. They retired to the eastward, drawing toward the Austrian claimant in Aragon. Reverse followed reverse, and on the 25th of April, 1707, the allied army was disastrously overthrown at Almansa, losing fifteen thousand men. All Spain fell back again into the power of Philip V., except the province of Catalonia, part of which also was subdued. The next year, 1708, the French made some progress in the same quarter, but were not able to attack Barcelona; Valencia and Alicante, however, were reduced.

The year 1707 was not marked by any naval event of importance. During the summer the allied fleets in the Mediterranean were diverted from the coast of Spain to support an attack upon Toulon made by the Austrians and Piedmontese. The latter moved from Italy along the

英、荷两个海洋大国同时控制并加以利用的又一个基地。这一次，从西面进攻比较成功；联军攻陷了埃斯特雷马杜拉省和莱昂省的多座城市，而联军将领们一听到巴塞罗那之围已解，随即便经由萨拉曼卡，开始向马德里步步进逼。菲利普五世在逃往法国之后，又经比利牛斯山西部返回了西班牙；可联军打过来之后，他便不得不再次出逃，任由联军占领西班牙首都了。1706年6月26日，葡萄牙人和联军一齐开进了马德里。而联合舰队在攻陷巴塞罗那之后，又占领了阿里坎特和卡塔赫纳两地。

如此一来，成功是无望的了；不过，西班牙人民的意愿一直被人误解，而西班牙人由该国自然特征所激励的目标和自豪感的力量，也仍然不为世人所理解。整个民族对于葡萄牙人的憎恨，以及在宗教上对于异教徒的反感，都被激发出来了；而在他们看来，那位英国将领本身就是一名信奉胡格诺教的流亡者。马德里及其周围乡村的民众都愤懑难抑，而南方地区则派人向那位波旁国王保证自己的忠心。所以，盟军不可能在这个充满敌意的城市里驻留下来，尤其是马德里周围的乡村根本找不到给养，并且到处都是游击队。于是，他们便向东撤退，向位于阿拉贡省的那位奥地利王子靠拢。联军接下来打了一场又一场的败仗，直到1707年的4月25日，联军又在阿尔曼萨大败，损失惨重，折损了15000兵力。西班牙全境，除了加泰罗尼亚，便重新回到了菲利普五世的势力之下，而该省也有部分地区被征服了。第二年，即1708年，法军在这一地区虽说推进了一点儿，但还是没能进攻巴塞罗那；然而，巴伦西亚和阿里坎特两地却被攻陷了。

1707年，并未发生什么重要的海战。在夏季，位于地中海的联合舰队调离了西班牙沿海，前去支援由奥地利人和皮埃蒙特人对土伦港发起的进攻。后者是沿着地中海海岸

coast of the Mediterranean, the fleet supporting the flank on the sea, and contributing supplies. The siege, however, failed, and the campaign was inconclusive. Returning home, the admiral, Sir Cloudesley Shovel, with several ships-of-the-line, was lost on the Scilly Islands, in one of those shipwrecks which have become historical.

In 1708 the allied fleets seized Sardinia, which from its fruitfulness and nearness to Barcelona became a rich storehouse to the Austrian claimant, so long as by the allied help he controlled the sea. The same year Minorca, with its valuable harbor, Port Mahon, was also taken, and from that time for fifty years remained in English hands. Blocking Cadiz and Cartagena by the possession of Gibraltar, and facing Toulon with Port Mahon, Great Britain was now as strongly based in the Mediterranean as either France or Spain; while, with Portugal as an ally, she controlled the two stations of Lisbon and Gibraltar, watching the trade routes both of the ocean and of the inland sea. By the end of 1708 the disasters of France by land and sea, the frightful sufferings of the kingdom, and the almost hopelessness of carrying on a strife which was destroying France, and easily borne by England, led Louis XIV. to offer most humiliating concessions to obtain peace. He undertook to surrender the whole Spanish monarchy, reserving only Naples for the Bourbon king. The allies refused; they demanded the abandonment of the whole Spanish Empire without exception by the Duke of Anjou, refusing to call him king, and added thereto ruinous conditions for France herself. Louis would not yield these, and the war went on.

During the remaining years the strenuous action of the sea power of the allies, which had by this time come to be that of Great Britain alone, with little help from Holland, was less than ever obtrusive, but the reality of its effect remained. The Austrian claimant, confined to Catalonia for the most part, was kept in communication with Sardinia and the Italian provinces

线，从意大利调过来的，由一支舰队在海上支援其侧翼，并且提供补给。然而，此次围攻失败了，并且此战也没带来什么效果。在返回途中，海军上将克劳兹利·沙吾尔勋爵连同数艘军舰在西西里群岛失踪，成了历史上的海难事故之一。

1708年，联合舰队攻陷了撒丁岛，此处由于土地肥沃且离巴塞罗那非常近便，所以变成了奥地利王子一处丰富的宝库，只要得到联军的协助，他便可以控制海洋了。同年，米诺卡岛连同马翁港这个重要港口也被联军占领了，并且自此以后，由英国掌控了50年。由于占领了直布罗陀，从而可以封堵加的斯和卡塔赫纳，又拥有了马翁港，可以对付土伦港，所以此时的大不列颠，在地中海地区的根基与法国或西班牙一样稳固了；并且，因为与葡萄牙结成了盟国，所以英国还控制着里斯本与直布罗陀这两个军事基地，监视着海洋上和内陆海域的贸易线路。到了1708年底，法国在海陆两方面所遭受的惨败，这个王国所承受的极大苦难，以及几乎无望再把这场正在毁灭法国、英国却泰然处之的战争继续进行下去，迫使路易十四不得不做出极为丢脸的让步来争取和平了。他同意交出整个西班牙王国，只将那不勒斯留给那位波旁国王。联军拒绝了这一条件；他们要求安茹公爵放弃整个西班牙帝国，不再称王，此外还向法国提出了许多造成严重后果的条件。路易十四是不会答应这些条件的，所以战争便继续进行下去。

在余下的那几年里，虽说盟国海军艰难的作战行动并不像以前那样显著了，但其影响的真实性却仍然存在；到了此时，这种作战已是主要由英国独自进行，荷兰很少协助了。大部分时间都被限制在加泰罗尼亚的那位奥地利王子，通过英国舰队与撒丁岛和德属意大利各省之间保持着联系；不过，法国海军完全消失了，而路易十四也明显无意在

of Germany by the English fleet; but the entire disappearance of the French navy and the evident intention on the part of Louis to keep no squadrons at sea, allowed some diminution of the Mediterranean fleet, with the result of greater protection to trade. In the years 1710 and 1711 expeditions were also made against the French colonies in North America. Nova Scotia was taken, but an attempt on Quebec failed.

During the winter of 1709 and 1710 Louis withdrew all the French troops from Spain, thus abandoning the cause of his grandson. But when the cause of France was at the very lowest, and it seemed as though she might be driven to concessions which would reduce her to a second-class power, the existence of the coalition was threatened by the disgrace of Marlborough, who represented England in it. His loss of favor with the queen was followed by the accession to power of the party opposed to the war, or rather to its further continuance. This change took place in the summer of 1710, and the inclination toward peace was strengthened both by the favorable position in which England then stood for treating, and by the heavy burden she was bearing; which it became evident could bring in no further advantages commensurate to its weight. The weaker ally, Holland, had gradually ceased to contribute her stipulated share to the sea forces; and although far-sighted Englishmen might see with complacency the disappearance of a rival sea power, the immediate increase of expense was more looked to and felt by the men of the day. The cost both of the continental and Spanish wars was also largely defrayed by England's subsidies; and while that on the continent could bring her no further gain, it was seen that the sympathies of the Spanish people could not be overborne in favor of Carlos III. without paying more than the game was worth. Secret negotiations between England and France soon began, and received an additional impulse by the unexpected death of the Emperor of Germany, the brother of the Austrian claimant of the Spanish throne. There being no other male heir,

海上部署小型舰队，使得英国的地中海舰队虽说规模稍减，但结果反而是增强了对贸易的保护力度。在1710年和1711年，英国还派遣了远征军，前去攻打北美的法国殖民地。远征军攻下了新斯科舍，但攻打魁北克却失败了。

在1709年至1710年间的这个冬季，路易十四从西班牙撤回了所有的法国军队，不再支持其孙儿的王业了。不过，正当法国的形势处于此种最低谷，似乎不得不做出让步，使得法国变成一个二流国家之时，英、荷、奥之间的同盟关系，却因在同盟中代表着英国的马尔伯勒失宠而受到了威胁。他失宠于英国女王之后，反对战争的那一派，或者更准确一点来说，就是反对继续进行战争的那一派上台掌权了。这一变故发生在1710年夏季，而英国当时正处在谈判的有利地位，同时承受着沉重的负担，故这两个方面都加强了整个国家渴望和平的那种趋势；很显然，这种形势不可能再给英国带来与之相应的什么优势。荷兰这个实力较弱的盟国，已经逐渐停止履行其对于联合海军应尽的义务了；尽管一些目光远大的英国人可能会满意地看到，一个与英国竞争的海洋大国将不复存在，但当时的人更关注的，却是英国的军费支出马上就因此而增加了。在欧洲大陆上进行的战争和西班牙战争中，联合省的费用主要也是由英国所提供的援助来支出的；而由于欧洲大陆上的战事无法再为英国带来进一步的利益，所以人们认为，西班牙人对波旁皇室的同情之心，是不可能在没有付出巨大代价的情况下，单纯为了支持卡洛斯三世而被压倒的。英、法两国间很快就开始了秘密谈判，而德意志皇帝的辞世又为谈判增加了一种动力；德意志皇帝正是身为西班牙国王的那位奥地利王子的哥哥。由于德皇没有其他的男性子嗣，所以卡洛斯马上就成了奥地利皇帝，并且随后不久即被推举为德意志皇

Carlos became at once emperor of Austria, and was soon after elected emperor of Germany. England had no more wish to see two crowns on an Austrian head than on that of a Bourbon.

The demands made by England, as conditions of peace in 1711, showed her to have become a sea power in the purest sense of the word, not only in fact, but also in her own consciousness. She required that the same person should never be king both of France and Spain; that a barrier of fortified towns should be granted her allies, Holland and Germany, as a defensive line against France; that French conquests from her allies should be restored; and for herself she demanded the formal cession of Gibraltar and Port Mahon, whose strategic and maritime value has been pointed out, the destruction of the port of Dunkirk, the home nest of the privateers that preyed on English commerce, the cession of the French colonies of Newfoundland, Hudson's Bay, and Nova Scotia, the last of which she held at that time, and finally, treaties of commerce with France and Spain, and the concession of the monopoly of the slave trade with Spanish America, known as the Asiento, which Spain had given to France in 1701.

Negotiations continued, though hostilities did not cease; and in June, 1712, a four months' truce between Great Britain and France removed the English troops from the allied armies on the continent, their great leader Marlborough having been taken from their head the year before. The campaign of 1712 was favorable to France; but in almost any event the withdrawal of Great Britain made the end of the war a question of but a short time. The remonstrances of Holland were met by the reply that since 1707 the Dutch had not furnished more than one third their quota of ships, and taking the war through, not over one half. The House of Commons in an address to the throne in 1712 complained that —

"The service at sea hath been carried on through the whole course of the war in a

帝。英国既不愿看到两顶王冠加于一位波旁皇室成员头上，同样也不愿看到两顶王冠加于一位哈布斯堡皇室成员的头上。

英国在1711年和约中所提的要求，表明该国已经成为了一个最纯粹的海洋大国；非但事实如此，而该国也已清醒地意识到了这一点。英国要求，法国和西班牙决不能由同一位国王来统治；应当允许荷兰和德国这两个盟国在一些市镇修筑工事，形成一道屏障，以此作为抵御法国进犯的防线；法国从英国盟邦掠夺得来的战利品应当归还；应当将直布罗陀和马翁港正式割让给英国——这两个地方在战略上和海洋上的重要性，前面我们已经指出来了；它还要求毁掉敦克尔克港，因为这儿是劫掠英国贸易的私掠者的老巢；应当割让纽芬兰、哈德逊湾以及新斯科舍等法属殖民地给英国，这是法国当时最后的几个殖民地；最后，英国要求与法国和西班牙分别签订贸易条约，还要求法国转让在拉丁美洲进行贩奴贸易的垄断权——此种垄断史称"贩奴权"，是1701年由西班牙授予给法国的。

尽管敌对行动不断，但谈判还是继续进行着；1712年6月，英法两国签订了一份为期4个月的停战协定，英国便将本国军队从欧洲大陆上的盟军中撤了出来，而英军的伟大领袖马尔伯勒早在前一年就不再担任盟军统帅了。1712年，战局对法国实际上是有利的；不过，在几乎每一场战事中，英军都退避三舍，使得战争结束只是一个时间早晚的问题了。荷兰提出的种种抗议，都得到了这样的回答：自1707年以来，荷兰一直就没有装备超过其应承担份额三分之一的舰船，就算从整场战争来看，它所装备的军舰也没有超过其应承担份额的一半。在1712年的一份奏章中，英国众议院发牢骚说：

manner highly disadvantageous to your Majesty's kingdom, for the necessity requiring that great fleets should be fitted out every year for maintaining a superiority in the Mediterranean and for opposing any force which the enemy might prepare either at Dunkirk or in the ports of west France; your Majesty's readiness, in fitting out your proportion of ships for all parts of that service, hath not prevailed with Holland, which has been greatly deficient every year in proportion to what your Majesty hath furnished. ... Hence your Majesty hath been obliged to supply those deficiencies with additional reinforcements of your own ships, and your Majesty's ships have been forced in greater numbers to continue in remote seas, and at unseasonable times of the year, to the great damage of the navy. This also hath straitened the convoys for trade; the coasts have been exposed for want of cruisers; and you have been disabled from annoying the enemy in their most beneficial commerce with the West Indies, whence they received those vast supplies of treasure, without which they could not have supported the expenses of the war."

In fact, between 1701 and 1716 the commerce of Spanish America had brought into France forty million dollars in specie. To these complaints the Dutch envoy to England could only reply that Holland was not in a condition to fulfil her compacts. The reverses of 1712, added to Great Britain's fixed purpose to have peace, decided the Dutch to the same; and the English still kept, amid their dissatisfaction with their allies, so much of their old feeling against France as to support all the reasonable claims of Holland. April 11, 1713, an almost general peace, known as the Peace of Utrecht, one of the landmarks of history, was signed between France on the one hand, and England, Holland, Prussia, Portugal, and Savoy on the other. The emperor still held out, but the loss of British subsidies fettered the movements of his armies, and with the withdrawal of the sea powers the continental war might have fallen of itself; but France with

"在此次战争的整个过程中，海军都是以一种极不利于陛下之王国的方式在作战，因为每一年我们都必须装备规模庞大的舰队，方能在地中海地区保持优势，方能对抗敌人可能在敦克尔克或者法国西部诸港部署的任何军队；陛下迅速装备了我国所承配额的舰船，参与了海战中的方方面面，但荷兰却并非如此，该国每年所装备之舰船数量，与陛下所装备之数量相较，都严重不足……因此，陛下不得不用我国的舰船，以及额外的兵力来进行补充，而陛下之舰船，也不得不以庞大的规模、并且在一年当中不合时宜的时候持续游弋于遥远之海域，从而给海军带来了极大的损失。此种情况，亦使得贸易护航任务节节吃紧；因为缺少巡洋舰，故我国沿海毫无防御；我们也无法骚扰敌方与西印度群岛之间那种获利巨大的贸易，敌人因此而获得了不菲之财源，倘若没有这种财源，他们是承受不了战争开支的。"

事实上，在1701年至1716年间，与西属拉丁美洲之间的贸易，为法国带来了4000万美元的收入。对于这些牢骚，荷兰驻英公使只是回应说，荷兰当时的形势是无法履行其约定义务的。1712年盟军数次战败，加上英国已经定下和谈目标，因此荷兰人也想进行和谈了；此时，尽管对其盟国有诸多不满，但英国人对法国仍然保持着以前的那种厌憎之情，所以还是支持了荷兰所有的合理要求。1713年4月11日，法国作为一方，与英、荷、普鲁士、葡萄牙以及萨伏伊的这一方，签订了一份几近全面、属于历史里程碑之一的和约，史称《乌特勒支和约》。奥地利皇帝仍在坚持，但英国不再拨款，使得他手下的军队寸步难行，并且随着各个海洋大国撤军，大陆战事很可能就只能由奥地利自己来支撑了；而法国呢，由于拳脚不再受缚，所以1713年在德国境内继续打了一场漂亮的胜

her hands freed carried on during 1713 a brilliant and successful campaign in Germany. On the 7th of March, 1714, peace was signed between France and Austria. Some embers of the war continued to burn in Catalonia and the Balearic Islands, which persisted in their rebellion against Philip V.; but the revolt was stifled as soon as the arms of France were turned against them. Barcelona was taken by storm in September, 1714; the islands submitted in the following summer.

The changes effected by this long war and sanctioned by the peace, neglecting details of lesser or passing importance, may be stated as follows:

1. The House of Bourbon was settled on the Spanish throne, and the Spanish empire retained its West Indian and American possessions; the purpose of William III. against her dominion there was frustrated when England undertook to support the Austrian prince, and so fastened the greater part of her naval force to the Mediterranean.

2. The Spanish empire lost its possessions in the Netherlands, Gelderland going to the new kingdom of Prussia and Belgium to the emperor; the Spanish Netherlands thus became the Austrian Netherlands.

3. Spain lost also the principal islands of the Mediterranean; Sardinia being given to Austria, Minorca with its fine harbor to Great Britain, and Sicily to the Duke of Savoy.

4. Spain lost also her Italian possessions, Milan and Naples going to the emperor. Such, in the main, were the results to Spain of the fight over the succession to her throne.

France, the backer of the successful claimant, came out of the strife worn out, and with considerable loss of territory. She had succeeded in placing a king of her own royal house on a neighboring throne, but her sea strength was exhausted, her population diminished, her financial condition ruined. The European territory surrendered was on her northern and eastern

仗。1714年3月7日，法、奥两国终于签订了和约。加泰罗尼亚和巴利阿里群岛等地仍有一些战火余烬，两地都在坚持反抗菲利普五世；不过，一待法军转而挥师两地，这次起义马上就被镇压下去了。巴塞罗那在1714年9月被彻底攻克；而到了第二年夏季，其余岛屿也都纷纷投降了。

由这场旷日持久的战争所导致、并在和约中所体现的变化，倘若不去考虑那些较不重要或不具长远重要性的细节，就可以归纳如下：

1. 波旁王室在西班牙王位上稳住了根基，而西班牙帝国则保住了西印度群岛和美洲的殖民地；英国开始支持那位奥地利王子，并因此而使得其大部分海军都被派往了地中海地区，因此之后威廉三世在此进攻西班牙领土的目标就无果而终了。

2. 西班牙帝国丧失了在尼德兰的领地，格尔德兰归了新的普鲁士王国，比利时则给了奥地利皇帝；于是，西属尼德兰便变成了奥属尼德兰。

3. 西班牙也不再拥有地中海上的一些重要岛屿：撒丁岛割让给了奥地利，米诺卡岛及其良港割让给了英国，而西西里岛则给了萨伏伊大公。

4. 西班牙还失去了意大利境内的领地：米兰和那不勒斯都割让给了奥地利皇帝。这些，就是王位继承战给西班牙带来的主要后果。

法国是支持菲利普五世成功地继承了王位的那一方，但从此次战争中脱身的时候，该国非但已经千疮百孔，还丧失了大量的领地。虽说法国成功地将一位属于同一皇室的国王成功地扶上了一个邻国的王位，但法国海军的实力已被消耗殆尽，人口数量大幅减少，财政状况也已严重受损。在欧洲大陆割让的领土，都位于法国北部与东部边境；而

boundaries; and she abandoned the use of the port of Dunkirk, the centre of that privateering warfare so dreaded by English merchants. In America, the cession of Nova Scotia and Newfoundland was the first step toward that entire loss of Canada which befell half a century later; but for the present she retained Cape Breton Island, with its port Louisburg, the key to the Gulf and River St. Lawrence.

The gains of England, by the treaty and the war, corresponded very nearly to the losses of France and Spain, and were all in the direction of extending and strengthening her sea power. Gibraltar and Port Mahon in the Mediterranean, and the colonies already mentioned in North America, afforded new bases to that power, extending and protecting her trade. Second only to the expansion of her own was the injury to the sea power of France and Holland, by the decay of their navies in consequence of the immense drain of the land warfare; further indications of that decay will be given later. The very neglect of Holland to fill up her quota of ships, and the bad condition of those sent, while imposing extra burdens upon England, may be considered a benefit, forcing the British navy to greater development and effort. The disproportion in military power on the sea was further increased by the destruction of the works at Dunkirk; for though not in itself a first-class port, nor of much depth of water, it had great artificial military strength, and its position was peculiarly adapted to annoy English trade. It was but forty miles from the South Foreland and the Downs, and the Channel abreast it is but twenty miles wide. Dunkirk was one of Louis' earliest acquisitions, and in its development was as his own child; the dismantling of the works and filling-in of the port show the depth of his humiliation at this time. But it was the wisdom of England not to base her sea power solely on military positions nor even on fighting-ships, and the commercial advantages she had now gained by the war and the peace were very great. The grant of the slave trade with Spanish America, in itself lucrative, became

法国也不再利用敦克尔克港了，尽管此处曾经是令英国商人闻风丧胆的那种私掠巡航战的中心。在美洲，割让新斯科舍和纽芬兰还只是第一步，半个世纪之后，法国便失去了整个加拿大；不过，目前法国还保留着布雷顿角岛以及岛上的路易斯堡港——此港是通往圣劳伦斯湾和圣劳伦斯河的门户。

英国通过此次战争以及所签条约而获得的好处，差不多等同于法国和西班牙两国所承受损失的总和，并且全部都是让英国朝着扩张和巩固其制海权的方向发展。地中海地区的直布罗陀和马翁港，以及前面已经提到的北美诸殖民地，都给英国的制海权提供了新的基地，使之能够扩张并且保护该国的贸易。程度仅次于英国海上实力扩张的，便是法国和荷兰因为陆上战争的巨大消耗而使得海军日渐衰落，从而给两国制海权带来的那种损害了；下文中我们还会给出两国海军衰落下去的更多迹象。荷兰疏于装备其应当派遣的舰船数量，以及该国所派舰船的糟糕状况，虽说给英国强加了额外的负担，但也可以说是一件好事，因为这迫使英国海军不得不做出更大的努力，不得不获取更大的发展。海上兵力的这种失衡，因敦克尔克港防御工事被毁而进一步加剧了；因为虽说敦克尔克本身并非一流港口，也非深水港，但其人为的军事实力极为强大，而其位置也尤其适合于阻挠英国的贸易往来。此处离南福兰和唐斯锚地仅有40英里，而整个英吉利海峡才20英里宽。敦克尔克是路易十四早期所占地区之一，而在此处发展起来的过程中，路易十四也像对待自己的孩子一样，对它倍加关注；所以，从拆除此处的防御工事并将港口填塞起来这一点上，就可以看出当时他所受屈辱的深切程度。不过，英国很明智，其制海权并非仅仅倚赖于军事要地，甚至也并非仅仅倚赖于战舰，所以，如今它通过此次战争与所签和约在商业贸易上

yet more so as the basis for an immense smuggling intercourse with those countries, which gave the English a partial recompense for their failure to obtain actual possession; while the cessions made to Portugal by France in South America were mainly to the advantage of England, which had obtained the control of Portuguese trade by the treaty of 1703. The North American colonies ceded were valuable, not merely nor chiefly as military stations, but commercially; and treaties of commerce on favorable terms were made both with France and Spain. A minister of the day, defending the treaty in Parliament, said: "The advantages from this peace appear in the addition made to our wealth; in the great quantities of bullion lately coined in our mint; by the vast increase in our shipping employed since the peace, in the fisheries, and in merchandise; and by the remarkable growth of the customs upon imports, and of our manufactures, and the growth of our country upon export;" in a word, by the impetus to trade in all its branches.

While England thus came out from the war in good running condition, and fairly placed in that position of maritime supremacy which she has so long maintained, her old rival in trade and fighting was left hopelessly behind. As the result of the war Holland obtained nothing at sea, — no colony, no station. The commercial treaty with France placed her on the same terms as England, but she received no concessions giving her a footing in Spanish America like that obtained by her ally. Indeed, some years before the peace, while the coalition was still maintaining Carlos, a treaty was made with the latter by the British minister, unknown to the Dutch, practically giving the British monopoly of Spanish trade in America; sharing it only with Spaniards, which was pretty much the same as not sharing it at all. This treaty accidentally became known, and made a great impression on the Dutch; but England was then so necessary to the coalition that she ran no risk of being left out by its other members.

所获得的优势就极其巨大了。西属拉丁美洲的贩奴特许权本身就很合算，而在此基础上与美洲国家进行大规模的走私活动之后，这种特许权就变得更是利润可观了，因为这些国家会因为自己没有获得实际的特许权而支付部分酬金给英国；法国在南美洲割让给葡萄牙的领地，基本上也是有利于英国的，因为英国通过1703年所签条约，已经掌控了葡萄牙的贸易。在北美地区割让给英国的那些殖民地，并非仅仅是作为军事要地、也并非主要是作为军事基地才显得重要，而是在商业贸易上，这些殖民地个个都重要得很；此外，英国还与法国和西班牙分别签署了贸易条约，其中的条款对英国都很有利。当时的一位大臣在国会里为《乌特勒支和约》进行辩护时，称："此和约所带来的好处，体现在我国财力的增长上；体现在我国造币厂里铸造的大量金条银条上；体现在自和约签订以来，渔业与商业领域雇用的我国船只数量有了巨大增长；体现在进口关税和我国制造业、对外贸易业的显著增长上，"总而言之，就是体现在英国各行各业都有了进行贸易的动力上。

这样，英国在发展状况良好的情况下摆脱了此次战争，并且安然坐稳了它已经长久维持下来的海洋霸主地位；而其宿敌法国，却在贸易上和战争中都毫无希望地落到了英国的后面。战争结束之后，荷兰在海洋上一无所获——既没有得到殖民地，也没有获得军事基地。虽说与法国所签商贸协定的条款跟英国一样，但法国并未割让领地给它，使它无法像其盟友英国那样，在西属拉丁美洲获得一处立足之地。实际上，在签订和约的数年之前，当盟国还在支持卡洛斯的时候，英国公使就已在荷兰人不知情的情况下，与卡洛斯签订了一份条约，事实上让英国垄断了西班牙在美洲所进行的商业贸易；英国只允许西班牙人参与贸易，这实际上跟西班牙人不参与贸易没什么两样。可一不小心，这份条约被人知道

The gain which Holland made by land was that of military occupation only, of certain fortified places in the Austrian Netherlands, known to history as the "barrier towns;" nothing was added by them to her revenue, population, or resources; nothing to that national strength which must underlie military institutions. Holland had forsaken, perhaps unavoidably, the path by which she had advanced to wealth and to leadership among nations. The exigencies of her continental position had led to the neglect of her navy, which in those days of war and privateering involved a loss of carrying-trade and commerce: and although she held her head high through the war, the symptoms of weakness were apparent in her failing armaments. Therefore, though the United Provinces attained the great object for which they began the war, and saved the Spanish Netherlands from the hands of France, the success was not worth the cost. Thenceforth they withdrew for a long period from the wars and diplomacy of Europe; partly, perhaps, because they saw how little they had gained, but yet more from actual weakness and inability. After the strenuous exertions of the war came a reaction, which showed painfully the inherent weakness of a State narrow in territory and small in the number of its people. The visible decline of the Provinces dates from the Peace of Utrecht; the real decline began earlier. Holland ceased to be numbered among the great powers of Europe, her navy was no longer a military factor in diplomacy, and her commerce also shared in the general decline of the State.

It remains only to notice briefly the results to Austria, and to Germany generally. France yielded the barrier of the Rhine, with fortified places on the east bank of the river. Austria received, as has been mentioned, Belgium, Sardinia, Naples, and the Spanish possessions in northern Italy; dissatisfied in other respects, Austria was especially discontented at her failure to obtain Sicily, and did not cease negotiating afterward, until she had secured that

了，使得荷兰人极为震惊；不过当时的同盟离不开英国，荷兰也承担不起被其他盟国冷落的风险。荷兰在陆地上的收获，只是军事占领了奥属尼德兰的一些要塞，即史称的"壁垒城镇"；这些地方，没有给荷兰的国家收入、人口数量或者资源带来任何增益，也没有增强荷兰的国家实力，而军事机构却正是建立在国家实力这一基础之上的。荷兰放弃了那条曾经通往国家富强和成为各国领袖的道路，或许也是必然的。它在欧洲大陆上那种岌岌可危的地位，使得它忽视了海军的发展，从而导致了在战争和私掠活动频发的那个年代，荷兰的海洋运输业和商业贸易遭受了重大损失：并且，尽管该国在整个战争中都依然趾高气扬，但其武器装备的缺乏与落后，已经明显地呈现出其衰落之兆了。因此，虽说荷兰共和国实现了其开战的大部分目标，并且从法国手中挽救了西属尼德兰，但这种成功，却是得不偿失的。自此以后，该国有很长一段时间淡出了欧洲的战争和外交舞台；虽然或许部分是因为该国看到自己所获甚少，但更多的却是因为该国实在是软弱无能。经过这场艰苦卓绝的战争之后，该国出现了一种保守之势，令人痛心地表现出了一个领土狭窄、人口不多的国家所固有的那种弱点。荷兰共和国明显的衰落之势，即是始于《乌特勒支和约》；而其真正的衰落，其实早就开始了。荷兰不再是欧洲列强中的一员，荷兰海军不再是欧洲外交中的一个军事因素，而荷兰的商业贸易也随着整个国家的全面衰落而衰败下去了。

其余方面，我们只需简单地注意一下此战给奥地利和德国带来的一般性结果就行了。法国放弃了莱茵河这道屏障，以及此河东岸上的各处要塞。前面已经说过，奥地利得到了比利时、撒丁岛和那不勒斯，以及西班牙在意大利北部的一些领地；虽说在其他方面很不满意，但令奥地利尤感不满的是，它没能得到西西里岛，所以后来一直都在谈判，直

island. A circumstance more important to Germany and to all Europe than this transitory acquisition of distant and alien countries by Austria was the rise of Prussia, which dates from this war as a Protestant and military kingdom destined to weigh in the balance against Austria.

Such were the leading results of the War of the Spanish Succession, "the vastest yet witnessed by Europe since the Crusades." It was a war whose chief military interest was on the land, — a war in which fought two of the greatest generals of all times, Marlborough and Prince Eugene, the names of whose battles, Blenheim, Ramillies, Malplaquet, Turin, are familiar to the most casual reader of history; while a multitude of able men distinguished themselves on the other theatres of the strife, in Flanders, in Germany, in Italy, in Spain. On the sea only one great battle, and that scarcely worthy of the name, took place. Yet looking only, for the moment, to immediate and evident results, who reaped the benefit? Was it France, whose only gain was to seat a Bourbon on the Spanish throne? Was it Spain, whose only gain was to have a Bourbon king instead of an Austrian, and thus a closer alliance with France? Was it Holland, with its barrier of fortified towns, its ruined navy, and its exhausted people? Was it, lastly, Austria, even though she had fought with the money of the sea powers, and gained such maritime States as the Netherlands and Naples? Was it with these, who had waged war more and more exclusively by land, and set their eyes more and more on gains on the land, or was it not rather with England, who had indeed paid for that continental war and even backed it with her troops, but who meanwhile was building up her navy, strengthening, extending, and protecting her commerce, seizing maritime positions, — in a word, founding and rearing her sea power upon the ruins of that of her rivals, friend and foe alike? It is not to depreciate the gains of others that the eye fixes on England's naval growth; their gains but bring out more clearly the immenseness

至它将该岛收入囊中才作罢。跟奥地利暂时获取这些遥远而陌生的地方相比，对德国和整个欧洲都更加重要的一种情况，便是普鲁士的崛起；作为一个信奉新教的军事王国，普鲁士注定会在反抗奥地利的过程中发挥重要的作用。

这些，就是西班牙王位继承战争的主要结果，而此次战争则是"欧洲自十字军东征以来最为浩大的一次战争"。这是一场军事意义主要是在陆地上的战争——在此次战争中，马尔伯勒和欧根亲王这两位有史以来最伟大的将领并肩作战，他们所进行的布伦海姆、拉米伊[7]、马尔普拉奎特[8]、都灵[9]等战役之名，即便是最为草率的历史读者，也都耳熟能详；而大量杰出人士也在此战中的其他一些战场上崭露头角，比如在佛兰德斯、在德国、在意大利、在西班牙。在海上，只发生过一场大规模的海战，并且此战也很难称得上是一场真正的海战。然而，此刻倘若只来看一看这场战争中那些直接而明显的结果，那么谁是赢家呢？是法国吗？该国的唯一收获，便是将一位波旁王室的国王扶上了西班牙王位。是西班牙吗？该国的唯一收获，便是用一位波旁王室的国王，取代了一位哈布斯堡王族的国王，从而与法国结成了更加亲密的同盟关系。是拥有了"壁垒城镇"，却使得海军败落、民穷财尽了的荷兰吗？最后，是用各个海洋大国的拨款来打仗、并且获得了尼德兰与那不勒斯这些海洋之邦的奥地利吗？是那些所进行的战争日益集中于陆上，而其目光也日益只盯着陆上利益的国家呢，还是英国？事实上，在欧洲大陆作战的经费都是由英国支出的，英国甚至还派出了军队，可该国在此期间也加强了自己的海军，巩固、扩张和保护了自己的贸易，占领了海上的军事要地——总而言之，就是在竞争对手、友邦和仇敌的废墟之上，创立并巩固了自己的制海权。我们关注英国

of hers. It was a gain to France to have a friend rather than an enemy in her rear, though her navy and shipping were ruined. It was a gain to Spain to be brought in close intercourse with a living country like France after a century of political death, and she had saved the greater part of her threatened possessions. It was a gain to Holland to be definitively freed from French aggression, with Belgium in the hands of a strong instead of a weak State. And it doubtless was a gain to Austria not only to have checked, chiefly at the expense of others, the progress of her hereditary enemy, but also to have received provinces like Sicily and Naples, which, under wise government, might become the foundation of a respectable sea power. But not one of these gains, nor all together, compared in greatness, and much less in solidity, with the gain to England of that unequalled sea power which started ahead during the War of the League of Augsburg, and received its completeness and seal during that of the Spanish Succession. By it she controlled the great commerce of the open sea with a military shipping that had no rival, and in the exhausted condition of the other nations could have none; and that shipping was now securely based on strong positions in all the disputed quarters of the world. Although her Indian empire was not yet begun, the vast superiority of her navy would enable her to control the communications of other nations with those rich and distant regions, and to assert her will in any disputes arising among the trading-stations of the different nationalities. The commerce which had sustained her in prosperity, and her allies in military efficiency, during the war, though checked and harassed by the enemy's cruisers (to which she could pay only partial attention amid the many claims upon her), started with a bound into new life when the war was over. All over the world, exhausted by their share of the common suffering, people were longing for the return of prosperity and peaceful commerce; and there was no country ready as England was in wealth, capital, and shipping to forward and reap the advantages of every enterprise by which

海军的发展情况，并非是要贬损别国所获得的利益；但这些国家的收获，不过是使英国所获利益之巨大，显得更加明显罢了。尽管法国的海军和海洋运输严重受损且一蹶不振了，但在自己的后方拥有了一个友邦而非仇敌，对法国来说，也是一种收获。在长达一个世纪的政治沉寂之后，再跟像法国这样活跃的国家进行密切往来，对于西班牙来说也是一种收获，并且，西班牙也保存下了大部分曾经受到威胁的领地。对于荷兰来说，收获就是最终摆脱了法国的进犯，并让比利时掌控在一个强国而非弱国的手中。而对于奥地利而言，该国非但主要通过牺牲别国的利益而遏制了其宿敌的发展，还获得了像西西里和那不勒斯这样的省份——它们在一个英明的政府治下，可能会为确立一种强大制海权而打下基础，所以这无疑是奥地利的一大收获。不过，这些收获中没有哪一种，甚至是这些收获加起来，也没法在规模上、更不用说在巩固性上与英国所获的利益相媲美；英国那种无可匹敌的制海权，在奥格斯堡同盟战争期间开始崭露头角，并在西班牙王位继承战争中得以完善并标志性地确立起来了。凭借这种制海权，该国用一支所向无敌的海军，掌控了公海之上的大规模贸易，而别的国家都已民穷财尽，不可能再拥有这样一支海军；并且，如今在全球各个有争议的地区，英国海军都有了牢固而强大的军事基地。尽管它的印度帝国此时还未成形，但其海军的巨大优势，使得英国既能够控制其他国家与那些富饶而遥远的地区所进行的贸易往来，还能在不同国家贸易站点之间产生的所有纠纷中，维护本国的意志。让该国在战争期间能够繁荣发展起来并让其盟国保持作战效率的贸易，虽说受到了敌方巡洋舰的阻挠和骚扰（由于要应对的问题繁多，英国无法全力去对付这些巡洋舰），但战争一结束，就必定会焕发出新的活力。世界各国都因承受此次

the interchange of commodities was promoted, either by lawful or unlawful means. In the War of the Spanish Succession, by her own wise management and through the exhaustion of other nations, not only her navy but her trade was steadily built up; and indeed, in that dangerous condition of the seas, traversed by some of the most reckless and restless cruisers France ever sent out, the efficiency of the navy meant safer voyages, and so more employment for the merchant-ships. The British merchant-ships, being better protected than those of the Dutch, gained the reputation of being far safer carriers, and the carrying-trade naturally passed more and more into their hands; while the habit of employing them in preference, once established, was likely to continue.

"Taking all things together," says an historian of the British navy, "I doubt whether the credit of the English nation ever stood higher than at this period, or the spirit of the people higher. The success of our arms at sea, the necessity of protecting our trade, and the popularity of every step taken to increase our maritime power, occasioned such measures to be pursued as annually added to our force. Hence arose that mighty difference which at the close of the year 1706 appeared in the Royal Navy; this, not only in the number but in the quality of the ships, was much superior to what it had been at the time of the Revolution or even before. Hence it was that our trade rather increased than diminished during the last war, and that we gained so signally by our strict intercourse with Portugal."

The sea power of England therefore was not merely in the great navy, with which we too commonly and exclusively associate it; France had had such a navy in 1688, and it shrivelled away like a leaf in the fire. Neither was it in a prosperous commerce alone; a few years after the date at which we have arrived, the commerce of France took on fair proportions, but the first blast of war swept it off the seas as the navy of Cromwell had once swept that of Holland.

战争所带来的共同苦难而疲惫不堪了，各国人民都渴望着重归繁荣，重新太太平平地进行贸易；没有哪一个国家像英国这样，在财力、资金和运输等方面都做好了准备，无论是通过合法途径还是非法手段，都能够推进并获取促进了商品交易的各行各业所带来的好处。在西班牙王位继承战争中，通过自身的高明管理以及消耗别国的财力，英国稳步地建立起了自己的海军和贸易；并且事实上，当时法国派出了史上最鲁莽、最不安分的一些巡逻舰越洋过海，在各个海域都危险重重的这种情况下，海军良好的作战效率就意味着航运更安全，也意味着商船上会因此而雇用更多的人。英国的商船因为比荷兰商船受到了更好的护卫，因此被人们称作是安全得多的承运者，而英国商船所承揽的运输业务自然也日益增加了；人们一旦养成了更喜欢雇用英国船只的习惯，这种习惯很可能就会保持下去。

"总体来看，"一位研究英国海军的历史学家称，"我认为英国这个民族的威望，或者说整个民族的精神状态，都在这个时期达到了巅峰。我国军队在海洋上所取得的成就，保护我国贸易的这种需求，以及所采取的每一步都因增强了我国制海权而广受欢迎，使得继续实行这些措施后，我国的实力年复一年地增强了。所以，1706年末皇家海军才呈现出了一种强大有力的不同面貌；此种不同，不仅体现在舰船数量上，而且体现在舰船质量上，这两个方面都大大超过了英国革命时期或者更早的皇家海军。因此，在上一次战争中，我国贸易才会不降反升，才会通过与葡萄牙之间的周密通商，取得如此突出的收获。"

所以，尽管我们经常都认为制海权只与海军相关，但英国的制海权并非仅仅体现在其庞大的海军上；法国在1688年也拥有这样一支海军，可这支海军却像火中之叶一样迅速枯萎了。英国的制海权也并非仅仅体现在商贸繁荣这一个方面；我们业已论述到的

It was in the union of the two, carefully fostered, that England made the gain of sea power over and beyond all other States; and this gain is distinctly associated with and dates from the War of the Spanish Succession. Before that war England was one of the sea powers; after it she was the sea power, without any second. This power also she held alone, unshared by friend and unchecked by foe. She alone was rich, and in her control of the sea and her extensive shipping had the sources of wealth so much in her hands that there was no present danger of a rival on the ocean. Thus her gain of sea power and wealth was not only great but solid, being wholly in her own hands; while the gains of the other States were not merely inferior in degree, but weaker in kind, in that they depended more or less upon the good will of other peoples.

Is it meant, it may be asked, to attribute to sea power alone the greatness or wealth of any State? Certainly not. The due use and control of the sea is but one link in the chain of exchange by which wealth accumulates; but it is the central link, which lays under contribution other nations for the benefit of the one holding it, and which, history seems to assert, most surely of all gathers to itself riches. In England, this control and use of the sea seems to arise naturally, from the concurrence of many circumstances; the years immediately preceding the War of the Spanish Succession had, moreover, furthered the advance of her prosperity by a series of fiscal measures, which Macaulay speaks of as "the deep and solid foundation on which was to rise the most gigantic fabric of commercial prosperity which the world had ever seen." It may be questioned, however, whether the genius of the people, inclined to and developed by trade, did not make easier the taking of such measures; whether their adoption did not at least partially spring from, as well as add to, the sea power of the nation. However that may be, there is seen, on the opposite side of the Channel, a nation which started ahead of England in the race, — a

那个时间的数年之后，虽说法国的商业贸易也相应地发展繁荣起来了，可战争的狂风一到，就把法国赶出了各个海域，就像克伦威尔治下的海军曾经横扫荷兰的贸易业一样。正是在两国精心培育的盟友关系中，英国才获得了远远优于其他国家的制海权；而这种收获，无疑与西班牙王位继承战争有关，且是始于这次战争。此战之前，英国只是海洋大国之一；而此战之后，它却成了唯一的海洋大国。这种制海权也由该国一手掌握，既无友邦共享，亦无仇敌遏制。该国一枝独秀，富有且独霸海洋，而其四通八达的航运业将众多的财富之源聚于手中，所以如今在海洋上已无出现竞争对手之虞。这样一来，该国所获的制海权和财力非但巨大，而且牢固，全都处于自己的掌控之下；其他国家所获得的利益，既在程度上大大不如英国，而性质上也较脆弱，因为它们或多或少，都有赖于其他民族的友好。

那么我们不妨问一问，这是否意味着，海权只是一个国家的伟大或者富裕所带来的结果呢？当然不是。正确地利用并掌控海洋，只是使财富得以积聚起来的商品交换链条上的一环罢了；不过，这是其中的中心环节，目的是让别的国家为掌控了海权的国家的利益而甘愿做出牺牲，并且历史似已肯定，这个环节的首先任务，无疑便是将财富聚集于该国。英国对海洋的此种掌控和利用，似乎是因为多种条件同时存在而自发形成的；此外，在西班牙王位继承战争之前的那些年里，一系列财政措施也推动了英国走向繁荣富强的步伐——麦考利曾称这些措施是"深厚而坚实之基础，在此之上，必将出现世间有史以来结构最为巨大的一种商业繁荣。"然而，人们或许会质疑，英国人民喜欢贸易并由贸易所培养的那种天赋，有没有使得采取这些措施变得更加容易；他们采取这

nation peculiarly well fitted, by situation and resources, for the control of the sea both by war and commerce. The position of France is in this peculiar, that of all the great powers she alone had a free choice; the others were more or less constrained to the land chiefly, or to the sea chiefly, for any movement outside their own borders; but she to her long continental frontier added a seaboard on three seas. In 1672 she definitely chose expansion by land. At that time Colbert had administered her finances for twelve years, and from a state of terrible confusion had so restored them that the revenue of the King of France was more than double that of the King of England. In those days France paid the subsidies of Europe; but Colbert's plans and hopes for France rested upon making her powerful on the sea. The war with Holland arrested these plans, the onward movement of prosperity ceased, the nation was thrown back upon itself, shut off from the outside world. Many causes doubtless worked together to the disastrous result which marked the end of the reign of Louis XIV.: constant wars, bad administration in the latter half of the period, extravagance throughout; but France was practically never invaded, the war was kept at or beyond her own frontiers with slight exceptions, her home industries could suffer little from direct hostilities. In these respects she was nearly equal to England, and under better conditions than her other enemies. What made the difference in the results? Why was France miserable and exhausted, while England was smiling and prosperous? Why did England dictate, and France accept, terms of peace? The reason apparently was the difference in wealth and credit. France stood alone against many enemies; but those enemies were raised and kept moving by English subsidies. The Lord Treasurer of England, writing in 1706 to Marlborough, says: —

"Though the land and trade of both England and Holland have excessive burthens upon

些措施，是否反而增强了该国的海权呢？无论怎样，我们都已看到，在英吉利海峡的另一边，还有一个在这场竞赛中起步比英国更早的国家——该国的位置与资源，都使得它尤其适合于通过战争或者贸易来称霸海洋。在这个方面，之所以说法国的位置非常独特，是因为在所有的海洋大国当中，只有该国可以自由选择；其他各国在本国疆域之外进行活动时，都或多或少，要么主要被限制在陆地上，要么主要被限制于海洋上；而法国呢，除了有一条漫长的大陆边疆，还有一个沿海地区，毗邻三大海域。1672年，该国明确无疑地决定经由陆地进行扩张。当时，柯尔贝尔掌管该国财政已有12年，已将法国财政从一种极端糟糕的混乱状态中恢复过来，使得法国国王的财政收入，变成了英王财政收入的两倍多。在那个时候，是法国向欧洲各国提供资助；但柯尔贝尔为法国所制定的计划和他对法国的期望，是建立在让法国变成一个海洋强国这一基础之上的。法荷战争阻碍了这些计划的实施，迈向繁荣富强的前进步伐停下了，而最后法国也被击退，回到了只能倚赖于自己且断绝了与外界联系的境地。无疑是诸多原因结合起来，才导致了此种标志着路易十四统治终结的可悲后果；这些原因有：战争频发，这一时期后半段的秕政，以及整个这一时期的奢侈浪费等。但是，法国从未被别国入侵过，除了极少数例外情况，战火也只是在该国边疆或者边境之外燃烧，而其国内工业，可能也很少因直接的战争而受损。在这些方面，法国几乎可以与英国相匹敌，而且条件比其他敌国也更加优越。那么，是什么让两国的结局大相径庭呢？为何法国会痛苦悲惨、民穷财尽，而英国却会喜气洋洋、繁荣一片呢？为何英国能够发号施令，而法国却只能接受和约的条款呢？个中原因，显然在于两国财力和威望的差距。法兰西孤立无援，独自面对着诸多敌人；而这些敌人，却是由英国的资助所培育，并在英国的资助之下发展起来的。英国的财务大臣在1706

them, yet the credit continues good both of them and us; whereas the finances of France are so much more exhausted that they are forced to give twenty and twenty-five per cent for every penny they send out of the kingdom, unless they send it in specie."

In 1712 the expenditure of France was 240,000,000 francs, while the taxes brought in only 113,000,000 gross, of which, after deducting losses and necessary expenses, only 37,000,000 remained in the treasury; the deficit was sought to be met by anticipating parts of the revenue for years ahead, and by a series of extraordinary transactions tedious to name or to understand.

"In the summer of 1715 [two years after the peace] it seemed as if the situation could not grow worse, — no more public nor private credit; no more clear revenue for the State; the portions of the revenue not pledged, anticipated on the following years. Neither labor nor consumption could be resumed for want of circulation; usury reigned on the ruins of society. The alternations of high prices and the depreciation of commodities finally crushed the people. Provision riots broke out among them, and even in the army. Manufactures were languishing or suspended; forced mendicity was preying upon the cities. The fields were deserted, the lands fallow for lack of instruments, for lack of manure, for lack of cattle; the houses were falling to ruin. Monarchical France seemed ready to expire with its aged king."

Thus it was in France, with a population of nineteen millions at that time to the eight millions of all the British Islands; with a land vastly more fertile and productive; before the great days, too, of coal and iron. "In England, on the contrary, the immense grants of Parliament in 1710 struck the French prodigiously; for while their credit was low, or in a manner quite gone, ours was at its zenith." During that same war "there appeared that

年写给马尔伯勒的一封信中，曾说：

"尽管英、荷两国的土地与贸易都承受着过重的负担，但荷兰与我国的信贷却都运行良好；法国由于财政枯竭的情况要严重得多，所以他们向国外寄钱时，每1便士都不得不支付20%和25%的手续费，除非他们寄的是金币。"

1712年，法国的财政支出是2亿4000万法郎，但税收总额却只有1亿1300万法郎，而且，这笔税收减去损耗和必要的支出之后，上交国库的就只剩下3700万法郎了；法国政府也曾试图通过预支未来数年的岁入，以及一系列名称冗长而难懂的临时交易，来平衡其财政赤字。

"1715年夏（即和约签订两年之后），法国的形势似乎已经到了无法再糟糕的地步了——没有了公共信贷和私人信贷；国家没有了清晰的收入来源；从未来数年所预支的那一部分财政收入也没有保障。生产活动和消费都因流通性匮乏而无法恢复；在社会败落的废墟之上，高利贷横行。物价飞涨和商品贬值轮番上阵，最终压榨着人民群众。因为供应品不足，民众甚至是军队当中都爆发了骚乱。生产企业都萧条得很，或者关门歇业了；被迫乞讨的人在各大城市里都遍地可见。农田荒废了，土地则由于没有农具、没有肥料、没有耕牛而闲置起来；房屋也纷纷倒塌，变成了废墟。实行君主制度的法国，似乎正准备同该国年老体衰的国王一起断气。"

这就是法国的形势。那时法国的人口数量是1900万，而英伦诸岛人口加起来才800万，而法国的土地，也比英国要富饶和丰产得多；并且，在这一伟大时期以前，法国还拥有丰富的煤、铁资源。"相反，在英国，1710年国会的一笔笔巨额拨款，极大地打击了法国；因为就在法国信贷低迷，或者说在某种程度上完全没有信贷的时候，我国的信

mighty spirit among our merchants which enabled them to carry on all their schemes with a vigor that kept a constant circulation of money throughout the kingdom, and afforded such mighty encouragement to all manufactures as has made the remembrance of those times grateful in worse."

"By the treaty with Portugal we were prodigious gainers. ... The Portuguese began to feel the comfortable effects of their Brazil gold mines, and the prodigious commerce that followed with us made their good fortune in great measure ours; and so it has been ever since; otherwise I know not how the expenses of the war had been borne. ... The running cash in the kingdom increased very considerably, which must be attributed in great measure to our Portuguese trade; and this, as I have made manifest, we owed wholly to our power at sea [which took Portugal from the alliance of the two crowns, and threw her upon the protection of the maritime powers]. Our trade with the Spanish West Indies by way of Cadiz was certainly much interrupted at the beginning of this war; but afterward it was in great measure restored, as well by direct communication with several provinces when under the Archduke, as through Portugal, by which a very great though contraband trade was carried on. We were at the same time very great gainers by our commerce with the Spaniards in the West Indies [also contraband]. ... Our colonies, though complaining of neglect, grew richer, more populous, and carried their trade farther than in former times. ... Our national end with respect to England was in this war particularly in great measure answered, — I mean the destruction of the French power at sea, for, after the battle of Malaga, we hear no more of their great fleets; and though by this the number of their privateers was very much increased, yet the losses of our merchants were far less in the latter than in the former reign. ... It is certainly a matter of great satisfaction that ... setting out at first with the sight of so great a naval power as the French

贷却是鼎盛之极。"就在这同一次战争中,"我国的商人表现出了一种强有力的精神,使得他们能够精力充沛地继续实施自己的各种计划——这些计划,让整个王国内部的资金保持着流通——并给所有企业提供了强大的激励,从而使得人们在回忆起那些形势更加糟糕的年代时,心中充满了欣慰之情。"

"通过与葡萄牙所达成的那份条约,我国获得了巨大的利益……葡萄牙人开始安逸地享受他们在巴西的那些金矿所带来的财富,而我国进行的大规模贸易,则使得他们的富有,在很大程度上也变成了我们的富有,并且此后一直都是这样;不然的话,我还真不知道我国进行战争的费用是从哪里来的呢……英国国内现金的流通量大幅增加了,这在很大程度上应当归功于我国与葡萄牙之间的贸易往来;而这一点,我已经阐述得非常明确,应当完全归功于我国的制海权(正是这种制海权,不但将葡萄牙拉出了两王同盟,而且还让它不得不倚赖于海洋大国的保护了)。我国经由加的斯与西属西印度群岛进行的贸易,在战争初期自然受到了很大的阻碍;不过,后来这种贸易大部分都恢复过来了,并且还通过葡萄牙,与当时正处于大公治下的数个省份进行直接联系,进行着一种虽说属于违禁但规模却相当巨大的贸易活动。同时,我们在与西印度群岛的西班牙人进行的贸易(也属于违禁活动)中,获利也极为丰厚……我国的各个殖民地,虽说埋怨母国疏于关注,但都日益富庶起来,人口渐增,还把贸易扩张到了比以前更远的那些地方……此次战争中,我们英格兰这个民族的目标,已经在很大程度上得到了明确的说明——我指的是摧毁法国的制海权,因为马拉加海战之后,我们就再也没有听说过他们的大型舰队了;尽管这样做使得他们的私掠船数量大增,但我国商人的损失,在法国私掠

king had assembled in 1688, while we struggled under such difficulties, and when we got out of that troublesome war, in 1697, found ourselves loaded with a debt too heavy to be shaken off in the short interval of peace, yet by 1706, instead of seeing the navy of France riding upon our coast, we sent every year a powerful fleet to insult theirs, superior to them not only in the ocean, but in the Mediterranean, forcing them entirely out of that sea by the mere sight of our flag. ... By this we not only secured our trade with the Levant, and strengthened our interests with all the Italian princes, but struck the States of Barbary with terror, and awed the awe from listening to any proposals from France. Such were the fruits of the increase of our naval power, and of the manner in which it was employed. ... Such fleets were necessary; they at once protected our flag and our allies, and attached them to our interest; and, what is of greater importance than all the rest, they established our reputation for maritime force so effectually that we feel even to this day [1740] the happy effects of the fame thus acquired."

It is needless to add more. Thus stood the Power of the Seas during the years in which the French historians tell us that their cruisers were battening on her commerce. The English writer admits heavy losses. In 1707, that is, in the space of five years, the returns, according to the report of a committee of the House of Lords, "show that since the beginning of the war England had lost 30 ships-of-war and 1146 merchant-ships, of which 300 were retaken; whereas we had taken from them, or destroyed, 80 ships-of-war, and 1346 merchantmen; 175 privateers also were taken." The greater number of the ships-of-war were probably on private venture, as has been explained. But, be the relative numbers what they may, no argument is needed beyond the statements just given, to show the inability of a mere cruising warfare, not based upon large fleets, to break down a great sea power. Jean Bart died in 1702; but in Forbin, Du Casse, and

船横行海上的时候，还是比法国大型舰队称霸海洋的时候要轻微得多……这当然是一件令人拍手称快的事情……我们刚开始起步的时候，看到的是法国国王在1688年集结起了一支强大无比的海军，而我们自己却是在艰难困苦中挣扎着；1697年，当我国终于从那场令人心烦的战争中脱身之后，却又发现自己负债累累，短暂的那一段和平时期根本无法让我们甩掉这些债务；可到了1706年，我们并没有看到法国海军驰骋于英国沿海，相反，却是我国每年都派遣一支强大的舰队前去袭扰法国的沿海地区，非但在大西洋上压倒了法国海军，还在地中海地区压制住了他们，迫使法国海军完全退出了地中海，从而让这一海域只有我国的国旗在飘扬……这样一来，不但确保了我国与黎凡特之间的贸易往来，巩固了我国在意大利各诸侯国的利益，还打得巴巴里诸国胆战心惊，令苏丹敬畏得不敢再听法国的任何建议。这些，就是我国海上实力增强的效果，也是我国利用此种制海权所取得的成果……这种舰队是必须保持的；它们曾经保护过我国的国威和盟友，还将这些方面同我国的利益结合起来；并且，最重要的是，它们有效地确立了我国海上力量的威名，以至于我们即便是如今（即1740年），也仍然能够感受到这种威望所带来的幸福影响。"

无需多言。正是在法国历史学家向我们夸耀说法国巡洋舰养肥了该国贸易的那些年里，英国如此成就了自己的海洋霸业。英国作家承认，这些年里英国也遭受了重大的损失。1707年，也就是说，自战争爆发以来的5年后，根据上议院一个委员会的报告，统计"表明自战争开始以来，英国已经损失了30艘军舰和1146艘商船，其中的300艘重新修好了；而我国也俘虏或者摧毁了敌方的80艘战舰，以及1346艘商船；此外，还俘虏了175艘私掠船。"前面我们已经说明，敌方损失的军舰数量更多，很可能是因为这些军舰被租赁

others, and above all in Duguay-Trouin, he left worthy successors, the equals of any commerce-destroyers the world has ever seen.

The name of Duguay-Trouin suggests the mention, before finally leaving the War of the Spanish Succession, of his greatest privateering expedition, carried to a distance from home rarely reached by the seamen of his occupation, and which illustrates curiously the spirit of such enterprises in that day, and the shifts to which the French government was reduced. A small French squadron had attacked Rio Janeiro in 1710, but being repulsed, had lost some prisoners, who were said to have been put to death. Duguay-Trouin sought permission to avenge the insult to France. The king, consenting, advanced the ships and furnished the crews; and a regular contract was drawn up between the king on the one hand and the company employing Duguay-Trouin on the other, stipulating the expenses to be borne and supplies furnished on either hand; among which we find the odd, business-like provision that for every one of the troops embarked who shall die, be killed, or desert during the cruise, the company should pay a forfeit of thirty francs. The king was to receive one fifth of the net profits, and was to bear the loss of any one of the vessels that should be wrecked, or destroyed in action. Under these provisions, enumerated in full in a long contract, Duguay-Trouin received a force of six ships-of-the-line, seven frigates, and over two thousand troops, with which he sailed to Rio Janeiro in 1711; captured the place after a series of operations, and allowed it to be ransomed at the price of something under four hundred thousand dollars, probably nearly equal to a million in the present day, besides five hundred cases of sugar. The privateering company cleared about ninety-two per cent on their venture. As two of the ships-of-the-line were never heard from after sailing on the return voyage, the king's profits were probably small.

给了私人企业所致。不过，无论其相对数量是多少，除了上述说明，我们不再需要任何理由来表明，一种不以大型舰队为基础的单纯的巡航战，是不可能瓦解掉一种伟大的制海权的。让·巴尔死于1702年；但他后继有人，留下了福尔班、杜·卡塞以及其他人，尤其是迪盖-特鲁安，这些私掠者都可与有史以来的任何贸易破坏者相匹敌。

既然提到了迪盖-特鲁安这个名字，那么我们在最终结束对西班牙王位继承战争的论述之前，不妨还来说一说他进行的一次最伟大的私掠远征行动。在此次远征中，他远离祖国，到达了其他私掠者绝少到达的遥远之地；因此，这次远征奇妙地说明了当时的人进行此种私掠活动的精神，以及法国政府衰落下去的种种转变过程。1710年，一支小型的法国舰队袭击了里约热内卢，但被击退了，损失了一批据说本应被处死的囚犯。迪盖-特鲁安想获得许可，去为法国报这一箭之仇。法国国王同意了，借给他船只并为这些船只配备了船员。法国国王作为一方，而雇用迪盖-特鲁安的那家公司则为另一方，拟定了一份例行合同，规定一方承担远征费用，另一方承担装备和给养的费用。从这份合同中，我们还看到了一条古怪的、商业化的条款，规定参与远征的部队在巡航过程中每自然死亡、战死或者逃跑一人，该公司就应当向法国国王支付30法郎的罚金。国王从远征队的净利润中提取五分之一，但应承担舰船沉没或者在作战中被毁的损失。根据这份长长的合同中详细列举的这些条款，迪盖-特鲁安得到了一支由60艘战舰、7艘护卫舰以及2000多兵力所组成的武装部队，然后就在1711年率领这支舰队向里约热内卢进发了；经过一系列作战行动之后，他攻取了该地，然后让当地人以大约不到40万美元的价格——大约相当于如今的100万美元——外加500箱食糖，将此地赎回去了。那家私掠公司在此次远征中的净利率大概达到

While the War of the Spanish Succession was engaging all western Europe, a strife which might have had a profound influence upon its issue was going on in the east. Sweden and Russia were at war, the Hungarians had revolted against Austria, and Turkey was finally drawn in, though not till the end of the year 1710. Had Turkey helped the Hungarians, she would have made a powerful diversion, not for the first time in history, in favor of France. The English historian suggests that she was deterred by fear of the English fleet; at all events she did not move, and Hungary was reduced to obedience. The war between Sweden and Russia was to result in the preponderance of the latter upon the Baltic, the subsidence of Sweden, the old ally of France, into a second-rate State, and the entrance of Russia definitively into European politics.

了92%；而因为有两艘战舰在返回途中失踪，所以法国国王所获利润很可能并不多。

虽说西欧诸国都卷入了西班牙王位继承战争，但与此同时，一场可能对此战之结果产生深远影响的冲突，也正在东欧进行着。瑞典和俄国正在交战，匈牙利人已经揭竿而起，反抗奥地利，最后把土耳其也拉了进来，但土耳其并未坚持到1710年末。倘若帮助了匈牙利人的话，土耳其可能就会发生一种有利于法国的强大逆转，这种情况在历史上本来就曾发生过。英国历史学家都认为，土耳其是因为害怕英国的舰队才没有那样做；但不论怎样，该国都没有轻举妄动，而匈牙利也不得不臣服于奥地利了。瑞典与俄国之间的战争，导致了后者称霸波罗的海；而作为法国老盟友的瑞典则衰落下去，变成了一个二流国家，还使得俄国最终登上了欧洲的历史舞台。

译者注：

[1] Flanders：佛兰德斯。中世纪西欧的一个国家，今为欧洲西北部的一个地区，在北海沿岸，包括法国西北部部分地区、现比利时的东佛兰德省、西佛兰德省以及荷兰的西南部分地区，是过去英、法长期争夺的目标。

[2] Port Royal：皇家港。南美牙买加的一个港市，亦译罗亚尔港。

[3] Duke of Parma：帕尔马公爵。帕尔马公国是以意大利城市帕尔马为中心的一个邦国，存在于1545年至1802年，以及1814年至1860年。西班牙国王菲利普五世的长子曾经统治过此公国。

[4] 这里是指1588年英、西之间的海战。此战中，西班牙"无敌舰队"先是在英国西南部海域惨败，然后又不得不绕道英国西北海岸返回西班牙，导致舰队几乎全军覆灭，也使得西班牙自此丧失了制海权。

[5] Marlborough：马尔伯勒（John Churchill, Duke of Marlborough, 1650～1722）。英国将领，在战略和战术上主张积极进攻，以攻势为主，惯以大量步兵钳制敌军，尔后投入骑兵突击胜。

[6] Prince Eugene：欧根亲王（Franois-Eugène, Prince of Savoy-Carignan, 1663～1736）。神圣罗马帝国元帅、军事委员会主席，是出色的战略家，也是懂得激励人心的领袖，被认为是当时最伟大的军人之一。

[7] Ramillies：拉米伊。尼德兰的一处村镇，今属比利时。1706年5月，马尔伯勒与欧根亲王率英、荷、奥盟军在此大败法军。

[8] Malplaquet：马尔普拉奎特。尼德兰的一处村镇，今属比利时。1709年9月，马尔伯勒与欧根亲王所率的英、荷、奥盟军在此经过顽强作战，打败了法军。此战以双方大量使用火炮而著名。亦译马尔普拉凯。

[9] Turin：都灵。意大利城市。1706年，欧根亲王率军在此以少胜多，打败了包围都灵的法军，结束了法国在北意大利的长期统治。

CHAPTER V The Regency in France

Alberoni in Spain. — Policies of Walpole and Fleuri. —
War of the Polish Succession. — English Contraband Trade in Spanish America. —
Great Britain Declares War against Spain. — 1715–1739.

The Peace of Utrecht was soon followed by the deaths of the rulers of the two countries which had played the foremost part in the War of the Spanish Succession. Queen Anne died August 1, 1714; Louis XIV. on the 1st of September, 1715.

The successor to the English throne, the German George I., though undoubtedly the choice of the English people, was far from being their favorite, and was rather endured as a necessary evil, giving them a Protestant instead of a Roman Catholic king. Along with the coldness and dislike of his own partisans, he found a very considerable body of disaffected men, who wished to see the son of James II. on the throne. There was therefore a lack of solidity, more apparent than real, but still real, in his position. In France, on the contrary, the succession to the throne was undisputed; but the heir was a child of five years, and there was much jealousy as to the possession of the regency, a power more absolute than that of the King of England. The regency was obtained and exercised by the next in succession to the throne, Philip, Duke of Orleans; but he had to apprehend, not only attempts on the part of rivals in France to shake his hold, but also the active enmity of the Bourbon king of Spain, Philip V., — an enmity which seems to

第五章 法国摄政时期

阿尔韦罗尼在西班牙；沃波尔和弗勒里的政策；
波兰王位继承战；英国在西属美洲的违禁贸易；
英国对西班牙宣战，1715–1739

《乌特勒支和约》签订后不久，曾在西班牙王位继承战争中担当主角的那两个国家的君主都相继去世了。安妮女王死于1714年8月1日；路易十四则是1715年9月1日辞世的。

继承英国大统的是德国的乔治一世；尽管这是英国人民的选择，但他们却并不喜欢乔治一世，把他当成是一种"必要之恶"而容忍着，因为这个国王信奉新教而不是信奉罗马天主教。除了效忠的臣民们显得很冷淡和嫌恶之外，他还发现了一大批心怀不满的人，这些人都希望由詹姆士二世的儿子来继承王位。所以，乔治一世的王位坐得很不牢靠，尽管更多的是在表面上而非真正的不牢靠，但实际上还是很不牢靠的。相反，法国在王位继承问题上毫无异议；但继承人是一位年方5岁的孩子，因此有很多人觊觎继承权——因为继承法国王位后，获得的将是一种比英国的王权更加绝对的权力。最后，第二继承人，即奥尔良大公菲利普获得了继承权，并开始大权独揽；但是，他也不得不既提防法国国内的对手动摇其统治的各种企图，又得提防西班牙那位属于波旁王室的国

have dated from an intrigue of Orleans, during the late war, to supplant Philip on the Spanish throne. There was therefore a feeling of instability, of apprehension, in the governments of England and France, which influenced the policy of both. As regards the relations of France and Spain, the mutual hatred of the actual rulers stood for a while in the way of the friendly accord Louis XIV. had hoped from family ties, and was injurious to the true interests of both nations.

The Regent Orleans, under the advice of the most able and celebrated French statesman of that day, the Abbé Dubois, made overtures of alliance to the King of Great Britain. He began first by commercial concessions of the kind generally acceptable to the English, forbidding French shipping to trade to the South Seas under penalty of death, and lowering the duties on the importation of English coal. England at first received these advances warily; but the regent would not be discouraged, and offered, further, to compel the Pretender, James III., to withdraw beyond the Alps. He also undertook to fill up the port at Mardyck, a new excavation by which the French government was trying to indemnify itself for the loss of Dunkirk. These concessions, all of which but one, it will be noted, were at the expense of the sea power or commercial interests of France, induced England to sign a treaty by which the two countries mutually guaranteed the execution of the treaties of Utrecht as far as their respective interests were concerned; especially the clause by which the House of Orleans was to succeed to the French throne, if Louis XV. died childless. The Protestant succession in England was likewise guaranteed. Holland, exhausted by the war, was unwilling to enter upon new engagements, but was at last brought over to this by the remission of certain dues on her merchandise entering France. The treaty, signed in January, 1717, was known as the Triple Alliance, and bound France to England for some years to come.

王——即菲利普五世———一直未消的仇怨：这种仇恨，似乎是因为在上一次战争中，奥尔良公爵曾耍过一次阴谋，想阻碍菲利普登上西班牙的王位。因此，英、法两国政府中都弥漫着一种不安和担忧的气氛，从而影响到了两国制定的政策。至于法国和西班牙的关系，因两国的现任君主彼此都很仇视，故一度阻挠了路易十四曾希望通过家族纽带来维持住的那种友好一致关系，从而给两国的真正利益带来了损害。

在当时最有能力、最有名望的杜布瓦主教[1]这位政治家的建议下，摄政王奥尔良大公开始向英王示好，提议与英国结成同盟。他先是在商业贸易上做出了让英国人全面接受的让步，禁止法国船只在南太平洋进行贸易，违者处以死刑，还降低了进口英国煤炭的关税。英国起初在接受这些主动示好行为的时候很警惕；但摄政王毫不气馁，又进一步提出并将詹姆士三世这位觊觎王位者赶到了阿尔卑斯山脉之外。他还在马尔迪克开始填造要塞；这个地方是新开挖出来的，法国政府试图用此地来弥补该国失去敦克尔克港的损失。我们会注意到，这些让步措施总的来说其实只有一点，那就是牺牲法国的海权或者贸易利益，诱使英国与之签订一个条约，从而让两国共同做出保证，执行在乌特勒支所签与两国利益相关的那些条约；尤其是执行下述这一条款：假如路易十五死后无嗣的话，应当由奥尔良大公家族来继承法国王位。而英国应由信奉新教的人来继任王位这一点，同样也会得到保证。被战争拖得筋疲力尽的荷兰不愿缔结新的协定，但法国承诺豁免荷兰商品的某些进口税费，最终还是让荷兰改变了立场，加入了这一条约。1717年1月所签署的这一条约，史称《三国同盟条约》；而在此后的数年间，这一条约都将法、英两国绑到了一起。

在法国向英国做出如此种种示好行为时，西班牙正在另一位能干的神职人员引领下，

While France was thus making overtures to England, Spain, under the guidance of another able churchman, was seeking the same alliance and at the same time developing her national strength with the hope of recovering her lost Italian States. The new minister, Cardinal Alberoni, promised Philip V. to put him in a position to reconquer Sicily and Naples, if granted five years of peace. He worked hard to bring up the revenues, rebuild the navy, and re-establish the army, while at the same time promoting manufactures, commerce, and shipping, and the advance made in all these was remarkable; but the more legitimate ambition of Spain to recover her lost possessions, and with them to establish her power in the Mediterranean, so grievously wounded by the loss of Gibraltar, was hampered by the ill-timed purpose of Philip to overthrow the regency of Orleans in France. Alberoni was compelled to alienate France, whose sea power, as well as that of Spain, was concerned in seeing Sicily in friendly hands, and, instead of that natural ally, had to conciliate the maritime powers, England and Holland. This he also sought to do by commercial concessions; promising promptly to put the English in possession of the privileges granted at Utrecht, concerning which Spain had so far delayed. In return, he asked favorable action from them in Italy. George I., who was at heart German, received coldly advances which were unfriendly to the German emperor in his Italian dominions; and Alberoni, offended, withdrew them. The Triple Alliance, by guaranteeing the existing arrangement of succession to the French throne, gave further offence to Philip V., who dreamed of asserting his own claim. The result of all these negotiations was to bind England and France together against Spain, — a blind policy for the two Bourbon kingdoms.

The gist of the situation created by these different aims and feelings, was that the Emperor of Austria and the King of Spain both wanted Sicily, which at Utrecht had been given to the

寻求同样的一种同盟关系；与此同时，该国还希望通过收复已经丧失的意大利各诸侯国，来增强自己的实力。新任大臣阿尔韦罗尼主教向菲利普五世承诺，假如给他5年的太平时间，他就让菲利普五世能够重新征服西西里和那不勒斯两地。他勤勤恳恳地工作着，努力提高国家的岁入，改造了海军，重新组建了陆军，同时还促进工业生产、贸易和运输业，并且在这些方面都获得了举世瞩目的进步；但西班牙要收复失地，要在这基础上确立该国在地中海地区的霸权——失去直布罗陀，极大地损害了该国的此种霸权——这种更为正当的雄心壮志，却因菲利普五世想要推翻奥尔良大公在法国的摄政政权这一不合时宜的目标，而受到了阻碍。阿尔韦罗尼主教不得不疏远法国；法国的海权与西班牙的海权一样，关键都在于让西西里掌控在友邦的手里，而且，西班牙并非需要获得法国这个天然盟友的支持，而是必须得到英、荷这两个海洋大国的支持。因此，阿尔韦罗尼主教也曾试图通过在贸易上做出让步来达到这一目的；他承诺让英国马上得到《乌特勒支和约》中所确定的各种特权，而对于这些特权，西班牙本来一直都在想方设法地拖延。作为回报，他要求英国在意大利实施有利于西班牙的行动。乔治一世本质上是德国人，所以他冷淡地接受了这些对德意志皇帝在意大利的诸领地不利的示好举措；阿尔韦罗尼主教很生气，便收回了这些承诺。三国同盟通过保证现有的法国王位继承办法，进一步羞辱了梦想着坚持自己的继承权利的菲利普五世。所有这些谈判的结果，便是使得英、法两国合起来对付西班牙——其实对于这两个波旁王国来说，此种做法都是一种很不理智的政策。

由这些不同的目标与意见所导致的局面，其实质就是奥地利皇帝和西班牙国王都想得到西西里，可在乌特勒支和会上，西西里却分给了萨伏伊大公；法、英两国都希望西

Duke of Savoy; and that France and England both wished for peace in western Europe, because war would give an opportunity to the malcontents in either kingdom. The position of George, however, being more secure than that of Orleans, the policy of the latter tended to yield to that of the former, and this tendency was increased by the active ill-will of the King of Spain. George, as a German, wished the emperor's success; and the English statesmen naturally preferred to see Sicily in the hands of their late ally and well-assured friend rather than in Spain's. France, contrary to her true policy, but under the urgency of the regent's position, entertained the same views, and it was proposed to modify the Treaty of Utrecht by transferring Sicily from Savoy to Austria, giving the former Sardinia instead. It was necessary, however, to consider Spain, which under Alberoni had already gained a degree of military power astounding to those who had known her weakness during the last war. She was not yet ready to fight, for only half of the five years asked by the cardinal had passed; but still less was she ready to forego her ambitions. A trifling incident precipitated an outbreak. A high Spanish official, travelling from Rome to Spain by land, and so passing through the Italian States of the emperor, was arrested as a rebellious subject by order of the latter, who still styled himself King of Spain. At this insult, Alberoni could not hold Philip back. An expedition of twelve ships of war and eighty-six hundred soldiers was sent against Sardinia, the transfer to Savoy not having yet taken effect, and reduced the island in a few months. This happened in 1717.

Doubtless the Spaniards would at once have moved on against Sicily; but France and England now intervened more actively to prevent the general war that seemed threatening. England sent a fleet to the Mediterranean, and negotiations began at Paris, Vienna, and Madrid. The outcome of these conferences was an agreement between England and France to effect the exchange of Sardinia and Sicily just mentioned, recompensing Spain by giving her Parma

欧保持和平，因为战争会给两国国内那些心怀不满的人带来兴风作浪的机会。然而，乔治一世的位置比奥尔良大公的位置要稳固得多，所以后者的政策往往会屈从于前者的政策，并且这一趋势还因西班牙国王不断表现出来的敌意而得到了强化。作为德国人，乔治一世很乐意见到德意志皇帝成功；而英国的政治家们，自然也更愿意看到西西里掌控在该国这个新的、令人放心的盟友手中，而不是掌控在西班牙手中。法国呢，虽说与其真实的政策背道而驰，但迫于摄政王地位不稳，所以也持有相同的观点；于是有人提议修改《乌特勒支和约》，让萨伏伊大公将西西里转让给奥地利，再把撒丁岛归给萨伏伊大公。然而，西班牙也得考虑，因为西班牙在阿尔韦罗尼主教的治理之下，已经拥有了一定的军事实力，令那些在上一次战争中得知西班牙软弱无能的人都惊讶不已。虽说该国还没做好开战准备，因为这位主教所要求的5年时间才过去了一半，但是，我们更不能说该国已经放弃了自己的种种野心。一个微不足道的小事件，就使得西班牙勃然大怒了。有位西班牙的高级官吏，在从罗马经由陆路前往西班牙时，途经了奥地利皇帝统治之下的意大利诸邦；奥地利皇帝却下令，将这名官吏作为反叛分子抓了起来，因为他仍然认为自己才是西班牙国王。受到了这种侮辱之后，阿尔韦罗尼根本就劝阻不了菲利普五世。于是，西班牙派遣一支由12艘战舰和8600名士兵所组成的远征军，前去攻打撒丁岛，并在数月之后攻陷了该岛；当时，撒丁岛还未正式转交给萨伏伊大公。此战发生于1717年。

西班牙人无疑也曾经去进攻过西西里；不过，此时法、英两国进行了更加积极主动的干预，以阻止这场看上去很危险的全面战争。英国派了一支舰队前往地中海，并在巴黎、维也纳和马德里三地展开了谈判。这些会议的成果，便是英、法之间达成了一项协

and Tuscany in northern Italy, and stipulating that the emperor should renounce forever his absurd but irritating claim to the Spanish crown. This arrangement was to be enforced by arms, if necessary. The emperor at first refused consent; but the increasing greatness of Alberoni's preparations at last decided him to accept so advantageous an offer, and the accession of Holland to the compact gave it the historical title of the Quadruple Alliance. Spain was obstinate; and it is significant of Alberoni's achievements in developing her power, and the eagerness, not to say anxiety, of George I., that the offer was made to purchase her consent by ceding Gibraltar. If the Regent Orleans knew this, it would partly justify his forwarding the negotiations.

Alberoni tried to back up his military power by diplomatic efforts extending all over Europe. Russia and Sweden were brought together in a project for invading England in the interest of the Stuarts; the signing of the Quadruple Alliance in Holland was delayed by his agents; a conspiracy was started in France against the regent; the Turks were stirred up against the emperor; discontent was fomented throughout Great Britain; and an attempt was made to gain over the Duke of Savoy, outraged by being deprived of Sicily. On the 1st of July, 1718, a Spanish army of thirty thousand troops, escorted by twenty-two ships-of-the-line, appeared at Palermo. The troops of Savoy evacuated the city and pretty nearly the whole island, resistance being concentrated in the citadel of Messina. Anxiety was felt in Naples itself, until the English admiral, Byng,[1] anchored there the day after the investment of Messina. The King of Sicily having now consented to the terms of the Quadruple Alliance, Byng received on board two thousand Austrian troops to be landed at Messina. When he appeared before the place, finding it besieged, he wrote to the Spanish general suggesting a suspension of arms for two months. This was of course refused; so the Austrians were landed again at Reggio, in Italy, and

定，按照上面所说的办法，将撒丁岛与西西里两地的归属进行交换，而将意大利北部的帕尔马和托斯卡纳划归西班牙以作补偿，还规定奥地利皇帝永远放弃他对西班牙王位那种荒唐而恼人的要求。倘有必要，可以武力执行这一协定。奥地利皇帝起初拒不同意，但阿尔韦罗尼的准备工作日益有力起来，最终还是让他决定接受这些如此有利的条件；而在荷兰加入这一条约之后，同盟便变成了史称的"四国同盟"。西班牙非常顽固；正是阿尔韦罗尼主教在发展壮大西班牙实力的过程中取得了重大成就，以及乔治一世非常热切，更不用说急不可耐了，才使得同盟提出用割让直布罗陀的条件来换取西班牙的同意。假如摄政王奥尔良大公明白这一点，那就可以部分地说明他之所以力促谈判的原因了。

阿尔韦罗尼主教试图通过在整个欧洲做出外交上的努力，来为该国的军事实力撑腰。在此期间，欧洲政治舞台风云变幻：俄国和瑞典曾经为了斯图亚特王室的利益，一起制订过一项入侵英国的计划；荷兰的代表曾经延迟签署"四国同盟"条约；法国国内开始密谋反对摄政王；土耳其人被煽动起来，反抗奥地利皇帝；英国各地民众的不满情绪都被激发起来了；他还试图拉拢因为被夺走了西西里而怒不可遏的萨伏伊大公。1718年7月1日，一支由30000兵力组成的西班牙陆军，在22艘军舰的护卫下，出现在巴勒莫[2]。萨伏伊大公的军队疏散了全城居民以及差不多整个西西里岛上的居民，抵抗则集中在墨西拿要塞进行。那不勒斯陷入了一片担忧之中，直至英国海军上将拜恩[1]在墨西拿被围的第二天率军抵达，这种恐慌才平息下来。由于西西里国王此时已经同意了"四国同盟"条约的条款，于是拜恩让2000名奥地利士兵上船，准备送他们前去登陆墨西拿。当他率军来到墨西拿，发现该地被围之后，便给西班牙主帅写了一封信，提出休

Byng passed through the Straits of Messina to seek the Spanish fleet, which had gone to the southward.

The engagement which ensued can scarcely be called a battle, and, as is apt to happen in such affairs, when the parties are on the verge of war but war has not actually been declared, there is some doubt as to how far the attack was morally justifiable on the part of the English. It seems pretty sure that Byng was determined beforehand to seize or destroy the Spanish fleet, and that as a military man he was justified by his orders. The Spanish naval officers had not made up their minds to any line of conduct; they were much inferior in numbers, and, as must always be the case, Alberoni's hastily revived navy had not within the same period reached nearly the efficiency of his army. The English approached threateningly near, one or more Spanish ships opened fire, whereupon the English, being to windward, stood down and made an end of them; a few only escaped into Valetta harbor. The Spanish navy was practically annihilated. It is difficult to understand the importance attached by some writers to Byng's action at this time in attacking without regard to the line-of-battle. He had before him a disorderly force, much inferior both in numbers and discipline. His merit seems rather to lie in the readiness to assume a responsibility from which a more scrupulous man might have shrunk; but in this and throughout the campaign he rendered good service to England, whose sea power was again strengthened by the destruction not of an actual but a possible rival, and his services were rewarded by a peerage. In connection with this day's work was written a despatch which has great favor with English historians. One of the senior captains was detached with a division against some escaping ships of the enemy. His report to the admiral ran thus: "Sir, — We have taken or destroyed all the Spanish ships upon this coast, the number as per margin. Respectfully, etc., G. Walton." One English writer makes, and another indorses, the uncalled-

战两个月。这一要求当然被西班牙主帅拒绝了；于是，这些奥地利士兵便在意大利的雷吉奥再次登陆，而拜恩则率舰队通过墨西拿海峡，搜索已经向南而去的西班牙舰队。

　　接下来的这场交战，很难称得上是一场战斗，并且正像在这种事态中很容易出现的那样，当双方都处于战争边缘、可又还未真正宣战的时候，英国人却开始怀疑，在道德上来看，发动进攻是不是正当的了。拜恩之前就已下定决心，要俘虏或者摧毁西班牙舰队，这一点似乎是确定无疑的，而作为一名军人，他也有理由下这样的命令。西班牙的海军将领，此时却还没有决定采取何种作战方针；他们的兵力大不如敌人，并且情况必定一向如此，阿尔韦罗尼主教匆匆忙忙地重新建立起来的海军，并未在同一时期内达到该国陆军那样的作战效率。英军开始咄咄逼人地迫近过来，一两艘西班牙军舰率先开了火；于是，处于上风位置的英军便顺势而行，消灭了这些舰船，只有少数几艘逃入了瓦莱塔港。这样，西班牙海军实际上就全军覆灭了。我们很难理解，一些史学家为何会认为拜恩在这个时候不顾战斗队形发动攻击的行为非常重要。他当时面对的，是一支杂乱无章、兵力和军纪都大不如英军的部队。他的功劳，似乎更在于他乐意承担起一种责任，因为一个更加谨慎小心的人，是有可能会逃避这种责任的；不过，在这一次以及整个战役中，他都为英国做出了很大的贡献，使得英国海军通过消灭一个虽说并非实际上的、却是一个潜在的对手，再一次巩固了该国的制海权，而他本人也因为此种贡献获得了奖赏，被封为贵族了。关于这一天的战斗，曾经被写成了一份极得英国史学家们喜爱的通讯报道。一位海军上校被派率领一支小型舰队，去追击数艘漏网的敌舰。他给海军司令的那份报告，是如此写的："阁下，我们已经在此处海岸俘虏或摧毁了所有的西班牙船只，数量请参见页面旁

for but characteristic fling at the French, that the ships thus thrust into the margin would have filled some pages of a French narration. It may be granted that the so-called "battle" of Cape Passaro did not merit a long description, and Captain Walton possibly felt so; but if all reports of naval transactions were modelled upon his, the writing of naval history would not depend on official papers.

Thus the Spanish navy was struck down on the 11th of August, 1718, off Cape Passaro. This settled the fate of Sicily, if it had been doubtful before. The English fleet cruised round the island, supporting the Austrians and isolating the Spaniards, none of whom were permitted to withdraw before peace was made. Alberoni's diplomatic projects failed one after the other, with a strange fatality. In the following year the French, in pursuance of the terms of the alliance, invaded the north of Spain and destroyed the dock-yards; burning nine large ships on the stocks, besides the materials for seven more, at the instigation of an English attaché accompanying the French headquarters. Thus was completed the destruction of the Spanish navy, which, says an English historian, was ascribed to the maritime jealousy of England.

"This was done," wrote the French commander, the Duke of Berwick, a bastard of the house of Stuart, "in order that the English government may be able to show the next Parliament that nothing has been neglected to diminish the navy of Spain." The acts of Sir George Byng, as given by the English naval historian, make yet more manifest the purpose of England at this time. While the city and citadel of Messina were being besieged by the Austrians, English, and Sardinians, a dispute arose as to the possession of the Spanish men-of-war within the mole. Byng, "reflecting within himself that possibly the garrison might capitulate for the safe return of those ships into Spain, which he was determined not to suffer; that on the other hand the right of possession might breed an inconvenient dispute at a critical juncture among the

注。致敬，G·沃尔顿。"一位英国作家说，如此被挤着标注在页边的那些船只，法国人很可能需要好几页才报告得完；而另一位英国作家也承认这一点，不过这种说法其实并无必要，不过是嘲讽法国的一个典型罢了。我们可以认为，这次在帕萨罗角的所谓"战斗"并不值得详述，而沃尔顿上校可能也是这么认为的；不过，倘若关于海军事务的所有报告都以他这种模式来写的话，那么整个海军历史就没法以官方文件为依据了。

这样一来，1718年8月11日，西班牙海军就在帕萨罗角海岸被英军击垮了。此战使得西西里的命运尘埃落定了——要是说它的命运此前还属未知之数的话。英国舰队绕着该岛巡逻，对奥地利人进行支援，并将西班牙人隔离起来，还下令在缔结和约之前，不允许任何一名西班牙人离开。阿尔韦罗尼主教的外交计划一个接一个地失败，带来了一种奇怪的致命性影响。第二年，法国根据同盟条约侵入了西班牙北部，摧毁了那儿的西班牙海军造船厂；在随同法军司令部的一位英国专员怂恿下，法军非但烧毁了西班牙正在建造中的9艘大型舰船，还烧掉了建造另外7艘多舰船的材料。这样，就彻底摧毁了西班牙的海军；据一位英国历史学家称，这种做法完全是由于英国忌惮西班牙的海上力量所致。当时的法军司令伯威克公爵是斯图亚特王室的一位私生子，他写道："这样做，是为了让英国政府可以向下一届议会表明，为了削弱西班牙海军的实力，政府已经尽了全力。"英国的海军历史学家们认为，乔治·拜恩勋爵的行为，则更清楚地表明了英国当时的目标。当墨西拿这个城市和要塞被奥地利军队、英军和撒丁岛的军队合围起来之时，三方因要塞中西班牙作战人员被俘后的归属问题发生了争执。拜恩"心中想到，该要塞可能会投降，并且提出让要塞内的舰船安全返回西班牙的条件，但这种条件他是决

princes concerned, and if it should at length be determined that they did not belong to England it were better they belonged to no one else, proposed to Count de Merci, the Austrian general, to erect a battery and destroy them as they lay." After some demur on the part of the other leaders, this was done. If constant care and watchfulness deserve success, England certainly deserved her sea power; but what shall be said of the folly of France at this time and in this connection?

The steady stream of reverses, and the hopelessness of contending for distant maritime possessions when without a navy, broke down the resistance of Spain. England and France insisted upon the dismissal of Alberoni, and Philip yielded to the terms of the Quadruple Alliance. The Austrian power, necessarily friendly to England, was thus firmly settled in the central Mediterranean, in Naples and Sicily, as England herself was in Gibraltar and Port Mahon. Sir Robert Walpole, the minister now coming into power in England, failed at a later day to support this favorable conjunction, and so far betrayed the traditional policy of his country. The dominion of the House of Savoy in Sardinia, which then began, has lasted; it is only within our own day that the title King of Sardinia has merged in the broader one of King of Italy.

Contemporaneously with and for some time after the short episode of Alberoni's ministry and Spain's ambition, a struggle was going on around the shores of the Baltic which must be mentioned, because it gave rise to another effectual illustration of the sea power of England, manifested alike in the north and south with a slightness of exertion which calls to mind the stories of the tap of a tiger's paw. The long contest between Sweden and Russia was for a moment interrupted in 1718, by negotiations looking to peace and to an alliance between the two for the settlement of the succession in Poland and the restoration of the Stuarts in

计不会接受的；另一方面，在此紧要关头，这些舰船的归属权也可能让相关侯爵之间发生极不合时宜的争执。所以，倘若这些船只最终被裁定不归英国所有的话，最好就不要归任何一方所有，而是交给奥军将领梅尔奇伯爵，由他建立一个炮台，将泊在要塞内的船只全部摧毁。"其他两方的将领犹豫了一阵子之后，便照此而行了。倘若持之以恒的谨慎和警惕能给人带来成功的话，英国确立其制海权就是当之无愧的；不过，对于法国此时在这个方面的愚笨，我们又该说什么呢？

持续不断的失败，以及没有了海军便无望争夺远洋殖民地的情况，彻底瓦解了西班牙的抵抗。英、法两国坚持要求将阿尔韦罗尼解职，菲利普也在"四国同盟"提出的条件下屈服了。必定会同英国保持友好关系的奥地利政权，就此在地中海中心地带的那不勒斯和西西里两地牢固地确立下来了，就像英国本身在直布罗陀和马翁港两地确立其政权那样。此时在英国上台掌权的大臣罗伯特·沃波尔勋爵，后来并没有维持好这一有利的同盟关系，从而极大地背离了英国的传统政策。萨伏伊王室在撒丁岛的统治自此开始，并且一直延续下去了；只是到了如今这个时代，"撒丁国王"这个称号才与更为广义的"意大利国王"合二为一。

在阿尔韦罗尼内阁执政、西班牙抱有野心这一短暂的时期内以及其后不久，波罗的海沿岸正在进行着一场战争；对此，我们必须提一提才行，因为它再一次有效地说明了英国的海权，表明该国在欧洲北方和南方一样毫不费力，从而让人想起虎爪轻叩的故事来。瑞典与俄国之间旷日持久的较量，在1718年暂时中断了；两国进行了和谈，想结成同盟，以解决波兰王位继承问题和在英国复辟斯图亚特王室的问题。这一计划，阿

England. This project, on which had rested many of Alberoni's hopes, was finally stopped by the death in battle of the Swedish king. The war went on; and the czar, seeing the exhaustion of Sweden, purposed its entire subjugation. This destruction of the balance of power in the Baltic, making it a Russian lake, suited neither England nor France; especially the former, whose sea power both for peace and war depended upon the naval stores chiefly drawn from those regions. The two western kingdoms interfered, both by diplomacy, while England besides sent her fleet. Denmark, which was also at war with her traditional enemy Sweden, readily yielded; but Peter the Great chafed heavily under the implied coercion, until at last orders were sent to the English admiral to join his fleet to that of the Swedes and repeat in the Baltic the history of Cape Passaro. The czar in alarm withdrew his fleet. This happened in 1719; but Peter, though baffled, was not yet subdued. The following year the interposition of England was repeated with greater effect, although not in time to save the Swedish coasts from serious injury; but the czar, recognizing the fixed purpose with which he had to deal, and knowing from personal observation and practical experience the efficiency of England's sea power, consented finally to peace. The French claim much for their own diplomacy in this happy result, and say that England supported Sweden feebly; being willing that she should lose her provinces on the eastern shore of the Baltic because Russia, thus brought down to the seashore, could more easily open to English trade the vast resources of her interior. This may very possibly be true, and certainty can be felt that British interests, especially as to commerce and sea power, were looked after; but the character of Peter the Great is the guarantee that the argument which weighed most heavily with him was the military efficiency of the British fleet and its ability to move up to his very doors. By this Peace of Nystadt, August 30, 1721, Sweden abandoned Livonia, Esthonia, and other provinces on the east side of the Baltic.

尔韦罗尼主教也曾寄予厚望，最终却因瑞典国王战死而终止了。于是，两国便继续战下去；俄国沙皇明白瑞典已是强弩之末，便打算完全征服瑞典。这种做法，会彻底打破波罗的海地区的势力均衡，使波罗的海变成俄国的一个内湖，这既不符合英国的利益，也不符合法国的利益；尤其是英国，因为该国的制海权无论是用于和平目的还是用于战争目的，都得倚赖主要源自波罗的海地区的海军物资。于是，这两个西欧王国都通过外交手段进行了干预，而英国还派出了自己的舰队。此时也正在与其宿敌瑞典交战的丹麦，很快就让了步；可彼得大帝却对两国这种不言而喻的高压态势深感气恼，直至最后，英国命令其海军司令率领舰队加入瑞典一方，准备在波罗的海上重现帕萨罗角海战的历史，沙皇这才惊慌失措，撤回了俄国舰队。这是1719年的事；彼得大帝虽说受了挫折，却并没有慑服。第二年，尽管没有及时救援瑞典沿海地区，没有使之免于遭受俄国的重大打击，但英国还是再次加大了干预的力度；而沙皇由于意识到自己不得不去对付英国此种坚定之目标，并且通过亲自观察和实战经验明白了英国海军的作战效率，所以最终同意议和了。对于这一令人满意的结果，法国人宣称主要应归功于他们的外交努力，还说英国对瑞典的支援软弱无力；说英国愿意放弃波罗的海东岸各个地区，因为俄国占领这些地区之后，便可以更加轻易地将该国广袤内陆的巨大资源对英国贸易进行开放。这一点，很可能并未言过其实，而英国所寻求的，无疑也是其自身的利益，尤其是其贸易和海权利益；不过，彼得大帝的性格，却决定了他最为重视的还是英国舰队的作战效率，以及英国舰队可以直接打到他家门口的作战能力。通过1721年8月30日签订的这份《尼斯塔德和约》，瑞典放弃了利沃尼亚[3]、爱沙尼亚以及波罗的海东部沿岸的其他

This result was inevitable; it was yearly becoming less possible for small States to hold their own.

It can readily be understood that Spain was utterly discontented with the terms wrung from her by the Quadruple Alliance. The twelve years which followed are called years of peace, but the peace was very uncertain, and fraught with elements of future wars. The three great grievances rankling with Spain were — Sicily and Naples in the possession of Austria, Gibraltar and Mahon in the hands of England, and lastly, the vast contraband trade carried on by English merchants and ships in Spanish America. It will be seen that England was the active supporter of all these injuries; England therefore was the special enemy of Spain, but Spain was not the only enemy of England.

The quiet, such as it was, that succeeded the fall of Alberoni was due mainly to the character and policy of the two ministers of France and England, who agreed in wishing a general peace. The policy and reasons of the French regent are already known. Moved by the same reasons, and to remove an accidental offence taken by England, Dubois obtained for her the further concession from Spain, additional to the commercial advantages granted at Utrecht, of sending a ship every year to trade in the West Indies. It is said that this ship, after being anchored, was kept continually supplied by others, so that fresh cargo came in over one side as fast as the old was sent ashore from the other. Dubois and the regent both died in the latter half of 1723, after an administration of eight years, in which they had reversed the policy of Richelieu by alliance with England and Austria and sacrificing to them the interests of France.

The regency and the nominal government of France passed to another member of the royal family; but the real ruler was Cardinal Fleuri, the preceptor of the young king, who was

地区。出现这种结果是必然的；因为当时这些小国已经越来越无法守住自己的领土了。

西班牙对"四国同盟"强迫它服从的那些条款极其不满，这一点是不难理解的。虽然接下来的12年被称为和平年代，但这种和平很不稳固，并且充满了导致日后爆发战争的各种因素。令西班牙难以释怀的三大不平之事就是：奥地利占领了西西里和那不勒斯，直布罗陀和马翁港在英国手里，以及英国商人和商船在西属美洲从事着巨大的走私贸易。我们会看到，英国正是这三大不平之事的积极支持者；因此，英国就是西班牙首要的敌人，而西班牙却并非英国唯一的敌人。

阿尔韦罗尼主教下台后西班牙的安定局面，实际上主要得益于法、英两国各自一位大臣的性格与政策，因为这两人都希望实现全面的和平。法国摄政王的政策以及实施此种政策的理由，我们都已经很清楚了。出于同样的理由，以及为了消除英国发动意外进攻的危险，杜布瓦还让西班牙进一步做出了妥协，在《乌特勒支和约》所规定的贸易优势之外，还允许英国每年派遣一艘船只前往西印度群岛进行贸易。据说这艘船只在泊港之后，其他船只就源源不断地将货物运到该船上，以至于新货物从一边装上船的速度跟旧货物从另一边卸下船的速度一样快。执政8年之后，杜布瓦主教和摄政王两人相继于1723年下半年去世了；在此期间，他们都彻底改变了黎塞留所制定的政策，既与英、奥两国结成了盟友，还为这两国牺牲了法国的利益。

法国的摄政权力和形同虚设的政府，转移到了皇室的另一位成员手中；不过，法国真正的统治者却是弗勒里大主教，他是此时年仅13岁的法国国王的导师。有些人曾经试图解除这位导师的职务，可结果却是不得不在1726年授予他大臣的头衔和权力。此时，

now thirteen years of age. Efforts to displace the preceptor resulted only in giving him the title, as well as the power, of minister in 1726. At this time Sir Robert Walpole had become prime minister of England, with an influence and power which gave him practically the entire guidance of the policy of the State. The chief wish of both Walpole and Fleuri was peace, above all in western Europe. France and England therefore continued to act together for that purpose, and though they could not entirely stifle every murmur, they were for several years successful in preventing outbreaks. But while the aims of the two ministers were thus agreed, the motives which inspired them were different. Walpole desired peace because of the still unsettled condition of the English succession; for the peaceful growth of English commerce, which he had ever before his eyes; and probably also because his spirit, impatient of equals in the government, shrank from war which would raise up stronger men around him. Fleuri, reasonably secure as to the throne and his own power, wished like Walpole the peaceful development of his country, and shrank from war with the love of repose natural to old age; for he was seventy-three when he took office, and ninety when he laid it down in death. Under his mild administration the prosperity of France revived; the passing traveller could note the change in the face of the country and of the people; yet it may be doubted whether this change was due to the government of the quiet old man, or merely to the natural elasticity of the people, no longer drained by war nor isolated from the rest of the world. French authorities say that agriculture did not revive throughout the country. It is certain, however, that the maritime prosperity of France advanced wonderfully, owing mainly to the removal of commercial restrictions in the years immediately following the death of Louis XIV. The West India islands in particular throve greatly, and their welfare was naturally shared by the home ports that traded with them. The tropical climate of Martinique, Guadeloupe, and Louisiana, and cultivation by slaves, lent themselves readily to

罗伯特·沃波尔勋爵已经就任英国首相，其影响力与权力使得他实际上完全领导着该国的政策走向。沃波尔和弗勒里的主要愿望都是和平，尤其是确保西欧的和平。因此，法、英两国便继续为此目标而共同进退，并且，尽管两国无法彻底压制住所有的怨言，但还是在数年间成功地制止了多次暴动。不过，虽说这两位大臣有着此种一致的目标，但他们怀有此种目标的动机却并不相同。沃波尔之所以希望和平，是因为英国王位继承问题仍然悬而未决，是因为摆在他面前的英国贸易需要和平崛起，并且很可能还是因为他的内心无法容忍英国政府中的那些对手，这才让他不愿再战，以免自己身边出现实力更强的人。弗勒里呢，则是由于法国国王的王位和他的权力都相当稳当，还像沃波尔一样希望自己的国家和平发展起来，以及出于老年人热爱平静的自然心态而不愿再战；因为他就任之时已有73岁，而在去世放权之时，则已是90高龄了。在他这种温和的执政时期，法国重新开始繁荣兴旺起来；就算是匆匆过客，也能注意到法国和法国人民面貌的改变。不过，此种改变究竟是应当归功于这位平和稳重的老人治下的政府呢，还是只应当归因于法国人民天生豁达开朗的性格，使得他们既不再为战争费神，也未与世界其他地区隔绝，这一点还是可以存疑的。法国当局声称，全国的农业生产并未恢复过来。然而完全可以确定的是，法国的海洋事业蓬勃发展起来且进步巨大，而其主要原因则是在路易十四死后的数年间废除了各种贸易限制政策。西印度群岛的发展尤其迅猛，与之进行贸易的母国港口，自然也会分享到这些地区的繁荣成果。马提尼克、瓜达鲁佩和路易斯安那的热带气候，以及由奴隶进行的农业耕作，都使得这些地区都很容易屈从于那种家长式的半军事制管理；虽说所有法属殖民地实行的都是这种行政方式，但在加拿大，却因为当地气候严寒而没有

the paternal, semi-military government which marks all French colonies, but which produced less happy results in the bitter weather of Canada. In the West Indies, France at this time obtained a decided preponderance over England; the value of the French half of Hayti was alone equal to that of all the English West Indies, and French coffee and sugar were driving those of England out of European markets. A like advantage over England in the Mediterranean and Levant trade is asserted by French historians. At the same time the East India Company was revived, and its French depot, whose name tells its association with the East, the Breton town of L'Orient, quickly became a splendid city. Pondicherry on the Coromandel coast, and Chandernagore on the Ganges, the chief seats of French power and commerce in India, grew rapidly; the Isle of Bourbon and the Isle of France, now the Mauritius, whose position is so well suited for the control of the Indian Ocean, became, the one a rich agricultural colony, the other a powerful naval station. The monopoly of the great company was confined to the trade between home and the chief Indian stations; the traffic throughout the Indian seas was open to private enterprise and grew more rapidly. This great movement, wholly spontaneous, and even looked on with distrust by the government, was personified in two men, Dupleix and La Bourdonnais; who, the former at Chandernagore and the latter at the Isle of France, pointed out and led the way in all these undertakings, which were building up the power and renown of the French in the Eastern seas. The movement was begun which, after making France the rival of England in the Hindustan peninsula, and giving her for a moment the promise of that great empire which has bestowed a new title on the Queen of Great Britain, was destined finally to falter and perish before the sea power of England. The extent of this expansion of French trade, consequent upon peace and the removal of restrictions, and not due in any sense to government protection, is evidenced by the growth of French merchant shipping from only three hundred vessels at the

取得令人满意的效果。在西印度群岛，法国此时已经获得了一种超过英国的决定性优势；仅仅是法国所占的那一半海地岛的产值，就相当于所有英属西印度群岛殖民地的总和，并且法国的咖啡和食糖，也正在将英国的这两种产品挤出欧洲市场。法国的史学家们还宣称，在与地中海地区和黎凡特的贸易中，法国也获得了压倒英国的类似优势。与此同时，东印度公司重新崛起，而它在法国的仓储地，"东方的布雷顿市"——从这个名字，就可以看出它与东方的关系——也迅速成为了一座声名显赫的城市。位于科罗曼德尔沿海的庞迪切里与位于恒河上的金德纳格尔这两处法国势力和贸易的中心，也迅速发展起来；波旁岛和法兰西岛（即如今的毛里求斯），也因为它们的位置十分有利于控制印度洋，所以其中之一变成了一处富庶的农业殖民地，而另一处则成为了一个强大的军港。这家庞大的公司手中的垄断权，只限于在本国与印度的主要军港之间进行贸易；而整个印度洋的贸易，则向私营企业开放，因而增长迅猛。这种伟大的发展完全是同时进行的，可法国政府甚至还以不信任的态度待之。此种发展以两个人物为代表，即杜普雷和拉·布尔多纳；前者在金德纳格尔，后者在法兰西岛，都为法国人指出了发展道路，并引导着他们在所有这些活动中前进，从而在东方诸海域确立起了法国的势力和声望。这一运动，自法国在印度半岛上变成了英国的竞争对手，并且暂时承诺让英国拥有那个已经以大不列颠女王之名授予了新封号的伟大帝国之后就开始了，但它注定最终会在英国的制海权面前不堪一击，并且消亡于无形。法国贸易的此种扩张，源于局势和平以及取消各种限制政策，并非源于政府的什么贸易保护意识，其发展程度可由法国商船运输业的增长看出来：路易十四去世的时候，法国只有300艘舰船，而20年后，法国已经拥有了1800艘商船。一位法国历史学家称，

death of Louis XIV., to eighteen hundred, twenty years later. This, a French historian claims, refutes "the deplorable prejudices, born of our misfortunes, that France is not fitted for sea commerce, the only commerce that indefinitely extends the power of a nation with its sphere of activity."

This free and happy movement of the people was far from acceptable to Fleuri, who seems to have seen it with the distrust of a hen that has hatched ducklings. Walpole and himself were agreed to love peace; but Walpole was obliged to reckon with the English people, and these were prompt to resent rivalry upon the sea and in trade, however obtained. Moreover, Fleuri had inherited the unfortunate policy of Louis XIV.; his eyes were fixed on the continent. He did not indeed wish to follow the course of the regency in quarrelling with Spain, but rather to draw near to her; and although he was not able for a time to do so without sacrificing his peace policy, because of Spain's restless enmity to England, yet his mind was chiefly bent upon strengthening the position of France on the land, by establishing Bourbon princes where he could, and drawing them together by family alliances. The navy was allowed to decay more and more. "The French government abandoned the sea at the very moment that the nation, through the activity of private individuals, was making an effort to regain it." The material force fell to fifty-four ships-of-the-line and frigates, mostly in bad condition; and even when war with England had been imminent for five years, France had but forty-five ships-of-the-line to England's ninety. This difference foreshadowed the results which followed a quarter of a century of war.

During the same period Walpole, relying upon Fleuri's co-operation, resolutely set his face against open war between England and Spain. The difficulties caused by the threatening and exasperating action of the latter country, and of such allies as she from time to time could raise,

这一事实驳斥了"那种因我们的不幸而产生出来的、说法国并不适于从事海洋贸易的可悲偏见，但海洋贸易却是无限扩大一国势力和活动范围的唯一一种贸易。"

不过，法国人民此种自由而满意的运动，却让弗勒里觉得完全无法接受；他似乎就像一只孵出了小鸭子的母鸡那样，对这种运动疑心重重。沃波尔和他本人都一样地热爱和平；但沃波尔却不得不认真对待英国民众，因为英国民众都坚决憎恨在海洋和贸易中的恩恩怨怨，无论此种恩怨是怎样结下的。此外，弗勒里还承袭了路易十四那种可悲的政策；他的关注点只是欧洲大陆。他并非真正愿意因袭摄政的老路，再去与西班牙纠纷不断，而是更愿意拉近法、西两国的关系；并且，尽管因为西班牙一直对英国恨恨不已，使得他曾经一度无法在不牺牲其和平政策的前提下做到这一点，但他的心思，主要还是倾向于通过在他能力所及的地方扶持波旁王族，并且通过家族联盟将这些王族团结起来，从而巩固法国在欧洲大陆上的地位。所以，他便任由法国海军日益衰败下去。"就在法国民众通过私人活动正努力恢复其海洋事业的这一刻，法国政府却已放弃了海洋。"法国海军的有形力量，减少到了54艘战列舰和护卫舰，并且大多数的状况都很糟糕；甚至是在英法战争一触即发的那5年间，法国也仅有45艘战列舰，而英国却有90艘。此种差异，其实早已预示了随后长达四分之一个世纪的那场战争的结局。

在同一时期，沃波尔由于依赖弗勒里的合作，所以坚决不让英国与西班牙开战。西班牙咄咄逼人和令人气恼的态度，以及它时常激怒一些盟国的做法所带来的种种麻烦局面，英国都用海军进行威慑的办法应付过去了，而且有时还应付得很成功——海军的威慑，是为了让这些国家记得，英国的那种制海权曾经让一国又一国感受深切并且甘拜

were met, and for a while successfully met, by naval demonstrations, — reminders of that sea power which one nation after another had felt and yielded to. In 1725, the Spanish king and the emperor agreed to sink their long-standing feud, and signed a treaty at Vienna, in which there was a secret clause providing that the emperor would support the claim of Spain to Gibraltar and Port Mahon, by arms if necessary. Russia also showed a disposition to join this confederacy. A counter-alliance was formed between England, France, and Prussia; and English fleets were sent, one to the Baltic to awe the czarina, another to the coast of Spain to check that government and protect Gibraltar, and a third to Porto Bello, on the Spanish Main, to blockade the fleet of galleons there assembled, and by cutting off the supplies remind the Spanish king at once of his dependence upon the specie of America, and of England's control of the highway by which it reached him. Walpole's aversion to war was marked by giving the admiral at Porto Bello the strictest orders not to fight, only to blockade; the consequence of which, through the long delay of the squadron upon the sickly coast, was a mortality among the crews that shocked the nation, and led, among other causes, to the minister's overthrow many years later. Between three and four thousand officers and men, including Admiral Hosier himself, died there. Walpole's aim, however, was reached; though Spain made a foolish attack by land upon Gibraltar, the presence of the English fleet assured its supplies and provisions and averted the formal outbreak of war. The emperor withdrew from the alliance, and under English pressure also revoked the charter of an East India company which he had authorized in the Austrian Netherlands, and which took its name from the port of Ostend. English merchants demanded the removal of this competitor, and also of a similar rival established in Denmark; both which concessions the English ministry, backed by Holland, obtained. So long as commerce was not seriously disturbed, Walpole's peace policy, accompanied as it naturally was by years of plenty and general content, was easily

下风。1725年，西班牙国王与奥地利皇帝同意放下两国的宿怨，并在维也纳签署了一个条约；其中有一项秘密条款，规定奥国皇帝应支持西班牙对直布罗陀和马翁港的主权声索，如有必要，还可使用武力。俄国也表现出了加入这一同盟的意向。而英、法、普鲁士三国则组成了一个反制联盟；英国还派出了三支舰队；其中一支前往波罗的海，以威慑俄国的那位女沙皇，另一支前往西班牙沿海，以遏制该国政府并保护直布罗陀，第三支则前往西班牙本土的拜尔罗港，以封锁那儿，不让西班牙的大帆船[4]集结，并且切断西班牙的物资供应，同时提醒西班牙国王：他离不开美洲运来的金币，而要运送这些金币，也离不开英国所控制的海上通道。沃波尔对战争的厌恶，从他严令在拜尔罗港的那位海军司令不许开战、只许封锁这一点即可见一斑；结果，这支小舰队却因为在疾病流行的沿海地区长久逗留，使得许多官兵都染病死去，情况之严重，令英国举国震惊；再加上其他的原因，便让这位首相多年之后终于被赶下了台。死于此处的官兵，人数在3000人至4000人之间，其中还包括海军司令霍西尔本人。不过，沃波尔的目的还是达到了；尽管西班牙愚蠢地在陆上对直布罗陀发动了一次进袭，但由于有英国舰队在此，确保了该地的军需和给养，所以两国间并未正式爆发战争。奥国皇帝退出了同盟，还在英国的施压之下取消了一家东印度公司的特许状；该公司曾由奥国皇帝授权，在奥属尼德兰地区从事贸易，并以奥斯坦德港为名。英国商人纷纷要求该国取缔这个竞争对手，以及在丹麦扶植起来的另一家与此相似的竞争对手；于是，在荷兰的支持下，英国政府便攫取了这两处的特许权。只要商业贸易没有受到严重的干扰，那么尽管西班牙不断威胁并傲慢地要求收复直布罗陀，但由于已经为英国带来多年的物资丰富，让英国民众普遍

maintained, even though Spain continued threatening and arrogant in her demands for Gibraltar; but unfortunately she now entered more deeply upon a course of annoyance to English trade. The concessions of the Asiento, or slave-trade, and of the annual ship to South America have been mentioned; but these privileges were but a part of the English commerce in those regions. The system of Spain with regard to the trade of her colonies was of the narrowest and most exclusive character; but, while attempting to shut them out from foreign traffic, she neglected to provide for their wants herself. The consequence was that a great smuggling or contraband trade arose throughout her American possessions, carried on mainly by the English, who made their lawful traffic by the Asiento and the yearly ship subserve also the unlawful, or at least unauthorized, trade. This system was doubtless advantageous to the great body of the Spanish colonists, and was encouraged by them, while colonial governors connived at it, sometimes for money, sometimes swayed by local public opinion and their own knowledge of the hardships of the case; but there were Spanish subjects who saw their own business injured by the use and abuse of English privileges, and the national government suffered both in pocket and in pride by these evasions of the revenue. It now began to pull the strings tighter. Obsolete regulations were revived and enforced. Words in which the action of Spain in this old controversy have been described are curiously applicable to certain recent disputes to which the United States has been a party. "The letter of the treaty was now followed, though the spirit which dictated it was abandoned. Although English ships still enjoyed the liberty of putting into Spanish harbors for the purpose of refitting and provisioning, yet they were far from enjoying the same advantages of carrying on a friendly and commercial intercourse. They were now watched with a scrupulous jealousy, strictly visited by guarda-costas, and every efficient means adopted to prevent any commerce with the colonies, except what was allowed by the annual ship." If Spain could

都感到满意,所以沃波尔的和平政策自然就很容易维持下去;可惜的是,西班牙如今已经开始更加繁复地侵害英国贸易了。"席位"特许权,即奴隶贸易特许权,以及每年派遣一艘船只前往南美进行贸易的特许权,我们在前文中都已经提及;这些特许权,不过是英国在这些地区所拥有的贸易特权中的一部分罢了。西班牙关于西属殖民地贸易的制度,是一种最为刻板、最为排他的制度;但是,在试图将外国贸易拒之于这些殖民地之外的同时,西班牙却忽视了这些殖民地对于本国贸易的需求。结果,在西属美洲诸殖民地中,出现了大规模的走私和违禁贸易活动;这些活动,主要都是英国人实施的,他们在进行合法的奴隶贸易和一年一船贸易的同时,也加大了进行非法贸易——或者说,起码是未经授权的贸易——的力度。此种制度,对于绝大部分西班牙殖民者来说,无疑都是有益的,因而得到了他们的支持;而各个殖民地的总督之所以纵容这一制度,有时是为了金钱,有时则是被当地的民意所左右,并且他们自己也知道时势艰难。不过,还是有一些西班牙人,看到了英国利用并滥用其贸易特权,损害到了西班牙人的贸易,而西班牙政府的岁入与自尊,也因这些侵害其税收的行为而受到了损害。于是,此时的西班牙政府,便开始更加严格地对这些殖民地进行管理了。一些本已废止的法律规定,又开始恢复和实行起来。奇怪的是,说明西班牙在这一古老争议中的做法的那些材料,对于合众国近来作为一方所卷入的某些争端,也很适用。"此时,条约的条款得到了执行,但贯穿该条约的精神却被抛弃了。尽管英国船只仍然可以自由驶入西属诸港进行整修或者获取给养,但它们并不享有与这些港口进行友好与贸易往来的同等优势。如今,这些英国船只被西班牙人谨慎而妒忌地盯着,有巡逻艇对它们严加盘查;西班牙人还采取了

have confined herself to closer watchfulness and to enforcing in her own waters vexatious customs regulations, not essentially different from those sanctioned by the general commercial ideas of that day, perhaps no further harm would have resulted; but the condition of things and the temper of her government would not let her stop there. It was not possible to guard and effectually seal a sea-coast extending over hundreds of miles, with innumerable inlets; nor would traders and seamen, in pursuit of gain which they had come to consider their right, be deterred by fears of penalties nor consideration for Spanish susceptibilities. The power of Spain was not great enough to enforce on the English ministry any regulation of their shipping, or stoppage of the abuse of the treaty privileges, in face of the feelings of the merchants; and so the weaker State, wronged and harassed, was goaded into the use of wholly unlawful means. Ships-of-war and guarda-costas were instructed, or at least permitted, to stop and search English ships on the high seas, outside of Spanish jurisdiction; and the arrogant Spanish temper, unrestrained by the weak central government, made many of these visits, both the lawful and the unlawful, scenes of insult and even violence. Somewhat similar results, springing from causes not entirely different, have occurred in the relations of Spanish officials to the United States and American merchant-ships in our own day. The stories of these acts of violence coming back to England, coupled with cases of loss by confiscation and by the embarrassment of trade, of course stirred up the people. In 1737 the West India merchants petitioned the House of Commons, saying, —

"For many years past their ships have not only frequently been stopped and searched, but also forcibly and arbitrarily seized upon the high seas, by Spanish ships fitted out to cruise, under the plausible pretext of guarding their own coasts; that the commanders thereof, with their crews, have been inhumanly treated, and their ships carried into some of the Spanish ports and there condemned with their cargoes, in manifest violation of the treaties subsisting between the

种种有效的手段，除了一年一船所允许进行的贸易外，禁止英国船只与殖民地有任何贸易往来。"倘若西班牙能够更加谨慎小心一点，只在本国所属的水域实行虽说无理苛刻、本质上却与当时普遍的贸易观念所赞同的那些做法并无二致的海关法规，那么，可能就不会给本国贸易带来进一步的损害了；但是，当时的形势和西班牙政府的倾向，却不容西班牙就此止步。要保卫并完全封锁长达数百英里且有着无数港湾的海岸线，是不可能的；而商人和海员为了追求他们认为属于自己权利的利益，也不会因为害怕受到惩处，或者因为考虑西班牙人的情感而退却。西班牙的实力，并未强大到足以迫使英国政府对其商船运输加以管束的地步，也无法阻止英国不顾商人的感受而滥用条约中所定特权的做法；于是，这个处于弱势地位国家，由于深感委屈和备受煎熬，便不得不开始使用全然非法的手段。军舰和缉私船都得到命令，或者说起码是获得了允许，可以在不属西班牙管辖的公海之上拦截和搜查英国船只；而西班牙人天性狂妄自大，软弱的中央政府又无力管束，所以这种拦截和搜查，不管是合法的还是非法的，很多都演变成了侮辱甚至是暴力伤害英国人的事件。如今，在与合众国以及美洲商船的关系当中，西班牙的政府官员也由于并非与此全然不同的原因，造成了多少点儿相似的后果。描述这些暴力行为的消息传回了英国，再加上因为西班牙没收以及阻挠贸易所造成的一起起损失，自然激起了英国民众的愤慨。1737年，西印度公司的商人向议院下院提交了请愿书，称：

"过去许多年以来，他们的船只非但经常遭到西班牙船只的拦截和搜查，还在公海之上遭到它们的武力威胁和随意查封；这些西班牙船只，都是打着保卫本国沿海的幌

two crowns; that the remonstrances of his Majesty's ministers at Madrid receive no attention, and that insults and plunder must soon destroy their trade."

Walpole struggled hard, during the ten years following 1729, to keep off war. In that year a treaty signed at Seville professed to regulate matters, restoring the conditions of trade to what they had been four years before, and providing that six thousand Spanish troops should at once occupy the territory of Tuscany and Parma. Walpole argued with his own people that war would lose them the commercial privileges they already enjoyed in Spanish dominions; while with Spain he carried on constant negotiations, seeking concessions and indemnities that might silence the home clamor. In the midst of this period a war broke out concerning the succession to the Polish throne. The father-in-law of the French king was one claimant; Austria supported his opponent. A common hostility to Austria once more drew France and Spain together, and they were joined by the King of Sardinia, who hoped through this alliance to wrest Milan from Austria and add it to his own territory of Piedmont. The neutrality of England and Holland was secured by a promise not to attack the Austrian Netherlands, the possession of any part of which by France was considered to be dangerous to England's sea power. The allied States declared war against Austria in October, 1733, and their armies entered Italy together; but the Spaniards, intent on their long-cherished projects against Naples and Sicily, left the others and turned southward. The two kingdoms were easily and quickly conquered, the invaders having command of the sea and the favor of the population. The second son of the King of Spain was proclaimed king under the title of Carlos III., and the Bourbon Kingdom of the Two Sicilies thus came into existence. Walpole's aversion to war, leading him to abandon a long-standing ally, thus resulted in the transfer of the central Mediterranean to a control necessarily unfriendly to Great Britain.

But while Walpole thus forsook the emperor, he was himself betrayed by his friend Fleuri.

子，被派出来巡逻的。因此，被查船只的指挥官和船员都遭到了很不人道的对待，而他们的船只则被拖进西班牙的一些港口，并因所携货物而获罪，这些做法明显违反了两国之间所签的协定；而陛下派驻马德里之公使的历次抗议，却并未得到西班牙政府的关注，所以此种侵害和掠夺，必将很快彻底地摧毁他们的贸易。"

自1729年后的那10年间，沃波尔使尽了浑身解数，以避免开战。就在那一年，英、西两国在塞维利亚又签署了一项协定，宣称将控制事态，将两国之间的贸易形势恢复到4年前的那种状态，并且规定，西班牙应当马上派遣6000士兵占领托斯卡纳和帕尔马两地。沃波尔对英国民众据理力争，说战争会让他们失去本已在西班牙诸领地上所享有的那些贸易特权；同时，他还不断与西班牙谈判，想要西班牙做出妥协并进行赔偿，以平息英国国内鼎沸的民怨。在此期间，因为波兰王位继承问题，爆发了一场战争。法国国王的岳父，乃是波兰的王位继承人之一；而奥地利支持的，却是法王岳父的政敌。于是，对于奥地利的一致敌视，便再次让法、西两国团结起来；后来，撒丁国王也加入进来了，因为撒丁国王希望通过这一同盟，从奥地利手中夺取米兰，并将米兰并入其位于皮埃蒙特的领土之中。英、荷两国表示中立，承诺不去进攻奥属尼德兰，不去进攻法国认为会危及英国海权的任何殖民地。盟国于1733年10月对奥宣战，而三国陆军也一齐开进了意大利；但西班牙人因觊觎那不勒斯和西西里已久，便与其余两国分道扬镳，转而南下了。那不勒斯和西西里这两个王国很快就被轻而易举地征服了；侵略者非但控制了海上，还获得了民众的支持。西班牙国王的二儿子被宣布为这两地的国王，号称卡洛斯三世，而两西里的波旁王朝也就此诞生了。沃波尔对战争的厌恶，让他抛弃了一个长久以来的盟友，从而使得

While making the open alliance with Spain against Austria, the French government agreed to a secret clause directed against England. This engagement ran as follows: "Whenever it seems good to both nations alike, the abuses which have crept into commerce, especially through the English, shall be abolished; and if the English make objection, France will ward off their hostility with all its strength by land and sea." "And this compact was made," as the biographer of Lord Hawke points out, "during a period of intimate and ostentatious alliance with England itself." "Thus the policy against which William III. had called on England and Europe to arm, at last came into existence." Had Walpole known of this secret agreement, it might have seemed to him an additional argument in favor of peace; for, his keen political sagacity warning him of the existence of a danger which he yet could not see, he told the House of Commons that "if the Spaniards had not private encouragement from powers more considerable than themselves, they would never have ventured on the insults and injuries which have been proved at your bar;" and he expressed the opinion that "England was not a match for the French and Spaniards too."

Fleuri had indeed given his old friend and fellow-statesman an ugly fall. The particular question which excited the two years' War of the Polish Succession, the choice of a ruler for a distracted kingdom fated soon to disappear from the list of European States, seems a small matter; but the turn imparted to European politics by the action of the powers engaged gives it a very different importance. France and Austria came to an arrangement in October, 1735, upon terms to which Sardinia and Spain afterward acceded, the principal points of which were as follows: The French claimant to the Polish throne gave up his claim to it, and received instead the duchies of Bar and Lorraine on the east of France, with the provision that upon his death they were to go to his son-in-law, the King of France, in full sovereignty; the two

地中海中心地带的控制权转移到了一个必然不会对大不列颠友好的国家手中。

不过，就在沃波尔如此弃奥国皇帝于不顾的时候，沃波尔本人也被自己的朋友弗勒里出卖了。在公开与西班牙结成同盟对抗奥地利的同时，法国政府同意了一项针对英国的秘密条款。这一条款，是如此表述的："无论何时，只要对两国同样有益，那么，业已存在于贸易活动当中的种种不正做法，尤其是英国人的不法行径，都应当加以彻底弃止；倘若英国人提出反对意见，法国则应当尽其海陆之力量，阻止英国人的敌对行为。"正如霍克勋爵的传记作者所指出的那样："这一协议，是在法国本身正与英国处于亲密且引人注目的同盟关系期间签订的。""因此，威廉三世曾经号召英国和欧洲应当加以防范的那种政策，终于出现了。"就算沃波尔得知了这项秘密协定的存在，他也很可能会认为，这不过是又为他提供了一个支持和平政策的理由罢了；因为，那种敏锐的政治远见会提醒他出现了一种此时还看不到的危险，故他曾对下议院说："要是西班牙人没有得到比该国强大得多的一些国家的私下怂恿，他们是决计不敢干出业已由你们审理并证实的种种侮辱和伤害行径的；"并且，他还表达了这样的观点："英国并非法、西两国的对手。"

弗勒里实际上是给了他这位老朋友和政客同仁用心险恶的一击。诱发长达两年的波兰王位继承战争的那个特殊问题，即为一个混乱不堪、注定很快会从欧洲国家名册中消失的王国选择君主，似乎只是一个小问题；但列强所卷入的行动，导致了欧洲政治格局的转变，却给这个问题带来了不一样的重要意义。法国和奥地利在1735年10月缔结了一项协定，后来撒丁王国与西班牙也都同意了其中的条款。该协定的要点如下：波兰王位的法国继承人放弃其继承要求，代之以给他位于法国东部的巴尔和洛林两个公国，条件

kingdoms of Sicily and Naples were confirmed to the Spanish Bourbon prince, Don Carlos; and Austria received back Parma. The Sardinian monarchy also got an increase to its Italian territory. France thus, under the peace-loving Fleuri, obtained in Bar and Lorraine an accession of strength which more warlike rulers had coveted in vain; and at the same time her external position was fortified at the expense of England, by the transfer of controlling positions in the central Mediterranean to an ally. Yet the heart of Fleuri might well have failed him as he remembered the secret agreement to check the commerce of England, and thought of her mighty sea power alongside of the decayed navy of France. That compact between France and Spain, to which the Two Sicilies acceded later, bore within it, in the then strained relations between England and Spain, the germ of the great wars between England and the House of Bourbon which issued in the creation of the British Empire and the independence of the United States.

The clamor in England over Spanish outrages continued, and was carefully nursed by the opposition to Walpole. The minister was now over sixty years of age, and scarcely able to change the settled convictions and policy of his prime. He was face to face with one of those irrepressible conflicts between nations and races toward which a policy of repression and compromise can be employed but for a short time. The English were bent upon opening the West Indies and Spanish America, the Spanish government equally bent upon obstructing them. Unfortunately for their policy of obstruction, they strengthened Walpole's enemies by unlawful search of English ships on the open sea, and possibly also by outrages to English seamen. Some of the latter were brought before the bar of the House of Commons, and testified that they had been not merely plundered, but tortured, shut up in prison, and compelled to live and work under loathsome conditions. The most celebrated case was that of a certain Jenkins, the master of a merchant-brig, who told that a Spanish officer had torn off one of his ears, bidding him carry

是他死后，这两处公国归他的女婿即法国国王所有，并且后者对这两个地方享有完整的统治权；确认西西里和那不勒斯两个王国归西班牙的波旁亲王唐·卡洛斯；而奥地利则重新获得了帕尔马。撒丁王国的国王也在意大利扩大了自己的领土范围。这样，在热爱和平的弗勒里治下，法国因获得了巴尔和洛林这两地而实力大增——此种实力上的增强，是一些更加好战的统治者垂涎不已却又无法做到的；同时，法国的外部地位，也因将地中海中部地区的要地转让给了一个盟国，以牺牲英国的利益为代价而得到了巩固。不过，弗勒里的内心深处完全没有勇气，因为他还记着遏制英国贸易的那份秘密协定，并且一想到业已衰落下去的法国海军，便会想起英国强大的海上力量来。由法、西两国签订、两西西里王国后来加入的那份协定，在当时英、西两国关系紧张的形势下，埋下了英国与波旁王朝历次大战的祸根；而正是这些大战，导致了大英帝国的诞生和合众国的独立。

英国国内因对西班牙人感到愤慨而产生的民怨仍在继续，并且被沃波尔的对手谨慎地加以利用。沃波尔这位大臣此时已经60多岁，几乎无法改变他在鼎盛时期确立下来的那些信念和政策了。摆在他面前的，是国家间和民族间那些无法约束的矛盾之一；而对于此种矛盾，任何高压加妥协的政策都只能是暂时有效的。英国人一心要打开西印度群岛和西属美洲的贸易大门，而西班牙政府则同样一心想对此加以阻挠。可惜的是，由于此种阻挠政策，西班牙人却通过在公海上非法搜查英国船只、并且可能还通过残暴对待英国海员，而使得沃波尔的政敌变得强大起来了。一些英国海员被带到下议院接受质询并且证实，他们非但受到了掠夺，还受到了虐待，被关进监狱，不得不在令人恶心的环境下生存和劳动。其中最有名的一个案件，便是有一位名叫詹金斯的双桅商船船主诉称，一名西班牙军

it to the king his master, and say that if he had been there he would have been served likewise. Being asked what were his feelings at such a moment of danger and suffering, he was said to have replied, "I commended my soul to God and my cause to my country." This well-turned dramatic utterance from the mouth of a man of his class throws a suspicion of high coloring over the whole story; but it can be readily imagined what a capital campaign-cry it would be in the heat of a popular movement. The tide of feeling swept away Walpole's patchwork of compromise, and war was declared against Spain by Great Britain on the 19th of October, 1739. The English ultimatum insisted upon a formal renunciation of the right of search as claimed and exercised by the Spaniards, and upon an express acknowledgment of the British claims in North America. Among these claims was one relating to the limits of Georgia, then a recently established colony, touching the Spanish territory of Florida.

How far the war thus urged on and begun by England, against the judgment of her able minister, was morally justifiable has been warmly argued on either side by English writers. The laws of Spain with regard to the trade of her colonies did not differ in spirit from those of England herself as shown by her Navigation Act, and Spanish naval officers found themselves in a position nearly identical with that of Nelson when captain of a frigate in the West Indies half a century later. American ships and merchants then, after the separation from the mother-country, continued the trade which they had enjoyed as colonists; Nelson, zealous for the commercial advantage of England as then understood, undertook to enforce the act, and in so doing found against him the feeling of the West Indians and of the colonial authorities. It does not seem that he or those supporting him searched unlawfully, for the power of England was great enough to protect her shipping interests without using irregular means; whereas Spain between 1730 and 1740, being weak, was tempted, as she has since been, to seize those whom she knew to have

官撕下了他的一只耳朵,命令他带着这只耳朵回到他的国王主子那里去,还说要是英国国王去那儿的话,也会受到此种对待。当问到他在这种危险与痛苦时刻的感受时,据说詹金斯是如此回答的:"我把灵魂交给了上帝,把事业交给了祖国。"像詹金斯这种阶层的人,能够说出文辞如此优美的话语,给这个故事增添了一种极其虚假的色彩,令人生疑;不过,我们不难想像,在英国民众运动如火如荼的时候,这句话会成为多么重要的一句运动口号。民情激愤如潮,毁掉了沃波尔让西班牙妥协的补救措施;于是,1739年10月19日,大不列颠向西班牙宣战了。英国发出了最后通牒,要求西班牙正式宣布终止该国所宣称并行使的搜查权,还应明确承认英国在北美洲的诸种权利。在这些权利中,有一种便是关于不久前才建立起来、并与西属殖民地佛罗里达接壤的佐治亚殖民地的边界问题。

英国违背沃波尔这位杰出首相的意见,如此力促并发动的这场战争,从道义上来看究竟有多少正当理由,英国作家们已经从这个问题的两个方面进行过激烈的讨论了。从实质来看,西班牙关于与该国殖民地进行贸易的法律规定,与英国通过《航海法案》所表现出来的那种精神并无二致;而西班牙的海军将领们也发现,自己所处的位置跟半个世纪后、时任西印度群岛一艘护卫舰舰长的纳尔逊差不多。当时,合众国脱离祖国独立后,该国的船只和商人仍然从事着殖民者所进行的那种贸易活动。纳尔逊因为急于保护当时人们所认为的那种英国的贸易优势,便开始实行《航海法案》;可在这样做的过程中,他却发现自己既让西印度群岛的民众不满,也为各个殖民地当局所不喜。他和那些支持他的人,似乎并没有在海上进行过非法搜查,这是因为英国实力强大,无需用非常手段即足以保护本国商船的利益;而1730年至1740年间的西班牙,实力却弱得很,所

injured her wherever she could find them, even outside her lawful jurisdiction.

After reading the entirely sympathetic presentation of the case of Walpole's opponents, urging war, which is given by Professor Burrows in his Life of Lord Hawke, a foreigner can scarcely fail to conclude that the Spaniards were grievously wronged, according to the rights of the mother-country over colonies as commonly admitted in that day; though no nation could tolerate the right of search as claimed by them. It chiefly concerns our subject to notice that the dispute was radically a maritime question, that it grew out of the uncontrollable impulse of the English people to extend their trade and colonial interests. It is possible that France was acting under a similar impulse, as English writers have asserted; but the character and general policy of Fleuri, as well as the genius of the French people, make this unlikely. There was no Parliament and no opposition to make known popular opinion in the France of that day, and very different estimates of Fleuri's character and administration have found voice since then. The English look rather at the ability which obtained Lorraine for France and the Sicilies for the House of Bourbon, and blame Walpole for being overreached. The French say of Fleuri that "he lived from day to day seeking only to have quiet in his old age. He had stupefied France with opiates, instead of laboring to cure her. He could not even prolong this silent sleep until his own death." When the war broke out between England and Spain, "the latter claimed the advantage of her defensive alliance with France. Fleuri, grievously against his will, was forced to fit out a squadron; he did so in niggardly fashion." This squadron, of twenty-two ships, convoyed to America the Spanish fleet assembled at Ferrol, and the reinforcement prevented the English from attacking.[2] "Still, Fleuri made explanations to Walpole and hoped for compromise, — an ill-founded hope, which had disastrous results for our sea interests, and prevented measures which would have given France, from the beginning

以它就像一直以来的那样，只要发现有船只危及到该国的利益，就忍不住要夺走这些船只，即便是这些船只并不在其合法的管辖范围内，也要这样做。

巴罗斯教授在其所著《霍克勋爵传记》一书中，对沃波尔的政敌的论辩持彻底支持的态度；看完这些之后，一位外国人也完全可以得出结论，说尽管没有哪个国家能够容忍西班牙宣称拥有的那种搜查权，但从当时普遍认可的、母国对殖民地所拥有的权利来看，西班牙人的确蒙受了极大的冤屈。与本书主题相关的方面，主要是我们应当注意，这一纷争本质上是一个海洋问题，起因则是英国人民急于扩张其贸易与殖民利益而表现出来的那种无法把持的冲动。法国可能也如英国作家所宣称的那样，是在一种类似的冲动驱使下行动的；不过，弗勒里的性格和他所制定的总体政策，连同法国人民的天赋，却使得他们不太可能是在冲动的驱使下行动。那个时代的法国，既无国会，也无反对派来将民意公之于众，并且自那时起，人们对于弗勒里的性格及其执政功过，就一直有着各种不同的评价。英国人宁愿看到他为法国获得了洛林、为波旁王室获得了两西西里的那种才能，并指责沃波尔上了他的当、受了他的骗。而法国人对于弗勒里，却说"他每日活着，只是为了让自己的暮年过得安静平稳。他只是用鸦片麻醉了法兰西，而不是努力去治好法兰西。他甚至无法让法兰西的这种昏睡持续到他自己去世的那一天。"英、西战争爆发后，"西班牙出于自身利益，宣称已与法国结成防守同盟。弗勒里痛苦地违背自己的意愿，不得不装备了一支小型舰队；他的这种做法很小气。"这支由22艘舰船组成的舰队，护送在费罗尔集结起来的西班牙船队前往美洲；正是这一增援阻止了英军，使之没有发动进攻[2]。"尽管如此，弗勒里还是向沃波尔进行了解释，并且希望

of the war, the superiority in eastern seas." But "upon Walpole's overthrow," says another Frenchman, "Fleuri perceived his mistake in letting the navy decay. Its importance had lately struck him. He knew that the kings of Naples and Sardinia forsook the French alliance merely because an English squadron threatened to bombard Naples and Genoa and to bring an army into Italy. For lack of this element of greatness, France silently swallowed the greatest humiliations, and could only complain of the violence of English cruisers, which pillaged our commerce, in violation of the law of nations," during the years of nominal peace that elapsed between the time when the French fleet was confined to protecting the Spanish against the English and the outbreak of formal war. The explanation of these differing views seems not very hard. The two ministers had tacitly agreed to follow lines which apparently could not cross. France was left free to expand by land, provided she did not excite the jealousy of the English people, and Walpole's own sense of English interests, by rivalry at sea. This course suited Fleuri's views and wishes. The one sought power by sea, the other by land. Which had been wiser, war was to show; for, with Spain as an ally to one party, war had to come, and that on the sea. Neither minister lived to see the result of his policy. Walpole was driven from power in 1742, and died in March, 1745. Fleuri died in office, January 29, 1743.

FOOTNOTES:
(1) Afterward Lord Torrington, father of Admiral John Byng, shot in 1757.
(2) The peculiar political relation which France bore toward England between 1739 and 1744, while the latter country was at war with Spain, needs to be explained, as it depended upon views of international duties which are practically obsolete. By her defensive alliance with Spain, France had bound herself to furnish a

做出妥协——此种希望，根本就站不住脚，给我国的海洋利益带来了灾难性的后果，并且妨碍了我国采取正确的措施，这些措施本来可以在战争伊始，就让法国在东方诸海域占据优势地位的。"不过，另一位法国人曾说："沃波尔一垮台，弗勒里就意识到了自己任由法国海军衰落下去的错误。不久之前，他终于认识到了海军的重要性。他明白，那不勒斯和撒丁两位国王抛弃法国这个盟友，仅仅是因为一小支英国舰队威胁他们说要炮击那不勒斯和热那亚，还要带一支陆军攻入意大利。"而在法国舰队只限于保护西班牙人免受英国人攻击，直到战争正式爆发这一段有名无实的和平时期，"由于没有这样一种伟大的力量，法兰西便只有默默吞下这种极大的耻辱，并且只能抗议英国巡逻艇劫掠我国商船、违反国际法的暴行了。"要解释这些截然不同的观点，似乎并不是很困难。沃波尔与弗勒里这两位大臣，都心照不宣地赞成并遵循着那些显然不能跨越的方针路线。法国可以自由地在欧洲大陆上进行扩张，只要不激起英国民众的猜忌就行，而沃波尔自己对于英国利益的认识，则在于通过海洋上的竞争来实现。这种路线，是符合弗勒里的观点与希望的。英国在海上争霸，法国在陆上称雄。究竟哪国更为聪明，战争自会给出分晓；因为法国既已与西班牙结盟，战争就无可避免，并且会发生在海洋之上。这两位大臣没能看到各自政策所带来的结果，便都离世而去了。沃波尔于1742年被赶下了台，并于1745年3月去世。弗勒里则于1743年1月29日在任上与世长辞。

原注：
（1）后来，海军司令约翰·拜恩之父多灵顿勋爵于1757年摧毁了该地。

contingent of specified force to the Spanish fleet when that country was involved in war of a certain kind. She claimed, however, that her sending these succors was not such an act of hostility to England as involved a breach of the peace existing between the two nations. The French ships-of-war, while thus serving with the Spanish fleet under the terms of the treaty, were enemies; but the French nation and all other armed forces of France, on sea and land, were neutrals, with all the privileges of neutrality. Of course England was not bound to accept this view of the matter, and could make the action of France a casus belli; but France claimed it was not justly so, and England practically conceded the claim, though the relation was likely to lead to formal war, as it did in 1744. A few years later the Dutch will be found claiming the same privilege of neutrality toward France while furnishing a large contingent to the Austrian army acting against her.

（2）关于1739年至1744年间法国同英国那种独特的政治关系——其时英国正同西班牙交战——我们需要解释一下。因为此种政治关系所依赖的，全都是那些几乎已经过时的关于国际义务的观点。法国已与西班牙订立防守同盟，所以，当西班牙卷入某种战争之后，法国便有义务向西班牙舰队派遣一支指定的武装力量。然而，法国却宣称，该国派遣这样的援军，并非是对英国开战，也并非破坏英、法两国间所签的和约。根据法、西所签协定之条款而在西班牙舰队中服役的那些法国军舰，确是英国的敌人；不过，法国以及法国其他所有的武装力量，无论是陆军还是海军，却都是中立的，都拥有中立国的所有权利。当然，在此问题上，英国并非一定要接受这种观点，也可以将法国的做法认为是一种宣战；可法国却称这样不公平，而尽管此种关系很可能会像1744年那样，导致英、法两国正式开战，但英国事实上却承认了法国的这一说辞。数年之后，荷兰也派遣了一支庞大的军队加入奥地利陆军对法作战，并向法国宣称它拥有同样的中立权利。

译者注：
[1] the Abbé Dubois：杜布瓦主教（Guillaume Dubois，1656～1723）。法国的枢机主教和政治家，是摄政时期的首席大臣和英法同盟的缔造者。Abbé在法语中是"神父"的意思，但亦有人音译为"阿贝·杜布瓦"。
[2] Palermo：巴勒莫。意大利的一个港口城市，位于西西里岛西北岸，为西西里首府。
[3] Livonia：利沃尼亚。波罗的海东岸的一个地区，原属俄国，1918年一战后分别划归拉脱维亚和爱沙尼亚。
[4] Galleons：西班牙大帆船。15～16世纪的主流舰船，可用做军舰或商船。直至18世纪初，欧洲仍有此种船只。此处显然是指西班牙的军舰。

CHAPTER VI War between Great Britain and Spain, 1739

War of the Austrian Succession, 1740. —
France Joins Spain against Great Britain, 1744. —
Sea Battles of Matthews, Anson, and Hawke. —
Peace of Aix–la–Chapelle, 1748.

We have now reached the opening of a series of great wars, destined to last with short intervals of peace for nearly half a century, and having, amid many misleading details, one broad characteristic distinguishing them from previous, and from many subsequent, wars. This strife embraced the four quarters of the world, and that not only as side issues here and there, the main struggle being in Europe; for the great questions to be determined by it, concerning the world's history, were the dominion of the sea and the control of distant countries, the possession of colonies, and, dependent upon these, the increase of wealth. Singularly enough it is not till nearly the end of the long contest that great fleets are found engaging, and the struggle transferred to its proper field, the sea. The action of sea power is evident enough, the issue plainly indicated from the beginning; but for a long time there is no naval warfare of any consequence, because the truth is not recognized by the French government. The movement toward colonial extension by France is wholly popular, though illustrated by a few great names; the attitude of the rulers is cold and mistrustful: hence came neglect of the navy, a foregone

第六章 1739年的英西战争

1740年的奥地利王位继承战争；1744年法国同西班牙对英作战；

马修斯、安森与霍克指挥的海战；

1748年的《亚琛和约》

现在，我们论述到一系列大规模战争的开端阶段了；这些大战注定会进行得断断续续，中间夹杂着短时的和平，持续了差不多半个世纪，并且除了一些令人误解的细节，它们还具有一个显著的特征，使之有别于以前的历次大战和后来的许多战争。这一系列战争，非但到处枝节横生，还波及到了整个世界；而其主战场则是在欧洲，因为战争所要解决的那些跟世界历史相关的重大问题，就是海洋霸权、控制那些与欧洲相距遥远的国家、攫取殖民地，以及在此基础上进行敛财聚富。而很奇怪的是，直到这一波旷日持久的战争接近尾声的时候，各国的大型舰队才开始参与进去，并将战争转移到其应有的战场，即海洋上。海权的作用是显而易见的，而战争伊始这一问题也早已表现得明明白白；可在很长一段时间内，却并没有发生过什么重大海战，因为法国政府还没有看清这一事实。尽管有一些伟大人物引领，但法国的殖民扩张运动，全然是一种民间行为；该国统治者的态度，是既冷淡、又不信任：这也正是法国统治者忽视海军，使得该国在海

conclusion of defeat on the main question, and destruction for the time of her sea power.

Such being the character of the coming wars, it is important to realize the relative positions of the three great powers in those quarters of the world, outside of Europe, where the strife was to engage.

In North America, England now held the thirteen colonies, the original United States, from Maine to Georgia. In these colonies was to be found the highest development of that form of colonization peculiar to England, bodies of free men essentially self-governing and self-dependent, still enthusiastically loyal, and by occupation at once agricultural, commercial, and sea-faring. In the character of their country and its productions, in its long sea-coast and sheltered harbors, and in their own selves, they had all the elements of sea power, which had already received large development. On such a country and such a people the royal navy and army were securely based in the western hemisphere. The English colonists were intensely jealous of the French and Canadians.

France held Canada and Louisiana, a name much more extensive in its application then than now, and claimed the entire valley of the Ohio and Mississippi, by right of prior discovery, and as a necessary link between the St. Lawrence and the Gulf of Mexico. There was as yet no adequate occupation of this intermediate country, nor was the claim admitted by England, whose colonists asserted the right to extend indefinitely westward. The strength of the French position was in Canada; the St. Lawrence gave them access to the heart of the country, and though Newfoundland and Nova Scotia had been lost, in Cape Breton Island they still held the key of the gulf and river. Canada had the characteristics of the French colonial system planted in a climate least suited to it. A government paternal, military, and monkish discouraged the development of individual enterprise and of free association for common ends. The colonists

权这个主要问题上不可避免地会以失败而告终，并且彻底毁掉其海上力量的原因。

即将爆发的这一系列战争具有此种特点，故看清三个大国在欧洲之外的其他地区的相对形势就很重要了，因为战争即将在这些地区打响。

在北美洲，此时英国已经拥有从缅因到佐治亚的13个殖民地，即最初的合众国。在这些殖民地中，英国所特有的那种殖民形式得到了极大的发展；自由民组成的那些团体，虽说实质上属于自治和自给自足，却仍然热切地忠于英国，同时从事着农业、商业和海运业。从这些殖民地所属国家和产品的特征、此处漫长的海岸线和诸多安全的海港以及这些自由民团体本身来看，他们都拥有了海权所需的一切要素，何况此时这种海权也已经得到了很大的发展。由于有这样一个国家和这样一个民族为后盾，所以英国海军和陆军在西半球的基础牢固得很。不过，英国殖民者对法国人和加拿大人都怀有强烈的嫉妒之心。

法国占领了加拿大和路易斯安那——当时的路易斯安那，范围比如今要广阔得多，还根据优先发现权，宣称拥有整个俄亥俄河和密西西比河河谷，并将其作为连接圣劳伦斯河与墨西哥湾必不可少的一环。其时，这处内陆乡村既未被人加以充分利用，而法国对此地的主权要求也未得到英国承认，因为英国殖民者坚称他们拥有向西无限扩张的权利。法国的实力本来都放在加拿大；而圣劳伦斯河则可以让他们深入这片乡村腹地，并且尽管失去了纽芬兰和新斯科舍，但法国人在布雷顿角岛上却仍然控制着圣劳伦斯湾和圣劳伦斯河的入口。加拿大带有一种特点，表现出法国殖民制度是应用在了一个最不适宜其应用的地区。该地的政府，是一个愚蠢的世袭政府，既不允许私营企业发展，也不允许私营企业为了共同的目标而自由联合起来。那里的法国殖民者放弃了贸易与农耕，只种植眼前所需的

abandoned commerce and agriculture, raising only food enough for immediate consumption, and were given to arms and hunting. Their chief traffic was in furs. There was so little mechanical art among them that they bought of the English colonies part of the vessels for their interior navigation. The chief element of strength was the military, arms-bearing character of the population; each man was a soldier.

Besides the hostility inherited from the mother-countries, there was a necessary antagonism between two social and political systems, so directly opposed, and lying one alongside the other. The remoteness of Canada from the West Indies, and the inhospitable winter climate, made it, from the naval point of view, of much less value to France than the English colonies to England; besides which the resources and population were greatly inferior. In 1750 the population of Canada was eighty thousand, that of the English colonies twelve hundred thousand. With such disparity of strength and resources, the only chance for Canada lay in the support of the sea power of France, either by direct control of the neighboring seas, or by such powerful diversion elsewhere as would relieve the pressure upon her.

On the continent of North America, in addition to Mexico and the countries south of it, Spain held Florida; under which name were embraced extensive regions beyond the peninsula, not accurately defined, and having little importance at any period of these long wars.

In the West Indies and South America, Spain held mainly what are still known as Spanish American countries, besides Cuba, Porto Rico, and part of Hayti; France had Guadeloupe, Martinique, and the western half of Hayti; England, Jamaica, Barbadoes, and some of the smaller islands. The fertile character of the soil, the commercial productions, and the less rigorous climate would seem to make these islands objects of particular ambition in a colonial war; but as a matter of fact no attempt was made, nor, except as to Jamaica, which Spain

粮食，并且沉迷于武器装备和狩猎。他们主要是进行皮毛贸易。这些人当中的机械人才极少，所以只得从英国殖民地购买部分船只来进行内陆航运。他们实力的主要因素，便是法国人那种尚武精神和兵役特点；可以说，此地的法国人是全民皆兵。

除了源于各自祖国的那种敌视态度之外，英、法两国殖民地所采取的两种社会和政治制度中，也存在着必然的对抗；这两种社会和政治制度相互直接对立，并且水火不容。加拿大与西印度群岛相距遥远，冬季气候严寒恶劣；所以从海军的角度来看，与英属殖民地对英国的意义相比，此地对法国的意义要逊色得多；此外，加拿大在资源和人口方面也大大不如那些英属殖民地。1750年时，加拿大才有80000人口，而英属殖民地则有120万人口。由于实力和资源如此悬殊，所以加拿大唯一有可能支持法国海权的方面，要么是直接控制附近海域，要么便是在其他地方进行有力的牵制，以减轻法国所承受的压力。

在北美大陆上，除了墨西哥及其以南的国家，西班牙还占领着佛罗里达。当时的佛罗里达，覆盖了佛罗里达半岛以外的广袤地区，并没有确定的界限；而在此次漫长的战争中，这一地区任何时候都没有起到过什么重要的作用。

在西印度群岛和南美洲，除了古巴、波多黎各以及海地部分地区以外，西班牙主要还占领着如今仍被称作"西语美洲"的那些国家；法国拥有瓜达鲁佩、马提尼克和海地西部；英国则占领了牙买加、巴巴多斯以及一些较小的岛屿。由于土地肥沃、物产丰富，气候也没那么严酷，故在一场殖民战争中，这些岛屿似乎就会成为那些独具野心的国家相互争夺的目标；可事实上，没有哪个国家曾经试图这样做，并且除了西班牙曾经想要收复牙买加之外，也没有哪个国家曾经想过去征服那些更大的岛屿。原因很可能是，海权虽说让

wished to recover, was any intention entertained of conquering any of the larger islands. The reason probably was that England, whose sea power made her the principal aggressor, was influenced in the direction of her efforts by the wishes of the great body of Englishmen on the North American continent. The smaller West India islands are singly too small to be strongly held except by a power controlling the sea. They had a twofold value in war: one as offering military positions for such a power; the other a commercial value, either as adding to one's own resources or diminishing those of the enemy. War directed against them may be considered as a war upon commerce, and the islands themselves as ships or convoys loaded with enemy's wealth. They will be found therefore changing hands like counters, and usually restored when peace comes; though the final result was to leave most of them in the hands of England. Nevertheless, the fact of each of the great powers having a share in this focus of commerce drew thither both large fleets and small squadrons, a tendency aided by the unfavorable seasons for military operations on the continent; and in the West Indies took place the greater number of the fleet-actions that illustrated this long series of wars.

In yet another remote region was the strife between England and France to be waged, and there, as in North America, finally decided by these wars. In India, the rival nations were represented by their East India companies, who directly administered both government and commerce. Back of them, of course, were the mother-countries; but in immediate contact with the native rulers were the presidents and officers appointed by the companies. At this time the principal settlements of the English were, — on the west coast, Bombay; on the east, Calcutta upon the Ganges, at some distance from the sea, and Madras; while a little south of Madras another town and station, known generally to the English as Fort St. David, though sometimes called Cuddalore, had been established later. The three presidencies of Bombay, Calcutta, and Madras were at this time mutually independent, and responsible only to the Court of Directors

英国成为了一个主要的侵略国，但北美大陆上绝大多数英国人的意愿，影响到了该国的主攻方向。西印度群岛上那些较小的岛屿，一个个都实在是太小了，除非具有掌控海洋的实力，否则便难以牢牢守住。这些岛屿，在战争中都具有双重的重要性：一方面，是为能够掌控海洋的大国提供军事基地；另一方面，则是具有贸易意义，即增加本国的资源或者削弱敌方的资源。直接对这些岛屿作战，可以认为是一种针对贸易的战争，这些岛屿本身也可看成是装载着敌方物资的船只或者船队。因此，它们会像筹码一样频繁易主，并在达成和约之后物归原主；但最终的结果，却还是大部分岛屿都掌控在英国手中。虽说如此，但每个大国在这个贸易中心区都有利益份额的事实，还是让各国都把大大小小的舰队派到了此处，而美洲大陆上并无实施军事行动的有利时机，也助长了这一趋势；所以，能够说明这一系列旷日持久的战争的大多数海战，自然也都发生在西印度群岛海域了。

还有另一处遥远的地区，英、法两国将在此处爆发冲突，并且此处会像北美洲那样，其最终归属将由这些战争来决定。在印度，两家直接掌管着行政与贸易的东印度公司，即代表了英、法这两个敌对国家。站在它们背后的，自然是各自的祖国；不过，直接与本国统治者进行联系的，都是公司所指定的总经理与官员。此时，英国在印度的主要殖民点，是西海岸的孟买、东部恒河上距海较远的加尔各答和马德拉斯；而在马德拉斯南边不远处，后来还建起了另一座城镇和基地，英国人通常称之为圣大卫堡，但有的时候也称其为古德洛尔。当时，孟买、加尔各答和马德拉斯这三地的管辖是相互独立的，并且都只对位于英国国内的董事会负责。

in England.

France was established at Chandernagore, on the Ganges, above Calcutta; at Pondicherry, on the east coast, eighty miles south of Madras; and on the west coast, far to the south of Bombay, she had a third station of inferior importance, called Mahé. The French, however, had a great advantage in the possession of the intermediate station already pointed out in the Indian Ocean, the neighboring islands of France and Bourbon. They were yet more fortunate in the personal character of the two men who were at this time at the head of their affairs in the Indian peninsula and the islands, Dupleix and La Bourdonnais, — men to whom no rivals in ability or force of character had as yet appeared among the English Indian officials. Yet in these two men, whose cordial fellow-working might have ruined the English settlement in India, there appeared again that singular conflict of ideas, that hesitation between the land and the sea as the stay of power, a prophecy of which seems to be contained in the geographical position of France itself. The mind of Dupleix, though not inattentive to commercial interests, was fixed on building up a great empire in which France should rule over a multitude of vassal native princes. In the pursuit of this end he displayed great tact and untiring activity, perhaps also a somewhat soaring and fantastic imagination; but when he met La Bourdonnais, whose simpler and sounder views aimed at sea supremacy, at a dominion based upon free and certain communication with the home country instead of the shifting sands of Eastern intrigues and alliances, discord at once arose. "Naval inferiority," says a French historian who considers Dupleix to have had the higher aims, "was the principal cause that arrested his progress;" but naval superiority was precisely the point at which La Bourdonnais, himself a seaman and the governor of an island, aimed. It may be that with the weakness of Canada, compared to the English colonies, sea power could not there have changed the actual issue; but in the condition of the rival nations in India everything depended upon controlling the sea.

法国则在恒河上位于加尔各答上游的金德纳格尔、东部海岸位于马德拉斯以南80英里的庞迪切里开辟了殖民地，而在西海岸位于孟买南边很远的地方，该国还建立了第三个重要性较小的基地，并称之为马埃。然而，法国人获得中间这一处基地，便拥有了巨大的优势，因为这种优势业已伸向印度洋，伸向法国和波旁王室所拥有的附近岛屿。从当时在印度半岛及各个岛屿上掌管法国事务的那两个人，即杜普雷和拉·布尔多纳的个人性格来看，他们也更幸运，因为这两个人的能力与人格力量，是英国派驻印度的那些官员们当中迄今都无人能敌的。不过，尽管他们的诚挚共事本可以毁掉英国在印度的殖民事业，但这两人之间再一次出现了那种古怪的观念冲突，即对于究竟是建立陆上霸权还是海上霸权犹豫不决；法国本身所处的地理位置，似乎早就预言了他们会这样做。杜普雷的心思虽说并非毫不关注贸易利益，但主要还是放在建立起一个伟大的帝国，使得法国能够统领大批本国诸侯这一点上。在追求这一目标的过程中，他表现出了极大的机智和不懈的积极性，或许还表现出了某种高涨而奇妙的想像力；不过，待他遇见拉·布尔多纳之后，分歧马上就产生了，因为后者的观点更简单、也更合理，旨在确立海洋霸权，确立一种以自由、可靠地与祖国进行交流为基础，而非以不可靠地与东方各国勾心斗角和结盟为基础的霸权。一位认为杜普雷拥有更高远目标的法国历史学家曾说："海军的劣势，是妨碍他实现理想的主要原因。"但是，让海军取得绝对优势，也正是本身即为海员、且是岛屿统治者的拉·布尔多纳的目标。或许，是由于加拿大不如那些英属殖民地，才使得制海权在北美洲无法改变一些实实在在的问题；但从殖民印度的这两个

Such were the relative situations of the three countries in the principal foreign theatres of war. No mention has been made of the colonies on the west coast of Africa, because they were mere trading stations having no military importance. The Cape of Good Hope was in possession of the Dutch, who took no active part in the earlier wars, but long maintained toward England a benevolent neutrality, surviving from the alliance in the former wars of the century. It is necessary to mention briefly the condition of the military navies, which were to have an importance as yet unrealized. Neither precise numbers nor an exact account of condition of the ships can be given; but the relative efficiency can be fairly estimated. Campbell, the English contemporary naval historian, says that in 1727 the English navy had eighty-four ships-of-the-line, from sixty guns up; forty 50-gun ships, and fifty-four frigates and smaller vessels. In 1734 this number had fallen to seventy ships-of-the-line and nineteen 50-gun ships. In 1744, after four years of war with Spain alone, the number was ninety ships-of-the-line and eighty-four frigates. The French navy at the same time he estimates at forty-five ships-of-the-line and sixty-seven frigates. In 1747, near the end of the first war, he says that the royal navy of Spain was reduced to twenty-two ships-of-the-line, that of France to thirty-one, while the English had risen to one hundred and twenty-six. The French writers consulted are less precise in their figures, but agree in representing not only that the navy was reduced to a pitiful number of ships, but that these were in bad condition and the dock-yards destitute of materials. This neglect of the navy lasted more or less throughout these wars, until 1760, when the sense of the nation was aroused to the importance of restoring it; too late, however, to prevent the most serious of the French losses. In England as well as in France discipline and administration had been sapped by the long peace; the inefficiency of the armaments sent out was notorious, and recalls the scandals that marked the outbreak of the Crimean War; while the very disappearance of the

敌对国家的情况来看，却是一切皆取决于制海权。

这就是在主要的海外战场进行交战的这三个国家的相对形势。我们没有提及非洲西海岸的各个殖民地，是因为它们都只是贸易据点，并非兵家必争之地。当时，好望角为荷兰人所占，他们并未积极参与早期的战争，而是长期对英国保持友好和中立，并在本世纪前期的战争中因与英国结盟而幸存了下来。我们还必须简要地说一说海军的情况，因为海军具有一种迄今为止人们尚未认识到的重要性。虽说我们既无法给出准确的舰船数量，也无法准确说明这些舰船的状况，但还是能够公平地估计一下它们相对的作战效率。英国的当代海军历史学家坎贝尔称，1727年时，英国海军拥有84艘战列舰，舰载火炮都在60门以上；还拥有40艘舰载火炮为50门的大船、54艘护卫舰以及一些较小的舰船。1734年，这一数字降到了只有70艘战列舰和19艘载有50门火炮的大船。到了1744年，与西班牙一国交战4年之后，英国海军的舰船数量，则变成了90艘战列舰和84艘护卫舰。他还估计，同一时期法国海军拥有45艘战列舰和67艘护卫舰。到了第一次战争即将结束的1747年，他说西班牙皇家海军的军舰数量减少到了22艘战列舰，法国海军的军舰减少到了31艘战列舰，而英国海军的战列舰则增加到了126艘。虽说他所请教的法国作家们给出的数字更不准确，但他们却一致指出，非但法国海军的军舰降到了少得可怜的地步，而且这些舰船的状况都很糟糕，造船厂里的材料也很匮乏。在差不多整个这一系列战争期间，法国政府对海军采取的都是这种漠然视之的态度，直到1760年，法国人民才清醒过来，认识到了重建海军的重要性；然而，此时已经太晚，无法阻止法国承受最惨重的损失了。在英、法两国，长久的和平都已让海军变得纪律涣散、管理松懈了；发放的武器装备不好用，当时是尽人皆知，

French ships led, by the necessity of replacing them, to putting afloat vessels superior singly, because more modern and scientific, to the older ships of the same class in England. Care must be had, however, in accepting too easily the complaints of individual writers; French authors will be found asserting that English ships are faster, while at the same period Englishmen complain that they are slower. It may be accepted as generally true that the French ships built between 1740 and 1800 were better designed and larger, class for class, than the English. The latter had the undoubted superiority both in the number and quality of the seamen and officers. Keeping some fleets always afloat, whether better or worse, the officers could not quite lose touch of their profession; whereas in France it is said that not one fifth of the officers were, in 1744, employed. This superiority was kept and increased by the practice, which henceforth obtained, of blockading the French military ports with superior force; the enemy's squadrons when they put to sea found themselves at once at a disadvantage in point of practical skill. On the other hand, large as was the number of English seamen, the demands of commerce were so great that war found them scattered all over the world, and part of the fleet was always paralyzed for lack of crews. This constant employment assured good seamanship, but the absence of so many men had to be supplied by an indiscriminate press, which dragged in a class of miserable and sickly men, sadly diluting the quality of the whole. To realize the condition of ships' companies of that day, it will be necessary only to read the accounts of those sent to Anson starting for a cruise round the world, or to Hawke when fitting out for war service; the statements are now almost incredible, and the results most deplorable. It was not a question of sanitation only; the material sent was entirely unfit to meet the conditions of sea life under the most favorable circumstances. In both the French and English service a great deal of weeding among the officers was necessary. Those were the palmy days of court and political influence;

也令我们想起标志着克里米亚战争爆发的那些耻辱来；而正是法国舰船渐渐损失殆尽，需要加以替换，才导致海上出现了一艘艘更加现代、更加科学、因而比英国同等的旧式舰船更加精良的船只。然而，我们必须小心，不要太过轻易地接受个别作家的埋怨；法国作家往往会坚称英国船只速度更快，而同一时期的英国人，却会埋怨说己方的船只速度更慢。大家都公认的一个事实，就是在1740年至1800年间建造的法国船只，比同级别的英国船只设计得更好，船体也更大。而英国海军在舰船数量、海员和官兵素质两个方面，则具有无可置疑的优势。无论舰船优劣，只要始终有舰队在海上航行，官兵们对自己的职业就不会太过生疏；而在法国，据说1744年在役的海军官兵还不到五分之一。此种优势，英国保持下来了，并且还在此后用优势兵力封锁法国诸军港的实践中得到了增强；因此，敌人的舰队一出海，马上便会发现他们在实战技能方面的明显劣势。而另一方面，尽管英国海员数量庞大，但商业贸易对海员的需求也很巨大，所以开战之后，由于这些海员散布在世界各地，因此英国的一部分舰队始终都因缺乏船员而动弹不得。虽说这种持续不断的在役确保了海军官兵的良好船艺，但由于要在一视同仁的紧迫压力之下装备如此之多的缺勤人员，连一些卑劣的或者有病的人也被强拉上船，这便可悲地削弱了整个海军的素质。要认识到当时那些船舶公司的情况，只需看一看安森开始巡逻全球的时候送给他的那些报告，或者是在霍克装备舰船准备作战时送给他的报告就可以了；如今看来，非但那些报告几乎令人难以置信，而结果也是令人极其可叹的。并非只有卫生条件差这一个问题；送来的材料，完全无法满足哪怕是最有利环境下的海上生活。英、法两国海军中，还需要对官兵进行大量的汰旧更新。可那个时代，议会与政治的影响正大行其道；而且，经历了长久的和平安

and, moreover, it is not possible, after a long peace, at once to pick out from among the fairest-seeming the men who will best stand the tests of time and exposure to the responsibilities of war. There was in both nations a tendency to depend upon officers who had been in their prime a generation before, and the results were not fortunate.

War having been declared against Spain by England in October, 1739, the first attempts of the latter power were naturally directed against the Spanish-American colonies, the cause of the dispute, in which it was expected to find an easy and rich prey. The first expedition sailed under Admiral Vernon in November of the same year, and took Porto Bello by a sudden and audacious stroke, but found only the insignificant sum of ten thousand dollars in the port whence the galleons sailed. Returning to Jamaica, Vernon received large reinforcements of ships, and was joined by a land force of twelve thousand troops. With this increased force, attempts were made upon both Cartagena and Santiago de Cuba, in the years 1741 and 1742, but in both wretched failures resulted; the admiral and the general quarrelled, as was not uncommon in days when neither had an intelligent comprehension of the other's business. Marryatt, when characterizing such misunderstandings by a humorous exaggeration, seems to have had in view this attempt on Cartagena: "The army thought that the navy might have beaten down stone ramparts ten feet thick; and the navy wondered why the army had not walked up the same ramparts, which were thirty feet perpendicular."

Another expedition, justly celebrated for the endurance and perseverance shown by its leader, and famous both for the hardships borne and singular final success, was sent out in 1740 under Anson. Its mission was to pass round Cape Horn and attack the Spanish colonies on the west coast of South America. After many delays, due apparently to bad administration, the squadron finally got away toward the end of 1740. Passing the Cape at the worst season of

逸之后，根本不可能马上从那些看似最佳的官兵中，挑选出最能经受住时间的考验、最能承担起战时责任的人来。两国都有着一种倾向，即倚重上一代人当中曾经取得过辉煌成就的那些官兵，因此，结果自然就没有那么侥幸了。

1739年10月，英国对西班牙宣战；而英国的第一波进击，自然便是针对西班牙在美洲的各个殖民地——个中原因，在于英国希望从中找到一处容易攻取的富庶之地。第一支远征军由海军上将弗农率领，于同年11月出征，并以迅雷不及掩耳之势，勇敢地攻下了拜尔罗港；可在西班牙大帆船起航的这处港口里，弗农却只找到了区区的10000美元。返回牙买加后，弗农的远征军兵力得到了扩充，非但增加了大批军舰，还增加了一支12000人的陆军。兵力大增之后，弗农便在1741年和1742年进攻了卡塔赫纳和古巴的圣地亚哥两地，但两次都以惨败而告终；于是，这位海军上将与那位陆军将领争吵了起来——此种情况，在海陆兵种互不了解彼此职责的那个时代，是很常见的。马里亚特[1]在用一种幽默夸张的语气描述此种不和的时候，似乎也想起了弗农对卡塔赫纳的这次进攻："陆军以为，海军本可以击毁厚达10英尺厚的石头城墙；而海军则不明白，陆军为何没有登上高达30英尺的同一道城墙。"

另一支远征军则由安森率领，于1740年出征；这支海军，既因其领导人所表现出来的耐力和毅力而赫赫有名，也因他们所承受的苦难和最终取得的非凡胜利而闻名于世。它的任务是绕过合恩角，去进攻南美洲西海岸的西属殖民地。因为明显的管理不善而耽搁了多次之后，这支舰队终于在1740年年底出发了。绕过合恩角的时候，正值一年中最糟糕的季节，所以这支远征军遭遇了一连串最猛烈的暴风雨；舰队被风暴冲得七零八

the year, the ships met a series of tempests of the most violent kind; the squadron was scattered, never all to meet again, and Anson, after infinite peril, succeeded in rallying a part of it at Juan Fernandez. Two ships had put back to England, a third was lost to the southward of Chiloe. With the three left to him he cruised along the South American coast, taking some prizes and pillaging the town of Payta, intending to touch near Panama and join hands with Vernon for the capture of that place and the possession of the isthmus, if possible. Learning of the disaster at Cartagena, he then determined to cross the Pacific and waylay the two galleons that sailed yearly from Acapulco to Manila. In the passage across, one of the two ships now left to him was found in such bad condition that she had to be destroyed. With the other he succeeded in his last undertaking, capturing the great galleon with a million and a half dollars in specie. The expedition, from its many misfortunes, had no military result beyond the terror and consequent embarrassment caused to the Spanish settlements; but its very misfortunes, and the calm persistency which worked out a great success from them all, have given it a well-deserved renown.

During the year 1740 happened two events which led to a general European war breaking in upon that in which Spain and England were already engaged. In May of that year Frederick the Great became king of Prussia, and in October the emperor Charles VI., formerly the Austrian claimant of the Spanish throne, died. He had no son, and left by will the sovereignty of his estates to his eldest daughter, the celebrated Maria Theresa, to secure whose succession the efforts of his diplomacy had been directed for many years. This succession had been guaranteed by the European powers; but the apparent weakness of her position excited the ambitions of other sovereigns. The Elector of Bavaria laid claim to the whole inheritance, in which he was supported by France; while the Prussian king claimed and seized the province of Silesia. Other

落，此后再也没有全部会合起来，但安森在经历了无数危险之后，最终还是在胡安费尔南德斯成功地将一部分舰船重新集结起来。有两艘军舰返回英国去了，还有一艘则在智鲁岛以南失踪。安森率领剩下的3艘军舰，开始沿着南美西海岸巡航，缴获了一些战利品，还劫掠了佩他城；他本想抵近巴拿马，与弗农联手攻下该地，并在可能的情况下占领巴拿马地峡。而得知了弗农在卡塔赫纳惨败的消息之后，他便决定横渡太平洋，伏击每年从阿卡普尔科[2]驶往马尼拉的两艘西班牙大帆船。在横渡太平洋的途中，此时他尚余的那两艘军舰当中，有一艘船况极其糟糕，只能毁掉了。但他率领最后一艘，却成功地完成了自己最后的任务，俘虏了那艘庞大的西班牙帆船，缴获了船上价值高达150万美元的金币。这次远征由于多灾多难，所以除了让西班牙的各个殖民地感到害怕和忍受必然的难堪之外，并没有在军事上取得什么成果；不过，正是由于这些灾难，以及安森在这些灾难当中保持着冷静和坚韧并最终取得重大胜利，此次远征才获得了当之无愧的美誉。

1740年还发生了两个事件，导致欧洲各国在西班牙和英国业已交战的地区，爆发了一场全面战争。就在这一年，腓特烈大帝登上了普鲁士王位，而原来想要继承西班牙王位的奥地利皇帝查理六世，则在这一年的10月去世了。查理六世没有儿子，便在遗嘱中将其领地的统治权留给了自己的大女儿，即那位有名的玛丽亚·特蕾西娅，以保证他致力于多年的那些外交政策能够由她继承下去。欧洲列强本已保证支持她继承王位；可她那种明显的脆弱地位，还是激起了其他一些君主的野心。巴伐利亚选帝侯要求继承整个奥地利，得到了法国的支持；而普鲁士国王则要求并夺取了西里西亚省。其他大大小小的国家，则分别与这两人沆瀣一气；而英国的态度却变得很复杂，因为英国国王也是汉诺威选帝侯，所以

powers, large and small, threw in their lot with one or the other; while the position of England was complicated by her king being also elector of Hanover, and in that capacity hurriedly contracting an obligation of neutrality for the electorate, although English feeling was strongly in favor of Austria. Meanwhile the failure of the Spanish-American expeditions and the severe losses of English commerce increased the general outcry against Walpole, who resigned early in 1742. England under the new ministry became the open ally of Austria; and Parliament voted not only a subsidy to the empress-queen, but also a body of troops to be sent as auxiliaries to the Austrian Netherlands. At the same time Holland, under English influence, and bound like England by previous treaties to support the succession of Maria Theresa, also voted a subsidy. Here occurs again that curious view of international relations before mentioned. Both of these powers thus entered the war against France, but only as auxiliaries to the empress, not as principals; as nations, except the troops actually in the field, they were considered to be still at peace. Such an equivocal situation could in the end have only one result. On the sea France had already assumed the same position of auxiliary to Spain, in virtue of the defensive alliance between the two kingdoms, while affecting still to be at peace with England; and it is curious to see the gravity with which French writers complain of assaults upon French by English ships, upon the plea that there was no open war between the two States. It has already been mentioned that in 1740 a French squadron supported a division of Spanish ships on their way to America. In 1741, Spain, having now entered the continental war as an enemy of Austria, sent a body of fifteen thousand troops from Barcelona to attack the Austrian possessions in Italy. The English admiral Haddock, in the Mediterranean, sought and found the Spanish fleet; but with it was a division of twelve French sails-of-the-line, whose commander informed Haddock that he was engaged in the same expedition and had orders to fight, if the Spaniards, though formally at war

尽管英国人都强烈支持奥地利，可他还是匆匆忙忙地承诺在选帝事宜上保持中立。在此期间，因为远征西语美洲失利和英国的商业贸易损失惨重，民众对沃波尔的抗议之声大增，使得沃波尔在1742年初便辞职了。新内阁执政下的英国，成了奥地利公开的盟国；国会非但通过投票决定给那位皇后兼女王拨款，还决定派遣一支军队作为外援前往奥属尼德兰。与此同时，处于英国势力范围之下的荷兰，因为像英国一样受到以前所签条约的约束而支持玛丽亚·特蕾西娅继承王位，也决定拨款。此时，便再一次出现了前面已经提到过的那种对于国际关系的古怪观点。英、荷两国虽说都如此加入了对法作战，可都只算是玛丽亚·特蕾西娅皇后的外援，而非当事方；除了实际参战的那些部队，作为国家来说，人们还是认为这两国与法国之间依然是处于和平状态。这样一种暧昧的形势，最终只可能出现一种结果。在海上，法国曾经采取过同样的态度，凭着两国间的防守同盟而做了西班牙的外援，却假装仍与英国保持着和平；所以，看到法国作家们借口两国间并未开战，而郑重其事地谴责英国海军攻击法国船只，着实令人奇怪。前面已经提到，1740年，在一批西班牙船只前往美洲的途中，有一支法国舰队对其进行了支援。到了1741年，此时已在欧洲大陆参战、成了奥地利之敌的西班牙，从巴塞罗那派了一支15000人的军队，前去进攻奥地利位于意大利的领土。正在地中海海域的英国海军上将哈多克，搜索并发现了这支运兵的西班牙舰队；可当时还有一支由15艘战列舰组成的法国舰队陪同，这支法国舰队的司令告诉哈多克说，他也参与了这一运送行动，并且得到了命令，尽管西班牙已正式与英国开战，但倘若这些西班牙人遭到攻击，他便会参战。由于法、西盟军的兵力几乎两倍于己，所以这位英国海军上将便不得不率军退回马翁港内。不久，他便被解职了；而新任海军上

with England, were attacked. As the allies were nearly double his force, the English admiral was obliged to go back to Port Mahon. He was soon after relieved; and the new admiral, Matthews, held at once the two positions of commander-in-chief in the Mediterranean and English minister at Turin, the capital of the King of Sardinia. In the course of the year 1742 an English captain in his fleet, chasing some Spanish galleys, drove them into the French port of St. Tropez, and following them into the harbor burned them, in spite of the so-called neutrality of France. In the same year Matthews sent a division of ships under Commodore Martin to Naples, to compel the Bourbon king to withdraw his contingent of twenty thousand troops serving with the Spanish army in northern Italy against the Austrians. To the attempts to negotiate, Martin replied only by pulling out his watch and giving the government an hour to come to terms. There was nothing for it but submission; and the English fleet left the harbor after a stay of twenty-four hours, having relieved the empress of a dangerous enemy. Henceforward it was evident that the Spanish war in Italy could only be maintained by sending troops through France; England controlled the sea and the action of Naples. These two last incidents, at St. Tropez and Naples, deeply impressed the aged Fleuri, who recognized too late the scope and importance of a well-founded sea power. Causes of complaint were multiplying on both sides, and the moment was fast approaching when both France and England must quit the pretence of being only auxiliaries in the war. Before it came to that, however, the controlling sea power and wealth of England again made itself felt by attaching the King of Sardinia to the Austrian cause. Between the dangers and advantages of the French or English alliance the king's action was determined by a subsidy and the promise of a strong English fleet in the Mediterranean; in return he engaged to enter the war with an army of forty-five thousand men. This compact was signed in September, 1743. In October, Fleuri being now dead, Louis XV. made with Spain a treaty, by which he engaged to declare war

将马修斯，则同时兼任地中海地区总司令和英国驻撒丁王国首都都灵的公使二职。1742年，马修斯所率舰队中有一名英国舰长在追击数艘西班牙的单层桨帆船的时候，把它们赶进了法国的圣特鲁佩斯港，然后尾随进入该港，并且不顾法国所谓的中立政策，焚毁了这些船只。同年，马修斯还派遣了一支分舰队，由马丁准将率领前往那不勒斯，以逼迫那位波旁国王，让他将派往西班牙军中效力、当时正在意大利北部对奥地利作战的那支20000人的部队撤回来。那不勒斯想与马丁进行谈判；对此，马丁准将的回应只是掏出手表，给了该国政府1个小时的时间来接受他的条件。除了投降，那不勒斯别无选择；于是，英国舰队在驻停了24个小时、为奥地利女王解决了一个极其危险的敌人之后，便离开了该港。自此以后，西班牙在意大利作战，显然就只能依靠法国派遣军队，才能维持下去了，因为英国控制了海上和那不勒斯的行动。最后这两个事件，即圣特鲁佩斯港事件和那不勒斯事件，给年老的弗勒里留下了不可磨灭的印象；他此时才认识到一种基础牢固的制海权所具有的力量和重要性，已经太迟了。双方相互指责的理由越来越多，而法、英两国都必须撕下在此次战争中只是外援的面具的那个时刻，也迅速到来了。然而在此之前，英国的海上霸权，在让撒丁王国加入奥地利一方的过程中，再一次显露出了强大的力量。撒丁国王曾在与英法任何一方结盟会带来何种危险和利益的问题上犹豫不决，而英国承诺给他拨款，并且答应在地中海海域常备一支强大的英国舰队后，他便做出了抉择；作为交换，他答应派遣一支45000人的军队参战。这份条约，签署于1743年9月。到了10月，此时弗勒里已经辞世，路易十五与西班牙签署了一份协定，承诺对英国和撒丁王国开战，并且支持西班牙在意大利的主权要求，以及它对直布罗陀、马翁港和佐治亚殖民地等地的主权声索。尽管

against England and Sardinia, and to support the Spanish claims in Italy, as also to Gibraltar, Mahon, and Georgia. Open war was thus near at hand, but the declaration was still deferred. The greatest sea fight that took place occurred while nominal peace yet existed.

In the latter part of 1743 the Infante Philip of Spain had sought to land on the coast of the Genoese Republic, which was unfriendly to the Austrians; but the attempt had been frustrated by the English fleet, and the Spanish ships forced to retreat into Toulon. They lay there for four months, unable to go out on account of the English superiority. In this dilemma the court of Spain applied to Louis XV. and obtained an order for the French fleet, under the command of Admiral de Court, — an old man of eighty years, a veteran of the days of Louis XIV., — to escort the Spaniards either to the Gulf of Genoa or to their own ports, it does not clearly appear which. The French admiral was ordered not to fire unless he was attacked. In order to secure the best co-operation of the Spaniards, whose efficiency he probably distrusted, De Court proposed, as Ruyter had done in days long gone by, to scatter their ships among his own; but as the Spanish admiral, Navarro, refused, the line-of-battle was formed with nine French ships in the van, in the centre six French and three Spaniards, in the rear nine Spanish ships; in all, twenty-seven. In this order the combined fleets sailed from Toulon February 19, 1744. The English fleet, which had been cruising off Hyères in observation, chased, and on the 22d its van and centre came up with the allies; but the rear division was then several miles to windward and astern, quite out of supporting distance. The wind was easterly, both fleets heading to the southward, and the English had the weather-gage. The numbers were nearly equal, the English having twenty-nine to the allied twenty-seven; but this advantage was reversed by the failure of the English rear to join. The course of the rear-admiral has been generally attributed to ill-will toward Matthews; for although he proved that in his separated position he made all sail to

开战已经迫在眉睫了，但开战宣言却一拖再拖。所以，规模最大的一场海战，便发生在有名无实的和平仍然存续的这一时期。

1743年下半年，西班牙的菲利普亲王试图在热那亚共和国沿海登陆，因为后者对奥地利很敌视；但这一企图被英国舰队挫败了，西班牙的舰船不得不撤入土伦港内。由于英国海军在兵力上具有优势，所以西班牙舰队只得在港内龟缩了4个月，无法出海。陷入此种困窘之中后，西班牙朝廷便向路易十五求助；后者则下令，由海军上将德·考尔指挥法国舰队，护送西班牙人前往热那亚湾或该国自己的港口——到底前往哪儿，命令并没有清楚说明；而德·考尔上将此时已是一位80高龄的老人，他曾是路易十四时代一名身经百战的将领。这位法国海军上将得到命令，除非他遭到攻击，否则就不要开火。为了确保西班牙人能够最好的加以配合（他很可能信不过西班牙军队的作战能力），德·考尔提出，像很久以前鲁伊特所做的那样，将西班牙船只散布于法国舰队之间；不过，由于西班牙海军上将纳瓦罗反对，所以最终的战斗队形便是9艘法国军舰任前锋，中军为6艘法国军舰和3艘西班牙军舰，后卫则是9艘西班牙军舰，总计27艘舰船。1744年2月19日，联合舰队便照此序列从土伦港起航了。一直在耶尔沿海巡逻监视的英国舰队展开了追击，其前锋和中军在22日便赶上了法、西盟军；但当时其后卫分队却处于下风，落后了数英里之远，根本无法进行支援。此时刮的是东风，两支舰队都是往南航行，而英国舰队处于上风位置。双方舰船数量差不多相等，英国是29艘，法、西盟军是27艘；不过，英军的这一优势，却因后卫分队未能赶上而逆转了。人们通常认为，英军后卫分队司令这样做，是因为他对马修斯怀有怨意；尽管他表明自己在战位上已经张开所有的帆，想赶上前去参战，但后来可以参战

join, he did not attack later on when he could, on the plea that the signal for the line-of-battle was flying at the same time as the signal to engage; meaning that he could not leave the line to fight without disobeying the order to form line. This technical excuse was, however, accepted by the subsequent court-martial. Under the actual conditions Matthews, mortified and harassed by the inaction of his lieutenant, and fearing that the enemy would escape if he delayed longer, made the signal to engage when his own van was abreast the enemy's centre, and at once bore down himself out of the line and attacked with his flag-ship of ninety guns the largest ship in the enemy's line, the "Royal Philip," of one hundred and ten guns, carrying the flag of the Spanish admiral. In doing this he was bravely supported by his next ahead and astern. The moment of attack seems to have been judiciously chosen; five Spanish ships had straggled far to the rear, leaving their admiral with the support only of his next ahead and astern, while three other Spaniards continued on with the French. The English van stood on, engaging the allied centre, while the allied van was without antagonists. Being thus disengaged, the latter was desirous of tacking to windward of the head of the English line, thus putting it between two fires, but was checked by the intelligent action of the three leading English captains, who, disregarding the signal to bear down, kept their commanding position and stopped the enemy's attempts to double. For this they were cashiered by the court-martial, but afterward restored. This circumspect but justifiable disregard of signals was imitated without any justification by all the English captains of the centre, save the admiral's seconds already mentioned, as well as by some of those in the van, who kept up a cannonade at long range while their commander-in-chief was closely and even furiously engaged. The one marked exception was Captain Hawke, afterward the distinguished admiral, who imitated the example of his chief, and after driving his first antagonist out of action, quitted his place in the van, brought to close quarters a fine

的时候，他却并未发起攻击，理由是舰队在发出作战信号的同时，还发出了保持战斗队列的信号；也就是说，他要离开队列去作战，便会违反保持队列的命令。然而，这种技术上的理由，却被随后的军事法庭采纳了。实际情况是，马修斯因其副将的拖拉无为而深感羞愧与恼火，还因担心拖延太久会让敌人逃脱，所以一待自己所率的前锋与敌人的中军并排开来，便发出了作战信号，然后马上抽身驶出队列，用自己装载有90门火炮的旗舰，对敌军阵列中最大的那一艘船发起了攻击；这艘军舰便是"皇家菲利普"号，它载有110门火炮，并且悬着西班牙海军司令的旗帜。在此期间，他得到了位于其前后两方舰船的英勇支援。发动进攻的时机，似乎是经过深思熟虑而选定的；有5艘西班牙军舰已经远远地落在后面，使得他们的海军司令只能得到前后紧挨着他的各一艘军舰支援，还有3艘西班牙军舰则继续同法国军舰待在一起。英军前锋保持着航向，向法、西盟军的中军发动进攻，而盟军的前锋则没有敌人。由于没有敌人攻击，盟军的前锋便想抢风航行，占领英军阵列前方的有利位置，从而将其置于两面火力的夹击之下；可三位领头的英国舰长，却以巧妙的机动阻止了他们的这一企图。这三位舰长不顾敌军逼近的信号，坚守着自己的指挥位置，使得敌人无法掉头航行。由于这一做法，他们还受到了军事法庭的撤职处分，不过后来又复职了。他们这种慎重而有理由地不服从旗语指挥的做法，却被英国舰队中军的所有舰长毫无理由地效仿，只有前面已经提到的、英国海军上将的那两位副手以及前锋中的数位舰长没有这样做，后者在他们的总司令靠近敌军、甚至与敌军猛烈交上火之后，仍然继续从远距离对敌人进行炮击。其中一个显著的例外，就是后来成为了一名杰出的海军上将的霍克上校；他效仿主帅的做法，在重创第一艘敌舰、使之无法战斗之后，便放弃了自己

Spanish ship that had kept at bay five other English ships, and took her, — the only prize made that day. The commander of the English van, with his seconds, also behaved with spirit and came to close action. It is unnecessary to describe the battle further; as a military affair it deserves no attention, and its most important result was to bring out the merit of Hawke, whom the king and the government always remembered for his share in it. The general inefficiency and wide-spread misbehavior of the English captains, after five years of declared war, will partly explain the failure of England to obtain from her undoubted naval superiority the results she might have expected in this war — the first act in a forty years' drama — and they give military officers a lesson on the necessity of having their minds prepared and stocked, by study of the conditions of war in their own day, if they would not be found unready and perhaps disgraced in the hour of battle.[1] It is not to be supposed that so many English seamen misbehaved through so vulgar and rare a defect as mere cowardice; it was unpreparedness of mind and lack of military efficiency in the captains, combined with bad leadership on the part of the admiral, with a possible taint of ill will toward him as a rude and domineering superior, that caused this fiasco. Attention may here fitly be drawn to the effect of a certain cordiality and good-will on the part of superiors toward their subordinates. It is not perhaps essential to military success, but it undoubtedly contributes to the other elements of that success a spirit, a breath of life, which makes possible what would otherwise be impossible; which reaches heights of devotion and achievement that the strictest discipline, not so enkindled, cannot attain. Doubtless it is a natural gift. The highest example of it possibly ever known among seamen was Nelson. When he joined the fleet just before Trafalgar, the captains who gathered on board the flag-ship seemed to forget the rank of their admiral in their desire to testify their joy at meeting him. "This Nelson," wrote Captain Duff, who fell in the battle, "is

在前锋中的战位，逼近一艘训练有素、阻挡住了英军舰队中其他五艘战舰去路的西班牙军舰，并且占领了这艘军舰——这是那天英军获得的唯一战利品。英军前锋的指挥官及其副手也表现得很英勇，与敌军短兵相接。我们无需再详细地描绘此次战斗了；作为一次军事行动，它并不值得我们加以注意，而其最重大的结果，也只是显示出了霍克的功绩，使得英王和英国政府始终都铭记着他在此战中的功劳罢了。开战5年之后，英军舰长们仍然存在着普遍的无能和大范围的不端行为，这既可以部分地解释英国为何没有凭借其无可置疑的海军优势，获得此次战争中本应获得的那种战果——这可是40年战争大戏中的第一幕——的原因，而且还给了军官们一个教训，那就是：倘若他们不想在战斗之时毫无准备，不想甚至可能蒙受耻辱，就必须通过研究所处时代的战争形势，让自己在思想上做好准备。[1]我们并不是说，如此多的英国海军官兵，都仅仅是因为像怯懦这种可鄙而罕见的弱点才表现不好；而是因为舰长们都没有做好充分的思想准备，并且缺乏军事才能，加上那位海军司令领导无方，以及下属对他这个粗鲁无礼、专横跋扈的长官可能怀有那么一点点怨意，才导致了这种惨痛的失败。在这里，我们不妨适当地注意一下，上级稍加亲切而友善地对待下级，会产生什么样的效果。虽说这样做可能并非军事上一个不可或缺的成功因素，但它无疑有助于军事成功的其他因素，为部队带来一种士气，带来一种让不可能完成的任务变成可能完成的那种不可或缺的精神；它能让军队达到高度的忠诚、取得高度的成就，而这种忠诚和成就，却是那种最为严厉、不能鼓舞士气的纪律根本无法实现的。毫无疑问，这是一种天赋。在这个方面，英国海军官兵中迄今所知的一个最杰出的榜样，大概要算纳尔逊了。他在特拉法尔加海战前夕入职英国舰队之后，集合到旗舰上来的那些

so lovable and excellent a man, so kindly a leader, that we all wish to exceed his desires and anticipate his orders." He himself was conscious of this fascination and its value, when writing of the battle of the Nile to Lord Howe, he said, "I had the happiness to command a band of brothers."

The celebrity attained by Matthews's action off Toulon, certainly not due to the skill with which it was managed, nor to its results, sprang from the clamor at home, and chiefly from the number and findings of the courts-martial that followed. Both the admiral and his second, and also eleven captains out of the twenty-nine, had charges preferred against them. The admiral was cashiered because he had broken the line; that is, because his captains did not follow him when he left it to get at the enemy, — a decision that smacks more of the Irish bull than of the Irish love of fighting. The second was acquitted on the technical grounds already given; he avoided the fault of breaking the line by keeping far enough away. Of the eleven captains one died, one deserted, seven were dismissed or suspended, two only were acquitted. Nor were the French and Spaniards better pleased; mutual recriminations passed. Admiral de Court was relieved from his command, while the Spanish admiral was decorated by his government with the title of Marquis de la Victoria, a most extraordinary reward for what was at best a drawn fight. The French, on the other hand, assert that he left the deck on the plea of a very slight wound, and that the ship was really fought by a French captain who happened to be on board.

To use a common expression, this battle, the first general action since that off Malaga forty years before, "woke up" the English people and brought about a healthful reaction. The sifting process begun by the battle itself was continued, but the result was reached too late to have its proper effect on the current war. It is rather by its deficient action, than by

舰长们，似乎都因为急切地想要表明自己见到他的欣喜之情，而忘记了这位海军上将的官衔。"这位纳尔逊，"参加了此战的达夫上校写道，"是如此讨人喜欢、如此优秀的一个人，又是如此和蔼的一位领导，因此我们都希望做得比他要求的更好，都期待着他向我们下达命令。"纳尔逊本人也清楚自己的这种魅力及其价值，在写给豪勋爵、报告尼罗河河口之战情况的信中，他说："能够指挥一帮兄弟，我感到很满足。"

马修斯在土伦海岸的行动带来了如此巨大的声誉，自然并非是由于其指挥才能，也并非是由于此战取得的战果，而是源于国内沸腾的民意，并且主要是随之而来的军事审判场次众多及其调查结果。这位海军上将和他的副指挥，还有29名舰长中的11位，都受到了指控。这位海军上将被解了职，因为他破坏了舰队阵列；也就是说，因为他手下的那些舰长们，在他离开阵列去进攻敌人的时候并未跟上他——因此，这一判决带有更多的爱尔兰人自相矛盾的味道[3]，而非爱尔兰人好斗的味道。他的副手，因为前面已经说明了的专业原因而被判无罪；他离得远远的，避免了破坏阵列的过错。那11名舰长中，1人死了，1人遭到流放，7人被解职或停职，只有2人被判无罪。法国人与西班牙人也好过不到哪里去；他们之间彼此指责、相互揭丑。德·考尔上将被解除了指挥权，西班牙的海军司令则被该国政府授予了"维多利亚侯爵"封号；对于一场打成了平局的战争来说，这可真算得上一种极其离奇的殊荣了。而另一方面，法国则坚称西班牙的这位海军司令借口受了一点儿轻伤便离开了甲板，他的座舰是由一名恰巧在那艘船上的法国军官指挥作战的。

用一种常见的说法来讲，此战作为自60年前的马拉加海战以来的首次常规作战，"唤醒"了英国民众，并且导致民众做出了有益的反应。虽说此战本身所开启的淘汰过程在继

such conspicuous successes as were attained in earlier and later times, that the general value of England's sea power is now shown; like some precious faculty, scarcely valued when possessed, but keenly missed when withdrawn. Mistress now of the seas rather by the weakness of her enemies than by her own disciplined strength, she drew from that mastery no adequate results; the most solid success, the capture of Cape Breton Island, in 1745, was achieved by the colonial forces of New England, to which indeed the royal navy lent valuable aid, for to troops so situated the fleet is the one line of communication. The misconduct off Toulon was repeated by officers high in command in the West and East Indies, resulting in the latter case in the loss of Madras. Other causes concurred with the effete condition of the naval officers to hamper the action of that sea power which launches out far from home. The condition of England itself was insecure; the cause of the Stuarts was still alive, and though a formidable invasion by fifteen thousand troops under Marshal Saxe, in 1744, was foiled, partly by the English Channel fleet, and partly by a storm which wrecked several of the transports assembled off Dunkirk, with the loss of many lives, yet the reality of the danger was shown in the following year, when the Pretender landed in Scotland with only a few men at his back and the northern kingdom rose with him. His successful invasion was carried well down into England itself; and sober historians have thought that at one time the chances of ultimate success were rather with than against him. Another serious fetter upon the full use of England's power was the direction given to the French operations on land and the mistaken means used to oppose them. Neglecting Germany, France turned upon the Austrian Netherlands, a country which England, out of regard to her sea interests, was not willing to see conquered. Her commercial preponderance would be directly threatened by the passing of Antwerp, Ostend, and the Scheldt into the hands of her great rival; and though her best check against this would have been to

续进行着，但这一过程却结束得太晚，并未对此时进行的这场战争产生应有的影响。正是因为作战中的不足，而非以前或以后那一场场引人注目的大捷，才使得英国那种制海权所具有的综合价值在此时得以显现出来；就像某种弥足珍贵的才能，一个人在拥有这种能力的时候很少重视，可失去之后却又极其怀念那样。此时的这位海洋霸主，与其说是因为它自身训练有素的实力所造就的，还不如说是因为其敌人的软弱无能所成就的，因而没有利用此种霸权获得充分的成就；连该国最为实在的一次成功，即1745年占领布雷顿角岛，也是新英格兰地区的殖民武装获得的，当然，英国皇家海军的确对这些殖民武装进行了大力支援，因为对于殖民武装当时的形势来说，英国舰队就是它唯一的交通补给线。那些曾经在西印度群岛和东印度群岛承担过高级指挥任务的将领，在土伦海战中再一次指挥无方，犯下了像在东印度群岛丢失马德拉斯那样的错误。除了海军官兵的颓败之势，还有其他的原因，共同妨碍了这支海上力量在离祖国非常遥远的地方作战。英国国内的形势也很不安全；斯图亚特王朝的余孽仍很活跃，并且，尽管1744年萨克斯元帅统领一支15000人的军队势如破竹地入侵英国时，一方面因英吉利海峡舰队进行了顽强抗击，另一方面因法国在敦克尔克沿岸集结的给养船中有几艘为风暴所毁，因而此次入侵被挫败了，但到了第二年，当王位觊觎者[4]只带着为数寥寥的支持者登陆苏格兰，而那个北方王国也起而随之的时候，现实的危险性就一览无遗了。查理的入侵很成功，之后他又稳稳当当地南下，侵入了英格兰境内，所以连一些稳重的历史学家也认为，此人一度很有可能获得最后的胜利。阻碍英国充分利用其实力的另一种严重束缚，便是它想控制法国在欧洲大陆上的军事行动，还采取了错误的方式来与法国进行对抗。法国无视德国的存在，进攻了奥属尼德

seize valuable French possessions elsewhere and hold them as a pledge, the weakness of her government and the present inefficiency of the navy prevented her doing so. The position of Hanover, again, controlled the action of England; for though united only by the tie of a common sovereign, the love of that sovereign for his continental dominion, his native country, made itself strongly felt in the councils of a weak and time-serving ministry. It was the disregard of Hanover by the first William Pitt, consequent upon his strong English feeling, that incensed the king and led him so long to resist the demands of the nation that he should be put at the head of affairs. These different causes — dissension at home, interest in the Netherlands, regard for Hanover — combined to prevent a subservient and second-rate ministry, divided also among themselves, from giving a proper direction and infusing a proper spirit into the naval war; but a better condition of the navy itself, more satisfactory results from it, might have modified even their action. As it was, the outcome of the war was almost nothing as regards the disputes between England and her special enemies. On the continent, the questions after 1745 reduced themselves to two, — what part of the Austrian possessions should be given to Prussia, Spain, and Sardinia, and how peace was to be wrenched by France from England and Holland. The sea countries still, as of old, bore the expenses of the war, which however now fell chiefly upon England. Marshal Saxe, who commanded the French in Flanders throughout this war, summed up the situation in half a dozen words to his king. "Sire," said he, "peace is within the walls of Maestricht." This strong city opened the course of the Meuse and the way for the French army into the United Provinces from the rear; for the English fleet, in conjunction with that of Holland, prevented an attack from the sea. By the end of 1746, despite the efforts of the allies, nearly all Belgium was in the hands of the French; but up to this time, although Dutch subsidies were supporting the Austrian government, and Dutch troops in the Netherlands were fighting

兰；英国出于对自身海洋利益的考虑，并不愿意看到该国被法国占领。倘若安特卫普、奥斯坦德和斯凯尔特河等地落入法国这个强大的敌人手中，就会直接威胁到英国的贸易优势；并且尽管英国遏制法国此种做法的最佳方式，本来应该是占领法国在其他地区一些重要的殖民地，并将它们当成质押，可政府的软弱以及海军此时的无能，使得英国根本就做不到这一点。汉诺威王室的态度，便再一次左右了英国的行动；尽管只是因为一个共同的君主统治而团结在一起，但这位君主非常热爱自己在欧洲大陆上的这处领土，热爱自己的祖国，从而使得德国在英国那个软弱而趋炎附势的内阁议会中具有了举足轻重的影响力。正是由于老威廉·皮特因为自己强烈的英式情感而忽视了德国汉诺威王室，才激怒了英国国王，使得他长久以来一直抵制国家的要求，并且拒绝优先考虑这些要求。这些不同的原因——国内的矛盾冲突、尼德兰地区的利益以及对汉诺威王室的考虑——结合起来，使得英国那个奴颜婢膝、平庸无能、内部也已分裂的内阁，根本无法正确地指导海战，也无法为海军注入一种正确的士气；倘若海军本身的情况好一点，获得更多令人满意的战果，或许也可以纠正他们的行为。可事实是，此次战争的结果，却跟英国与其具体的敌人之间的纷争几乎毫无关系。在欧洲大陆上，各国间的争议在1745年之后便归结成了两个方面，即应当将奥地利领土中的哪些地区分别划给普鲁士、西班牙和撒丁王国，以及法国将如何迫使英、荷两国与该国媾和。虽说这些海洋国家仍然像以前那样承负着战争的代价，然而，如今这种代价主要却是由英国来承担了。此次战争中一直在佛兰德斯统帅法军的萨克斯元帅，用寥寥数语，便向法国国王概括说明了当时的形势。"陛下，"他说，"和平在于马斯特里赫特的城墙之内。"这座坚固的城市，既打开了默兹河的航道，也打开了法国陆军

for it, there was nominal peace between the United Provinces and France. In April, 1747, "the King of France invaded Dutch Flanders, announcing that he was obliged to send his army into the territory of the republic, to arrest the protection granted by the States-General to the Austrian and English troops; but that he had no intention of breaking with it, and that the places and provinces occupied would be restored to the United Provinces as soon as they gave proof that they had ceased to succor the enemies of France." This was actual, but not formal, war. Numerous places fell during the year, and the successes of the French inclined both Holland and England to come to terms. Negotiations went on during the winter; but in April, 1748, Saxe invested Maestricht. This forced a peace.

Meanwhile, though languishing, the sea war was not wholly uneventful. Two encounters between English and French squadrons happened during the year 1747, completing the destruction of the French fighting navy. In both cases the English were decidedly superior; and though there was given opportunity for some brilliant fighting by particular captains, and for the display of heroic endurance on the part of the French, greatly outnumbered but resisting to the last, only one tactical lesson is afforded. This lesson is, that when an enemy, either as the result of battle or from original inequality, is greatly inferior in force, obliged to fly without standing on the order of his flying, the regard otherwise due to order must be in a measure at least dismissed, and a general chase ordered. The mistake of Tourville in this respect after Beachy Head has already been noted. In the first of the cases now under discussion, the English Admiral Anson had fourteen ships against eight French, weaker individually as well as in total number; in the second, Sir Edward Hawke had fourteen against nine, the latter being somewhat larger, ship for ship, than the English. In both cases the signal was made for a general chase, and the action which resulted was a mêlée. There was no opportunity for anything else; the

从其背后进入联合省王国的道路；因为当时英国舰队与荷兰舰队携手，使得法国无法从海上发起攻击。到了1746年年底，尽管英、荷盟军做出了努力，但整个比利时几乎都已落入法国手中；不过，虽说荷兰拨了款来支援奥地利政府，而荷兰军队也在尼德兰地区为奥地利作战，但直到此时，联合省王国和法国之间仍然保持着名义上的和平关系。1747年4月，"法国国王入侵了荷兰的佛兰德斯，声称自己是不得已才将法军派到这个共和国境内，目的是阻止荷兰议会为奥、英两国军队提供保护；不过，他无意与荷兰决裂，因此，一旦荷兰证明自己不再保护法国的敌人，法国占领的那些地区和省份便会归还给联合省王国。"这是一种事实上的战争，而非正式的战争。这一年里，许多地方都被法军占领了；而法国的节节胜利，也让英、荷两国都准备让步，准备接受法国的条件了。这一年的整个冬季都在谈判；但1748年4月，萨克斯元帅包围了马斯特里赫特，迫使英、荷两国与法国缔结了和约。

在此期间，尽管日趋衰弱，但海战也并不是全然平淡无奇的。英国和法国的两支小型舰队，在1747年间爆发过两次遭遇战，从而彻底消灭了法国能够用于作战的海军力量。在这两次海战中，英国一方都占有绝对优势；尽管对于个别舰长来说，有着打上一场漂亮胜仗的机会，而对于兵力大大不如敌方却坚持到了最后的法军来说，也有表现出其英勇无畏、坚忍不拔的精神，但从这两次海战中，我们却只能汲取到一种战术上的教训。这个教训就是，当敌人或是因为战斗受损，或是因为力量原本就不对等，兵力上大大劣于己方，因而不得不逃跑，且不再坚持撤退秩序的时候，那么，我方在某种程度上至少也必须放弃对于秩序的其他考虑，下令进行全面追击才行。比奇角海战之后，图维尔在这个方面所犯的失误，已经是众所周知的了。在我们如今所讨论的这两个战例中，第一战中是英国的安

one thing necessary was to overtake the running enemy, and that can only certainly be done by letting the fleetest or best situated ships get ahead, sure that the speed of the fastest pursuers is better than that of the slowest of the pursued, and that therefore either the latter must be abandoned or the whole force brought to bay. In the second case the French commander, Commodore l'Étenduère, did not have to be followed far. He had with him a convoy of two hundred and fifty merchant-ships; detaching one ship-of-the-line to continue the voyage with the convoy, he placed himself with the other eight between it and the enemy, awaiting the attack under his topsails. As the English came up one after another they divided on either side of the French column, which was thus engaged on both sides. After an obstinate resistance, six of the French ships were taken, but the convoy was saved. The English had been so roughly handled that the two remaining French men-of-war got back safely to France. If, therefore, Sir Edward Hawke showed in his attack the judgment and dash which always distinguished that remarkable officer, it may be claimed for Commodore l'Étenduère that fortune, in assigning him the glorious disadvantage of numbers, gave him also the leading part in the drama, and that he filled it nobly. A French officer justly remarks that "he defended his convoy as on shore a position is defended, when the aim is to save an army corps or to assure an evolution; he gave himself to be crushed. After an action that lasted from mid-day till eight P.M. the convoy was saved, thanks to the obstinacy of the defence; two hundred and fifty ships were saved to their owners by the devotion of l'Étenduère and of the captains under his orders. This devotion cannot be questioned, for eight ships had but few chances of surviving an action with fourteen; and not only did the commander of the eight accept an action which he might possibly have avoided, but he knew how to inspire his lieutenants with trust in him; for all supported the strife with honor, and yielded at last, showing the most indisputable proofs of their fine and energetic defence.

森上将率14艘战舰对法国的8艘战舰，后者非但在总数上不如前者，而且每艘战舰的实力也不如前者；在第二个战例中，是爱德华·霍克勋爵率14艘战舰对9艘法舰，后者的单艘战舰舰体都比英舰要大一点儿。在两次战斗中，英军都发出了全面追击的信号，可接下来的作战，却都是一场混战。根本就没有机会来考虑其他什么东西，因为唯一要做的事情，便是必须赶上逃跑的敌军；而要做到这一点，自然就只能让那些速度最快或者状况最佳的舰船驶在最前面，并且确保担任追击任务的那些最快战舰的速度，超过了被追者中最慢舰船的速度，从而使得敌人要么必须抛弃那些最慢的舰船，要么便让整支敌军陷入包围当中。在第二个战例中，对法军指挥官拉埃腾杜尔准将进行追击为时并不是很久。他还率领着一队有250艘船的商船队；他派一艘战列舰护送这队商船继续航行，而自己则率其余8艘战舰，挡在了商船队和敌人之间，等待着敌人向他们发动攻击。英军战舰相继赶上来之后，便在法国舰队的两侧分散开来，使之陷入了两面夹击的境地。经过顽强的抵抗之后，6艘法舰被俘，但整个商船队却得救了。英国舰队也遭到了重创，以至于剩下的那两艘法舰竟然安全地返回了法国。所以，倘若爱德华·霍克勋爵在此次进攻中，表现出了这位非凡的将领一直都因之而著称的那种判断力与勇猛的话，那么就只能说拉埃腾杜尔准将是命运使然，让他虽说兵力严重不如敌军，却在此战中扮演了主角，而他也很英勇地完成了自己的使命。有一位法国军官，曾经很公正地说："他保护那支商船队，就像在海滩上保护一处阵地，目标是保护一支陆军或者确保部队机动似的；他让自己处在首当其冲的位置。战斗从正午一直持续到晚上8点，多亏他顽强抵抗，商船队才得以脱险；由于拉埃腾杜尔及其手下将士的献身精神，那250艘商船才安然回到了各自的主人手中。这种献身精

Four ships were entirely dismasted, two had only the foremast standing." The whole affair, as conducted on both sides, affords an admirable study of how to follow up an advantage, original or acquired, and of the results that may be obtained by a gallant, even hopeless defence, for the furtherance of a particular object. It may be added that Hawke, disabled from further pursuit himself, sent a sloop of war express to the West Indies, with information of the approach of the convoy, — a step which led to the capture of part of it, and gives a touch of completeness to the entire transaction, which cannot fail to be gratifying to a military student interested in seeing the actors in history fully alive to and discharging to the utmost their important tasks.

Before bringing to a close the story of this war and mentioning the peace settlement, an account must be given of the transactions in India, where France and England were then on equal terms. It has been said that affairs there were controlled by the East India companies of either nation; and that the French were represented in the peninsula by Dupleix, in the islands by La Bourdonnais. The latter was appointed to his post in 1735, and his untiring genius had been felt in all the details of administration, but especially in converting the Isle of France into a great naval station, — a work which had to be built up from the foundations. Everything was wanting; everything was by him in greater or less measure supplied, — storehouses, dock-yards, fortifications, seamen. In 1740, when war between France and England became probable, he obtained from the East India Company a squadron, though smaller than he asked, with which he proposed to ruin the English commerce and shipping; but when war actually began in 1744, he received orders not to attack the English, the French company hoping that neutrality might exist between the companies in that distant region, though the nations were at war. The proposition

神是无可置疑的，因为8艘军舰与14艘军舰对战，几乎不可能幸存下来；而指挥这8艘军舰的拉埃腾杜尔准将非但勇敢地面对了这场他本可以避开的战斗，而且还知道如何激励自己的手下，让他们相信自己——因为所有将士都光荣地支持战斗，直到最后才投降，最无可争辩地证明了他们的防守杰出而有力。有4艘军舰的桅杆彻底折断了，还有两艘则只剩下前桅还挺立着。"整个这一次战斗，从双方的表现来看，都为我们提供了研究如何利用优势——无论这种优势是一开始便拥有，还是后来获得的——的极佳机会，以及研究为了促成某一特定目标而进行虽说无望却很英勇的防御作战可能会取得何种战果的极佳机会。还应当补充一点，那就是霍克虽说因自身受创而无法继续追击，但他派了一艘快速战船，带着西班牙商船队即将抵达的情报前往西印度群岛——所以，英军后来还是俘虏了这支商船队中的一部分船只，从而让这次海战变得有点儿完整了；这样一来，那些喜欢看到历史参与者充分意识到并最大限度地履行其重要职责的军事学者，就不会感到不满意了。

在结束描绘此次海战的过程并提及战后的和平协定之前，我们还必须说明一下印度的情况，当时英、法两国在印度可以说是势均力敌的。据说，当时的形势均由两国的东印度公司所掌控；法国在印度半岛的代表是杜普雷，在印度群岛的代表则是拉·布尔多纳。后者是1735年被委派此任的；他那种不懈的天才，在其行政的各个方面都发挥了重要作用，尤其是他将法兰西岛变成了一个庞大的海军基地——这一任务，是必须打好基础才能完成的。当时，什么都很匮乏；一切都是由他或多或少地想办法解决的——仓库、船坞、防御工事、水兵，等等。1740年，当英、法两国间很可能爆发战争的时候，他从本国的东印度公司获得了一支小型舰队；尽管规模比他所求的要小，他还是想用这支舰队去摧毁英国的贸易和商船运输业。不过，1744年战争真的爆发之后，他却接到命令，不准去进

does not seem absurd in view of the curious relations of Holland to France, nominally at peace while sending troops to the Austrian army; but it was much to the advantage of the English, who were inferior in the Indian seas. Their company accepted the proffer, while saying that it of course could bind neither the home government nor the royal navy. The advantage won by the forethought of La Bourdonnais was thus lost; though first, and long alone, on the field, his hand was stayed. Meanwhile the English admiralty sent out a squadron and began to seize French ships between India and China; not till then did the company awake from its illusion. Having done this part of its work, the English squadron sailed to the coast of India, and in July, 1745, appeared off Pondicherry, the political capital of French India, prepared to sustain an attack which the governor of Madras was about to make by land. La Bourdonnais' time was now come.

Meanwhile, on the mainland of the Indian peninsula, Dupleix had been forming wide views and laying broad foundations for the establishment of French preponderance. Having entered the service of their company at first in a subordinate clerical position, his ability had raised him by rapid steps to be head of the commercial establishments at Chandernagore, to which he gave a very great enlargement, seriously affecting, it is said even destroying, parts of the English trade. In 1742 he was made governor-general, and as such removed to Pondicherry. Here he began to develop his policy, which aimed at bringing India under the power of France. He saw that through the progress and extension of the European races over the seas of the whole world the time had come when the Eastern peoples must be brought into ever-increasing contact with them; and he judged that India, so often conquered before, was now about to be conquered by Europeans. He meant that France should win the prize, and saw in England the only rival. His plan was to meddle in Indian politics: first, as head of a foreign and independent colony, which

攻英国人；因为法属东印度公司希望，尽管英、法两国正在交战，但在这个与欧洲相距甚远的地区，两家公司可以保持中立。既然荷兰可以与法国保持那种古怪的关系，在名义上处于和平的时候却派遣部队加入奥地利军队，那么法属东印度公司的这一计划看上去也就并不荒唐了；不过，这个计划倒是很有利于英国人，因为英军在印度海域并不是法军的对手。所以，英属东印度公司便接受了这一提议，但同时又说，这一提议对英国政府和英国皇家海军都并不具有约束力。于是，因拉·布尔多纳的深谋远虑而获得的优势，就这样化为乌有了；虽说一开始并且长久以来，他都在致力于获得此种优势。与此同时，英国海军部派出了一支舰队，开始扣押位于印度和中国两国海域之间的法国船只；直到此时，法属东印度公司才从幻想中醒悟过来。在完成了这一部分任务之后，那支英国舰队便驶往印度海岸，并于1745年7月抵达了法属印度的政治首都庞迪切里，准备支援马德拉斯总督即将从陆上对此处发动的进攻。于是，拉·布尔多纳大显身手的时候便到来了。

在此期间，在印度半岛大陆上，杜普雷一直都在纵观全局，一直都在为确立法国的优势地位而打下广泛的基础。他入职法属东印度公司之初，还只是一个低级办事员，但其杰出的才干，使得他迅速跃升成为了金德纳格尔各商号的领导人；他极大地扩充了这些商号的规模，严重地影响到了——据说甚至还彻底压垮了——英国的部分贸易机构。1742年，他被任命为总督，并以此种身份移居庞迪切里。在这儿，他开始实行自己的政策，目标是将整个印度都置于法国的势力之下。他认识到，由于欧洲各国对世界海洋霸权的竞争越来越白热化，范围也越来越广，东方各国人民势必与欧洲各国的联系越来越密切；因此他认为，过去经常被外族征服的印度，如今必定会再次被欧洲列强所征服。他觉得应当由法国来拔此头筹，所以将英国视作唯一的对手。他的计划，是干预印度的政治：首先是成

he already was; and second, as a vassal of the Great Mogul, which he intended to become. To divide and conquer, to advance the French lines and influence by judicious alliances, to turn wavering scales by throwing in on one side or the other the weight of French courage and skill, — such were his aims. Pondicherry, though a poor harbor, was well adapted for his political plans; being far distant from Delhi, the capital of the Mogul, aggressive extension might go on unmarked, until strong enough to bear the light. Dupleix's present aim, therefore, was to build up a great French principality in southeast India, around Pondicherry, while maintaining the present positions in Bengal.

Let it be noted, however, — and the remark is necessary in order to justify the narration of these plans in connection with our subject, a connection perhaps not at first evident, — that the kernel of the question now before Dupleix was not how to build up an empire out of the Indian provinces and races, but how to get rid of the English, and that finally. The wildest dreams of sovereignty he may have entertained could not have surpassed the actual performance of England a few years later. European qualities were bound to tell, if not offset by the opposition of other Europeans; and such opposition on the one side or the other depended upon the control of the sea. In a climate so deadly to the white races the small numbers whose heroism bore up the war against fearful odds on many a field must be continually renewed. As everywhere and always, the action of sea power was here quiet and unperceived; but it will not be necessary to belittle in the least the qualities and career of Clive the English hero of this time and the founder of their empire, in order to prove the decisive influence which it exerted, despite the inefficiency of the English naval officers first engaged, and the lack of conclusive results in such naval battles as were fought.[2] If during the twenty years following 1743, French fleets instead of English had controlled the coasts of the peninsula and the seas between it and Europe, can it

为这个地处英国国外的独立殖民地的领袖，这一点他业已做到；其次，他还打算成为大莫卧儿王朝[5]的一个诸侯。分化瓦解和征服印度，通过谨慎的联合促进法国的方针政策和影响力，并且凭借法国人的勇敢与才能，平衡印度那种左摇右摆的政治天平———这些，就是他的目标。尽管庞迪切里是一个微不足道的港口，但正适合于他实施自己的政治计划；因为庞迪切里远离莫卧儿王朝的首都德里，他便可以神不知鬼不觉地进行积极的扩张，直至变得势力强大，可以不惧公之于众的时候。因此，杜普雷当下的目标，就是以庞迪切里为中心，在印度东南部建立起一个庞大的法属诸侯国，同时保持好孟加拉目前的局面。

然而，我们应当注意——为了看清这些计划与本书主题的联系，我们也有必要说明这一点，因为此种联系初看上去可能不是很明显——此时摆在杜普雷面前的这个问题的核心，并非如何在印度的省份和民众当中建立起一个帝国，而是如何赶走英国人，并且是一劳永逸地赶走他们。就算杜普雷统治印度的野心再大，也不可能超过了数年之后英国的实际做法。倘若没有因为其他欧洲国家的敌对而抵消掉，欧洲人的本领必定是大有用武之地的；而此种敌对，无论是哪个方面的，都取决于对海洋的掌控。在一个对白种人如此不利的地区，那一小部分有着英雄气概、在许多方面都是以寡敌众地承受着战争危险的人，必须不断地加以更替才行。跟其他任何地方、任何时候都一样，海权在此处的作用也是潜移默化、感觉不出来的；但这一点，并不一定意味着我们就要贬损英国当时的英雄人物、英帝国的奠基者克莱夫的才干和成就，才能证明海权所产生的决定性影响——尽管起初英国海军官兵在作战时确实很无能，而且在前面所述的那些海战中也并未获得什么重大战果[2]。倘若在1743年以后的20年间，是法国舰队而非英国舰队控制

be believed that the schemes of Dupleix would have utterly failed? "Naval inferiority," justly says a French historian, "was the principal cause that arrested the progress of Dupleix. The French royal navy did not make its appearance in the East Indies" in his day. It remains to tell the story briefly.

The English, in 1745, made preparations to besiege Pondicherry, in which the royal navy was to support the land forces; but the effects of Dupleix's political schemes were at once seen. The Nabob of the Carnatic threatened to attack Madras, and the English desisted. The following year La Bourdonnais appeared on the scene, and an action took place between his squadron and that under Commodore Peyton; after which, although it had been a drawn fight, the English officer deserted the coast, taking refuge in Ceylon, and leaving the control at sea with the French. La Bourdonnais anchored at Pondicherry, where quarrels between him and Dupleix soon arose, and were aggravated by the conflicting tone of their instructions from home. In September he went to Madras, attacked by land and sea, and took the place, but made with the governor the stipulation that it might be ransomed; and a ransom of two million dollars was accordingly paid. When Dupleix heard of this he was very angry, and claimed to annul the terms of capitulation on the ground that, once taken, the place was within his jurisdiction. La Bourdonnais resented this attempt as dishonorable to him after the promise given. While the quarrel was going on, a violent cyclone wrecked two of his ships and dismasted the rest. He soon after returned to France, where his activity and zeal were repaid by three years' imprisonment under charges, from the effects of which treatment he died. After his departure Dupleix broke the capitulation, seized and kept Madras, drove out the English settlers, and went on to strengthen the fortifications. From Madras he turned against Fort St. David, but the approach of an English squadron compelled him to raise the siege in

了印度半岛沿海以及印度半岛与欧洲之间的海域，那么我们还能认为杜普雷的计划最终会彻底失败么？一位法国历史学家曾经公正地说："阻碍杜普雷前进步伐的主要原因，便在于法国海军的劣势地位。"在杜普雷所处的那个时代，"在东印度群岛，连法国皇家海军的影子都见不到。"因此接下来，我们还需简要地叙述一下当时的情况。

1745年，英军已经做好了围攻庞迪切里的准备，英国海军的任务则是为其地面部队提供支援；不过，杜普雷政治计谋的效果，同时也显现出来了。卡那提克的行政长官威胁英国，说要进攻马德里斯；于是英军只得断了围困庞迪切里的念头。第二年，拉·布尔多纳登场了，他所率的舰队与佩顿准将所率的英国舰队间爆发了一场战斗；之后，尽管此战双方打了个平手，但这位英军将领还是逃离了庞迪切里海岸，前往锡兰躲避，从而将此处海域的控制权拱手送给了法国人。拉·布尔多纳率领舰队泊入庞迪切里之后，他与杜普雷之间很快便产生了龃龉，并且因为他们各自收到的国内命令相互矛盾，从而使得二人的争执日益激烈起来。是年9月，他率军前往马德拉斯，从海陆两路同时进攻，占领了该地，却又与当地总督缔结协定，说英军可以赎回马德拉斯。杜普雷得知此事后怒不可遏，宣布拉·布尔多纳所签协议无效，理由是一旦占领，该地即应由他杜普雷来管辖。拉·布尔多纳对杜普雷的这一做法大为不满，认为这是出尔反尔，丢了他的脸。就在他们为此争论不休的时候，一场巨大的飓风刮沉了他的两艘舰船，还折断了其余舰船的桅杆。于是，他不久后就回法国去了；他的积极和热心，回国后换来的却是受到指控和3年监禁，后来又因为受到此种不公对待，郁郁而终。他一离开，杜普雷便撕毁协议，攻占了马德拉斯，赶走了此处的英国人，并且开始加固该地的防御工事。后来，他还从马德拉斯出发，去攻打圣

March, 1747.

During this year the disasters to the French navy in the Atlantic, already related, left the English undisturbed masters of the sea. In the following winter they sent to India the greatest European fleet yet seen in the East, with a large land force, the whole under the command of Admiral Boscawen, who bore a general's commission in addition to his naval rank. The fleet appeared off the Coromandel coast in August, 1748. Pondicherry was attacked by land and sea, but Dupleix made a successful resistance. The English fleet in its turn suffered from a hurricane, and the siege was raised in October. Shortly after came the news of the Peace of Aix-la-Chapelle, which ended the European war. Dupleix, with his home communications restored, could now resume his subtle and persevering efforts to secure a territorial base which should, as far as possible, shelter him from the chances of sea war. Pity that so much genius and patience should have been spent in an effort wholly vain; nothing could protect against that sea attack but a naval aid, which the home government could not give. One of the conditions of the peace was that Madras should be restored to the English in exchange for Louisburg, the prize won by the North American colonists and released by them as reluctantly as Madras was by Dupleix. This was indeed illustrating Napoleon's boast that he would reconquer Pondicherry on the bank of the Vistula; yet, although the maritime supremacy of England made Louisburg in her hands much stronger than Madras, or any other position in India, when held by the French, the gain by the exchange was decidedly on the side of Great Britain. The English colonists were not men to be contented with this action; but they knew the naval power of England, and that they could do again what they had done once, at a point not far distant from their own shores. They understood the state of the case. Not so with Madras. How profound must have been the surprise of the native princes at this surrender, how injurious to the personality of Dupleix and

大卫堡；不过，因为来了一支英国舰队，他才不得不在1747年3月放弃了对此地的围攻。

就在这一年里，法国海军在大西洋上接连大败——这一点，我们已经叙述过了——使得英国毫无干扰地成为了海上霸主。在接下来的这个冬天，英国向印度派遣了一支舰队——这可是东方诸国所见到的一支最大的欧洲舰队——和一支庞大的陆军部队，统由海军上将兼陆军上将的博斯科恩指挥。这支舰队于1748年8月抵达科罗曼德尔沿海。庞迪切里遭到了海陆两面的夹击，但杜普雷成功地进行了抵抗。这一次，英国舰队也因飓风而受损严重，所以10月份庞迪切里之围便解除了。不久之后，传来了《亚琛和约》签订、欧洲战争结束的消息。杜普雷恢复了与国内的联系，此时又可以重新开始实施他那种狡猾而不懈的计划，来建立一个可以最大限度地让他不受海战打击的陆上基地了。他花费了如此之多的精力和耐心，来从事一项全属徒劳的事业，实在是令人同情；因为除非获得海军支援，否则任何措施都是无法在遭到海上攻击之时保全一个陆上基地的，可法国政府却无法给杜普雷提供这种支援。和约缔结时的条件之一，便是将马德拉斯归还给英国，以换取路易斯堡；后者是北美殖民者占领的，他们在归还此地时，跟杜普雷归还马德拉斯一样很不情愿。这的确证明了拿破仑说自己会在维斯瓦河上再次征服庞迪切里的那句豪言壮语；不过，虽说英国的海洋霸主地位使得该国对路易斯堡的掌控，要比法国人对马德拉斯或印度其他地方的掌控更加牢固，但在此次交换中收获最大的，毫无疑问还是大不列颠。英国殖民者并不是只满足于这一次胜利的人；他们知道英国海军的实力，知道他们可以像以前那样，在离本国沿海不远的地方再次获得胜利。他们明白当时的形势。但对于马德拉斯，他们却没有那么深刻的认识。放弃这个地方，会让当地的

the influence he had gained among them, to see him, in the very hour of victory, forced, by a power they could not understand, to relinquish his spoil! They were quite right; the mysterious power which they recognized by its working, though they saw it not, was not in this or that man, king or statesman, but in that control of the sea which the French government knew forbade the hope of maintaining that distant dependency against the fleets of England. Dupleix himself saw it not; for some years more he continued building, on the sand of Oriental intrigues and lies, a house which he vainly hoped would stand against the storms that must descend upon it.

The Treaty of Aix-la-Chapelle, ending this general war, was signed April 30, 1748, by England, France, and Holland, and finally by all the powers in October of the same year. With the exception of certain portions shorn off the Austrian Empire, — Silesia for Prussia, Parma for the Infante Philip of Spain, and some Italian territory to the east of Piedmont for the King of Sardinia, — the general tenor of the terms was a return to the status before the war. "Never, perhaps, did any war, after so many great events, and so large a loss of blood and treasure, end in replacing the nations engaged in it so nearly in the same situation as they held at first." In truth, as regarded France, England, and Spain, the affair of the Austrian succession, supervening so soon upon the outbreak of war between the two latter, had wholly turned hostilities aside from their true direction and postponed for fifteen years the settlement of disputes which concerned them much more nearly than the accession of Maria Theresa. In the distress of her old enemy, the House of Austria, France was easily led to renew her attacks upon it, and England as easily drawn to oppose the attempts of the French to influence or dictate in German affairs, — a course the more readily followed from the German interests of the king. It may be questioned whether the true policy for France was to direct the war upon

贵族感到多么震惊,会给杜普雷的人格和他已在当地贵族当中确立起来的威望带来多大的耻辱啊!这些贵族看到的,是他在胜利的那一刻却因一种他们所不理解的力量而不得不拱手放弃自己的战利品。他们的看法是对的。这些当地贵族并未亲眼看到的这种神秘力量,只是感受到了这种力量的作用;而这种力量并非掌握在某一个人手里,也并非掌握在哪个国王或政治家手里,而是完全在于制海权。法国政府已经明白,这种制海权使得它根本不要指望与英国舰队对抗并守住这一处遥远的属地。杜普雷本人并没有看清这一点;因为此后多年间,他仍然在东方这处充斥着阴谋与谎言的散沙之上,建起了一座空中楼阁,并且徒劳地寄望它能够承受起必将倾注其上的暴风骤雨。

结束此次大战的《亚琛和约》,最初由英、法、荷三国签署于1748年4月30日;后来,所有列强在同年10月份都签署了这一和约。除了奥地利帝国割让了一部分地区——西里西亚归普鲁士,帕尔马归西班牙的菲利普亲王,意大利皮埃蒙特以东的一些领土则归撒丁国王,和约条款的主旨便是让欧洲回到战前的形势。"或许,还从未有过一场战争,在经过了这么多的大战、损失了如此之多的生命和财富之后,以让交战各国回复到几乎跟战前一模一样的局面而告终。"实际上,对于法、英和西班牙来说,紧随英、西两国间战争而来的奥地利王位继承问题,已经让战争全然背离了它们的真正目标,并且使得它们之间的一些纠纷推迟了15年才得以解决;它们对这些纠纷的关注,可以说远超过对玛丽亚·特蕾西娅继承王位这个问题的关心。由于自己的宿敌哈布斯堡王朝正处在危难之中,法国便轻而易举地被牵着鼻子,再次对它发动了进攻;而英国也轻而易举地被牵着鼻子,加入了反对法国企图影响或决定德意志事务的这场战争——由于英王在

the heart of the Austrian Empire, by way of the Rhine and Germany, or, as she finally did, upon the remote possessions of the Netherlands. In the former case she rested on friendly territory in Bavaria, and gave a hand to Prussia, whose military power was now first felt. Such was the first theatre of the war. On the other hand, in the Netherlands, whither the chief scene of hostilities shifted later, France struck not only at Austria, but also at the sea powers, always jealous of her intrusion there. They were the soul of the war against her, by their subsidies to her other enemies and by the losses inflicted on her commerce and that of Spain. The misery of France was alleged to the King of Spain by Louis XV., as forcing him to conclude peace; and it is evident that the suffering must have been great to induce him to yield such easy terms as he did, when he already held the Netherlands and parts of Holland itself by force of arms. But while so successful on the continent, his navy was annihilated and communication with the colonies thus cut off; and though it may be doubted whether the French government of that day cherished the colonial ambitions ascribed to it by some, it is certain French commerce was suffering enormously.

While this was the condition of France, impelling her to peace, England in 1747 found that, from disputes about trade in Spanish America and through the inefficient action of her navy, she had been led away into a continental war, in which she had met with disaster, incurred nearly £80,000,000 of debt, and now saw her ally Holland threatened with invasion. The peace itself was signed under a threat by the French envoy that the slightest delay would be the signal for the French to destroy the fortifications of the captured towns and at once begin the invasion. At the same time her own resources were drained, and Holland, exhausted, was seeking to borrow from her. "Money," we are told, "was never so scarce in the city, and

德国拥有利益，他就更容易走上这条道路了。法国的真正政策，究竟是不是要经由莱茵河和德国对奥地利帝国的中心地带发动战争，或者像该国最终所做的，对荷兰那些遥远的领地发动战争，这一点是可以质疑的。在前一种情况下，法国依赖的是巴伐利亚那些友好的领地；该国还帮助了普鲁士，而普鲁士的军事实力此时也是首次让人见识到。这就是第一战场。另一方面，在主战场后来转移到了此处的尼德兰，法国则不仅进攻奥地利，还向一直嫉妒法国入侵该地区的英、荷发动了进攻。英、荷是此次对法作战的主要推手，非但向法国的其他敌人提供拨款，还通过损害法国和西班牙的贸易而让这两个国家损失惨重。路易十五将法国的困境归咎于西班牙国王，因为后者迫使他不得不缔结和约；很显然，这种痛苦必定极其强大，才使得他在已经通过武力占领了尼德兰和荷兰部分地区之后，还以如此宽松的条件做出让步。不过，尽管他在欧洲大陆获得了成功，但其海军却覆灭了，从而使得法国与其殖民地之间的联系就此中断；并且，尽管当时的法国政府是否像有些人所认为的那样，是否因为在欧洲大陆取得了胜利而抱有殖民野心，这一点仍值得怀疑，但可以肯定的是，当时法国的贸易业正在遭受着巨大的损失。

当时法国的形势就是这样，使得该国不得不缔结和约；而英国在1747年却发现，由于西属美洲的贸易争端以及英国海军的无能，该国已经被拖入了一场大陆战争——在这场战争中，英国惨遭失败，非但产生了8000万英镑的债务，此时还眼看着自己的盟国荷兰陷入了被法国入侵的危险之中。和约本身是在法国公使的威胁之下签订的；这位公使称，哪怕再耽搁一点儿时间，也会发出让法国摧毁所占城镇的防御工事并马上开始入侵荷兰的信号。与此同时，英国自己的资源也已枯竭，而弹尽粮绝的荷兰，却仍在向英国借款。我们得知，当时"城市中从未像如今这样缺少资金，即便是12%的利息也贷不到

cannot be had at twelve per cent." Had France, therefore, at this time had a navy able to make head against that of England, even though somewhat inferior in strength, she might, with her grip on the Netherlands and Maestricht, have exacted her own conditions. England, on the other hand, though driven to the wall on the continent, was nevertheless able to obtain peace on equal terms, through the control of the sea by her navy.

The commerce of all three nations had suffered enormously, but the balance of prizes in favor of Great Britain was estimated at £2,000,000. Stated in another way, it is said that the combined losses of French and Spanish commerce amounted during the war to 3,434 ships, the English to 3,238; but in considering such figures, the relation they bear to the total merchant shipping of either nation must not be forgotten. A thousand vessels were a very much larger fraction of French shipping than of English, and meant more grievous loss.

"After the disaster to the squadron of l'Étenduère," says a French writer, "the French flag did not appear at sea. Twenty-two ships-of-the-line composed the navy of France, which sixty years before had one hundred and twenty. Privateers made few prizes; followed everywhere, unprotected, they almost always fell a prey to the English. The British naval forces, without any rivals, passed unmolested over the seas. In one year they are said to have taken from French commerce £7,000,000 sterling. Yet this sea power, which might have seized French and Spanish colonies, made few conquests from want of unity and persistence in the direction given them."

To sum up, France was forced to give up her conquests for want of a navy, and England saved her position by her sea power, though she had failed to use it to the best advantage.

款。"因此，倘若此时法国有一支海军，能够迎头痛击英国海军的话，就算实力上稍有不如，法国也能够在掌控了尼德兰和马斯特里赫特的前提下，迫使其他国家接受其苛刻条件。而另一方面，英国之所以尽管在欧洲大陆上被逼得走投无路，却仍然能够以平等的条件缔结和约，就是因为英国海军控制了海洋。

这三个国家的商业贸易，都遭受了巨大的损失；不过据估计，损失与战利品两相抵消之后，英国还赚了200万英镑。换种方式来看，据说法、西两国在此战中贸易上的合并损失是3434艘船，而英国则是3238艘船；不过，在研究这些数据的时候，我们不能忘记各国商船在总商船数中所占的份额。对于法国的商船运输业来说，1000艘船所占的比重要远远大于英国，这也意味着法国的损失比英国的损失要严重得多。

"拉埃腾杜尔所率舰队惨遭失败之后，"一位法国作家说，"在海洋上就看不到法国国旗了。此时，法国海军整个家当都只有22艘战列舰，可就在60年前，它都还有120艘哩。私掠船并没有夺到多少战利品；它们到处都受到跟踪，并且无人保护，往往成为了英国舰队的牺牲品。而英国海军却无人可敌，畅通无阻地在各个海域来来去去。据说，它们一年之内就从法国的贸易业中攫取了700万标准英镑。不过，此种本可以用于占领法属、西属诸殖民地的制海权，却因为缺乏统一的指挥和不懈的精神，而使得英国海军并没有征服过多少殖民地。"

总而言之，法国是因为没有一支强大的海军，而不得不放弃东征西讨；英国虽说凭借其制海权挽救了自己的地位，却没有充分利用好这种制海权。

FOOTNOTES:

(1) There is not in modern naval history a more striking warning to the officers of every era, than this battle of Toulon. Coming as it did after a generation of comparative naval inactivity, it tried men's reputation as by fire. The lesson, in the judgment of the author, is the danger of disgraceful failure to men who have neglected to keep themselves prepared, not only in knowledge of their profession, but in the sentiment of what war requires. The average man is not a coward; but neither is he endowed by nature only with the rare faculty of seizing intuitively the proper course at a critical moment. He gains it, some more, some less, by experience or by reflection. If both have been lacking to him, indecision will follow; either from not knowing what to do, or from failure to realize that utter self-devotion of himself and his command are required. Of one of the captains cashiered it is said: "No man had ever lived with a fairer or more honorable character previous to the unfortunate event which did such irreparable injury to his reputation. Many of his contemporaries, men in the highest popular estimation, who knew him well, could scarcely credit what were indisputably established as facts, and declared, with the utmost astonishment, 'they believed it next to impossible for Captain Burrish to behave otherwise than as a man of gallantry and intrepidity.'" He had been twenty-five years in service, and eleven afloat as a captain (Charnock's Biographia Navalis). Others of the condemned men bore fair characters; and even Richard Norris, who absconded to avoid trial, had been of respectable repute.

(2) "Notwithstanding the extraordinary effort made by the French in sending out M. Lally with a considerable force last year, I am confident before the end of this [1759] they will be near their last gasp in the Carnatic unless some very unforeseen event interpose in their favor. The superiority of our squadron and the plenty of money and supplies of all kinds which our friends on that coast will be furnished with from this province [Bengal], while the enemy are in total want of everything, without any visible means of redress, are such advantages as, if properly attended to, cannot fail of wholly effecting their ruin in that as well as in every other part of India" (Letter of Clive to Pitt, Calcutta, January 7, 1759; Gleig's Life of Lord Clive). It will be

原注：

（1）在现代海军历史上，还没有哪一次海战像这次土伦之战那样，为每个时代的海军将领提出了如此醒目的警示。它是在经历了海军活动相对不那么活跃的一代之后爆发的，像烈火一样考验了人们的荣誉。在笔者看来，此战的教训就是，倘若忽视了备战——非但忽视了专业知识的准备，还忽视了战争所需的那种态度，就会有遭受可耻之失败的危险。一般的人都并非懦夫；但一般的人也并非天生就具有某种罕见的本领，能够在关键时刻凭借直觉，抓住正确的机会。一般的人，或多或少都是通过经验或者通过反思获得这一本领的。倘若既无经历又无反思，那他就会优柔寡断；要么是因为不知道要干什么，要么便是因为没有认识到战争需要自己拥有彻底的献身精神和掌控能力。有人曾经如此描述一位被解职的舰长，说："在这次不幸的事件给他的名望带来无可挽回的损害之前，他的人格之清白与可敬，堪称是前无古人。许多跟他同时代的、极受民众敬重且熟悉他的人，都难以相信那些被确定为无可辩驳的事实，并且带着极度的震惊强调，'他们认为，贝尔瑞什舰长除了英勇无畏地作战，是不可能有其他不齿行径的。'"这位舰长已经服役了25年，还曾11次以舰长身份率舰出海（参见查诺克的《海军将领生平》一书）。其他被定罪的人，也都有着清白的名声；就连偷偷潜逃以躲过审判的理查德·诺里斯，也一直有着令人敬重的名望。

（2）"尽管法国做出了非凡的努力，去年派出了由莱利元帅所率的一支庞大的部队，但我坚信，今年（指1759年）年底前，他们在卡那提克便会变得奄奄一息，除非发生某种不可预见的、有利于他们的事件。我方舰队在兵力占有优势，资金充足，我们的友军在沿海也会得到这个省份（指孟加拉）提供的各种补给品，而敌人却什么也没有，看不到任何支援措施；此种优势，倘若恰当加以保持，是绝对可以彻底消灭此处之敌，乃至印度每一处之敌的。"（参见1759年1月7日克莱夫自加尔各答写给皮特的信，以及葛莱格的《克莱夫勋爵传记》一书）我们应当记住，直到不久前，英

remembered that the control and use of Bengal, upon which Clive here counts, had only lately been acquired by the English; in the days of Dupleix they did not possess them. As will be seen later, Clive's predictions in this letter were wholly fulfilled.

国才像克莱夫在此所期待的那样,控制并利用了孟加拉;而在杜普雷那个时代,英国人还没有做到这一点。我们过后就会看到,克莱夫在此信中做出的预计,完全都实现了。

译者注:

[1] 马里亚特(Frederick Marryatt, 1792~1848)。英国海军上校、皇家科学院成员和作家。他是航海类型小说的创始人,著有《加拿大黎民》、《新森林的孩子们》等作品。

[2] Acapulco:阿卡普尔科。墨西哥南部港口,如今为世界闻名的旅游城市。

[3] Irish bull:自相矛盾的说法,荒唐可笑的说法。这是一个俗语,原本特指爱尔兰人,因为自恃有文化有教养的英格兰人认为爱尔兰人说话不合逻辑、荒唐可笑(bull在古语中指"逻辑上的错误")。

[4] Pretender:觊觎王位者。指英国意图复辟斯图亚特王朝的詹姆士二世的儿子和孙子,有"老觊觎者"和"小觊觎者"之分,此处是指其孙子查理(Charles Edward Louis John Casimir Silvester Maria Stuart, 1720~1788),即"小觊觎者"。1745年,他在法国的支持下,率两艘舰船同7位支持者在苏格兰的埃里什凯登陆,并开始招兵买马,准备复辟。

[5] Great Mogul:大莫卧儿王朝。16世纪初到19世纪中期统治印度的一个王朝。

CHAPTER VII   Seven Years' War, 1756-1763

England's Overwhelming Power and Conquests on the Seas, in North America, Europe, and East and West Indies. —
Sea Battles: Byng off Minorca; Hawke and Conflans;
Pocock and D'Aché in East Indies.

The urgency with which peace was desired by the principal parties to the War of the Austrian Succession may perhaps be inferred from the neglect to settle definitely and conclusively many of the questions outstanding between them, and notably the very disputes about which the war between England and Spain began. It seems as though the powers feared to treat thoroughly matters that contained the germs of future quarrels, lest the discussion should prolong the war that then existed. England made peace because the fall of Holland was otherwise inevitable, not because she had enforced, or surrendered, her claims of 1739 against Spain. The right of uninterrupted navigation in West Indian seas, free from any search, was left undetermined, as were other kindred matters. Not only so, but the boundaries between the English and French colonies in the valley of the Ohio, toward Canada, and on the land side of the Nova Scotian peninsula, remained as vague as they had before been. It was plain that peace could not last; and by it, if she had saved Holland, England surrendered the control of the sea which she had won. The true character of the strife, shrouded for a moment by the continental

第七章   1756–1763年的"七年战争"

英国在诸海域、北美、欧洲以及东、西印度群岛上的压倒性实力和征战；
海战：拜恩在米诺卡岛指挥的海战；霍克和孔夫兰；
波考克和德阿克在东印度群岛的海战

奥地利王位继承战争中主要交战方都在迫切地渴望着和平；这一点，或许从他们不顾一切而最终性地解决各国间的许多重要问题，尤其是解决导致英、西两国开战的纠纷这种态度上，就可以推断出来。看上去，各个列强似乎都害怕彻底解决那些可能会导致日后产生争端的问题，以免在这些问题上争来辩去会拖延当时正在进行的这场战争。英国之所以缔结和约，是因为不这样的话，荷兰必然会陷于敌手，而不是因为它坚持或者放弃了1739年对西班牙提出的要求。在西印度群岛海域进行自由航行、不受任何一国搜查的权利问题，跟同类的许多其他问题一样，并未得到解决。非但如此，连英、法两国殖民地在俄亥俄河流域朝加拿大一方的边界，以及在新斯科舍半岛上沿大陆一侧的边界，也仍像以前那样不明确。很显然，此种和平维持不了多久；并且，就算英国通过此种和平挽救了荷兰，该国其实也是放弃了自己已经赢得的制海权。此次战争的实质，一度为陆上战争所遮掩，此时却通过这种所谓的和平显示出来了；尽管形式上有所缓和，

war, was revealed by the so-called peace; though formally allayed, the contention continued in every part of the world.

In India, Dupleix, no longer able to attack the English openly, sought to undermine their power by the line of policy already described. Mingling adroitly in the quarrels of surrounding princes, and advancing his own power while so doing, he attained by rapid steps to the political control, in 1751, of the southern extremity of India, — a country nearly as large as France. Given the title of Nabob, he now had a place among the princes of the land. "A merely commercial policy was in his eyes a delusion; there could be no middle course between conquest and abandonment." In the course of the same year further grants extended the French power through extensive regions to the north and east, embracing all the coast of Orissa, and made Dupleix ruler of a third of India. To celebrate his triumphs, perhaps also in accordance with his policy of impressing the native mind, he now founded a town and put up a pillar setting forth his successes. But his doings caused the directors of the company only disquietude; instead of the reinforcements he asked for they sent him exhortations to peace; and at about this time Robert Clive, then but twenty-six years old, began to show his genius. The success of Dupleix and his allies became checkered with reverses; the English under Clive's leadership supported the native opponents of the French. The company at home was but little interested in his political schemes, and was annoyed at the failure of dividends. Negotiations were opened at London for a settlement of difficulties, and Dupleix was summoned home; the English government, it is said, making his recall an absolute condition of continued peace. Two days after his departure, in 1754, his successor signed a treaty with the English governor, wholly abandoning his policy, stipulating that neither company should interfere in the internal politics of India, and that all possessions acquired during the war in the Carnatic should be

但对于海权的竞争，却仍在世界各地继续着。

在印度，杜普雷因为无法再公开进攻英国人，便竭力通过前述政策削弱英国人的势力。他巧妙地介入周围诸省之间的争端，并在这样做的同时增强自己的实力，使得自己很快便在1751年掌控了印度最南端的政治——这个国家，面积差不多跟法国一样大。由于他获得了地方长官的名号，所以如今在地方贵族当中，他就拥有了一席之地。"单纯的贸易政策，在他看来就是一种幻想；他认为，在征服和放弃之间，并无第三条道路。"同一年间，杜普雷获得了更多的许可，将法国的势力经由广袤的地区扩张到了印度的北部和东部，覆盖了整个奥里萨邦沿海，他也因此而成为了统治印度的三号人物。为了庆祝他所获得的胜利，或许同时也是按照他在当地人心中留下不可磨灭之印象的那种政策，他便建起了一座城市，并在该市中心竖起了一根柱子，上面铭刻着他的丰功伟绩。不过，他的这些做法，却让东印度公司的董事们深感不安；所以，他们并未按照杜普雷的要求给他派遣援军，而是派人去规劝他保持此地的和平与安定；而大约也就是这个时候，当时年仅26岁的罗伯特·克莱夫开始崭露头角了。杜普雷及其支持者的发财之路，开始遭遇各种挫折；因为英国人在克莱夫的领导下，向对抗法国的那些当地人提供支持。法国国内的东印度公司对杜普雷的政治计划并不感兴趣，却因股东回报减少而懊恼不已。于是，英、法两国开始在伦敦进行谈判，以求解决争端，而杜普雷也被召回了法国；据说，英国政府把召回杜普雷当成是继续保持和平的先决条件。1754年，就在杜普雷离任的两天之后，他的继任者与英国总督签订了一份条约，完全抛弃了他的政策，规定两家公司都不得干预印度的内政，而在卡提那克战争中所获得的领土，也应全部归

given back to the Mogul. What France thus surrendered was in extent and population an empire, and the mortification of French historians has branded the concession as ignominious; but how could the country have been held, with the English navy cutting off the eagerly desired reinforcements?

In North America, the declaration of peace was followed by renewed agitation, which sprang from and betokened the deep feeling and keen sense of the situation had by the colonists and local authorities on either side. The Americans held to their points with the stubbornness of their race. "There is no repose for our thirteen colonies," wrote Franklin, "so long as the French are masters of Canada." The rival claims to the central unsettled region, which may accurately enough be called the valley of the Ohio, involved, if the English were successful, the military separation of Canada from Louisiana; while on the other hand, occupation by the French, linking the two extremes of their acknowledged possessions, would shut up the English colonists between the Alleghany Mountains and the sea. The issues were apparent enough to leading Americans of that day, though they were more far-reaching than the wisest of them could have foreseen; there is room for curious speculation as to the effect, not only upon America, but upon the whole world, if the French government had had the will, and the French people the genius, effectively to settle and hold the northern and western regions which they then claimed. But while Frenchmen upon the spot saw clearly enough the coming contest and the terrible disadvantage of unequal numbers and inferior navy under which Canada must labor, the home government was blind alike to the value of the colony and to the fact that it must be fought for; while the character and habits of the French settlers, lacking in political activity and unused to begin and carry through measures for the protection of their own interests, did not remedy the neglect of the mother-country. The paternal centralizing system of French rule

还给莫卧儿王室。法国因此而放弃的，其实是一个面积广大、人口众多的帝国，故法国的历史学家将这次让步看成是一种可耻的屈辱；不过，由于英国海军切断了法国人所迫切需要的支援，法国又怎么可能守住这个帝国呢？

在北美地区，和约宣告之后，纷争又开始死灰复燃了；这种纷争，既起源于、也标志着两国殖民者和殖民地政府的深切情感以及对当时形势的敏锐感觉。美国人的观点，带有这一民族的倔强与顽强。"我们这13个殖民地，"富兰克林曾经写道，"只要法国人掌控着加拿大，便没有安稳之日。"双方争夺的是北美中部无人定居的那些地区，精确一点来说，可以称之为俄亥俄河流域；并且，倘若英国获胜，就还涉及到从军事上将加拿大与路易斯安那隔离开来的问题；而另一方面，这一地区倘由法国占领，便会将他们业已确定的两处殖民地连接起来，并将英国殖民者堵在阿利根尼山脉和大西洋之间。这些问题都很明显，足以影响到当时的美国人，尽管它们的意义极其深远，但就算是当时最睿智的美国人，也不可能有此远见；我们完全可以好奇地猜测一下，倘若法国政府有此决心，法国人民有此才干，能够在当时他们所要求的北部和西部地区大力殖民，并且有效地占领这些地区的话，会给美洲以及整个世界带来什么样的影响。不过，尽管身处北美的法国人清楚地认识到了即将到来的争夺，认识到了兵力不等、海军势弱给他们带来的巨大劣势，并且加拿大必将受害于此种劣势，但法国政府对这一殖民地的价值和必须为之而战的事实，却都视而不见；法国的殖民者呢，也由于自身的性格和习气，由于缺乏政治积极性，由于不习惯制定和贯彻实施保护自身利益的政策措施，而没有纠正本国政府这种漠然视之的态度。法国惯常采用家长式的中央集权制度，使得殖民者已经

had taught the colonists to look to the mother-country, and then failed to take care of them. The governors of Canada of that day acted as careful and able military men, doing what they could to supply defects and weaknesses; it is possible that their action was more consistent and well-planned than that of the English governors; but with the carelessness of both home governments, nothing in the end could take the place of the capacity of the English colonists to look out for themselves. It is odd and amusing to read the conflicting statements of English and French historians as to the purposes and aims of the opposing statesmen in these years when the first murmurings of the storm were heard; the simple truth seems to be that one of those conflicts familiarly known to us as irrepressible was at hand, and that both governments would gladly have avoided it. The boundaries might be undetermined; the English colonists were not.

The French governors established posts where they could on the debatable ground, and it was in the course of a dispute over one of these, in 1754, that the name of Washington first appears in history. Other troubles occurred in Nova Scotia, and both home governments then began to awake. In 1755 Braddock's disastrous expedition was directed against Fort Duquesne, now Pittsburg, where Washington had surrendered the year before. Later in the year another collision between the English and French colonists happened near Lake George. Although Braddock's expedition had been first to start, the French government was also moving. In May of the same year a large squadron of ships-of-war, mostly armed en flute[1], sailed from Brest with three thousand troops, and a new governor, De Vaudreuil, for Canada. Admiral Boscawen had already preceded this fleet, and lay in wait for it off the mouth of the St. Lawrence. There was as yet no open war, and the French were certainly within their rights in sending a garrison to their own colonies; but Boscawen's orders were to stop them. A fog which scattered the

习惯了唯祖国马首是瞻，因而无法自行应对这些问题。当时加拿大的各省总督都是谨慎而能干的军人，都曾竭尽所能地去弥补他们的缺陷和弱点，并且他们的这些做法，可能比英国那些殖民地总督的做法更加一贯，也更加周密；但由于两国政府的漠视与疏忽，所以英国殖民者自立自强的能力，最终便成了一种无可取代的优势。对于在美洲这种大动荡的惊雷之声远远传来的那些年间两国政治家们的意图和目标，英国的历史学家和法国的历史学家说得都相互矛盾，读来既令人觉得奇怪，又让人觉得很有意思；唯一的事实，似乎就是我们所熟知的那种难以约束的冲突之一即将爆发，而倘若能够避免这一冲突，两国政府便会皆大欢喜。边界问题可以悬而未决，而英国殖民者却并不优柔寡断。

法国总督竭尽所能地在争议之地上建立据点，而这种做法，正值1754年两国就其中的一处地方发生争执的过程中；也正是这一年，"华盛顿"这个名称在历史上首次出现了。在新斯科舍还存在着其他的问题，因此两国政府也开始清醒过来。1755年，布拉多克进行了一次损失惨重的远征，针对的就是杜魁斯要塞，即如今的匹兹堡；一年之前，华盛顿曾在此投降。这一年的下半年，英、法两国殖民者在乔治湖附近又爆发了一次冲突。虽说布拉多克的远征军率先出发，但法国政府也在行动。同年5月，法国派遣一支数量庞大的军舰舰队，其中绝大多数都装有分离式火炮[1]，连同3000士兵和新任总督德·沃德勒伊，从布雷斯特起航前往加拿大。博斯科恩上将早已赶在这支舰队前头，抵达圣劳伦斯河河口海域设伏等候了。直到此时，两国之间尚未公开爆发过战斗，法国自然也有权利向自己的殖民地派遣卫戍部队；不过，博斯科恩上将所受命令，却是阻击这支部队。一场大雾让法国舰队分散开来，还为它通过圣劳伦斯河河口提供了掩护；不

French squadron also covered its passage; but two of the ships were seen by the English fleet and captured, June 8, 1755. As soon as this news reached Europe, the French ambassador to London was recalled, but still no declaration of war followed. In July, Sir Edward Hawke was sent to sea with orders to cruise between Ushant and Cape Finisterre, and to seize any French ships-of-the-line he might see; to which were added in August further orders to take all French ships of every kind, men-of-war, privateers, and merchantmen, and to send them into English ports. Before the end of the year, three hundred trading vessels, valued at six million dollars, had been captured, and six thousand French seamen were imprisoned in England, — enough to man nearly ten ships-of-the-line. All this was done while nominal peace still existed. War was not declared until six months later.

France still seemed to submit, but she was biding her time, and preparing warily a severe stroke for which she had now ample provocation. Small squadrons, or detachments of ships, continued to be sent to the West Indies and to Canada, while noisy preparations were made in the dock-yard of Brest, and troops assembled upon the shores of the Channel. England saw herself threatened with invasion, — a menace to which her people have been peculiarly susceptible. The government of the day, weak at best, was singularly unfit for waging war, and easily misled as to the real danger. Besides, England was embarrassed, as always at the beginning of a war, not only by the numerous points she had to protect in addition to her commerce, but also by the absence of a large number of her seamen in trading-vessels all over the world. The Mediterranean was therefore neglected; and the French, while making loud demonstrations on the Channel, quietly equipped at Toulon twelve ships-of-the-line, which sailed on the 10th of April, 1756, under Admiral La Galissonière, convoying one hundred and fifty transports with fifteen thousand troops, commanded by the Duke of Richelieu. A week later

过，竟在1755年6月8日，法国舰队中的两艘军舰还是被英国舰队发现并俘虏了。这一消息传到欧洲之后，法国立即召回了派驻伦敦的大使，但随后还是没有对英国宣战。7月份，爱德华·霍克勋爵率军出海，受命前往韦桑岛与菲尼斯特雷角之间的海域巡逻，同时还受命可以夺取他所看到的任何一艘法国军舰；8月份，英国政府又进一步命令他，可以夺取法国的任何船只，无论是军舰、私掠船还是商船，并将这些船只送往英国的港口。这一年年底之前，英国俘虏了300艘法国商船，其价值高达600万美元，还将6000名法国海员囚禁在英国——这些人，差不多足够装备10艘战列舰了。这一切，都发生在两国间名义上还保持着和平关系的时期。直到6个月之后，两国才正式宣战。

法国虽说看上去仍在忍气吞声，但它正在等待时机，并且小心地备战，因为此时该国已经受够了挑衅，准备重重地反戈一击了。该国继续派遣小型舰队或独立的分舰队前往西印度群岛和加拿大，而布雷斯特的造船厂也正如火如荼地进行着准备，陆军则在英吉利海峡沿岸集结起来。英国看到本土有被法国入侵的危险了——对于这种恐吓，英国民众尤为敏感。当时的英国政府极其软弱，非常不适于发动战争，并且很容易受到误导，从而陷入真正的危险中去。此外，英国在战争初期一向都是狼狈得很，非但要保护本国的贸易和为数众多的地点，还因为本国海员都在商船上满世界跑，所以没有数量庞大的海员来装备其军舰。于是，该国便只能不管地中海地区了；这样一来，法国一面在英吉利海峡大张旗鼓地示威，一面则在土伦港悄无声息地装备了12艘战列舰，并在1756年4月10日派拉·加里森尼尔上将统帅这支舰队，护卫由150艘运兵船运送、由黎塞留公爵指挥的15000兵力起航了。一个星期之后，这支部队在米诺卡岛安全登陆，并且包围

the army was safely landed in Minorca, and Port Mahon invested, while the fleet established itself in blockade before the harbor.

Practically this was a complete surprise; for though the suspicions of the English government had been at last aroused, its action came too late. The garrison had not been reinforced, and numbered a scant three thousand men, from which thirty-five officers were absent on leave, among them the governor and the colonels of all the regiments. Admiral Byng sailed from Portsmouth with ten ships-of-the-line only three days before the French left Toulon. Six weeks later, when he reached the neighborhood of Port Mahon, his fleet had been increased to thirteen ships-of-the-line, and he had with him four thousand troops. It was already late; a practicable breach had been made in the fortress a week before. When the English fleet came in sight, La Galissonière stood out to meet it and bar the entrance to the harbor.

The battle that followed owes its historical celebrity wholly to the singular and tragic event which arose from it. Unlike Matthews's battle off Toulon, it does afford some tactical instruction, though mainly applicable to the obsolete conditions of warfare under sail; but it is especially linked to the earlier action through the effect produced upon the mind of the unfortunate Byng by the sentence of the court-martial upon Matthews. During the course of the engagement he repeatedly alluded to the censure upon that admiral for leaving the line, and seems to have accepted the judgment as justifying, if not determining, his own course. Briefly, it may be said that the two fleets, having sighted each other on the morning of the 20th of May, were found after a series of manoeuvres both on the port tack, with an easterly wind, heading southerly, the French to leeward, between the English and the harbor. Byng ran down in line ahead off the wind, the French remaining by it, so that when the former made the signal to engage, the fleets were not parallel, but formed an angle of from thirty to forty degrees. The

了马翁港，而拉·加里森尼尔上将统帅的这支舰队，则停在马翁港前进行封锁。

事实上，这一行动让英国彻底地大吃了一惊；因为，尽管英国政府在最后一刻还是起了疑心，但此时再采取应对行动，已经太迟了。港内的守军一直没有得到增援，兵力空缺达到了3000人，同时还有35名军官请了假，其中还包括该地总督以及各团团长。拜恩上将率领10艘战舰从朴茨茅斯起航，只比法军从土伦港出发早了3天。6个星期之后，当他抵达马翁港附近海域的时候，他所率舰队的战船数量已经增加到了13艘，并且他手中还握有4000兵力。然而为时已晚；一周之前，要塞就已经被攻开了一处缺口。英国舰队出现之后，拉·加里森尼尔便率舰出港迎击，堵住了马翁港的入口。

接下来的这场海战之所以在历史上赫赫有名，全在于此战中一桩非凡而悲惨的事件。跟马修斯在土伦海域指挥的那场海战不同，此战的确具有某种战术上的教训，尽管这种教训主要是适用于帆船时代那种过时的战争条件；不过，这位倒霉的拜恩上将之前因为军事法庭判决马修斯，使得他的思想受到了冲击，由此而导致的那些行为，却与这方面紧密相关。在交战过程中，他不停地提及马修斯这位上将因为离开了队列而受到责难这件事，并且似乎已经承认此种指责，认为就算此种指责没有限制自己的行动，也会使他的行动有理可依。简而言之就是，这两支舰队于5月20日清晨遭遇之后，都是左舷抢风，进行了一系列机动，然后便借着东风向南而行，法军处于下风，楔在英军和马翁港之间。拜恩率舰队成纵列顺风而下，而法军也仍在航行，所以当英军发出交战信号时，两支舰队不是并排相向，而是有一个30°到40°的夹角。按照拜恩自己的说法，他本打算让每艘战舰都去进攻自己对面敌军阵列中的战船，但这种进攻在任何情况下都是

attack which Byng by his own account meant to make, each ship against its opposite in the enemy's line, difficult to carry out under any circumstances, was here further impeded by the distance between the two rears being much greater than that between the vans; so that his whole line could not come into action at the same moment. When the signal was made, the van ships kept away in obedience to it, and ran down for the French so nearly head-on as to sacrifice their artillery fire in great measure; they received three raking broadsides, and were seriously dismantled aloft. The sixth English ship, counting from the van, had her foretopmast shot away, flew up into the wind, and came aback, stopping and doubling up the rear of the line. Then undoubtedly was the time for Byng, having committed himself to the fight, to have set the example and borne down, just as Farragut did at Mobile when his line was confused by the stopping of the next ahead; but according to the testimony of the flag-captain, Matthews's sentence deterred him. "You see, Captain Gardiner, that the signal for the line is out, and that I am ahead of the ships 'Louisa' and 'Trident' [which in the order should have been ahead of him]. You would not have me, as the admiral of the fleet, run down as if I were going to engage a single ship. It was Mr. Matthews's misfortune to be prejudiced by not carrying down his force together, which I shall endeavor to avoid." The affair thus became entirely indecisive; the English van was separated from the rear and got the brunt of the fight. One French authority blames Galissonière for not tacking to windward of the enemy's van and crushing it. Another says he ordered the movement, but that it could not be made from the damage to the rigging; but this seems improbable, as the only injury the French squadron underwent aloft was the loss of one topsail yard, whereas the English suffered very badly. The true reason is probably that given and approved by one of the French authorities on naval warfare. Galissonière considered the support of the land attack on Mahon paramount to any destruction of the English fleet, if

无法实施的，而在这儿，又因双方舰队后翼之间的距离远远大于前锋之间的距离而受到了妨碍；因此，他的整个阵列便不可能同时发动进攻。发出交战信号之后，前锋舰船便服从命令远离阵列，并顺风向法军冲去，几乎完全是面对敌人，在很大程度上就像是要牺牲于敌人的炮火之下似的；这几艘军舰侧面受到了三次重击，桅杆严重受损。从前锋舰船算起的第六艘战舰，因为前主桅被火炮轰掉且飘向了空中，便掉转头来停下，并入了阵列后翼之中。接下来，无疑便是一心沉浸在战斗当中的拜恩大显身手、树立榜样且全力以赴的时候了，就像法拉格特在莫比尔河之战中，当他所率阵列在再次跑到敌军前面而乱成一团时那样；不过，据其旗舰舰长的证词，马修斯的判决还是让他打消了这个念头。"你看，加德纳上校，保持阵列的信号已经发出，而我却还在'路易莎'号和'三叉戟'号的前面（按照命令，这两艘战船本来应当位于他的前面）。你不应当让我这个舰队司令率舰冲在前面，好像我打算去跟单艘敌舰交火似的。马修斯先生的不幸，在于被人误认为是抛弃了他的部下，而我应当尽力避免这一点。"这样一来，整个战斗便完全变得拖泥带水了；英军的前锋同后翼脱了节，独自承受了战斗的压力。有位法国的权威人士，曾经指责加里森尼尔上将没有左舷抢风，去迎击敌人的前锋并将其消灭。而另一位权威人士则说，加里森尼尔上将曾经下达了此种调遣命令，只是由于其座舰索具受损，无法执行这一命令罢了；不过，这种情况似乎不太可能，因为法国舰队甲板以上所遭受的唯一损毁，便是损坏了一根中桅榆，而英国舰队的损失则极为惨重。真正的原因，很可能就是法国一位研究海战的权威人士所指出并加以证实的那样。加里森尼尔认为，从陆地上对马翁港进攻的重要性超过了摧毁英国舰队的重要性，就算他因此而让

he thereby exposed his own. "The French navy has always preferred the glory of assuring or preserving a conquest to that more brilliant perhaps, but actually less real, of taking some ships, and therein has approached more nearly the true end that has been proposed in war." The justice of this conclusion depends upon the view that is taken of the true end of naval war. If it is merely to assure one or more positions ashore, the navy becomes simply a branch of the army for a particular occasion, and subordinates its action accordingly; but if the true end is to preponderate over the enemy's navy and so control the sea, then the enemy's ships and fleets are the true objects to be assailed on all occasions. A glimmer of this view seems to have been present to Morogues when he wrote that at sea there is no field of battle to be held, nor places to be won. If naval warfare is a war of posts, then the action of the fleets must be subordinate to the attack and defence of the posts; if its object is to break up the enemy's power on the sea, cutting off his communications with the rest of his possessions, drying up the sources of his wealth in his commerce, and making possible a closure of his ports, then the object of attack must be his organized military forces afloat; in short, his navy. It is to the latter course, for whatever reason adopted, that England owed a control of the sea that forced the restitution of Minorca at the end of this war. It is to the former that France owed the lack of prestige in her navy. Take this very case of Minorca; had Galissonière been beaten, Richelieu and his fifteen thousand troops must have been lost to France, cooped up in Minorca, as the Spaniards, in 1718, were confined to Sicily. The French navy therefore assured the capture of the island; but so slight was the impression on the ministry and the public, that a French naval officer tells us: "Incredible as it may seem, the minister of marine, after the glorious affair off Mahon, instead of yielding to the zeal of an enlightened patriotism and profiting by the impulse which this victory gave to France to build up the navy, saw fit to sell the ships and rigging which we still had in our

自己所率的舰队遭受敌人的打击，也是如此。"法国海军向来都偏爱确保或维持某种战利品，并且使之达到一种或许更加华丽、事实上却不实在的高度所带来的荣耀，比如俘虏某些船只；因而在这个方面，他们也就更加接近于战争中所提的真正目标。"这一结论是否公正，取决于海战真正的目标是什么的观点。倘若海战的真正目标只是确保岸上的一处或多处战略要地，那么海军就会变成只是陆军用于某种特定场合的一个分支，而其行动也会相应地从属于陆军的行动；但是，倘若其真正目标是胜过敌方的海军并因而掌控海洋，那么在任何情况下，敌方的船只和舰队便都会成为正确的攻击目标。莫罗盖在写下"海洋之上并无可守之战场、亦无可占之地"等语句的时候，心中似乎已经模模糊糊地有了这一观点。倘若海战是一种争夺战略要地的战争，那么，舰队的作战行动就必须服从进攻或防守这些要地的要求；倘若海战的目标是粉碎敌人的海上实力、切断敌方与其他领土之间的交通补给、耗尽敌人在贸易领域的财力之源并且在可能的时候封锁敌人的港口，那么我方海军进攻的目标，就必定是敌方海上有组织的军事武装；简而言之，便是敌方的海军。英国正是根据后一种方针——无论是它出于什么原因采取的——才掌控了海洋，并在此次战争结束时迫使法国归还了米诺卡岛的。而前一种做法，也正是导致法国海军毫无威望的原因。就以米诺卡岛之战为例；倘若加里森尼尔上将战败，那么法国就必定会折损掉黎塞留公爵和他所率的那15000名士兵，他们会被封锁在米诺卡岛上，就像1718年西班牙人被阻在西西里岛上那样。结果，法国海军确保占领了该岛；可这件事情并未对内阁和公众产生多大的影响，以至于一位法国海军将领如此告诉我们："看上去可能令人难以置信，但海军大臣在马翁港海战取得了辉煌战果之后，既不是满怀开明的爱国热情，

ports. We shall soon see the deplorable consequences of this cowardly conduct on the part of our statesmen." Neither the glory nor the victory is very apparent; but it is quite conceivable that had the French admiral thought less of Mahon and used the great advantage luck had given him to take, or sink, four or five of the enemy, the French people would have anticipated the outbreak of naval enthusiasm which appeared too late, in 1760. During the remainder of this war the French fleets, except in the East Indies, appear only as the pursued in a general chase.

The action imposed upon the French fleets was, however, consistent with the general policy of the French government; and John Clerk was probably right in saying that there is apparent in this action off Minorca a tactics too well defined to be merely accidental, — a tactics essentially defensive in its scope and aim. In assuming the lee-gage the French admiral not only covered Mahon, but took a good defensive position, imposing upon his enemy the necessity of attacking with all the consequent risks. Clerk seems to bring evidence enough to prove that the leading French ships did, after roughly handling their assailants, astutely withdraw thus forcing the latter to attack again with like results. The same policy was repeatedly followed during the American war twenty years later, and with pretty uniform success; so much so that, although formal avowal of the policy is wanting, it may be concluded that circumspection, economy, defensive war, remained the fixed purpose of the French authorities, based doubtless upon the reasons given by Admiral Grivel, of that navy: —

"If two maritime powers are at strife, the one that has the fewest ships must always avoid doubtful engagements; it must run only those risks necessary for carrying out its missions, avoid action by manoeuvring, or at worst, if forced to engage, assure itself of favorable conditions. The attitude to be taken should depend radically upon the power of your opponent. Let us not tire of

也未充分利用此战给法兰西上下带来的动力，来增强法国海军的实力，而是认为此时正是卖掉当时我国港口中仍有的那些船只和索具的大好时候。不久之后我们就会看到，这些政客此种卑劣行径带来的可悲下场了。"当然，此种辉煌也好、胜利也罢，都不是很明显；但可想而知的是，倘若那位法国上将少考虑一点儿马翁港，而是利用上苍赐予给他的巨大优势，俘虏或者击沉四五艘敌舰，那么法国人民很可能早就爆发出对海军的那种热情了，待1760年才出现此种热情，已经太晚了。而在此次战争的后一时期，除了在东印度群岛海域，法国舰队便只是在一场全面的追击战中现过身，而且还被追得东躲西藏了。

然而，强加于法国舰队身上的作战行动，与法国政府的总体政策却是一致的。约翰·克拉克曾说，米诺卡海战中显然有着一种战术，只是此种战术太过明确，故不能说是纯属偶然——他很可能说得对，这种战术从范围和目标上来看，本质上都属于防御战术。占据下风战位后，这位法国的海军上将不但保护了马翁港，还采取了一种良好的防御态势，使敌人不得不承担大举进攻所带来的一切不测后果。克拉克似乎还提出了证据，足以证明法国舰队中打头阵的那几艘战舰在重创来犯之敌后，的确敏捷地撤了回来，迫使敌军不得不再次进击，并再次吃到同样的苦头。在20年后的美洲战争中，法国海军再次遵循了同样的政策，并且差不多一律都大获成功；以至于尽管此种政策没有正式公之于众，但我们还是可以得出结论，说谨慎、节约和防御战争仍是法国当局的坚定目标。至于其中的原因，无疑则是法国海军上将格里维尔所述的下述理由：

"倘若两个海洋大国交战，那么舰船数量较少的一方必须始终确保不打无把握之仗才行；它只能在执行其他任务所必需的情况下，才能去冒险，故应当通过谋略避免作

repeating, according as she has to do with an inferior or superior power, France has before her two distinct strategies, radically opposite both in means and ends, — Grand War and Cruising War."

Such a formal utterance by an officer of rank must be received with respect, and the more so when it expresses a consistent policy followed by a great and warlike nation; yet it may be questioned whether a sea power worthy of the name can thus be secured. Logically, it follows from the position assumed, that combats between equal forces are to be discouraged, because the loss to you is greater than the loss to your opponent. "In fact," says Ramatuelle, upholding the French policy, "of what consequence to the English would be the loss of a few ships?" But the next inevitable step in the argument is that it is better not to meet the enemy. As another Frenchman, previously quoted, says, it was considered a mishap to their ships to fall in with a hostile force, and, if one was met, their duty was to avoid action if possible to do so honorably. They had ulterior objects of more importance than fighting the enemy's navy. Such a course cannot be consistently followed for years without affecting the spirit and tone of the officers charged with it; and it led directly to as brave a man as ever commanded a fleet, the Comte de Grasse, failing to crush the English under Rodney when he had the chance, in 1782. On the 9th of April of that year, being chased by the English among the Windward Islands, it happened to him to have sixteen of their fleet under his lee while the main body was becalmed under Dominica. Though greatly superior to the separated ships, during the three hours that this state of things lasted, De Grasse left them undisturbed, except by a distant cannonade by his own van; and his action was justified by the court which tried him, in which were many officers of high rank and doubtless of distinction, as being "an act of prudence on the part of the admiral, dictated to him by the ulterior projects of the cruise." Three days later he was

战，就算在最坏的情况下不得不交战，那也要确保自己拥有有利的条件。至于要采取的态度，则应当完全取决于敌人的实力。我们无需厌烦，而应当一再指出，不论要应对的是一个弱国还是一个强国，法国面前都有两种不同的战略，其手段和目标都是截然相反的——这就是大规模战争和巡航战争。"

这样正式的话语，由一位高级军官说出来，我们必须敬而受之才是，尤其是因为，他的这些话表达出了一个伟大、好战的国家所遵循的一贯政策；不过，一个名副其实的海洋大国能否因此而确保无虞，这一点却尚可质疑。从逻辑上来说，倘若采取如此一种姿态，那么在兵力相等的情况下，就不该与敌作战，因为我方的损失会比对方的损失更大。"事实上，"支持法国此种政策的拉马杜埃尔说，"损失数艘舰船，对英国来说又算得了什么呢？"不过，此种论战中必然涉及的下一步，便是最好不要与敌遭遇。正如前面引述过的另一位法国人曾说，人们认为，让己方的船只落入敌军之手是一种灾难，因此，倘若遇上了敌人，那么在可以体面地做到的情况下，他们就有责任去避而不战。他们有着长远的、比与敌人海军作战更加重要的目标。这样一种方针，是不可能在多年间一贯遵循而不影响到海军官兵们的精神和风气的；因此，它直接导致了像曾经指挥过一支舰队的德·格拉斯伯爵这样英勇的人，也会在1782年自己有机会的情况下没能摧毁罗德尼所率的英国舰队。那一年的4月9日，正在温德华群岛中受到英军追击的过程中，他突然发现，英军舰队中有16艘船处在自己的下风向，而英军主力则因为海上无风而滞留在南边的多米尼加岛。尽管他的兵力远远超过了这些离开了主力的英国军舰，但在接下来形势一直如此的那3个小时中，德·格拉斯却始终没去进攻，只是让自己的前锋舰

signally beaten by the fleet he had failed to attack at disadvantage, and all the ulterior projects of the cruise went down with him.

To return to Minorca, after the action of the 20th, Byng called a council of war, which decided that nothing more could be done, and that the English fleet should go to Gibraltar and cover that place from an attack. At Gibraltar, Byng was relieved by Hawke and sent home to be tried. The court-martial, while expressly clearing him of cowardice or disaffection, found him guilty of not doing his utmost either to defeat the French fleet or to relieve the garrison at Mahon; and, as the article of war prescribed death with no alternative punishment for this offence, it felt compelled to sentence him to death. The king refused to pardon, and Byng was accordingly shot.

The expedition against Minorca was begun while nominal peace still lasted. On the 17th of May, three days before Byng's battle, England declared war, and France replied on the 20th of June. On the 28th, Port Mahon surrendered, and Minorca passed into the hands of France.

The nature of the troubles between the two nations, and the scenes where they occurred, pointed out clearly enough the proper theatre of the strife, and we should by rights now be at the opening of a sea war, illustrated by great naval actions and attended with great modifications in the colonial and foreign possessions of the two powers. Of the two, England alone recognized the truth; France was again turned aside from the sea by causes which will shortly be given. Her fleets scarcely appeared; and losing the control of the sea, she surrendered one by one her colonies and all her hopes in India. Later in the struggle she drew in Spain as her ally, but it was only to involve that country in her own external ruin. England, on the other hand, defended and nourished by the sea, rode it everywhere in triumph. Secure and prosperous at home, she

队进行远距离炮击；后来审判他的军事法庭认为，他这样做是正当的，而法庭上许多级别很高、声名显赫的将领，也都认为"作为司令，因受命巡航并实施隐秘之目标，故为审慎之行为。"三天之后，他就被自己未趁其处于劣势之时进攻的这支舰队打了个落花流水，而巡航中所有的隐秘之目标，便都随着他一齐葬身水下了。

在20日的海战过后返回米诺卡的过程中，拜恩召开了一次作战会议；会议决定，由于在此已无可作为，故英国舰队应当前往直布罗陀，以保护该港不受攻击。在直布罗陀，拜恩却被霍克免了职并送回国内受审。军事法庭在明确澄清他没有怯战和叛国的同时，却宣判他有罪，因为他既没有尽力击败法国舰队，也没有尽力支援马翁港内的守军；并且，由于战争法案规定，此种罪行只有死刑，没有其他选择，因此军事法庭不得不判处拜恩死刑。英国国王拒绝赦免，于是拜恩便被枪决了。

远征米诺卡，是在英、法两国名义上仍然保持着和平关系的同时开始的。5月17日，也就是拜恩指挥的那次海战爆发的三天之前，英国对法宣战，而法国则在6月20日正式应战。28日，马翁港投降，而米诺卡岛也落入了法国的手中。

英、法两国间争端的性质，以及发生争端的那些地点，都足够清晰地指出了此次战争的真正舞台；因此按理来说，我们如今开始研究的，本来应当是一场海洋战争的初期——这场战争，既有大规模海上作战的战例可资说明，我们还能看到这两个大国的殖民地和海外领地发生巨大变化的情况。在这两个国家中，只有英国认识到了这一现实；法国则再一次置海洋于不顾，至于原因，我们将简单地加以说明。法国的舰队，几乎全都不再露面了；由于失去了制海权，该国丢掉了一个又一个殖民地，在印度的希望也全都落了空。在战争后期，法国将西班牙拉进来做了盟友，可这不过是让西班牙也陷入了该国

supported with her money the enemies of France. At the end of seven years the kingdom of Great Britain had become the British Empire.

It is far from certain that France could have successfully contended with England on the sea, without an ally. In 1756 the French navy had sixty-three ships-of-the-line, of which forty-five were in fair condition; but equipments and artillery were deficient. Spain had forty-six ships-of-the-line; but from the previous and subsequent performances of the Spanish navy, it may well be doubted if its worth were equal to its numbers. England at this time had one hundred and thirty ships-of-the-line; four years later she had one hundred and twenty actually in commission. Of course when a nation allows its inferiority, whether on land or sea, to become as great as that of France now was, it cannot hope for success.

Nevertheless, she obtained advantages at first. The conquest of Minorca was followed in November of the same year by the acquisition of Corsica. The republic of Genoa surrendered to France all the fortified harbors of the island. With Toulon, Corsica, and Port Mahon, she now had a strong grip on the Mediterranean. In Canada, the operations of 1756, under Montcalm, were successful despite the inferiority of numbers. At the same time an attack by a native prince in India took from the English Calcutta, and gave an opportunity to the French.

Yet another incident offered a handle for French statesmanship to strengthen her position on the ocean. The Dutch had promised France not to renew their alliance with England, but to remain neutral. England retaliated by declaring "all the ports of France in a state of blockade, and all vessels bound to those ports liable to seizure as lawful prize." Such a violation of the rights of neutrals can only be undertaken by a nation that feels it has nothing to fear from their rising against it. The aggressiveness, born of the sense of power, which characterized England,

海外势力日趋没落的境地罢了。而另一方面，英国则通过海洋捍卫和强化了本国实力，并且凭借制海权在世界各地耀武扬威。由于国内安全稳固、兴旺富足，该国还用自己的资金扶持了法国的敌人。到了第7年年底，"大不列颠王国"便已变成"不列颠帝国"了。

倘若没有盟友，法国是否能够成功地在海上与英国展开角逐，这一点是谁也没有把握的。1756年，法国海军拥有63艘战列舰，其中45艘的船况相当好；不过，装备和弹药却不足。西班牙拥有46艘战舰；但从西班牙海军以前及后来的表现来看，我们完全可以怀疑，这些战舰的作战能力是否配得上它们的数量。此时英国拥有130艘战列舰；4年过后，实际在役的就只有120艘了。自然，倘若一个国家像此时的法国那样，任由自己的劣势变得巨大无比，那么这个国家就是不可能指望获得成功的。

尽管如此，法国在最初还是努力获得了一些优势。攻克米诺卡岛之后，同年11月份，法国又占领了科西嘉岛。热那亚共和国将该岛上所有筑有防御工事的海港，全都割让给了法国。由于拥有了土伦、科西嘉和马翁港，故法国此时便有力地控制了地中海地区。在加拿大，1756年蒙特卡姆指挥过数次战斗，虽说兵力不如敌人，但都取得了胜利。与此同时，印度一位当地贵族也指挥进行了一次袭击，从英国人手中夺取了加尔各答，从而给了法国人一个机会。

还有另外一件事情，为法国的政客们加强该国在海洋上的地位提供了口实。荷兰已经向法国做出承诺，不再重新与英国结盟，而是保持中立。作为报复，英国宣布"法国的所有港口都处于封锁状态，所有开往这些港口的船只，都可以扣押作为合法战利品。"此种违反中立国权利的行为，只有一个认为自己对其他任何反对力量都无所畏惧的国家，才做得出来。由这种实力感而产生出来的、属于英国特色的那种咄咄逼人的气势，法国本来是

might have been used by France to draw Spain and possibly other States into alliance against her.

Instead of concentrating against England, France began another continental war, this time with a new and extraordinary alliance. The Empress of Austria, working on the religious superstitions of the king and upon the anger of the king's mistress, who was piqued at sarcasms uttered against her by Frederick the Great, drew France into an alliance with Austria against Prussia. This alliance was further joined by Russia, Sweden and Poland. The empress urged that the two Roman Catholic powers should unite to take Silesia away from a Protestant king, and expressed her willingness to give to France a part of her possessions in the Netherlands, which France had always desired.

Frederick the Great, learning the combination against him, instead of waiting for it to develop, put his armies in motion and invaded Saxony, whose ruler was also King of Poland. This movement, in October, 1756, began the Seven Years' War; which, like the War of the Austrian Succession, but not to the same extent, drew some of the contestants off from the original cause of difference. But while France, having already on hand one large quarrel with her neighbor across the Channel, was thus needlessly entering upon another struggle, with the avowed end of building up that Austrian empire which a wiser policy had long striven to humble, England this time saw clearly where her true interests lay. Making the continental war wholly subsidiary, she turned her efforts upon the sea and the colonies; at the same time supporting Frederick both with money and cordial sympathy in the war for the defence of his kingdom, which so seriously diverted and divided the efforts of France. England thus had really but one war on hand. In the same year the direction of the struggle was taken from the hands of a weak ministry and given into those of the bold and ardent William Pitt, who retained his office

可以加以利用，将西班牙以及其他可能的国家全都拉拢过来，组成一个反英同盟的。

可法国并未把精力集中于对抗英国上，而是开始了另一场大陆战争；不过，这一次它有了一个新的、了不起的盟友。奥地利皇后一直用宗教迷信影响国王，并且对国王的情妇大为光火，又被腓特烈大帝挖苦讽刺的话语所激怒，于是便拉拢法国，使之与奥地利结成同盟，来对抗普鲁士。后来，俄国、瑞典和波兰也先后加入了这一同盟。奥地利皇后敦促这两个信奉罗马天主教的大国应当团结起来，从那个信奉新教的国王手中夺取西里西亚，并且还说愿意将她在尼德兰的一部分领地割让给法国，而这一点，正是法国一直梦寐以求的。

腓特烈大帝得知法、奥联合起来对抗普鲁士的消息之后，并没有等待这个同盟逐渐发展壮大，而是立即调兵遣将，入侵了萨克森，因为此地的统治者同时也是波兰国王。这一事件发生于1756年10月，从而拉开了"七年战争"的大幕；此次战争，跟奥地利王位继承战争一样，只是程度不同，也让一些交战国不再关注它们之间产生争端的初始原因了。不过，对于法国来说，由于它业已与英吉利海峡对面的邻邦全面反目，所以根本没有必要再卷入另一场战争，何况这场战争的目的众所周知，便是增强那个因受一种更明智的政策约束而一直不得不低声下气的奥地利帝国的实力；而这一次，英国则看清了自己的真正利益所在。英国对欧洲大陆上进行的此次战争毫不在意，而是将自己的精力转向了海洋和各个殖民地；与此同时，还用资金和真挚的同情支持腓特烈大帝在战争中保卫他的王国，从而严重地转移了法国的注意力，并分散了法国的力量。这样一来，英国参与的，实际上就只是一场战争。同一年，战争的指挥权从一个软弱的内阁转移到了英勇而忠诚的威廉·皮

till 1761, by which time the ends of the war had practically been secured.

In the attack upon Canada there were two principal lines to be chosen, — that by the way of Lake Champlain, and that by the way of the St. Lawrence. The former was entirely inland, and as such does not concern our subject, beyond noting that not till after the fall of Quebec, in 1759, was it fairly opened to the English. In 1757 the attempt against Louisburg failed; the English admiral being unwilling to engage sixteen ships-of-the-line he found there, with the fifteen under his own command, which were also, he said, of inferior metal. Whether he was right in his decision or not, the indignation felt in England clearly shows the difference of policy underlying the action of the French and English governments. The following year an admiral of a higher spirit, Boscawen, was sent out accompanied with twelve thousand troops, and, it must in fairness be said, found only five ships in the port. The troops were landed, while the fleet covered the siege from the only molestation it could fear, and cut off from the besieged the only line by which they could look for supplies. The island fell in 1758, opening the way by the St. Lawrence to the heart of Canada, and giving the English a new base both for the fleet and army.

The next year the expedition under Wolfe was sent against Quebec. All his operations were based upon the fleet, which not only carried his army to the spot, but moved up and down the river as the various feints required. The landing which led to the decisive action was made directly from the ships. Montcalm, whose skill and determination had blocked the attacks by way of Lake Champlain the two previous years, had written urgently for reinforcements; but they were refused by the minister of war, who replied that in addition to other reasons it was too probable that the English would intercept them on the way, and that the more France sent, the more England would be moved to send. In a word, the possession of Canada depended upon sea

特手中；他直到1761年才卸任，此时英国的战争目标实际上已经确保实现了。

在进攻加拿大的时候，有两条主要的进军路线可供选择———一是取道尚普兰湖，二是取道圣劳伦斯河。前者完全位于内陆，所以与本书的主题无关，但我们要注意，直到1759年魁北克陷落之后，尚普兰湖才完全对英国开放。1757年，英军进攻路易斯堡失利；因为英军的舰队司令不愿指挥自己所率的15艘战舰与那儿的16艘敌舰交战，还说他所率战舰的钢甲不如敌舰结实。无论他的决定正确与否，英国国内对这一事件的愤慨，都清楚地表明了法、英两国政府据以行动的政策并不相同。第二年，英国派出了斗志更为昂扬的博斯科恩上将，以及12000名陆军；而我们必须公正地说，他抵达时发现路易斯堡港内只有5艘舰船。陆军上了岸，而舰队则掩护陆军进行围攻，并切断了被围守军唯一的补给线。该岛于1758年陷落，从而打通了经由圣劳伦斯河通往加拿大腹地的水路，也使英国的舰队和陆军获得了一个新的基地。

第二年，沃尔夫所率的远征军被派去进攻魁北克。他的所有作战行动，都没有离开过舰队的支持；英国舰队非但将沃尔夫手下的军队运送到了战场之上，还根据不同的佯攻需要，在圣劳伦斯河上来来回回地进行机动。在具有决定意义的那一战中，陆军是在军舰之上直接登岸的。曾经凭借自己的本领与决心，在前两年里阻止了英军取道尚普兰湖发起的多次进击的蒙特卡姆，便向国内写信紧急求援；可战争大臣却拒发援兵，回复说增援部队很有可能在路上遭到英军截击，并且法国派的人越多，英国派的人也就会越多，还有许多其他的理由。总而言之，便是控制加拿大完全取决于制海权。

因此，蒙特卡姆由于虑及英军肯定会从圣劳伦斯河上对魁北克发动进攻，便不得不

power.

Montcalm, therefore, in view of the certain attack upon Quebec by the river, was compelled to weaken his resistance on the Champlain route; nevertheless, the English did not get farther than the foot of the lake that year, and their operations, though creditable, had no effect upon the result at Quebec.

In 1760, the English, holding the course of the St. Lawrence, with Louisburg at one end and Quebec at the other, seemed firmly seated. Nevertheless, the French governor, De Vaudreuil, still held out at Montreal, and the colonists still hoped for help from France. The English garrison at Quebec, though inferior in numbers to the forces of the Canadians, was imprudent enough to leave the city and meet them in the open field. Defeated there, and pursued by the enemy, the latter nearly entered Quebec pell-mell with the English troops, and trenches were opened against the city. A few days later an English squadron came in sight, and the place was relieved. "Thus," says the old English chronicler of the navy, "the enemy saw what it was to be inferior at sea; for, had a French squadron got the start of the English in sailing up the river, Quebec must have fallen." Wholly cut off now, the little body of Frenchmen that remained in Montreal was surrounded by three English armies, which had come, one by way of Lake Champlain, the others from Oswego and from Quebec. The surrender of the city on the 8th of September, 1760, put an end forever to the French possession of Canada.

In all other quarters of the world, after the accession of Pitt to power, the same good fortune followed the English arms, checkered only at the first by some slight reverses. It was not so on the continent, where the heroism and skill of Frederick the Great maintained with difficulty his brilliant struggle against France, Austria, and Russia. The study of the difficulties of his position, of the military and political combinations attending it, do not belong to our subject. Sea power does not appear directly in its effects upon the struggle, but indirectly it was felt in two

在尚普兰湖这条路线上降低抵抗力度；尽管如此，那一年里，英军也没有越过该湖南端，并且他们的作战行动虽说值得称颂，但对魁北克之战的结果却并没有产生什么影响。

1760年，由于掌控了一端为路易斯堡、另一端为魁北克的整个圣劳伦斯河，英军似乎已经牢牢地扎下了根基。尽管如此，法国总督德·沃德勒伊却仍然坚守着蒙特利尔，而法国殖民者也仍然指望着国内派兵前来救援。魁北克的英国守军虽说在数量上不如加拿大军队，却很鲁莽地出城去与之在开阔地带交战。英国守军战败之后，敌人便追击而至，差点就跟英军混杂在一起入了城；之后，敌军又开始修筑战壕，准备进攻魁北克。数天之后，一小支英国舰队抵达，此处才得以解围。"这样一来，"原先那位海军编年史家说，"敌人就明白了海上力量处于弱势的后果；因为，倘若有一支法国舰队先于英军沿河而上，魁北克就必定已被攻下。"此时仍然坚守蒙特利尔的那一小支法国军队已被完全孤立起来，并被三支英军包围了；这三支英军，一支取道尚普兰湖而来，其余两支则来自奥斯维戈与魁北克。1760年9月8日，蒙特利尔投降，从而永久性地结束了法国占领加拿大的历史。

自皮特上台掌权以后，英国军队在世界其他地方也都交上了同样的好运，只是起初遭遇过一些轻微的波折罢了。但在欧洲大陆上却并非这样，腓特烈大帝正凭自己的英雄气概和本领，一直艰难地同法、奥、俄三国进行着非凡的战斗。研究他的处境、军事和政治方面的种种艰难，并不属于本书的主题。制海权的作用，并非直接体现在它对此次战争所产生的影响，而是间接地体现在两个方面：首先，体现在英国国力雄厚、信用良好，使得它可以给腓特烈大帝拨款，而这些拨款在既节俭又能干的腓特烈大帝手里，能够发挥出更大

ways, — first, by the subsidies which the abundant wealth and credit of England enabled her to give Frederick, in whose thrifty and able hands they went far; and second, in the embarrassment caused to France by the attacks of England upon her colonies and her own sea-coast, in the destruction of her commerce, and in the money — all too little, it is true, and grudgingly given — which France was forced to bestow on her navy. Stung by the constant lashing of the Power of the sea, France, despite the blindness and unwillingness of the rulers, was driven to undertake something against it. With a navy much inferior, unable to cope in all quarters of the world, it was rightly decided to concentrate upon one object; and the object chosen was Great Britain itself, whose shores were to be invaded. This decision, soon apprehended by the fears of the English nation, caused the great naval operations to centre for some years around the coast of France and in the Channel. Before describing them, it will be well to sum up the general plan by which England was guided in the use of her overwhelming sea power.

Besides the operations on the North American continent already described, this plan was fourfold: —

1. The French Atlantic ports were watched in force, especially Brest, so as to keep the great fleets or small squadrons from getting out without fighting.

2. Attacks were made upon the Atlantic and Channel coasts with flying squadrons, followed at times by the descent of small bodies of troops. These attacks, the direction of which could not be foreseen by the enemy, were chiefly intended to compel him to keep on hand forces at many points, and so to diminish the army acting against the King of Prussia. While the tendency would certainly be that way, it may be doubted whether the actual diversion in favor of Frederick was of much consequence. No particular mention will be made of these operations, which had but little visible effect upon the general course of the war.

3. A fleet was kept in the Mediterranean and near Gibraltar to prevent the French Toulon

的作用；其次，体现在英国进攻法国的殖民地和法国本土沿海，这样做既摧毁了法国的贸易，使之疲于应付，也让该国在不得不投入海军的军费方面捉襟见肘——的确，法国海军军费非但少得可怜，政府在支出海军军费的时候也很不情愿。不断地受到这个海洋霸主痛击之后，尽管法国的统治者既无知、也不愿意这样做，他们还是不得不开始采取行动来对抗英国了。因为海军实力相当之弱，无法在世界各地作战，所以，集中力量打击一个目标，就是很正确的决定；而法国选择的这个目标，就是大不列颠本土，准备入侵其沿海地区。这一决定，很快便引起了英国人的担忧和惧怕，从而导致了以法国沿海和英吉利海峡为中心的、长达数年的大规模海军作战行动。在描述这些作战行动之前，我们不妨先来总结一下英国在利用其势不可挡的制海权的过程中，那种引领英国前进的总体规划。

除了前文已经叙述过的、在北美大陆上进行的那些军事行动，这一规划由四个部分所组成：

1. 全力监视大西洋沿岸的法属港口，尤其是布雷斯特，以使本国的大型舰队或小型分舰队无需作战即可出海。

2. 用机动舰队进攻法国的大西洋和英吉利海峡沿岸地区，偶尔派出小股陆军部队登陆袭扰。由于敌人不可能预测出进攻方向，所以这些袭扰的目的，主要在于迫使敌人不得不在多处地点部署兵力，从而减少敌人用于对付普鲁士国王的兵力。尽管英国的意图自然如此，但这种有利于腓特烈大帝的实际牵制是不是具有什么重大意义，这一点我们是可以存疑的。我们不会具体提及这些军事行动中的哪一次，因为它们对于整个战争

fleet from getting round to the Atlantic. It does not appear that any attempt was seriously made to stop communications between France and Minorca. The action of the Mediterranean fleet, though an independent command, was subsidiary to that in the Atlantic.

4. Distant foreign expeditions were sent against the French colonies in the West India Islands and on the coast of Africa, and a squadron was maintained in the East Indies to secure the control of those seas, thereby supporting the English in the Peninsula, and cutting off the communications of the French. These operations in distant waters, never intermitted, assumed greater activity and larger proportions after the destruction of the French navy had relieved England from the fear of invasion, and when the ill-advised entrance of Spain into the war, in 1762, offered yet richer prizes to her enterprise.

The close blockade of the enemy's fleet in Brest, which was first systematically carried out during this war, may be considered rather a defensive than an offensive operation; for though the intention certainly was to fight if opportunity offered, the chief object was to neutralize an offensive weapon in the enemy's hands; the destruction of the weapon was secondary. The truth of this remark is shown by the outburst of fear and anger which swept over England when an unavoidable absence of the blockading fleet in 1759 allowed the French to escape. The effect of the blockade in this and after wars was to keep the French in a state of constant inferiority in the practical handling of their ships, however fair-showing their outward appearance or equal their numerical force. The position of the port of Brest was such that a blockaded fleet could not get out during the heavy westerly gales that endangered the blockaders; the latter, therefore, had the habit of running away from them to Torbay or Plymouth, sure, with care, of getting back to their station with an east wind before a large and ill-handled fleet could get much start of them.

的进程而言，都只有微不足道的影响。

3. 在靠近直布罗陀的地中海海域部署一支舰队，以阻遏法国的土伦舰队趁机前往大西洋。英国似乎并没有认真采取过什么措施，来阻断法国本土与米诺卡岛之间的交通联络。地中海舰队的作战行动，虽说是独立指挥，却从属于英国在大西洋上的作战。

4. 派出进行远距离海外作战的远征军，前去攻打法国在西印度群岛和非洲海岸的那些殖民地，还在东印度群岛海域常备一支分舰队，以确保控制那些海域，从而支援印度半岛上的英军，并且切断法军的交通补给。这些在距英国很遥远的海域进行的军事行动从未中断过，而在法国海军被摧毁、从而解除了遭受法国入侵的担忧之后，这样的军事行动进行得更加活跃，也占据了英军作战行动中的较大比例；待1762年西班牙轻率地参战之后，这些行动还让英国为其海洋霸权获得了更加丰富的战利品。

将布雷斯特的敌方舰队封锁在港内，是此次战争中英军首次有组织地实施的军事行动，可以说是一种防御性的而非进攻性的行动。因为，尽管英军想在机会到来的时候与之交战，但其主要目标，还是让敌人手中那种进攻性武器无用武之地；至于摧毁这一武器，则在其次。1759年执行封锁任务的那支舰队不得不撤走，让法国舰队得以逃脱，使得英国上下一片担忧和愤慨之声，由此即可看出这种说法是正确的。此次封锁和战后所进行的封锁，都是为了让法国在实际利用其舰船这个方面始终都处在一种劣势之中，无论该国让舰队外表看上去有多好，或是让兵力与英国相等。布雷斯特港的位置，使得一支被封锁的舰队，即便是在有强劲的西风危及执行封锁任务的英国舰队时，也无法出港；因此，后者便经常会抛下被封锁的法国舰队，避往托贝港或者普利茅斯，但当然是在谨慎地确信自己能够及时顺着东风赶回驻地，不会让某支庞大而指挥不当的法国舰队

In the latter part of 1758, France, depressed by the sense of failure upon the continent, mortified and harassed by English descents upon her coasts, which had been particularly annoying that year, and seeing that it was not possible to carry on both the continental and sea wars with her money resources, determined to strike directly at England. Her commerce was annihilated while the enemy's throve. It was the boast of London merchants that under Pitt commerce was united with and made to flourish by war; and this thriving commerce was the soul also of the land struggle, by the money it lavished on the enemy of France.

At this time a new and active-minded minister, Choiseul, was called into power by Louis XV. From the beginning of 1759, preparations were made in the ocean and Channel ports. Flat-boats to transport troops were built at Havre, Dunkirk, Brest, and Rochefort. It was intended to embark as many as fifty thousand men for the invasion of England, while twelve thousand were to be directed upon Scotland. Two squadrons were fitted out, each of respectable strength, one at Toulon, the other at Brest. The junction of these two squadrons at Brest was the first step in the great enterprise.

It was just here that it broke down, through the possession of Gibraltar by the English, and their naval superiority. It seems incredible that even the stern and confident William Pitt should, as late as 1757, have offered to surrender to Spain the watch-tower from which England overlooks the road between the Mediterranean and the Atlantic, as the price of her help to recover Minorca. Happily for England, Spain refused. In 1759, Admiral Boscawen commanded the English Mediterranean fleet. In making an attack upon French frigates in Toulon roads, some of his ships were so damaged that he sailed with his whole squadron to Gibraltar to refit; taking the precaution, however, to station lookout frigates at intervals, and to arrange signals by

抢先出港的情况下，英军才会这样做。

1758年下半年，法国因为在欧洲大陆接连失败而沮丧不已，又因英国进攻其沿海地区而深受侮辱、烦恼至极——英国在这一年里对法国沿海的袭扰尤其恼人，还因为明白本国财力不可能同时在欧洲大陆和海上作战，便决心直接进攻英国。此时，法国的贸易已经被完全摧毁，而英国的贸易却繁荣兴旺得很。让伦敦商人引以为傲的是，在皮特的领导下，英国的商业贸易团结一致，并且通过战争而获得了长足的发展；而此种繁荣的商业贸易，又通过给法国的敌人提供大笔大笔的资金，成为了大陆战争的主要推动者。

就在此时，路易十五召来了一位新的、头脑灵活的大臣舒瓦瑟尔，让他上台执政。从1759年初开始，法国便在大西洋和英吉利海峡沿岸各港备战了。勒阿弗尔、敦克尔克、布雷斯特和罗什福尔等港市都建造了运送部队的平底船。法国想要运送多达50000人的兵力入侵英格兰，同时派遣12000兵力直接进攻苏格兰。法国还装备了两支分舰队，每一支的实力都不弱，一支位于土伦，另一支位于布雷斯特。让两支舰队在布雷斯特集结起来，便是实施这一宏伟计划的第一步。

然而，计划正是毁在了这个地方，因为英国占据着直布罗陀，而其海军实力也大大优于法国海军。就连如此坚定自信的威廉·皮特，也会在1757年提出，将英军俯瞰地中海与大西洋间水道的那座瞭望塔让给西班牙，以换取西班牙帮助英国收复米诺卡岛，这一点似乎令人难以置信。但让英国幸运的是，西班牙拒绝了皮特的这一提议。1759年，博斯科恩上将担任了英国地中海舰队的司令。在进击驶往土伦海域的法国护卫舰时，他手下的数艘舰船受损严重，于是他便率领整支舰队前往直布罗陀进行整修；然而，他也采取了预防措施，时不时地派出监视船，并且规定，当敌军靠近时，应当及时用枪炮给

guns to notify him betimes of the enemy's approach. Taking advantage of his absence, and in obedience to orders, the French commodore, De la Clue, left Toulon with twelve ships-of-the-line on the 5th of August, and on the 17th found himself at the Straits of Gibraltar, with a brisk east wind carrying him out into the Atlantic. Everything seemed propitious, a thick haze and falling night concealing the French ships from the land, while not preventing their sight of each other, when an English frigate loomed up in the near distance. As soon as she saw the fleet, knowing they must be enemies, she hauled in for the land and began firing signal-guns. Pursuit was useless; flight alone remained. Hoping to elude the chase he knew must follow, the French commodore steered west-northwest for the open sea, putting out all lights; but either from carelessness or disaffection, — for the latter is hinted by one French naval officer, — five out of the twelve ships headed to the northward and put into Cadiz when on the following morning they could not see the commodore. The latter was dismayed when at daylight he saw his forces thus diminished. At eight o'clock some sails made their appearance, and for a few minutes he hoped they were the missing ships. Instead of that, they were the lookouts of Boscawen's fleet, which, numbering fourteen ships-of-the-line, was in full pursuit. The French formed their order on one of the close-hauled lines, and fled; but of course their fleet-speed was less than that of the fastest English ships. The general rule for all chases where the pursuer is decidedly superior, namely, that order must be observed only so far as to keep the leading ships within reasonable supporting distance of the slower ones, so that they may not be singly overpowered before the latter can come up, was by this time well understood in the English navy, and that is certainly the fitting time for a mélêe. Boscawen acted accordingly. The rear ship of the French, on the other hand, nobly emulated the example of l'Étenduère when he saved his convoy. Overtaken at two o'clock by the leading English ship, and soon after surrounded by four others, her captain

他发信号。法国准将德·拉·克鲁趁着博斯科恩离开的这一机会，奉命率领12艘战舰于8月5日离开了土伦港，并于17日抵达了直布罗陀海峡，顺着猛烈的东风进入了大西洋。一切似乎都顺利得很，厚厚的雾霾和夜幕使得岸上的人看不到法国舰队的行踪；但一艘英国的护卫舰从近处突如其来地冒了出来，彼此都看到了对方。英国的那艘护卫舰一看到法国舰队，便明白这必定是敌方舰船，于是一面驶向岸边，一面开始鸣炮示警。去追击这艘护卫舰是毫无用处的；于是法国舰队便只有逃跑了。这位法国准将明白英军必定前来追击，而为了躲避追击，他便转舵西北偏西，驶往公海，并且熄灭了船上所有的灯火；可或是因为粗心，或是由于不忠——法国一位海军将领曾经暗示过后一种原因——12艘战舰中有5艘驶向了北方，并在第二天早上找不到德·拉·克鲁准将的情况下，驶进了加的斯。天亮之后，看到手下舰队一下子少了那么多艘舰船，德·拉·克鲁准将惊慌失措了。到了8点钟，一些舰船出现了，德·拉·克鲁准将一度希望那是他手下失踪的战舰。不过事与愿违，这些都是博斯科恩所率舰队派出来的警戒船，包括14艘战舰，此时正在全速追击法军。法国舰队在迎风一侧排列成阵，然后开始逃跑；但是，它们的整体速度自然比不过英国最快的那些舰船。对于在所有的追击战中，当追击者占有绝对优势之时应当遵循的一般性准则——也就是说，只是在为了让领先的那些舰船保持在较慢船只能够支援的合理距离之内的时候，才必须服从秩序，以使它们不至于在后面的舰船尚未赶上的时候落单并被敌人以优势兵力打垮——如今的英国海军已经理解得很透彻了，所以，此时便理所当然地是进行混战的最佳时机。博斯科恩上将正是按照这一准则行动的。而另一方面，法军的那艘后卫军舰则勇敢地效仿了拉埃腾杜尔救援商船队时的

made for five hours a desperate resistance, from which he could hope, not to save himself, but to delay the enemies long enough for the better sailers to escape. He so far succeeded that — thanks to the injury done by him and their better speed — they did that day escape action at close quarters, which could only have ended in their capture. When he hauled down his flag, his three topmasts were gone, the mizzen-mast fell immediately after, and the hull was so full of water that the ship was with difficulty kept afloat. M. de Sabran — his name is worthy to be remembered — had received eleven wounds in this gallant resistance, by which he illustrated so signally the duty and service of a rearguard in retarding pursuit. That night two of the French ships hauled off to the westward, and so escaped. The other four continued their flight as before; but the next morning the commodore, despairing of escape, headed for the Portuguese coast, and ran them all ashore between Lagos and Cape St. Vincent. The English admiral followed and attacked them, taking two and burning the others, without regard to the neutrality of Portugal. For this insult no amend was made beyond a formal apology; Portugal was too dependent upon England to be seriously considered. Pitt, writing to the English minister to Portugal about the affair, told him that while soothing the susceptibilities of the Portuguese government he must not allow it to suppose that either the ships would be given up or the distinguished admiral censured.

The destruction or dispersal of the Toulon fleet stopped the invasion of England, though the five ships that got into Cadiz remained a matter of anxiety to Sir Edward Hawke, who cruised before Brest. Choiseul, balked of his main object, still clung to the invasion of Scotland. The French fleet at Brest, under Marshal de Conflans, a sea officer despite his title, numbered twenty sail-of-the-line, besides frigates. The troops to be embarked are variously stated at fifteen to twenty thousand. The original purpose was to escort the transports with only five

做法。这艘军舰在2点钟的时候被冲在最前面的那艘英舰追上，不久之后又陷入了其他4艘英舰的包围，但该舰舰长指挥手下进行了5个小时的殊死抵抗；他这样做，并非是希望挽救自己，而是为了尽可能久地拖住敌人，好让那些船况更好的军舰逃脱。当时，他成功地做到了这一点——多亏了他给敌舰造成的损害，以及其他舰船速度也更快——所以那一天其他法舰的确从短兵相接的战斗中逃脱了，可最终却还是免不了被俘虏的结局。当这位舰长放下自己的旗帜时，船上的三根中桅已经无影无踪，而后桅随后也倒了，整个船体都浸满了水，艰难地漂浮在海面上。这位M·德·萨布朗——他的名字，值得人们永远铭记——在此次英勇的抵抗中，身上受了11处伤；通过此次抵抗，他也非凡地说明了在阻遏追击时后卫力量的义务与职责。那天晚上，有两艘法舰向西退却，因而逃脱了。其余4艘则继续像之前那样逃窜；可第二天早上，这支舰队的临时司令感到逃脱无望，便率舰向葡萄牙沿海驶去，并且全都在拉各斯和圣文森特角之间搁了浅。英军司令率军尾随而来，向法国舰队发起攻击，俘虏了其中的两艘，并且烧毁了其余两艘，根本就没有考虑过葡萄牙的中立国地位。对于这种无礼行径，英国除了正式道歉之外，并没有进行什么纠正；葡萄牙太过依赖英国，所以英国无需严肃地去顾及该国的感受。皮特在就此事写给荷兰驻英公使的信中对后者说，尽管葡萄牙政府脆弱的感情需要安抚，但他决不会答应葡萄牙政府提出让英国放弃缴获之舰船或谴责那位杰出的英国海军司令的要求。

土伦舰队的覆灭或消失，挫败了法国对英国的入侵企图，但逃入加的斯港的那5艘舰船，却仍然让爱德华·霍克勋爵寝食难安，所以他便率领舰队在布雷斯特港外游弋。舒瓦瑟尔虽说自己的主要目标受阻，却仍然坚持入侵苏格兰。法国的布雷斯特舰队除了

ships-of-the-line, besides smaller vessels. Conflans insisted that the whole fleet ought to go. The minister of the navy thought that the admiral was not a sufficiently skilful tactician to be able to check the advance of an enemy, and so insure the safe arrival of the convoy at its destination near the Clyde without risking a decisive encounter. Believing therefore that there would be a general action, he considered that it would be better to fight it before the troops sailed; for if disastrous, the convoy would not be sacrificed, and if decisively victorious, the road would then be clear. The transports were assembled, not at Brest, but in the ports to the southward as far as the mouth of the Loire. The French fleet therefore put to sea with the expectation and purpose of fighting the enemy; but it is not easy to reconcile its subsequent course with that purpose, nor with the elaborate fighting instructions issued by the admiral before sailing.

About the 5th or 6th of November there came on a tremendous westerly gale. After buffeting it for three days, Hawke bore up and ran into Torbay, where he waited for the wind to shift, keeping his fleet in readiness to sail at once. The same gale, while keeping back the French already in Brest, gave the chance to a small squadron under M. Bompart, which was expected from the West Indies, to slip in during Hawke's absence. Conflans made his preparations with activity, distributed Bompart's crews among his own ships, which were not very well manned, and got to sea with an easterly wind on the 14th. He stood at once to the southward, flattering himself that he had escaped Hawke. The latter, however, had sailed from Torbay on the 12th; and though again driven back, sailed a second time on the 14th, the same day that Conflans left Brest. He soon readied his station, learned that the enemy had been seen to the southward steering east, and easily concluding that they were bound to Quiberon Bay, shaped his own course for the same place under a press of sail. At eleven P.M. of the 19th the French admiral estimated his position to be seventy miles southwest by west from Belle Isle;

护卫舰外，还拥有20艘战舰，由德·孔夫兰元帅指挥——别看他号称陆军"元帅"，其实却是一位海军将领。准备运送的陆军兵力说法各异，应在15000至20000人之间。法国最初的想法是，只用5艘战舰和一些小型舰船护送运兵船只。而孔夫兰元帅却坚持说，整支舰队都应当前去护航。海军大臣认为孔夫兰这位司令并不是一个老练的战术家，不足以阻遏敌人的进击，因而要确保护送的兵力安全抵达位于克莱德河附近的目的地，就免不了要冒爆发一场重大遭遇战的危险。由于孔夫兰相信英、法之间可能会爆发一场大战，所以认为，最好是在部队出发之前打上一仗；这样一来，倘有重大损失，要运送的这支陆军也不至于白白牺牲掉，而倘若取得决定性胜利的话，那么一路上也就畅通无阻了。那些运兵船的集结地并非布雷斯特，而是南部远至卢瓦尔河河口的一些港口。于是，法国舰队便带着与敌人作战的希望与目标出海了；可之后的过程，却很难说是心想事成，与这位海军司令在出发前下达的那些煞费苦心的作战命令，也很难说是保持了一致。

大概是11月5日或6日，海上刮起了猛烈的西风。在与肆虐的海风搏斗了三天之后，霍克率舰队转向下风，驶入了托贝港，等待着风向改变，并让舰队做好了随时起航的准备。这场大风，虽说阻碍了布雷斯特的法军出发，却给M·波姆巴特所率的一支小型舰队提供了机会；法军正盼着从西印度群岛而来的这支舰队，此时它便趁霍克所率舰队不在而溜进了布雷斯特。孔夫兰进行了积极的备战，将波姆巴特的手下全都编入了他自己那支人员配备不足的舰队之中，然后便在14日趁着东风起航了。他一度朝南航行，自以为摆脱了霍克所率的英军。然而，霍克其实12日就已从托贝出发；并且，尽管再次被海风赶了回来，但在14日，即孔夫兰离开布雷斯特的同一天，他又率军出发了。他迅速部

and the wind springing up fresh from the westward, he stood for it under short sail, the wind continuing to increase and hauling to west-northwest. At daybreak several ships were seen ahead, which proved to be the English squadron of Commodore Duff, blockading Quiberon. The signal was made to chase; and the English, taking flight, separated into two divisions, — one going off before the wind, the other hauling up to the southward. The greater part of the French fleet continued its course after the former division, that is, toward the coast; but one ship hauled up for the second. Immediately after, the rear French ships made signal of sails to windward, which were also visible from aloft on board the flag-ship. It must have been about the same moment that the lookout frigate in advance of the English fleet informed her admiral of sails to leeward. Hawke's diligence had brought him up with Conflans, who, in his official reports, says he had considered it impossible that the enemy could have in that neighborhood forces superior or even equal to his own. Conflans now ordered his rear division to haul its wind in support of the ship chasing to the southward and eastward. In a few moments more it was discovered that the fleet to windward numbered twenty-three ships-of-the-line to the French twenty-one, and among them some three-deckers. Conflans then called in the chasing ships and got ready for action. It remained to settle his course under circumstances which he had not foreseen. It was now blowing hard from the west-northwest, with every appearance of heavy weather, the fleet not far from a lee shore, with an enemy considerably superior in numbers; for besides Hawke's twenty-three of the line, Duff had four fifty-gun ships. Conflans therefore determined to run for it and lead his squadron into Quiberon Bay, trusting and believing that Hawke would not dare to follow, under the conditions of the weather, into a bay which French authorities describe as containing banks and shoals, and lined with reefs which the navigator rarely sees without fright and never passes without emotion. It was in the midst of these ghastly dangers that

署好了舰队的战位，通过侦察获知了敌人在南面转舵向东的情报，轻而易举地推知敌人的目的地是基伯龙湾，便调整了自己的航线，满帆全速赶往基伯龙湾。19日晚上11点，法国这位海军司令估计自己的位置是在贝尔岛西南偏西约70英里的地方；此时由于西风正猛，他便低帆顶风前进，可风力一直在增强，将法国舰队吹得转向西北偏西而去。天亮之后，法军前面出现了数艘舰船，细究之下，却是达夫准将所率的一支英国舰队，堵住了前往基伯龙湾的去路。法军发出了进行追击的信号；英军一边逃逸，一边分成了两支分队———一支顺风逃窜，另一支则掉头向南而去。法国舰队的主力保持着航向，跟在第一支英军分队后面追击，也就是驶向海岸；只有一艘军舰转向去追击第二支英军分队。旋即，法国后卫舰船发出了抢风航行的信号，在旗舰甲板上也能看到。一定也就是在这个时候，先于英国舰队抵达的侦察船向英军司令报告了顺风航行的消息。霍克的勤勉，让他终于赶上了孔夫兰；而孔夫兰在自己的正式报告中称，他认为敌方在这一带不可能部署有优于法军的兵力，甚至也不可能部署有与法军相等的兵力。此时，孔夫兰下令其后卫分队转向抢风，支援向南、向东执行追击任务的那艘法国军舰。片刻之后，他却发现，上风位置的那支英国舰队有23艘战舰，并且其中还有数艘三层甲板的炮舰，而法军却只有21艘战舰。于是，孔夫兰召回了正在追击敌人的舰船，准备开战。然而，由于他并未预见到此种情况，所以他的作战方针尚未确定下来。此时，西北偏西的海风刮得正猛，天气马上就会变得极其恶劣，舰队处在离下风处的海岸不远的地方，而敌人兵力又大大优于己方；因为除了霍克所率的那23艘战舰，达夫准将手下还有4艘载有50门火炮的军舰。所以，孔夫兰决定迅速摆脱敌人，率领舰队进入基伯龙湾；因为他相信，在这种恶劣的天气条件下，霍

forty-four large ships were about to engage pell-mell; for the space was too contracted for fleet manoeuvres. Conflans flattered himself that he would get in first and be able to haul up close under the western shore of the bay, forcing the enemy, if he followed, to take position between him and the beach, six miles to leeward. None of his expectations were fulfilled. In the retreat he took the head of his fleet; a step not unjustifiable, since only by leading in person could he have shown just what he wanted to do, but unfortunate for his reputation with the public, as it placed the admiral foremost in the flight. Hawke was not in the least, nor for one moment, deterred by the dangers before him, whose full extent he, as a skilful seaman, entirely realized; but his was a calm and steadfast as well as a gallant temper, that weighed risks justly, neither dissembling nor exaggerating. He has not left us his reasoning, but he doubtless felt that the French, leading, would serve partially as pilots, and must take the ground before him; he believed the temper and experience of his officers, tried by the severe school of the blockade, to be superior to those of the French; and he knew that both the government and the country demanded that the enemy's fleet should not reach another friendly port in safety. On the very day that he was thus following the French, amid dangers and under conditions that have made this one of the most dramatic of sea fights, he was being burnt in effigy in England for allowing them to escape. As Conflans, leading his fleet, was rounding the Cardinals, — as the southernmost rocks at the entrance of Quiberon Bay are called, — the leading English ships brought the French rear to action. It was another case of a general chase ending in a mêlée, but under conditions of exceptional interest and grandeur from the surrounding circumstances of the gale of wind, the heavy sea, the lee shore, the headlong speed, shortened canvas, and the great number of ships engaged. One French

克不敢追击,进入一个法国当局称之为布满浅滩、礁石林立、航海者睹之恐惧、过之动容的海湾。可就是在如此恐怖和危险的情况下,44艘大型舰船即将展开一场混战;因为此处的空间狭小,舰队根本无法机动。孔夫兰自以为是地认为,他会率先进入基伯龙湾,从而在紧挨着港湾西岸下面的地方转向,倘若敌人追击而至的话,这样做就会迫使敌人处在他和下风6英里外的海滩之间的战位。可他的希望全都落空了。在撤退的时候,他的座舰位于舰队之首;这样做并不是没有道理的,因为只有亲自领头,才能准确地表明自己的意图,但可惜的是,这却给他在公众中带来了恶名,因为人们认为,这位海军司令是在率先逃跑。面对这些危险的时候,尽管霍克这个老练的水兵完全认识到了它们的危险程度,可他却没有丝毫和片刻的退缩;他生性沉着冷静、坚定不移而又英勇无畏,能够正确地权衡危险,既不会虚饰太平,也不会夸大其辞。他当时的想法我们不得而知,但他无疑是觉得,领头进入海湾的法军,会部分地充当英军的领航员,并且必定会在英军之前搁浅;他认为,手下将士们的情绪和经验都优于法军将士,因为他的手下都经过了执行封锁任务时的严酷考验;并且他也明白,英国政府和民众都要求他,再也不能让敌人的这支舰队安全地进入另一个与法国保持友好关系的港口了。这一天,他就这样在重重危险之中、在种种不利条件之下,尾随着法国舰队——正是这些危险和不利条件,使得此次战斗成为了史上最具戏剧性的海战之一;而在英格兰,民众却纷纷焚烧霍克的肖像,说他任由法国舰队逃脱了。当孔夫兰率领法国舰队绕过"枢机主教"礁——即基伯龙湾入口处最南端的礁石——时,领头的数艘英军战舰开始与法军后卫舰队交起火来。这是全面追击以混战结束的又一个战例;只不过此战是在有着非凡意义的条件下发生的,并且从海风狂暴、海涛汹涌、海岸背风、船速迅猛、船帆尽收、交战舰船数量众多等战场情况来看,此战的场面也

seventy-four, closely pressed and outnumbered, ventured to open her lower-deck ports; the sea sweeping in carried her down with all on board but twenty men. Another was sunk by the fire of Hawke's flag-ship. Two others, one of which carried a commodore's pennant, struck their colors. The remainder were dispersed. Seven fled to the northward and eastward, and anchored off the mouth of the little river Vilaine, into which they succeeded in entering at the top of high water in two tides, — a feat never before performed. Seven others took refuge to the southward and eastward in Rochefort. One, after being very badly injured, ran ashore and was lost near the mouth of the Loire. The flag-ship bearing the same name as that of Tourville burned at La Hougue, the "Royal Sun," anchored at nightfall off Croisic, a little to the northward of the Loire, where she rode in safety during the night. The next morning the admiral found himself alone, and, somewhat precipitately it would seem, ran the ship ashore to keep her out of English hands. This step has been blamed by the French, but needlessly, as Hawke would never have let her get away. The great French fleet was annihilated; for the fourteen ships not taken or destroyed were divided into two parts, and those in the Vilaine only succeeded in escaping, two at a time, between fifteen months and two years later. The English lost two ships which ran upon a shoal, and were hopelessly wrecked; their losses in action were slight.

All possibility of an invasion of England passed away with the destruction of the Brest fleet. The battle of November 20, 1759, was the Trafalgar of this war; and though a blockade was maintained over the fractions that were laid up in the Vilaine and at Rochefort, the English fleets were now free to act against the colonies of France, and later of Spain, on a grander scale than ever before. The same year that saw this great sea fight and the fall of Quebec witnessed

相当壮观。一艘满员74人的法国军舰，由于被多艘英国战舰逼得太紧，竟然冒险打开了其下层舱门；海水一涌而入，这艘战舰便连同船上的人一起葬身海底了，只救上来了20人。另一艘则为霍克的旗舰所击沉。还有两艘战舰投了降，其中的一艘还悬挂着一位准将的旗帜。其余的法国战舰，全都四散奔逃。其中有7艘向北和向东逃窜，停在了维莱纳这条小河的河口海面，并趁着两次大潮涨得最高的时候，成功地遁入了此河——这可真是一次前无古人的壮举。另有7艘战舰往南，逃到了罗什福尔以东。还有一艘受到重创的法国战舰搁了浅，后来在卢瓦尔河河口附近海域失踪了。法军的旗舰，与图维尔在拉和岬海战中被烧毁的那艘旗舰的名字一样，都叫"皇家太阳"号；黄昏时分它在距卢瓦尔河以北不远的海面停了下来，漂浮着安全地度过了那个晚上。第二天早上，这位法国的海军司令发现自己变成了孤家寡人，便在仓皇之中让这艘旗舰搁了浅，以免它落入英军手中。法国人纷纷谴责他的这一做法；不过，根本就没有必要再去谴责他，因为霍克是决计不会让这艘船逃脱的。于是，这支庞大的法国舰队就此覆灭了；因为那14艘未被俘虏或击毁的战舰分成了两支，而那些进入维莱纳河的舰船都只能说是成功逃跑了而已，后来每次逃出两艘，持续了15个月到两年的时间才全部脱身。英军损失了两艘战舰，都是因为撞上了暗礁、受损严重而毁掉的；而他们在战斗中遭受的损失，可以说是微不足道的。

布雷斯特舰队覆灭之后，法国便不可能再有入侵英格兰的机会了。1759年11月20日发生的这场海战，便是特拉法尔加海战；尽管英军仍然对躲在维莱纳河和罗什福尔的那些法国战舰维持着封锁，但如今英国舰队可以自由地用一种比以前更大的规模，去进攻法国的、后来又加上了西班牙的那些殖民地了。就在发生此次伟大海战和魁北克陷落的同一年，英国还攻陷了西印度群岛的瓜达鲁佩、非洲西海岸的格雷岛，而法国则在经

also the capture of Guadeloupe in the West Indies, of Goree on the west coast of Africa, and the abandonment of the East Indian seas by the French flag after three indecisive actions between their commodore, D'Aché, and Admiral Pocock, — an abandonment which necessarily led to the fall of the French power in India, never again to rise. In this year also the King of Spain died, and his brother succeeded, under the title of Charles III. This Charles had been King of Naples at the time when an English commodore had allowed one hour for the court to determine to withdraw the Neapolitan troops from the Spanish army. He had never forgotten this humiliation, and brought to his new throne a heart unfriendly to England. With such feelings on his part, France and Spain drew more readily together. Charles's first step was to propose mediation, but Pitt was averse to it. Looking upon France as the chief enemy of England, and upon the sea and the colonies as the chief source of power and wealth, he wished, now that he had her down, to weaken her thoroughly for the future as well as the present, and to establish England's greatness more firmly upon the wreck. Later on he offered certain conditions; but the influence of Louis's mistress, attached to the Empress of Austria, prevailed to except Prussia from the negotiations, and England would not allow the exception. Pitt, indeed, was not yet ready for peace. A year later, October 25, 1760, George II. died, and Pitt's influence then began to wane, the new king being less bent on war. During these years, 1759 and 1760, Frederick the Great still continued the deadly and exhausting strife of his small kingdom against the great States joined against him. At one moment his case seemed so hopeless that he got ready to kill himself; but the continuance of the war diverted the efforts of France from England and the sea.

  The hour was fast approaching for the great colonial expeditions, which made the last year of the war illustrious by the triumph of the sea power of England over France and Spain united.

历了由该国的德阿克准将与英国的波考克上将指挥的三次不具决定意义的战斗之后，放弃了对东印度群岛海域的掌控——这种放弃，必然会导致法国在印度的势力垮台，再也无法重新崛起了。也是在这一年，西班牙国王辞世了，他的弟弟继承了王位，号称查理三世。这个查理，曾经是那不勒斯国王，就是有位英国准将[1]给了那不勒斯朝廷1个小时、让他们将那不勒斯的军队从西班牙军队中撤回来那个时候的那不勒斯国王。对于这次受辱，他一直都耿耿于怀，所以在登上西班牙王位后，便一心要与英国为敌。由于他带有这种态度，法国和西班牙就更容易联合起来了。查理的第一步，便是提出为英、法国两国进行居间调停，可皮特却不愿意调停。他将法国视为英国的头号敌人，将海洋和殖民地视为英国首要的实力和财力之源；既然已经将法国打败，他就希望彻底削弱法国当下和未来的实力，并在法国受损的基础上让英国的伟大变得更加稳固。后来，他提出了一些条件；但由于路易十五情妇的影响，以及路易十五对奥地利皇后的爱慕之心，使得法国打算将普鲁士拒之于谈判之外，英国却不允许此种排斥。实际上，是因为皮特此时还没有做好和谈的准备。一年之后的1760年10月25日，乔治二世驾崩，皮特的影响力开始衰落，并且新任国王也不那么热衷于战争了。在1759年至1760年这两年间，腓特烈大帝仍然领导着自己那个小小的王国，与联合起来反对他的那些大国做着殊死而筋疲力尽的斗争。曾经有一段时间，他的情况看上去极为不妙，以至于他都准备自杀了；不过，战争持续进行，让法国把注意力转移到英国和海洋上去了。

  进行大规模殖民远征的时候很快就到来了，它使得此次战争的最后一年，因英国的制海权战胜了法、西两国的联合力量而变得非凡无比。首先，我们有必要叙述一下英国

It is first necessary to tell the entirely kindred story of the effect of that sea power in the East Indian peninsula.

The recall of Dupleix and the entire abandonment of his policy, which resulted in placing the two East India companies on equal terms, have already been told. The treaty stipulations of 1754 had not, however, been fully carried out. The Marquis de Bussy, a brave and capable soldier who had been a second to Dupleix, and was wholly in accord with his policy and ambitions, remained in the Deccan, — a large region in the southern central part of the peninsula, over which Dupleix had once ruled. In 1756, troubles arose between the English and the native prince in Bengal. The nabob of that province had died, and his successor, a young man of nineteen, attacked Calcutta. The place fell, after a weak resistance, in June, and the surrender was followed by the famous tragedy known as that of the Black Hole of Calcutta. The news reached Madras in August, and Clive, whose name has already been mentioned, sailed with the fleet of Admiral Watson, after a long and vexatious delay. The fleet entered the river in December and appeared before Calcutta in January, when the place fell into English hands again as easily as it had been lost.

The nabob was very angry, and marched against the English; sending meanwhile an invitation to the French at Chandernagore to join him. Although it was now known that England and France were at war, the French company, despite the experience of 1744, weakly hoped that peace might be kept between it and the English. The native invitation was therefore refused, and offers of neutrality made to the other company. Clive marched out, met the Indian forces and defeated them, and the nabob at once asked for peace, and sought the English alliance, yielding all the claims on the strength of which he had first attacked Calcutta. After some demur his offers were accepted. Clive and Watson then turned upon Chandernagore and

这种制海权在东印度半岛发挥作用的整个过程。

杜普雷被召回法国后，他的政策也被彻底抛弃，使得英、法两家东印度公司获得了平等的地位，这一点前面已经叙述过了。然而，1754年所签条约的规定并未完全得到了执行。马奎斯·德·比西是一位英勇而能干的战士，曾经是杜普雷的副手，并且全心全意支持杜普雷的政策与雄心，他此时仍然留在德干高原上——这是印度半岛南部中央杜普雷曾经统治过的一个广袤地区。1756年，孟加拉的英国人与当地贵族发生了纠纷。该省的地方长官已经去世，而其继任者是一个19岁的年轻人，他率军进攻了加尔各答。进行了无力的抵抗之后，该地于6月被攻陷了；而投降之后，就发生了一件著名的惨案，史称"加尔各答黑洞"[2]。这一消息于8月传到了马德拉斯，前面已经提及的那位克莱夫，便随沃森上将所率的舰队，经过了漫长而令人烦恼的耽搁之后出发了。12月，这支舰队驶入了孟加拉河，并于第二年1月兵临加尔各答城下；随后，该地又像之前被攻陷那样，轻而易举地回到了英国人手中。

孟加拉省那位新任地方长官恼羞成怒，便率军前去攻打英军；与此同时，他还派人去要求位于金德纳格尔的法军参战。尽管此时英、法两国正在交战这一事实已是尽人皆知，但法属东印度公司却无视1744年的教训，怯懦地指望着该公司与英国人之间仍然可以和平相处。因此，该公司拒绝了当地土著的要求，并且向英属东印度公司表示中立。克莱夫便率军出击，与印度军队狭路相逢，并击败了印度军队；那位地方长官马上求和，想与英国结成盟友，完全放弃了起初进攻加尔各答时提出的所有要求。英军在遭遇了内部的一些反对意见之后，还是接受了他的这一提议。克莱夫和沃森随后便转而进攻

compelled the surrender of the French settlement.

The nabob, who had not meant to allow this, took umbrage, and entered into correspondence with Bussy in the Deccan. Clive had full knowledge of his various intrigues, which were carried on with the vacillation of a character as weak as it was treacherous; and seeing no hope of settled peace or trade under the rule of this man, entered into an extensive conspiracy for his dethronement, the details of which need not be given. The result was that war broke out again, and that Clive with three thousand men, one third of whom were English, met the nabob at the head of fifteen thousand horse and thirty-five thousand foot. The disproportion in artillery was nearly as great. Against these odds was fought and won the battle of Plassey, on the 23d of June, 1757, — the date from which, by common consent, the British empire in India is said to begin. The overthrow of the nabob was followed by placing in power one of the conspirators against him, a creature of the English, and dependent upon them for support. Bengal thus passed under their control, the first-fruits of India. "Clive," says a French historian, "had understood and applied the system of Dupleix."

This was true; yet even so it may be said that the foundation thus laid could never have been kept nor built upon, had the English nation not controlled the sea. The conditions of India were such that a few Europeans, headed by men of nerve and shrewdness, dividing that they might conquer, and advancing their fortunes by judicious alliances, were able to hold their own, and more too, amidst overwhelming numerical odds; but it was necessary that they should not be opposed by men of their own kind, a few of whom could turn the wavering balance the other way. At the very time that Clive was acting in Bengal, Bussy invaded Orissa, seized the English factories, and made himself master of much of the coast regions between Madras and Calcutta; while a French squadron of nine ships, most of which, however, belonged to the East

金德纳格尔，迫使这个法属殖民地不得不缴械投降了。

那位地方长官并不允许英军这样做，所以心中恼怒，便与身处德干高原的比西联系。克莱夫已经料定他会耍各种各样的阴谋诡计，因为这个人性格使然，在耍阴谋诡计的时候总是犹豫不决、摇摆不定，既软弱无能，又奸巧狡诈；看到在这个人的统治之下，英国无望与之和平相处或者安稳地进行贸易之后，克莱夫便开始制定一个巨大的计谋，想要将这个地方长官赶下台去，其详细情况我们自然无需赘述。结果便是战争再次爆发，克莱夫率领3000士兵，其中三分之一为英国人，与那位地方长官所率的15000骑兵和35000步兵对垒。双方拥有的火炮数量，几乎跟他们之间的兵力一样悬殊。尽管困难重重，但英军还是赢得了1757年6月23日的这场普拉西之战——人们一致认为，英国在印度建立起来的那个帝国，据说就是从这个时候开始的。推翻了那位地方长官的统治之后，英军便扶持了密谋反对者中的一位上台掌权；这个人完全是英国人的走狗，离不开英国人的支持。孟加拉就这样转到了英国的掌控之下，也成了英国在印度的最初收获。"克莱夫，"一位法国历史学家说，"理解并应用了杜普雷的政策。"

确实如此；不过，即便如此，我们还是可以说，倘若英国没有掌控海洋，那么如此打下的基础，英国既不可能维持下去，也不可能加以依赖。虽说印度的形势如此，使得在一些勇敢、精明之人的领导下分散开来攻城掠地，并审慎寻找盟友以加速其成功的少数欧洲人，能够在无数机遇中抓住自己和其他更多人的命运，但必不可少的一个前提就是，他们不能自相残杀，因为一少撮自己人就能让本已摇摆不定的天平倒向另一个方向。正当克莱夫在孟加拉作战时，比西侵入了奥里萨邦，占领了英国人的工厂，掌控了

India Company and were not first-rate men-of-war, was on its way to Pondicherry with twelve hundred regular troops, — an enormous European army for Indian operations of that day. The English naval force on the coast, though fewer in numbers, may be considered about equal to the approaching French squadron. It is scarcely too much to say that the future of India was still uncertain, and the first operations showed it.

The French division appeared off the Coromandel coast to the southward of Pondicherry on the 26th of April, 1758, and anchored on the 28th before the English station called Fort St. David. Two ships kept on to Pondicherry, having on board the new governor, Comte de Lally, who wished to go at once to his seat of government. Meanwhile, the English admiral, Pocock, having news of his enemy's coming, and fearing specially for this post, was on his way to it, and appeared on the 29th of April, before the two ships with the governor were out of sight. The French at once got under way and stood out to sea on the starboard tack, heading to the northward and eastward, the wind being southeast, and signals were made to recall the ship and frigate escorting Lally; but they were disregarded by the latter's order, an act which must have increased, if it did not originate, the ill-will between him and Commodore D'Aché, through which the French campaign in India miscarried. The English, having formed to windward on the same tack as the French, made their attack in the then usual way, and with the usual results. The seven English ships were ordered to keep away together for the French eight, and the four leading ships, including the admiral's, came into action handsomely; the last three, whether by their own fault or not, were late in doing so, but it will be remembered that this was almost always the case in such attacks. The French commodore, seeing this interval between the van and the rear, formed the plan of separating them, and made signal to wear together, but in his impatience did not wait for an answer. Putting his own helm up, he wore round, and was

马德拉斯和加尔各答之间的大片沿海地区。同时，一支由9艘舰船组成的法国舰队——然而，因为其中大部分舰船都属于东印度公司，所以都不是一流的战舰——也带着一支1200人的常规陆军部队，往庞迪切里而来；那个时候，这可算是在印度作战的一支庞大的欧洲陆军了。驻庞迪切里沿海的英国海军虽说兵力较少，但我们可以认为其实力与即将到来的法国舰队差不多旗鼓相当。此时，说印度的未来仍然多变不定，无论怎么说也不过分，因为最初的交战便表明了这一点。

1758年4月26日，法国舰队抵达了庞迪切里南边的科罗曼德尔海域，并于28日在英军的圣大卫堡基地外泊了锚。有两艘舰船继续前往庞迪切里，新任总督德·拉利伯爵也在船上，他希望马上赶到自己的任所。在此期间，英军的波考克上将得知了敌人正在前来的消息，因为特别担忧这一据点，所以也正在赶来，并于4月29日抵达了圣大卫堡，看到了乘有法国总督的那两艘舰船。法军马上出动，右舷抢风出港，朝北方和东方而行，此时正刮东南风，法军还发出信号，提醒护送拉利伯爵的那两艘军舰和护卫舰；不过，拉利下令不要理睬，他的这一做法就算不是导致他和德阿克准将之间相互嫌恶的原因，也势必加重了二人之间的怨气，从而使得法国在印度的战役失败了。英国舰队已经跟法国人一样右舷抢风列好了阵势，用那时常见的方式发动了进攻，也收到了常见的效果。7艘英舰受命散开，拦住了法国的8艘战舰，而4艘领先的战舰，包括波考克上将的座舰，则井然有序地投入了战斗；最后3艘呢，不管是否因为其自身的过错，反正没有及时参战，不过我们要记住，在此种进攻中这种现象是常有的事。法军准将德阿克看到英军前锋与后卫之间留有空挡，便制定了将英军分隔开来的计划，并且发出了一起转向下风的信号；不过，因为他太过性

followed in succession by the rear ships, while the van stood on. The English admiral, who had good reason to know, gives D'Aché more credit than the French writers, for he describes this movement thus: —

"At half-past four P.M. the rear of the French line had drawn pretty close up to their flagship. Our three rear ships were signalled to engage closer. Soon after, M. D'Aché broke the line, and put before the wind; his second astern, who had kept on the 'Yarmouth's' [English flag-ship] quarter most part of the action, then came up alongside, gave his fire, and then bore away; and a few minutes after, the enemy's van bore away also."

By this account, which is by no means irreconcilable with the French, the latter effected upon the principal English ship a movement of concentration by defiling past her. The French now stood down to their two separated ships, while the English vessels that had been engaged were too much crippled to follow. This battle prevented the English fleet from relieving Fort St. David, which surrendered on the 2d of June.

After the fall of this place, the two opposing squadrons having refitted at their respective ports and resumed their station, a second action was fought in August, under nearly the same conditions and in much the same fashion. The French flag-ship met with a series of untoward accidents, which determined the commodore to withdraw from action; but the statement of his further reasons is most suggestive of the necessary final overthrow of the French cause. "Prudence," a writer of his own country says, "commanded him not to prolong a contest from which his ships could not but come out with injuries very difficult to repair in a region where it was impossible to supply the almost entire lack of spare stores." This want of so absolute a requisite for naval efficiency shows in a strong light the fatal tendency of that economy which always characterized French operations at sea, and was at once significant and

急,所以等不及部下做出回应,便将自己的座舰满舵掉头转向下风,后卫舰船纷纷跟随,可前锋舰船却还是保留着原有的航向。英国的波考克上将亲历并且完全了解这次海战,他对德阿克准将的评价比法国作家的评价更高,因为他是如此描述这次海战的:

"下午四点半,法军阵列中的后卫离他们的旗舰已经相当近了。我方的3艘后卫战舰收到了近距离交战的信号。不久之后,主帅德阿克改换了阵形,开始顺风航行;他后面的第二艘军舰,在战斗中的大多数时间都处于'雅茅斯'号(即英军的旗舰)的尾舷方向,此时靠拢过来,开了火,然后便转向了下风;几分钟过后,敌人的前锋舰船也都转向下风了。"

这一描述绝非与法国人的描述相矛盾;从中可以看出,法军是想通过排成纵队超过英军,从而让英军的主舰进行集结机动。此时法军已经顺风驶向他们那两艘落了单的战舰,而参战的英军舰船则受损严重,无法追击了。此战使得英国舰队并没有减轻圣大卫堡的压力,所以6月2日圣大卫堡便投降了。

此地陷落之后,双方舰队便在各自的港口进行了整修,分别返回了基地,并于8月在差不多相同的条件下、以差不多相同的方式爆发了第二次战斗。法军的旗舰遭遇了一系列不幸的意外,使得德阿克准将决定撤出战斗;不过,对其深层原因的剖析,却极其含蓄地表明了法国的目标最终必然会被英国粉碎的这种结局。"节俭,"一位法国作家曾说,"使得他不会长久作战,以免最后自己手下的舰船受损严重,因为这种受损,在印度这个差不多完全没有富余材料可提供的地区,是很难维修的。"连海军作战所必需的维修保障都没有,这就极其明显地表现出了法国人那种致命的节俭之性;而此种节俭习气,始终都是法国人进行海战的一大特色,同时也是一种重大而不利的特色。

ominous.

Returning to Pondicherry, D'Aché found that, though the injuries to the masts and rigging could for this time be repaired, there was lack of provisions, and that the ships needed calking. Although his orders were to remain on the coast until October 15, he backed himself with the opinion of a council of war which decided that the ships could not remain there longer, because, in case of a third battle, there was neither rigging nor supplies remaining in Pondicherry; and disregarding the protests of the governor, Lally, he sailed on the 2d of September for the Isle of France. The underlying motive of D'Aché, it is known, was hostility to the governor, with whom he quarrelled continually. Lally, deprived of the help of the squadron, turned his arms inland instead of against Madras.

Upon arriving at the islands, D'Aché found a state of things which again singularly illustrates the impotence and short-sightedness characteristic of the general naval policy of the French at this time. His arrival there was as unwelcome as his departure from India had been to Lally. The islands were then in a state of the most complete destitution. The naval division, increased by the arrival of three ships-of-the-line from home, so exhausted them that its immediate departure was requested of the commodore. Repairs were pushed ahead rapidly, and in November several of the ships sailed to the Cape of Good Hope, then a Dutch colony, to seek provisions; but these were consumed soon after being received, and the pressure for the departure of the squadron was renewed. The situation of the ships was no less precarious than that of the colony; and accordingly the commodore replied by urging his entire lack of food and supplies. The condition was such that, a little later, it was necessary to make running rigging out of the cables, and to put some of the ships on the bottom, so as to give their materials to others. Before returning to India, D'Aché wrote to the minister of the navy that

返回庞迪切里之后，德阿克发现，尽管此战中受损的桅杆和索具这一次可以维修好，但没有给养，而且所有舰船还得填隙防水才行。虽然他下令舰队在沿海地区坚持到10月15日，但他召开了一次作战会议，会议认为，这些舰船不可能在此坚持那么久的时间，因为万一发生第三次海战，庞迪切里就既无索具，也无给养了；于是，他便以此为由，不顾总督拉利伯爵的抗议，于9月2日率领舰队起航往法兰西岛而去了。人们都知道，德阿克此举的潜在原因，是因为他经常跟拉利总督发生争执，从而对后者心怀敌意。而拉利总督由于没有了舰队的支援，便率军向内陆进发，不再攻打马德拉斯了。

抵达法兰西群岛之后，德阿克的处境便再一次奇特地说明了法国在这个时候所采取的一般性海军政策，是多么的无效和鼠目寸光。该地并不欢迎他的到来，就像拉利总督不想让他离开印度那样。法兰西群岛当时正处在一种几乎赤贫的形势之中。德阿克所率的这支海军，加上国内又派来的那3艘战舰，已让各岛不堪重负，于是他们便要求德阿克准将立即率军离开。因此维修工作不得不在仓促之中进行；到了11月，数艘舰船便驶往当时仍为荷属殖民地的好望角寻求补给去了。不过，得到的给养很快便被消耗完了，所以诸岛又开始催促舰队离开。这些舰船的处境，跟印度这个殖民地的处境一样岌岌可危；因此，德阿克准将只得强调自己完全没有食物和给养，以此来回复诸岛民众。不久之后，情况变得更糟，他们只能用锚索来做活动吊索，只能将一些船只清空，好把上面的部件用于其他舰船了。在回印度去之前，德阿克给海军大臣写了一封信，说他"打算离开，只是为了不让船员饿死，并且倘若不送给养过来，就不要指望这支舰队能够完成什么任务，因为这支舰队的人员和情况都糟糕透顶。"

he "was about to leave, only to save the crews from dying of hunger, and that nothing need be expected from the squadron if supplies were not sent, for both men and things were in a deplorable state."

Under these circumstances D'Aché sailed from the islands in July, 1759, and arrived off the Coromandel coast in September. During his year of absence Lally had besieged Madras for two months, during the northeast monsoon. Both squadrons were absent, that season being unfit for naval operations on this coast; but the English returned first, and are said by the French to have caused, by the English to have hastened, the raising of the siege. D'Aché, upon his return, was much superior in both number and size of ships; but when the fleets met, Pocock did not hesitate to attack with nine against eleven. This action, fought September 10, 1759, was as indecisive as the two former; but D'Aché retreated, after a very bloody contest. Upon it Campbell, in his "Lives of the Admirals," makes a droll, but seemingly serious, comment: "Pocock had reduced the French ships to a very shattered condition, and killed a great many of their men; but what shows the singular talents of both admirals, they had fought three pitched battles in eighteen months without the loss of a ship on either side." The fruits of victory, however, were with the weaker fleet; for D'Aché returned to Pondicherry and thence sailed on the 1st of the next month for the islands, leaving India to its fate. From that time the result was certain. The English continued to receive reinforcements from home, while the French did not; the men opposed to Lally were superior in ability; place after place fell, and in January, 1761, Pondicherry itself surrendered, surrounded by land and cut off from the sea. This was the end of the French power in India; for though Pondicherry and other possessions were restored at the peace, the English tenure there was never again shaken, even under the attacks of the skilful and bold Suffren, who twenty years later met difficulties as great

就是在这样的形势下，德阿克于1759年7月从法兰西群岛率领舰队起航，并于9月抵达了科罗曼德尔沿海。在他离开的这一年里，拉利总督曾经在东北季风期包围了马德拉斯两个月。双方舰队都不在场，因为那个季节此处沿海并不适于进行海战；但英国舰队先返回来，据法国人称，正是英国舰队率先赶回来，才解了马德拉斯之围。德阿克返回印度之后，在兵力和战舰规模两个方面都大大胜过了英国舰队；可当两支舰队遭遇之后，波考克却毫不犹豫地率领9艘战舰对法国的11艘战舰发动了攻击。此战发生于1759年9月10日，跟前两次海战一样并无决定性意义；不过，这一次是德阿克在经过了一场殊死搏斗之后又撤退了。关于此战，坎贝尔在《海军上将生平》一书中，曾经进行过虽说诙谐、表面上却很严肃的评论："波考克将法国舰船打得七零八落，并且歼灭了大量敌军；不过，体现出了双方司令非凡天才的是，他们在18个月内打了3场高调的海战，双方却没有损失一艘船只。"然而，胜利的果实却由实力较弱的那支舰队来享受；因为德阿克返回了庞迪切里，并在10月1日从此处起航驶往了法兰西群岛，任由印度自生自灭去了。从那个时候起，印度半岛的结局就已经定下来了。英军不断得到国内的支援，而法军却没有；跟拉利伯爵打仗的人，都比这位总督有能力得多；所以，各地接连陷落，而到了1761年1月，庞迪切里也因为陆上被包围、海上被封锁而投降了。法国统治印度的历史就此终结；尽管后来法国根据和约收回了庞迪切里和其他殖民地，但英国占有印度的局面却再也没有动摇过。即便是受到经验丰富、勇猛无畏的苏弗朗进攻时，形势也没有什么改观；20年之后，苏弗朗在印度遇到的重重困难都与德阿克一样，但他表现出来的那种气势和品德，德阿克在此时形势更为乐观的情况下，却并未表现出来。

as D'Aché's with a vigor and conduct which the latter at a more hopeful moment failed to show.

France having thus lost both Canada and India by the evident failure of her power to act at a distance by sea, it would seem scarcely possible that Spain, with her own weak navy and widely scattered possessions, would choose this moment for entering the war. Yet so it was. The maritime exhaustion of France was plain to all, and is abundantly testified to by her naval historians. "The resources of France were exhausted," says one; "the year 1761 saw only a few single ships leave her ports, and all of them were captured. The alliance with Spain came too late. The occasional ships that went to sea in 1762 were taken, and the colonies still remaining to France could not be saved." Even as early as 1758, another Frenchman writes, "want of money, the depression of commerce given over to English cruisers, the lack of good ships, the lack of supplies, etc., compelled the French ministry, unable to raise large forces, to resort to stratagems, to replace the only rational system of war, Grand War, by the smallest of petty wars, — by a sort of game in which the great aim is not to be caught. Even then, the arrival of four ships-of-the-line at Louisburg, by avoiding the enemy, was looked on as a very fortunate event. ... In 1759 the lucky arrival of the West India convoy caused as much surprise as joy to the merchants. We see how rare had become such a chance in seas ploughed by the squadrons of England." This was before the disasters of La Clue and Conflans. The destruction of French commerce, beginning by the capture of its merchant-ships, was consummated by the reduction of the colonies. It can hardly, therefore, be conceded that the Family Compact now made between the two courts, containing, as it did, not only an agreement to support each other in any future war, but also a secret clause binding Spain to declare war against England within a year, if peace were not made, "was honorable to the wisdom of the two governments." It is hard to

这样一来，由于海军明显无法在距本国很远的海域作战，法国非但丢了加拿大，还丢了印度，所以本国海军实力也很弱、殖民地又遍布世界各地的西班牙，似乎不可能选择在这个时候参战。然而，西班牙却参战了。法国海军实力的衰落，世人都清楚得很，并且法国海军历史学家们也都充分地证实了这一点。"法国的资源已经枯竭，"有位海军历史学家称，"1761年法国只有为数寥寥的舰船离港出海，并且全都被英国俘虏了。法国与西班牙结成同盟，已经太迟。1762年偶尔出海的那些舰船，也都被英国夺走了，所以此时仍然属于法国的那些殖民地，是不可能幸免的。"甚至早在1758年，另一位法国人也曾写道："缺乏资金，由于英国巡逻舰船的袭扰而导致的贸易萧条、没有优质舰船、缺乏装备补给等等，都迫使无法招募大规模兵力的法国政府不得不从策略方面去想办法，把进行大规模作战这种唯一合理的战争方法，变成一系列规模最小的小型战争——变成一种最高目标就是避免被俘的游戏。就连4艘战舰避开敌人抵达了路易斯堡，都被认为是一件极其幸运的事情……1759年那支护航队幸运地到达了西印度群岛，让法国的商人既高兴，又惊讶。我们知道，英国舰队在海洋上横冲直撞的时代，此种机会是多么的珍贵。"这还是在拉·克鲁和孔夫兰惨败之前的情况。法国海上贸易的覆灭过程，始于其商船被英国俘获，以其殖民地数量减少而告终。因此，对于此时法、西两国王室所签订的《家族盟约》——事实上，盟约中既包括了一项在未来的任何战争中相互支援的协定，还含有一项秘密条款，规定倘若一年后英、法两国还未停战议和，那么西班牙就必须对英宣战，因此，我们很难承认这份盟约"是为两国政府的明智增了光"。对于西班牙政府，甚至还有法国诱惑一个同宗的民族加入这样一桩糟糕交易的做

pardon, not only the Spanish government, but even France for alluring a kindred people into such a bad bargain. It was hoped, however, to revive the French navy and to promote an alliance of neutral powers; many of which, besides Spain, had causes of complaint against England. "During the war with France," confesses an English historian, "the Spanish flag had not always been respected by British cruisers." "During 1758," says another, "not less than one hundred and seventy-six neutral vessels, laden with the rich produce of the French colonies or with military or naval stores, fell into the hands of the English." The causes were already at work which twenty years later gave rise to the "armed neutrality" of the Baltic powers, directed against the claims of England on the sea. The possession of unlimited power, as the sea power of England then really was, is seldom accompanied by a profound respect for the rights of others. Without a rival upon the ocean, it suited England to maintain that enemy's property was liable to capture on board neutral ships, thus subjecting these nations not only to vexatious detentions, but to loss of valuable trade; just as it had suited her earlier in the war to establish a paper blockade of French ports. Neutrals of course chafed under these exactions; but the year 1761 was ill-chosen for an armed protest, and of all powers Spain risked most by a war. England had then one hundred and twenty ships-of-the-line in commission, besides those in reserve, manned by seventy thousand seamen trained and hardened by five years of constant warfare afloat, and flushed with victory. The navy of France, which numbered seventy-seven ships-of-the-line in 1758, lost as prizes to the English in 1759 twenty-seven, besides eight destroyed and many frigates lost; indeed, as has been seen, their own writers confess that the navy was ruined, root and branch. The Spanish navy contained about fifty ships; but the personnel, unless very different from the days before and after, must have been very inferior. The weakness of her empire, in the absence of an efficient navy, has before been pointed out. Neutrality, too, though

法，我们也很难原谅。然而，两国希望以此来复兴法国的海军实力，并且促成一个中立同盟；除了西班牙，还有很多国家都对英国感到不满。"在英、法战争期间，"一位英国历史学家承认，"英国的巡逻舰船一向都没有尊重西班牙的主权。"另一位历史学家则称："在1758年这一年里，有不下于176艘装载法属殖民地丰富物产或海陆军备的中立国船只落入了英国手中。"这些原因此时已经产生了作用，从而导致波罗的海各国在20年后组成了"武装中立"，来对抗英国的海上强权。无限权力之拥有，很少是通过极其尊重他人的权利而获得的；当时英国的制海权实际上就是这样一种无限之权力。由于在海洋上所向无敌，所以英国自然会认为中立国船只所装载的敌方物资应当夺取，从而使得这些国家非但要忍受本国船只被扣押的烦恼，而且还失去了宝贵的贸易机会；英国在此战早期，曾宣布对法国诸港进行纸上封锁，体现的也正是这种理所当然的态度。这些巧取豪夺的做法，自然会激怒各个中立国；不过，它们选择在1761年进行武装对抗，时机却并不合适，而在这些国家中，西班牙因为直接参战，所以冒的风险最大。当时英国有120艘现役军舰，还有一些备用舰船，装备了70000名训练有素的水兵，他们在过去5年来不断进行的海战中都得到了锻炼，成了久经沙场的老手，并且因节节取胜而意气风发。法国海军在1758年时拥有77艘战舰，而在1759年有27艘为英国所俘，还被击毁了8艘，损失了许多护卫舰；实际上，正如我们已经看到的那样，法国的作家也都承认，此时法国海军已经彻底覆灭了。西班牙海军拥有大约50艘舰船；但在人员配备上，除非与此前或后来的情况大相径庭，否则就必定是非常之差。西班牙帝国因为没有一支强有力的海军，所以衰弱得很，这一点，我们在前面已经指出过了。保持中立，虽说有时候

at times outraged, had been of great advantage to her, permitting her to restore her finances and trade and to re-establish her internal resources; but she needed a still longer period of it. Nevertheless, the king, influenced by family feeling and resentment against England, allowed himself to be drawn on by the astute Choiseul, and the Family Compact between the two crowns was signed on the 15th of August, 1761. This compact, into which the King of Naples was also to enter, guaranteed their mutual possessions by the whole power of both kingdoms. This in itself was a weighty undertaking; but the secret clause further stipulated that Spain should declare war against England on the 1st of May, 1762, if peace with France had not then been made. Negotiations of this character could not be kept wholly secret, and Pitt learned enough to convince him that Spain was becoming hostile in intention. With his usual haughty resolve, he determined to forestall her by declaring war; but the influence against him in the councils of the new king was too strong. Failing to carry the ministry with him, he resigned on the 5th of October, 1761. His prevision was quickly justified; Spain had been eager in professing good-will until the treasure-ships from America should arrive laden with the specie so needed for carrying on war. On the 21st of September the Flota of galleons anchored safely in Cadiz; and on the 2d of November the British ambassador announced to his government that "two ships had safely arrived with very extraordinary rich cargoes from the West Indies, so that all the wealth that was expected from Spanish America is now safe in old Spain," and in the same despatch reports a surprising change in the words of the Spanish minister, and the haughty language now used. The grievances and claims of Spain were urged peremptorily, and the quarrel grew so fast that even the new English ministry, though ardently desiring peace, recalled their ambassador before the end of the year, and declared war on the 4th of January, 1762; thus adopting Pitt's policy, but too late to reap the advantages at which he had aimed.

让该国备受欺凌，但也有着巨大的好处，可以让该国恢复金融和贸易业，并且重新部署国内的各种资源；不过，该国还需要更长的一段时期才能做到这一点。尽管如此，西班牙国王出于家族感情和对英国的怨恨，还是任由狡猾的舒瓦瑟尔牵着鼻子走，所以法、西两国便于1761年8月15日签署了《家族盟约》。那不勒斯国王也加入了这一盟约；盟约规定，法、西两国都应举全国之力，来保护两国的共同财产。这本身是一种意义重大的承诺，但盟约中的秘密条款却进而规定，倘若英、法之间在1762年5月1日还未议和，那么西班牙就应当在此日对英宣战。此种性质的谈判是不可能做到完全神不知鬼不觉的，所以皮特很快就得知并确信，西班牙正准备对英国图谋不轨。带着他惯常的那种高傲之气，皮特决定先发制人，对西班牙宣战；不过，新任国王手下幕僚们反对他的势力实在是太过强大了。由于没能争取到内阁的支持，皮特便于1761年10月5日辞去了职务。他的先见之明很快便得到了印证；虽然西班牙一直都急切地宣称它与英国关系亲善，可一旦发动战争所急需的资金由宝船从美洲运送到国内，该国马上就变脸了。9月21日，西班牙的帆船舰队安全泊靠加的斯；而在11月2日，英国大使对政府报告称，"有两艘船，携带着西印度群岛异常丰富的货物安全抵达了西班牙，使得西班牙期待着的西属美洲的全部财富，如今都安然运送到了国内，"而在同一批到达的报告中，西班牙公使的口气也发生了惊人的变化，因为此时他的语气开始变得傲慢无礼了。西班牙盛气凌人地强调自己的不平之气，并坚持自己的要求；两国间的争端发展得如此之快，以至于英国新上任的这一届政府内阁虽说极为渴望和平，也不得不在是年年底前召回了驻西班牙大使，并于1762年1月4日对西班牙宣战；这样一来，他们便采纳了皮特的政策，只不过有点太晚，达不到皮特所力求的效果了。

However, no such delay on the part of England could alter the essential inequality, in strength and preparation, between the two nations. The plans formed by Pitt were in the main adopted by his successor, and carried out with a speed which the readiness of the English navy permitted. On the 5th of March, Pocock, who had returned from the East Indies, sailed from Portsmouth, convoying a fleet of transports to act against Havana; in the West Indies he was reinforced from the forces in that quarter, so that his command contained nineteen ships-of-the-line besides smaller vessels, and ten thousand soldiers.

In the previous January, the West India fleet, under the well-known Rodney, had acted with the land forces in the reduction of Martinique, the gem and tower of the French islands and the harbor of an extensive privateering system. It is said that fourteen hundred English merchantmen were taken during this war in the West Indian seas by cruisers whose principal port was Fort Royal in Martinique. With this necessary base fell also the privateering system resting upon it. Martinique was surrendered February 12, and the loss of this chief commercial and military centre was immediately followed by that of the smaller islands, Grenada, Sta. Lucia, St. Vincent. By these acquisitions the English colonies at Antigua, St. Kitts, and Nevis, as well as the ships trading to those islands, were secured against the enemy, the commerce of England received large additions, and all the Lesser Antilles, or Windward Islands, became British possessions.

Admiral Pocock was joined off Cape St. Nicholas by the West Indian reinforcement on the 27th of May, and as the season was so far advanced, he took his great fleet through the old Bahama channel instead of the usual route around the south side of Cuba. This was justly considered a great feat in those days of poor surveys, and was accomplished without an accident. Lookout and sounding vessels went first, frigates followed, and boats

然而，英国的这种延误，决不会改变两国间在力量和准备方面那种根本性的势不均、力不敌的情况。皮特的后任基本上采纳了他所制定的政策，并且以英国海军做好准备所允许的速度实施着。3月5日，已从东印度群岛返回英国的波考克，率军从朴茨茅斯起航，护送着一支运兵船队，前去攻打哈瓦那；到了西印度群岛之后，他又得到了当地驻军的支援，故此时他所指挥的，已是一支拥有19艘战舰、一些小型舰船以及10000兵力的大军了。

在之前的1月份，赫赫有名的罗德尼曾指挥西印度舰队，携同陆军攻取了马提尼克；马提尼克是法属诸岛中最重要的一处堡垒，也是法国那些覆盖面广的私掠船只的庇护所。据说在此次战争期间，有1400艘英国商船在西印度群岛海域被法国的巡逻舰俘虏，而这些巡逻舰的主要港口，便是马提尼克岛上的皇家要塞。随着这一不可或缺的基地而陷落的，还有依赖这一基地的那种私掠制度。马提尼克于2月12日投降，而丢掉了这个主要的贸易和军事中心之后，格林纳达、圣卢西亚和圣文森特这些较小的岛屿随即也纷纷陷落了。占领了这些地方后，英国在安提瓜岛、圣基茨岛和尼维斯岛上的殖民地，以及与这些岛屿之间进行贸易的英国舰船，便都可以用来对付敌人了；英国的商业贸易也得到了大幅加强，而小安的列斯群岛或温德华群岛，则全都变成了英国的殖民地。

5月27日，波考克上将在圣尼古拉斯角海域与西印度群岛的援军汇合了；由于季节已晚，他便率领这支庞大的舰队穿过了原来的巴哈马海峡，而没有沿着惯常所走的、绕过古巴南边的那条水路。在勘测工作很落后的那个时代，人们完全有理由认为这是一种伟大的壮举，因为舰队没出任何意外地通过了这条海峡。侦察船和测深船先行，护卫舰随后，而小型船只或单桅帆船则停泊在浅水区，并且昼夜都分别有一套精心布置的旗

or sloops were anchored on shoals with carefully arranged signals for day or night. Having good weather, the fleet got through in a week and appeared before Havana. The operations will not be given in detail. After a forty days' siege the Moro Castle was taken on the 30th of July, and the city surrendered on the 10th of August. The Spaniards lost not only the city and port, but twelve ships-of-the-line, besides £3,000,000 in money and merchandise belonging to the Spanish king. The importance of Havana was not to be measured only by its own size, or its position as centre of a large and richly cultivated district; it was also the port commanding the only passage by which the treasure and other ships could sail from the Gulf of Mexico to Europe in those days. With Havana in an enemy's hands it would be necessary to assemble them at Cartagena and from there beat up against the trade-winds, — an operation always difficult, and which would keep ships long in waters where they were exposed to capture by English cruisers. Not even an attack upon the isthmus would have been so serious a blow to Spain. This important result could only be achieved by a nation confident of controlling the communications by its sea power, to which the happy issue must wholly be ascribed, and which had another signal illustration in the timely conveying of four thousand American troops to reinforce the English ranks, terribly wasted by battle and fever. It is said that only twenty-five hundred serviceable fighting men remained on foot when the city fell.

While the long reach and vigor of England's sea power was thus felt in the West Indies, it was receiving further illustration in Portugal and in the far East. The allied crowns in the beginning had invited Portugal to join their alliance against those whom they had taken to calling the "tyrants of the seas," reminding her how the English monopoly of her trade was draining the country of gold, and recalling the deliberate violation of her neutrality by

语。由于天气状况良好，所以舰队一周内便穿过了海峡，出现在哈瓦那面前。接下来的战斗，我们无需详尽描述。总之，被围40天之后，莫罗城堡于7月30日被攻陷，而整个哈瓦那城也于8月10日投降了。西班牙人非但丢城弃港，还损失了12艘战舰，以及本属于西班牙国王的、价值300万英镑的现金和货物。哈瓦那的重要性，不能仅以其本身的大小来衡量，也不能仅以它位于一片广袤而作物丰富的地区的中心来衡量；因为它还是一处港口，扼守着当时的运宝船和其他船只从墨西哥湾前往欧洲的唯一通道。倘若哈瓦那位于敌人手里，这些船只就必须在卡塔赫纳集结，然后从那里出发，并且一路上与信风对抗——这一点，非但一向都困难重重，还会让这些船只长久地航行在极易被英国巡逻舰所俘虏的那些海域。在中美地峡还从未有过一场进袭，对西班牙的打击如此之严重。这一重大战果，只有一个自信能够通过其制海权掌控海上交通补给的国家才能实现；所以英国获得这样完美的结局，完全应当归功于其制海权，而将4000美洲兵力及时运送过去支援因战斗和热病而折损严重的英军，也是说明英国制海权的另一个显著例子。据说，攻陷哈瓦那城的时候，英军竟然只剩下2500名能够作战的士兵了。

尽管英国这种势力远达、强大有力的制海权在西印度群岛发挥了如此巨大的作用，但在葡萄牙和远东地区，该国制海权的作用则得到了进一步的说明。战争伊始，法、西这两个盟国就已邀请葡萄牙加入同盟，来共同对抗它们称之为"海洋暴君"的英国；两国提醒葡萄牙，英国垄断海上贸易后是如何榨取葡萄牙的黄金的，并让葡萄牙记起了博斯科恩指挥的舰队是如何故意侵害其中立权利的。当时的葡萄牙首相完全了解这一切，并且感受也很深切；不过，尽管这种邀请同时也明白无误地表明葡萄牙此后不能再继续保持

the fleet under Boscawen. The Portuguese minister of the day well knew all this, and keenly felt it; but though the invitation was accompanied by the plain statement that Portugal would not be allowed to continue a neutrality she could not enforce, he judged rightly that the country had more to fear from England and her fleet than from the Spanish army. The allies declared war and invaded Portugal. They were for a time successful; but the "tyrants of the seas" answered Portugal's call, sent a fleet and landed at Lisbon eight thousand soldiers, who drove the Spaniards over the frontiers, and even carried the war into Spain itself.

Simultaneous with these significant events, Manila was attacked. With so much already on hand, it was found impossible to spare troops or ships from England. The successes in India and the absolute security of the establishments there, with the control of the sea, allowed the Indian officials themselves to undertake this colonial expedition. It sailed in August, 1762, and reaching Malacca on the 19th, was supplied at that neutral port with all that was needed for the siege about to be undertaken; the Dutch, though jealous of the English advance, not venturing to refuse their demands. The expedition, which depended entirely upon the fleet, resulted in the whole group of Philippine Islands surrendering in October and paying a ransom of four million dollars. At about the same time the fleet captured the Acapulco galleon having three million dollars on board, and an English squadron in the Atlantic took a treasure-ship from Lima with four million dollars in silver for the Spanish government.

"Never had the colonial empire of Spain received such blows. Spain, whose opportune intervention might have modified the fate of the war, entered it too late to help France, but in time to share her misfortunes. There was reason to fear yet more. Panama and San Domingo were threatened, and the Anglo-Americans were preparing for the invasion of Florida and Louisiana. ... The conquest of Havana had in great measure interrupted the communications

中立——该国事实上也无能保持这种所谓的中立——但他还是正确地认为，相比于西班牙的陆军来说，英国以及英国舰队更令葡萄牙担忧。法、西盟军便宣战并入侵了葡萄牙。两国曾经一度节节取胜；但是，"海洋暴君"答应了葡萄牙的要求，派了一支舰队，运送8000陆军在里斯本登陆，将西班牙人赶过了边境，甚至还将战火烧到了西班牙本国境内。

在这些重大战事的同时，马尼拉却遭到了攻击。此时业已四面作战的英国，国内不可能再抽调出部队或舰船了。不过，由于英军在印度获得了胜利，并且通过掌控海洋而完全确保了此处殖民地的安全，所以驻印度的英军将领便可以开始此次殖民远征了。此处的英军于1762年8月起航，19日抵达了马六甲，并在这个中立港口获得了即将进行的围攻所必需的全部给养；荷兰人尽管忌惮英军的扩张，却不敢拒绝他们的要求。于是，这支完全依赖于舰队的远征军大获全胜，于10月攻克了整个菲律宾群岛，并且勒索了400万美元的赎金。大约也就在此时，英国舰队俘虏了装有300万美元的阿卡普尔科邮船[3]，而另一支分舰队还在大西洋上夺取了一艘从利马为西班牙政府运送400万美元银币的运宝船。

"西班牙所建立的殖民帝国，还从未受到过如此沉重的打击。倘若西班牙适时地加以干预，本来可以改变此次战争的结局，但它参战援助法国的时间太迟了，只落得个赶上了分担法国不幸的结局。然而，西班牙要担忧的，还远不止于此。巴拿马和圣多明哥都受到了威胁，而英裔美洲人也正准备入侵佛罗里达和路易斯安那……哈瓦那的陷落，在很大程度上中断了富裕的西属美洲殖民地与欧洲之间的交通联系。如今失去菲律宾群岛，又将西班牙排除在亚洲之外了。所以，这就严重地削减了西班牙的一切贸易收入，

between the wealthy American colonies of Spain and Europe. The reduction of the Philippine Islands now excluded her from Asia. The two together severed all the avenues of Spanish trade and cut off all intercourse between the parts of their vast but disconnected empire."

The selection of the points of attack, due to the ministry of Pitt, was strategically good, cutting effectually the sinews of the enemy's strength; and if his plans had been fully carried out and Panama also seized, the success would have been yet more decisive. England had lost also the advantage of the surprise he would have effected by anticipating Spain's declaration of war; but her arms were triumphant during this short contest, through the rapidity with which her projects were carried into execution, due to the state of efficiency to which her naval forces and administration had been brought.

With the conquest of Manila ended the military operations of the war. Nine months, counting from the formal declaration by England in January, had been sufficient to shatter the last hope of France, and to bring Spain to a peace in which was conceded every point on which she had based her hostile attitude and demands. It seems scarcely necessary, after even the brief summary of events that has been given, to point out that the speed and thoroughness with which England's work was done was due wholly to her sea power, which allowed her forces to act on distant points, widely apart as Cuba, Portugal, India, and the Philippines, without a fear of serious break in their communications.

Before giving the terms of peace which ought to summarize the results of the war, but do so imperfectly, owing to the weak eagerness of the English ministry to conclude it, it is necessary to trace in outline the effect of the war upon commerce, upon the foundations of sea power and national prosperity.

One prominent feature of this war may be more strongly impressed upon the mind by a startling, because paradoxical, statement that the prosperity of the English is shown by the

并且完全割断了其广袤却并不相连的殖民帝国各个地区的联系。"

对于进攻地点的选择，应当归功于皮特的手段；从战略角度来看，这些选择都是很不错的，都有效地切断了敌人实力所赖的主要资源；而他的计划倘若得到了充分实施，将巴拿马也攻取下来的话，那么这种胜利就将更具决定性意义了。英国也已失去了一次先机：皮特本来是打算抢先对西班牙宣战，打西班牙一个措手不及的；不过，英国军队还是通过快速执行所制定的计划，在这次短暂的战争中大获全胜，而这一点，无疑则应当归功于引领英国海军和英国政府的那种作战效率。

这次战争中的军事行动，以攻取马尼拉而告终。此战自1月份英国正式宣战始，历时9个月，足以粉碎法国的最后一丝幻想，并且让西班牙缔结和约，使它在每个方面做出让步，而这些方面正是让该国从态度和要求上都与英国为敌所倚赖的基础。即便是如此简要地总结了前述战事之后，我们似乎也没有必要再来指出，英国之所以能够迅速而彻底地实现自己的目标，完全在于该国掌控了制海权；正是这种制海权，使得英国的军队可以在距本国很遥远的地方作战，并且就算这些地方分散如古巴、葡萄牙、印度和菲律宾，也不用担心军队的交通补给跟不上。

在说明和约的条款——这些条款本来应当确定此次战争的结果，不过，由于英国政府并不急于缔结和约，因此在这一点上做得很不完善——之前，我们还必须概括勾勒一下此次战争对贸易、对制海权的基础和国家富强等方面所产生的影响。

此战的一个显著特点，可能就是下述这种因为矛盾而令人觉得极其震惊的说法：英

magnitude of their losses.

"From 1756 to 1760," states a French historian, "French privateers captured from the English more than twenty-five hundred merchantmen. In 1761, though France had not, so to speak, a single ship-of-the-line at sea, and though the English had taken two hundred and forty of our privateers, their comrades still took eight hundred and twelve English vessels. The explanation of the number of these prizes lies in the prodigious growth of the English shipping. In 1760 it is claimed that the English had at sea eight thousand sail; of these the French captured nearly one tenth, despite escorts and cruisers. In the four years from 1756 to 1760 the French lost only nine hundred and fifty vessels."

But this discrepancy is justly attributed by an English writer "to the diminution of the French commerce and the dread of falling into the hands of the English, which kept many of their trading-vessels from going to sea;" and he goes on to point out that the capture of vessels was not the principal benefit resulting from the efficiency of England's fleets. "Captures like Duquesne, Louisburg, Prince Edward's Island, the reduction of Senegal, and later on of Guadeloupe and Martinique, were events no less destructive to French commerce and colonies than advantageous to those of England." The multiplication of French privateers was indeed a sad token to an instructed eye, showing behind them merchant shipping in enforced idleness, whose crews and whose owners were driven to speculative pillage in order to live. Nor was this risk wholly in vain. The same Englishman confesses that in 1759 the losses of merchantmen showed a worse balance than the ships-of-war. While the French were striving in vain to regain equality upon the sea and repair their losses, but to no purpose, for "in building and arming vessels they labored only for the English fleet," yet, "notwithstanding the courage and vigilance of English cruisers, French privateers so swarmed that in this year they took

国在此战中所遭受的巨大损失，恰恰表现出了该国的繁荣富强。

"自1756年至1760年，"一位法国历史学家曾说，"法国的私掠者只从英国手中俘虏了2500多艘商船。1761年，尽管法国可以说没有派遣一艘战舰出海，尽管英国俘获了我国的240艘私掠船，但其他私掠者还是俘虏了812艘英国船只。这些战利品的数量，说明了英国航运业的惊人增长。1760年，据说英国有8000艘船只在海上航行；法国所俘获的，无论是护航舰还是巡逻舰，都仅占其中的十分之一。而在1756年至1760年这4年间，法国只损失了950艘舰船。"

不过，一位英国作家却将此种矛盾，合理地归因于"法国的商业贸易萎缩了，以及由于对落入英国手中心存恐惧，所以许多的贸易船只都并未出海"这两个原因；他还进一步指出，俘获船只并非是英国舰队发挥作用所导致的最重要的结果。"攻取像杜魁斯要塞、路易斯堡、爱德华王子岛这些地方，攻下塞内加尔以及后来的瓜达鲁佩和马提尼克，既让法国的贸易和殖民地全面覆灭，又有利于英国贸易和殖民地的发展。"法国私掠者的增加，在明眼人看来，实际上是一种可悲的预兆，表明其背后的商船运输业处于一种被迫的、无事可做的状态，表明其船员和船主们都不得不通过投机性的劫掠来活命。当然，这种冒险也并非全然一无用处。这位英国作家同时也承认，1759年英国商船的损失表现出了一种比战舰损失更不平衡的状况。虽说法国竭尽全力想要在海洋上重新与英国平起平坐并且弥补自己的损失，却完全是徒劳无用的，因为"他们建造和装备船只，不过都是为英国做嫁衣裳罢了"，但"尽管英国的巡逻舰船英勇而警惕，可法国私掠者众多，所以在这一年里，他们竟然俘获了240艘英国舰船，其中主要都是巡逻船和

two hundred and forty British vessels, chiefly coasters and small craft." In 1760 the same authority gives the British loss in trading-vessels at over three hundred, and in 1761 at over eight hundred, three times that of the French; but he adds: "It would not have been wonderful had they taken more and richer ships. While their commerce was nearly destroyed, and they had few merchant-ships at sea, the trading-fleets of England covered the seas. Every year her commerce was increasing; the money which the war carried out was returned by the produce of her industry. Eight thousand vessels were employed by the traders of Great Britain." The extent of her losses is attributed to three causes, of which the first only was preventable: 1. The inattention of merchant-ships to the orders of the convoying vessels; 2. The immense number of English ships in all seas; 3. The enemy's venturing the whole remains of his strength in privateering. During the same year, 1761, the navy lost one ship-of-the-line, which was retaken, and one cutter. At the same time, notwithstanding the various exchanges, the English still held twenty-five thousand French prisoners, while the English prisoners in France were but twelve hundred. These were the results of the sea war.

Finally, in summing up the commercial condition of the kingdom at the end of the war, after mentioning the enormous sums of specie taken from Spain, the writer says: —

"These strengthened trade and fostered industry. The remittances for foreign subsidies were in great part paid by bills on merchants settled abroad, who had the value of the drafts in British manufactures. The trade of England increased gradually every year, and such a scene of national prosperity while waging a long, costly, and bloody war, was never before shown by any people in the world."

No wonder, with such results to her commerce and such unvarying success attending her arms, and seeing the practical annihilation of the French navy, that the union of France and

小型船只。"这位权威人士还指出，英国在1760年损失了300多艘贸易舰船，1761年损失了800多艘，是法国损失的3倍；不过，他又补充说："法国俘获了数量更多、质量更好的船只，并不是什么好事。就在该国贸易几近毁灭、出海的商船寥寥可数之时，英国的一支支贸易舰队却遍布了各个海域。英国的贸易每年都在增长；战争所消耗的资金，又从其工业产品中赚了回来。大不列颠的贸易商总计雇用了8000艘船只。"英国的损失，主要归结于三个原因，其中只有第一个原因是可以避免的：1.商船没有注意到护航舰船发出的命令；2.英国船只遍布各个海域，数量庞大；3.敌人倾尽全力，冒险进行私掠活动。就在1761年这一年，海军损失了一艘战舰（后来又重新夺回了）和一艘巡逻舰。与此同时，尽管进行了多次交换，但英国仍然拘押着25000名法国囚徒，而法国拘押的英国囚犯却只有1200名。这些，都是海战所导致的结果。

最后，在提及英国从西班牙获取了巨额现金之后，作者总结了此次战争结束时英国的贸易形势，说：

"这些方面都巩固了商业贸易，促进了工业生产。为外国拨款所需的汇款，很大一部分均系用商人在外国结算的凭单进行支付，而这些商人则会获得与汇票等价的英国工业产品。英国的贸易业年复一年地逐渐增长起来，而此种一边进行着一场旷日持久、代价高昂、血腥无比的战争，一边却是国家繁荣兴旺的景象，是世界上其他任何民族都前所未有过的。"

英国获得了商业贸易上的这些战果，同时拥有如此一贯的成功，并且看到法国海军几近覆灭之后，对于曾经一度威胁到英国未来并让整个欧洲为之畏惧的法、西同盟，英

Spain, which was then lowering on her future and had once excited the fears of all Europe, was now beheld by Great Britain alone without the smallest fear or despondency. Spain was by her constitution and the distribution of her empire peculiarly open to the attack of a great sea people; and whatever the views of the government of the day, Pitt and the nation saw that the hour had come, which had been hoped for in vain in 1739, because then years of peace and the obstinate bias of a great minister had relaxed the muscles of her fleet. Now she but reached forth her hand and seized what she wished; nor could there have been any limit to her prey, had not the ministry again been untrue to the interests of the country.

The position of Portugal with reference to Great Britain has been alluded to, but merits some special attention as instancing an element of sea power obtained not by colonies, but by alliance, whether necessary or prudential. The commercial connection before spoken of "was strengthened by the strongest political ties. The two kingdoms were so situated as to have little to fear from each other, while they might impart many mutual advantages. The harbors of Portugal gave shelter as well as supplies to the English fleet, while the latter defended the rich trade of Portugal with Brazil. The antipathy between Portugal and Spain made it necessary for the former to have an ally, strong yet distant. None is so advantageous in that way as England, which in her turn might, and always has, derived great advantages from Portugal in a war with any of the southern powers of Europe."

This is an English view of a matter which to others looks somewhat like an alliance between a lion and a lamb. To call a country with a fleet like England's "distant" from a small maritime nation like Portugal is an absurdity. England is, and yet more in those days was, wherever her fleet could go. The opposite view of the matter, showing equally the value of the alliance, was well set forth in the memorial by which, under the civil name of an invitation, the

国如今毫不害怕和感到悲观，这一点就不足为怪了。西班牙本身的特点，以及西班牙殖民帝国的分布方式，都让该国特别容易受到一个伟大的海洋民族的攻击；而无论当时英国政府有着什么样的观点，皮特和整个英国都明白这种时机已经到来——自1739年后，他们就一直徒然地期待着这一时机，因为这些年来的和平形势以及那位伟大首相的顽固成见，都已大大削弱了英国舰队的实力。而如今，英国只要伸出手去，抓住自己希望得到的东西就行了；倘若政府内阁没有再一次置整个国家利益于不顾的话，那么英国攫取利益的范围就是毫无限制的了。

葡萄牙相对于大不列颠的形势，虽说前面已经提及，但还是值得我们特别加以注意，因为这是一个例证，说明了一种不是通过殖民地、而是通过结盟来获得的制海权要素——无论这种结盟是迫不得已还是经过了深谋远虑的。前文所说的那种贸易联系，"为此种最强大的政治纽带所巩固了。英、葡两个王国间的位置，使得它们彼此几乎不用心怀担忧，却可以相互分享诸多的共同利益。葡萄牙的各个港口，既可为英国舰队提供庇护之所，又可为其提供给养，而英国则保护着葡萄牙与巴西之间那种利润颇丰的贸易。葡萄牙与西班牙之间相互厌憎，使得葡萄牙必须要有一个强大而相距甚远的盟国。在这个方面，没有哪个国家比英国更为合适的了；而反过来，英国无论与欧洲南部哪一个大国爆发战争，都总能从葡萄牙那里获得极大的利益。"

这是英国人的观点；而在其他人看来，这种结盟看上去似乎有点儿像是狮子和羊所结成的联盟。说一个像英国那样拥有强大舰队的国家，与像葡萄牙这样的海洋小国相距"甚远"，是很荒谬可笑的。凡是舰队可去之地，就是英国；这种情况现在如此，在

crowns of France and Spain ordered Portugal to declare against England.

The grounds of that memorial — namely, the unequal benefit to Portugal from the connection and the disregard of Portuguese neutrality — have already been given. The King of Portugal refused to abandon the alliance, for the professed reason that it was ancient and wholly defensive. To this the two crowns replied: —

"The defensive alliance is actually an offensive one by the situation of the Portuguese dominions and the nature of the English power. The English squadrons cannot in all seasons keep the sea, nor cruise on the principal coasts of France and Spain for cutting off the navigation of the two countries, without the ports and assistance of Portugal; and these islanders could not insult all maritime Europe, if the whole riches of Portugal did not pass through their hands, which furnishes them with the means to make war and renders the alliance truly and properly offensive."

Between the two arguments the logic of situation and power prevailed. Portugal found England nearer and more dangerous than Spain, and remained for generations of trial true to the alliance. This relationship was as useful to England as any of her colonial possessions, depending of course upon the scene of the principal operations at any particular time.

The preliminaries of peace were signed at Fontainebleau, November 3, 1762; the definitive treaty on the 10th of the following February, at Paris, whence the peace takes its name.

By its terms France renounced all claims to Canada, Nova Scotia, and all the islands of the St. Lawrence; along with Canada she ceded the valley of the Ohio and all her territory on the east side of the Mississippi, except the city of New Orleans. At the same time Spain, as an equivalent for Havana, which England restored, yielded Florida, under which name were comprised all her continental possessions east of the Mississippi. Thus England obtained a

那个时候就更是如此了。而在法国和西班牙命令葡萄牙对英国宣战、并且礼貌地称之为"邀请"的那份备忘录中，则阐述了另一种同样表现出了结盟重要性的对立观点。

出现这份备忘录的理由——也就是说，葡萄牙从英、葡关系中所获利益上的不平等，以及英国舰队毫不尊重葡萄牙中立国权利的做法——前面已经交代过了。葡萄牙国王不愿背弃英、葡之间的同盟关系，理由则是众所周知的，因为这一同盟关系历史悠久，并且全然是一种防御同盟。对这一点，法、西两国是如此回应的：

"所谓的防守同盟，从葡萄牙领土的位置与英国实力之本质来看，实际上就是一种进攻同盟。倘若没有葡萄牙的港口与协助，英国舰队就不可能时时掌控海洋，也不可能在法、西两国重要的沿海地区巡逻，来切断这两国的海上航运；倘若不是葡萄牙举国之财全都转移到了英国人手中，使得他们拥有了发动战争的财力，并将英、葡之间的同盟变成一种真正而彻底的进攻同盟，那么这些岛民是不可能欺凌所有沿海之欧洲国家的。"

在这两种论调中，位置和实力逻辑占据了上风。葡萄牙发现，英国比西班牙距自己更近，也更危险，并且此种说法的正确性业已经过英、葡两国同盟数个世代的验证。这种关系对于英国来说，就像是该国任何一处殖民地那样有利，因为这种关系所依赖的，自然是在某一特定时期进行主要作战行动所处的位置。

1762年11月3日，在枫丹白露签署了和约的初步条款；而最终的条约，则是第二年的2月10日在巴黎签订的，故此条约即被称之为《巴黎和约》。

和约规定，法国放弃加拿大、新斯科舍以及圣劳伦斯河口所有岛屿的全部主权；除了加拿大，法国还割让了俄亥俄河流域以及密西西比河东岸的所有领地，只有新奥尔

colonial empire embracing Canada, from Hudson's Bay, and all of the present United States east of the Mississippi. The possibilities of this vast region were then only partially foreseen, and as yet there was no foreshadowing of the revolt of the thirteen colonies.

In the West Indies, England gave back to France the important islands of Guadeloupe and Martinique. The four so-called neutral islands of the Lesser Antilles were divided between the two powers; Sta. Lucia going to France, St. Vincent, Tobago, and Dominica to England, which also retained Grenada.

Minorca was given back to England; and as the restoration of the island to Spain had been one of the conditions of the alliance with the latter, France, unable to fulfil her stipulation, ceded to Spain Louisiana west of the Mississippi.

In India, France recovered the possessions she had held before Dupleix began his schemes of aggrandizement; but she gave up the right of erecting fortifications or keeping troops in Bengal, and so left the station at Chandernagore defenceless. In a word, France resumed her facilities for trading, but practically abandoned her pretensions to political influence. It was tacitly understood that the English company would keep all its conquests.

The right of fishing upon the coasts of Newfoundland and in parts of the Gulf of St. Lawrence, which France had previously enjoyed, was conceded to her by this treaty; but it was denied to Spain, who had claimed it for her fishermen. This concession was among those most attacked by the English opposition.

The nation at large and Pitt, the favorite of the nation, were bitterly opposed to the terms of the treaty. "France," said Pitt, "is chiefly formidable to us as a maritime and commercial power. What we gain in this respect is valuable to us above all through the injury to her which results from it. You leave to France the possibility of reviving her navy." In

良除外。与此同时，英国将哈瓦那归还给西班牙，而作为等价交换，西班牙则将佛罗里达让与英国——此处包括了西班牙在北美大陆上密西西比河以东的所有殖民地。这样一来，英国就得到了一个殖民帝国，涵盖了始于哈德逊湾的加拿大，以及如今合众国境内密西西比河以东的全部地区。当时，人们还只是部分预见到了这片广袤区域中所蕴含的机会；而到此时为止，也还没有出现那13个殖民地会爆发革命的任何预兆。

在西印度群岛，英国将瓜达鲁佩和马提尼克这两个重要岛屿归还给了法国。小安的列斯群岛中那4个所谓的中立岛屿，由英、法两国瓜分了；圣卢西亚归法国，而圣文森特、多巴哥和多米尼加岛则归英国，并且英国还保留着格林纳达。

米诺卡岛归还给了英国；由于将该岛归还给西班牙是西班牙与法国结盟的条件之一，所以没能履行这一条件的法国，便将密西西比河以西的路易斯安那割让给了西班牙。

在印度，法国收复了杜普雷开始实施其扩张计划以前的那些法属殖民地；不过，法国放弃了在孟加拉建立防御工事和保留军队的权利，让金德纳格尔这个基地变得毫无防御了。总而言之，法国虽说重新获得了从事贸易的环境，可实际上却是放弃了在该地施加政治影响的要求。英国的东印度公司会继续征服整个印度，这一点大家都是心照不宣的。

在纽芬兰沿海以及圣劳伦斯湾部分海域捕鱼的权利，法国之前一直享有，而这份条约又正式将此种权利让与了法国；西班牙也替本国渔民提出了在此打鱼的要求，却遭到了拒绝。这次让与，正是那些持反对态度的英国人抨击得最厉害的让与措施之一。

英国上下，连同皮特这个英国民族的宠儿，全都强烈反对这一条约的条款。皮特曾经说道："法国主要是我国一个强大的海洋和贸易对手。我们在这个方面所取得的成

truth, from the point of view of sea power and of the national jealousies which the spirit of that age sanctioned, these words, though illiberal, were strictly justifiable. The restoration to France of her colonies in the West Indies and her stations in India, together with the valuable right of fishery in her former American possessions, put before her the possibility and the inducement to restore her shipping, her commerce, and her navy, and thus tended to recall her from the path of continental ambition which had been so fatal to her interests, and in the same proportion favorable to the unprecedented growth of England's power upon the ocean. The opposition, and indeed some of the ministry, also thought that so commanding and important a position as Havana was poorly paid for by the cession of the yet desolate and unproductive region called Florida. Porto Rico was suggested, Florida accepted. There were other minor points of difference, into which it is unnecessary to enter. It could scarcely be denied that with the commanding military control of the sea held by England, grasping as she now did so many important positions, with her navy overwhelmingly superior in numbers, and her commerce and internal condition very thriving, more rigorous terms might easily have been exacted and would have been prudent. The ministry defended their eagerness and spirit of concession on the ground of the enormous growth of the debt, which then amounted to £122,000,000, a sum in every point of view much greater then than now; but while this draft upon the future was fully justified by the success of the war, it also imperatively demanded that the utmost advantages which the military situation made attainable should be exacted. This the ministry failed to do. As regards the debt, it is well observed by a French writer that "in this war, and for years afterward, England had in view nothing less than the conquest of America and the progress of her East India Company. By these two countries her manufactures and commerce acquired more than sufficient outlets, and repaid her for the

就，尤其是通过给该国带来损害而获得的成就，对我们来说弥足珍贵。而你们，却让法国有了重建其海军的可能性。"事实上，从制海权的观点来看，从当时的时代精神所鼓励的那种民族忌惮之心来看，这些话尽管显得气量狭窄，却完全是无可非议的。将西印度群岛的殖民地以及印度的基地，连同该国以前在美洲的殖民地海域那种宝贵的捕鱼权利全都归还给法国，等于将机会送到了该国面前，会诱使该国去复兴航运业、贸易业和海军，从而有可能让法国清醒过来，从而不再在大陆扩张的道路上继续走下去；而这条道路，既严重危及了法国的利益，又同等比例地有利于英国海洋实力的空前增长。反对的这一方事实上也包括了一些内阁成员，他们还认为，像哈瓦那这样险要的地方，用当时还很荒芜、没有物产的那个叫佛罗里达的地区来交换，未免太不划算了。当时英国曾提出要波多黎各，可最终接受的却是佛罗里达。其间还有一些细微的分歧，但我们无需去加以详述了。不可否认，由于英国对海洋拥有强大的军事控制权，并且像此时这样掌握着如此之多的要地，海军在兵力上占有无与匹敌的优势，商业贸易和国内形势也都蒸蒸日上，所以该国本来是可以轻而易举地强迫敌人签下一些更加严苛的条款，而在条款的内容上本来也是可以做到谨慎精明的。政府内阁辩称说，他们之所以急于签订和约并且如此大度，是因为英国债务大幅增长，当时已经高达12200万英镑了；从哪方面来看，这一总额都要比如今所负的债务要高得多。不过，在此次战争的胜利充分说明了这种寅吃卯粮的做法有道理的同时，它也必然要求该国榨取其军事形势业已使之能够获取的最大利益。可英国政府却没有做到这一点。至于说债务，一位法国作家说得好："在此次战争期间以及战后数年里，英国一心扑在征服美洲和扩大英国的东印度公司上。在法、

numerous sacrifices she had made. Seeing the maritime decay of Europe, — its commerce annihilated, its manufactures so little advanced, — how could the English nation feel afraid of a future which offered so vast a perspective?" Unfortunately the nation needed an exponent in the government; and its chosen mouthpiece, the only man, perhaps, able to rise to the level of the great opportunity, was out of favor at court.

Nevertheless, the gains of England were very great, not only in territorial increase, nor yet in maritime preponderance, but in the prestige and position achieved in the eyes of the nations, now fully opened to her great resources and mighty power. To these results, won by the sea, the issue of the continental war offered a singular and suggestive contrast. France had already withdrawn, along with England, from all share in that strife, and peace between the other parties to it was signed five days after the Peace of Paris. The terms of the peace were simply the status quo ante bellum. By the estimate of the King of Prussia, one hundred and eighty thousand of his soldiers had fallen or died in this war, out of a kingdom of five million souls; while the losses of Russia, Austria, and France aggregated four hundred and sixty thousand men. The result was simply that things remained as they were. To attribute this only to a difference between the possibilities of land and sea war is of course absurd. The genius of Frederick, backed by the money of England, had proved an equal match for the mismanaged and not always hearty efforts of a coalition numerically overwhelming. What does seem a fair conclusion is, that States having a good seaboard, or even ready access to the ocean by one or two outlets, will find it to their advantage to seek prosperity and extension by the way of the sea and of commerce, rather than in attempts to unsettle and modify existing political arrangements in countries where a more or less long possession of power has conferred acknowledged rights, and created national allegiance or political ties. Since

西两国，英国的产品和贸易有了不止是长足的销路，因而弥补了该国曾经遭受的无数损失。看到欧洲各个海洋国家都在衰落——它们的商业贸易都已彻底摧毁，它们的制造业几乎毫无进步——对一种有着如此巨大希望的未来，英国又怎可能会感到担心呢？"可惜的是，英国政府里需要有一位这样的倡导者才行；但英国人民所选择的那位代言人，或许也是唯——一个能够达到这一巨大机遇水平的人，此时却在英国宫廷里失宠了。

尽管如此，英国的收获还是非常巨大的；它不但增加了殖民地、增强了海上优势，而且在其他国家眼中的声望和地位也都提高了——这些国家，如今都被英国的巨大资源和强大实力打开了大门。相对于英国通过海洋实力获得的这些战果而言，欧洲大陆战争的结果，却与此形成了一种很奇特、也颇具启发意义的反差。法国，连同英国，都已经退出此次战争，而其他各方也在《巴黎和约》签订之后的5天里都签署了这份和约。和约的条款很简单，只是让各国恢复到了战前的状态。据普鲁士国王估计，在此次战争中该国有18万名士兵被俘或者战死，而这个王国的总人口才500万；而普、奥、法三国的伤亡人数总计则高达46万。可此次战争的结果，却只是让一切都恢复原样罢了。仅将这一点归因于爆发陆上战争和海洋战争两种可能性之间的差异，自然是很荒谬的。腓特烈大帝的天赋加上英国的资金支持，业已证明了他足以与一帮数量上占绝对多数、但指挥不善且并非始终都全心全意地努力的盟国相匹敌。我们似乎可以得出下面这样一个公正的结论：那些有着优良的沿海地区、甚至通过一两个河口便可轻而易举地出海的国家会发现，通过海洋、通过贸易来实现国家富强和势力扩张的做法，对它们来说是很有利的；它们无需试图动摇或者纠正某些国家中现存的政治制度，来形成国家间的相互支持或者政治纽带，因为那些国家

the Treaty of Paris in 1763, the waste places of the world have been rapidly filled; witness our own continent, Australia, and even South America. A nominal and more or less clearly defined political possession now generally exists in the most forsaken regions, though to this statement there are some marked exceptions; but in many places this political possession is little more than nominal, and in others of a character so feeble that it cannot rely upon itself alone for support or protection. The familiar and notorious example of the Turkish Empire, kept erect only by the forces pressing upon it from opposing sides, by the mutual jealousies of powers that have no sympathy with it, is an instance of such weak political tenure; and though the question is wholly European, all know enough of it to be aware that the interest and control of the sea powers is among the chief, if not the first, of the elements that now fix the situation; and that they, if intelligently used, will direct the future inevitable changes. Upon the western continents the political condition of the Central American and tropical South American States is so unstable as to cause constant anxiety about the maintenance of internal order, and seriously to interfere with commerce and with the peaceful development of their resources. So long as — to use a familiar expression — they hurt no one but themselves, this may go on; but for a long time the citizens of more stable governments have been seeking to exploit their resources, and have borne the losses arising from their distracted condition. North America and Australia still offer large openings to immigration and enterprise; but they are filling up rapidly, and as the opportunities there diminish, the demand must arise for a more settled government in those disordered States, for security to life and for reasonable stability of institutions enabling merchants and others to count upon the future. There is certainly no present hope that such a demand can be fulfilled from the existing native materials; if the same be true when the demand arises, no theoretical positions, like

或多或少都早已通过协商而获得了各国公认的权利。自1763年签署《巴黎和约》之后，世界上的那些不毛之地很快都得到了拓殖开发；我们所处的北美洲、澳大利亚，甚至是南美洲，即是一个明证。如今，即便是最荒芜的那些地区，也普遍存在着一种名义上的、多多少少得到了清晰界定的政治占有制度，尽管关于这一说法还有着一些明显的例外情况；不过，这种政治占有在许多地方都是有名无实，而在其他地区也很势弱，是无法仅凭自身来为这些地区提供支持或者保护的。大家都很熟悉的一个著名实例，便是土耳其帝国；恰恰是因为敌对各方施加给该国的压力，以及反对它的各国都共同忌惮，这个帝国才维持着没有垮塌，也正好说明了此种政治占有制度的软弱无力。尽管这个问题全然属于欧洲内部的问题，但所有人都很清楚得很，明白在如今扭转局面的那些因素当中，海洋大国的利益和掌控就算不是首要因素，也是重要的因素之一；并且，倘若将这些因素巧加利用，就会引导着未来发生必然的改变。至于西方大陆，中美洲和属于热带气候的南美各国政治形势都很不稳定，既使得人们始终都要担忧这些地区能否维持好国内秩序，也严重地妨碍了这一地区的商业贸易，妨碍了各国资源的和平开发。用一句老话来说，只要它们除了危害自身，不会危及别人，那就可以由它们去；但是，只是由于那些更为稳定的国家当中的人民长久以来都想开发这些国家的资源，他们才会因这些国家的混乱状况遭受损失。北美洲和澳大利亚如今仍然为移民和企业提供了大量机会；但是，这些机会正在迅速减少，而由于机会减少，就会产生出在那些混乱无序的各国间成立一个更加稳固的政府的需求，以使人民生活安定，并保持制度的相对稳定，并让商人和其他人都对未来充满希望。我们目前自然不要指望能够以国内现存的资源来满足这样一种需要，而倘若这种需求出现的时候形势

the Monroe doctrine, will prevent interested nations from attempting to remedy the evil by some measure, which, whatever it may be called, will be a political interference. Such interferences must produce collisions, which may be at times settled by arbitration, but can scarcely fail at other times to cause war. Even for a peaceful solution, that nation will have the strongest arguments which has the strongest organized force. It need scarcely be said that the successful piercing of the Central American Isthmus at any point may precipitate the moment that is sure to come sooner or later. The profound modification of commercial routes expected from this enterprise, the political importance to the United States of such a channel of communication between her Atlantic and Pacific seaboards, are not, however, the whole nor even the principal part of the question. As far as can be seen, the time will come when stable governments for the American tropical States must be assured by the now existing powerful and stable States of America or Europe. The geographical position of those States, the climatic conditions, make it plain at once that sea power will there, even more than in the case of Turkey, determine what foreign State shall predominate, — if not by actual possession, by its influence over the native governments. The geographical position of the United States and her intrinsic power give her an undeniable advantage; but that advantage will not avail if there is a great inferiority of organized brute-force, which still remains the last argument of republics as of kings. Herein lies to us the great and still living interest of the Seven Years' War. In it we have seen and followed England, with an army small as compared with other States, as is still her case to-day, first successfully defending her own shores, then carrying her arms in every direction, spreading her rule and influence over remote regions, and not only binding them to her obedience, but making them tributary to her wealth, her strength, and her reputation. As she loosens the grasp and neutralizes the influence of France

依然如此,那么就没有哪一种理论上的立场——比如门罗主义——能够阻止一些利益相关的国家企图采取某种措施来革除此种弊端的做法了;无论这些国家把此种措施称作什么,它实际上都会是一种政治干预。这样的干预必定会产生出各种冲突来;虽说这些冲突有时可以通过仲裁加以解决,但可能更多的却会导致战争,这一点已经是屡试不爽的了。即便是在和平解决这些冲突的过程中,理由最为有力的,也是那些有组织的力量最为强大的国家。我们无需言明,不管是从什么地方成功地突破中美地峡,可能都会产生出一种在将来或迟或早必定出现的契机。打通中美地峡,有望彻底改变现有的贸易线路,而在合众国的大西洋沿岸地区和太平洋沿岸地区之间存在这样一条交通要道,对该国也有着极其重要的政治意义;但是,这二者并非整个问题的全部,甚至也不是这一问题的主要方面。我们能够看到的是,这样一个时刻即将到来:美洲或欧洲现有的那些强大而稳固的国家,必定会确保美洲的热带国家全都建立起一个稳固的政府。这些美洲国家的地理位置和气候条件,使得我们马上就可以看出,倘若不是实际占领、不是直接影响当地政府的话,那么制海权在这里将完全决定由哪个外国来占据主导地位,其决定性程度甚至超过了土耳其帝国的情形。合众国的地理位置与内在动力,使得它在这方面拥有了无可争辩的优势;但是,倘若它在有组织的武装实力方面大不如人,那么这一优势就会毫无用处——可武力却仍然是各个共和国和各个王国都最不愿意提起的一种论调。在这个方面,"七年战争"对我们仍然有着巨大而鲜活的意义。在此次战争中,我们业已看到,虽说英国那时的陆军跟别的国家相比规模很小(现在也仍然如此),但它先是成功地保卫了该国的沿海地区,然而又将双手伸向四面八方,将自己的规矩与势力扩张到了那些遥远的地区,非但让这些

and Spain in regions beyond the sea, there is perhaps seen the prophecy of some other great nation in days yet to come, that will incline the balance of power in some future sea war, whose scope will be recognized afterward, if not by contemporaries, to have been the political future and the economical development of regions before lost to civilization; but that nation will not be the United States if the moment find her indifferent, as now, to the empire of the seas.

The direction then given to England's efforts, by the instinct of the nation and the fiery genius of Pitt, continued after the war, and has profoundly influenced her subsequent policy. Mistress now of North America, lording it in India, through the company whose territorial conquests had been ratified by native princes, over twenty millions of inhabitants, — a population larger than that of Great Britain and having a revenue respectable alongside of that of the home government, — England, with yet other rich possessions scattered far and wide over the globe, had ever before her eyes, as a salutary lesson, the severe chastisement which the weakness of Spain had allowed her to inflict upon that huge disjointed empire. The words of the English naval historian of that war, speaking about Spain, apply with slight modifications to England in our own day.

"Spain is precisely that power against which England can always contend with the fairest prospect of advantage and honor. That extensive monarchy is exhausted at heart, her resources lie at a great distance, and whatever power commands the sea, may command the wealth and commerce of Spain. The dominions from which she draws her resources, lying at an immense distance from the capital and from one another, make it more necessary for her than for any other State to temporize, until she can inspire with activity all parts of her enormous but disjointed empire."

地区服从英国的统治，还让这些地区成了附庸，让它们为英国的财富、实力与声望做出了贡献。由于它动摇了法、西两国对海外地区的掌控，削弱了两国在这些地区的势力，故我们或许会看到这样一种预兆，那就是：日后可能会出现某个别的大国，打破未来某种海战中的实力平衡；就算当代的人认识不到，后人也会认识到，此种海战的影响范围，就是那些地区在未开化之前的政治未来和经济发展。不过，要是那个时候的合众国仍然跟如今一样，对成为海洋帝国不感兴趣的话，这个大国就绝对不会是合众国。

英格兰民族和皮特那种炽热的天赋，给当时的英国赋予了努力的方向，而这一方向在此次战争过后仍然保持着，并且深刻地影响到了该国后来的政策。英国如今已经成了北美霸主，又通过东印度公司在当地王公的批准之下所进行的领地征战，以及统治着2000多万人口，从而称霸了印度——这一人口数量，非但超过了大不列颠本国的人口，还为该国带来了可与国内政府相比肩的可观岁入；并且，英国还拥有诸多散布于世界各地的、富庶的殖民地。但是，英国面前却一直有着一个有益的教训，那就是西班牙的软弱无能，使得英国能够损害这个支离破碎的庞大帝国，从而给它以沉重打击。研究此战的英国海军历史学家在谈及西班牙时所说的话，对如今我们所处的这个时代而言，依然只需稍加修改便会符合英国的情况。

"西班牙正是英国始终都可与之相争并最有可能占据优势和获得荣耀的那种国家。这个面积广袤的君主之国，本质上早已羸弱不堪，且其资源都地处远方，所以无论哪个国家掌控了海洋，便都可以掌控西班牙的财力和贸易。该国赖以获得资源的那些领地，非但离西班牙首都极其遥远，而这些领地彼此之间也相距甚远，从而使得西班牙在能够充分激发

It would be untrue to say that England is exhausted at heart; but her dependence upon the outside world is such as to give a certain suggestiveness to the phrase.

This analogy of positions was not overlooked by England. From that time forward up to our own day, the possessions won for her by her sea power have combined with that sea power itself to control her policy. The road to India — in the days of Clive a distant and perilous voyage on which she had not a stopping-place of her own — was reinforced as opportunity offered by the acquisition of St. Helena, of the Cape of Good Hope, of the Mauritius. When steam made the Red Sea and Mediterranean route practicable, she acquired Aden, and yet later has established herself at Socotra. Malta had already fallen into her hands during the wars of the French Revolution, and her commanding position, as the corner-stone upon which the coalitions against Napoleon rested, enabled her to claim it at the Peace of 1815. Being but a short thousand miles from Gibraltar, the circles of military command exercised by these two places intersect. The present day has seen the stretch from Malta to the Isthmus of Suez, formerly without a station, guarded by the cession to her of Cyprus. Egypt, despite the jealousy of France, has passed under English control. The importance of that position to India, understood by Napoleon and Nelson, led the latter at once to send an officer overland to Bombay with the news of the battle of the Nile and the downfall of Bonaparte's hopes. Even now, the jealousy with which England views the advance of Russia in Central Asia is the result of those days in which her sea power and resources triumphed over the weakness of D'Aché and the genius of Suffren, and wrenched the peninsula of India from the ambition of the French.

"For the first time since the Middle Ages," says M. Martin, speaking of the Seven

起广袤却不相连的帝国各地的昂扬斗志之前，比其他任何国家都更需要姑息和妥协。"

我们自然不能说英国在本质上也羸弱不堪；不过，由于该国极其依赖于外部世界，所以这句话还是有着某种启发意义的。

英国并未忽视它与西班牙在处境上的这种相似性。从那时起，直到如今这个时代，制海权让英国获取的那些殖民地，都与此种制海权本身紧密地结合起来了，从而控制了该国的政策走向。通往印度的航路——在克莱夫所处的那个时代，这是一条遥远而危机四伏的航线，因为一路上英国没有属于本国的落脚之处——得到了巩固，因为取得圣海伦那、好望角和毛里求斯之后，英国就有了巩固这一航线的条件。蒸汽轮船使得红海与地中海之间可以通航后，英国又攻取了亚丁，不过后来该国还是在索科特拉岛上才扎下根来的。马耳他在法国革命战争期间就已落入英国手中；而英国的统治地位，非但是反拿破仑同盟形成的基础，也使得它能够在《1815年和约》中坚持得到了马耳他。由于马耳他距直布罗陀仅有短短的1000英里，所以这两个地方的军事指挥范围便交织在一起了。如今我们已经看到，英国的势力已从马耳他扩张到了苏伊士地峡；以前，苏伊士地峡上并无英军驻地，而是由割让给英国的塞浦路斯来守卫的。埃及无视法国的妒忌，也转到了英国的控制之下。这一位置对于印度的重要性，拿破仑和纳尔逊都很清楚；正是因为这一点，纳尔逊才能在尼罗河河口之战爆发、拿破仑希望破灭之后，马上派遣一名军官，将此消息经由陆路送往孟买。即便是现在，英国因俄罗斯进至中亚地区而表现出来的那种忌惮之心，也是源自该国凭借制海权和资源击败了软弱的德阿克和聪明的苏弗朗，并从野心勃勃的法国手中夺取了印度半岛的那个时代。

"自中世纪以来，"M·马丁在谈及"七年战争"时曾说，"英国第一次在几乎没

Years' War, "England had conquered France single-handed almost without allies, France having powerful auxiliaries. She had conquered solely by the superiority of her government."

Yes! But by the superiority of her government using the tremendous weapon of her sea power. This made her rich, and in turn protected the trade by which she had her wealth. With her money she upheld her few auxiliaries, mainly Prussia and Hanover, in their desperate strife. Her power was everywhere that her ships could reach, and there was none to dispute the sea to her. Where she would she went, and with her went her guns and her troops. By this mobility her forces were multiplied, those of her enemies distracted. Ruler of the seas, she everywhere obstructed its highways. The enemies' fleets could not join; no great fleet could get out, or if it did, it was only to meet at once, with uninured officers and crews, those who were veterans in gales and warfare. Save in the case of Minorca, she carefully held her own sea-bases and eagerly seized those of the enemy. What a lion in the path was Gibraltar to the French squadrons of Toulon and Brest! What hope for French succor to Canada, when the English fleet had Louisburg under its lee?

The one nation that gained in this war was that which used the sea in peace to earn its wealth, and ruled it in war by the extent of its navy, by the number of its subjects who lived on the sea or by the sea, and by its numerous bases of operations scattered over the globe. Yet it must be observed that these bases themselves would have lost their value if their communications remained obstructed. Therefore the French lost Louisburg, Martinique, Pondicherry; so England herself lost Minorca. The service between the bases and the mobile force between the ports and the fleets is mutual.[2] In this respect the navy is essentially a light corps; it keeps open the communications between its own ports, it obstructs those of the enemy;

有盟友、而法国却有着强大帮手的情况下，独自击败了法国。它完全是凭借英国政府的优秀而打败法国的。"

的确如此！不过，在英国政府的优秀之外，还要加上运用了制海权这种巨大武器这一点才行。这种武器使得英国日益富裕，反过来又保护了属于英国财富之源的贸易。英国还用本国的资金，在为数不多的那几个帮手——主要是普鲁士和汉诺威——所进行的殊死斗争中，对它们进行了支持。英国的势力，渗透到了该国船只能够到达的所有地区，而在海洋之上，则无人能够与之争锋。该国的舰船想去哪儿就去哪儿，并且随之而去的，还有该国的枪炮和军队。有了这样一种机动能力之后，英国的兵力激增，而其敌人的兵力则分散开来了。由于英国是海洋霸主，所以它在哪儿都可以堵住属于它的那些交通要道。敌人的舰队无法汇合；大型舰队无法出海，而就算出海的话，它们那些毫无经验的官兵和船员，马上便会遭到闯荡过狂风暴雨、经历过战争考验的英军的痛击。除了米诺卡岛那次海战，其他情况下该国都谨慎地据守着自己的海上基地，并且渴望着夺取敌人的海上基地。对于土伦港和布雷斯特的法国舰队来说，直布罗陀是多么凶狠的一只拦路虎呀！而当英国舰队将路易斯堡置于其保护之下后，法国派往加拿大的援军还能抱有什么指望呢？

此次战争中唯一获得胜利的，便是英国这个在和平时期利用海洋来获取财富，而在战争时期又利用其海军的规模、利用其生活于海上或海边的臣民、利用散布于全球各地数不胜数的作战基地来统治海洋的国家。不过，我们还须注意到，倘若这些基地之间的交通联系一直都不通畅的话，那么它们就没有价值了。正是因为这个原因，法国才失去了路易斯堡、马提尼克和庞迪切里，而英国本身也曾失去了米诺卡岛。基地之间需要相互支援，港口与舰队之间需要机动部队，道理都是一样的。[2] 从这个方面来看，海军

but it sweeps the sea for the service of the land, it controls the desert that man may live and thrive on the habitable globe.

FOOTNOTES:

(1) That is, with the guns on board, but for the most part not mounted on their carriages, in order to give increased accommodation for troops. When the troops were landed, the guns were mounted.

(2) These remarks, always true, are doubly so now since the introduction of steam. The renewal of coal is a want more frequent, more urgent, more peremptory, than any known to the sailing-ship. It is vain to look for energetic naval operations distant from coal stations. It is equally vain to acquire distant coaling stations without maintaining a powerful navy; they will but fall into the hands of the enemy. But the vainest of all delusions is the expectation of bringing down an enemy by commerce-destroying alone, with no coaling stations outside the national boundaries.

本质上应当是一支轻型队伍；它不但应当保持己方港口之间的交通联系，还须阻断敌方港口之间的交通联系；不过，它横扫海洋的目的是服务于陆地，而它控制海洋，也是为了让人类可以在这个适于居住的地球上生活下去并茁壮成长。

原注：

（1）也就是说，船上虽说装有火炮，但大多数火炮都并未装上炮架，目的是增加舱位来运送部队。部队登陆后，这些火炮便会安装到炮架上。

（2）这些说法一向都是对的，而如今由于出现了蒸汽轮船，则更是如此了。汽轮需要加煤；跟人们所知的帆船的任何一种需要相比，这种需要都更加频繁、更加紧迫和更加绝对。指望在远离燃煤基地的地方进行积极有力的海战，是徒劳无益的。而想要取得一些与本国相距遥远的煤炭基地，却没有保持一支强大的海军，同样也是毫无意义的；因为这些煤炭基地最终只会落入敌人的手中。不过，所有痴心妄想中最为无益的，还是在国境之外根本没有燃煤基地，却指望通过单纯的贸易破坏战来彻底打垮敌人。

译者注：

［1］即英国的马丁准将。参见第六章。

［2］Black Hole of Calcutta：加尔各答黑洞。指1756年孟加拉的纳瓦布在加尔各答用地牢囚禁了146名英国俘虏、其中仅有23名得以生还的惨案。后多用于指小型地牢。

［3］Acapulco galleon：阿卡普尔科邮船。指从墨西哥南部港口阿卡普尔科开往马尼拉的西班牙邮船，亦称"马尼拉邮船"（Manila- Acapulco galleon）。

CHAPTER VIII
Course of Events from the Peace of Paris to 1778

Maritime War consequent upon the American Revolution. — Sea Battle off Ushant.

If England had reason to complain that she had not reaped from the Treaty of Paris all the advantages that her military achievements and position entitled her to expect, France had every cause for discontent at the position in which the war left her. The gain of England was nearly measured by her losses; even the cession of Florida, made to the conqueror by Spain, had been bought by France at the price of Louisiana. Naturally the thoughts of her statesmen and of her people, as they bent under the present necessity to bear the burden of the vanquished, turned to the future with its possibilities of revenge and compensation. The Duc de Choiseul, able though imperious, remained for many years more at the head of affairs, and worked persistently to restore the power of France from the effects of the treaty. The Austrian alliance had been none of his seeking; it was already made and working when he came to office in 1758; but he had even at the first recognized that the chief enemy was England, and tried as far as could be to direct the forces of the nation against her. The defeat of Conflans having thwarted his projects of invasion, he next sought, in entire consistency with his main purpose, to stir up Spain and gain her alliance. The united efforts of the two kingdoms with their fine seaboards could, under good administration and with time for preparation, put afloat a navy that would

第八章 自《巴黎和约》到1778年间形势的发展

美国革命战争引发的海战；韦桑岛海战

要说英国都有理由埋怨，觉得自己没有从《巴黎和约》中获得该国军事实力和地位使之应当能够得到的所有利益，那么法国就完全有理由对战争给它带来的地位感到不满了。英国的收获，差不多可以用法国的损失来衡量；即便是由西班牙割让给英国这个征服者的佛罗里达，也曾是法国以路易斯安那为代价购买得来的。由于当下不得不低头承受被征服的重负，所以该国的政治家和民众的心思，自然就转向在将来对英国进行报复和索取补偿的可能性了。舒瓦瑟尔公爵虽说能干，却很专横，此后又继续担任了多年的政府首脑；自该条约生效后，他一直都在孜孜不倦地想让法国再次强大起来。与奥地利结盟，并非他所追求的目标；在他上台执政的1758年，法、奥同盟就已经形成并开始生效了；不过，他一开始就认识到，英国才是法国的主要敌人，于是他便竭尽全力，引导着整个法国的力量来与英国进行对抗。孔夫兰战败，挫败了他入侵英国的计划，所以他接下来便谋求煽动西班牙并与之结成盟国，这一点与他的主要目标是完全一致的。法、西这两个王国都有着完美的沿海地区，倘若联合起来，善加管理并假以时日的话，便能建立起一支完全可以与英国海军相抗衡的海军来。而那些实力较弱的海洋国家，倘若看

be a fair counterpoise to that of England. It was also doubtless true, that weaker maritime States, if they saw such a combination successfully made and working efficiently, would pluck up heart to declare against a government whose greatness excited envy and fear, and which acted with the disregard to the rights and welfare of others common to all uncontrolled power. Unhappily for both France and Spain, the alliance came too late. The virtual annihilation of the French fleet in 1759 was indeed followed by an outburst of national enthusiasm for the navy, skilfully fostered and guided by Choiseul. "Popular feeling took up the cry, from one end of France to the other, 'The navy must be restored.' Gifts of cities, corporations, and private individuals raised funds. A prodigious activity sprang up in the lately silent ports; everywhere ships were building and repairing." The minister also recognized the need of restoring the discipline and tone, as well as the material of the navy. The hour, however, was too late; the middle of a great and unsuccessful war is no time to begin preparations. "Better late than never" is not so safe a proverb as "In time of peace prepare for war." The condition of Spain was better. When war broke out, the English naval historian estimates that she had one hundred ships of all sizes; of these, probably sixty were of the line. Nevertheless, although the addition of Spain to her numerous enemies might make the position of England seem critical, the combination in her favor of numbers, skill, experience, and prestige, was irresistible. With seventy thousand veteran seamen, she had only to maintain a position already won. The results we know.

After the peace, Choiseul wisely remained faithful to his own first ideas. The restoration of the navy continued, and was accompanied and furthered by a spirit of professional ambition and of desire to excel, among the officers of the navy, which has been before mentioned, and which, in the peculiar condition of the United States navy at the present day, may be

到这样一种同盟成功结成并且成效显著的话，便都会鼓起勇气来对抗英国政府，这一点毫无疑问也是正确的；因为非但英国政府的伟大激起了各国的嫉妒和担忧，同时这个政府还像所有权力失控的国家一样，无视其他国家的权利和福祉。令法国和西班牙两国遗憾的是，这种同盟出现得太迟了。1759年法国舰队事实上全军覆灭之后，在舒瓦瑟尔的巧妙助长和引导下，法国的确爆发出了一阵全民支持重建海军的热潮。"从南到北，法国的民众纷纷喊出了'必须重建海军'的口号。各个城市、公司和私人都踊跃捐款，募集资金。不久前还死气沉沉的各个港口，一下子爆发出了惊人的积极性；到处都在建造或者维修舰船。"这位首相也认识到，除了恢复海军的物质设备，还需要重新确立海军的纪律和士气才行。然而，此时开始已经太迟；这场大规模的、令法国节节败退的战争已经进行过半，根本就没有时间再让法国开始做准备了。"亡羊补牢，为时未晚"这句谚语，其实并不如"居安思危"这句谚语来得可靠。西班牙的形势则稍微好一点儿。据英国的海军历史学家估计，战争爆发的时候，西班牙拥有各种型号的舰船100艘；其中，大约有60艘是战舰。不过，尽管西班牙加入了英国众多的敌国阵营，让英国的形势看上去岌岌可危，但英军在兵力、技术、经验和名望等方面都有优势，它们结合起来，便使得英军势不可挡了。由于拥有70000名经验丰富的海员，因此英国早已立于不败之地。至于结局，我们都知道了。

和约签署之后，舒瓦瑟尔英明地继续坚持着其最初的那些目标。重建海军的工作继续进行着，同时海军官兵们当中还洋溢着一种事业心和好胜精神，从而大大促进了重建工作；这种精神前面已经提到过，而在合众国海军目前这种独特的形势下，我们也可以将这种精神当成榜样。建造战舰的工作继续如火如荼、大规模地进行着。多亏了始于

commended as a model. The building of ships-of-war continued with great activity and on a large scale. At the end of the war, thanks to the movement begun in 1761, there were forty ships-of-the-line in good condition. In 1770, when Choiseul was dismissed, the royal navy numbered sixty-four of the line and fifty frigates afloat. The arsenals and storehouses were filled, and a stock of ship-timber laid up. At the same time the minister tried to improve the efficiency of the officers by repressing the arrogant spirit of those of noble birth, which showed itself both toward superiors and toward another order of officers, not of the nobility, whose abilities made them desired on board the fleet. This class-feeling carried with it a curious sentiment of equality among officers of very different grades, which injuriously affected the spirit of subordination. Members, all, of a privileged social order, their equality as such was more clearly recognized than their inequality as junior and senior. The droll story told by Marryatt of the midshipman, who represented to his captain that a certain statement had been made in confidence, seems to have had a realization on the French quarter-deck of that day. "Confidence!" cried the captain; "who ever heard of confidence between a post-captain and a midshipman!" "No sir," replied the youngster, "not between a captain and a midshipman, but between two gentlemen." Disputes, arguments, suggestions, between two gentlemen, forgetful of their relative rank, would break out at critical moments, and the feeling of equality, which wild democratic notions spread throughout the fleets of the republic, was curiously forestalled by that existing among the members of a most haughty aristocracy. "I saw by his face," says one of Marryatt's heroes, "that the first lieutenant did not agree with the captain; but he was too good an officer to say so at such a moment." The phrase expresses one of the deepest-rooted merits of the English system, the want of which is owned by French writers: —

1761年的这场运动,到此次战争结束的时候,法国才保留着40艘船况良好的战舰。1770年舒瓦瑟尔被解职的时候,法国皇家海军已经拥有了64艘战舰和50艘护卫舰。各个军械库和仓库都得到了充实,还存储了一批造船所用的木料。与此同时,这位首相还试图通过压制贵族出身的海军将领的傲慢自大之心,来提高海军官兵的作战效率;那些贵族出身的海军将领,非但对上级傲慢无礼,对其他等级、非贵族出身、具有才干而渴望在舰队中服役的军官也是这种态度。而此种等级感情,同时还让不同级别的海军官兵间形成了一种古怪的平等观念,极为不利地影响到了绝对服从的精神。这种特权阶层中的所有成员,对他们之间的平等地位都认识得一清二楚,但对于他们在海军中的上下级关系,却并未有着如此清晰的界限。海军准尉马里亚特曾经讲述过一次很滑稽的亲身经历,似乎正是体现出了那时法国海军军官们的思想。他向舰长指出,自己的某句话是跟后者推心置腹地说的。"推心置腹!"那位舰长大声呵斥道,"谁听说过上校舰长和准尉之间会有什么推心置腹!"这位年轻的准尉回答道:"不,先生,不是舰长和准尉之间,而是两位绅士之间。"倘若忘记了各自的职衔,那么两位绅士在关键时刻就会产生分歧、争执和不同意见;但由狂热的民主思想散布到每一支共和国舰队中的那种平等观念却奇怪得很,被这种极为傲慢的贵族阶层成员中业已存在的那种平等观念所阻断了。"从他的脸上,"马里亚特手下的一位勇士说,"我看得出这位中尉并不赞同舰长的意见;不过,他是一位如此优秀的军官,因而不会在这样一个时候反对自己的上级。"这句话,表达出了英国海军制度中那些根深蒂固的优点之一,而法国的作家们也承认,法国海军正是缺乏这样一种优点:

"Under Louis XVI. the intimacy and fellowship existing between the chief and the subordinate led the latter to discuss the orders which were given him. ... The relaxation of discipline and the spirit of independence were due also to another cause than that pointed out; they can be partly attributed to the regulation of the officers' messes. Admiral, captain, officers, midshipmen, ate together; everything was in common. They thee-and-thou'd each other like chums. In handling the ship, the inferior gave his opinion, argued, and the chief, irritated, often preferred to yield rather than make enemies. Facts of this kind are asserted by witnesses whose truthfulness is above suspicion."

Insubordination of this character, to which weaker men gave way, dashed in vain against the resolute and fiery temper of Suffren; but the spirit of discontent rose almost to the height of mutiny, causing him to say in his despatches to the minister of the navy, after his fourth battle: "My heart is pierced by the most general defection. It is frightful to think that I might four times have destroyed the English fleet, and that it still exists." Choiseul's reforms broke against this rock, which only the uprising of the whole nation finally removed; but in the personnel of the crews a great improvement was made. In 1767 he reorganized the artillery of the fleet, forming a body of ten thousand gunners, who were systematically drilled once a week during the ten years still to intervene before the next war with England.

Losing sight of no part of his plans, Choiseul, while promoting the naval and military power of France, paid special attention to the alliance with Spain and judiciously encouraged and furthered the efforts of that country in the path of progress under Charles III., the best of her kings of the Bourbon line. The Austrian alliance still existing was maintained, but his hopes were chiefly fixed upon Spain. The wisdom and insight which had at once fastened upon England as the centre of enmity to France had been justified and further enlightened by the

"在路易十六统治时期，主帅和下级之间相互熟悉、互有交情，使得下级在接受命令的时候会跟上级讨价还价……除了已经指出的这个方面，海军纪律涣散和各自为政的思想还有另外一个原因；其中部分原因就在于军官集体用膳的这一制度。上将、上校、军官、见习军官，统统都在一起用膳；吃的东西也都是一样的。用膳之时，他们彼此之间都是'你'啊'你'的，就像好朋友似的。在指挥舰艇的时候，下级会提出自己的意见并与上级争辩，而主帅不耐烦了之后，往往便宁愿顺从下级的意思，而不愿与下级为敌。许多有着无可置疑之诚实品质的见证者，都曾坚称这是法国海军中的真实情况。"

此种不服从上级的习气，既让那些较为软弱的人退避三舍，也曾在碰上苏弗朗那种果断而暴烈的脾气时，变得毫无用处；但是，苏弗朗部下的不满情绪却日渐累积，差点儿酿成兵变，使得他指挥了第四次海战之后，在战报中对海军大臣如此说道："我的心，完全被我军当中那种最为普遍的不尽职责之行为伤透了。我本来四次都可以摧毁英国舰队，可时至今日，英国舰队却仍然存在，想想都觉得可怕。"舒瓦瑟尔的改革措施曾给这种坚若磐石的习气带来了冲击；虽说只有全国上下群起而攻之，才能最终消除这种弊端，但他的措施还是让整个海军队伍有了巨大的进步。1767年，他对舰队中的炮兵进行了整顿，组成了一支10000人的炮兵队伍，并让他们在再次与英国开战之前的那10年间，每周都有组织地训练一次。

舒瓦瑟尔并没有忽视自己所定计划中的任何一个方面。他在提升法国海军和陆军实力的同时，还尤为关注法国与西班牙之间的同盟关系，并且审慎地鼓励和促进该国在查理三世治下沿着发展道路所做出的努力；后者正是波旁皇室中最优秀的一位西班牙君

whole course of the Seven Years' War. In Spain was the surest, and, with good administration, the most powerful ally. The close proximity of the two countries, the relative positions of their ports, made the naval situation particularly strong; and the alliance which was dictated by sound policy, by family ties, and by just fear of England's sea power, was further assured to France by recent and still existing injuries that must continue to rankle with Spain. Gibraltar, Minorca, and Florida were still in the hands of England; no Spaniard could be easy till this reproach was wiped out.

It may be readily believed, as is asserted by French historians, that England viewed with disquietude the growth of the French navy, and would gladly have nipped it betimes; but it is more doubtful whether she would have been willing to force a war for that purpose. During the years succeeding the Peace of Paris a succession of short ministries, turning mainly upon questions of internal policy or unimportant party arrangement, caused her foreign policy to present a marked contrast to the vigorous, overbearing, but straightforward path followed by Pitt. Internal commotions, such as are apt to follow great wars, and above all the controversy with the North American colonies, which began as early as 1765 with the well-known Stamp Act, conspired with other causes to stay the hand of England. Twice at least during the years of Choiseul's ministry there occurred opportunities which a resolute, ready, and not too scrupulous government might easily have converted into a cause of war; the more so as they involved that sea power which is to England above all other nations the object of just and jealous concern. In 1764 the Genoese, weary of their unsuccessful attempts to control Corsica, again asked France to renew the occupation of the ports which had been garrisoned by her in 1756. The Corsicans also sent an ambassador to France in order to solicit recognition of the independence of the island, in consideration of a tribute equivalent to that which they had formerly paid to Genoa.

主。虽说还维持着现存的法、奥同盟关系，不过他的希望主要还是放在西班牙身上。"七年战争"的整个过程，已经证明并进一步阐述了他从一开始就坚持将英国视作法国主要敌人的那种睿智与远见。而西班牙只要治理得当，便是法国最可靠、最强大的盟友。两国紧密相邻的地理形势和两国海港的相对位置，都让海军的形势显得极其稳固；而通过明智的政策、家族纽带以及对英国制海权的合理担忧而确定下来的这种同盟关系，又因英国近来仍然在损害西班牙且必定会让西班牙继续心生怨恨，而让法国获得了进一步的保证。直布罗陀、米诺卡和佛罗里达仍然掌握在英国手中；在洗刷掉这一耻辱之前，任何西班牙人都是不会心安理得的。

人们很容易像法国历史学家所宣称的那样，认为英国对法国海军实力的增长感到忧心忡忡，并且很想及早将其铲除掉；不过，英国会不会愿意因此而对法国发动一场战争，这一点却更值得我们怀疑。《巴黎和约》签订之后的那些年间，由于主要都是受制于国内政策或者那些不重要的党争问题，历届政府任期都很短暂，故英国此时的外交政策与皮特所遵循的那种强势、专横而明确的外交路线相比，便形成了一种鲜明的对照。国内的种种骚乱，都极易引发大规模战争，而首当其冲的就是英国与北美各殖民地之间的纷争；此种纷争，早在1765年就因为那部著名的《印花税法案》而开始了，再加上其他的一些原因，使得北美各殖民地都不愿意再接受英国的统治了。在舒瓦瑟尔任期内，倘若英国政府果断、毫不犹豫且不是太过保守谨慎的话，本可以趁机将这种纷争变成发动战争的理由，并且这种情况至少出现过两次；因为那些纷争都涉及到了制海权，而对于英国来说，制海权是超越其他任何国家、值得它合理地去加以提防的目标，所以该

The latter, feeling its inability to reconquer the island, at length decided practically to cede it. The transaction took the shape of a formal permission for the King of France to exercise all the rights of sovereignty over all the places and harbors of Corsica, as security for debts owing to him by the republic. This cession, disguised under the form of a security in order to palliate the aggrandizement of France in the eyes of Austria and England, recalls the conditional and thinly veiled surrender of Cyprus to England nine years ago, — a transfer likely to be as final and far-reaching as that of Corsica. England then remonstrated and talked angrily; but though Burke said, "Corsica as a province of France is terrible to me," only one member of the House of Commons, the veteran admiral Sir Charles Saunders, was found to say "that it would be better to go to war with France than consent to her taking possession of Corsica." Having in view the then well-recognized interests of England in the Mediterranean, it is evident that an island so well situated as Corsica for influencing the shores of Italy and checking the naval station at Minorca, would not have been allowed to go into the hands of a strong master, if the nation had felt ready and willing for war.

Again, in 1770, a dispute arose between England and Spain relative to the possession of the Falkland Islands. It is not material to state the nature of either claim to what was then but a collection of barren islands, destitute of military as well as of natural advantages. Both England and Spain had had a settlement, on which the national colors were flying; and at the English station a captain in the navy commanded. Before this settlement, called Port Egmont, there suddenly appeared, in June, 1770, a Spanish expedition, fitted out in Buenos Ayres, of five frigates and sixteen hundred soldiers. To such a force the handful of Englishmen could make no serious resistance; so after a few shots, exchanged for the honor of the flag, they

国就更有可能这样做了。1764年，由于厌倦了在试图控制科西嘉的过程中屡战屡败的局面，热那亚人便再次要求法国重新占领1756年法国曾派兵驻守的那些港口。科西嘉也派了一位大使前往法国，想请求法国承认该岛独立，因为之前他们已经向热那亚支付了与此等值的赎金。热那亚因为觉得本国无法重新征服科西嘉岛，所以最终决定将科西嘉岛事实上割让出去。两国所签协定采取的形式是，正式允许法兰西国王在科西嘉的所有领土和海港行使全部的统治权，以此作为热那亚共和国所欠法国国王款项的抵押。这次领土割让以抵押的形式作外衣，是为了掩盖法国的扩张，骗过奥地利和英国的眼睛，故令人想起了9年之前让塞浦路斯有条件地、不加掩饰地向英国投降的情形——这是一种很可能像科西嘉那样不可更改而且影响深远的转让。所以英国表示反对，并且言辞激烈；不过，虽然伯克说过："科西嘉变成法国的一个省，在我看来糟糕得很，"但我们发现，只有一个下议院议员，即退役的海军上将查尔斯·桑德斯爵士，说了"同法国开战要比同意该国占领科西嘉好"这样的话。考虑到当时英国在地中海地区有着公认的利益，那么，倘若该国觉得自己准备好了且愿意开战的话，那么它就决不会允许一个像科西嘉这样位置险要、能够控制意大利沿海并遏制米诺卡海军基地的岛屿，落入到一个强大的敌人手中去。

再则，在1770年，英、西两国因福克兰群岛的归属问题产生了纠纷。说明两国所提的要求属于什么性质并不重要，因为两国所争的这个地方，当时还只是一群荒无人烟的岛屿，既无军事利益，又无自然利益。英国和西班牙在此处各有一个殖民地，都悬挂着各自的国旗；英国的基地由一位海军上校指挥。1770年6月，一支西班牙远征军突然出现在这个叫做埃格蒙特港的英国殖民地；这支远征军是在布宜诺斯艾利斯装备起来的，包括5艘护卫舰和1600名士兵。面对这样一支兵力，为数寥寥的英军是不可能做出什么顽强抵抗

capitulated.

The news of this transaction, which reached England in the following October, showed by its reception how much more serious is an insult than an injury, and how much more bitterly resented. The transfer of Corsica had scarcely occasioned a stir outside the offices of statesmen; the attack on Port Egmont roused the people and Parliament. The minister to Madrid was ordered to demand the immediate restoration of the islands. with a disavowal of the action of the officer who had ordered the attack. Without waiting for a reply, ships were ordered into commission, press-gangs swept the streets, and in a short time a powerful fleet was ready at Spithead to revenge the insult. Spain, relying upon the Bourbon family compact and the support of France, was disposed to stand firm; but the old king, Louis XV., was averse to war, and Choiseul, among whose enemies at court was the last mistress, was dismissed. With his fall disappeared the hopes of Spain, which at once complied with the demands of England, reserving, however, the question as to the rights of sovereignty. This conclusion shows clearly that England, though still wielding an effective sea power able to control Spain, was not eager for a war merely in order to break down the rival navies.

It is not wholly alien to the question of sea power to note, without dwelling upon it, a great event which now happened, seemingly utterly removed from all relation to the sea. The first partition of Poland between Prussia, Russia, and Austria, carried out in 1772, was made easier by the preoccupation of Choiseul with his naval policy and the Spanish alliance. The friendship and support of Poland and Turkey, as checks upon the House of Austria, were part of the tradition received from Henry IV. and Richelieu; the destruction of the former was a direct blow to the pride and interest of France. What Choiseul would have done had he been in office,

的；因此，为了国家荣誉而象征性地开了数炮之后，守卫此地的英军便缴械投降了。

发生这一事件的消息在随后的10月传到了英国，而英国对这一消息的反应表明，一种耻辱会比一种损害要严重得多，而受辱者的不满也要强烈得多。科西嘉易手，几乎没有在英国的政治家圈子之外引发什么骚动；可进攻埃格蒙特港，却既激怒了英国民众，也激怒了英国国会。驻马德里的英国公使接到命令，要求西班牙马上归还福克兰群岛，并且不得承认下令发动攻击的那名军官的行为。不待西班牙做出答复，英国政府又下令舰船做好战斗准备，征兵广告贴满了大街小巷，于是在很短的时间内，一支强大的舰队便在斯皮特海德整装待发，准备去洗雪耻辱了。西班牙倚仗着波旁皇室所签订的《家族盟约》以及法国的支持，打算坚定立场、毫不退缩；不过，太上皇路易十五反对战争，而舒瓦瑟尔也被解职了——他在宫廷中的对手之一，便是路易十五的最后一位情妇。随着舒瓦瑟尔倒台，西班牙也就没有了坚定立场的指望；于是，该国马上遵照英国的要求行事，不过还将福克兰群岛统治权的问题推到了以后再解决。这一结果清楚地表明，尽管英国还是能够利用其有效的制海权来控制西班牙，但该国并不希望仅仅为了摧毁敌方的海军便发动战争。

我们注意到，此时还发生了一件大事；虽说它似乎与海洋毫无关联，我们不会去详加描述，但它与制海权问题也并非全然是格格不入的。俄、普、奥三国于1772年对波兰的第一次瓜分，因为舒瓦瑟尔把精力全都放在该国的海军政策与法、西两国的同盟关系上，所以变得更简单了。争取波兰和土耳其两国的友好与支持，将其当成遏制哈布斯堡王室的力量，是法国从亨利四世和黎塞留时代继承下来的传统政策的一部分；所以，波兰的瓦解，对于法国的自尊和利益来说都是一种直接的打击。倘若舒瓦瑟尔还在任上，他会怎么做，我们不得而知；不过，倘若"七年战争"是一种不同的结局，那么法国可

cannot be known; but if the result of the Seven Years' War had been different, France might have interfered to some purpose.

On the 10th of May, 1774, Louis XV. died, at the time when the troubles in the North American colonies were fast coming to a head. Under his youthful successor, Louis XVI., the policy of peace on the continent, of friendly alliance with Spain, and of building up the navy in numbers and efficiency, was continued. This was the foreign policy of Choiseul, directed against the sea power of England as the chief enemy, and toward the sea power of France as the chief support, of the nation. The instructions which, according to a French naval author, the new king gave to his ministers show the spirit with which his reign up to the Revolution was inspired, whether or not they originated with the king himself: —

"To watch all indications of approaching danger; to observe by cruisers the approaches to our islands and the entrance to the Gulf of Mexico; to keep track of what was passing on the banks of Newfoundland, and to follow the tendencies of English commerce; to observe in England the state of the troops and armaments, the public credit and the ministry; to meddle adroitly in the affairs of the British colonies; to give the insurgent colonists the means of obtaining supplies of war, while maintaining the strictest neutrality; to develop actively, but noiselessly, the navy; to repair our ships of war; to fill our storehouses and to keep on hand the means for rapidly equipping a fleet at Brest and at Toulon, while Spain should be fitting one at Ferrol; finally, at the first serious fear of rupture, to assemble numerous troops upon the shores of Brittany and Normandy, and get everything ready for an invasion of England, so as to force her to concentrate her forces, and thus restrict her means of resistance at the extremities of the empire."

Such instructions, whether given all at once as a symmetrical, well-thought-out plan, or

能便会对瓜分波兰进行有效的干预了。

1774年5月10日，路易十五驾崩，此时正是北美殖民地问题迅速达到了紧要关头的时候。在年轻的继任者路易十六治下，法国继续实行在欧洲大陆保持和平、同西班牙结成友好盟邦以及加强海军兵力和效率等政策。这些都是舒瓦瑟尔的外交政策，它们非但直接针对首敌英国的制海权，还旨在确立法国的制海权，并将此种制海权当成支撑国家的主要力量。据一位法国海军作家称，新任国王给大臣们下达的指示，表明他直到大革命爆发之前的统治一直都为一种精神所激励着，无论这些指示是不是源自这位国王本人：

"应当警惕即将到来的种种危险之迹象；应当派遣巡逻舰对通往我国内陆及进入墨西哥湾的水路加以警戒；应当掌握经过纽芬兰沿海的船只货物，密切注意英国的贸易趋势；应当注意英国国内军队和军备、政府信用和内阁的情况；应当巧妙干预英属殖民地的事务；应当为叛乱殖民者提供获取战争物资的渠道，同时最为严格地保持中立；应当积极但悄无声息地发展海军；应当维修好我国的战舰；应当充实我国的仓库，确保能够在布雷斯特和土伦快速装备一支舰队，而西班牙也应当在费罗尔装备一支舰队；最后，一旦出现关系破裂的严重担忧，就应当在布列塔尼和诺曼底沿海地区集结大批兵力，做好入侵英国的一切准备，以迫使该国将兵力集中起来，从而限制该国兵力在大英帝国边远地区所进行的抵抗。"

这些命令，无论是作为一种系统的、经过深思熟虑的计划而一次性下达的，还是随着形势变化而不时下达的，都表明法国已经准确地预计到了当时的形势，并且流露出了一种坚定的信念——倘若早点儿抱有这种信念的话，就会极大地改变英、法两国的历

from time to time, as occasion arose, showed that an accurate forecast of the situation had been made, and breathed a conviction which, if earlier felt, would have greatly modified the history of the two countries. The execution was less thorough than the conception.

In the matter of developing the navy, however, fifteen years of peace and steady work showed good results. When war openly broke out in 1778, France had eighty ships-of-the-line in good condition, and sixty-seven thousand seamen were borne on the rolls of the maritime conscription. Spain, when she entered the war in 1779 as the ally of France, had in her ports nearly sixty ships-of-the-line. To this combination England opposed a total number of two hundred and twenty eight ships of all classes, of which about one hundred and fifty were of the line. The apparent equality in material which would result from these numbers was affected, to the disadvantage of England, by the superior size and artillery of the French and Spaniards; but on the other hand her strength was increased by the unity of aim imparted by belonging to one nation. The allies were destined to feel the proverbial weakness of naval coalitions, as well as the degenerate administration of Spain, and the lack of habit — may it not even be said without injustice, of aptitude for the sea — of both nations. The naval policy with which Louis XVI. began his reign was kept up to the end; in 1791, two years after the assembly of the States-General, the French navy numbered eighty-six ships-of-the-line, generally superior, both in dimensions and model, to English ships of the same class.

We have come, therefore, to the beginning of a truly maritime war; which, as will be granted by those who have followed this narrative, had not been seen since the days of De Ruyter and Tourville. The magnificence of sea power and its value had perhaps been more clearly shown by the uncontrolled sway, and consequent exaltation, of one belligerent; but the lesson thus given, if more striking, is less vividly interesting than the spectacle of

史。当然，法国在执行这些命令的时候，并没有说起来那么彻底。

然而，在发展壮大海军这个方面，15年的和平与不懈努力，还是带来了良好的效果。1778年英、法战争正式爆发的时候，法国已经拥有80艘船况良好的战舰，而海军的征兵名册上，也登记着67000名水兵。西班牙在1779年作为法国的盟国参战时，各海港中也泊有差不多60艘战舰。与这一组合进行对抗的英国，各类舰船总计有228艘，其中差不多150艘都是战舰。从这些数据来看，双方装备表面上是平等的，还因为法国和西班牙两国在兵力和火炮上占有优势，从而不利于英国；但从另一方面来看，英国的实力也因兵力属于一个国家、作战目标一致而得到了增强。法、西盟军注定会感受到不同的海军联合作战时那种尽人皆知的弱点，同时还会尝到西班牙海军那种颓废的管理方式以及两国海军都没有形成良好习惯——要是不公正一点，甚至可以说没有海上作战的资格——所带来的苦果。路易十六登基后开始实行的海军政策，一直维持到了最后；而到了1791年，即三级会议召集的两年之后，法国海军已经拥有了86艘战舰，而且综合性能都很好，在大小和样式两个方面都要优于英国的同类战舰。

因此，我们接下来要说明的，便是一场真正的海洋战争的初期了；这场战争，正如那些一直紧随本书脉络的读者所承认的那样，是自德·鲁伊特和图维尔那个时代以来所没过的一场海战。虽说一个交战国那种势不可挡的统治地位以及因此而来的趾高气扬，或许更加清晰地表明了制海权的辉煌及其价值，但由此而得到的教训，若说更为显著的话，也不会像那个海上强国遭遇一个值得它去刀剑相拼的仇敌，然后热血沸腾地拼尽全力与之战斗的场面那样生动有趣——这场战争，非但危及到了该国最为重要的殖民

that sea power meeting a foe worthy of its steel, and excited to exertion by a strife which endangered, not only its most valuable colonies, but even its own shores. Waged, from the extended character of the British Empire, in all quarters of the world at once, the attention of the student is called now to the East Indies and now to the West; now to the shores of the United States and thence to those of England; from New York and Chesapeake Bay to Gibraltar and Minorca, to the Cape Verde Islands, the Cape of Good Hope, and Ceylon. Fleets now meet fleets of equal size, and the general chase and the mêlée, which marked the actions of Hawke, Boscawen, and Anson, though they still occur at times, are for the most part succeeded by wary and complicated manoeuvres, too often barren of decisive results as naval battles, which are the prevailing characteristic of this coming war. The superior tactical science of the French succeeded in imparting to this conflict that peculiar feature of their naval policy, which subordinated the control of the sea by the destruction of the enemy's fleets, of his organized naval forces, to the success of particular operations, the retention of particular points, the carrying out of particular ulterior strategic ends. It is not necessary to endeavor to force upon others the conviction of the present writer that such a policy, however applicable as an exception, is faulty as a rule; but it is most desirable that all persons responsible for the conduct of naval affairs should recognize that the two lines of policy, in direct contradiction to each other, do exist. In the one there is a strict analogy to a war of posts; while in the other the objective is that force whose destruction leaves the posts unsupported and therefore sure to fall in due time. These opposing policies being recognized, consideration should also be had of the results of the two as exemplified in the history of England and France.

It was not, however, with such cautious views that the new king at first sought to impress

地，甚至还危及到了其本土上的沿海地区。由于不列颠帝国具有范围广袤的特点，所以战争同时在世界各地展开，而研究者的注意力一会儿需要转向东印度群岛，一会儿又要转向西方；一会儿需要注意合众国沿海地区，一会儿又要转向英国的沿海地区；还需要从纽约和切萨皮克湾转到直布罗陀和米诺卡，再转到佛得角群岛、好望角和锡兰。舰队方面，如今是规模相似的舰队相互遭遇，而曾经标志着霍克、博斯科恩和安森等人一场场战斗的那种全面追击和混战，尽管仍然会偶尔出现，但多半已为谨慎而复杂的机动所代替，并且海战往往没有产生出具有决定性的结果；这一点，就是即将发生的这场战争的显著特点。法国人高超的战术技巧，成功地让这次战争带上了法国海军政策的独特特征，那就是：通过摧毁敌方舰队及其有组织的海军力量而获得的制海权，须服从确保打赢特定战斗、守卫特定地点以及实现特定长远战略目标的需要。本书作者没有必要强迫他人接受自己的观点，说无论在例外情况下如何适用，此种政策通常都是一种败笔；不过，所有负责处理海军事务的人都应当认识到的确存在两种彼此直接对立的政策路线，说明这一点却是极有必要的。在其中的一种政策下，双方完全就像是在打一种要塞攻守战；而在另一种政策中，战争目标则是摧毁敌人的有生力量，使得要塞得到不增援，从而确保要塞在恰当的时候陷落。认识到了这两种相互对立的政策之后，我们还应当去思考英、法两国这两种政策导致的不同结果；这些结果，在两国历史上都已有例证。

然而，法国那位新任国王最初要让手下的海军将领牢记的，却并不是这些谨慎的观点。在发给奥尔维利埃伯爵、命令他统帅第一支从布雷斯特出发的舰队的指示中，海军大臣代表国王说：

his admirals. In the instructions addressed to the Count D'Orvilliers, commanding the first fleet sent out from Brest, the minister, speaking in the name of the king, says: —

"Your duty now is to restore to the French flag the lustre with which it once shone; past misfortunes and faults must be buried out of sight; only by the most illustrious actions can the navy hope to succeed in doing this. His Majesty has the right to expect the greatest efforts from his officers. ... Under whatever circumstances the king's fleet may be placed, his Majesty's orders, which he expressly charges me to impress upon you, as well as upon all officers in command, are that his ships attack with the greatest vigor, and defend themselves, on all occasions, to the last extremity."

More follows to the same effect; upon which a French officer, who has not before been quoted in connection with this phase of French naval policy, says: —

"How different this language from that held to our admirals during the last war; for it would be an error to believe that they followed by choice and temper the timid and defensive system which predominated in the tactics of the navy. The government, always finding the expenses exacted by the employment of the navy excessive, too often prescribed to its admirals to keep the sea as long as possible without coming to pitched battles, or even to brushes, generally very expensive, and from which might follow the loss of ships difficult to replace. Often they were enjoined, if driven to accept action, carefully to avoid compromising the fate of their squadron by too decisive encounters. They thought themselves, therefore, obliged to retreat as soon as an engagement took too serious a turn. Thus they acquired the unhappy habit of voluntarily yielding the field of battle as soon as an enemy, even inferior, boldly disputed it with them. Thus to send a fleet to meet the enemy, only to retire shamefully from his presence; to receive action instead of offering it; to begin battles only to end them with the semblance of

"你如今的职责，便是让法国国旗恢复其原有的辉煌；不准再让人看到过去的种种灾难和失误；只有通过最为辉煌的战斗，海军才有望成功地做到这一点。陛下有权希望自己手下的官兵做出最大的努力……陛下向我下达了明确指示，要你和你所指挥的官兵都牢牢记住，无论国王的舰队身处何种境地，陛下的命令都是：所有舰船须一往无前地进攻和防御，并且始终都须坚持到最后一刻。"

他还说了许多大意相同的话；关于这一点，我们在前文中说明法国此阶段的海军政策时并未引述过的一位法国将领，曾经如是说：

"这些话，与上一次战争中下达给我国海军将领的那些命令是多么的截然不同啊；要是认为这些海军将领是经过自主选择和出于本性，才遵循支配着海军战术的那种谨慎的防御政策，那你就错了。法国政府一向都认为海军所耗军费过多，所以海军将领们往往都尽可能久地在海上航行，而不愿与敌人去激战，甚至也不愿发生小战，因为只要开战，通常都会付出高昂代价，还有可能导致出现难以更替的舰船损失。倘若不得不与敌作战，舰队通常也会接到命令，要小心地避免打重大遭遇战，以免危及各支分舰队。因此，一旦战斗形势发生过于重大的转变，海军将领们自然就会认为自己必须撤退。于是，他们便形成了一种不好的习惯，一旦敌军勇敢无畏地与之作战，哪怕兵力不如他们，他们也会自动退出战场。这样一来，派遣舰队前去迎击敌人，就只会变成敌人一出现、法国舰队就令人惭愧地撤退的局面；它们只会被动地接受战斗，而不会主动出击；倘若发动战斗，那么只会落得个近乎失败的结局；为了挽救有形的作战力量，却毁掉了无形的道德力量——正如M·查尔斯·迪潘很有见地地说的那样，这就是引导着那个时

defeat; to ruin moral force in order to save physical force, — that was the spirit which, as has been very judiciously said by M. Charles Dupin, guided the French ministry of that epoch. The results are known."

The brave words of Louis XVI. were followed almost immediately by others, of different and qualifying tenor, to Admiral D'Orvilliers before he sailed. He was informed that the king, having learned the strength of the English fleet, relied upon his prudence as to the conduct to be followed at a moment when he had under his orders all the naval force of which France could dispose. As a matter of fact the two fleets were nearly equal; it would be impossible to decide which was the stronger, without detailed information as to the armament of every ship. D'Orvilliers found himself, as many a responsible man has before, with two sets of orders, on one or the other of which he was sure to be impaled, if unlucky; while the government, in the same event, was sure of a scape-goat.

The consideration of the relative force of the two navies, material and moral, has necessarily carried us beyond the date of the opening of the American Revolutionary War. Before beginning with that struggle, it may be well to supplement the rough estimate of England's total naval force, given, in lack of more precise information, by the statement of the First Lord of the Admiralty made in the House of Lords in November, 1777, a very few months before the war with France began. Replying to a complaint of the opposition as to the smallness of the Channel fleet, he said: —

"We have now forty-two ships-of-the-line in commission in Great Britain (without counting those on foreign service), thirty-five of which are completely manned, and ready for sea at a moment's warning. ... I do not believe that either France or Spain entertains any hostile disposition toward us; but from what I have now submitted to you, I am authorized to affirm that

代的法国政府的精神。结局我们都知道了。"

路易十六这些勇敢的话语，几乎马上得到了其他人的追捧，并且带着各种不同的意思，在奥尔维利埃上将率军出发之前，到达了他的耳朵里。他被告知，法国国王已经了解到英国舰队的实力，所以下令将法国能够调动的海军力量全都置于他的指挥之下后，法国国王所仰仗的，便是他在随后行动中的谨慎小心了。事实上，英、法两国舰队差不多势均力敌；倘若不知道每艘战舰上武器装备的详细情况，那就不可能判断哪支舰队实力更强。像以前许多有责任心的人一样，奥尔维利埃上将发现自己收到了两道命令，要是运气不好的话，无论按照哪道命令来行事，他都肯定会进退维谷、左右为难；而倘若运气不好，那么法国政府肯定也会成为替罪羊。

比较两支海军在装备和士气上的相对实力，必定已经让我们想到了美国革命战争爆发的那个时候。在开始描述此次战争之前，我们不妨还补充一点，粗略估计一下英国的全部海军力量；由于没有更为精确的材料，所以这种估计是从1777年11月，即英法战争爆发前数月，海军大臣在上议院的发言中得出的。在回答反对派说海峡舰队规模太小的指责时，他说：

"我们在大不列颠现有42艘现役战舰（不包括那些在国外执行任务的），其中有35艘为满员装备，一有警报便可出海作战……我认为法国和西班牙对我国并不怀有任何敌意；不过，从我此刻提交给各位的数据来看，我完全可以确定，整个波旁皇室的海军都不是我国海军的敌手。"

然而，我们必须说，在第二年3月凯珀尔上将受命指挥并用"水兵的眼光"（这是

our navy is more than a match for that of the whole House of Bourbon."

It must, however, be said that this pleasing prospect was not realized by Admiral Keppel when appointed to command in the following March, and looking at his fleet with (to use his own apt expression) "a seaman's eye;" and in June he went to sea with only twenty ships.

It is plainly undesirable to insert in a narrative of this character any account of the political questions which led to the separation of the United States from the British Empire. It has already been remarked that the separation followed upon a succession of blunders by the English ministry, — not unnatural in view of the ideas generally prevalent at that day as to the relations of colonies to the mother-country. It needed a man of commanding genius to recognize, not only the substantial justice of the American claims, — many did that, — but also the military strength of their situation, as before indicated. This lay in the distance of the colonies from home, their nearness to each other independently of the command of the sea, the character of the colonists, — mainly of English and Dutch stock, — and the probable hostility of France and Spain. Unfortunately for England, the men most able to cope with the situation were in the minority and out of office.

It has been said before that, had the thirteen colonies been islands, the sea power of Great Britain would have so completely isolated them that their fall, one after the other, must have ensued. To this it may be added that the narrowness of the strip then occupied by civilized man, and the manner in which it was intersected by estuaries of the sea and navigable rivers, practically reduced to the condition of islands, so far as mutual support went, great sections of the insurgent country, which were not large enough to stand alone, yet too large for their fall not to have been a fatal blow to the common cause. The most familiar case is that of the line of the Hudson, where the Bay of New York was held from the first by the British, who also took the

他的习惯说法）看着这支舰队的时候，他可没有看到这种令人愉快的前景；这一年6月他率军出海时，手下仅有20艘舰船。

在进行此种性质的叙述过程中，插叙导致合众国脱离不列颠帝国的那些政治问题，显然是不可取的。前面已经说过，合众国是在英国政府犯下了一连串的重大错误之后，才要脱离不列颠帝国的——但从当时普遍流行的、关于殖民地与母国关系的观念来看，英国政府的那些错误却都是合情合理的。当时需要一个具有统帅之才的人，既承认美洲殖民者的要求从本质上来说是公平合理的——许多人都认识到了这一点——又要认识到前面已经表明的、殖民者所处位置在军事上的优势。这种优势，在于各殖民地都远离英国，在于它们彼此接近，不受制海权的制约，在于殖民者的特点——他们主要都是英国或荷兰血统，以及法国和西班牙很可能采取敌视的态度。可惜的是，英国那些最具才干、能够应对这一局面的人，既属于少数派，又全都并不掌权。

前文已经说过，倘若这13个殖民地都是岛屿的话，大不列颠的制海权就可以彻底将它们孤立开来，使得它们一个接一个地相继陷落。对于这个方面，我们还可以补充一点，那就是当时文明人所占的区域非常狭长，且河流入海口和可通航的河流在这些地区之间纵横交错，使得各个地区的状况几乎跟岛屿差不多；至于相互支援这个方面，因为叛乱地区虽说为数众多，且各自面积都不够大，无法独自支撑下去，但加起来面积却又太大，倘若不能相互支援，它们的共同事业就会受到致命打击。大家都熟悉的一个例子便是哈德逊河防线；从一开始英军就占领了那里的纽约湾，后来又在《独立宣言》发布后两个月的1776年9月占领了纽约市。当时驾驶帆船在这样一条河流上来去，无疑比有

city in September, 1776, two months after the Declaration of Independence. The difficulties in the way of moving up and down such a stream were doubtless much greater to sailing vessels than they now are to steamers; yet it seems impossible to doubt that active and capable men wielding the great sea power of England could so have held that river and Lake Champlain with ships-of-war at intervals and accompanying galleys as to have supported a sufficient army moving between the head-waters of the Hudson and the lake, while themselves preventing any intercourse by water between New England and the States west of the river. This operation would have closely resembled that by which in the Civil War the United States fleets and armies gradually cut in twain the Southern Confederacy by mastering the course of the Mississippi, and the political results would have been even more important than the military; for at that early stage of the war the spirit of independence was far more general and bitter in the section that would have been cut off, — in New England, — than in New York and New Jersey, perhaps than anywhere except in South Carolina.[1]

In 1777 the British attempted to accomplish this object by sending General Burgoyne from Canada to force his way by Lake Champlain to the Hudson. At the same time Sir Henry Clinton moved north from New York with three thousand men, and reached West Point, whence he sent by shipping a part of his force up the river to within forty miles of Albany. Here the officer in command learned of the surrender of Burgoyne at Saratoga, and returned; but what he did at the head of a detachment from a main body of only three thousand, shows what might have been done under a better system. While this was happening on the Hudson, the English commander-in-chief of the troops acting in America had curiously enough made use of the sea power of his nation to transport the bulk of his army — fourteen thousand men — from New York to the head of Chesapeake Bay, so as to take Philadelphia in the rear. This eccentric movement was successful as regarded its objective, Philadelphia; but it was determined by political

了汽轮的如今要困难得多;不过,一些积极而能干的人士,倘若利用英国那种伟大的制海权,本来能够凭借战舰时不时地掌控哈德逊河与尚普兰湖,并用单桅帆船帮助运送足够多的陆军往返于哈德逊上游与尚普兰湖之间,同时自身还能阻断新英格兰与哈德逊河以西诸州之间的水路交通,这一点似乎是不容置疑的。这种做法,跟美国内战中合众国的舰队和陆军通过控制密西西比航道、逐渐将南部邦联隔成两半的做法本来是极其相似的,并且其政治效果会比军事效果重大得多;因为在此次战争的初期阶段,在本可以孤立起来的这一地区,即新英格兰,民众的独立风气要比纽约和新泽西更普遍、更强烈,或许甚至比除了南卡罗莱纳以外的其他任何地区都要更普遍、更强烈。[1]

1777年,英国想要实现这一目标,便派博戈因将军率军从加拿大出发,准备强行打通经由尚普兰河通往哈德逊河的通道。与此同时,亨利·柯林顿勋爵率领3000士兵从纽约北上,到达了西点,并在此处用船只运送一部分兵力溯河而上,抵达了距阿尔巴尼不到40英里的地方。就在此处,这支分队的指挥官得知了博戈因将军在萨拉托加投降的消息,便退了回来;不过,作为一支主力只有3000士兵的分队指挥官,他的做法却表明,倘若有着一种更好的制度,这支分队本来是可以有更大作为的。尽管这一切都发生在哈德逊河上,但很奇怪的是,在美洲作战的英军总司令却利用英国的制海权,将自己的大部分陆军——14000兵力——从纽约运送到了切萨皮克湾的岬角上,以便占领岬角后端的费城;不过,这是由政治方面的考量决定的——因为费城是合众国国会所在地——与正确的军事政策却完全背道而驰。因此,占领后的费城很快又陷落了;但是,占领费城

considerations, because Philadelphia was the seat of Congress, and was contrary to sound military policy. The conquest therefore was early lost; but it was yet more dearly won, for by this diversion of the British forces the different corps were placed out of mutual support, and the control of the water-line of the Hudson was abandoned. While Burgoyne, with seven thousand regular troops, besides auxiliaries, was moving down to seize the head-waters of the river, fourteen thousand men were removed from its mouth to the Chesapeake. The eight thousand left in or near New York were consequently tied to the city by the presence of the American army in New Jersey. This disastrous step was taken in August; in October Burgoyne, isolated and hemmed in, surrendered. In the following May the English evacuated Philadelphia, and after a painful and perilous march through New Jersey, with Washington's army in close pursuit, regained New York.

This taking of the British fleet to the head of the Chesapeake, coupled with the ascent of the Potomac in 1814 by English sailing-frigates, shows another weak line in the chain of the American colonies; but it was not, like that of the Hudson and Champlain, a line both ends of which rested in the enemy's power, — in Canada on the one hand, on the sea on the other.

As to the sea warfare in general, it is needless to enlarge upon the fact that the colonists could make no head against the fleets of Great Britain, and were consequently forced to abandon the sea to them, resorting only to a cruising warfare, mainly by privateers, for which their seamanship and enterprise well fitted them, and by which they did much injury to English commerce. By the end of 1778 the English naval historian estimates that American privateers had taken nearly a thousand merchant-ships, valued at nearly £2,000,000; he claims, however, that the losses of the Americans were heavier. They should have been; for the English cruisers were both better supported and individually more powerful, while the extension of American commerce had come to be the wonder of the statesmen of the mother-country. When the war

却让英国付出了高昂的代价，因为分兵此处之后，英军的其他部队便无法相互支援，从而放弃了对哈德逊河水道的控制。就在博戈因率7000正规兵力以及后备力量南下，准备攻取哈德逊河上游的时候，却有14000兵力从哈德逊河河口调往了切萨皮克湾。于是，留在纽约市内或附近地区的那8000英军，便被新泽西的美国军队困在了当地。这一毁灭性的做法，是在8月份出现的；而到了10月，博戈因将军因为孤立无援、陷入了重重包围，便投降了。第二年5月，英军撤离了费城；因华盛顿所率部队紧追不舍，所以他们费了九牛二虎之力才穿过了危机四伏的新泽西，并重新占领了纽约。

将英国舰队调往切萨皮克湾岬角，连同1814年英国的帆船护卫舰溯波托马克河而上，还表现出了美洲殖民地链条上的另一处薄弱防线；不过，它与哈德逊河与尚普兰湖防线不同，并非两端都处在敌人的势力之下——它的一端在加拿大境内，一端则是海洋。

至于海上战争的概况，我们无需再来详述这样一种事实：殖民者无法与大不列颠舰队硬碰硬，故不得不让海洋任由英军掌控，只能求助于巡航战，并且主要是由私掠者来进行，因为私掠者的航海技术与冒险精神很适合于干这个，而他们的私掠活动，也给英国贸易带来了严重的损害。那位英国海军历史学家估计，到1778年年底，美国的私掠者差不多已经俘获了1000艘商船，价值大约200万英镑；然而，他还称，美国人的损失更惨重。这是理所当然的，因为英国的巡逻舰非但有着更好的援兵，单艘舰船的作战能力也更强大；而美国贸易的扩张，也逐渐开始成为英国的政治家们大惑不解的一件事情。战争爆发的时候，美国贸易的规模，已经达到了英国在本世纪初的贸易规模。

broke out, it was as great as that of England herself at the beginning of the century.

An interesting indication of the number of the seafaring population of North America at that time is given by the statement in Parliament by the First Lord of the Admiralty, "that the navy had lost eighteen thousand of the seamen employed in the last war by not having America," — no inconsiderable loss to a sea power, particularly if carried over to the ranks of the enemy.

The course of warfare on the sea gave rise, as always, to grievances of neutrals against the English for the seizures of their ships in the American trade. Such provocation, however, was not necessary to excite the enmity and the hopes of France in the harassed state of the British government. The hour of reckoning, of vengeance, at which the policy of Choiseul had aimed, seemed now at hand. The question was early entertained at Paris what attitude should be assumed, what advantage drawn from the revolt of the colonies. It was decided that the latter should receive all possible support short of an actual break with England; and to this end a Frenchman named Beaumarchais was furnished with money to establish a business house which should supply the colonists with warlike stores. France gave a million francs, to which Spain added an equal sum, and Beaumarchais was allowed to buy from government arsenals. Meanwhile agents were received from the United States, and French officers passed into its service with little real hindrance from their government. Beaumarchais' house was started in 1776; in December of that year Benjamin Franklin landed in France, and in May, 1777, Lafayette came to America. Meanwhile the preparations for war, especially for a sea war, were pushed on; the navy was steadily increased, and arrangements were made for threatening an invasion from the Channel, while the real scene of the war was to be in the colonies. There France was in the position of a man who has little to lose. Already despoiled of Canada, she had

英国海军大臣在国会发言时，曾经很有意思地暗示出了当时北美殖民地从事航海事业的人口数量："由于没有了美洲，海军损失了在上一次战争中所雇用的18000名海员。"对于一个海洋大国来说，这种损失可不是无足轻重的，而倘若这些海员转而充实到敌方队伍中去，则尤其是一种重大损失了。

像以前一样，海上战争使得各个中立国家都对英国心生怨恨，因为英军扣押了各国与美洲进行贸易的船只。然而此种挑衅，并不是在英国政府处于筋疲力尽的时候激起中立国家的敌意、并让法国生出希望的必要条件。舒瓦瑟尔所定政策之目标，即进行清算和报复英国的时候，此时似乎即将到来了。巴黎早就在考虑这一问题，考虑该采取一种什么样的态度，考虑法国能够从北美殖民地革命当中获得什么样的好处。法国政府决定，应当给各殖民地提供一切可能的、同时又不足以同英国真正决裂的支援；为了实现这一目的，法国政府给一个名叫博马舍的法国人提供资金，让他成立了一家商行，来向北美殖民者供应战争物资。法国和西班牙各拨了100万法郎的款项，并且允许博马舍从政府开设的兵工厂里进行采购。与此同时，来自合众国的政府代表也得到了法国的承认，而法国官员在为合众国服务的时候，法国政府也很少真正加以阻挠。博马舍的商行于1776年开业；是年12月，本杰明·富兰克林抵达法国，而1777年5月，拉斐特也来到了美洲。在此期间，法国还在加紧备战，尤其是准备进行一场海战；该国海军的实力已得到稳步增强，还做出了部署，准备威胁英国，说要从英吉利海峡入侵英国，而真正的战场，其实却是在北美殖民地。在北美殖民地，法国就像是个光棍，不会有什么损失。加拿大业已被英国夺走，故法国完全有理由认为，因为欧洲的中立国和美国人是友非

every reason to believe that a renewal of war, with Europe neutral and the Americans friends instead of enemies, would not rob her of her islands. Recognizing that the Americans, who less than twenty years before had insisted upon the conquest of Canada, would not consent to her regaining it, she expressly stipulated that she would have no such hopes, but exacted that in the coming war she should retain any English West Indian possessions which she could seize. Spain was differently situated. Hating England, wanting to regain Gibraltar, Minorca, and Jamaica, — no mere jewels in her crown, but foundation-stones of her sea power, — she nevertheless saw that the successful rebellion of the English colonists against the hitherto unrivalled sea power of the mother-country would be a dangerous example to her own enormous colonial system, from which she yearly drew so great subsidies. If England with her navy should fail, what could Spain achieve? In the introductory chapter it was pointed out that the income of the Spanish government was drawn, not as a light tax upon a wealthy sea power, built upon the industry and commerce of the kingdom, but from a narrow stream of gold and silver trickling through a few treasure-ships loaded with the spoils of colonies administered upon the narrowest system. Spain had much to lose, as well as to gain. It was true still, as in 1760, that she was the power with which England could war to the greatest advantage. Nevertheless, existing injuries and dynastic sympathy carried the day. Spain entered upon the secretly hostile course pursued by France.

To this explosive condition of things the news of Burgoyne's surrender acted as a spark. The experience of former wars had taught France the worth of the Americans as enemies, and she was expecting to find in them valuable helpers in her schemes of revenge; now it seemed that even alone they might be able to take care of themselves, and reject any alliance. The tidings reached Europe on the 2d of December, 1777; on the 16th the French foreign minister informed the commissioners of Congress that the king was ready to recognize the independence

敌，所以继续同英国作战，自然不会让法国再失去那些殖民地岛屿了。由于美国人在20年前曾坚持要求英国攻下加拿大，所以在认识到他们不会同意法国收复该地之后，法国政府便明确保证，说该国没有收复加拿大的打算，而是要求在接下来的这场战争里，英属西印度群岛的殖民地中，凡是法军能够占领的，都应当归法国所有。西班牙的处境则不一样。虽说该国憎恨英国，并且想要收复直布罗陀、米诺卡和牙买加——这几个地方非但是西班牙王冠上的明珠，还是其确立制海权的基石——但它也明白，英裔殖民者反抗迄今为止具有无可匹敌之制海权的祖国倘若获得成功的话，就会成为一个危险的例子，危及到西班牙本国那种巨大的殖民体系，而西班牙每年都从这一体系中获得了不菲的利益。要是英国有着强大的海军都失败了，那么西班牙又能获得什么呢？在"导论"那一章中我们已经指出，西班牙政府的岁入，并不是以国内工业和贸易为基础，建立起一个富裕的海洋大国，然后征取轻徭薄赋得来的，而是在那种狭窄的殖民体系管控之下，从各个殖民地掠夺赃物，再用为数不多的运宝船一点一点地将金银运回西班牙而获得的。因此，西班牙既会损失巨大，也会收获良多。不过，跟1760年的情况一样，倘若英、西两国交战，那么英国仍然会占尽优势。尽管如此，英国业已对该国造成的损害和法、西两国王室的共同情感，还是占据了上风。于是，西班牙也加入了法国实行的那种暗中与英国作对的道路。

对于此时一触即发、极其危险的形势来说，博戈因投降的消息便成为了导火索。过去历次战争的经验，让法国懂得了曾经与之为敌的美国人的价值，所以法国便希望在美国人当中寻找到得力的帮手，来帮助它实施报复英国的计划；可如今看来，即便是单打独斗，美国人也游刃有余，并且不会与任何国家结盟了。美国独立的消息于1777年12月2

of the United States, and to make with them a commercial treaty and contingent defensive alliance. The speed with which the business was done shows that France had made up her mind; and the treaty, so momentous in its necessary consequences, was signed on the 6th of February, 1778.

It is not necessary to give the detailed terms of the treaty; but it is important to observe, first, that the express renunciation of Canada and Nova Scotia by France foreshadowed that political theory which is now known as the Monroe doctrine, the claims of which can scarcely be made good without an adequate sea-force; and next, that the alliance with France, and subsequently with Spain, brought to the Americans that which they above all needed, — a sea power to counterbalance that of England. Will it be too much for American pride to admit that, had France refused to contest the control of the sea with England, the latter would have been able to reduce the Atlantic seaboard? Let us not kick down the ladder by which we mounted, nor refuse to acknowledge what our fathers felt in their hour of trial.

Before going on with the story of this maritime war, the military situation as it existed in the different parts of the world should be stated.

The three features which cause it to differ markedly from that at the opening of the Seven Years' War, in 1756, are — 1. the hostile relation of America to England; 2. the early appearance of Spain as the ally of France; and 3. the neutrality of the other continental States, which left France without preoccupation on the land side.

On the North American continent the Americans had held Boston for two years. Narragansett Bay and Rhode Island were occupied by the English, who also held New York and Philadelphia. Chesapeake Bay and its entrance, being without strong posts, were in the power of any fleet that appeared against them. In the South, since the unsuccessful attack upon

日传到了欧洲；16日，法国外交大臣便通知美国的国会委员，说法国国王准备承认合众国独立，并且准备与合众国签署贸易条约，结成可能的防守同盟。法国处理此事的速度表明它已经下定了决心；而这份意义必然重大的贸易条约，则于1778年2月6日签署了。

我们无需细述这份条约的具体条款；不过，重要的是要注意到下述两个方面：首先，法国明确放弃加拿大和新斯科舍的做法，是如今我们所知的"门罗主义"的先声，因为倘若没有一支恰当的海军力量，法国是很难成功地要回这两个地方的；其次，与法国结盟以及后来又与西班牙结成盟国，使得美国人获得了他们最需要的东西——那就是一种能够与英国相抗衡的制海权。承认倘若法国不愿与英国争夺制海权的话，英国本来是能够攻取大西洋沿岸北美各地的，难道还会损害到美国人的自尊心吗？我们既不能过河拆桥，也不能否认我们的先辈们在历经磨难时的感受。

在继续描述这次海战的经过之前，我们还应当说明一下世界各地当时的军事形势。

此次战争，与1756年爆发的"七年战争"有着显著不同的三大特点：1. 美洲与英国为敌；2. 西班牙很早就与法国结成了同盟；3. 欧洲大陆上其他国家都采取中立态度，使得法国在欧洲大陆上没有急需应对的问题。

在北美大陆上，美国人已经占领波士顿两年了。英国人占领着纳拉干塞特湾和罗德岛，同时还占领着纽约和费城。切萨皮克湾及其入口由于没有强大的据点，所以哪支舰队前来攻打，便处于哪支舰队的掌控之下。在南方，自1776年进攻查尔斯顿失利之后，英军并未进行什么重大行动；直到法国宣战之前，主要战事都是发生在切萨皮克湾（的巴尔的摩）以北。而另一方面，美国人攻取加拿大失利，所以直到战争最后，加拿大一

Charlestown in 1776, no movement of importance had been made by the English; up to the declaration of war by France the chief events of the war had been north of the Chesapeake (of Baltimore). In Canada, on the other hand, the Americans had failed, and it remained to the end a firm base to the English power.

In Europe the most significant element to be noted is the state of preparedness of the French navy, and to some extent of the Spanish, as compared with previous wars. England stood wholly on the defensive, and without allies; while the Bourbon kings aimed at the conquest of Gibraltar and Port Mahon, and the invasion of England. The first two, however, were the dear objects of Spain, the last of France; and this divergence of aims was fatal to the success of this maritime coalition. In the introductory chapter allusion was made to the strategic question raised by these two policies.

In the West Indies the grip of the two combatants on the land was in fact about equal, though it should not have been so. Both France and England were strongly posted in the Windward Islands, — the one at Martinique, the other at Barbadoes. It must be noted that the position of the latter, to windward of all others of the group, was a decided strategic advantage in the days of sail. As it happened, the fighting was pretty nearly confined to the neighborhood of the Lesser Antilles. Here, at the opening of the struggle, the English island of Dominica lay between the French Martinique and Guadeloupe; it was therefore coveted and seized. Next south of Martinique lay Sta. Lucia, a French colony. Its strong harbor on the lee side, known as Gros Ilot Bay, was a capital place from which to watch the proceedings of the French navy in Fort Royal, Martinique. The English captured the island, and from that safe anchorage Rodney watched and pursued the French fleet before his famous action in 1782. The islands to the southward were of inferior military consequence. In the greater islands, Spain should have

直都是英军一处坚实的基地。

在欧洲，我们需加以注意的一个最重要的方面，便是跟以前的历次战争相比，法国海军这一次有了充分的准备，而西班牙海军也做好了一定程度的准备。英国完全处于守势，并且没有盟友；而法、西两位波旁国王的目标，则是攻取直布罗陀和马翁港，并且入侵英国。不过，前面两个其实是西班牙最热切的目标，后者才是法国的目标；所以，这种目标上的分歧，便成了导致这次两国在海上结成联盟未能获胜的致命原因。在《导论》一章中，我们已经提及了法、西两国政策不同而引发的战略问题。

在西印度群岛，交战双方在陆地上的实力事实上相差无几，尽管形势本来不应当是这样。法、英两国在温德华群岛上都拥有强大的据点——法国据守着马提尼克，而英国则牢牢掌控着巴巴多斯。我们必须注意到，巴巴多斯地处其他各个岛屿的上风位置，这在帆船时代是一种具有决定意义的优势。巧合的是，两国之间的战斗几乎全都限于小安的列斯群岛附近海域。战争刚刚爆发的时候，英属多米尼加岛正位于法属马提尼克岛和瓜达鲁佩之间；所以法国一直觊觎并且攻下了此处。紧邻马提尼克南边的是圣卢西亚，它也是法国的殖民地。此处背风位置有一个牢固的海港，叫格罗斯岛湾，它是一处要地，能够监视马提尼克岛皇家要塞内法国海军的动静。英军攻取了这个岛屿；罗德尼则在1782年那场著名的海战之前，一直以这个安然稳固的海港为锚地，监视并追击法国舰队。再往南的那些岛屿，都没有什么大的军事重要性。在那些较大的岛屿上，西班牙本来可以压制住英国，像控制古巴、波多黎各两地并跟法国一起控制海地那样，独自来对抗牙买加的。然而西班牙却认为，此处对它来说毫无价值，只是一种累赘罢了；更何

outweighed England, holding as she did Cuba, Porto Rico, and, with France, Hayti, as against Jamaica alone. Spain, however, counted here for nothing but a dead-weight; and England had elsewhere too much on her hands to attack her. The only point in America where the Spanish arms made themselves felt was in the great region east of the Mississippi, then known as Florida, which, though at that time an English possession, did not join the revolt of the colonies.

In the East Indies it will be remembered that France had received back her stations at the peace of 1763; but the political predominance of the English in Bengal was not offset by similar control of the French in any part of the peninsula. During the ensuing years the English had extended and strengthened their power, favored in so doing by the character of their chief representatives, Clive and Warren Hastings. Powerful native enemies had, however, risen against them in the south of the peninsula, both on the east and west, affording an excellent opportunity for France to regain her influence when the war broke out; but her government and people remained blind to the possibilities of that vast region. Not so England. The very day the news of the outbreak of war reached Calcutta, July 7, 1778, Hastings sent orders to the governor of Madras to attack Pondicherry, and set the example by seizing Chandernagore. The naval force of each nation was insignificant; but the French commodore, after a brief action, forsook Pondicherry, which surrendered after a siege by land and sea of seventy days. The following March, 1779, Mahé, the last French settlement, fell, and the French flag again disappeared; while at the same time there arrived a strong English squadron of six ships-of-the-line under Admiral Hughes. The absence of any similar French force gave the entire control of the sea to the English until the arrival of Suffren, nearly three years later. In the mean while Holland had been drawn into the war, and her stations, Negapatam on the Coromandel coast, and the very important harbor of Trincomalee in Ceylon, were both captured, the latter in January, 1782, by

况，英军在别的地方已经压得它喘不过气来，所以该国根本就无暇再来攻打牙买加。西班牙军队在美洲唯一产生过重要作用的地方，便是在密西西比河以东、时称佛罗里达的那片广袤地区；此处那时虽说也是英国的殖民地，但并未与其他殖民地一起反叛。

在东印度群岛，我们应当还记得，法国通过1763年所签和约，收复了该国原有的那些军事基地；不过，法国虽说还控制着印度半岛上的其他地区，却并未因此而抵消掉英国在孟加拉的政治优势。随后的那些年间，在其首席代表克莱夫和沃伦·黑斯廷斯的支持之下，英国的势力得到了扩张和巩固。但是，在印度半岛的南方地区，东西两面都有强大的本地敌对势力起来反抗英军，从而使得此次战争爆发之后，法国有了恢复其势力范围的绝佳机会；可法国政府和民众，对这一广袤地区的发展潜力却仍然视而不见。英国可不是这样。1778年7月7日，当战争爆发的消息一传到加尔各答，黑斯廷斯便派人命令马德拉斯总督进攻庞迪切里，还率先攻下了金德纳格尔以作示范。两国部署在东印度群岛的海军兵力都微不足道，但法国准将在匆匆小战之后，便放弃了庞迪切里；海陆两面都被围困70天之后，该地最终还是投降了。1779年3月，法国的最后一个殖民地马埃岛陷落，于是法国国旗在东印度群岛再次消失了；与此同时，休斯上将也率领一支由6艘战舰组成的强大舰队，来到了此处。由于法国在此地并没有与之抗衡的海军力量，因此整个海域便完全处在英军的掌控之下，直到差不多3年后苏弗朗率军前来，才改变这一局面。在此期间，荷兰也被拖入了战争之中，该国的两处军事基地，即科罗曼德尔沿海的奈伽帕塔姆以及位于锡兰的亭可马里这个重要港口，都被英军占领了；后者是在1782年1月被英国的海陆两军联合攻下的。成功占领这两处要地，使得苏弗朗在一个月

the joint forces of the army and navy. The successful accomplishment of these two enterprises completed the military situation in Hindostan at the time when the arrival of Suffren, just one month later, turned the nominal war into a desperate and bloody contest. Suffren found himself with a decidedly stronger squadron, but without a port, either French or allied, on which to base his operations against the English.

Of these four chief theatres of the war, two, North America and the West Indies, as might be expected from their nearness, blend and directly affect each other. This is not so obviously the case with the struggles in Europe and India. The narrative therefore naturally falls into three principal divisions, which may to some extent be treated separately. After such separate consideration their mutual influence will be pointed out, together with any useful lessons to be gathered from the goodness or badness, the success or failure, of the grand combinations, and from the part played by sea power.

On the 13th of March, 1778, the French ambassador at London notified the English government that France had acknowledged the independence of the United States, and made with them a treaty of commerce and defensive alliance. England at once recalled her ambassador; but though war was imminent and England at disadvantage, the Spanish king offered mediation, and France wrongly delayed to strike. In June, Admiral Keppel sailed from Portsmouth, with twenty ships, on a cruise. Falling in with two French frigates, his guns, to bring them to, opened the war. Finding from their papers that thirty-two French ships lay in Brest, he at once returned for reinforcements. Sailing again with thirty ships, he fell in with the French fleet under D'Orvilliers to the westward of Ushant, and to windward, with a westerly wind. On the 27th of July was fought the first fleet action of the war, generally known as the battle of Ushant.

This battle, in which thirty ships-of-the-line fought on either side, was wholly indecisive in

后率军抵达此处时，印度斯坦的军事形势已经完全掌控在英军手里，从而让一场有名无实的战争，变成了一场孤注一掷而血腥无比的争夺战。苏弗朗虽说拥有一支极其强大的舰队，可此地却没有法国及其盟友的一处港口，使他能够以之为基地来对英军作战。

在此次战争的四大主要战场中，北美洲和西印度群岛两处因为相距甚近，故可想而知，它们之间可以相互协调并且直接影响到彼此。在欧洲和印度，战争形势则并没有如此明显。因此，我们的叙述自然便会集中于三个主要的方面；而从某种程度上来说，对这三个方面，也可以彼此独立地来加以研究。经过这种个别研究之后，我们还会指出它们的共同影响，并且从大规模联合作战的好坏与成败，以及制海权所起的作用这两个方面，总结出一些有益的教训来。

1778年3月13日，驻伦敦的法国大使通知英国政府，说法国已经承认合众国独立，并同合众国签署了一份贸易和防守同盟条约。英国马上召回了驻法大使；不过，虽说战争迫在眉睫且英国处于不利地位，但西班牙国王还是提出进行居间调停，所以法国错误地耽搁了发动进攻的时机。6月，凯珀尔上将率领20艘舰船从朴茨茅斯起航去巡逻。途中遭遇了两艘法国护卫舰，他想让这两艘护卫舰停船，便下令开了两炮，从而打响了此次战争。他从这两艘船上缴获的文件中发现，法国在布雷斯特有32艘舰船，马上便返回去请援兵。率领30艘战舰再次起航之后，他在韦桑岛以西海域遇上了奥尔维利埃指挥的法国舰队；当时正刮西风，法军处于上风位置。于是，7月27日便打响了此次战争中第一场由两国舰队参与的海战，史称韦桑岛海战。

此次海战中，虽说双方都有30艘战舰参战，但结果却全然不具决定性意义。没有一

its results. No ship was taken or sunk; both fleets, after separating, returned to their respective ports. The action nevertheless obtained great celebrity in England from the public indignation at its lack of result, and from the storm of naval and political controversy which followed. The admiral and the officer third in command belonged to different political parties; they made charges, one against the other, and in the following courts-martial all England divided, chiefly on party lines. Public and naval sentiment generally favored the commander-in-chief, Keppel.

Tactically, the battle presents some interesting features, and involves one issue which is still living to-day. Keppel was to leeward and wished to force an action; in order to do this he signalled a general chase to windward, so that his fastest ships might overtake the slower ones of the enemy. Granting equal original fleet-speed, this was quite correct. D'Orvilliers, to windward, had no intention of fighting except on his own terms. As will generally be the case, the fleet acting on the offensive obtained its wish. At daybreak of the 27th both fleets were on the port tack, heading west-northwest, with a steady breeze at southwest. The English rear had fallen to leeward, and Keppel consequently made signal to six of its ships to chase to windward, so as to place them in a better position to support the main body if it could get into action. D'Orvilliers observed this movement, and construed it to show an intention to attack his rear with a superior force. The two fleets being then from six to eight miles apart, he wore his fleet in succession, by which he lost ground to leeward, but approached the enemy, and was able to see them better. At the completion of this evolution the wind hauled to the southward, favoring the English; so Keppel, instead of going about, stood on for half an hour more, and then tacked together in wake of the French. This confirmed D'Orvilliers' suspicions, and as the wind, which certainly favored the English that morning, now hauled back again to the westward, permitting them to lay up for the French rear, he wore his fleet together, thus bringing the rest to aid the

艘舰船被俘或者被击沉；两支舰队分开后，便都返回了各自的港口。尽管如此，由于此战一无所获，英国民众愤慨不已，并且随后在海军内部引发了一场巨大的动荡和政治争论，英国海军还是变得大名鼎鼎了。凯珀尔上将与舰队的第三指挥官分属不同的政党；他们都相互指责对方，而在随后召开的军事审判中，所有英国人都分了组、站了队，并且主要都是根据政党的路线来站队的。不过，民众和海军内部的意见普遍都是支持舰队总司令，即凯珀尔上将的。

从战术上来看，此次海战还具有一些很有意思的特点，并且涉及到了一个如今仍然有效的问题。凯珀尔率舰队驶向下风，希望迫使法军与之交战；为了达到这一目的，他发出了迎风进行全面追击的信号，以使己方速度最快的战舰能够赶上敌方速度较慢的舰船。假定双方舰队起初的速度相同，那么这一命令是相当正确的。可处在上风位置的奥尔维利埃，除非按照他自己的条件来，否则便无意交战。据通常情况来看，主动进击的舰队一般都会如愿以偿。到了27日拂晓，两支舰队都已是左舷抢风，在平稳的西南风下向西北偏西航行。英军后翼已经落在了下风向，于是凯珀尔便下令由6艘战舰迎风追击，以便在舰队主力能够与敌交战的时候，让这些战舰处在较为有利的位置，来支援主力舰队。奥尔维利埃注意到了英军的这种调动，以为这是英军准备用优势兵力进攻其后翼分队。两支舰队当时相距大约6至8英里，他便命令舰队鱼贯转向下风，这样一来，他便失去有利位置而处于下风向了；不过，这样也使他接近了敌军，看得更清楚了。完成这一机动之后，风向却转为南风，有利于英军了；于是凯珀尔不再转向，而是保持着航向航行了半个多小时，然后便紧随着法国舰队一起抢风行驶。这让奥尔维利埃更加确信自己的怀疑了，而由于那天上

rear, now become the van, and preventing Keppel from concentrating on or penetrating it. The two fleets thus passed on opposite tacks,[2] exchanging ineffective broadsides, the French running free to windward and having the power to attack, but not using it. D'Orvilliers then made the signal for his van, formerly the rear, to wear to leeward of the English rear, which was to leeward of its own main body, intending himself to remain to windward and so attack it on both sides; but the commander of that division, a prince of the blood royal, did not obey, and the possible advantage was lost. On the English side the same manoeuvre was attempted. The admiral of the van and some of his ships tacked, as soon as out of fire, and stood after the French rear; but for the most part the damage to rigging prevented tacking, and wearing was impossible on account of the ships coming up behind. The French now stood to leeward and formed line again, but the English were not in condition to attack. This was the end of the battle.

It has been said that there are some interesting points about this resultless engagement. One is, that Keppel's conduct was approved throughout, on oath before the court-martial, by one of the most distinguished admirals England has brought forth, Sir John Jervis, who commanded a ship in the fleet. It does not indeed appear what he could have done more; but his lack of tactical understanding is shown by a curious remark in his defence. "If the French admiral really meant to come to action," says he, "I apprehend he would never have put his fleet on the contrary tack to that on which the British fleet was approaching." This remark can only proceed from ignorance or thoughtlessness of the danger to which the rear of the French fleet would have been exposed, and is the more curious as he himself had said the English were lying up for it. Keppel's idea seems to have been that the French should have waited for him to come up abreast, and then go at it, ship for ship, in

午确实有利于英军的风向此时再一次转为了西风，使得英军可以停下来等候法军的后翼，所以奥尔维利埃便令舰队一起转向下风；这样一来，既可让其他舰船支援此时已经变为前锋的后翼舰队，也可阻碍凯珀尔集中兵力进击或者楔入法国舰队当中。这样，两支舰队便对舷相向而行，[2] 彼此都开了数发毫无用处的舷炮之后，法军便自然转到了上风位置，并且能够发动进攻了，可法军却没有利用这一机会。奥尔维利埃随后便向之前的后卫、如今的前锋舰队发出信号，令其转向当时正处于英军主力下风位置的英军后翼的下风向，并且打算自己继续保持上风位置，从而对英军进行两面夹击；可担任这支前锋舰队指挥官的那位皇室亲王没有服从命令，于是法军这种可能的优势便不复存在了。英国舰队也尝试着进行了相同的机动。一待脱离火力范围，前锋司令便率手下的数艘战舰抢风行驶，紧随在法军后翼之后；不过，由于船上的索具大部分都已损坏，所以难以抢风，而待后面的战舰纷纷赶了上来后，前锋也不可能再转向下风了。法军此时已是背风，并且重新排成了一列；可在这种情况下，英军却不宜进击了。于是，这场海战便就此结束。

据说，这场一无所获的交战还是具有数处很有意思的地方。其中之一便是，英国最杰出的海军上将之一、曾在这支舰队中指挥过一艘战舰的约翰·杰维斯勋爵，曾在军事法庭上赌咒发誓，始终认可凯珀尔的指挥。实际上，这样做并未显示出他本来可以发挥什么样的更大作用；不过，他在为自己辩护的时候，说了一句很古怪的话语，表明他缺乏战术上的判断力。"假如法国的海军司令的确想要交战的话，"他说，"我认为，他决不会把自己的舰队置于迎着英国舰队正在前来的航向上。"这样的话，只有可能是出于不知道或者没有想到法国舰队后翼可能面临的危险才说得出来；而更奇怪的是，他

what was to him the good old style; D'Orvilliers was too highly trained to be capable of such action.

The failure of the Duc de Chartres, commanding the French van during the firing, to wear in obedience to orders, whether due to misunderstanding or misconduct, raises the question, which is still debated, as to the proper position for a naval commander-in-chief in action. Had D'Orvilliers been in the van, he could have insured the evolution he wished. From the centre the admiral has the extremities of his fleet equally visible, or invisible, as it may be. At the head he enforces his orders by his example. The French toward the end of this war solved the question by taking him out of the line altogether and putting him on board a frigate, for the avowed reasons that he could thus better see the movements of his fleet and of the enemy without being blinded by smoke or distracted by the occurrences on board his own ship, and that his signals could be better seen.[3] This position, resembling somewhat that of a general on shore, being remote from personal risk, was also assumed by Lord Howe in 1778; but both that officer and the French abandoned the practice later. Nelson at Trafalgar, the end of his career, led his column; but it may be doubted whether he had any other motive than his ardor for battle. The two other great attacks in which he commanded in chief were directed against ships at anchor, and in neither did he take the head of the column; for the good reason that, his knowledge of the ground being imperfect, the leading ship was in most danger of grounding. The common practice in the days of broadside sailing-ships, except when a general chase was ordered, was for the admiral to be in the line, and in the centre of it. The departure from this custom on the part of both Nelson and Collingwood, each of whom led his own columns at Trafalgar, may have had some reason, and an ordinary man rather shrinks from criticising the action of officers of their eminence. The danger to which were

自己也曾说过英军当时正严阵以待。凯珀尔的想法，似乎是法军本来应当等待着他率舰队与之并排行驶，然后再向他发动舰对舰的攻击，因为在他看来，这才是正宗的传统战法；可奥尔维利埃经验却极为丰富，是不可能采取这样的行动的。

在交火过程中，指挥法军后翼舰队的德·夏特尔公爵没有服从命令转向下风，无论他是出于误解还是出于渎职，都引发了一个如今仍然存有争议的问题，那就是在战斗中海军总司令的正确位置在哪儿的问题。倘若奥尔维利埃身处前锋舰队，那么他就能够保证实现自己想要进行的那种战术机动。倘若身处中军，那么舰队的两端海军司令都看得见，当然也有可能两端都看不到。身处前锋舰队的时候，他可以通过前锋的示范来执行自己的命令。到此次战争结束的时候，法军已经解决了这个问题：让海军总司令完全身处战阵之外，待在一艘护卫舰上指挥；其理由是公认的，因为这样一来，他就可以更加清楚地看到手下舰队和敌方舰队的运动，不会被炮火的烟雾遮住双眼，或者因座舰上发生的事情而分神，而手下也能更好地看清他所发出的信号了。[3]这一位置，有点儿像是岸上陆军将领所处的位置，因远离战场，故总司令个人不会有危险，故豪勋爵在1778年也曾采用过这样的位置；不过，豪勋爵和法军后来都放弃了这种做法。纳尔逊在结束其职业生涯的特拉法尔加海战中，就是待在前锋舰队，身先士卒地率领着手下的舰队作战的；不过，除了热衷于作战之外，他还有没有其他动机，这一点却是值得怀疑的。他担任总司令一职的其他两次大规模战斗，针对的都是停泊着的舰船，而在这两次战斗中，他都并未率先冲在整个舰队的前面；最充分的理由便是，他并不完全了解这两处战场的情况，而冲在最前面的舰船，会有搁浅的极大危险。在帆船上安装舷炮的那个时代，通常的做法便是让海军司

exposed the two senior officers of the fleet, upon whom so much depended, is obvious; and had any serious injury befallen their persons, or the head of their columns, the lack of their influence would have been seriously felt. As it was, they were speedily obliterated, as admirals, in the smoke of the battle, leaving to those who came after them no guidance or control except the brilliancy of their courage and example. A French admiral has pointed out that the practical effect of the mode of attack at Trafalgar, two columns bearing down upon a line at right angles to them, was to sacrifice the head of the columns in making two breaches in the enemy's line. So far, very well; the sacrifice was well worth while; and into these breaches came up the rear ships of each column, nearly fresh, forming in fact a reserve which fell upon the shattered ships of the enemy on either side of the breaks. Now this idea of a reserve prompts a thought as to the commander-in-chief. The size of his ship was such as precluded its being out of the order; but would it not have been well had the admiral of each column been with this reserve, keeping in his hands the power of directing it according to the chances of the action, making him a reality as well as a name for some time longer, and to a very useful purpose? The difficulty of arranging any system of signals or light despatch-boats which could take the place of the aids or messengers of a general, coupled with the fact that ships cannot stand still, as divisions of men do, waiting orders, but that they must have steerage-way, precludes the idea of putting an admiral of a fleet under way in a light vessel. By so doing he becomes simply a spectator; whereas by being in the most powerful ship of the fleet he retains the utmost weight possible after action is once engaged, and, if this ship be in the reserve, the admiral keeps to the latest possible moment the power of commander-in-chief in his own hands. "Half a loaf is better than no bread;" if the admiral cannot, from the conditions of sea warfare, occupy the calmly watchful position of his brother on shore, let

令的座舰入列，并处在整个阵列的中枢位置，除非是在下令进行全面追击的时候。纳尔逊与柯林伍德两人都背弃了这一传统做法，在特拉法尔加海战中都身处各自所率舰队的前头，可能是有某种原因的，而普通人也宁愿不去指摘这些杰出将领的行为。双方舰队中，这两位高级将领所面临的危险是显而易见的，而各自的整个舰队也全都依赖于他们来指挥；倘若他们人身受到什么伤害，或者整个前锋舰队遭受什么损失，从而失去了他们的指挥的话，就会导致严重的后果。结果却是，他们作为海军司令的身份，很快就在战斗的硝烟中被人遗忘了；所以，除了勇猛和身先士卒的辉煌之外，他们并未给追随他们的那些将领留下什么指引和约束之力。一位法国的海军司令曾经指出，特拉法尔加海战的进攻模式，即让舰船排成两列，并以各自合适的角度冲向敌军阵线，其实际效果便是牺牲掉两列舰船中打头阵的战舰，从而在敌方阵线上撕开两条口子。迄今为止，这种做法都没什么不妥，这种牺牲都是很值得的；每队的后翼舰船都能从这些缺口中插入敌阵，并且差不多全都精神抖擞，事实上形成了一种向缺口两侧被冲散的敌舰发动进攻的预留力量。如今，这种预留力量的观念又引发出了一种关于舰队总司令的思想。总司令座舰的大小，决定了他的座舰不可能脱离阵列；但是，倘若每队战舰的司令都有这样一种预留力量，使之能够根据战斗当中出现的机会而直接指挥这支力量，使之非但是名义上、而且是实实在在地拥有更长的时间来实现一种有益的目标，这样不是会更好吗？部署能够取代陆军将领手下之副将或信使的信号系统和轻型通信船都很困难，再加上船只无法像陆军部队那样停下来等候命令，而是必须有航速，所以是不可能让一位司令乘坐轻型船只随舰队航行的。倘若这样做，舰队司令便会变成一位旁观者；而倘若身处舰队中最强大的那艘战舰上，那么

there be secured for him as much as may be. The practice of Farragut after New Orleans and Vicksburg, that is to say, in the latter part of his career, when it may be believed experience had determined his views, was to lead in person. It is known that he very reluctantly, at the solicitation of various officers, yielded his convictions in this matter at Mobile so far as to take the second place, and afterward freely expressed his regrets for having done so. It may, however, be argued that the character of all the actions in which Farragut commanded had a peculiarity, differentiating them from battles in the strict sense of the word. At New Orleans, at Vicksburg, at Port Hudson, and at Mobile, the task was not to engage, but to pass fortifications which the fleet confessedly could not stand up to; and the passage was to be made under conditions mainly of pilotage upon ground as to which, unlike Nelson, he had good knowledge. There was thus imposed upon the commander-in-chief the duty of leadership in the literal, as well as the military, sense of the term. So leading, he not only pointed out to the fleet the safe road, but, drawing continually ahead of the smoke, was better able to see and judge the path ahead, and to assume the responsibility of a course which he may have prescribed and intended throughout, but from which a subordinate might shrink. It has not perhaps been commonly noted, that at Mobile the leaders, not only of one but of both columns, at the critical point of the road hesitated and doubted as to the admiral's purpose; not that they had not received it clearly, but because circumstances seemed to them to be different from what he had supposed. Not only Alden in the "Brooklyn," but Craven also in the "Tecumseh," departed from the admiral's orders and left the course dictated to them, with disastrous results. There is no necessity to condemn either captain; but the irresistible inference is that Farragut was unqualifiedly right in his opinion that the man who alone has the highest responsibility should, under the conditions of his battles, be in the front. And here

战斗一旦打响，他就有可能发挥出举足轻重的作用，并且倘若这艘座舰也属于预留力量的话，他便能够牢牢掌握作为总司令对整个舰队的指挥权，直到战斗的最后一刻。俗话说得好，"聊胜于无"；虽说海战的情况复杂，使得舰队司令无法像陆军一样处于岸上那种能够冷静地进行观察的位置，但我们还是应当尽量确保他有这样做的机会才是。法拉格特在新奥尔良之战和维克斯堡之战后——也就是说，在其职业生涯的后半部分，在人们可以认为其经验已经决定了其见解的时候，他的战法正是身先士卒。众所周知，在莫比尔海战中，是由于各级军官极力恳请，他才很不情愿地放弃自己的信条并退居二线的；并且此战过后，他又直率地表达出了对自己这样做的遗憾之情。然而我们可以说，法拉格特指挥过的所有战斗都具有一种独特的特点，使之不同于严格意义上的海战。在新奥尔良、维克斯堡、哈德逊港和莫比尔河口，他的任务都并非与敌交战，而是越过舰队明显无法与之对抗的敌方工事；通过这些防御工事，主要取决于领航技术，而他对这个方面了如指掌，跟纳尔逊完全不一样。这样一来，舰队总司令的职责便既包括字面意思上的"领导"，也有军事意义上的"领导"了。如此"领导"舰队的时候，他非但可以为舰队指出安全的路径，还因为自己一直位于硝烟之前，所以视野更清晰，也能更好地判断前面的航路，并且承担起引导舰队按照他可能已经规定好并打算通过、而其部下却可能退缩的路线前进的职责。人们或许通常都没有注意到，在莫比尔之战中，两列舰队的指挥官在前进的关键之处都犹豫不决，都对舰队司令的目的心存疑虑；原因并非在于他们没有清楚地接收到命令，而是因为在他们看来，战场形势似乎与这位舰队司令所预想的不一样。指挥"布鲁克林"号的奥尔登和指挥"特库姆塞"号的克雷文都没有理会舰队司令的命令，驶离了规定

it must be remarked that at such critical moments of doubt any but the highest order of mind tends to throw off the responsibility of decision upon the superior, though from the instancy of the case hesitation or delay may be fatal. A man who as the commissioned chief would act intelligently, as the mere subordinate will balk. Nelson's action at St. Vincent will rarely be emulated, a truth which is strongly shown by the fact that Collingwood was immediately in his rear that day, and did not imitate his action till signalled by the commander-in-chief; yet after receiving the authority of the signal, he particularly distinguished himself by his judgment and daring.[4] It will be recalled, also, in connection with this question of pilot-ground battles, that a central position nearly lost the flag-ship at New Orleans, owing to the darkness and to the smoke from the preceding ships; the United States fleet came near finding itself without its leader after the passage of the forts. Now as the mention of a reserve prompted one set of considerations, so the name of pilotage suggests certain ideas, broader than itself, which modify what has been said of keeping the admiral with the reserve. The ease and quickness with which a steam fleet can change its formation make it very probable that a fleet bearing down to attack may find itself, almost at the very moment of collision, threatened with some unlooked-for combination; then where would be the happiest position for an admiral? Doubtless in that part of his own order where he could most readily pilot his ships into the new disposition, or direction, by which he would meet the changed conditions; that is, in the position of leading. It would seem that there are always two moments of greatest importance in a sea-fight; one which determines the method of the main attack, the other the bringing up and directing the effort of the reserve. If the first is more important, the second perhaps requires the higher order of ability; for the former may and should proceed on a before-determined plan, while the latter may, and often must, be shaped to meet unforeseen

的航线，从而导致了灾难性的后果。我们无需再来谴责这两位舰长；不过，由此我们可以得出一个无可辩驳的结论，那就是法拉格特的观点是完全正确的，在他所处的那种战斗形势下，担负最高指挥职责的人应当冲在最前面。在这里我们还须指出，在此令人心存疑虑的关键时刻，倘若没有那种最崇高的服从命令的精神，任何东西都有可能让部下把做出决断的责任扔给上级；虽然在这个战例中，犹豫或拖延都可能带来严重的后果。一个受命担任长官的人会随机应变，而只有那些仅仅把自己当成下级的人才会推诿犹豫。纳尔逊在圣文森特海战中的做法，很少有人会去效仿；而当天柯林伍德虽说就在后翼舰队中紧紧跟随，但直到舰队总司令向他发出信号，他也没有效仿其做法，这个事实就已有力地表明了这一点。不过，虽说收到了上级的旗语命令，他却仍然根据自己的判断和胆识行事，这样做倒是让他自己脱颖而出、声名远播了。[4] 关于取决于领航技术的海战这个问题，我们还会记起，在舰队司令处在中枢位置的新奥尔良之战中，由于天色昏暗以及前面舰船喷出的浓烟阻挡了视线，所以旗舰都差点儿毁掉了；合众国舰队逼近敌军之后才发现，通过那些要塞之后，舰队司令竟然不见了。如今因为提及预留力量而引发出了一系列的注意事项，所以"领航"这个词也含有了广于其本义的一些思想，会修正我们之前提到的要让舰队司令与预留力量待在一起的说法。汽轮舰队能够轻易而快速地改变队形，使得一支逼近敌军准备进攻的舰队很有可能会发现，就在战斗打响的那一刻，己方却面临着一种出乎意料的战术组合的威胁；那么，舰队司令的最佳位置又会是哪儿呢？毫无疑问，应当是在己方阵列中最容易引领手下舰船进行新的部署或者转向新的航向、从而满足战场已变形势需要的位置；也就是说，应当是在舰队中领头的位置。海战中，似乎始终都存

exigencies. The conditions of sea-battles of the future contain one element that land battles cannot have, — the extreme rapidity with which encounters and changes of order can take place. However troops may be moved by steam to the field of battle, they will there fight on foot or on horseback, and with a gradual development of their plan, which will allow the commander-in-chief time to make his wishes known (as a rule, of course), in case of a change in the enemy's attack. On the other hand, a fleet, comparatively small in numbers and with its component units clearly defined, may be meditating an important change of which no sign can appear until it begins, and which will occupy but a few minutes. So far as these remarks are sound, they show the need of a second in command thoroughly conversant with not only the plans, but with the leading principles of action of his chief, — a need plain enough from the fact that the two extremities of the order-of-battle may be necessarily remote, and that you want the spirit of the leader at both extremities. As he cannot be there in person, the best thing is to have an efficient second at one end. As regards Nelson's position at Trafalgar, mentioned at the beginning of this discussion, it is to be noted that the "Victory" did nothing that another ship could not have done as well, and that the lightness of the wind forbade the expectation of any sudden change in the enemy's order. The enormous risk run by the person of the admiral, on whose ship was concentrated the fire of the enemy's line, and which led several captains to implore a change, was condemned long before by Nelson himself in one of his letters after the battle of the Nile: —

"I think, if it had pleased God I had not been wounded, not a boat would have escaped to have told the tale; but do not believe that any individual in the fleet is to blame. ... I only mean to say that if my experience could in person have directed those individuals, there was every

在着两个极其重要的关键时刻；一是决定主攻方式，二是调动并指挥预留力量作战。倘若说前者更重要，那么后者可能就需要更大的本领才行；因为前者可以也应当根据预先决定的作战计划来进行，而后者则可能并且经常不得不加以调整，才能满足无法预见的种种紧急情况。未来海战的形势，将会含有一种陆上战争所无法拥有的要素，那就是遭遇战与改变阵列能够极为快速地发生。无论陆军部队可以如何由汽轮运送，他们在战场之上都是靠步行或在马背上战斗，并且逐渐形成作战计划，使得在敌人的进攻方式有所变化的情况下，总司令有时间来让部下得知自己的作战意图（当然，这也是一种规定）。而另一方面，一支舰队因为数量相对较少，而其作战单元也有明确界定，故能够介入一种毫无先兆、只需片刻即可发生的重大变故。只要这些论断是正确合理的，那么它们就表明，一名下级指挥官非但需要彻底了解作战计划，还需要了解其上级首要的作战原则才行——从战斗序列的首尾两端必定会相距遥远、两端都需要指挥者的鼓舞这一事实，便可看出这种需要是显而易见的。由于指挥官不可能亲自分身两端，所以最好的办法就是在两端各安排一名能干的副指挥官。至于前面已经提及的、纳尔逊在特拉法尔加海战中所处的位置，我们必须注意，"维多利亚"号并未做到其他舰船不可做到的事情，而风力不大也让敌人的阵列不可能发生什么突然的变化。这位海军司令自身冒着巨大风险的做法——因为敌军阵列的火力全都集中于其座舰上，使得数名舰长都恳求他改变位置——在尼罗河河口之战后纳尔逊自己所写的一封信里，他早就自责过了：

"我认为，倘若上帝眷顾，我没有受伤的话，那么就不会有一艘舰船能够逃走，来告诉人们这次绝处逢生的经历了；不过，我并不认为舰队中有哪一个人应当为此负责。……我只是想说，倘若我的亲历亲为能够引导那些人的话，那么万能的上帝肯定会

appearance that Almighty God would have continued to bless my endeavors," etc.

Yet, notwithstanding such an expression of opinion based upon experience, he took the most exposed position at Trafalgar, and upon the loss of the leader there followed a curious exemplification of its effects. Collingwood at once, rightly or wrongly, avoidably or unavoidably, reversed Nelson's plans, urged with his last breath. "Anchor! Hardy, do you anchor!" said the dying chief. "Anchor!" said Collingwood. "It is the last thing I should have thought of."

FOOTNOTES:
(1) "A candid view of our affairs, which I am going to exhibit, will make you a judge of the difficulties under which we labor. Almost all our supplies of flour and no inconsiderable part of our meat are drawn from the States westward of Hudson's River. This renders a secure communication across that river indispensably necessary, both to the support of your squadron and the army. The enemy, being masters of that navigation, would interrupt this essential intercourse between the States. They have been sensible of these advantages.... If they could by any demonstration in another part draw our attention and strength from this important point, and by anticipating our return possess themselves of it, the consequences would be fatal. Our dispositions must therefore have equal regard to co-operating with you [at Boston] in a defensive plan, and securing the North River, which the remoteness of the two objects from each other renders peculiarly difficult." — Washington to D'Estaing, Sept. 11, 1778.

(2) The leading ships of the two fleets diverged from each other, which is, by the French, attributed to the English van keeping away; by the English it is said that the French van luffed.

(3) The capture of the French commander-in-chief on board his flag-ship, in the battle of April 12, 1782,

继续保佑我所做出的努力……"等等。

不过，尽管此种观点是基于其亲身经历，但他在特拉法尔加海战中还是选择了最为暴露的位置；而失去了这位指挥官之后，他的做法却产生出了一种奇怪的榜样效果。不管是对是错，也不管是为了逃避还是迫不得已，柯林伍德都马上推翻了纳尔逊在奄奄一息时强烈要求实行的那个作战计划。"停下！哈迪，请停下！"这位临死的海军司令说。"停下！"柯林伍德说，"这才是我最不想考虑的事情哩。"

原注：
（1）"坦率地来看待我们的形势，正是我接下来打算表明的，会让您对我们所苦的种种困难有所了解。我们几乎所有的面粉供应和绝大部分肉食，全都来自于哈德逊河以西的各州。这使得我们必须拥有一条越过此河的安全交通线，才能支援您所率的舰队和陆军。敌人掌控着这条航线，所以会阻碍各州间这种必需的交通联系。他们已经明白自己拥有这些优势了……倘若他们可以在别的地方进行佯动，将我们的注意力和兵力引离这个重要位置，并且抢在我们返回之前占领这个地方，那么后果就会很严重。因此，我们的部署就必须同时考虑到配合你们（在波士顿）实施防御计划，以及确保北河[1]的安全才是；可这两个目标相距甚远，使得我们实施起来异常困难。"——1778年9月11日华盛顿写给德斯坦的信。

（2）两支舰队领先的舰船彼此背道而驰。在法国人看来，这是因为英军前锋防着不让他们接近，而在英国人看来，据说则是因为法军前锋抢风航行所致。

（3）1782年4月12日法国海军总司令在其旗舰上被俘，也是出现此种新阵列的一个原因。

（4）下面这次发生在1782年4月罗德尼率军追击德·格拉斯过程中的事件，表明了下级严格服

was also a motive for this new order.

(4) The following incident, occurring during Rodney's chase of De Grasse, in April, 1782, shows how far subordination may be carried. Hood was one of the finest of the British officers; nor does the author undertake to criticise his action. He was some miles from Rodney at the time. "The separated French ship in the N.W., having got the breeze at the same time as our van division, boldly stood for and endeavored to weather the British advanced ships; that being the only way to regain her own fleet, then to windward. To such a length did she carry her audacity that she compelled the Alfred, the headmost ship of Sir Samuel Hood's division, to bear up in order to allow her to pass. Every eye was fixed upon the bold Frenchman, excepting those who were anxiously looking out on the commander-in-chief to make the signal to engage, but who, most likely from not supposing it could be an enemy, did not throw out the ardently looked-for signal, and therefore not a gun was fired. This is mentioned to show the state of discipline on board the ships composing Sir Samuel Hood's division, and that he, though second in command, would not fire a single shot until directed to do so by his commander-in-chief. 'It is more than probable that Sir S. Hood's reason for having waited for the signal to engage from his commander-in-chief, ere he would fire, arose from the supposition that had he been the occasion of prematurely bringing on an action under the above circumstances, he would have been responsible for the results.'" (White's Naval Researches, p. 97.)

Hood may have been influenced by Rodney's bearing toward inferiors whose initiative displeased him. The relations of the two seem to have been strained.

从上级能够产生出什么样的效果。胡德是英军中最优秀的将领之一；而笔者在此也并非是要批评他的做法。当时他距罗德尼有数英里远。"西北方向上那艘落了单的法国战舰，跟我方的前锋舰队同时碰上了逆风，它大胆地绕行，极力想绕过逼近的英舰；那是它重新回到法国舰队、然后占据上风位置的唯一途径。这艘战舰是如此的英勇无畏，以至于萨缪尔·胡德勋爵所率舰队中领头的'阿尔弗雷德'号不得不驶向下风，好让这艘战舰通过。除了那些正在焦急地瞭望、等待舰队总司令发出交战信号的人，可以说每个人的目光全都集中在那位鲁莽大胆的法国人身上；可英军总司令极有可能是认为这艘战舰并非是敌舰，并未发出部下所热切期待的信号，因此在这一过程中，英军一炮未发。提及这一点，是为了表明萨缪尔·胡德所率舰队的纪律情况，并且尽管他是副司令，倘若没有接到总司令的命令，他也是不会擅发一炮的。'萨缪尔·胡德勋爵之所以在开火之前要等候总司令发出交战的信号，很可能源于这样一种看法：假如他在上述情况下过早发动战斗，那么他就会为此行动所带来的后果负责。'"（参见怀特的《海军研究》，第97页）

胡德很可能是受了罗德尼对待下级的态度所影响，因为后者不喜欢下级过于主动。他们两人之间的关系，似乎一直都很紧张。

译者注：

[1] North River：北河。美国哈德逊河的一段。

CHAPTER IX
Maritime War in North America and West Indies, 1778-1781

Its Influence upon the Course of the American Revolution. —
Fleet Actions off Grenada, Dominica, and Chesapeake Bay.

On the 15th of April, 1778, Admiral Comte d'Estaing sailed from Toulon for the American continent, having under his command twelve ships-of-the-line and five frigates. With him went as a passenger a minister accredited to Congress, who was instructed to decline all requests for subsidies, and to avoid explicit engagements relative to the conquest of Canada and other British possessions. "The Cabinet of Versailles," says a French historian, "was not sorry for the United States to have near them a cause of anxiety, which would make them feel the value of the French alliance." While acknowledging the generous sympathy of many Frenchmen for their struggle, Americans need not blind themselves to the self-interestedness of the French government. Neither should they find fault; for its duty was to consider French interests first.

D'Estaing's progress was very slow. It is said that he wasted much time in drills, and even uselessly. However that may be, he did not reach his destination, the Capes of the Delaware, until the 8th of July, — making a passage of twelve weeks, four of which were spent in reaching the Atlantic. The English government had news of his intended sailing; and in fact, as soon as

第九章 1778-1781年间北美和西印度群岛的海上战争

它对美国革命进程的影响

格林纳达、多米尼加和切萨皮克湾海域的舰队作战

1778年4月15日，海军上将德斯坦伯爵率领着由12艘战舰和5艘护卫舰组成的舰队从土伦起航，驶往北美洲。随之前往的还有一名乘客，那就是合众国国会认可的一位公使，法国政府指示他拒绝合众国所有的拨款要求，并且避免卷入到明显涉及攻取加拿大与其他英属殖民地的战争中去。"凡尔赛内阁，"一位法国历史学家称，"对合众国焦头烂额的处境并不同情，因为这种处境会让美国人感受到与法国结盟的重要性。"虽说承认许多法国人对合众国的独立斗争充满同情之心，但美国人也不必对法国政府的自私自利视而不见。当然，美国人也不应当吹毛求疵；因为优先考虑法国的利益，正是法国政府的职责所在。

德斯坦的行进非常缓慢。据说他在训练上浪费了许多时间，甚至是一无用处的训练。无论是出于何种原因，他直到7月8日才抵达了目的地特拉华角——他一路上航行了12周，其中用了4周才进入大西洋。英国政府得知了他准备率军前往美洲的消息；事实上，一召回驻巴黎的大使，英国政府就派人前往美洲，命令英军撤出费城，将兵力集结

they recalled their ambassador at Paris, orders were sent to America to evacuate Philadelphia, and concentrate upon New York. Fortunately for them, Lord Howe's movements were marked by a vigor and system other than D'Estaing's. First assembling his fleet and transports in Delaware Bay, and then hastening the embarkation of stores and supplies, he left Philadelphia as soon as the army had marched from there for New York. Ten days were taken up in reaching the mouth of the bay;[1] but he sailed from it the 28th of June, ten days before D'Estaing arrived, though more than ten weeks after he had sailed. Once outside, a favoring wind took the whole fleet to Sandy Hook in two days. War is unforgiving; the prey that D'Estaing had missed by delays foiled him in his attempts upon both New York and Rhode Island.

The day after Howe's arrival at Sandy Hook the English army reached the heights of Navesink, after an harassing march through New Jersey, with Washington's troops hanging upon its rear. By the active co-operation of the navy it was carried up to New York by the 5th of July; and Howe then went back to bar the entrance to the port against the French fleet. As no battle followed, the details of his arrangements will not be given; but a very full and interesting account by an officer of the fleet can be found in Ekins's "Naval Battles." Attention, however, may well be called to the combination of energy, thought, skill, and determination shown by the admiral. The problem before him was to defend a practicable pass with six sixty-four-gun ships and three of fifty, against eight of seventy-four guns or over, three sixty-fours, and one fifty, — it may be said against nearly double his own force.

D'Estaing anchored outside, south of the Hook, on the 11th of July, and there remained until the 22d, engaged in sounding the bar, and with every apparent determination to enter. On the 22d a high northeast wind, coinciding with a spring tide, raised the water on the bar to thirty feet. The French fleet got under way, and worked up to windward to a point fair for crossing the

于纽约。幸好，豪勋爵麾下的部队调动，以不同于德斯坦的雷厉风行和制度健全而著称。他首先是在特拉华湾将舰队和运兵船集结起来，接着加紧装载军备和给养，待陆军开拔前往纽约后，他也马上率领舰队离开了费城。他花了10天时间，率军抵达了特拉华湾入海口；[1]不过，他是在6月28日，即德斯坦到达之前的10天离开此处的，尽管此时离德斯坦起航已经过去了十几个星期。一旦出了海，整支舰队便在两天之内顺风抵达了桑迪岬。战争是毫无情面可讲的；由于延误，德斯坦非但错过了到手的猎物，还使得他进击纽约和罗德岛的企图全都付之东流了。

豪勋爵率军抵达桑迪岬的第二天，英国的陆军部队也人困马乏地穿过了新泽西，在华盛顿所率部队的追击之下，抵达了纳瓦辛克高地。在海军的积极配合下，这支部队于7月5日被运送到了纽约；然后豪勋爵便返回来，拦击法国舰队进入纽约港。由于接下来并未发生战斗，所以我们无需详细说明他的部署；不过，在艾金斯的《海战》一书中，可以看到英国舰队中一位将领对此所进行的详细而有趣的描述。然而，我们的注意力还是应当放在这位海军上将所表现出来的整体领导才能、思想、技巧和决心上。他所面临的问题，是凭借6艘装有64门火炮的战舰以及3艘装有50门火炮的军舰，来防守这个可通航的河口并对抗拥有8艘装有74门及以上火炮、3艘装有64门火炮以及1艘装有50门火炮的战舰的法军——可以说，后者的兵力几乎是他手下兵力的两倍。

7月11日，德斯坦在桑迪岬以南的海面上泊锚，尔后在此停到了22日，以探测沙洲的深度，并且显然下定了决心，要攻进纽约港。22日，海上刮起了猛烈的东北风，同时潮水大涨，使得海水涨到了沙洲之上30英尺。法国舰队就此开拔，并且逐渐迎风驶到了

bar. Then D'Estaing's heart failed him under the discouragement of the pilots; he gave up the attack and stood away to the southward.

Naval officers cannot but sympathize with the hesitation of a seaman to disregard the advice of pilots, especially on a coast foreign to him; but such sympathy should not close their eyes to the highest type of character. Let any one compare the action of D'Estaing at New York with that of Nelson at Copenhagen and the Nile, or that of Farragut at Mobile and Port Hudson, and the inferiority of the Frenchman as a military leader, guided only by military considerations, is painfully apparent. New York was the very centre of the British power; its fall could not but have shortened the war. In fairness to D'Estaing, however, it must be remembered that other than military considerations had to weigh with him. The French admiral doubtless had instructions similar to those of the French minister, and he probably reasoned that France had nothing to gain by the fall of New York, which might have led to peace between America and England, and left the latter free to turn all her power against his own country. Less than that would have been enough to decide his wavering mind as to risking his fleet over the bar.

Howe was more fortunate than D'Estaing, in having no divided purposes. Having escaped from Philadelphia and saved New York by his diligence, he had in store the further honor of saving Rhode Island by the like rapid movements. Scattered ships-of-war from a fleet despatched from England now began to arrive. On the 28th of July Howe was informed that the French fleet, which had disappeared to the southward, had been seen heading for Rhode Island. In four days his fleet was ready for sea, but owing to contrary winds did not reach Point Judith till the 9th of August. There he anchored, and learned that D'Estaing had run the batteries the day before and anchored between Gould and Canonicut Islands;[2] the Seakonnet and Western

一个完全可以越过那处沙洲的地方。可接下来，领航员们的劝阻使德斯坦失去了信心；于是，他便不再进攻，而是离开了此地，向南而去。

虽说一名水兵不可能不考虑领航员的建议，尤其是在自己不熟悉的海岸，而海军将领们对此也都深有同感，但即便有着这样的同感，也不应该让他们对那些具有最崇高品质的人不加注意。不论是谁，只要将德斯坦在纽约的做法，与纳尔逊在哥本哈根以及尼罗河河口的做法，或者法拉格特在莫比尔河与哈德逊港的表现比较一下，那么德斯坦这个法国军事指挥官只会从军事方面来考虑问题的能力缺陷，就是极其明显的了。纽约正是英国势力的中枢；攻陷此处，完全可以缩短此次战争的时间。然而，为了做到公正地来评价德斯坦，我们也必须记住，除了军事上的考虑，他还得权衡其他方面的问题。这位法国的海军上将，无疑也收到了与那位法国公使相似的命令，所以他很可能认为，攻陷纽约并不会让法国获得什么好处，因为这样可能会令美国和英国议和，从而使得英国可以放心大胆地将该国所有兵力都用于与法国作战了。就算到不了此种程度，这也足以让他犹豫不决，不想冒险率领手下的舰队越过那道沙洲了。

豪勋爵比德斯坦的运气好一些，因为他并无相互抵触的目标。逃离费城并凭借迅速行动而挽救了纽约之后，不久他又凭借同样迅速的调兵遣将，进一步获得了保全罗德岛的辉煌荣誉。英国从一支舰队中分派出来的数艘战舰，此时也开始抵达美洲了。7月28日，豪勋爵得到情报，说有人看到那支往南而去的法国舰队正在驶向罗德岛。4天之后，他手下的舰队便做好了出海准备，可由于风向不对，这支舰队直到8月9日才抵达尤迪斯角。他在那里泊停下来，得知德斯坦前一天已经炮击过罗德岛，此时正停在古尔德

passages had also been occupied by French ships, and the fleet was prepared to sustain the American army in an attack upon the British works.

The arrival of Howe, although his reinforcements did not raise the English fleet to over two thirds the strength of the French, upset D'Estaing's plans. With the prevailing summer southwest breezes blowing straight into the bay, he was exposed to any attempts his adversary might make. That same night the wind shifted unexpectedly to the northward, and D'Estaing at once got under way and stood out to sea. Howe, though surprised by this unlooked-for act, — for he had not felt himself strong enough to attack, — also made sail to keep the weather-gage. The next twenty-four hours passed in manoeuvring for the advantage; but on the night of the 11th of August a violent gale of wind dispersed the fleets. Great injury was done to the vessels of both, and among others the French flag-ship "Languedoc," of ninety guns, lost all her masts and her rudder. Immediately after the gale two different English fifty-gun ships, in fighting order, fell in, the one with the "Languedoc," the other with the "Tonnant," of eighty guns, having only one mast standing. Under such conditions both English ships attacked; but night coming on, they ceased action, intending to begin again in the morning. When morning came, other French ships also came, and the opportunity was lost. It is suggestive to note that one of the captains was Hotham, who as admiral of the Mediterranean fleet, seventeen years later, so annoyed Nelson by his cool satisfaction in having taken only two ships: "We must be contented; we have done very well." This was the immediate occasion of Nelson's characteristic saying, "Had we taken ten sail, and allowed the eleventh to escape, being able to get at her, I could never have called it well done."

The English fell back on New York. The French rallied again off the entrance of Narragansett Bay; but D'Estaing decided that he could not remain on account of the damage to

岛和坎农尼科特岛之间[2]；西肯雷特和西部水道也被法国舰船占领了，而这支法国舰队还准备进攻英军的工事，为美国的陆军提供支援。

尽管带来的援军并未让英国舰队的兵力超过法国兵力的三分之二，但豪勋爵的到来还是打乱了德斯坦的计划。当时正值夏季，西南风盛行且直接吹入海湾，所以他极易受到敌人的攻击。那天晚上，风向出乎意料地转成了北风，于是德斯坦立即率领舰队起航，停到了外海上。豪勋爵虽说对德斯坦这种出人意料的做法感到奇怪——因为他觉得自己兵力不足，没法进攻——但也率军起航，以保持有利位置。接下来的24个小时，双方都在为抢占有利位置而进行机动；不过，8月11晚上刮起了大风，把两支舰队都打散了。双方舰船都遭受了巨大的损失，其中，法军装有90门火炮的旗舰"朗格多克"号桅杆尽失，船舵也没了。就在这场大风过后，两艘各装有50门火炮、排成战斗队形的英国战舰中，一艘遭遇了"朗格多克"号，另一艘遭遇了装有80门火炮、此时只剩一根桅杆的"轰鸣"号。在这种情况下，这两艘英舰便都发动了攻击；但夜幕马上降临了，它们便停止了行动，准备第二天早上再战。第二天早上，其他的法国战舰也都赶了过来，所以英舰便失去了进攻的机会。大家不妨注意一下，这两艘英舰中有一艘的舰长便是霍瑟姆，17年之后他还当上了地中海舰队的司令；此战中只击败了两艘法舰，可他却无动于衷，还感到很满意："我们必须知足才是；因为我们已经干得很漂亮了。"这让纳尔逊大为光火，也是导致纳尔逊说出下面这句典型话语的直接原因："就算我们击败了10艘船，却在能够做到的情况下放跑了第11艘，那我是决不会说自己干得很漂亮的。"

英国舰队于是撤退到了纽约。法国舰队则在纳拉干塞特湾入海口重新集结起来；不

the squadron, and accordingly sailed for Boston on the 21st of August. Rhode Island was thus left to the English, who retained it for a year longer, evacuating then for strategic reasons. Howe on his part diligently repaired his ships, and sailed again for Rhode Island when he heard of the French being there; but meeting on the way a vessel with word of their going to Boston, he followed them to that harbor, in which they were too strongly placed to be attacked. Taking into consideration his enforced return to New York, the necessary repairs, and the fact that he was only four days behind the French at Boston, it may be believed that Howe showed to the end the activity which characterized the beginning of his operations.

Scarcely a shot had been exchanged between the two fleets, yet the weaker had thoroughly outgeneralled the stronger. With the exception of the manoeuvres for the weather-gage after D'Estaing left Newport, which have not been preserved, and of Howe's dispositions to receive the expected attack in New York Bay, the lessons are not tactical, but strategic, and of present application. Chief among them undoubtedly stands the value of celerity and watchfulness, combined with knowledge of one's profession. Howe learned of his danger by advices from home three weeks after D'Estaing sailed from Toulon. He had to gather in his cruisers from the Chesapeake and outside, get his ships-of-the-line from New York and Rhode Island, embark the supplies of an army of ten thousand men, move down the Delaware, — which unavoidably took ten days, — and round to New York again. D'Estaing was ten days behind him at the Delaware, twelve days at Sandy Hook, and only one day ahead of him in entering Newport, outside which harbor he had lain ten days before sailing in. An English narrator in the fleet, speaking of the untiring labor between June 30, when the English army reached Navesink, and the arrival of the French fleet on the 11th of July, says: "Lord Howe attended in person as usual, and by his presence animated the zeal and quickened the industry of officers and

过德斯坦认为，由于舰队遭受了重创，不宜再留在此处，便于8月21日起航，往波士顿而去。这样一来，罗德岛便留给了英军，他们又在此地盘踞了一年，后来出于战略原因才撤出了这里。豪勋爵努力修理好了舰队，并在得知法军位于罗德岛的消息之后，再一次驶往此处；但在半路上遇到了一艘船只，说法国舰队已经往波士顿而去，于是他便尾随法国舰队，来到了这个港口——法军在该港实力强大，难以遭到攻击。考虑到他已经返回纽约对舰队进行了必要的修理，以及他只比法国舰队晚了4天就抵达了波士顿这一事实，我们可以认为，豪勋爵始终都表现出了标志着他发起作战行动之初的那种积极性。

尽管这两支舰队几乎还没有互开一炮，但实力较弱的英军在战略战术上早已完全胜过了实力较强的法军。除了德斯坦在离开纽波特后为抢占上风位置而指挥舰队进行的机动——他并没有保住这一上风位置——以及豪勋爵在纽约湾中为应对预期的进攻而进行的部署之外，此战留给我们的教训都并非战术上的，而是战略上的，并且如今仍然适用。其中最主要的教训，无疑就是快速、谨慎和专业知识都很重要这几个方面。德斯坦从土伦港起航3个星期之后，豪勋爵即通过来自国内的消息得知了自己的危险处境。他必须召回切萨皮克湾和外海上的巡逻舰，必须将纽约和罗德岛的战舰集结起来，必须装备好10000陆军兵力的给养，并沿特拉华河而下——这必然要花上10天的时间才能办到——然后再转到纽约。德斯坦比他晚了10天才抵达特拉华湾，晚了12天才到达桑迪岬，并且只比他早一天进入纽波特，而在该港之外，他还驻停了10天才入港。英国舰队中的一个人，说到英国陆军在抵达纳瓦辛克的6月30日至法国舰队抵达的7月11日这几天里的不懈辛劳时，是如此说的："豪勋爵像往常一样亲自参与，而他的亲历亲为，既鼓舞了士气，也加快了官兵们

men." In this quality he was a marked contrast to his amiable but indolent brother, General Howe.

The same industry and watchfulness marked his remaining operations. As soon as the French ships hauled off to the southward, lookout vessels followed them, and preparations continued (notably of fireships) for pursuit. The last ship that joined from England crossed the bar at New York on the 30th of July. On the 1st of August the fleet was ready for sea, with four fire-ships. The accident of the wind delayed his next movements; but, as has been seen, he came up only one day after the entrance of the enemy into Newport, which his inferior force could not have prevented. But the object of the enemy, which he could not oppose, was frustrated by his presence. D'Estaing was no sooner in Newport than he wished himself out. Howe's position was strategically excellent. With his weatherly position in reference to the prevailing winds, the difficulty of beating a fleet out through the narrow entrance to the harbor would expose the French ships trying it to be attacked in detail; while if the wind unluckily came fair, the admiral relied upon his own skill to save his squadron.

Cooper, in one of his novels, "The Two Admirals," makes his hero say to a cavilling friend that if he had not been in the way of good luck, he could not have profited by it. The sortie of the French, the subsequent gale, and the resulting damage were all what is commonly called luck; but if it had not been for Howe's presence off Point Judith threatening them, they would have ridden out the gale at their anchors inside. Howe's energy and his confidence in himself as a seaman had put him in the way of good luck, and it is not fair to deny his active share in bringing it about. But for him the gale would not have saved the British force in Newport.[3]

D'Estaing, having repaired his ships, sailed with his whole force for Martinique on the

的行动。"在这种品德上,他跟自己那位和蔼却很懒散的兄弟豪将军形成了鲜明的对照。

在接下来的作战行动中,豪勋爵也表现出了同样的勤勉与谨慎。法国舰队转而向南退去之后,他马上派遣瞭望船进行尾随,并且继续备战(尤其是准备了火攻船),打算进行追击。英国派遣的最后一艘增援舰于7月30日通过了纽约港的那处沙洲。8月1日,英国舰队准备出海了,其中还包括4艘火攻船。风向突变,耽搁了他的后续行动;不过,正如我们已经看到的那样,他紧追慢赶,只比敌人进入纽波特晚了一天,而他兵力较弱,本来也没法阻止敌军进入该港。虽说无法与敌对抗,但他的到来却挫败了敌人的意图。德斯坦一进入纽波特港,就想率领舰队重新出海了。可豪勋爵所占据的位置,在战略上却无懈可击。从盛行的风向来看,他处于能够抢风航行的位置,而经由进入该港的狭窄水道去进击一支舰队非但困难重重,还会让出击的法国舰船陷入被敌人逐一消灭的危险;倘若风向偏巧转为顺风的话,那么这位海军司令便只有依靠自己的本领,才能挽救手下的舰队了。

在库珀所著的《海军两司令》这部小说中,主人公曾对一位百般挑剔的朋友说,倘若他不把鸿运拦住的话,便不会因鸿运而受益。法国舰队的突围、接下来的大风以及最终的受创,都是人们通常所称的"运气";不过,倘若不是豪勋爵在尤迪斯角海域威胁到了他们,法军就会泊在港内,安然无恙地避过这场大风了。正是豪勋爵具有作为一名水兵的精神和内心的自信,才使得他拦住了鸿运;而要否认他也积极地创造了条件,从而给自己带来了这种鸿运,则是不公平的。不过对他来说,假如是在纽波特,那么这场大风是挽救不了英军的。[3]

德斯坦将所有舰船都修理妥当之后,便在11月4日率全部兵力前往马提尼克;就在

4th of November; on the same day Commodore Hotham left New York for Barbadoes, with five sixty-four and fifty-gun ships and a convoy of five thousand troops, destined for the conquest of Sta. Lucia Island. On the way a heavy gale of wind injured the French fleet more than the English, the French flag-ship losing her main and mizzen topmasts. The loss of these spars, and the fact that twelve unencumbered ships-of-war reached Martinique only one day before the convoy of fifty-nine English transports reached Barbadoes, a hundred miles farther on, tells badly for the professional skill which then and now is a determining feature in naval war.

Admiral Barrington, commanding at Barbadoes, showed the same energy as Howe. The transports arrived on the 10th; the troops were kept on board; sailed on the morning of the 12th for Sta. Lucia, and anchored there at three P.M. the 13th. The same afternoon half the troops were landed, and the rest the next morning. They seized at once a better port, to which the admiral was about to move the transports when the appearance of D'Estaing prevented him. All that night the transports were being warped inside the ships-of-war, and the latter anchored across the entrance to the bay, especial care being taken to strengthen the two extremities of the line, and to prevent the enemy from passing inside the weather end, as the English ships in after years did at the battle of the Nile. The French was much more than double the English fleet; and if the latter were destroyed, the transports and troops would be trapped.

D'Estaing stood down along the English order twice from north to south, cannonading at long range, but did not anchor. Abandoning then his intentions against the fleet, he moved to another bay, landed some French soldiers, and assaulted the position of the English troops. Failing here also, he retired to Martinique; and the French garrison, which had been driven into the interior of the island, surrendered.

同一天，霍瑟姆准将也率领5艘装有64门火炮和50门火炮的军舰，以及一支运送5000陆军的船队，从纽约动身前往巴巴多斯，准备去攻打圣卢西亚岛。在途中，他们遇上了暴风，法国舰队的损失比英国舰队要严重，法军旗舰的主桅和后桅全都吹折了。这种船桅的损失，以及那12艘丝毫未受到阻碍的战舰，也只比英军那59艘运兵船队抵达100英里外的巴巴多斯提早了一天到达了马提尼克的事实，都严重地说明了法国海军缺乏职业本领的情况；而无论是在当时还是在如今，职业本领都是海战中的一个有着决定意义的特征。

在巴巴多斯指挥作战的巴林顿上将，他表现出了与豪勋爵相同的干劲。运兵船队于10日抵达了巴巴多斯；部队被留在船上，而12日晨便又起航前往圣卢西亚，并在13日下午3点抵达了该地。这天下午，陆军中的一半登上了岸，余下的那一半则是第二天早上登陆的。他们马上便攻占了一处较好的港口，巴林顿上将正打算让运兵船队进入该港，可德斯坦所率的舰队出现了，所以他只得放弃了。那天晚上，整支运兵船队全都躲在军舰后面，军舰则横着泊在海湾入口，还小心地加强了舰队头尾的力量，以防敌军从上风一端通过并进入港湾；英军在随后的数年中都沿用了这一做法，就像在尼罗河河口之战中那样。法军的兵力是英国舰队的两倍多；倘若英国舰队被击败，那么整支运兵船队和陆军部队便会陷入绝境。

德斯坦率领舰队沿着英军阵列，由北向南来回航行了两次，并且进行了远距离炮击，不过并未泊锚。接下来，他放弃了进攻这支舰队的企图，转而驶往了另一处海湾，让一部分法军登陆，并袭击了英军的阵地。由于在此处的作战也失利了，他便撤回了马提尼克；于是，已被驱赶到了圣卢西亚岛内陆的法军便只能缴械投降了。

我们似乎无需指出巴林顿上将的勤勉作风是多么令人钦佩，而他本人也将这一重大

It seems scarcely necessary to point out the admirable diligence of Admiral Barrington, to which and to the skill of his dispositions he owed this valuable strategic success; for such it was. Sta. Lucia was the island next south of Martinique, and the harbor of Gros Ilot at its northern end was especially adapted to the work of watching the French depot at Fort Royal, their principal station in the West Indies. Thence Rodney pursued them before his great action in 1782.

The absence of precise information causes hesitation in condemning D'Estaing for this mortifying failure. His responsibility depends upon the wind, which may have been light under the land, and upon his power to anchor. The fact, however, remains that he passed twice along the enemy's line within cannon-shot, yet did not force a decisive action. His course was unfavorably criticised by the great Suffren, then one of his captains.

The English had thus retrieved the capture of Dominica, which had been taken on the 8th of September by the French governor of the West India Islands. There being no English squadron there, no difficulty had been met. The value of Dominica to the French has been pointed out; and it is necessary here to use the example of both Dominica and Sta. Lucia to enforce what has before been said, that the possession of these smaller islands depended solely upon the naval preponderance. Upon the grasp of this principle held by any one will depend his criticism upon the next action of D'Estaing, to be immediately related.

Six months of almost entire quiet followed the affair of Sta. Lucia. The English were reinforced by the fleet of Byron, who took chief command; but the French, being joined by ten more ships-of-the-line, remained superior in numbers. About the middle of June, Byron sailed with his fleet to protect a large convoy of merchant-ships, bound for England, till they were clear of the islands. D'Estaing then sent a very small expedition which seized St. Vincent, June

的战略成功，归因于自己的勤勉与在兵力部署上的本领；因为事实就是如此。圣卢西亚是靠近马提尼克南边的一个岛屿，而其北端的格罗斯岛湾这个海港，又尤其适合于监视皇家要塞这个军事基地的动向，后者还是法国在西印度群岛上最主要的一个基地。从此时起到1782年那场伟大的海战爆发之前，罗德尼一直都在致力于夺取这些地方。

由于没有准确的资料，所以我们在指责德斯坦遭受此种令人痛心的失败之时，不免会心存犹疑。他的责任，取决于在陆地上可能并不重要的风向以及泊锚的本领。然而事实仍是，他两次进入到了敌军阵线的火炮射程之内，却并未果断发起进攻。那位伟大的苏弗朗，当时还是其手下的一名舰长，就曾极其激烈地批评过德斯坦的这种做法。

这样一来，英国就重新占领了多米尼加；此处是法国的西印度群岛总督于9月8日攻占的。当时那里并无英国舰队，因此法军未费吹灰之力。前面我们已经指出多米尼加对法国的重要性了；此处则有必要再用多米尼加和圣卢西亚这两个例子，再来强调一下前面的观点：占领这些小岛，完全依赖于海军所占的优势。任何人理解了这一原则，便都会对德斯坦接下来的行为加以批评；我们随后就会论述到这一点。

圣卢西亚之战后，接下来有6个月，双方几乎都没有丝毫动静。英军得到了由拜伦担任总司令的那支舰队增援；但法军由于又增加了10艘战舰，故在兵力上仍然占有优势。6月中旬左右，拜伦率领舰队，前去护送一支驶往英国的大型商船队离开西印度群岛。于是，德斯坦便派了一支兵力极少的远征队，在1779年6月16日毫不费力地夺取了圣文森特；而在6月30日，他又率领整支舰队前去攻打格林纳达。7月2日在乔治敦海域泊锚之后，他命令士兵登陆；7月4日，700名英国守军缴械投降，交出了该岛。在此期

16, 1779, without difficulty; and on the 30th of June he sailed with his whole fleet to attack Grenada. Anchoring off Georgetown on the 2d of July, he landed his soldiers, and on the 4th the garrison of seven hundred men surrendered the island. Meanwhile Byron, hearing of the loss of St. Vincent and probable attack on Grenada, sailed with a large convoy of vessels carrying troops, and with twenty-one ships-of-the-line, to regain the one and relieve the other. Receiving on the way definite information that the French were before Grenada, he kept on for it, rounding the northwest point of the island at daybreak of July 6. His approach had been reported the day before to D'Estaing, who remained at anchor, fearing lest with the currents and light winds he might drop too far to leeward if he let go the bottom. When the English came in sight, the French got under way; but the confused massing of their ships prevented Byron from recognizing at once the disparity of numbers, they having twenty-five ships-of-the-line. He made signal for a general chase, and as the disorder of the French fleet forced it to form on the leewardmost ships, the English easily retained the advantage of the wind with which they approached. As the action began, therefore, the French were to the westward with a partly formed line, on the starboard tack, heading north, the rear in disorder, and to windward of the van and centre. The English stood down with a fair wind, steering south by west on the port tack, between the island and the enemy, their leading ships approaching at a slight angle, but heading more directly for his yet unformed rear; while the English convoy was between its own fleet and the island, under special charge of three ships, which were now called in. As the signal so far commanded a general chase, the three fastest of the English, among which was the flag of the second in command, Admiral Barrington, came under fire of the French centre and rear, apparently unsupported, and suffered much from the consequent concentration of fire upon them. When they reached the sternmost ships they wore upon the same tack with them and stood north, after and to windward

间，拜伦得知了圣文森特陷落、格林纳达很可能会遭到攻击的消息，便率领21艘战舰，带着一支运送部队的大型运输船队起航，准备收复圣文森特并救援格林纳达。在途中他得到确切的情报，说法军正在围攻格林纳达，便继续往前，并于7月6日绕过了该岛的西北角。德斯坦在前一天便已获知他前来的消息；当时他仍然停泊在乔治敦海域，正在担心要是起锚的话，洋流和微风会让舰队顺风漂得太远。不过，法国舰队的阵势混乱得很，使得拜伦一时间并没有立即看清双方兵力上的悬殊，因为法军此时拥有25艘战舰。于是，拜伦发出了全面追击的信号；由于法国舰队毫无秩序，不得不由处于最下风的舰船组成阵列，所以英军轻而易举地保持住了风向优势，一路逼向敌军。因此，战斗打响之后，法国舰队的西边是一种不完整的阵列，右舷受风，头朝北方，后翼则乱成一团，并且处于前锋和中军的上风位置。英军顺风而下，左舷受风，航向西南，楔在敌军和格林纳达岛之间，其先头舰船正以微小角度逼近，不过更是直接冲向法军尚未形成的后翼；而英军的运兵船队则位于英军舰队与格林纳达岛之间，由此时才召回的3艘战舰加以专门护卫。由于发出全面追击的信号时两军相距甚远，所以英军中那3艘速度最快的战舰——副司令巴林顿上将的旗舰也在其中——明显没有支援地冲到了法国舰队中军的火力之下，并因随后法军密集的火力而吃了不少苦头。赶上法军落在最后面的那些舰船后，它们便调转方向，与敌舰同舷抢风，保持向北而行，跟在敌舰后面并占领着上风位置；差不多就在此时，之前并不知道格林纳达守军已经投降的拜伦，看到了要塞上方飘扬着的法国国旗。于是，他便发出了连续转向、让先头舰船排成阵列以相互支援的信号，从而结束了引发这次海战的全面追击。就在舰队主力仍然保持左舷抢风向南航行的时候，有3艘战舰，即"康沃尔"号、"格拉夫

of them; and at about the same time Byron, who had not before known of the surrender, saw the French flag flying over the forts. Signals followed to wear in succession, and for the advanced ships to form line for mutual support, ceasing the general chase under which the engagement had hitherto been fought. While the main body was still standing south on the port tack, three ships, — "Cornwall," "Grafton," and "Lion" , — obeying literally the signal for close action, had passed much to leeward of the others, drawing upon themselves most of the fire of the enemy's line. They thus suffered very severely in men and spars; and though finally relieved by the advanced ships, as these approached from the southward on the opposite tack, they were unable, after wearing, to keep up with the fleet, and so dropped astern and toward the French. The bulk of the injury sustained by the English fell upon these three, upon the three advanced ships under Barrington, and upon two others in the rear, which, seeing the van so heavily engaged, did not follow the successive movement, but bore down straight out of the order, and took their places at the head of the column, — an act strongly resembling that which won Nelson such high renown at Cape St. Vincent, but involving less responsibility.[4]

So far Byron had conducted his attack, using the initiative permitted him by the advantage of the wind and the disorder of the French rear. It will be observed that, though it was desirable to lose no time in assailing the latter while in confusion, it is questionable whether Barrington's three ships should have been allowed to separate as far as they seem to have done from the rest of the fleet. A general chase is permissible and proper when, from superiority of numbers, original or acquired, or from the general situation, the ships first in action will not be greatly outnumbered, or subjected to overpowering concentration before support comes up, or when there is probability that the enemy may escape unless promptly struck. This was not so here. Nor should the "Cornwall," "Grafton," and "Lion" have been permitted to take a course which allowed, almost compelled, the enemy to concentrate rather

顿"号和"莱昂"号，因为完全服从短兵相接的信号，已经顺风越过了其他舰船，因而吸引了敌军阵列的大部分火力。这样，它们在人员和桅帆方面都受到了重创；并且，尽管最终被从另一侧由南而来的前锋战舰所解救，但在转向下风之后，它们却没法再赶上己方舰队，因而落在后面，漂向了法国舰队。英军所遭受的大部分损失，都在这3艘战舰和巴林顿所率的那3艘打头阵的战舰，以及后翼舰队中的另外2艘战舰上；那两艘后翼舰船看到前锋舰船战斗得如此猛烈，便没有遵循顺次机动，而是径直冲出了阵列，插到了阵列最前头的位置——这一行为，与在圣文森特角海战中让纳尔逊赢得了巨大威望的做法极其相似，只是没有纳尔逊那么大的责任感罢了。[4]

至此，拜伦利用风向优势以及法军后翼的混乱所赋予的主动权，实施了进攻。我们会注意到，尽管趁着敌人乱成一团的时候抓紧时间对其进行攻击的做法是可取的，但任由巴林顿的那3艘战舰脱离整个舰队那么远，好像凭它们就可以完成整个舰队的任务似的，这种做法却是值得质疑的。倘若兵力上占有优势——无论是一开始就有还是后来获得的，或者是从整体形势来看具有优势——使得率先作战的舰船不会寡不敌众，不会在援兵赶到之前遭受敌方压倒性火力的集中攻击，或者倘若不立即发起攻击，敌人很可能就会逃走，那么发动全面追击既是可以的，也是正确的做法。但在此处，情况却并非如此。英军也不应当任由"康沃尔"号、"格拉夫顿"号与"莱昂"号采取一种允许、甚至是迫使敌军集中火力而不是分散火力向它们进攻的航向。由于此战的详细情况不甚准确，故我们除了指出这些失误，指出不必将这些失误全都归咎于拜伦这位海军上将的过

than diffuse his fire. The details of the affair are not precise enough to warrant more comment than naming these mistakes, without necessarily attributing them to fault on the part of the admiral.

The French had up to this time remained strictly on the defensive, in accordance with their usual policy. There was now offered an opportunity for offensive action which tested D'Estaing's professional qualities, and to appreciate which the situation at the moment must be understood. Both fleets were by this on the starboard tack, heading north, the French to leeward. The latter had received little injury in their motive power, though their line was not in perfect order; but the English, owing to the faulty attack, had seven ships seriously crippled, four of which — the "Monmouth", "Grafton," "Cornwall", and "Lion" — were disabled. The last three, by three P.M., were a league astern and much to leeward of their line, being in fact nearer the French than the English; while the speed of the English fleet was necessarily reduced to that of the crippled ships remaining in line. These conditions bring out strongly the embarrassments of a fleet whose injuries are concentrated upon a few ships, instead of being distributed among all; the ten or twelve which were practically untouched had to conform to the capabilities of the others. D'Estaing, with twenty-five ships, now had Byron to windward of him with seventeen or eighteen capable of holding together, but slower and less handy than their enemies, and saw him tactically embarrassed by the care of a convoy to windward and three disabled ships to leeward. Under these circumstances three courses were open to the French admiral: 1. He might stretch ahead, and, tacking in succession, place himself between Byron and the convoy, throwing his frigates among the latter; 2. He might tack his fleet together and stand up to the English line to bring on a general action; or 3. he could, after going about, cut off the three disabled ships, which might bring on a general action with less exposure.

None of these did he do. As regards the first, he, knowing the criticisms of the fleet, wrote

错之外，就无法进行更多的评述了。

在此之前，法军一直都保持着严格意义上的防御态势，固守着他们那种一贯的政策。如今，此战则提供了一个采取进攻态势来检验德斯坦的职业本领，以及领会我们必须了解的当时形势的机会。在此战中，双方舰队都是右舷抢风、向北而行，法国舰队处在下风位置。尽管阵列不是很有秩序，但由于机动能力强，所以法军并未遭受什么损失；而英军呢，由于发动了错误的进攻，使得7艘战舰遭受重创，其中有4艘——"蒙默斯"号、"格拉夫顿"号、"康沃尔"号和"莱昂"号——则全然损毁了。余下的3艘，到下午3点钟的时候，已经一齐落在了后面，远远处于己方阵列的下风，实际上它们距法军比距英军更近；而英军舰队的速度，就必然会降到与仍然留在阵列中的那些受损舰船的速度了。这些情况，导致出现了一支舰队因受损情况集中于少数几艘舰船而非所有舰船分而受之带来的种种尴尬局面；所以，英军那10艘或12艘几乎完好无损的战舰，就不得不根据其他舰船的状况来行动了。此时，拥有25艘战舰的德斯坦已让拜伦处于他的向风位置，当时他率领着17艘或18艘能够集结拢来的战舰，不过在速度和敏捷方面不如敌人；同时，他也看到拜伦陷入了战术上的尴尬境地：既要照料一支处于迎风位置的运输船队，又要照料处于下风向的3艘已损战舰。在这种情况下，德斯坦这位法国海军上将有3种方案可以选择：1. 他可以将舰队向前展开，接连抢风航行，楔入拜伦和那支运输船队之间，并让自己的护卫舰去对付那支运输船队；2. 他可以让自己的舰队抢风集结起来，勇敢面对英军阵列，发起全面作战；3. 他可以在改变方向后，将那3艘

home that his line was too much disordered to allow it. Whatever the technical irregularity, it is difficult to believe that, with the relative power of motion in the two fleets, the attempt was hopeless. The third alternative probably presented the greatest advantage, for it insured the separation between the enemy's main body and the crippled ships, and might very probably exasperate the British admiral into an attack under most hazardous conditions. It is stated by English authorities that Byron said he would have borne down again, had any attack been made on them. At three P.M. D'Estaing tacked all together, forming line on the lee ship, and stood to the southward again.

The English imitated this movement, except the van ship "Monmouth", which being too badly hurt to manoeuvre kept on to the northward, and the three separated ships. Two of these kept on north and passed once more under the French broadsides; but the "Lion", unable to keep to the wind, kept broad off before it across the bows of the enemy, for Jamaica, a thousand miles away. She was not pursued; a single transport was the sole maritime trophy of the French. "Had the admiral's seamanship equalled his courage," wrote the celebrated Suffren, who commanded the French van ship, "we would not have suffered four dismasted vessels to escape." "D'Estaing, at the age of thirty, had been transferred from the army to the navy with the premature rank of rear-admiral. The navy did not credit him with nautical ability when the war broke out, and it is safe to say that its opinion was justified by his conduct during it."

"Brave as his sword, D'Estaing was always the idol of the soldier, the idol of the seaman; but moral authority over his officers failed him on several occasions, notwithstanding the marked protection extended to him by the king."

Another cause than incapacity as a seaman has usually been assigned by French historians

受损舰船隔开，从而可以在减少危险的前提下发动全面作战。

可他根本没有这样做。关于第一种选择，德斯坦在得知人们对其舰队的指摘之后，曾写信回国，辩解说是因为他的阵列太过混乱，根本就不允许他这样去做。无论从专业角度来说这是一种什么样的不规范行为，我们都很难相信，在两支舰队中法军拥有相对较大机动能力的情况下，这种尝试会完全无望成功。第三种选择很可能具有最大的优势，因为这样做，确保了将敌人的主力与受损舰船隔离开来，并且极有可能激怒那位英军司令，使之在极为冒险的情况下发动进攻。据英国当局称，拜伦曾经说过，倘若法军进攻这些受损舰船的话，他是会再次向敌军进逼的。下午3点，德斯坦命令所有舰船抢风集结起来，向下风方向形成阵列，然后便再次往南而去。

除了前锋舰船"蒙默斯"号因受损太过严重、无法机动而继续向北漂去，以及那3艘落了单的战舰，英军也照样进行了机动。那3艘战舰中，有两艘继续漂在北边，并且再次遭到了法军的舷炮齐射；但"莱昂"号由于无法迎风航行，故一直斜着横过敌军阵前，往1000英里以外的牙买加而去了。它没有受到敌人的追击；法军在此战中的唯一战利品，便是一艘运输船。"倘若司令的航海技术比得上他的勇敢，"著名的苏弗朗当时正指挥着法军的前锋战舰，他如此写道，"那么我们便不会让4艘没有桅杆的舰船逃走了。" "德斯坦时年30岁，乃是从陆军转入海军的，并且过快地被提升成了海军少将。所以，战争爆发之后，海军官兵都信不过他的海战本领；而根据他在此次战争中的表现，我们也完全可以说海军官兵的这种观点是有道理的。" "由于英勇无畏，所以德斯坦一向都既是陆军士兵们的偶像，也是海军官兵们的偶像；不过，这种凌驾于官兵们之上的道德典范，也让他多次辜负了人们的期望，尽管如此，法国国王还是明显地袒护了他。"

for the impotent action of D'Estaing on this occasion. He looked upon Grenada, they say, as the real objective of his efforts, and considered the English fleet a very secondary concern. Ramatuelle, a naval tactician who served actively in this war and wrote under the Empire, cites this case, which he couples with that of Yorktown and others, as exemplifying the true policy of naval war. His words, which probably reflect the current opinion of his service in that day, as they certainly do the policy of French governments, call for more than passing mention, as they involve principles worthy of most serious discussion: —

"The French navy has always preferred the glory of assuring or preserving a conquest to that, more brilliant perhaps, but actually less real, of taking a few ships; and in that it has approached more nearly the true end to be proposed in war. What in fact would the loss of a few ships matter to the English? The essential point is to attack them in their possessions, the immediate source of their commercial wealth and of their maritime power. The war of 1778 furnishes examples which prove the devotion of the French admirals to the true interests of the country. The preservation of the island of Grenada, the reduction of Yorktown where the English army surrendered, the conquest of the island of St. Christopher, were the result of great battles in which the enemy was allowed to retreat undisturbed, rather than risk giving him a chance to succor the points attacked."

The issue could not be more squarely raised than in the case of Grenada. No one will deny that there are moments when a probable military success is to be foregone, or postponed, in favor of one greater or more decisive. The position of De Grasse at the Chesapeake, in 1781, with the fate of Yorktown hanging in the balance, is in point; and it is here coupled with that of D'Estaing at Grenada, as though both stood on the same grounds. Both are justified alike;

法国历史学家们通常都认为，此战中德斯坦之所以作战不力，除了没有海战才能，还有另外一个原因。他们说，德斯坦认为格林纳达才是他所做努力的真正目标，因此英国舰队在他心中居于非常次要的地位。海军战术家拉马杜埃尔曾积极参与了此次战争，并写作出了《帝国》一书；在书中他引用了这个战例，并将其与约克镇之战和其他海战相提并论，以此来说明真正的海战政策。他的说法很可能反映了当时海军中的普遍观点，自然也反映出了历届法国政府的政策；由于其中含有一些值得我们极其认真地来加以讨论的原则，因此我们不能只是简单提及：

"法国海军向来都更愿意确保占领某地或者守住所占之地，而不愿意只是夺取数艘舰船，尽管后者可能会显得更加辉煌，但实际上却并没有前者那样实在；在这一点上，法国海军的做法更加接近于战争的真正目标。事实上，损失几艘舰船，对于英国来说又有什么大不了的呢？首要之处，便是在英属殖民地对他们发动进攻，因为殖民地正是英国贸易财富和制海权的直接来源。1778年战争为我们提供了诸多例子，证明了法国海军将领们为了国家的真正利益做出了巨大的贡献。守住格林纳达岛，攻陷约克镇并使得那里的英军投降，占领圣克里斯托弗岛，都是大规模作战的结果；在这些战斗中，法军都是任由敌人安然撤退，而不是冒着风险，给敌人以增援被攻之地的机会。"

格林纳达岛之战，最直接地提出了这一问题。无可否认，有的时候为了支持一种更大的或者更具决定意义的军事行动，我们会提前或者推迟进行某种很有可能获胜的军事行动。1781年切萨皮克湾海战中，由于约克镇前途未卜，所以德·格拉斯的处境正是如此；他与格林纳达岛之战中的德斯坦相差无几，仿佛两人所站的立场完全相同似的。两人的做法也都有道理；但并不是指他们各自在应对具体情况时的功过相同，而是指他

not on their respective merits as fitting the particular cases, but upon a general principle. Is that principle sound? The bias of the writer quoted betrays itself unconsciously, in saying "a few ships." A whole navy is not usually to be crushed at a blow; a few ships mean an ordinary naval victory. In Rodney's famous battle only five ships were taken, though Jamaica was saved thereby.

In order to determine the soundness of the principle, which is claimed as being illustrated by these two cases (St. Christopher will be discussed later on), it is necessary to examine what was the advantage sought, and what the determining factor of success in either case. At Yorktown the advantage sought was the capture of Cornwallis's army; the objective was the destruction of the enemy's organized military force on shore. At Grenada the chosen objective was the possession of a piece of territory of no great military value; for it must be remarked that all these smaller Antilles, if held in force at all, multiplied large detachments, whose mutual support depended wholly upon the navy. These large detachments were liable to be crushed separately, if not supported by the navy; and if naval superiority is to be maintained, the enemy's navy must be crushed. Grenada, near and to leeward of Barbadoes and Sta. Lucia, both held strongly by the English, was peculiarly weak to the French; but sound military policy for all these islands demanded one or two strongly fortified and garrisoned naval bases, and dependence for the rest upon the fleet. Beyond this, security against attacks by single cruisers and privateers alone was needed.

Such were the objectives in dispute. What was the determining factor in this strife? Surely the navy, the organized military force afloat. Cornwallis's fate depended absolutely upon the sea. It is useless to speculate upon the result, had the odds on the 5th of September, 1781, in favor of De Grasse, been reversed; if the French, instead of five ships more, had had five ships

们所遵循的普遍原则相同。那么，这种原则正确吗？前面这位作者在说"数艘舰船"的时候，就已经不自觉地暴露出了自己的成见。一次打击，通常都是无法摧毁一整支海军的；摧毁数艘舰船，则意味着获得一次普普通通的海战胜利。在罗德尼那次著名的海战中，只击毁了5艘战舰，可牙买加却因此而得以保全了。

为了判断我们说这两次战例（圣克里斯托弗海战将在后面讨论）业已证明的这一原则的合理性，我们必须来审视一下，这两个战例中法军所追求的优势和获胜的决定性因素是什么。在约克镇之战中，法军所追求的优势是俘虏康华里的军队，而目标则是在海滩上摧毁敌人有组织的军事力量。在格林纳达，法军选择的目标是占领一处并无重大军事意义的领土；因为我们必须注意到，倘若用武力占领小安的列斯群岛中的所有岛屿，那么就会使所派大型部队的数量成倍增长，而这些部队又完全依赖于海军进行相互支援。倘若没有海军的支援，那么这些大型部队就有可能被敌人逐一消灭；而要让己方的海军保持优势，就必须消灭敌人的海军。格林纳达离英军牢牢据守的巴巴多斯和圣卢西亚两地都很近，并且位于它们的下风位置，因此对于法军来说，此处异常地不牢固；但是，要想针对所有这些岛屿制定出正确合理的军事政策，那么就需要一两处筑有牢固工事且有驻军防守的海军基地才行，而其余方面则需要依赖舰队。除此之外，还需确保此地不受到零散巡逻舰或者私掠船的攻击。

这些都是交战双方争夺的目标。那么，此次战争中的决定性因素又是什么呢？自然就是海军，即海上有组织的军事力量。康华里的命运，就是完全取决于海军。假设1781年9月5日有利于德·格拉斯的胜算逆转了，假设法军不是比英军多5艘战舰，而是比英

less than the English. As it was, De Grasse, when that fight began, had a superiority over the English equal to the result of a hard-won fight. The question then was, should he risk the almost certain decisive victory over the organized enemy's force ashore, for the sake of a much more doubtful advantage over the organized force afloat? This was not a question of Yorktown, but of Cornwallis and his army; there is a great deal in the way things are put.

So stated, — and the statement needs no modifications, — there can be but one answer. Let it be remarked clearly, however, that both De Grasse's alternatives brought before him the organized forces as the objective.

Not so with D'Estaing at Grenada. His superiority in numbers over the English was nearly as great as that of De Grasse; his alternative objectives were the organized force afloat and a small island, fertile, but militarily unimportant. Grenada is said to have been a strong position for defence; but intrinsic strength does not give importance, if the position has not strategic value. To save the island, he refused to use an enormous advantage fortune had given him over the fleet. Yet upon the strife between the two navies depended the tenure of the islands. Seriously to hold the West India Islands required, first, a powerful seaport, which the French had; second, the control of the sea. For the latter it was necessary, not to multiply detachments in the islands, but to destroy the enemy's navy, which may be accurately called the army in the field. The islands were but rich towns; and not more than one or two fortified towns, or posts, were needed.

It may safely be said that the principle which led to D'Estaing's action was not, to say the least, unqualifiedly correct; for it led him wrong. In the case of Yorktown, the principle as stated by Ramatuelle is not the justifying reason of De Grasse's conduct, though it likely enough was the real reason. What justified De Grasse was that, the event depending upon the

军少5艘战舰，然后再来推测此战的结果，是没有任何益处的。事实是，战斗打响之时，德·格拉斯虽说兵力优于英军，可最终的结局，却只能说是胜利来之不易。那么问题就是，他该不该为了那种胜过英国海军却不确定得多的优势，而拿胜过敌人沿海陆军的那种几乎肯定且具有决定意义的胜利去冒险呢？虽说如何来应对这种形势的方法多种多样，但这并非是约克镇之争，而是康华里及其陆军之争。

所以说——并且这种说法无需再加修正——答案只可能有一个。不过，让我们说得更加清楚明了一点，那就是：德·格拉斯这两种选择，都让他把敌人有组织的武装力量当成了己方的作战目标。

但格林纳达岛之战中的德斯坦却并非如此。他在兵力上对英军的优势，差不多跟德·格拉斯那时一样；而他可以选择的目标，则是有组织的英国海军和一个虽说肥沃却在军事上并不重要的小岛。据说格林纳达是个可以牢固防守的地方；不过，倘若此处并无战略价值，那么内在的牢固也不会赋予它什么重要性。为了保住这个小岛，他拒绝利用上天赋予他在舰队兵力上占有的那种巨大优势。不过，英、法两支海军都是通过此次战争来决定这些岛屿的归属的。要想严肃认真地占领西印度群岛，首先需要有一个强大的海港，这方面法国已经具备了；其次，则是需要掌控海洋。对于后面这一点来说，法国所必需的，不是向各个岛屿增派部队，而是应当摧毁敌人的海军；更准确一点来说，就是应当摧毁敌人的作战部队。这些岛屿，不过是富庶的城镇罢了；法国所需要的，不过就是一两个筑有防御工事的城镇或者据点罢了。

我们可以有把握地说，导致德斯坦如此表现的这一原则，至少并非是完全正确的；

unshaken control of the sea, for a short time only, he already had it by his greater numbers. Had the numbers been equal, loyalty to the military duty of the hour must have forced him to fight, to stop the attempt which the English admiral would certainly have made. The destruction of a few ships, as Ramatuelle slightingly puts it, gives just that superiority to which the happy result at Yorktown was due. As a general principle, this is undoubtedly a better objective than that pursued by the French. Of course, exceptions will be found; but those exceptions will probably be where, as at Yorktown, the military force is struck at directly elsewhere, or, as at Port Mahon, a desirable and powerful base of that force is at stake; though even at Mahon it is doubtful whether the prudence was not misplaced. Had Hawke or Boscawen met with Byng's disaster, they would not have gone to Gibraltar to repair it, unless the French admiral had followed up his first blow with others, increasing their disability.

Grenada was no doubt very dear in the eyes of D'Estaing, because it was his only success. After making the failures at the Delaware, at New York, and at Rhode Island, with the mortifying affair at Sta. Lucia, it is difficult to understand the confidence in him expressed by some French writers. Gifted with a brilliant and contagious personal daring, he distinguished himself most highly, when an admiral, by leading in person assaults upon intrenchments at Sta. Lucia and Grenada, and a few months later in the unsuccessful attack upon Savannah.

During the absence of the French navy in the winter of 1778-79, the English, controlling now the sea with a few of their ships that had not gone to the West Indies, determined to shift the scene of the continental war to the Southern States, where there was believed to be a large number of loyalists. The expedition was directed upon Georgia, and was so far successful that Savannah fell into their hands in the last days of 1778. The whole State speedily submitted.

因为这一原则误导了他。在约克镇之战中，拉马杜埃尔所称的那种原则，也并非是开释德·格拉斯行为的理由，尽管他的理由很可能确实如此。而能够为德·格拉斯进行辩护的，便在于战争所依赖的是无可动摇的制海权，只需暂时掌控海洋就行，但他因为兵力较强，已经做到了这一点。倘若双方兵力相等，那么，当时对军事职责的忠诚之心必定会迫使他去与敌作战，以挫败英国海军司令自然会有的那种企图。拉马杜埃尔轻描淡写地指出的损毁数艘舰船，恰恰会带来此种优势，从而令约克镇之战获得了令人满意的结果。作为一般原则，与法国所追求的目标相比，这种目标无疑更好。当然，也会有例外情况；但那些例外情况，很可能都发生在像约克镇之战中有军队在别的地方直接受到攻击的情形下，或者像在马翁港海战中有一处优良而强大的军事基地岌岌可危的时候；但即便是在马翁港海战中，法军的谨慎是不是用错了地方，这一点也仍是值得怀疑的。要是霍克或博斯科恩遭遇了拜恩这样的惨败，他们是不会去直布罗陀修理舰船的；除非法国的海军司令对他们穷追猛打，使之越来越无力还击，他们才会这样做。

毫无疑问，德斯坦非常重视格林纳达，因为这是他唯一的战果。但德斯坦在特拉华河、纽约和罗德岛接连惨败，还经历了圣卢西亚那可耻的一战之后，有些法国作家却仍然表示对他很有信心，这一点实在令人很难理解。德斯坦天生有着一种杰出而具感染力的英勇之气，他担任海军上将之后，是通过圣卢西亚和格林纳达两战，以及数月后进攻萨凡纳无果的那一战中，身先士卒地进攻敌人的堑壕而让自己获得了极高声誉的。

1778年至1779年间的冬季，就在法国海军离去的这一段时间里，此时已用数艘未去西印度群岛的舰船控制了海上的英军，决定将陆上战争的战场转移到南方诸州；因为他们认为，在南方诸州有着大量反对美国独立的人。于是，他们派遣远征军，前去攻打佐治亚，

Operations were thence extended into South Carolina, but failed to bring about the capture of Charleston.

Word of these events was sent to D'Estaing in the West Indies, accompanied by urgent representations of the danger to the Carolinas, and the murmurings of the people against the French, who were accused of forsaking their allies, having rendered them no service, but on the contrary having profited by the cordial help of the Bostonians to refit their crippled fleet. There was a sting of truth in the alleged failure to help, which impelled D'Estaing to disregard the orders actually in his hands to return at once to Europe with certain ships. Instead of obeying them he sailed for the American coast with twenty-two ships-of-the-line, having in view two objects, — the relief of the Southern States and an attack upon New York in conjunction with Washington's army.

Arriving off the coast of Georgia on the 1st of September, D'Estaing took the English wholly at unawares; but the fatal lack of promptness, which had previously marked the command of this very daring man, again betrayed his good fortune. Dallying at first before Savannah, the fleeting of precious days again brought on a change of conditions, and the approach of the bad-weather season impelled him, too slow at first, into a premature assault. In it he displayed his accustomed gallantry, fighting at the head of his column, as did the American general; but the result was a bloody repulse. The siege was raised, and D'Estaing sailed at once for France, not only giving up his project upon New York, but abandoning the Southern States to the enemy. The value of this help from the great sea power of France, thus cruelly dangled before the eyes of the Americans only to be withdrawn, was shown by the action of the English, who abandoned Newport in the utmost haste when they learned the

并且节节取胜，使得萨凡纳在1778年的最后几天也落入了英军手中。整个佐治亚州赶紧归降了。英军的作战行动，随后又从那里延伸到了南卡罗莱纳，但并未夺得查尔斯顿。

这些战况都报告给了身处西印度群岛的德斯坦，还有南、北卡罗莱纳两州面临危险的紧急呈文，以及民众对于法国人的怨言——他们指责法国人背弃了盟友，没有向他们提供帮助，反而是利用了波士顿人的热忱相助，整修好了自己受损的舰船。他们说法国人没有帮助他们，还是有一点儿事实依据的，因此德斯坦才没有去理会当时已经送达他手中、让他率领某些舰船立即返回欧洲的命令。他没有服从这些命令，而是率领22艘战舰驶往了美国沿海；当时，他有两个目标，一是驰援南方各州，一是联合华盛顿所率的陆军进攻纽约。

德斯坦率军于9月1日抵达了佐治亚沿海，完全打了英军一个措手不及；不过，以前一直标志着这位勇敢之人指挥风格的那种致命的拖延习气，再一次辜负了他的好运。他的舰队一开始是逗留在萨凡纳海域，无所事事；宝贵的时间一天天飞逝，使得形势发生了变化，而气候恶劣的冬季也日渐逼近，迫使他在起初速度太慢的情况下仓促地发动了进攻。在此战中，他表现出了一贯的勇敢之气，处在阵列的最前头作战，就像美国的陆军将领那样；可一场恶战之后，结果却是他被击退了。围攻一结束，德斯坦马上便起航返回法国，非但放弃了进攻纽约的目标，也让南方各州任由敌人去宰割了。此种由法国强大制海权所提供的支援，就这样无情地悬在美国人眼前，结果却又撤走了；而英军一听说法国舰队到来，便极其仓促地放弃了纽波特，他们的行动则正好表明了此种支援的重要性。虽说撤离是预先就决定好了的，但德斯坦的到来，却将这种撤退变成了逃跑。

德斯坦一离去，也意味着整支法国舰队都离去了，因为那些没有返回欧洲的舰船，全都返回西印度群岛去了；所以，英军在行动暂停了一段时间之后，又开始再次进击南

presence of the French fleet. Withdrawal had been before decided upon, but D'Estaing's coming converted it into flight.

After the departure of D'Estaing, which involved that of the whole French fleet, — for the ships which did not go back to France returned to the West Indies, — the English resumed the attack upon the Southern States, which had for a moment been suspended. The fleet and army left New York for Georgia in the last weeks of 1779, and after assembling at Tybee, moved upon Charleston by way of Edisto. The powerlessness of the Americans upon the sea left this movement unembarrassed save by single cruisers, which picked up some stragglers, — affording another lesson of the petty results of a merely cruising warfare. The siege of Charleston began at the end of March, — the English ships soon after passing the bar and Fort Moultrie without serious damage, and anchoring within gunshot of the place. Fort Moultrie was soon and easily reduced by land approaches, and the city itself was surrendered on the 12th of May, after a siege of forty days. The whole State was then quickly overrun and brought into military subjection.

The fragments of D'Estaing's late fleet were joined by a reinforcement from France under the Comte de Guichen, who assumed chief command in the West Indian seas March 22, 1780. The next day he sailed for Sta. Lucia, which he hoped to find unprepared; but a crusty, hard-fighting old admiral of the traditional English type, Sir Hyde Parker, had so settled himself at the anchorage, with sixteen ships, that Guichen with his twenty-two would not attack. The opportunity, if it were one, did not recur. De Guichen, returning to Martinique, anchored there on the 27th; and the same day Parker at Sta. Lucia was joined by the new English commander-in-chief, Rodney.

This since celebrated, but then only distinguished, admiral was sixty-two years old at the

方各州了。在1779年的最后几周里，英国舰队和陆军先是从纽约出发前往佐治亚，并在泰碧岛集结之后，取道艾迪斯托河向查尔斯顿进发。美国人在海上毫无力量可言，使得英军的行动畅通无阻，只有个别巡逻舰前来袭扰，偶尔夺取一些掉了队的舰船——这又是一种教训，说明纯粹的巡航战不过是小打小闹罢了，只能获得微不足道的战果。3月底，英军开始围攻查尔斯顿；而英国的舰船，随后不久也通过了沙洲和莫尔特里堡，没有受到什么重创，然后泊到了火炮射程能够覆盖此地的地方。英军在陆上很快且轻而易举地攻下了莫尔特里堡，而查尔斯顿城则在被围40天之后，于5月12日投降了。接下来，英军很快便横扫整个佐治亚州，对该州进行了军事征服。

德斯坦不久前所率舰队中留下来的那一部分舰船，与法国派遣的、由基申伯爵所率的援军会合了；1780年3月22日，基申伯爵就任法国驻西印度群岛海军总司令一职。第二天，他便率领舰队起航前往圣卢西亚，以为那儿的英军可能毫无防备；但是，海德·帕克勋爵这位脾气暴躁、打过许多硬仗、属于传统型的英国老将，却率领着16艘战舰驻扎在此处，使得率有22艘战舰的基申伯爵也不敢进攻。要说这是一次机会的话，那么这样的机会后来就再也没有出现过了。基申伯爵返回了马提尼克，并于27日泊锚；就在同一天，圣卢西亚的帕克勋爵与新任英军总司令罗德尼会师了。

这位此后名震天下、而当时却只是卓越高贵的海军上将，在担任此地司令一职时已经62岁；而正是在此地，他即将为自己赢得不朽的功名。他有着非凡的勇气和职业才能，却有着挥霍无度——倘若不能说是不合规矩的话——的习惯，故在此次战争爆发之初，因为囊中羞涩，他还在法国耽搁了好一阵子。他曾经夸口说，倘若条件允许他回到英国，他定

time of assuming a command where he was to win an undying fame. Of distinguished courage and professional skill, but with extravagant if not irregular habits, money embarrassments had detained him in exile in France at the time the war began. A boast of his ability to deal with the French fleet, if circumstances enabled him to go back to England, led a French nobleman who heard it to assume his debts, moved by feelings in which chivalry and national pique probably bore equal shares. Upon his return he was given a command, and sailed, in January, 1780, with a fleet of twenty ships-of-the-line, to relieve Gibraltar, then closely invested. Off Cadiz, with a good luck for which he was proverbial, he fell in with a Spanish fleet of eleven ships-of-the-line, which awkwardly held their ground until too late to fly.[5] Throwing out the signal for a general chase, and cutting in to leeward of the enemy, between them and their port, Rodney, despite a dark and stormy night, succeeded in blowing up one ship and taking six. Hastening on, he relieved Gibraltar, placing it out of all danger from want; and then, leaving the prizes and the bulk of his fleet, sailed with the rest for his station.

Despite his brilliant personal courage and professional skill, which in the matter of tactics was far in advance of his contemporaries in England, Rodney, as a commander-in-chief, belongs rather to the wary, cautious school of the French tacticians than to the impetuous, unbounded eagerness of Nelson. As in Tourville we have seen the desperate fighting of the seventeenth century, unwilling to leave its enemy, merging into the formal, artificial — we may almost say trifling — parade tactics of the eighteenth, so in Rodney we shall see the transition from those ceremonious duels to an action which, while skilful in conception, aimed at serious results. For it would be unjust to Rodney to press the comparison to the French admirals of his day. With a skill that De Guichen recognized as

然能够对付法国舰队；一位法国绅士听说了之后，很可能一半是被他的骑士精神所感动，一半是这位绅士本身对法国感到不满，便承担了他的债务。一返回英国，他便被委以司令之职，并于1780年1月率领一支由20艘军舰所组成的舰队，动身前去解救当时正被敌人紧紧包围的直布罗陀。在加的斯海域，由于他那种众所周知的好运，他遇上了一支有11艘军舰的西班牙舰队，后者愚笨地坚守着阵地，而到最后想要逃跑的时候却为时已晚了。[5] 发出全面追击的信号并抢先插入敌军下风位置、阻断敌军撤向港内的退路之后，罗德尼不顾这是一个漆黑而风高浪大的夜晚，成功地炸毁了一艘敌舰，并且俘虏了6艘敌舰。之后他又加速前进，解除了直布罗陀之围，并且使之不再有任何危险；接下来，他便留下所有的战利品和舰队中的大部分船只，并率领其余战舰动身前往自己的驻地了。

尽管他有着非凡的个人勇气和职业本领——从战术的角度来看，他的职业才能已经远远超过了同时代的英国将领——但身为总司令的罗德尼，与其说属于拥有冲动急躁、无限热情的纳尔逊那一类人，还不如说他属于机警谨慎的法国战术家一类。由于我们在图维尔身上看到了17世纪那种拼死力战、不愿舍敌而去的做法，逐渐融入了18世纪那种形式上的、不自然的——甚至几乎可以说是毫无意义的——炫耀式战术，因此在罗德尼身上，我们会看到那些讲究形式的决斗，过渡到了一种虽说构思很巧妙、但目的却旨在获取重大战果的作战行动。硬将他与同时代的法国海军将领来进行比较，对罗德尼并不公平。两军一交锋，基申伯爵就领教到了罗德尼的本领，所以罗德尼的目的就是损及对方，而不是只想摆摆那种毫无意义的花架子。无论一路上命运给他带来了多少意外的帮助，但他的目光从未偏离过的那个目标，就是法国舰队，也就是敌人在海上有组织的军

soon as they crossed swords, Rodney meant mischief, not idle flourishes. Whatever incidental favors fortune might bestow by the way, the objective from which his eye never wandered was the French fleet, — the organized military force of the enemy on the sea. And on the day when Fortune forsook the opponent who had neglected her offers, when the conqueror of Cornwallis failed to strike while he had Rodney at a disadvantage, the latter won a victory which redeemed England from the depths of anxiety, and restored to her by one blow all those islands which the cautious tactics of the allies had for a moment gained, save only Tobago.

De Guichen and Rodney met for the first time on the 17th of April, 1780, three weeks after the arrival of the latter. The French fleet was beating to windward in the Channel between Martinique and Dominica, when the enemy was made in the southeast. A day was spent in manoeuvring for the weather-gage, which Rodney got. The two fleets being now well to leeward of the islands, both on the starboard tack heading to the northward and the French on the lee bow of the English, Rodney, who was carrying a press of sail, signalled to his fleet that he meant to attack the enemy's rear and centre with his whole force; and when he had reached the position he thought suitable, ordered them to keep away eight points (90°) together. De Guichen, seeing the danger of the rear, wore his fleet all together and stood down to succor it. Rodney, finding himself foiled, hauled up again on the same tack as the enemy, both fleets now heading to the southward and eastward. Later, he again made signal for battle, followed an hour after, just at noon, by the order (quoting his own despatch), "for every ship to bear down and steer for her opposite in the enemy's line." This, which sounds like the old story of ship to ship, Rodney explains to have meant her opposite at the moment, not her opposite in numerical order. His own words are: "In a slanting position, that my leading

事力量。就在命运之神抛弃了基申伯爵这个忽视其好意的敌手,就在战胜了康华里的基申伯爵让罗德尼处于劣势后却没有对其发动进击的那一天,后者获得了大捷,从而将整个英国从极度的焦虑中解救了出来,还一鼓作气地为英国收复了西印度群岛中除多巴哥以外的所有岛屿;而法、美盟军凭借谨慎的战略,却只是短暂地占有过这些岛屿罢了。

基申伯爵与罗德尼第一次交锋,是在1780年的4月17日,即罗德尼抵达圣卢西亚的3个星期之后。正当法国舰队在马提尼克和多米尼加之间的海峡逆风航行时,东南方出现了敌人。双方一整天都在不停地机动,以抢占有利位置;最终还是罗德尼占了上风。此时,两支舰队都已经完全处在两个岛屿的下风向,全都是右舷抢风朝北,并且法军处于英军船头的下风向;正在满帆行驶的罗德尼向舰队发出信号,打算集中全部力量进攻敌军的后翼与中军;而当他到达自认为合适的位置之后,他便命令舰队一起偏离8个罗经点[1](即90°)。基申伯爵看到了己方后翼所面临的危险,便令舰队一齐转向下风,冲过去支援后翼。罗德尼见到自己进击受阻,便再次与敌军同舷抢风,逆风行驶,所以两支舰队此时便都朝向东南了。后来,他又一次发出了交战信号;一个小时之后,已是正午了,他又下了一道命令(引自他自己的电文):"每艘战舰都应竭尽全力,转向正对着自己的那艘敌舰。"这道命令,听上去像是古老的舰对舰打法;对此,罗德尼解释说,他指的是当时每艘军舰正面对着的敌舰,而不是按照数字顺序来算与自己对应的敌舰。他的原话是这样的:"处于一种斜向位置的时候,我方打头阵的战舰,可以进攻敌方中军里领头的那些舰船,所以整支英国舰队所面对的,只是敌军三分之二的兵力。"随后执行这一命令所遇到的困难和部下对这一命令的误解,似乎主要都是源于旗语手册

ships might attack the van ships of the enemy's centre division, and the whole British fleet be opposed to only two thirds of the enemy". The difficulty and misunderstanding which followed seem to have sprung mainly from the defective character of the signal book. Instead of doing as the admiral wished, the leading ships carried sail so as to reach their supposed station abreast their numerical opposite in the order. Rodney stated afterward that when he bore down the second time, the French fleet was in a very extended line of battle; and that, had his orders been obeyed, the centre and rear must have been disabled before the van could have joined.

There seems every reason to believe that Rodney's intentions throughout were to double on the French, as asserted. The failure sprang from the signal-book and tactical inefficiency of the fleet; for which he, having lately joined, was not answerable. But the ugliness of his fence was so apparent to De Guichen, that he exclaimed, when the English fleet kept away the first time, that six or seven of his ships were gone; and sent word to Rodney that if his signals had been obeyed he would have had him for his prisoner.[6] A more convincing proof that he recognized the dangerousness of his enemy is to be found in the fact that he took care not to have the lee-gage in their subsequent encounters. Rodney's careful plans being upset, he showed that with them he carried all the stubborn courage of the most downright fighter; taking his own ship close to the enemy and ceasing only when the latter hauled off, her foremast and mainyard gone, and her hull so damaged that she could hardly be kept afloat.

An incident of this battle mentioned by French writers and by Botta, who probably drew upon French authorities, but not found in the English accounts, shows the critical nature of the attack in the apprehension of the French. According to them, Rodney, marking a gap in their

的问题。英军领头的那些战舰并未像罗德尼所希望的那样去做，而是张起船帆，以便赶到按照阵列中的数字顺序来算与自己对应的敌舰位置。后来罗德尼曾说，当他第二次逼近敌军的时候，法国舰队已经完全展开，形成了战斗阵列；倘若部下执行了他的命令，那么不待敌军的前锋加入进来，其中军和后翼一定早就被击溃了。

我们完全有理由相信，罗德尼自始至终都是想夹击法国舰队，就像他自己所坚称的那样。而没能做到这一点的原因，则在于旗语手册不完善，以及英国舰队在战术上效率低下；对于这个方面，由于他不久前才加入海军，所以不应当为此负责。不过，罗德尼的战术之险恶，对基申伯爵来说是显而易见的，所以后者惊呼，当英国舰队第一次阻断的时候，他手下就有6、7艘战舰不见了；后来他还派人传话给罗德尼，说倘若部下服从了罗德尼的命令，那么基申伯爵就会成为罗德尼的阶下之囚。[6] 还有一个令人信服的证据，表明基申伯爵看出了敌军的危险性；这就是在后来的遭遇战中，他都小心得很，不让自己再处于敌军的下风位置。虽说罗德尼的精心计划被打乱了，但他在这些计划中，表现出了属于最纯正之斗士的那种顽强不屈的勇气；在战斗中，他让自己的座舰紧逼敌军，直到敌军退却才罢手，故其座舰失去了前桅和主帆桁，而船体也严重受创，几乎无法浮在水上了。

法国的作家和博塔[2] 都曾提到过此战中的一个小插曲——博塔很可能是引用了法国的官方资料，但我们在英国人的报道中却看不到；这个小插曲表明，在法国人看来，此次进击具有极大的危险性。据他们说，罗德尼注意到，由于法国海军司令后面的一艘战舰离开了编队位置，所以法国阵列中出现了一处缺口，于是他便试图强行楔入这个缺口；但"德斯廷"号战舰上那位74岁的舰长下令船帆尽张，竭力赶了过去，横在英军那

order due to a ship in rear of the French admiral being out of station, tried to break through; but the captain of the "Destin," seventy-four, pressed up under more sail and threw himself across the path of the English ninety-gun ship.

"The action of the 'Destin' was justly praised," says Lapeyrouse-Bonfils. "The fleet ran the danger of almost certain defeat, but for the bravery of M. de Goimpy. Such, after the affair, was the opinion of the whole French squadron. Yet, admitting that our line was broken, what disasters then would necessarily threaten the fleet? Would it not always have been easy for our rear to remedy the accident by promptly standing on to fill the place of the vessels cut off? That movement would necessarily have brought about a mêlée, which would have turned to the advantage of the fleet having the bravest and most devoted captains. But then, as under the empire, it was an acknowledged principle that ships cut off were ships taken, and the belief wrought its own fulfilment."

The effect of breaking an enemy's line, or order-of-battle, depends upon several conditions. The essential idea is to divide the opposing force by penetrating through an interval found, or made, in it, and then to concentrate upon that one of the fractions which can be least easily helped by the other. In a column of ships this will usually be the rear. The compactness of the order attacked, the number of the ships cut off, the length of time during which they can be isolated and outnumbered, will all affect the results. A very great factor in the issue will be the moral effect, the confusion introduced into a line thus broken. Ships coming up toward the break are stopped, the rear doubles up, while the ships ahead continue their course. Such a moment is critical, and calls for instant action; but the men are rare who in an unforeseen emergency can see, and at once take the right course, especially if, being subordinates, they incur responsibility. In such a scene of confusion the English, without presumption, hoped to

艘装有90门火炮的战舰前头，挡住了它的去路。

"'德斯廷'号的做法得到了理所当然的颂扬，"拉佩鲁斯·邦费斯曾说，"倘若没有这位勇敢的M·德·戈因姆比，法国舰队就有必然战败之虞了。此事之后，整个法国舰队全都是这样认为的。不过，就算我方阵列被英军突破了，又有什么样的大难一定会危及到整个舰队呢？我方的后翼舰船，不是一向都能轻而易举地补救这种意外，都能迅速保持航向，补上被隔开的那些船的位置吗？那种调动，必定会引发混乱，从而变成舰长们最勇猛、最有献身精神的那支舰队的优势。但从另一方面来说，就像在法兰西帝国时期那样，掉队的舰船都算被俘舰船是一条公认的准则，而这种信条也会使人们自行去加以履行的。"

突破敌军阵列或战斗序列的效果，取决于若干条件。其基本思想就是通过楔入我方在敌军阵列中发现或者制造出来的缺口，从而将敌军分隔开来，然后再集中兵力，进攻最难获得另一部支援的那一部分敌军。在战舰纵列中，这样的部分通常都是后翼舰船。受击阵列中舰船的密集程度、被隔离开来的舰船数量，以及隔离这些舰船并以众敌寡的时间，全都会影响到这种战法的结果。而这个问题中还有一个非常重要的因素，那就是士气效果；这样突破敌阵，会让整个敌阵陷入慌乱之中。赶来填补缺口的舰船受到阻击，后翼受到夹击，而领头的那些舰船却仍在继续航行。这种时候最为关键，需要立即采取行动才行；不过，在此种没有预料到的紧急情况下，能够看清形势并立即采取正确行动的人不多，尤其是作为下级，因为下级会因此而承担责任。在这样一种混乱状况中，英军并未自以为是，而是希望通过他们更好的航海技术来获得优势；因为当时发挥作用的，除了"勇气和献身精神"，还有技术。"打乱敌军阵列"这一战法的所有效

profit by their better seamanship; for it is not only "courage and devotion," but skill, which then tells. All these effects of "breaking the line" received illustration in Rodney's great battle in 1782.

De Guichen and Rodney met twice again in the following month, but on neither occasion did the French admiral take the favorite lee-gage of his nation. Meanwhile a Spanish fleet of twelve ships-of-the-line was on its way to join the French. Rodney cruised to windward of Martinique to intercept them; but the Spanish admiral kept a northerly course, sighted Guadeloupe, and thence sent a despatch to De Guichen, who joined his allies and escorted them into port. The great preponderance of the coalition, in numbers, raised the fears of the English islands; but lack of harmony led to delays and hesitations, a terrible epidemic raged in the Spanish squadron, and the intended operations came to nothing. In August De Guichen sailed for France with fifteen ships. Rodney, ignorant of his destination, and anxious about both North America and Jamaica, divided his fleet, leaving one half in the islands, and with the remainder sailing for New York, where he arrived on the 12th of September. The risk thus run was very great, and scarcely justifiable; but no ill effect followed the dispersal of forces. Had De Guichen intended to turn upon Jamaica, or, as was expected by Washington, upon New York, neither part of Rodney's fleet could well have withstood him. Two chances of disaster, instead of one, were run, by being in small force on two fields instead of in full force on one.

Rodney's anxiety about North America was well grounded. On the 12th of July of this year the long expected French succor arrived, — five thousand French troops under Rochambeau and seven ships-of-the-line under De Ternay. Hence the English, though still superior at sea, felt forced to concentrate at New York, and were unable to strengthen their operations

果，在1782年罗德尼指挥的那次伟大海战中都得到了充分的说明。

在第二个月里，基申伯爵和罗德尼又遭遇过两次，但这位法国海军司令两次都没有占据该国海军所喜欢的下风位置。在此期间，一支由12艘战舰组成的西班牙舰队正在前来，准备与法军会合。罗德尼巡航到了马提尼克的上风向，打算截击这支西班牙船队；不过，那位西班牙海军司令领着舰队一直都是向北航行，待看到了瓜达鲁佩之后，才派人去通知基申伯爵，而待双方会合之后，基申伯爵又护送着这支西班牙舰队进入了港口。法、西联合舰队在兵力上大大优于英国舰队，使得英属各岛上的人都开始担忧起来；但是，由于法军与西班牙人相处得并不融洽，故法、西两军都在拖延和犹豫，随后西班牙舰队中又爆发了一场可怕的瘟疫，所以那些预定的作战行动便无一实施了。是年8月，基申伯爵便率领15艘舰船，动身返回法国去了。罗德尼由于不知道基申伯爵要去哪里，又担心北美地区和牙买加的安危，便将手下舰队分成了两支，一半留在西印度群岛，自己则率余下的那一半舰船驶往纽约，并于9月12日抵达了那里。他这样做，是冒了极为巨大的风险，并且也是没有什么道理的；不过，虽说兵力分散了，却并没有造成什么不良后果。倘若基申伯爵打算去进攻牙买加的话，或者像华盛顿所期待的那样去进攻纽约，那么罗德尼的任何一支分舰队都是没法很好地抵挡住他的。将兵力分散至两处，而不是集中兵力于一处，就有可能遭受两次失败，而不仅仅是一次了。

罗德尼担心北美地区的安危，是有充分理由的。这一年的7月12日，期盼已久的法国援兵终于到来了——就是罗尚博所率的5000法国陆军，以及德·泰尔奈所率的7艘战舰。因此，尽管在海上仍然占有优势，但英军还是觉得必须将兵力集结于纽约，因而无

in Carolina. The difficulty and distance of movements by land gave such an advantage to sea power that Lafayette urged the French government further to increase the fleet; but it was still naturally and properly attentive to its own immediate interests in the Antilles. It was not yet time to deliver America.

Rodney, having escaped the great hurricane of October, 1780, by his absence, returned to the West Indies later in the year, and soon after heard of the war between England and Holland; which, proceeding from causes which will be mentioned later, was declared December 20, 1780. The admiral at once seized the Dutch islands of St. Eustatius and St. Martin, besides numerous merchant-ships, with property amounting in all to fifteen million dollars. These islands, while still neutral, had played a role similar to that of Nassau during the American Civil War, and had become a great depot of contraband goods, immense quantities of which now fell into the English hands.

The year 1780 had been gloomy for the cause of the United States. The battle of Camden had seemed to settle the English yoke on South Carolina, and the enemy formed high hopes of controlling both North Carolina and Virginia. The treason of Arnold following had increased the depression, which was but partially relieved by the victory at King's Mountain. The substantial aid of French troops was the most cheerful spot in the situation. Yet even that had a checkered light, the second division of the intended help being blocked in Brest by the English fleet; while the final failure of De Guichen to appear, and Rodney coming in his stead, made the hopes of the campaign fruitless.

A period of vehement and decisive action was, however, at hand. At the end of March, 1781, the Comte de Grasse sailed from Brest with twenty-six ships-of-the-line and a large convoy. When off the Azores, five ships parted company for the East Indies, under Suffren, of

法加强他们在卡罗莱纳的作战行动了。部队在陆地上机动困难重重且路途遥远，让海军拥有了极大的优势，所以拉斐特便不断敦促法国政府，要求进一步增强法国舰队的实力；但是，此时法国政府却更关注该国在安的列斯群岛的直接利益，而这也仍然属于一种自然而正确的态度。因为现在还没到解救美国的时候。

由于当时不在西印度群岛，所以罗德尼躲过了1780年10月的那场大飓风，并在这一年的年底才返回此处，而不久之后，他便得知了英、荷两国开战的消息；两国是在1780年12月20日开战的，至于交战原因，后文自会提及。这位海军司令马上便夺取了圣尤斯泰西厄斯和圣马丁这两个荷属岛屿，还俘虏了无数的荷兰商船，所掠财产价值总计高达1500万美元。这两个岛屿虽说当时仍然处于中立，但其作用类似于美国内战中的拿骚[3]，因而成为了一个大型的违禁物资集散地，而这些堆积如山的违禁物资，如今全都落到了英军手里。

对于合众国的独立事业来说，1780年是极其绝望的一年。卡姆登[4]之战，似乎让南卡罗莱纳再也摆脱不了英国的束缚了；而敌人则有了更大的希望，还想控制北卡罗莱纳和弗吉尼亚。接下来的阿诺德[5]叛国案，让美国上下更感沮丧，直到获得国王山大捷[6]，此种沮丧之情才稍有减轻。法国军队提供了重要的支援，这是当时形势下最令人高兴的一点。不过，即便是这个方面，也是坎坷不断，因为打算前来支援的法军第二师被英国舰队封锁在布雷斯特，基申伯爵也将遭遇到一生中的最后一次惨败，并将由罗德尼取而代之；这些，都使得美国人因此次大捷而燃起的希望，全都化成了泡影。

然而，一段战斗激烈且具有决定性意义的时期很快就要到来了。1781年3月底，德·格拉斯伯爵率领26艘战舰以及一支运输船队从布雷斯特起航了。到了亚速尔群岛海

whom more will be heard later on. De Grasse came in sight of Martinique on the 28th of April. Admiral Hood (Rodney having remained behind at St. Eustatius) was blockading before Fort Royal, the French port and arsenal on the lee side of the island, in which were four ships-of-the-line, when his lookouts reported the enemy's fleet. Hood had two objects before him, — one to prevent the junction of the four blockaded ships with the approaching fleet, the other to keep the latter from getting between him and Gros Ilot Bay in Sta. Lucia. Instead of effecting this in the next twenty-four hours, by beating to windward of the Diamond Rock, his fleet got so far to leeward that De Grasse, passing through the channel on the 29th, headed up for Fort Royal, keeping his convoy between the fleet and the island. For this false position Hood was severely blamed by Rodney, but it may have been due to light winds and the lee current. However that be, the four ships in Fort Royal got under way and joined the main body. The English had now only eighteen ships to the French twenty-four, and the latter were to windward; but though thus in the proportion of four to three, and having the power to attack, De Grasse would not do it. The fear of exposing his convoy prevented him from running the chance of a serious engagement. Great must have been his distrust of his forces, one would say. When is a navy to fight, if this was not a time? He carried on a distant cannonade, with results so far against the English as to make his backwardness yet more extraordinary. Can a policy or a tradition which justifies such a line of conduct be good?

The following day, April 30, De Grasse, having thrown away his chance, attempted to follow Hood; but the latter had no longer any reason for fighting, and his original inferiority was increased by the severe injuries of some ships on the 29th. De Grasse could not overtake him, owing to the inferior speed of his fleet, many of the ships not being coppered, — a fact worthy of note, as French vessels by model and size were generally faster than English;

域后，有5艘战舰在苏弗朗的指挥下，一齐驶往了东印度群岛；关于这个苏弗朗，后文还会涉及到更多的内容。4月28日，德·格拉斯抵达了马提尼克附近海域。当时，胡德上将正率军封锁着皇家要塞（罗德尼那时仍然留在圣尤斯泰西厄斯），这个法属港口和海军船坞位于马提尼克岛背风的那一侧，港内泊有4艘战舰；就在此时，胡德上将的瞭望队向他报告了敌方舰队到来的消息。摆在胡德面前的，是两个目标：一是阻止封锁在港内的那4艘战舰与正在前来的敌方舰队会合，二是不让敌方舰队楔入己方舰队与圣卢西亚的格罗斯岛湾之间。可在接下来的24个小时中，胡德上将却并未通过率先抢风赶到钻石崖来实现这两个目标，相反，因为他所率舰队处于下风位置太远，故德·格拉斯率军于29日穿过了此处海峡，并让运输船队处在舰队和马提尼克岛之间，驶往了皇家要塞。由于采取了如此不正确的战法，后来胡德上将还受到了罗德尼的严厉批评；不过，有可能因为当时风力不大，而洋流也是流向下风向，所以才造成这样的局面。不管是什么原因，反正皇家要塞内的那4艘战舰都驶出了港口，加入了主力舰队当中。此时英军只有18艘战舰，而法军则有24艘，并且处在上风位置；不过，尽管法、英兵力比达到了4∶3，且有实力发起进攻，但德·格拉斯也不会那样做。由于担心运输船队的安危，所以他不会冒险与英军进行真正的交锋。有人会说，他肯定是极其信不过自己手下的部队。否则，要说这都不是时机的话，那么一支海军的作战时机又是什么呢？他进行了远距离炮击，非但没有伤及英军，反而使得他的畏缩显得更加奇怪了。一种认为这样的行动准则都是合理的政策或传统，能是一种好的政策和传统吗？

第二天，即4月30日，业已放弃了机会的德·格拉斯，却又试图去追击胡德；不

but this superiority was sacrificed through the delay of the government in adopting the new improvement.

Hood rejoined Rodney at Antigua; and De Grasse, after remaining a short time at Fort Royal, made an attempt upon Gros Ilot Bay, the possession of which by the English kept all the movements of his fleet under surveillance. Foiled here, he moved against Tobago, which surrendered June 2, 1781. Sailing thence, after some minor operations, he anchored on the 26th of July at Cap Français (now Cape Haytien), in the island of Hayti. Here he found awaiting him a French frigate from the United States, bearing despatches from Washington and Rochambeau, upon which he was to take the most momentous action that fell to any French admiral during the war.

The invasion of the Southern States by the English, beginning in Georgia and followed by the taking of Charleston and the military control of the two extreme States, had been pressed on to the northward by way of Camden into North Carolina. On the 16th of August, 1780, General Gates was totally defeated at Camden; and during the following nine months the English under Cornwallis persisted in their attempts to overrun North Carolina. These operations, the narration of which is foreign to our immediate subject, had ended by forcing Cornwallis, despite many successes in actual encounter, to fall back exhausted toward the seaboard, and finally upon Wilmington, in which place depots for such a contingency had been established. His opponent, General Greene, then turned the American troops toward South Carolina. Cornwallis, too weak to dream of controlling, or even penetrating, into the interior of an unfriendly country, had now to choose between returning to Charleston, to assure there and in South Carolina the shaken British power, and moving northward again

过，胡德上将已无再战的理由，并且其起初的兵力劣势，又因29日有数艘舰船遭受了重创而加剧了。由于所率舰队中许多船只的船体都未包铜，速度不如英国舰队，所以德·格拉斯根本就不可能赶上胡德——这一事实值得我们加以注意，因为法国舰船的样式和大小更合理，使得它们的速度通常都要快过英国战舰；不过，这种优势却因法国政府迟迟不肯采用新的改良工艺而白白地浪费掉了。

胡德在安提瓜与罗德尼会合了；而德·格拉斯在皇家要塞稍事停留之后，就前去攻打格罗斯岛湾——因为英军占领着此处，所以他所率舰队的一举一动，全都处在英军的监视之下。由于进攻此地受阻，所以他转而进击多巴哥；1781年6月2日，多巴哥投降了。然后，他又从此处率军起航，在经历了数次小规模战斗之后，于7月26日停靠在海地岛上的法兰西角（即如今的海地角）。在这里，他发现有一艘从合众国而来、带着华盛顿与罗尚博二人急函的法国护卫舰正在等候着他；按照这些急函的要求，他准备发起此战中所有法国海军司令采取过的一场最为重大的作战行动。

英军入侵南方各州始于佐治亚，继而是夺取了查尔斯顿以及对两个激进州进行军事管制，然后再取道卡姆登，一步步向北推进到了北卡罗莱纳境内。1780年8月16日，盖茨将军在卡姆登之战中彻底战败；而在随后的9个月里，康华里所率的英军一直都坚持不懈，想要踏平北卡罗莱纳。这些作战行动的详细情况，与我们的直接主题无关；而最终结果是，尽管在实际的遭遇战中获取过多次胜利，但康华里还是不得不筋疲力尽地撤退到了沿海地区，最后到达了威明顿，那里已经为防止出现这种意外情况而建起了数座补给站。于是，他的对手格林将军便率领美国军队转而攻向南卡罗莱纳。康华里手下兵

into Virginia, there to join hands with a small expeditionary force operating on the James River under Generals Phillips and Arnold. To fall back would be a confession that the weary marching and fighting of months past had been without results, and the general readily convinced himself that the Chesapeake was the proper seat of war, even if New York itself had to be abandoned. The commander-in-chief, Sir Henry Clinton, by no means shared this opinion, upon which was justified a step taken without asking him. "Operations in the Chesapeake," he wrote, "are attended with great risk unless we are sure of a permanent superiority at sea. I tremble for the fatal consequences that may ensue." For Cornwallis, taking the matter into his own hands, had marched from Wilmington on the 25th of April, 1781, joining the British already at Petersburg on the 20th of May. The forces thus united numbered seven thousand men. Driven back from the open country of South Carolina into Charleston, there now remained two centres of British power, — at New York and in the Chesapeake. With New Jersey and Pennsylvania in the hands of the Americans, communication between the two depended wholly upon the sea.

Despite his unfavorable criticism of Cornwallis's action, Clinton had himself already risked a large detachment in the Chesapeake. A body of sixteen hundred men under Benedict Arnold had ravaged the country of the James and burned Richmond in January of this same year. In the hopes of capturing Arnold, Lafayette had been sent to Virginia with a nucleus of twelve hundred troops, and on the evening of the 8th of March the French squadron at Newport sailed, in concerted movement, to control the waters of the bay. Admiral Arbuthnot, commanding the English fleet lying in Gardiner's Bay,[7] learned the departure by his lookouts, and started in pursuit on the morning of the 10th, thirty-six hours later. Favored either by diligence or luck,

力太弱,根本不会指望去控制、甚至是深入到一个敌对国家的腹地;如今他面临着两种选择:一是返回查尔斯顿,以保护那里与南卡罗莱境内摇摇欲坠的英国势力,二是向北挺进,再次进入弗吉尼亚,在那儿与菲利普将军和阿诺德将军所率、正在詹姆士河上作战的一小支远征部队联起手来。倘若撤退,那就意味着承认过去数月间实施的疲惫进军与作战都无果而终;而这位将军,也早已毫无困难地让自己相信,切萨皮克湾才是真正的战场,即便是纽约,也必须放弃才行。可总司令亨利·柯林顿爵士却毫不认同这种观点,认为不过问他便采取行动是没有理由的。他写道:"除非我们确保在海上拥有永久性的优势,否则的话,切萨皮克湾的作战行动就会伴随着极大的风险。一想到那样做可能发生的致命后果,我就不寒而栗。"对于这个问题,康华里已经擅自做出了决定,已于1781年4月25日从威明顿出发,并于5月20日同已在彼得斯堡的英军会师了。这样会合起来的英军,兵力达到了7000人。由于英军已经被美国军队从南卡罗莱纳的开阔乡村赶回了查尔斯顿,所以英国势力如今只留下了两个中心:纽约和切萨皮克湾。而新泽西和宾夕法尼亚两州都在美军手里,所以在纽约和切萨皮克湾这两处之间的通信联络就完全依赖于海路了。

尽管不留情面地指责康华里的行动,但柯林顿爵士自己也已冒着风险,往切萨皮克湾派遣了一支大部队。本尼迪克特·阿诺德指挥的一支1600人的部队已经劫掠了詹姆士河两岸的乡村,并在同一年的1月份纵火焚毁了里士满。法军想要活捉阿诺德,便派拉斐特率领一支1200人的精锐部队前往弗吉尼亚,而在3月8日傍晚,驻纽波特的法国舰队也已起航,协同行动,以控制切萨皮克湾海域。泊于加德纳湾的英国舰队由阿巴思诺特上将指挥,[7]他从瞭望哨得知了法国舰队离去的消息,便在10日上午开始追击;此时

he made such good time that when the two fleets came in sight of each other, a little outside of the capes of the Chesapeake, the English were leading[8]. They at once went about to meet their enemy, who, on his part, formed a line-of-battle. The wind at this time was west, so that neither could head directly into the bay.

The two fleets were nearly equal in strength, there being eight ships on each side; but the English had one ninety-gun ship, while of the French one was only a heavy frigate, which was put into the line. Nevertheless, the case was eminently one for the general French policy to have determined the action of a vigorous chief, and the failure to see the matter through must fall upon the good-will of Commodore Destouches, or upon some other cause than that preference for the ulterior objects of the operations, of which the reader of French naval history hears so much. The weather was boisterous and threatening, and the wind, after hauling once or twice, settled down to northeast, with a big sea, but was then fair for entering the bay. The two fleets were by this time both on the port tack standing out to sea, the French leading, and about a point on the weather bow of the English. From this position they wore in succession ahead of the latter, taking the lee-gage, and thus gaining the use of their lower batteries, which the heavy sea forbade to the weather-gage. The English stood on till abreast the enemy's line, when they wore together, and soon after attacked in the usual manner, and with the usual results. The three van ships were very badly injured aloft, but in their turn, throwing their force mainly on the two leaders of the enemy, crippled them seriously in hulls and rigging. The French van then kept away, and Arbuthnot, in perplexity, ordered his van to haul the wind again. M. Destouches now executed a very neat movement by defiling. Signalling his van to haul up on the other tack, he led the rest of his squadron by the disabled English ships, and after giving them the successive broadsides of his comparatively fresh

已是法国舰队出发的36个小时之后了。或是因为行动迅速，或是因为运气好，反正他行进得很快，以至于当两支舰队在切萨皮克湾海角以外不远处看得见彼此的时候，英国舰队竟然还领先了。[8]两军马上各自组成战斗序列，准备交战。此时正刮西风，所以双方谁也无法直接驶向切萨皮克湾内。

这两支舰队的兵力差不多相等，每一边都是8艘战舰；不过，英军拥有一艘装有90门火炮的战舰，而法军与之对应的，只是一艘也被编入了战斗序列的重型护卫舰。尽管如此，此次海战仍是体现出了法国那种总体政策的一个显著战例；正是这种政策，决定了一位精力充沛的主帅的行动以及他未能看透这一问题的责任，必定会归咎于德图什准将的良好愿望，或者归咎于其他理由，而不是归咎于此种政策对作战行动的隐秘目标的偏好；可凡是阅读过法国海军历史的人，都对这种所谓的隐秘目标耳熟能详了。当时天气恶劣、风雨欲来，而风向转过一两次之后，便稳定下来往东北直刮，海面上风高浪大，不过当时很适合于舰队进入海湾。到了此时，两支舰队都是左舷抢风向着大海，法国舰队在前，距英国舰队向风的船首大约1个罗经点。它们从这个位置上依次转向下风，驶在英国舰队前面，并且占领了下风位置，这样就可以利用其下层舰炮了——因为海上风浪太大，下层舰炮不能在上风位置使用。英国舰队保持航向，直到与敌军阵列并排，然后便一齐转向下风，并且很快开始用惯常的方式发起攻击，而结果也与平常并无二致。法军3艘前锋战舰的高处遭到了重创，不过轮到它们攻击的时候，它们的火力主要都落在2艘领头的敌舰上，重创了敌舰的船体与索具。于是，法国的前锋舰船便偏离航向，而乱成一团的阿巴思诺特却命令其前锋舰船再一次逆风行驶。此时，M·德图什指挥

ships, wore, and out to sea. This was the end of the battle, in which the English certainly got the worst; but with their usual tenacity of purpose, being unable to pursue their enemy afloat, they steered for the bay, made the junction with Arnold, and thus broke up the plans of the French and Americans, from which so much had been hoped by Washington. There can be no doubt, after careful reading of the accounts, that after the fighting the French were in better force than the English, and they in fact claimed the victory; yet the ulterior objects of the expedition did not tempt them again to try the issue with a fleet of about their own size.[9]

The way of the sea being thus open and held in force, two thousand more English troops sailing from New York reached Virginia on the 26th of March, and the subsequent arrival of Cornwallis in May raised the number to seven thousand. The operations of the contending forces during the spring and summer months, in which Lafayette commanded the Americans, do not concern our subject. Early in August, Cornwallis, acting under orders from Clinton, withdrew his troops into the peninsula between the York and James rivers, and occupied Yorktown.

Washington and Rochambeau had met on the 21st of May, and decided that the situation demanded that the effort of the French West Indian fleet, when it came, should be directed against either New York or the Chesapeake. This was the tenor of the despatch found by De Grasse at Cap Français, and meantime the allied generals drew their troops toward New York, where they would be on hand for the furtherance of one object, and nearer the second if they had to make for it.

In either case the result, in the opinion both of Washington and of the French government, depended upon superior sea power; but Rochambeau had privately notified the admiral that his

舰队排成纵列前进，实施了一次非常巧妙的机动。他用旗语命令前锋舰船改成另一侧迎风行驶，然后率领其余相对完好战舰驶过并用舷炮连续猛轰那些已经动弹不得的英国战舰之后，便转向下风驶向了外海。这场海战就此结束了，其中英军的损失无疑最为严重；不过，由于他们一贯有着顽强的目标，此时不能出海去追击敌军，所以他们便转而驶向切萨皮克湾，与阿诺德会合，从而粉碎了法军和美军的计划，也让华盛顿对这些计划所寄予的厚望落了空。在仔细阅读了这些描述之后，我们无疑便会得知，此战过后，法军的兵力要优于英军，而法军实际上也宣称他们在此战中取胜了；不过这支远征军的隐秘目标，却并未让他们再跟一支规模与他们自己不相上下的舰队去较量，来验证这一结果了。

如此一来，英军打通并以武力掌控了海上，从纽约便又赶来了2000兵力，并于3月26日抵达了弗吉尼亚，而随后康华里也于5月来到这里，使得英军总数上升到了7000人。双方在这一年春季与夏季的作战行动，与本书论述的主题并不相关；其中，美军是由拉斐特指挥作战的。8月上旬，康华里按照柯林顿勋爵的命令，将军队撤入了位于纽约和詹姆士河之间的半岛上，然后夺取了约克镇。

华盛顿与罗尚博于5月21日见了面，并且认为，此时的形势需要法国西印度群岛舰队来发挥作用，待这支舰队到来后，就可用它来进攻纽约或者切萨皮克湾。这就是德·格拉斯在法兰西角收到的那份电文的意思；而与此同时，这两位联军将领将各自的陆军调往纽约，准备在那里实现俘虏康华里的这个目标，并且倘若他们必须实现第二个目标的话，这样也会更快一些。

华盛顿和法国政府都一致认为，在这两种情况下，战局都取决于制海权方面的优

own preference was for the Chesapeake as the scene of the intended operations, and moreover the French government had declined to furnish the means for a formal siege of New York. The enterprise therefore assumed the form of an extensive military combination, dependent upon ease and rapidity of movement, and upon blinding the eyes of the enemy to the real objective, — purposes to which the peculiar qualities of a navy admirably lent themselves. The shorter distance to be traversed, the greater depth of water and easier pilotage of the Chesapeake, were further reasons which would commend the scheme to the judgment of a seaman; and De Grasse readily accepted it, without making difficulties or demanding modifications which would have involved discussion and delay.

Having made his decision, the French admiral acted with great good judgment, promptitude, and vigor. The same frigate that brought despatches from Washington was sent back, so that by August 15th the allied generals knew of the intended coming of the fleet. Thirty-five hundred soldiers were spared by the governor of Cap Français, upon the condition of a Spanish squadron anchoring at the place, which De Grasse procured. He also raised from the governor of Havana the money urgently needed by the Americans; and finally, instead of weakening his force by sending convoys to France, as the court had wished, he took every available ship to the Chesapeake. To conceal his coming as long as possible, he passed through the Bahama Channel, as a less frequented route, and on the 30th of August anchored in Lynnhaven Bay, just within the capes of the Chesapeake, with twenty-eight ships-of-the-line. Three days before, August 27, the French squadron at Newport, eight ships-of-the-line with four frigates and eighteen transports under M. de Barras, sailed for the rendezvous; making, however, a wide circuit out to sea to avoid the English. This course was the more necessary as the French siege-artillery was with it. The troops under Washington and Rochambeau had crossed the

势；不过，罗尚博曾经私下跟德·格拉斯上将说，他本人更想在切萨皮克湾打响拟定的战斗，并且法国政府也拒绝提供装备，来正式围攻纽约。因此，他们只能采取陆军大范围联合作战的形式，依赖于灵活而快速的机动，并且蒙蔽敌人，让敌人不知道他们的真正目标———一支海军能够放下架子，支持这样的作战目标，是很值得称道的。部队调动距离较短，切萨皮克湾航道较深，并且较易领航，这些也是导致这位水兵做出此种判断、支持这一计划的深层理由；所以，德·格拉斯欣然同意了这个作战计划，既未刁难，也未要求修改——倘若他再刁难改动的话，势必会讨论来讨论去，从而耽搁计划的实施。

下定决心之后，这位法国海军上将便开始极其准确地审时度势，迅速而干劲十足地行动起来。他将送来华盛顿急函的那艘护卫舰派了回去，因此到8月15日时，华盛顿与罗尚博这两位联军将领都得知了法国舰队即将前来的消息。在有一支西班牙舰队泊在法兰西角的情况下，德·格拉斯还是从该地总督手中得到了3500名士兵。他还从哈瓦那总督那里，募集到了美军所急需的资金；最后，他也没有按照法国朝廷的要求，分兵护送运输船队返回法国，而是率领着所有舰船前往切萨皮克湾。为了尽可能久地掩盖其前往切萨皮克湾的行踪，他经由舰船较少通航的巴哈马海峡，率领28艘战舰在8月30日抵达了位于切萨皮克湾海角内的林黑文湾。而3天前的8月27日，纽波特那支由8艘战舰、4艘护卫舰和18艘运输舰所组成的法国分舰队，在M·德·巴拉斯的率领下，也已起航前往集结地；不过，这支舰队为了避开英军，还在海上绕了一个大圈子。这样做是很有必要的，因为这支舰队携带着法军的攻城大炮。华盛顿和罗尚博指挥的部队已于8月24日渡过了哈德逊河，正向切萨皮克湾前端挺进。这样，海陆两支不同的武装力量便合二为

Hudson on the 24th of August, moving toward the head of Chesapeake Bay. Thus the different armed forces, both land and sea, were converging toward their objective, Cornwallis.

The English were unfortunate in all directions. Rodney, learning of De Grasse's departure, sent fourteen ships-of-the-line under Admiral Hood to North America, and himself sailed for England in August, on account of ill health. Hood, going by the direct route, reached the Chesapeake three days before De Grasse, looked into the bay, and finding it empty went on to New York. There he met five ships-of-the-line under Admiral Graves, who, being senior officer, took command of the whole force and sailed on the 31st of August for the Chesapeake, hoping to intercept De Barras before he could join De Grasse. It was not till two days later that Sir Henry Clinton was persuaded that the allied armies had gone against Cornwallis, and had too far the start to be overtaken.

Admiral Graves was painfully surprised, on making the Chesapeake, to find anchored there a fleet which from its numbers could only be an enemy's. Nevertheless, he stood in to meet it, and as De Grasse got under way, allowing his ships to be counted, the sense of numerical inferiority — nineteen to twenty-four — did not deter the English admiral from attacking. The clumsiness of his method, however, betrayed his gallantry; many of his ships were roughly handled, without any advantage being gained. De Grasse, expecting De Barras, remained outside five days, keeping the English fleet in play without coming to action; then returning to port he found De Barras safely at anchor. Graves went back to New York, and with him disappeared the last hope of succor that was to gladden Cornwallis's eyes. The siege was steadily endured, but the control of the sea made only one issue possible, and the English forces were surrendered October 19, 1781. With this disaster the hope of subduing the colonies died in England. The conflict flickered through a year longer, but no serious operations were

一，全都向康华里这个目标扑去。

英军在各个方面都很倒霉。获知德·格拉斯离去的消息后，罗德尼派胡德上将率领14艘战舰前往北美地区，而他自己则因为生病，于8月动身回英国治疗去了。胡德走的是直路，故比德·格拉斯早3天到达了切萨皮克湾；他派人侦察，发现湾内空空荡荡的，便继续率军驶向纽约。在纽约海域，他遇上了格雷夫斯上将所率的5艘战舰；后者是位高级将领，指挥着这支部队于8月31日起航前往切萨皮克湾，想截击德·巴拉斯，使之无法与德·格拉斯会合。直到两天之后，亨利·柯林顿爵士才确信美、法联军已经前去进击康华里部，可此时再来动身追赶，为时已晚了。

格雷夫斯上将在率军抵达切萨皮克湾时大吃了一惊，发现那里竟然泊有一支舰队，而从舰船数量来看，只可能是敌方的舰队。尽管如此，他还是率军驶上前去，而当德·格拉斯拔营起航，任由敌人清点其舰船数量之后，兵力上的劣势——19艘战舰对24艘战舰——却并未让这位英国的海军上将打消进击的念头。不过，他的进攻方式笨拙不灵，却有负于他的勇敢；他手下的许多战舰指挥得都很糟糕，没有争取到任何优势。德·格拉斯因为要等德·巴拉斯，所以在切萨皮克湾外的海面上停留了5天，将这支英国舰队当作消遣，并未与其交战；而待他返回泊地时，却发现德·巴拉斯已经安全抵达了。格雷夫斯便返回了纽约，而康华里获取支援的最后一线希望，也随着格雷夫斯的返回而破灭了。虽然他一直顽强地抵抗着美、法联军的围攻，可由于后者控制了海面，结局只可能有一种，所以英军便于1781年10月19投降了。这次惨败，使得英国征服美洲各殖民地的希望完全化为了乌有。这场战争断断续续地又进行了一年多，但后来并没有再出现什么重大的作战行动了。

undertaken.

In the conduct of the English operations, which ended thus unfortunately, there was both bad management and ill fortune. Hood's detachment might have been strengthened by several ships from Jamaica, had Rodney's orders been carried out. The despatch-ship, also, sent by him to Admiral Graves commanding in New York, found that officer absent on a cruise to the eastward, with a view to intercept certain very important supplies which had been forwarded by the American agent in France. The English Court had laid great stress upon cutting off this convoy; but, with the knowledge that he had of the force accompanying it, the admiral was probably ill-advised in leaving his headquarters himself, with all his fleet, at the time when the approach of the hurricane season in the West Indies directed the active operations of the navies toward the continent. In consequence of his absence, although Rodney's despatches were at once sent on by the senior officer in New York, the vessel carrying them being driven ashore by enemy's cruisers, Graves did not learn their contents until his return to port, August 16. The information sent by Hood of his coming was also intercepted. After Hood's arrival, it does not appear that there was avoidable delay in going to sea; but there does seem to have been misjudgment in the direction given to the fleet. It was known that De Barras had sailed from Newport with eight ships, bound probably for the Chesapeake, certainly to effect a junction with De Grasse; and it has been judiciously pointed out that if Graves had taken up his cruising-ground near the Capes, but out of sight of land, he could hardly have failed to fall in with him in overwhelming force. Knowing what is now known, this would undoubtedly have been the proper thing to do; but the English admiral had imperfect information. It was nowhere expected that the French would bring nearly the force they did; and Graves lost information, which he ought to have received, as to their numbers, by the carelessness of his

在英军以惨败而告终的这次作战行动中，既有指挥不当的原因，也有运气不好的因素。倘若罗德尼的命令得到了执行，那么胡德所率的分队，本来是可以获得来自牙买加的一些战舰增援的。而罗德尼派往纽约舰队司令格雷夫斯上将处的那艘通讯船抵达纽约后，却发现这位将领不在；因为他当时率军往东边巡逻去了，打算截击由身处法国的美国政府代表运送过来的一批极其重要的补给物资。英国政府已经给他施加了巨大的压力，严令要他截取这支运输船队；不过，在了解自己手下部队实力的情况下，这位海军上将很可能是因为考虑不周，才会在西印度群岛海域的飓风季节即将到来、并会让海军的主动作战转向大陆作战的这个时候，亲自率领整支舰队离开自己的司令部。由于他不在，尽管留守纽约的那位高级将领马上派船将罗德尼的公函给他送去，但送信的那艘船，却被敌人的巡逻舰赶回了岸边；所以，格雷夫斯直到8月16日回港后才得知这些公函的内容。胡德上将发出的、关于他即将到来的情报，也被敌人截获了。胡德抵达纽约后，他们在率军出海这一点上似乎并没有出现什么可以避免的延误；不过，他们下达给舰队的命令，却似乎的确出现了判断失误的情况。我们都知道，德·巴拉斯此时已经率领8艘战舰从纽波特出发，很可能是驶往切萨皮克湾，自然是想与德·格拉斯所率的舰队会合；而前文也已明智地指出，假如格雷夫斯是在切萨皮克湾海角附近看不见陆地的海域巡逻的话，他很可能会遇上德·巴拉斯，并以压倒性的兵力击溃后者。倘若了解了我们如今所知的这些情况，那么这无疑就是格雷夫斯应当采取的正确行动；可当时这位海军上将的情报太不完善了。他决计想不到，法军兵力会跟他们差不多；何况，格雷夫斯又因为自己派驻切萨皮克湾海域的那些巡逻舰太过疏忽，而没有获知本应得到的、关于法军舰船数量的情报。他本已下命令这

cruisers stationed off the Chesapeake. These had been ordered to keep under way, but were both at anchor under Cape Henry when De Grasse's appearance cut off their escape. One was captured, the other driven up York River. No single circumstance contributed more to the general result than the neglect of these two subordinate officers, by which Graves lost that all-important information. It can readily be conceived how his movements might have been affected, had he known two days earlier that De Grasse had brought twenty-seven or twenty-eight sail of the line; how natural would have been the conclusion, first, to waylay De Barras, with whom his own nineteen could more than cope. "Had Admiral Graves succeeded in capturing that squadron, it would have greatly paralyzed the besieging army [it had the siege train on board], if it would not have prevented its operations altogether; it would have put the two fleets nearly on an equality in point of numbers, would have arrested the progress of the French arms for the ensuing year in the West Indies, and might possibly have created such a spirit of discord between the French and Americans[10] as would have sunk the latter into the lowest depths of despair, from which they were only extricated by the arrival of the forces under De Grasse." These are true and sober comments upon the naval strategy.

In regard to the admiral's tactics, it will be enough to say that the fleet was taken into battle nearly as Byng took his; that very similar mishaps resulted; and that, when attacking twenty-four ships with nineteen, seven, under that capable officer Hood, were not able to get into action, owing to the dispositions made.

On the French side De Grasse must be credited with a degree of energy, foresight, and determination surprising in view of his failures at other times. The decision to take every ship with him, which made him independent of any failure on the part of De Barras; the passage

两艘巡逻舰起航，可是当德·格拉斯率军出现并切断它们的逃跑路线时，两船却都还停泊在亨利角下。其中一艘成了俘虏，其余那艘则被赶进了约克河。这两位下级将领的疏忽，使得格雷夫斯没有获知这一重大情报，因而是导致英军失败的最大原因。倘若他早两天得知德·格拉斯率有27艘或28艘战舰的话，他的调遣部署将会受到多大的影响，这一点是我们可想而知的；而结果又会是多么的自然而然啊——首先便是伏击德·巴拉斯，因为用他自己所率的那19艘战舰来对付德·巴拉斯，完全是绰绰有余的。"假如格雷夫斯上将成功地俘虏了那支分舰队，就算不会完全阻断围攻纽约之陆军的作战行动，也会极大地削弱其进攻力量（因为这支分舰队携带着攻城装备）；这样的话，就会使双方舰队在兵力上变得差不多势均力敌，就会阻碍第二年法国陆军在西印度群岛的进击，并且可能会使法军与美军之间产生不和，[9] 从而让后者陷入绝望的深渊中去——而德·格拉斯所率部队的到来，则是他们唯一得以跳出此种深渊的机会。"这些，都是关于海军战略的中肯而冷静的评价。

至于格雷夫斯这位海军上将的战术，我们只要明白下述几点就够了：他所率的舰队加入战斗，跟拜恩让手下舰队加入战斗的情况差不多；惨败的结果也极其相似；还有，在用19艘战舰进攻24艘战舰的过程中，虽说胡德这位能干的将领率有7艘战舰，却因格雷夫斯的既定部署而无法参与战斗。

而在法军这一方，考虑到德·格拉斯在其他战役中的种种不足，因此他在此战中表现出了一定程度的领导才能、远见卓识和坚决果断，既令人惊讶，也必须加以称颂。他果断地率全部舰船行动，使得德·巴拉斯的任何失败，都不会波及到他；他率军通过巴哈马海峡，隐藏了自己的行踪；他老练机智地从西班牙和法国的军事当局那里，获得了所

through the Bahama Channel to conceal his movements; the address with which he obtained the money and troops required, from the Spanish and the French military authorities; the prevision which led him, as early as March 29, shortly after leaving Brest, to write to Rochambeau that American coast pilots should be sent to Cap Français; the coolness with which he kept Graves amused until De Barras's squadron had slipped in, are all points worthy of admiration. The French were also helped by the admiral's power to detain the two hundred merchant-ships, the "West India trade," awaiting convoy at Cap Français, where they remained from July till November, when the close of operations left him at liberty to convoy them with ships-of-war. The incident illustrates one weakness of a mercantile country with representative government, compared with a purely military nation. "If the British government," wrote an officer of that day, "had sanctioned, or a British admiral had adopted, such a measure, the one would have been turned out and the other hanged." Rodney at the same time had felt it necessary to detach five ships-of-the-line with convoys, while half a dozen more went home with the trade from Jamaica.

It is easier to criticise the division of the English fleet between the West Indies and North America in the successive years 1780 and 1781, than to realize the embarrassment of the situation. This embarrassment was but the reflection of the military difficulty of England's position, all over the world, in this great and unequal war. England was everywhere outmatched and embarrassed, as she has always been as an empire, by the number of her exposed points. In Europe the Channel fleet was more than once driven into its ports by overwhelming forces. Gibraltar, closely blockaded by land and sea, was only kept alive in its desperate resistance by the skill of English seamen triumphing over the inaptness and discords of their combined enemies. In the East Indies, Sir Edward Hughes met in Suffren an opponent as superior to

需的资金和军队；他有先见之明，早在刚离开布雷斯特不久的3月29日便写信给罗尚博，说应当将美国的海岸领航员派到法兰西角去；他冷静地戏弄着格雷夫斯，直到德·巴拉斯所率的分舰队悄无声息地进入切萨皮克湾；这些，都是值得称道的方面。此外，这位海军上将还颇具魄力，将当时正在法兰西角等候他来护送的"西印度群岛贸易队"那200条商船扣留下来，让它们从7月份一直等到了11月份——此时作战行动已经结束，他可以随心所欲地用军舰来护送这些商船了；这一点，对法军也起到了有益的作用。这件事情，还说明了采用代议制政体的贸易国与纯粹的军事制国家相比的一个弱点。当时的一位将领曾经如此写道："倘若英国政府支持这样一种措施，倘若哪个英国海军将领采取这样一种措施，那么，政府会被推翻，而将领则会被绞死。"与此同时，罗德尼也认为，有必要派遣5艘战舰护送运输船队，此外还有6艘战舰也随牙买加的贸易船队返回了英国。

我们常常会批评英国舰队在1780和1781这连续的两年间分兵于西印度群岛和北美地区的做法，却很难认识到当时形势的窘迫。这种窘迫局面，不过是反映出了这场重大而不对等的战争中，英国在全世界的军事形势都遇到了困难罢了。英国在各个地区都遭到了失败，狼狈不堪，因为它是一个帝国，受到敌人攻击的地方实在太多。在欧洲，英国的海峡舰队曾经不止一次被敌人用优势兵力赶回了自己的港口。直布罗陀被敌人从海陆两面紧紧地封锁着，只是因为英国水兵殊死抵抗，他们训练有素，胜过联合起来的那些不熟练且相互不和的敌军，才得以苟延残喘。在东印度群岛，爱德华·休斯爵士的敌手，是兵力强过他的苏弗朗，就像胡德的敌手是兵力胜过他的德·格拉斯一样；而苏弗朗的本领，也远远超过了爱德华·休斯爵士。英国政府放弃了米诺卡岛，使得它在敌人

him in numbers as was De Grasse to Hood, and of far greater ability. Minorca, abandoned by the home government, fell before superior strength, as has been seen to fall, one by one, the less important of the English Antilles. The position of England from the time that France and Spain opened their maritime war was everywhere defensive, except in North America; and was therefore, from the military point of view, essentially false. She everywhere awaited attacks which the enemies, superior in every case, could make at their own choice and their own time. North America was really no exception to this rule, despite some offensive operations which in no way injured her real, that is her naval, foes.

Thus situated, and putting aside questions of national pride or sensitiveness, what did military wisdom prescribe to England? The question would afford an admirable study to a military inquirer, and is not to be answered off-hand, but certain evident truths may be pointed out. In the first place, it should have been determined what part of the assailed empire was most necessary to be preserved. After the British islands themselves, the North American colonies were the most valuable possessions in the eyes of the England of that day. Next should have been decided what others by their natural importance were best worth preserving, and by their own inherent strength, or that of the empire, which was mainly naval strength, could most surely be held. In the Mediterranean, for instance, Gibraltar and Mahon were both very valuable positions. Could both be held? Which was more easily to be reached and supported by the fleet? If both could not probably be held, one should have been frankly abandoned, and the force and efforts necessary to its defence carried elsewhere. So in the West Indies the evident strategic advantages of Barbadoes and Sta. Lucia prescribed the abandonment of the other small islands by garrisons as soon as the fleet was fairly outnumbered, if not before. The case of so large an island as Jamaica must be studied separately, as well as with reference to the general question.

的优势兵力之下陷落了，就像之前我们看到那些重要性较低的英属安的列斯群岛一个接一个地陷于敌手一样。自法国和西班牙开始与之进行海上战争以来，英国在各个地方都转入了防御态势，只有北美地区除外；因此，从军事角度来看，这种态势在本质上就是错误的。该国在各个地区都是被动挨打，而敌人每次都是利用兵力优势，按照自己的方式和时间来进攻。实际上，该国在北美地区也是这种情况，只进行了寥寥几次主动进攻的作战行动，根本就没有损及真正的敌人，也就是敌方的海军力量。

形势既然如此，倘若撇开民族自尊或敏感心理这个问题不谈，那么在兵法智慧方面，人们又给英国开出了什么样的药方呢？这个问题，尽管可以让军事研究者做出一项令人钦佩的研究，且不是一个能够即兴回答的问题，但我们还是能够指出一些显而易见的事实来。首先，我们应当判断，受敌攻击的大英帝国，哪些地区最不值得加以保留。在当时的英国看来，除了不列颠群岛本身，北美各个殖民地就是该国最重要的领地了。其次，我们应当根据各地固有的重要性，判断其他哪些地方最值得去加以保护，并且根据各地的内在实力，或者根据整个帝国的内在实力——主要是海军实力，来判断能够最可靠地守住其他哪些地方。比方说，在地中海地区，直布罗陀和马翁港都是极其重要的战略要地。这两个地方都能守住吗？舰队最容易到达和支援哪个地方呢？假如两地都很可能守不住的话，那么显然应当放弃其中之一，而将防守该地的兵力和精力放到其他地方去。因此在西印度群岛，既然巴巴多斯和圣卢西亚具有明显的战略优势，那么即便不是预先就放弃，也应当在敌军兵力一超过英国舰队实力的时候，放弃驻守其他小岛。牙买加岛面积广大，必须单独加以研究才行，并且应当参照全面的问题来进行研究。这样的岛屿或许能够保护自身，顶

Such an island may be so far self-supporting as to defy any attack but one in great force and numbers, and that would rightly draw to it the whole English force from the windward stations at Barbadoes and Sta. Lucia.

With the defence thus concentrated, England's great weapon, the navy, should have been vigorously used on the offensive. Experience has taught that free nations, popular governments, will seldom dare wholly to remove the force that lies between an invader and its shores or capital. Whatever the military wisdom, therefore, of sending the Channel fleet to seek the enemy before it united, the step may not have been possible. But at points less vital the attack of the English should have anticipated that of the allies. This was most especially true of that theatre of the war which has so far been considered. If North America was the first object, Jamaica and the other islands should have been boldly risked. It is due to Rodney to say that he claims that his orders to the admirals at Jamaica and New York were disobeyed in 1781, and that to this was owing the inferiority in number of Graves's fleet.

But why, in 1780, when the departure of De Guichen for Europe left Rodney markedly superior in numbers during his short visit to North America, from September 14 to November 14, should no attempt have been made to destroy the French detachment of seven ships-of-the-line in Newport? These ships had arrived there in July; but although they had at once strengthened their position by earthworks, great alarm was excited by the news of Rodney's appearance off the coast. A fortnight passed by Rodney in New York and by the French in busy work, placed the latter, in their own opinion, in a position to brave all the naval force of England. "We twice feared, and above all at the time of Rodney's arrival," wrote the chief of staff of the French squadron, "that the English might attack us in the road itself; and there was a space of time during which such an undertaking would not have been an act of rashness.

得住敌人的进击，除非敌人是用大量兵力进击；而在这种情况下，将英国处于上风位置的巴巴多斯和圣卢西亚这两个基地里的全部兵力都派往此处，就是正确的做法了。

因为防守力量如此密集，故英国最厉害的武器，即英国海军，就应当大力用于进攻才是。经验已经表明，自由国家和民选政府很少敢于撤走楔在入侵之敌与己方沿海或首都之间的兵力。因此，派遣海峡舰队在敌军联合起来之前去搜索敌人，无论用的是什么样的兵法智慧，这种做法可能都是行不通的。不过，在一些不那么至关重要的地方，英军是可以先于联军发起进攻的。对于迄今为止我们所研究的那个战场来说，这一点尤为正确。倘若北美地区是英军的第一目标，那么牙买加和其他岛屿就应当大胆地冒一冒险。罗德尼曾称，1781年牙买加和纽约两位海军司令都没有服从他所下达的命令；而这一点，又是由于格雷夫斯所率舰队的兵力处于劣势所致。

但在1780年，当基申伯爵启程返回欧洲，使得在9月14日至11月14日短暂造访北美的罗德尼兵力明显占有优势之后，为何他却没有想过进攻并摧毁位于纽波特的那支由7艘战舰组成的法军舰队呢？这些舰船7月份就已抵达纽波特；尽管法军随后马上用土木工事加固了己方的阵地，但一听说罗德尼所率舰队来到此处沿海，还是让法军大惊失色。罗德尼在纽约过了两个星期；而法国人也在阵地上忙碌了两个星期——据他们自己说，这两个星期过后，法军已经变得能够勇敢地面对英国的所有海军力量了。"我们有两次都很担心，尤其是罗德尼抵达美洲的那一次，"法国舰队司令如此写道，"担心英军可能会在半路上伏击我们；好在还有一段时间，使得这种备战措施不至于变成一种仓促的行为。现在（即10月20日），我们的锚地修建了防御工事，因而能够勇敢地面对英

Now [October 20], the anchorage is fortified so that we can there brave all the naval force of England."

The position thus taken by the French was undoubtedly very strong.[11] It formed a re-entrant angle of a little over ninety degrees, contained by lines drawn from Goat Island to what was then called Brenton's Point, the site of the present Fort Adams on the one side, and to Rose Island on the other. On the right flank of the position Rose Island received a battery of thirty-six 24-pounders; while twelve guns of the same size were placed on the left flank at Brenton's Point. Between Rose and Goat islands four ships, drawn up on a west-northwest line, bore upon the entrance and raked an approaching fleet; while three others, between Goat Island and Brenton's Point, crossed their fire at right angles with the former four.

On the other hand, the summer winds blow directly up the entrance, often with great force. There could be no question even of a considerably crippled attacking ship reaching her destined position, and when once confused with the enemy's line, the shore batteries would be neutralized. The work on Rose Island certainly, that on Brenton's Point probably, had less height than the two upper batteries of a ship-of-the-line, and could be vastly outnumbered. They could not have been casemated, and might indisputably have been silenced by the grapeshot of the ships that could have been brought against them. Rose Island could be approached on the front and on the west flank within two hundred yards, and on the north within half a mile. There was nothing to prevent this right flank of the French, including the line of ships, being enfiladed and crushed by the English ships taking position west of Rose Island. The essential points of close range and superior height were thus possible to the English fleet, which numbered twenty to the enemy's seven. If successful in destroying the shipping and reducing Rose Island, it could find anchorage farther up the bay and

国的所有海军力量了。"[10]

法国人如此加固的阵地无疑是极其牢固的。[11]它形成了一个略大于90°的凹角,被从山羊岛起,一边延伸到当时称作布伦顿岬(即如今的亚当斯要塞),另一边延伸到罗斯岛的防线所包围。在阵地右翼的罗斯岛上,配有由36门发射24磅重炮的火炮组成的炮阵,而左翼的布伦顿岬上也安有12门同样大小的火炮。在罗斯岛和山羊岛之间,有4艘战舰排成西偏西北的一列纵阵,全都瞄准入口,可对来犯的舰队进行扫射;还有3艘则部署在山羊岛和布伦顿岬之间,它们的火力与前面那4艘的火力成直角交叉。

而另一方面,在夏季,海风会径直吹向纽波特港入口,并且经常风力强劲。毫无疑问,就算是一艘受损极其严重的进击战舰,一旦到达其预定位置、混入敌军阵列,那么岸上的炮阵威力也会大打折扣。罗斯岛上的工事自然没有战舰上的两组上层火炮那样高,而布伦顿岬上的工事很可能也是这样,因此可能会出现严重的寡不敌众的情况。这两处不可能设有炮楼,故毋庸置疑,倘若敌舰可以对其发动攻击的话,数发霰弹就可将它们打哑。进攻罗斯岛,既可以从正面进击,也可以从不到200英尺远的西侧进击,还可以从相距不到半英里远的北侧进击。倘若英军抢占了罗斯岛以西的阵地,那么法军的这一右翼就会无可避免地受到英军的纵向炮击,就会无可避免地被英军消灭。这样一来,拥有20艘战舰对阵敌方7艘战舰的英国舰队,就有可能获得"近距离"与"高优势"这两个关键因素。假如成功地摧毁法军舰船并且攻克罗斯岛,那么英国舰队便可以在这个海湾更深之处找到锚地,等待有利的风向来撤退。在当时一位杰出的、极为熟悉此处战场的英国海军将领看来,[12]倘若发动进攻的话,英军定会取胜;所以,他曾屡

await a favorable wind to retire. In the opinion of a distinguished English naval officer of the day,[12] closely familiar with the ground, there was no doubt of the success of an attack; and he urged it frequently upon Rodney, offering himself to pilot the leading ship. The security felt by the French in this position, and the acquiescence of the English in that security, mark clearly the difference in spirit between this war and the wars of Nelson and Napoleon.

It is not, however, merely as an isolated operation, but in relation to the universal war, that such an attempt is here considered. England stood everywhere on the defensive, with inferior numbers. From such a position there is no salvation except by action vigorous almost to desperation. "It is impossible for us," wrote with great truth the First Lord of the Admiralty to Rodney, "to have a superior fleet in every part; and unless our commanders-in-chief will take the great line, as you do, and consider the king's whole dominions under their care, our enemies must find us unprepared somewhere, and carry their point against us." Attacks which considered in themselves alone might be thought unjustifiable, were imposed upon English commanders. The allied navy was the key of the situation, and its large detachments, as at Newport, should have been crushed at any risk. The effect of such a line of action upon the policy of the French government is a matter of speculation, as to which the present writer has no doubts; but no English officer in chief command rose to the level of the situation, with the exception of Hood, and possibly of Howe. Rodney was now old, infirm, and though of great ability, a careful tactician rather than a great admiral.

The defeat of Graves and subsequent surrender of Cornwallis did not end the naval operations in the western hemisphere. On the contrary, one of the most interesting tactical

次向罗德尼力陈此事，并且提出由他自己给那艘打头阵的舰船领航。法军对于此处阵地的安全感，以及英军允许法国人拥有这种安全感，都清楚地表明了纳尔逊和拿破伦之间的数次战争在精神风气上与此战之间的不同之处。

然而，此处我们考虑这样一种意图，并非仅仅是将其作为一次孤立的作战行动，而是涉及到了全球战争。由于兵力上处于劣势，因此英国在世界各地都是采取防御态势。在这种形势下，除了斗志昂扬、甚至是孤注一掷地战斗，此外并无其他挽救之法。英国海军大臣在给罗德尼的信中，极为诚实地写道："我们不可能在每个地区都拥有一支出众的舰队；除非我们的海军总司令个个都像您这样坚持着伟大的方针，将国王的所有领土都置于自己的精心照管之下，否则的话，我们的敌人必定会在某个地方攻我们之不备，将他们的刀枪刺向我们的。"发动那些他们内心可能认为并没有正当理由的进攻，则是强加给英军指挥官的。联军的海军是此种局面的关键，因此像联军泊在纽波特那样的大型舰队，本应当不惜任何代价加以消灭的。根据法国政府的政策来采取这样一种作战方针的效果，是一个需要深思的问题，如今的作家对此毫不怀疑了；但是，除了胡德，可能还有豪励爵之外，当时并没有哪一个担任总司令之职的英国将领达到了看清形势的高度。罗德尼此时已经年老体衰；他虽说能力出众，却只能说是一个谨慎的战术家，而不再是一位伟大的海军上将了。

格雷夫斯的战败和随后康华里的投降，并未结束各国海军在西半球的军事行动。相反，英国还将在整个这场战争中完成最有意思的一桩战术壮举，并获得最辉煌的一次胜利，从而给该国在西印度群岛的国旗增色不少；但约克镇事件之后，美国人就不再有热

feats and the most brilliant victory of the whole war were yet to grace the English flag in the West Indies; but with the events at Yorktown the patriotic interest for Americans closes. Before quitting that struggle for independence, it must again be affirmed that its successful ending, at least at so early a date, was due to the control of the sea, — to sea power in the hands of the French, and its improper distribution by the English authorities. This assertion may be safely rested on the authority of the one man who, above all others, thoroughly knew the resources of the country, the temper of the people, the difficulties of the struggle, and whose name is still the highest warrant for sound, quiet, unfluttered good-sense and patriotism.

The keynote to all Washington's utterances is set in the "Memorandum for concerting a plan of operations with the French army," dated July 15, 1780, and sent by the hands of Lafayette: —

"The Marquis de Lafayette will be pleased to communicate the following general ideas to Count de Rochambeau and the Chevalier de Ternay, as the sentiments of the underwritten:

"I. In any operation, and under all circumstances, a decisive naval superiority is to be considered as a fundamental principle, and the basis upon which every hope of success must ultimately depend."

This, however, though the most formal and decisive expression of Washington's views, is but one among many others equally distinct. Thus, writing to Franklin, December 20, 1780, he says: —

"Disappointed of the second division of French troops [blockaded in Brest], but more especially in the expected naval superiority, which was the pivot upon which everything turned, we have been compelled to spend an inactive campaign after a flattering prospect at the opening

爱母国的那种热情了。在结束描述这次美国独立战争之前，我们必须再一次强调，美国在此战中之所以最终获胜，或者起码说，美国在此战中如此之早地获得胜利，原因就在于制海权——在于法军所掌控的海权，以及英国当局对自己手中制海权的不正确部署。这一论断，因为一个人的威望而显得非常可靠；这个人比其他任何人都更加彻底地了解该国的资源、民众的脾性和此次战争的艰辛，而华盛顿的名字，如今也仍然是正确、谦逊且不骄不躁之判断力以及爱国主义的最高证明。

华盛顿所有言论的要旨，在所注日期为1780年7月15日、经拉斐特之手发出的那份《协同法国陆军制定作战计划之备忘录》中，得到了体现：

"拉斐特侯爵深感荣幸，就下述总体思路与罗尚博伯爵以及泰尔奈勋爵进行交流，并达成如下意见：

"第一，在任何作战行动中，在任何情况下，都应将保持海军之决定性优势，视为一条基本之原则，视为获得胜利最终必须倚赖之基础。"

不过，虽说这是华盛顿所持观点最正式和最明确的表述，但它只是许多同样明确无误的表述中的一种。比如，1780年12月20日在给富兰克林的信中，他如此写道：

"由于对法军第二师（被封锁在布雷斯特）感到失望，尤其是对我们所预期的、一切皆取决于这一中心的海军优势感到失望，所以我们不得不带着一开始时那种令人高兴的前景，而将精力浪费在这场消极的战役上。……近来我们又不得不当起了旁观者，看着一支又一支陆军分队在康华里勋爵的协助之下来到纽约；而我们海军的软弱无力，以及我国大部分陆军在政治上都处于一盘散沙的状态，使得我们在南方根本就无力抵抗英

of it. ... Latterly we have been obliged to become spectators of a succession of detachments from the army at New York in aid of Lord Cornwallis; while our naval weakness, and the political dissolution of a large part of our army, put it out of our power to counteract them at the southward, or to take advantage of them here."

A month later, January 15, 1781, in a memorandum letter to Colonel Laurens, sent on a special mission to France, he says: —

"Next to a loan of money, a constant naval superiority upon these coasts is the object most interesting. This would instantly reduce the enemy to a difficult defensive. ... Indeed, it is not to be conceived how they could subsist a large force in this country, if we had the command of the seas to interrupt the regular transmission of supplies from Europe. This superiority, with an aid in money, would enable us to convert the war into a vigorous offensive. With respect to us it seems to be one of two deciding points."

In another letter to the same person, then in Paris, dated April 9, he writes: —

"If France delays a timely and powerful aid in the critical posture of our affairs, it will avail us nothing, should she attempt it hereafter. ... Why need I run into detail, when it may be declared in a word that we are at the end of our tether, and that now or never our deliverance must come? How easy would it be to retort the enemy's own game upon them, if it could be made to comport with the general plan of the war to keep a superior fleet always in these seas, and France would put us in condition to be active by advancing us money."

Ships and money are the burden of his cry. May 23, 1781, he writes to the Chevalier de la Luzerne: "I do not see how it is possible to give effectual support to the Southern States, and avert the evils which threaten, while we are inferior in naval force in these seas." As

军，也无法在此处占得英军的便宜。"

一个月后的1781年1月15日，在写给当时正被派往法国执行特殊任务的劳伦斯上校的一封备忘信中，他又说道：

"除了贷款，在这些海岸部署一支兵力占有优势的常备海军，就是最令我们关注的一个目标了。这会不断地削弱敌人的实力，使之难以招架。……事实上，倘若我们能够掌控各个海域，阻断欧洲定期运送过来的给养物资，那么英国就别指望能够在我国维持一支庞大的军队了。这种优势加上资金援助，会让我们将此次战争变成一场强有力的进攻战。对于我们而言，这似乎是两个关键点中的一个。"

而在写给当时身处巴黎的劳伦斯上校、所署日期为4月9日的另一封信中，他又写道：

"假如法国拖拖拉拉，不在这个关键的时候帮助我们的话，那么就算日后法国想这样做，对我们来说也没什么用处了。……在一句话就可以说明我们到了山穷水尽的地步，并且我们获得解放必定是一件机不可失之事的时候，我为什么还要再去详加解释呢？倘若法国恪守我们达成的关于此次战争的总体规划，在这些海域常备一支优势舰队，并且贷款给我国，让我们能够主动进攻的话，那么以敌人之道、还治敌人之身会是一件多么容易的事情啊。"

他这种呼吁的主旨，就是舰船和资金。1781年5月23日，他在写给拉吕泽尔勋爵的信中说："我不明白，在这些海域我们的海军实力不如敌军的情况下，如何可能对南方诸州进行有效支援，同时又避免可能出现的危险和损失。"由于适合主动作战的季节正在临近，所以他的言论就越发频繁，语气也越发紧迫了。1781年6月1日，他写信给当

the season for active operations advances, his utterances are more frequent and urgent. To Major General Greene, struggling with his difficulties in South Carolina, he writes, June 1, 1781: "Our affairs have been attentively considered in every point of view, and it was finally determined to make an attempt upon New York, in preference to a Southern operation, as we had not decided command of the water." To Jefferson, June 8: "Should I be supported in the manner I expect, by the neighboring States, the enemy will, I hope, be reduced to the necessity of recalling part of their force from the southward to support New York, or they will run the most imminent risk of being expelled from that post, which is to them invaluable; and should we, by a lucky coincidence of circumstances, gain a naval superiority, their ruin would be inevitable. ... While we remain inferior at sea ... policy dictates that relief should be attempted by diversion rather than by sending reinforcements immediately to the point in distress," that is, to the South. To Rochambeau, June 13: "Your Excellency will recollect that New York was looked upon by us as the only practicable object under present circumstances; but should we be able to secure a naval superiority, we may perhaps find others more practicable and equally advisable." By the 15th of August the letters of De Grasse announcing his sailing for the Chesapeake were received, and the correspondence of Washington is thenceforth filled with busy preparations for the campaign in Virginia, based upon the long-delayed fleet. The discouragement of De Grasse, and his purpose to go to sea, upon learning that the English fleet in New York had been reinforced, drew forth an appealing letter dated September 25, which is too long for quotation; but the danger passed, Washington's confidence returns. The day after the capitulation he writes to De Grasse: "The surrender of York ... the honor of which belongs to your Excellency, has greatly anticipated [in time] our most sanguine anticipations." He then goes on to urge further operations in the

时正在南卡罗莱纳苦苦挣扎、疲于应付的格林少将，说："我们已经全面而仔细地考虑过了目前的事态，并且最终决定先对纽约发动进击，然后再在南方作战，因为我们尚未掌控海上。"6月8日，他写信给杰斐逊说："假如相邻各州按照我所期待的方式来支援我，那么我希望削弱敌军的实力，使得敌人必须从南方召回部分兵力来支援纽约，否则的话，敌人就会面临被我们逐出这一据点的最为紧迫的危险，因为这个据点对敌人来说十分重要；而倘若我们运气好，海军碰巧获得了优势的话，那么敌人的灭亡就是不可避免的了。……当我们在海上实力仍然不如敌人的时候，谋略决定了我们只能通过调虎离山的办法来解围，而不是直接向处于危险当中的那些地方派遣援军，"也就是说，向南方派遣援军。6月13日，他给罗尚博写信说："阁下想必还记得，我们都曾认为，在目前之形势下，纽约是我们唯一可行之目标；不过，倘若我们能够确保我方海军占有兵力优势，那么我们或许还可以找出其他更加可行、同样适宜夺取的目标来。"到了8月15日，华盛顿收到了德·格拉斯通知说他已经率军起航前往切萨皮克湾的信件；从那以后，华盛顿的信件当中，就全是以这支耽搁已久的舰队为基础，忙于准备发动弗吉尼亚战役的内容了。德·格拉斯得知纽约的英国舰队得到了增援后就泄了气，打算出海离去，使得华盛顿在9月25日给他写了一封言辞恳切的信，只是此信很长，我们无法引述；不过，危险过去之后，华盛顿又恢复了信心。就在纽约英军投降的第二天，他给德·格拉斯写信说："纽约受降……荣耀归于阁下，已经（在时间上）极大地先于我们最乐观的预期而实现了。"接下来，他看到天气良好、适于作战的季节才过了一小半，便敦促法军在南方实施进一步的作战行动："在阁下到来之前，英国海军的总体优势使

South, seeing so much of the good season was still left: "The general naval superiority of the British, previous to your arrival, gave them decisive advantages in the South, in the rapid transport of their troops and supplies; while the immense land marches of our succors, too tardy and expensive in every point of view, subjected us to be beaten in detail. It will depend upon your Excellency, therefore, to terminate the war." De Grasse refusing this request, but intimating an intention to co-operate in the next year's campaign, Washington instantly accepts: "With your Excellency I need not insist upon the indispensable necessity of a maritime force capable of giving you an absolute ascendency in these seas. ... You will have observed that, whatever efforts are made by the land armies, the navy must have the casting vote in the present contest." A fortnight later, November 15, he writes to Lafayette, who is on the point of sailing for France: —

"As you expressed a desire to know my sentiments respecting the operations of the next campaign, I will, without a tedious display of reasoning, declare in one word that it must depend absolutely upon the naval force which is employed in these seas, and the time of its appearance next year. No land force can act decisively unless accompanied by a maritime superiority. ... A doubt did not exist, nor does it at this moment, in any man's mind, of the total extirpation of the British force in the Carolinas and Georgia, if Count de Grasse could have extended his co-operation two months longer."

Such, in the opinion of the revered commander-in-chief of the American armies, was the influence of sea power upon the contest which he directed with so much skill and such infinite patience, and which, amidst countless trials and discouragements, he brought to a glorious close.

It will be observed that the American cause was reduced to these straits, notwithstanding

得他们在南方有着许多重要的有利条件，能够快速运送部队和给养物资；而我们的援军只能经由陆路进行长距离行军，从各个方面来看都太过缓慢且花费巨大，使得我军处处掣肘，从而被敌人一一消灭。因此，只有仰仗阁下，才能结束此次战争。"德·格拉斯拒绝了这一要求，但同时也暗示说，在第二年的战争中他打算与美军合作，而华盛顿马上就认可了这一点："对于阁下，我无需再强调一支海军必然能够让您在这些海域占有绝对优势的问题了。……您会注意到，在目前所进行的这次战争中，无论陆军做出何种巨大的努力，最终的决定权都掌握在海军的手里。"两个星期后的11月15日，他写信给当时正准备动身前往法国的拉斐特说：

"您说想知道我对于下一场战役中的作战行动有什么看法，我不会啰啰嗦嗦地摆出一大堆理由，而只会说一句话，那就是：我们必须依赖于目前正在这些海域活动的海军力量，掌握好明年将这支海军投入作战的时机。除非同时拥有海上优势，否则陆军是不可能果断作战的。……任何人在过去和此时都不曾怀疑，倘若德·格拉斯伯爵能够与我们再合作两个月的话，那么南、北卡罗莱纳和佐治亚两州的英军就会被我们彻底歼灭。"

在这位受人敬重的美军总司令看来，制海权对于美国独立战争的影响就是上述这些方面；他极其老练而无限耐心地领导着美国人民，在经历了无数的考验和挫折之后，最终无比辉煌地结束了此次战争。

我们还会注意到，尽管英国的商业贸易因为联军的巡逻舰和美国的私掠船而遭受了世人公认的巨大损失，但与此同时，美国的独立革命也陷入了上述重重困境之中。这一事实，加上由贸易破坏战观点所主导的全面战争并未获得什么重大战果，都有力地表

the great and admitted losses of British commerce by the cruisers of the allies and by American privateers. This fact, and the small results from the general war, dominated as it was by the idea of commerce-destroying, show strongly the secondary and indecisive effect of such a policy upon the great issues of war.

FOOTNOTES:

(1) This delay was due to calms. Howe's Despatch, Gentleman's Magazine, 1778.

(2) Most accounts say between Goat Island and Canonicut; but the position given seems more probable. The names "Goat" and "Gould" (often written "Gold") are easily confused. Since writing the above, the author has been favored with the sight of a contemporary manuscript map obtained in Paris, which shows the anchorage as near Canonicut and abreast Coaster's Harbor Island; the latter being marked "L'Isle d'Or ou Golde Isle." The sketch, while accurate in its main details, seems the more authentic from its mistakes being such as a foreigner, during a hurried and exciting stay of twenty-four hours, might readily make.

(3) "The arrival of the French fleet upon the coast of America is a great and striking event; but the operations of it have been injured by a number of unforeseen and unfavorable circumstances, which, though they ought not to detract from the merit and good intention of our great ally, have nevertheless lessened the importance of its services in a great degree. The length of the passage, in the first instance, was a capital misfortune; for had even one of common length taken place, Lord Howe, with the British ships-of-war and all the transports in the river Delaware, must inevitably have fallen; and Sir Henry Clinton must have had better luck than is commonly dispensed to men of his profession under such circumstances, if he and his troops had not shared at least the fate of Burgoyne. The long passage of Count d'Estaing was succeeded by an unfavorable discovery at the Hook, which hurt us in two respects, — first, in a defeat of the enterprise upon New York and the shipping and troops at that place, and next in the delay occasioned in ascertaining the depth of water over

明，对于战争中的重大问题来说，此种政策只会产生次要和非决定性的作用。

原注：

（1）这种耽误是由于海面平静无风所致。参见1778年《绅士杂志》上豪勋爵的电文。

（2）绝大多数文献都是说位于山羊岛和坎农尼科特岛之间；不过，本书所给位置显得更有可能性。"山羊"（Goat）和"古尔德"（Gould，经常拼作Gold）两个名称很容易搞混。在写作本书的过程中，笔者有幸看到了从巴黎得到的一张当代的手稿原图，此图表明，锚地位于坎农尼科特岛附近，且与考斯特港岛并排；后者在图上被标为"L'Isle d'Or ou Golde Isle"。这张草图虽说主要细节很准确，却是因其错误而显得更加可信的，因为这是一个外国人在来去匆匆、兴奋不已的24个小时中画成的，故很容易犯这种错误。

（3）"法国舰队抵达美洲海岸是一件重大而令人震惊的事情；不过，许多没有预见到的不利情况妨碍到了法国舰队的作战行动。虽说这些作战行动不应有损我们这位伟大盟友的功劳和善意，但还是在很大程度上削弱了法国舰队在此战中所起的作用。首先，从法国到美洲这段漫长的行程便是一种严重的不幸；因为要是由豪勋爵率领英国舰队和所有运输舰船在特拉华河上航行的话，哪怕是普普通通的一段航程，豪勋爵必定也免不了一死；而对于亨利·柯林顿勋爵来说，要是他和手下部队的命运起码不像博戈因那样的话，那么在这种情况下，他必定会比其他海军将领的运气要好。德斯坦伯爵完成远距离航行之后，在桑迪岬却发现形势不利于己方，使我们在两个方面感到痛心：首先是进攻纽约失利，此处的舰船和陆军都被敌人击败了；其次是他为了探测进入纽约港所必经的那道沙洲处的水深而耽搁了行动。此外，在业已制定了进攻罗德岛的作战计划并且就在准备实施这一计划的时候，豪勋爵却率领英国舰队插了进来；他的目的只是声东击西，想将法国舰队引离罗德

the bar which was essential to their entrance into the harbor of New York. And, moreover, after the enterprise upon Rhode Island had been planned and was in the moment of execution, that Lord Howe with the British ships should interpose merely to create a diversion and draw the French fleet from the island was again unlucky, as the Count had not returned on the 17th to the island, though drawn off from it on the 10th; by which means the land operations were retarded, and the whole subjected to a miscarriage in case of the arrival of Byron's squadron." — Washington's Letter, Aug. 20, 1778.

(4) Of one of these, the "Monmouth," sixty-four, it is said that the officers of the French flag-ship drank to the health of the captain of the "little black ship." Ships' names, like those of families, often have a marked career. A former "Monmouth," twenty years before, had attacked and taken, practically single-handed, the "Foudroyant," eighty-four, one of the finest ships in the French navy. She was then commanded by a Captain Gardiner, who, having commanded Byng's ship in the battle which led to his execution, was moved by his mortification at the result of that affair to dare such desperate odds, and thereby lost his life. The same ship, here punished so severely off Grenada, will be found in like sturdy fight, under another captain, three years later in India.

(5) Drinkwater, in his history of the siege of Gibraltar, explains that the Spanish admiral believed that Rodney would not accompany the convoy to the Straits, but had separated from it. He did not detect his mistake until too late.

(6) In a severe reprimand addressed to Captain Carkett, commanding the leading ship of the English line, by Rodney, he says: "Your leading in the manner you did, induced others to follow so bad an example; and thereby, forgetting that the signal for the line was at only two cables' length distance from each other, the van division was led by you to more than two leagues distance from the centre division, which was thereby exposed to the greatest strength of the enemy and not properly supported" (Life, vol. i. p. 351). By all rules of tactical common-sense it would seem that the other ships should have taken their distance from their next astern, that

岛。这又是一件运气不好的事情，因为虽说10日就已撤离罗德岛，但这位伯爵却直到17日都没有返回该岛；这意味着地面作战被推迟了，而万一拜伦所率舰队抵达这里，那么整个作战计划就流产了。"（参见华盛顿的《书信集》，1778年8月20日。）

（4）关于其中的一艘，即装有64门火炮的"蒙默斯"号，据说法军旗舰上的官兵都曾举杯，祝这艘"小黑船"的舰长健康长寿。舰船的名称就像家族名称一样，通常都有着非凡的历史。20年前就有一艘"蒙默斯"号战舰，几乎是单枪匹马地进攻并俘虏了属于法国海军中精锐战舰之一、装有84门火炮的"闪电"号。当时，"蒙默斯"号由一位加德纳舰长指挥；因为曾经在导致拜恩被判处死刑的那次海战中指挥过拜恩的座舰，这位加德纳舰长为那次海战结果所受的耻辱驱动，才敢于不顾一切地战斗，从而献出了自己的生命。在格林纳达海域受到重创的同一艘战舰，3年以后在另一位舰长的指挥下又在印度海域进行了类似的顽强战斗。

（5）德林克沃特在其关于围攻直布罗陀的历史著述中解释说，那位西班牙海军司令认为罗德尼不会陪同护航队前往直布罗陀海峡，而是与护航队分道扬镳了。后来他发现自己判断失误，可为时已晚了。

（6）罗德尼在对指挥英军阵列中那艘前导战舰的卡科特上校进行严厉申斥时，说："因为你用这种方式打头阵，使得其他人有了一个如此糟糕的榜样；你忘记了旗语是命令阵列各部彼此之间保持2链[7]的距离，而将前锋分队领到了距中军2里格[8]多的地方，从而让中军暴露于强大的敌军面前，并且得不到恰当的支援。"（参见《传记》第一卷，第351页）根据战术常识的所有规则来看，似乎其余舰船本来应当从相邻的船尾处开始拉开距离，也就是说，应当是向中军靠拢才是。在跟未参与此次作战的吉尔伯特·布莱恩进行交谈时，罗德尼曾称法军阵列展开后长达4里格之远，"好像基申伯爵以为我们会从他的面前逃走似的。"（参见《海军编年史》第十五卷，第402页）

is, should have closed toward the centre. In conversation with Sir Gilbert Blane, who was not in this action, Rodney stated that the French line extended four leagues in length, "as if De Guichen thought we meant to run away from him" (Naval Chronicle, vol. xxv. p. 402).

(7) At the eastern end of Long Island.

(8) The French ascribe this disadvantage to the fact that some of their ships were not coppered.

(9) That the French government was not satisfied with M. Destouches's action can be safely inferred from its delay to reward the officers of the squadron, which called forth much feeling and very lively remonstrances. The French asserted that Arbuthnot was hooted in the streets of New York and recalled by his government. The latter is a mistake, as he went home by his own request; but the former is likely enough. Both commanders reversed in this case the usual naval policy of their nations.

(10) De Barras had been unwilling to go to the Chesapeake, fearing to be intercepted by a superior force, and had only yielded to the solicitation of Washington and Rochambeau.

(11) Diary of a French officer, 1781; Magazine of American History for March, 1880. The works at the time of Rodney's visit to New York were doubtless less complete than in 1781. This authority, a year later, gives the work on Rose Island twenty 36-pounders.

(12) Sir Thomas Graves, afterward second in command to Nelson in the attack at Copenhagen in 1801, — an enterprise fully as desperate and encompassed with greater difficulties of pilotage than the one here advocated. See biographical memoir, Naval Chronicle, vol. viii.

（7）位于长岛东端。

（8）法国人将此种劣势归咎于他们的一些舰船外部没有包铜。

（9）法国政府对M·德图什的作战行动很不满意；这一点，从它迟迟不肯奖励德图什所率舰队的将领，使得这些将领大为不满，还进行了强烈抗议的事实，便完全可以推断出来。法国人曾经声称，阿巴斯诺特在纽约大街上被民众轰赶，随后即被英国政府召回了国内。后面半句说得不对，阿巴斯诺特是自己要求回国的；但前半句说得很可能是对的。在此战中，双方的指挥官都违反了两国一贯的海军政策。

（10）德·巴拉斯担心受到敌人优势兵力的截击，本不愿意前往切萨皮克湾，只是因为华盛顿与罗尚博二人苦苦相求才率军前往的。

（11）引自1781年一位法国将领的日记，《美国历史》杂志1880年3月号。罗德尼造访纽约时的工事，无疑并没有1781年所造工事那样全面。一年之后，这位权威人士为罗斯岛之战配备了20门发射36磅炮弹的火炮。

（12）即托马斯·格雷夫斯爵士，后来他在1801年进击哥本哈根之战中，曾担任纳尔逊的副司令；此战完全是殊死之战，在领航时遇到的困难比此处所提出的困难要大得多。参见《海军编年史》第八卷中他的传记体回忆录。

译者注：

［1］Point：罗经点。航海学中的角度术语，1罗经点相当于11.25°。

［2］博塔（Carlo Giuseppe Guglielmo Botta, 1766~1837）。旅居法国的意大利历史学家，曾在法国陆军中当过军医，著有4卷本的《意大利历史（1789~1814）》等作品。

［3］Nassau：拿骚。巴哈马联邦的首都，是有名的海滨旅游与疗养胜地。

［4］Camden：卡姆登。美国新泽西州西南部的一个港口城市。1780年8月16日，美国军队在此被康华里所率的英军打败。

［5］阿诺德（Benedict Arnold, 1741~1801）。美国独立战争时期的军事将领，作战英勇，曾

官至少将。后因生活奢侈而破坏军规,并向英国出卖情报。其通敌阴谋于1780年9月败露,他本人虽说逃脱,但仍被华盛顿判处缺席死刑,其名字也成了"叛徒"的美式代名词。

　　[6] King's Mountain:国王山。美国南卡罗莱纳州的一处地名。1780年10月7日,美国军队在此打败英军。此役是美国独立战争中最重要的一次胜利,被托马斯·杰斐逊称为"成功的转折点"。

　　[7] Cable's length:链。海上测距单位,相当于十分之一海里(美国海军定为219米,而英国海军则定为185米)。亦拼作cable length。

　　[8] League:里格。长度单位,1里格大约相当于3英里或3海里。

CHAPTER X   Maritime War in Europe, 1779-1782

The last chapter closed with the opinions of Washington, expressed in many ways and at many times, as to the effect of sea power upon the struggle for American independence. If space allowed, these opinions could be amply strengthened by similar statements of Sir Henry Clinton, the English commander-in-chief.[1] In Europe the results turned yet more entirely upon the same factor. There the allies had three several objectives, at each of which England stood strictly upon the defensive. The first of these was England herself, involving, as a preliminary to an invasion, the destruction of the Channel fleet, — a project which, if seriously entertained, can scarcely be said to have been seriously attempted; the second was the reduction of Gibraltar; the third, the capture of Minorca. The last alone met with success. Thrice was England threatened by a largely superior fleet, thrice the threat fell harmless. Thrice was Gibraltar reduced to straits; thrice was it relieved by the address and fortune of English seamen, despite overpowering odds.

After Keppel's action off Ushant, no general encounter took place between fleets in European seas during the year 1778 and the first half of 1779. Meantime Spain was drawing toward a rupture with England and an active alliance with France. War was declared by her on the 16th of June, 1779; but as early as April 12, a treaty between the two Bourbon kingdoms, involving active war upon England, had been signed. By its terms the invasion of Great Britain or Ireland was to be undertaken, every effort made to recover for Spain, Minorca, Pensacola, and

第十章   1779—1782年间的欧洲海战

在上一章中，我们以华盛顿的观点结尾，阐述了制海权在各个方面、不同时期对美国独立战争所产生的影响。如果不是限于篇幅的话，我们还可以引用英军总司令亨利·柯林顿许多类似的话语，来充分强调这些观点。[1]在欧洲，战局则更加完全倚赖于制海权这一相同的因素。联军在欧洲有着三大目标，而英国对其中的任何一个目标都是完全处于防御态势。联军的第一个目标，便是英国本土，以及消灭其海峡舰队，为入侵英国本土做准备——倘若严肃对待的话，我们是很难说联军曾经认真尝试过这一目标的；第二个目标，是攻取直布罗陀；第三个目标，便是夺取米诺卡岛。联军只实现了最后一个目标。英国被兵力极其强大的舰队威胁了三次，可这三次威胁都平安解除了。直布罗陀也三次陷入了重重危机之中，而尽管每次都几无胜算，但这三次危机也都因为英国海军的骁勇善战和好运气而得以化解了。

自凯珀尔指挥的韦桑岛海战之后，在1778年一整年和1779年上半年，双方舰队在欧洲海域并未发生过什么全面的遭遇战。与此同时，西班牙与英国决裂，并同法国结成了有力的同盟。1779年6月16日，该国对英宣战；不过，早在4月12日，法、西这两个波旁王国便已签署了一份条约，其中就有主动对英国宣战的内容。根据条约的规定，两国同意侵入大不列颠或爱尔兰，尽最大努力让西班牙收复米诺卡、彭萨科拉和莫比尔，并且

Mobile, and the two courts bound themselves to grant neither peace, nor truce, nor suspension of hostilities, until Gibraltar should be restored.

The declaration of war was withheld until ready to strike; but the English government, doubtless, should have been upon its guard in the strained relations of the two countries, and prepared to prevent a junction of the two fleets. As it was, no efficient blockade of Brest was established, and twenty-eight French sail-of-the-line went out unopposed[2] June 3, 1779, under D'Orvilliers, Keppel's opponent of the year before. The fleet steered for the coasts of Spain, where it was to find the Spanish ships; but it was not till the 22d of July that the full contingent joined. Seven precious summer weeks thus slipped by unimproved, but that was not all the loss; the French had been provisioned for only thirteen weeks, and this truly great armada of sixty-six ships-of-the-line and fourteen frigates had not more than forty working-days before it. Sickness, moreover, ravaged the fleet; and although it was fortunate enough to enter the Channel while the English were at sea, the latter, numbering little more than half their enemies, succeeded in passing within them. The flabbiness of coalitions increased the weakness due to inefficient preparation; a great and not unnatural panic on the English Channel coast, and the capture of one ship-of-the-line, were the sole results of a cruise extending, for the French, over fifteen weeks.[3] The disappointment, due to bad preparation, mainly on the part of Spain, though the French ministry utterly failed to meet the pressing wants of its fleet, fell, of course, upon the innocent Admiral D'Orvilliers. That brave and accomplished but unfortunate officer, whose only son, a lieutenant, had died of the pestilence which scourged the allies, could not support the odium. Being of a deeply religious character, the refuge which Villeneuve after Trafalgar found in suicide was denied him; but he threw up his command and retired into a religious house.

两国朝廷还约定，在收复直布罗陀之前，决不同英国议和、休战或者暂停战事。

直到做好进攻准备，西班牙才对英宣战；英国政府本来应当警惕两国业已紧张的关系，并且做好防止法、西两国舰队联合的准备才是。可事实却是，英国并未有效地封锁布雷斯特，因此1779年6月3日，前一年与凯珀尔对过阵的奥尔维利埃率领28艘法国战舰，如入无人之境地出了港，扬长而去了。[2] 这支舰队随后转而驶向西班牙沿海，去与那儿的西班牙舰船会合；不过，直到7月22日，两国所派舰队才完全集结起来。夏季7个星期的宝贵时间就这样未加利用而浪费掉了，但这还不是两国全部的损失；根据规定，法军只有13个星期的准备时间，因此，这支由66艘战舰和14艘护卫舰组成的、确实庞大无比的舰队，真正拥有的工作日就已不足40天了。此外，整支舰队中还疾病肆虐；并且，尽管舰队的运气相当好，是在英国舰队出海的时候进入英吉利海峡的，但兵力只有敌军一半多的英国舰队，却成功地从敌人的舰队中穿插过去了。联军的优柔寡断，使得因为备战效率低下而导致的软弱变得非常明显了；所以，在15个多星期的时间里，法军扩大巡航战的唯一战果，便是让英吉利海峡沿岸地区出现了大范围不足为怪的恐慌情绪，以及俘虏了一艘英国战舰。[3] 由于准备不充分——主要是西班牙这一方，但法国政府也完全没有满足其舰队的迫切需要——率直的奥尔维利埃上将自然会萌生出沮丧情绪。这是一位勇猛、老练却又很不幸运的将领，他唯一的儿子，一名海军上尉，也死于联军中肆虐的瘟疫，所以他再也无法忍受对战争的憎恶之情了。他是一个宗教信仰极为虔敬的人，没法像特拉法尔加海战之后的维尔纳夫那样，以自杀来获得解脱；但他辞去了司令之职，遁入了空门。

The scanty maritime interest of the year 1780, in Europe, centres round Cadiz and Gibraltar. This fortress was invested by Spain immediately upon the outbreak of war, and, while successfully resisting direct attack, the supply of provisions and ammunition was a matter of serious concern to England, and involved both difficulty and danger. For this purpose, Rodney sailed on the 29th of December, 1779, having under his command twenty ships-of-the-line with a large convoy and reinforcements for Gibraltar and Minorca, as well as the West India trade. The latter parted company on the 7th of January, under the care of four frigates, and the following morning the fleet fell in with and captured a Spanish squadron of seven ships-of-war and sixteen supply-ships. Twelve of the latter being laden with provisions were carried on to Gibraltar. A week later, at one P.M. of the 16th, a Spanish fleet of eleven sail-of-the-line was seen in the southeast. They held their ground, supposing the approaching vessels to be only supply-ships for Gibraltar, without a strong force of men-of-war, — an unfortunate error from which they did not awake until too late to escape, owing to the yet more unfortunate oversight of having no lookout frigates thrown out. When the Spanish admiral, Don Juan de Langara, recognized his mistake, he attempted to escape; but the English ships were copper-bottomed, and Rodney making the signal for a general chase overtook the enemy, cut in between him and his port, regardless of a blowy night, lee shore, and dangerous shoals, and succeeded in capturing the commander-in-chief with six ships-of-the-line. A seventh was blown up. The weather continuing very tempestuous, one of the prizes was wrecked, and one forced into Cadiz; several of the English ships were also in great danger, but happily escaped, and within a few days the entire force entered Gibraltar Bay. The convoy for Minorca was at once despatched, and immediately after the return of the ships-of-war guarding it, on the 13th of February, Rodney sailed for the West Indies with four ships-of-the-line, sending the rest of

1780年欧洲唯一让我们关注海洋的地区，全都集中在加的斯和直布罗陀两地。战争一爆发，直布罗陀这处要塞就被西班牙派兵包围了，并且，尽管成功地抵挡了敌人的直接进攻，但给养和武器装备供应却是让英国大伤脑筋、实施起来既困难又危险的一个问题。为了这个，1779年12月29日，罗德尼率领20艘战舰，护送一支庞大的船队及援兵起航前往直布罗陀和米诺卡，然后还要去西印度群岛进行贸易。接受护送的船队于1月7日与舰队分道扬镳，由4艘护卫舰接着护送，而罗德尼所率舰队在第二天上午即遭遇并俘虏了一支由7艘战舰和16艘补给船所组成的西班牙分舰队。其中12艘装载着给养的运输船，被英军带往了直布罗陀。一个星期之后，16日的下午1点，东南海面又出现了一支由11艘战舰所组成的西班牙舰队。西班牙人坚守阵地，以为逼近的这支舰队只是驶往直布罗陀的补给船队，并没有强大的兵力护送——他们直到为时已晚、无法逃脱的时候，才意识到这是一种不幸的失误，原因在于他们太过疏忽大意，竟然没有派出瞭望船。西班牙上将胡安·德·兰加拉先生意识到了自己所犯的错误之后，曾经试图率军逃跑；不过，英国战舰的底部都包了铜，所以罗德尼在发出全面追击的信号之后，英军便赶上了这支西班牙船队，切断了后者逃进该国港口的去路，并且尽管当晚海风肆虐、海岸处于下风向且有着危险重重的暗礁，英军还是成功地俘虏了这位西班牙海军司令及其手下的6艘战舰，还有一艘西班牙战舰被炸毁了。由于海上仍然狂风大作、暴雨如注，所以被俘的战舰中，有一艘被吹沉了，另一艘则被冲进了加的斯港；英军中有几艘战舰也陷入了极大的危险当中，不过还是幸运地逃过了一劫。数日之后，整支英军便进入了直布罗陀湾。驶往米诺卡的运输船队随即出发了，而一待护送这支运输船队的战舰返回直布罗

his force, with the prizes, to England under Admiral Digby.

The state of politics and parties in England at this time was such that, combined with the unavoidable inferiority of the Channel fleet, it was difficult to find an admiral willing to accept the chief command. An admirable officer, Barrington, the captor of Sta. Lucia, refused the first place, though willing to serve as second, even to a junior. The allied fleet, to the number of thirty-six sail-of-the-line, assembled at Cadiz. Their cruises, however, were confined to the Portuguese coast; and their only service, a most important one, was the capture of an entire convoy, largely laden with military stores, for the East and West Indies. The entrance of sixty English prizes, with nearly three thousand prisoners, into Cadiz, was a source of great rejoicing to Spain. On the 24th of October, De Guichen, returning from his contest with Rodney, came into the same port with his West Indian squadron, of nineteen ships-of-the-line; but the immense armament thus assembled did nothing. The French ships returned to Brest in January, 1781.

While thus unproductive of military results in Europe, the war in 1780 gave rise to an event which cannot wholly be passed over by any history of sea power. This was the Armed Neutrality, at the head of which stood Russia, joined by Sweden and Denmark. The claim of England to seize enemy's goods in neutral ships bore hard upon neutral powers, and especially upon those of the Baltic and upon Holland, into whose hands, and those of the Austrian Netherlands, the war had thrown much of the European carrying-trade; while the products of the Baltic, naval stores and grain, were those which England was particularly interested in forbidding to her enemies. The declarations finally put forth by Russia, and signed by Sweden and Denmark, were four in number:

1. That neutral vessels had a right, not only to sail to unblockaded ports, but also from port

陀，即2月13日，罗德尼便率领4艘战舰动身前往西印度群岛，而让其余战舰带着缴获的战利品，在迪格比上将的指挥下返回英国去了。

此时，英国国内的政治形势严峻，党派纷争严重，加上海峡舰队难免兵力较弱，使得英国政府很难找到一位乐意担任舰队总司令一职的人选。巴林顿这位可敬的将领曾率军攻取了圣卢西亚；他虽然拒绝担任总司令，却愿意当这支舰队的副司令，哪怕是给一名后辈当副司令也行。法、西联合舰队的兵力达到了36艘战舰，并在加的斯集结起来了。不过，联合舰队的巡逻范围，却只限于葡萄牙沿海；而这支舰队唯一一次发挥了重大作用的行动，便是俘虏了敌人一整支满载着军用物资驶往东、西印度群岛的运输船队。60艘英国被俘船只和近3000名俘虏被押入加的斯，使得西班牙举国上下一片欢腾。10月24日，同罗德尼交过手的基申伯爵回师了，他率领由19艘战舰组成的那支西印度群岛舰队，也驶入了加的斯港；不过，如此集结起来的这支庞大的兵力，随后却什么也没干。1781年1月，法国舰队便返回了布雷斯特。

虽说欧洲战事是如此的徒劳无果，但1780年这场战争却引发了一件海权历史完全无法忽视的事件。这就是《武装中立条约》，其中领头的是俄国，参与国则有瑞典和丹麦。英国声称自己有权扣押中立国船只运送的敌方物资，这种做法压迫和掌控了各个中立国，尤其是波罗的海沿岸各国和荷兰，以及奥属尼德兰地区，而此次战争，又使得欧洲的国际运输业务大部分都落入了英国手中；波罗的海沿岸各国的产品，即海军物资和粮食，正是英国尤其想禁止敌国获得的那些物资。成立"武装中立同盟"的宣言最终由俄国提出，并与瑞典、丹麦两国共同签署；宣言包括4点内容：

to port of a belligerent nation; in other words, to maintain the coasting trade of a belligerent.

2. That property belonging to the subjects of a power at war should be safe on board neutral vessels. This was the principle involved in the now familiar maxim, "Free ships make free goods."

3. That no articles are contraband, except arms, equipments, and munitions of war. This ruled out naval stores and provisions unless belonging to the government of a belligerent.

4. That blockades, to be binding, must have an adequate naval force stationed in close proximity to the blockaded port.

The contracting parties being neutral in the present war, but binding themselves to support these principles by a combined armed fleet of a fixed minimum number, the agreement received the name of the Armed Neutrality. The discussion of the propriety of the various declarations belongs to International law; but it is evident that no great maritime State, situated as England then was, would submit to the first and third as a matter of right. Policy only could induce her to do so. Without meeting the declarations by a direct contradiction, the ministry and the king determined to disregard them, — a course which was sustained in principle even by prominent members of the bitter opposition of that day. The undecided attitude of the United Provinces, divided as in the days of Louis XIV. between the partisans of England and France, despite a century of alliance with the former, drew the especial attention of Great Britain. They had been asked to join the Armed Neutrality; they hesitated, but the majority of the provinces favored it. A British officer had already gone so far as to fire upon a Dutch man-of-war which had resisted the search of merchant-ships under its convoy; an act which, whether right or wrong, tended to incense the Dutch generally against England. It was determined by the latter that if the United Provinces acceded to the coalition of neutrals, war should be declared. On the 16th of

1. 中立国船只非但拥有驶往未封锁港口的权利，也拥有在交战国诸港间航行的权利；换言之，即有权维持交战国的沿海贸易。

2. 应当确保中立国船只上属于交战国国民财产的安全。这一点，就是如今我们熟悉的"船只中立，货物也中立"这一准则中所包含的原则。

3. 除了武器、装备和军需物品，其余商品都不属于战时禁运品。这一条将海军物资和给养等排除在禁运物资之外，除非它们属于某个交战国政府。

4. 进行封锁时，必须在被封锁港口附近派驻一支兵力充足的海军，否则此种封锁就不具有约束力。

虽说在此次战争中，签署这一条约的三方都属于中立国，但为了约束自身并支持上述原则，三国还组建了一支联合武装舰队，维持着最低限度的固定兵力，因此该协定即得名《武装中立条约》。对上述各条声明的性质进行探讨，属于国际法学的范畴；不过很显然，没有哪一个处在当时英国那种位置上的海洋大国，会承认第1点和第3点是一种重要权利的。该国的政策，只是促成了这种做法罢了。英国政府和英王都没有直接否定这一声明，而是决定不予理会——即便是当时态度最为激烈的反对党，也在原则上支持了这种应对方针。联合省王国的态度犹豫不定，虽说它与英国结盟已达一个世纪，但在路易十四时期，各省就已分裂成了亲英和亲法两派，因而英国尤为关注。俄、瑞、丹三国曾经要求该国加入《武装中立条约》；各省虽说犹疑不定，但大多数省份还是赞同加入。有位英军将领曾经做得太过分，向一艘拒绝英军搜查其护送商船的荷兰军舰开火；这种行为不论是对是错，都会激怒荷兰人，使之群起而对抗英国。英国决定，倘若联合省王国加入"武装中

December, 1780, the English ministry was informed that the States-General had resolved to sign the declarations of the Armed Neutrality without delay. Orders were at once sent out to Rodney to seize the Dutch West India and South American possessions; similar orders to the East Indies; and the ambassador at the Hague was recalled. England declared war four days later. The principal effect, therefore, of the Armed Neutrality upon the war was to add the colonies and commerce of Holland to the prey of English cruisers. The additional enemy was of small account to Great Britain, whose geographical position effectually blocked the junction of the Dutch fleet with those of her other enemies. The possessions of Holland fell everywhere, except when saved by the French; while a bloody but wholly uninstructive battle between English and Dutch squadrons in the North Sea, in August, 1781, was the only feat of arms illustrative of the old Dutch courage and obstinacy.

The year 1781, decisive of the question of the independence of the United States, was marked in the European seas by imposing movements of great fleets followed by puny results. At the end of March De Grasse sailed from Brest with twenty-six ships-of-the-line. On the 29th he detached five under Suffren to the East Indies, and himself continued on to meet success at Yorktown and disaster in the West Indies. On the 23d of June De Guichen sailed from Brest with eighteen ships-of-the-line for Cadiz, where he joined thirty Spanish ships. This immense armament sailed on the 22d of July for the Mediterranean, landed fourteen thousand troops at Minorca, and then moved upon the English Channel.

The English had this year first to provide against the danger to Gibraltar. That beset fortress had had no supplies since Rodney's visit, in January of the year before, and was now in sore want, the provisions being scanty and bad, the biscuits weevilly, and the meat tainted. Amid the horrors and uproar of one of the longest and most exciting sieges of history, the sufferings

立同盟",那么英国就应当对其宣战。1780年12月16日,英国政府得知,荷兰议会决定马上签署《武装中立条约》。于是,英国政府立即派人向罗德尼下令,要他攻取西印度群岛和南美洲的荷属殖民地;东印度群岛的英军,也接到了同样的命令;同时,政府还召回了驻海牙的英国大使。4天之后,英国对荷宣战。因此,《武装中立条约》对于此次战争的主要影响,便是让英国的巡逻舰下,多了荷兰的殖民地与贸易这一牺牲品。对于英国来说,多出来的这个敌人并无太大价值,因为该国的地理位置,实际上使得荷兰舰队不可能与其他两个敌国的舰队联合起来。各地的荷属殖民地纷纷陷落,除非有法军救援才能保全;而1781年8月,英、荷两国舰队在北海海域进行的那场伤亡惨重却毫无益处的海战,便成了说明荷兰人原来那种勇敢无畏和顽强不屈之精神的唯一一件战功。

1781年是美国独立进程中关键的一年,这一年在欧洲则以交战舰队规模庞大、交战结果却微不足道为标志。3月底,德·格拉斯率26艘战舰从布雷斯特起航。29日,他派苏弗朗率5艘战舰前往东印度群岛,而他自己则继续向美洲进发,在约克镇获得了胜利,但在西印度群岛遭到了惨败。6月23日,基申伯爵率18艘战舰,从布雷斯特动身前往加的斯,并在那里与30艘西班牙舰船会合了。这支庞大的海军部队于7月22日出发驶往地中海,并在米诺卡岛放下了14000陆军,然后便向英吉利海峡逼进。

在这一年中,英国首先必须防范直布罗陀遭遇危险。由于遭到围攻,这处要塞自前一年1月份罗德尼率军到过之后,就一直没有获得给养,此时已经到了山穷水尽的地步,存粮既少又差,饼干长了虫,肉类也全都腐臭了。这是历史上持续时间最久、力度最大的围困之一,士兵们身处恐惧和骚动之中,而城中还有许多老百姓,包括这些士兵和军官们的

of the combatants were intensified by the presence of many peaceful inhabitants, including the wives and families of soldiers as well as of officers. A great fleet of twenty-eight ships-of-the-line sailed from Portsmouth on the 13th of March, convoying three hundred merchant-ships for the East and West Indies, besides ninety-seven transports and supply-ships for the Rock. A delay on the Irish coast prevented its falling in with De Grasse, who had sailed nine days after it. Arriving off Cape St. Vincent, it met no enemy, and looking into Cadiz saw the great Spanish fleet at anchor. The latter made no move, and the English admiral, Derby, threw his supplies into Gibraltar on the 12th of April, undisturbed. At the same time he, like De Grasse, detached to the East Indies a small squadron, which was destined before long to fall in with Suffren. The inaction of the Spanish fleet, considering the eagerness of its government about Gibraltar and its equal if not superior numbers, shows scanty reliance of the Spanish admiral upon himself or his command. Derby, having relieved Gibraltar and Minorca, returned to the Channel in May.

Upon the approach of the combined fleet of nearly fifty sail in August following, Derby fell back upon Torbay and there anchored his fleet, numbering thirty ships. De Guichen, who held chief command, and whose caution when engaged with Rodney has been before remarked, was in favor of fighting; but the almost unanimous opposition of the Spaniards, backed by some of his own officers, overruled him in a council of war,[4] and again the great Bourbon coalition fell back, foiled by their own discord and the unity of their enemy. Gibraltar relieved, England untouched, were the results of these gigantic gatherings; they can scarcely be called efforts. A mortifying disaster closed the year for the allies. De Guichen sailed from Brest with seventeen sail, protecting a large convoy of merchantmen and ships with military supplies. The fleet was pursued by twelve English ships under Admiral Kempenfeldt, an officer whose high professional abilities have not earned the immortality with which poetry has graced his tragical

家属，让士兵们更是苦不堪言。3月13日，一支由28艘战舰组成的大型舰队从朴茨茅斯起航，护送着300艘商船前往东、西印度群岛，以及97艘驶往直布罗陀的运输船和补给船。由于在爱尔兰沿海耽搁了，所以这支舰队并未遇到在它9天之后起航的德·格拉斯所率舰队。抵达圣文森特角海域后，英国舰队并未遇到敌军，而向加的斯港内看去，却发现那支庞大的西班牙舰队此时正泊在港内。西班牙舰队并未采取行动，因此英军司令德比便顺顺当当地在4月12日将所载给养投入了直布罗陀。与此同时，他像德·格拉斯那样，派了一支小型舰队前往东印度群岛，而这支分队注定不久以后就会遇上苏弗朗。鉴于西班牙政府急不可耐地想要得到直布罗陀，而西班牙舰队就算不占优势，兵力也与英军相等，所以这支西班牙舰队的不作为，表明那位西班牙海军司令对自己和自己的指挥都毫无信心。德比上将在解除了直布罗陀与米诺卡岛之围后，便于5月返回英吉利海峡去了。

在接下来的8月份，由于拥有近50艘战舰的法、西联合舰队步步紧逼，德比撤退到了托贝，率领手下那支拥有30艘战舰的舰队泊在此港。担任联合舰队总司令的基申伯爵赞同交战，在前文中我们已经指出过，他与罗德尼交战时抱着极其谨慎的态度；可由于西班牙人几乎全都反对，而他本人手下的一些将领也支持西班牙人，故他的交战决定在作战会议上被否决了，[4] 而这支由两个波旁王国联合组成的庞大舰队，也因为受阻于其内部的不和与敌人的团结，再一次退却了。直布罗陀之围解了，英国本土毫发无损，就是两国声势浩大地集结兵力所获得的成果；事实上，它们根本就称不上是什么成果。这一年年底，法、西联军还遭受了一次令人羞愧的惨败。基申伯爵率领17艘战舰从布雷斯特出发，护送一支大型的商船队，其中还有运送军用物资的舰船。这支舰队，遭到了

death. Falling in with the French one hundred and fifty miles west of Ushant, he cut off a part of the convoy, despite his inferior numbers.[5] A few days later a tempest dispersed the French fleet. Only two ships-of-the-line and five merchantmen out of one hundred and fifty reached the West Indies.

The year 1782 opened with the loss to the English of Port Mahon, which surrendered on the 5th of February, after a siege of six months, — a surrender induced by the ravages of scurvy, consequent upon the lack of vegetables, and confinement in the foul air of bombproofs and casemates, under the heavy fire of an enemy. On the last night of the defence the call for necessary guards was four hundred and fifteen, while only six hundred and sixty men were fit for duty, thus leaving no reliefs.

The allied fleets assembled this year in Cadiz, to the number of forty ships-of-the-line. It was expected that this force would be increased by Dutch ships, but a squadron under Lord Howe drove the latter back to their ports. It does not certainly appear that any active enterprise was intended against the English coast; but the allies cruised off the mouth of the Channel and in the Bay of Biscay during the summer months. Their presence insured the safe arrival and departure of the homeward and outward bound merchantmen, and likewise threatened English commerce; notwithstanding which, Howe, with twenty-two ships, not only kept the sea and avoided an engagement, but also succeeded in bringing the Jamaica fleet safe into port. The injury to trade and to military transportation by sea may be said to have been about equal on either side; and the credit for successful use of sea power for these most important ends must therefore be given to the weaker party.

Having carried out their orders for the summer cruise, the combined fleets returned to Cadiz. On the 10th of September they sailed thence for Algesiras, on the opposite side of the

一支由凯姆本菲尔特上将指挥、包括12艘战舰的英国舰队的追击；这位将领具有杰出的职业能力，虽说没有获得不朽之声望，但诗歌中却优雅地传颂着他那种悲剧性的牺牲。在韦桑岛以西150英里的海域与法军狭路相逢之后，尽管在兵力上不如敌军，但他还是率军将法国护航船队的一部分与其主力隔离开来了。[5]数天之后，一场暴风雨打散了法国舰队。在这150艘舰船中，只有2艘战舰和5艘商船最终抵达了西印度群岛。

1782年伊始，英国就丢掉了马翁港；此处是在被围6个月之后，于2月5日向法、西联军缴械投降的——港内守军之所以投降，是因缺乏果蔬而导致坏血病肆虐，加之又在敌军强大的炮击之下整天躲在掩体与炮台里，呼吸着污浊的空气所迫。在顽强抵抗的最后一夜，需要450名士兵担任必要的警戒任务，可港内能够执勤的将士总共才有650名，所以根本就无人换岗。

这一年，法、西联军舰队再次在加的斯集结起来，兵力达到了40艘战舰。两国都等着荷兰舰队加入，以便壮大这支兵力；可豪勋爵率领的一支分舰队将荷兰舰队赶回去了。自然，这支兵力似乎并不打算主动向英国沿海发动进击；不过，联军整个夏季都在英吉利海峡峡口和比斯开湾海域进行巡航。有这支兵力在此，就确保了回国或者出海的商船在到达和出发时的安全，同时还对英国商船构成了威胁；尽管如此，豪勋爵率领着20艘战舰，非但一直在海上游弋，还成功地领着牙买加舰队安全地泊入了港口。可以说，双方海上贸易和海上军事运输所遭受的损失都差不多；因此，成功地利用制海权实现了这些极其重要之目标的荣誉，自然应当归于兵力较弱的英国这一方才是。

在执行完夏季巡逻的命令之后，联合舰队便返回了加的斯。9月10日，联合舰队从

bay from Gibraltar, to support a grand combined attack by land and sea, which, it was hoped, would reduce to submission the key to the Mediterranean. With the ships already there, the total rose to nearly fifty ships-of-the-line. The details of the mighty onslaught scarcely belong to our subject, yet cannot be wholly passed by, without at least such mention as may recognize and draw attention to their interest.

The three years' siege which was now drawing to its end had been productive of many brilliant feats of arms, as well as of less striking but more trying proofs of steadfast endurance, on the part of the garrison. How long the latter might have held out cannot be said, seeing the success with which the English sea power defied the efforts of the allies to cut off the communications of the fortress; but it was seemingly certain that the place must be subdued by main force or not at all, while the growing exhaustion of the belligerents foretold the near end of the war. Accordingly Spain multiplied her efforts of preparation and military ingenuity; while the report of them and of the approaching decisive contest drew to the scene volunteers and men of eminence from other countries of Europe. Two French Bourbon princes added, by their coming, to the theatrical interest with which the approaching drama was invested. The presence of royalty was needed adequately to grace the sublime catastrophe; for the sanguine confidence of the besiegers had determined a satisfactory dénouement with all the security of a playwright.

Besides the works on the isthmus which joins the Rock to the mainland, where three hundred pieces of artillery were now mounted, the chief reliance of the assailants was upon ten floating batteries elaborately contrived to be shot and fire proof, and carrying one hundred and fifty-four heavy guns. These were to anchor in a close north-and-south line along the west face of the works, at about nine hundred yards distance. They were to be supported by forty gunboats and as many bomb vessels, besides the efforts of the ships-of-the-line to cover the attack and

加的斯出发，驶往与直布罗陀隔着海湾相望的阿尔赫西拉斯[1]，准备支援发动一次规模浩大的海陆联合进攻；他们希望通过此种进攻，迫使直布罗陀这个进出地中海地区的要冲投降。连同已经抵达此处的舰船，联合舰队的总兵力达到了将近50艘战舰。这次猛攻的详细情况虽说并不属于本书主题的范畴，但也不能全然忽略，起码应当说一说那些可以让我们看清并注意到此战重要性的细节情况才行。

对直布罗陀长达3年之久的围攻，此时已经接近尾声；而英国守军在此也获得了许多辉煌显赫的战功，还有许多不那么令人瞩目、却更加证明了英军具有坚定不移之耐力的成就。看到英国利用其制海权，一次又一次成功地挫败了联军切断这处要塞的交通补给的企图后，我们没法说联军究竟还能坚持多久；但毫无疑问的是，由于交战双方都日益疲惫不堪，预示着此次战争即将结束，所以直布罗陀要么必定被联军主力攻克，要么就是安然无恙。于是，西班牙便加紧了准备工作和军事谋略研究；而对于这些方面和即将爆发的这场决定性战役的报道，则吸引了欧洲其他国家中的许多志愿者与杰出人士，使得他们纷纷走上了战场。波旁皇族另有两位亲王也加入了此战，从而为即将到来的这幕大戏增加了戏剧性效果。为了美化这次惨败，必须要有皇族的参与才行；因为像一个剧作家所保证的那样，围攻者乐观的信心已经决定了这幕大戏会有一个圆满的结局。

除了在连接直布罗陀与西班牙本土之间的地峡上修筑的那些工事——此时这里已经部署了300门火炮，联军主要依赖10艘炮舰；它们都经过精心设计，尽量做到防弹防火，并且总共携带了154门重炮。这些战舰都沿着那些工事西面而泊，排成严密的南北阵列，彼此之间相距大约900码[2]。除了用战舰掩护并转移守军的火力之外，还有40艘

distract the garrison. Twelve thousand French troops were brought to reinforce the Spaniards in the grand assault, which was to be made when the bombardment had sufficiently injured and demoralized the defenders. At this time the latter numbered seven thousand, their land opponents thirty-three thousand men.

The final act was opened by the English. At seven o'clock on the morning of September 8, 1782, the commanding general, Elliott, began a severe and most injurious fire upon the works on the isthmus. Having effected his purpose, he stopped; but the enemy took up the glove the next morning, and for four days successively poured in a fire from the isthmus alone of six thousand five hundred cannon-balls and one thousand one hundred bombs every twenty-four hours. So approached the great closing scene of September 13. At seven A.M. of that day the ten battering-ships unmoored from the head of the bay and stood down to their station. Between nine and ten they anchored, and the general fire at once began. The besieged replied with equal fury. The battering-ships seem in the main, and for some hours, to have justified the hopes formed of them; cold shot glanced or failed to get through their sides, while the self-acting apparatus for extinguishing fires balked the hot shot.

About two o'clock, however, smoke was seen to issue from the ship of the commander-in-chief, and though controlled for some time, the fire continued to gain. The same misfortune befell others; by evening, the fire of the besieged gained a marked superiority, and by one o'clock in the morning the greater part of the battering-ships were in flames. Their distress was increased by the action of the naval officer commanding the English gunboats, who now took post upon the flank of the line and raked it effectually, — a service which the Spanish gunboats should have prevented. In the end, nine of the ten blew up at their anchors, with a loss estimated at fifteen hundred men, four hundred being saved from the midst of the fire by the

小炮艇以及许多的岸轰艇来支援这些炮舰。法国派出了12000名陆军，来增援这场大规模进攻中的西班牙军队；等到炮击让英国守军充分受到重创并失去士气之后，他们就会发动这场大规模的进攻战了。此时英国守军有7000人，而与之对阵的联军，光是陆军便达到了33000兵力。

决战是由英军发起的。1782年9月8日早上7点，英军主将埃利奥特开始向直布罗陀地峡上的联军工事发动猛烈炮击，使之受损严重。在达到了目的之后，他便下令停止炮击；可敌军却在第二天早上开始应战，而在接下来的4天内，光是从直布罗陀地峡上的联军阵地，每一天都向英军发射了6500发重炮炮弹和1100枚炸弹。这样，就到了9月13日那场伟大的结局之战了。那天早上7点钟，10艘炮舰从阿尔赫西拉斯湾顶端拔锚起航，南下到达了各自的战斗位置。它们在9点到10点间泊锚扎阵，随后马上就开始对英军全面开火。被围英军则回之以同样猛烈的火力。在数个小时的炮击中，这些炮舰似乎基本上能够实现它们的作战意图；英军的冷弹要么是与它们擦肩而过，要么就是根本没打到它们附近，而炮舰上的自动灭火装置，也使英军的热弹没起到应有的作用。

然而，下午大约2点钟的时候，炮舰舰队总司令的座驾开始冒起浓烟，尽管控制了一段时间，可火势还是继续蔓延开来。其他炮舰也开始遭受同样的噩运；到了傍晚时分，被围英军的火力开始明显占据了上风，而到了凌晨1点的时候，大部分炮舰全都火光冲天了。让他们更倒霉的是，指挥英军炮艇的那位海军将领开始采取行动，他此时已经占领了联军炮舰阵列的右翼位置，有效地对这些炮舰进行猛击——西班牙的炮艇本来应当阻挡住英军，不让英军有机可乘的。结果，这10艘炮舰中有9艘还没拔锚便被炸毁了，伤亡估

English seamen. The tenth ship was boarded and burned by the English boats. The hopes of the assailants perished with the failure of the battering-ships.

There remained only the hope of starving out the garrison. To this end the allied fleets now gave themselves. It was known that Lord Howe was on his way out with a great fleet, numbering thirty-four ships-of-the-line, besides supply vessels. On the 10th of October a violent westerly gale injured the combined ships, driving one ashore under the batteries of Gibraltar, where she was surrendered. The next day Howe's force came in sight, and the transports had a fine chance to make the anchorage, which, through carelessness, was missed by all but four. The rest, with the men-of-war, drove eastward into the Mediterranean. The allies followed on the 13th; but though thus placed between the port and the relieving force, and not encumbered, like the latter, with supply-ships, they yet contrived to let the transports, with scarcely an exception, slip in and anchor safely. Not only provisions and ammunition, but also bodies of troops carried by the ships-of-war, were landed without molestation. On the 19th the English fleet repassed the straits with an easterly wind, having within a week's time fulfilled its mission, and made Gibraltar safe for another year. The allied fleet followed, and on the 20th an action took place at long range, the allies to windward, but not pressing their attack close. The number of ships engaged in this magnificent spectacle, the closing scene of the great drama in Europe, the after-piece to the successful defence of Gibraltar, was eighty-three of the line, — forty-nine allies and thirty-four English. Of the former, thirty-three only got into action; but as the duller sailers would have come up to a general engagement, Lord Howe was probably right in declining, so far as in him lay, a trial which the allies did not too eagerly court.

Such were the results of this great contest in the European seas, marked on the part of the allies by efforts gigantic in size, but loose-jointed and flabby in execution. By England,

计达1500人，还有400人则是被英军从火海中救出来的。第10艘炮舰则被英国用小艇攻到了船上，然后放火烧毁了。随着这支炮舰舰队的覆灭，进攻者的希望也化为了泡影。

于是，就只剩下一种指望了，那就是饿死驻守的英军。为了实现这一目标，联合舰队此时开始付出代价了。他们得知，豪勋爵率领一支包括34艘战舰和给养船只的舰队，正在前来的路上。10月10日，一场猛烈的西风让联合舰队损失惨重，将其中一艘吹得在直布罗陀的炮阵之下搁了浅，然后就缴械投降了。第二天，豪勋爵所率舰队出现了，那些运输船本来有着大好的机会入港泊锚，可由于疏忽大意，除了其中的4艘，其余舰船都没有把握住这个机会。其余运输船便同战舰一起，向东驶入了地中海。联合舰队在13日开始追击；可是，就算如此楔在直布罗陀港与英国援军之间，并且像英国援军那样，己方的给养船只丝毫没有受到阻碍，可他们仍然让英国的运输舰船总能偷偷地溜过去，并且安全地泊入直布罗陀港。非但是给养和弹药，甚至是军舰所运载的兵力，也都毫不受阻地运送到了直布罗陀。19日，英国舰队趁着东风，再一次通过了直布罗陀海峡，在一个星期内就完成了运送给养与援兵的使命，使得直布罗陀又可以安然牢固地支撑上一年了。联合舰队追击而至，20日爆发了一场远距离交火；当时联合舰队处于上风位置，可没有逼近敌军发起进攻。在这次场面壮观、属于欧洲这场战争大戏的闭幕式和直布罗陀守卫战尾声的交火中，参战兵力为83艘战舰，其中联军49艘，英军34艘。联军战舰中，只有34艘采取了行动；可豪勋爵并未像一些较愚钝的海军将领那样与敌人全面交战，这一做法很可能是正确的，因为联军并不急于冒险与他所率的舰队进行全面交锋。

欧洲海域所进行的这场大规模海战的结果就是这些；其中令人瞩目的是，联军的

so heavily overmatched in mere numbers, were shown firmness of purpose, high courage, and seamanship; but it can scarcely be said that the military conceptions of her councils, or the cabinet management of her sea forces, were worthy of the skill and devotion of her seamen. The odds against her were not so great — not nearly so great — as the formidable lists of guns and ships seemed to show; and while allowance must justly be made for early hesitations, the passing years of indecision and inefficiency on the part of the allies should have betrayed to her their weakness. The reluctance of the French to risk their ships, so plainly shown by D'Estaing, De Grasse, and De Guichen, the sluggishness and inefficiency of the Spaniards, should have encouraged England to pursue her old policy, to strike at the organized forces of the enemy afloat. As a matter of fact, and probably from the necessities of the case, the opening of every campaign found the enemies separated, — the Spaniards in Cadiz, the French in Brest.[6] To blockade the latter in full force before they could get out, England should have strained every effort; thus she would have stopped at its head the main stream of the allied strength, and, by knowing exactly where this great body was, would have removed that uncertainty as to its action which fettered her own movements as soon as it had gained the freedom of the open sea. Before Brest she was interposed between the allies; by her lookouts she would have known the approach of the Spaniards long before the French could know it; she would have kept in her hands the power of bringing against each, singly, ships more numerous and individually more effective. A wind that was fair to bring on the Spaniards would have locked their allies in the port. The most glaring instances of failure on the part of England to do this were when De Grasse was permitted to get out unopposed in March, 1781; for an English fleet of superior force had sailed from Portsmouth nine days

行动在规模上浩大无比，但实施起来却松弛涣散、优柔寡断。而英军在兵力屈指可数、实力大大不如敌军的情况下，却表现出了坚定不移的目标、高度的勇敢和高超的海战本领；不过，英国议会的军事观念或者内阁对海军的管理，却很难说配得上英国海军官兵们的才干和奉献。战胜该国的机会并没有——甚至远不及——联军火炮和舰船那种压倒性的数量看上去显示的那样大；尽管应当允许他们在战争早期犹豫不决，但过去这些年来，联军的优柔寡断和效率低下，本来就已将其弱点暴露在英国面前了。德斯坦、德·格拉斯和基申伯爵等人，都明显暴露出法国人不愿让自己的舰船承担风险的心态，而西班牙人则拖拉怠惰、低效无能，本来也应当促使英国继续实行其原有的政策，去打击敌人有组织的海上力量才是。事实上，很可能是由于形势所迫，故每次战役开始的时候，敌军都是不在一起的——西班牙海军位于加的斯，法国海军则在布雷斯特。[6]英国本应想尽办法，全力封锁法国海军，使之无法出港；这样，英国就会从源头阻断联军实力的主要来源，并且在对这支海军力量身处何处了如指掌的前提下，消除阻碍英国海军在公海上自由行动的不确定性。坚守布雷斯特海域，英军实际上就是像一颗钉子似的楔在了联军之间；通过瞭望哨，英军会提早获知西班牙人前来的情报，而法国人则要很久以后才会得知；英军会将主动权掌握在自己手中，决定用兵力更多的舰船、更有效地逐个对敌人采取行动。倘若风向有利于西班牙船队前来，那么这种风向也会将其盟军阻在港内。英国没能做到这一点的一个最为显著的例子，便是1781年3月竟然任由德·格拉斯毫无阻碍地率军出港；一支兵力上占有优势的英国舰队本来在他动身9天之前便从朴茨茅斯起航，却在爱尔兰沿海被海军部耽搁了；[7]还有就是在这一年年底，派凯姆本菲尔特上将率不如敌方的兵力前去阻截基申伯爵，可本来足以扭转战局的舰船，却被留在了国内。凯姆本菲尔特动身

before him, but was delayed by the admiralty on the Irish coast;[7] and again at the end of that year, when Kempenfeldt was sent to intercept De Guichen with an inferior force, while ships enough to change the odds were kept at home. Several of the ships which were to accompany Rodney to the West Indies were ready when Kempenfeldt sailed, yet they were not associated with an enterprise so nearly affecting the objects of Rodney's campaign. The two forces united would have made an end of De Guichen's seventeen ships and his invaluable convoy.

Gibraltar was indeed a heavy weight upon the English operations, but the national instinct which clung to it was correct. The fault of the English policy was in attempting to hold so many other points of land, while neglecting, by rapidity of concentration, to fall upon any of the detachments of the allied fleets. The key of the situation was upon the ocean; a great victory there would have solved all the other points in dispute. But it was not possible to win a great victory while trying to maintain a show of force everywhere.[8]

North America was a yet heavier clog, and there undoubtedly the feeling of the nation was mistaken; pride, not wisdom, maintained that struggle. Whatever the sympathies of individuals and classes in the allied nations, by their governments American rebellion was valued only as a weakening of England's arm. The operations there depended, as has been shown, upon the control of the sea; and to maintain that, large detachments of English ships were absorbed from the contest with France and Spain. Could a successful war have made America again what it once was, a warmly attached dependency of Great Britain, a firm base for her sea power, it would have been worth much greater sacrifices; but that had become impossible. But although she had lost, by her own mistakes, the affection of the colonists, which would have supported

时，计划护送罗德尼前往西印度群岛的数艘战舰本来已经准备就绪，可这些战舰，却没有用于此次几乎影响到了罗德尼那场战役之目标的作战行动。倘若这两支兵力合二为一，本来是可以让基申伯爵所率的那17战舰，以及他护送的那支价值连城的运输队全军覆灭的。

虽说直布罗陀的确对英军的作战行动有着举足轻重的作用，但英国不放弃此地的直觉也是正确的。英国政策上的失误，便是在试图掌控许多其他地方的过程中，忽视了迅速集中兵力进击联军舰队的所有分队。当前形势的关键，乃在于海洋；在海上获得一次大捷，便可以解决其他的所有争端。但是，倘若同时还想到处展示出自己的实力，那么英国就是不可能获得此种大捷的。(8)

北美也是一种更加沉重的阻碍，而英国对于北美的态度，无疑也是错误的；英国坚持在北美作战，是出于自尊，而非出于理智。无论法、西等盟国的国内民众和不同阶层具有什么样的同情之心，这些盟国政府所看重的，都是美国人的反叛会削弱英国的实力。正如前面所述，北美作战行动所依赖的就是制海权；而为了维持北美地区的作战行动，大量与法国和西班牙较量的英国舰船，便都被吸引到了北美地区。假如英国在北美进行的战争取得了胜利，使得美国回复到原来的那种状态，回复到那种高度依赖英国的状态，回复成英国制海权一处牢固的基地，那么，英国就算做出更大的牺牲也是值得的；可这一切都是不可能的了。不过，尽管由于自身的错误而失去了殖民者的热爱——这种热爱本来可以支持并确保英国继续固守北美诸港口和沿海地区的——但在哈利法克斯、百慕大和西印度群岛，英国仍然拥有一些足够强大的军事据点；作为海军基地，这些地方不过就是比那些被资源丰富、人口众多的友好国家所包围的强大海港要差一点儿罢了。不再在北美争雄，会让英国的实力大大增强，且增强程度也会大大超过法、西等

and secured her hold upon their ports and sea-coast, there nevertheless remained to the mother-country, in Halifax, Bermuda, and the West Indies, enough strong military stations, inferior, as naval bases, only to those strong ports which are surrounded by a friendly country, great in its resources and population. The abandonment of the contest in North America would have strengthened England very much more than the allies. As it was, her large naval detachments there were always liable to be overpowered by a sudden move of the enemy from the sea, as happened in 1778 and 1781.

To the abandonment of America as hopelessly lost, because no military subjection could have brought back the old loyalty, should have been added the giving up, for the time, all military occupancy which fettered concentration, while not adding to military strength. Most of the Antilles fell under this head, and the ultimate possession of them would depend upon the naval campaign. Garrisons could have been spared for Barbadoes and Sta. Lucia, for Gibraltar and perhaps for Mahon, that could have effectually maintained them until the empire of the seas was decided; and to them could have been added one or two vital positions in America, like New York and Charleston, to be held only till guarantees were given for such treatment of the loyalists among the inhabitants as good faith required England to exact.

Having thus stripped herself of every weight, rapid concentration with offensive purpose should have followed. Sixty ships-of-the-line on the coast of Europe, half before Cadiz and half before Brest, with a reserve at home to replace injured ships, would not have exhausted by a great deal the roll of the English navy; and that such fleets would not have had to fight, may not only be said by us, who have the whole history before us, but might have been inferred by those who had watched the tactics of D'Estaing and De Guichen, and later on of De Grasse. Or, had even so much dispersal been thought unadvisable, forty ships before Brest would have left the sea open to the Spanish fleet to try conclusions with the rest of the English navy when the

盟国。可事实却是，英国派到北美的一支支大型海军，往往会被从海上突然出现的敌人所打垮，就像1778年和1781年的情况那样。

除了由于军事镇压不可能再挽回诸殖民地原来那种忠诚之心而不得不绝望地放弃美国之外，英国本来还应当暂时放弃所有的军事占领地，因为这些地方既阻碍了英国集中兵力，同时又没有增强英国的军事实力。安的列斯群岛中的大多数地区都属于这一类，而最终能否守住这些地方，则取决于海军的作战情况。这些地方的守军，本来是可以腾出来派往巴巴多斯、圣卢西亚、直布罗陀等地，或许还可派往马翁港，从而可以有效地守住这些地方，直到英国确立其海洋帝国地位的那一天的；在这些地方之外，还可以再加上美洲一两个至关重要的位置，比如纽约和查尔斯顿，直到美国保证民众中反对独立的那些人切实得到了英国所规定的那种善意对待，才可以不再占领这些地方。

如此甩掉所有的包袱之后，英国接下来便应当为了进攻而将兵力快速地集中起来。在欧洲沿海部署60艘战舰，一半放在加的斯海域，一半放在布雷斯特海域，并在国内保持一支后备舰队来置换受损舰船，并不会因为海军兵力太过庞大而耗尽英国的资源；并且，这些舰队并非一定需要前去作战——我们这些了解整个历史的人可以这样说，而那些关注过德斯坦、基申伯爵以及后来德·格拉斯等的战术的人，可能也会得出同样的结论。或者，倘若有人认为将兵力如此分散开来不妥的话，那么在布雷斯特海域部署40艘战舰，就会让海上变得畅通无阻，而待直布罗陀与马翁港两地的控制权这个问题需要决断的时候，便可以让西班牙舰队来与英国剩下的海军力量决一雌雄了。倘若了解我们对

question of controlling Gibraltar and Mahon came up for decision. Knowing what we do of the efficiency of the two services, there can be little question of the result; and Gibraltar, instead of a weight, would, as often before and since those days, have been an element of strength to Great Britain.

The conclusion continually recurs. Whatever may be the determining factors in strifes between neighboring continental States, when a question arises of control over distant regions, politically weak, — whether they be crumbling empires, anarchical republics, colonies, isolated military posts, or islands below a certain size, — it must ultimately be decided by naval power, by the organized military force afloat, which represents the communications that form so prominent a feature in all strategy. The magnificent defence of Gibraltar hinged upon this; upon this depended the military results of the war in America; upon this the final fate of the West India Islands; upon this certainly the possession of India. Upon this will depend the control of the Central American Isthmus, if that question take a military coloring; and though modified by the continental position and surroundings of Turkey, the same sea power must be a weighty factor in shaping the outcome of the Eastern Question in Europe.

If this be true, military wisdom and economy, both of time and money, dictate bringing matters to an issue as soon as possible upon the broad sea, with the certainty that the power which achieves military preponderance there will win in the end. In the war of the American Revolution the numerical preponderance was very great against England; the actual odds were less, though still against her. Military considerations would have ordered the abandonment of the colonies; but if the national pride could not stoop to this, the right course was to blockade the hostile arsenals. If not strong enough to be in superior force before both, that of the more powerful nation should have been closed. Here was the first fault of the English admiralty; the statement of the First Lord as to the available force at the outbreak of

这两种情况下作战效果所做的推断，那么结果就是毫无疑问的了；而直布罗陀也不会再是一种负担，而是会像那时之前与之后一样，成为英国实力的一个组成部分了。

结局总是不断地重现。倘若相邻的大陆国家之间发生战争，那么无论战争的决定性因素是什么，当一个有关于控制与本国相距遥远、政治上比较软弱的地方——不论是摇摇欲坠的帝国、无政府主义盛行的共和国、殖民地、孤立的军事据点还是低于一定规模的岛屿——的问题出现之后，这个问题最终必定会由制海权来解决，由有组织的海上力量来解决；而这种有组织的海上力量，则代表着在一切战略中形成了如此显著特征的交通补给。辉煌壮烈的直布罗陀保卫战，依赖的就是这一点；美国独立战争在军事上所取得的成果，依赖的就是这一点；西印度群岛的最终命运，取决于这一点；而占领印度，当然也是取决于这一点。倘若从军事角度来看的话，控制中美地峡也将取决于这一点；并且，尽管会因土耳其的大陆性位置和环境而有所变化，但这种相同的制海权，在决定欧洲关于近东问题结局走向的过程中，必定也会成为一个重要的因素。

果真如此的话，那么既涉及时间、又涉及资金的军事智慧与经济情况，便会决定下面这两点：所有问题都将尽快地在广阔的海洋之上得以解决，而那些在海洋上获得了军事优势的国家，最终则必定会获胜。在美国革命战争中，兵力优势这方面对英国极为不利；可敌人实际的胜算却并不大，尽管这种胜算还是对英国不利。军事上的种种考虑，本来是会促使该国放弃这些殖民地的；不过，要是民族自尊感实在让英国无法如此忍辱负重的话，那么正确的方针便应当是封锁敌人的海军船坞。倘若海军不够强大，无法

the war was not borne out by facts. The first fleet, under Keppel, barely equalled the French; and at the same time Howe's force in America was inferior to the fleet under D'Estaing. In 1779 and 1781, on the contrary, the English fleet was superior to that of the French alone; yet the allies joined unopposed, while in the latter year De Grasse got away to the West Indies, and Suffren to the East. In Kempenfeldt's affair with De Guichen, the admiralty knew that the French convoy was of the utmost importance to the campaign in the West Indies, yet they sent out their admiral with only twelve ships; while at that time, besides the reinforcement destined for the West Indies, a number of others were stationed in the Downs, for what Fox justly called "the paltry purpose" of distressing the Dutch trade. The various charges made by Fox in the speech quoted from, and which, as regarded the Franco-Spanish War, were founded mainly on the expediency of attacking the allies before they got away into the ocean wilderness, were supported by the high professional opinion of Lord Howe, who of the Kempenfeldt affair said: "Not only the fate of the West India Islands, but perhaps the whole future fortune of the war, might have been decided, almost without a risk, in the Bay of Biscay." Not without a risk, but with strong probabilities of success, the whole fortune of the war should at the first have been staked on a concentration of the English fleet between Brest and Cadiz. No relief for Gibraltar would have been more efficacious; no diversion surer for the West India Islands; and the Americans would have appealed in vain for the help, scantily given as it was, of the French fleet. For the great results that flowed from the coming of De Grasse must not obscure the fact that he came on the 31st of August, and announced from the beginning that he must be in the West Indies again by the middle of October. Only a providential combination of circumstances prevented a repetition to Washington, in 1781, of

同时在法、西两国海军船坞前保持优势兵力，那么，就应当首先完全封锁住实力更强的那个国家的海军船坞。这正是英国海军部所犯下的第一个错误；海军大臣在战争爆发之初关于英国可用兵力的说法，并不是实事求是的。凯珀尔所指挥的第一支舰队，自然无法与法国舰队相匹敌；而与此同时，豪勋爵在美洲所率之兵力，也不如德斯坦所指挥的那支舰队。相反，在1779年和1781年，英国舰队的兵力却优于法国海军；可法、西联军却毫无阻碍地会师一处了，而且1781年德·格拉斯又出发去了西印度群岛，苏弗朗则率军去了东印度群岛。在凯姆菲尔特上将与基申伯爵的较量中，海军部明知法国那支运输船队对西印度群岛的战事极其重要，但还是让凯姆菲尔特这位海军上将率领屈屈12艘战舰前去阻截；而就在那时，除了准备前往西印度群岛进行增援的舰船，还有其他许多舰船都泊在唐斯锚地，为的是袭扰荷兰的海上贸易——对此，福克斯曾恰当地将其称之为"毫无价值的目的"。福克斯在其引用并涉及法、西战争的讲话中所提出的各种指摘，主要理由便是应该抓住有利时机进攻联军，以免联军逃到茫茫大海上；这些看法，得到了豪勋爵那种高度职业观点的支持，他在谈及凯姆菲尔特的那次战事时，曾经这样说过："不但是西印度群岛的归属问题，而且可能还有整个战争未来的走向，本来都是可以几无悬念地在比斯开湾确定下来的。"虽说并非毫无悬念，但也很有可能成功；而对于这场战争的整体命运，首先就应当赌上一把，将英国舰队集中部署于布雷斯特和加的斯之间才是。这样一来，就会最有效地解救直布罗陀之围，也可最有保障地分兵西印度群岛了；而美国人则会求救无门，不会像事实那样得到法国舰队的帮助。因为德·格拉斯率军前来而取得的重大战果，不应掩盖这样一种事实：他是8月31日到来的，并且从一开始就宣布自己在10月中旬必须再回到西印度群岛去。只是种种情况有如神助般地结

the painful disappointments by D'Estaing and De Guichen in 1778 and 1780.

FOOTNOTES:

(1) The curious reader can consult Clinton's letters and notes, in the "Clinton Cornwallis Controversy," by B.F. Stevens. London, 1888.

(2) Although the English thus culpably failed to use their superiority to the French alone, the Channel fleet numbering over forty of the line, the fear that it might prevent the junction caused the Brest fleet to sail in haste and undermanned, — a fact which had an important effect upon the issue of the cruise. (Chevalier, p. 159.)

(3) The details of the mismanagement of this huge mob of ships are so numerous as to confuse a narrative, and are therefore thrown into a foot-note. The French fleet was hurried to sea four thousand men short. The Spaniards were seven weeks in joining. When they met, no common system of signals had been arranged; five fair summer days were spent in remedying this defect. Not till a week after the junction could the fleet sail for England. No steps were taken to supply the provisions consumed by the French during the seven weeks. The original orders to D'Orvilliers contemplated a landing at Portsmouth, or the seizure of the Isle of Wight, for which a large army was assembled on the coast of Normandy. Upon reaching the Channel, these orders were suddenly changed, and Falmouth indicated as the point of landing. By this time, August 16, summer was nearly over; and Falmouth, if taken, would offer no shelter to a great fleet. Then an easterly gale drove the fleet out of the Channel. By this time the sickness which raged had so reduced the crews that many ships could be neither handled nor fought. Ships companies of eight hundred or a thousand men could muster only from three to five hundred. Thus bad administration crippled the fighting powers of the fleet; while the unaccountable military blunder of changing the objective from a safe and accessible roadstead to a fourth-rate and exposed harbor completed the disaster by taking away the only hope of a secure base of operations during the fall and winter

合起来，才使得华盛顿在1781年避免了再次经历1778年和1780年分别由德斯坦和基申伯爵所带来的那种极度的失望。

原注：

（1）喜欢刨根问底的读者，可以参阅B·F·史蒂文斯所著《柯林顿与康华里之争》（1888年，伦敦）一书中柯林顿的书信和注释。

（2）尽管英国如此疏忽大意地没有利用其优势兵力单独对付法国，但其海峡舰队兵力却达到了40多艘战舰；由于担心这支舰队会阻碍法、西联军会合，所以法国驻布雷斯特的舰队便急急忙忙，在人员不足的情况下出了港——这一事实，对于巡航问题产生了重大影响。（参见《希瓦利埃》，第159页）。

（3）这样一支庞大而混乱的舰队，在处置不当方面的问题数不胜数，连本书作者也搞混了，故将其放在此处加以说明。法国舰队是在缺员4000人的情况下仓皇出海的。西班牙船队在7个星期之后才与法军会合。会师之前，两国并未制定出一套共同的旗语；于是，他们又在这个晴朗的夏季花了5天时间来弥补这一不足。所以，直到会师一个星期之后，这支联合舰队才动身驶往英格兰。在这7个星期中，法国竟然没有采取为法国舰队提供给养的任何措施。奥尔维利埃最初接受的命令，是打算在朴茨茅斯登陆，或者攻取怀特岛；为此，法国在诺曼底海滩上集结了一支庞大的陆军。到达英吉利海峡之后，命令突然变了，登陆地点改成了法尔茅斯。到了这个时候，即8月16日，夏季已经快结束了；就算是占领了法尔茅斯，这儿也容不下一支大型的舰队。接下来，一场猛烈的东风将舰队吹出了英吉利海峡。到了此时，由于疾病盛行，舰队减员厉害，使得许多舰船既无人指挥，也没法参与作战了。那些原本满员为800或1000人的战舰编队，只能召拢300至500人。如此糟糕的管理，大大削弱了这支舰队的战斗力；而将作战目标从一个稳妥而容易到达的锚地变成一

months. France then had no first-class port on the Channel; hence the violent westerly gales which prevail in the autumn and winter would have driven the allies into the North Sea.

(4) Beatson gives quite at length (vol. v. p. 395) the debate in the allied council of war. The customary hesitation of such councils, in face of the difficulties of the situation, was increased by an appeal to the delusion of commerce-destroying as a decisive mode of warfare. M. de Beausset urged that "the allied fleets should direct their whole attention to that great and attainable object, the intercepting of the British homeward-bound West India fleets. This was a measure which, as they were now masters of the sea, could scarcely fail of success; and it would prove a blow so fatal to that nation, that she could not recover it during the whole course of the war." The French account of Lapeyrouse-Bonfils is essentially the same. Chevalier, who is silent as to details, justly remarks: "The cruise just made by the allied fleet was such as to injure the reputation of France and Spain. These two powers had made a great display of force which had produced no result." The English trade also received little injury. Guichen wrote home: "I have returned from a cruise fatiguing but not glorious."

(5) This mishap of the French was largely due to mismanagement by De Guichen, a skilful and usually a careful admiral. When Kempenfeldt fell in with him, all the French ships-of-war were to leeward of their convoy, while the English were to windward of it. The former, therefore, were unable to interpose in time; and the alternative remedy, of the convoy running down to leeward of their escort, could not be applied by all the merchant-ships in so large a body.

(6) "In the spring of 1780 the British admiralty had assembled in the Channel ports forty-five ships-of-the-line. The squadron at Brest was reduced to twelve or fifteen. ... To please Spain, twenty French ships-of-the-line had joined the flag of Admiral Cordova in Cadiz. In consequence of these dispositions, the English with their Channel fleet held in check the forces which we had in Brest and in Cadiz. Enemy's cruisers traversed freely the space between the Lizard and the Straits of Gibraltar." (Chevalier, p. 202.)

个毫无价值、毫无保护的海港，既是一种不可理喻的军事失误，还因舰队无法再拥有一个在秋、冬两季作战的牢固基地，而让此次行动以惨败而告终了。当时的法国在英吉利海峡沿岸还没有一流的港口；所以，秋、冬两季盛行的强劲西风，会将整支舰队都吹到北海去。

（4）比特森相当详尽地描述了联军这次作战会议上所进行的争论（第五卷，第395页）。在面对艰难形势时，这种作战会议通常都会久拖不决；而当时因为有人呼吁将贸易破坏战当成是一种具有决定意义的战争模式，故这种幻想便让此次作战会议更是久久无法做出决定了。M·德·博塞坚持说，"联合舰队应当将全部注意力放在伟大而可实现的目标上，即截击从西印度群岛驶往国内的英国舰队。由于联合舰队此时正是海洋霸主，故这一方案绝无不成功之理；并且，此举将会给英国以重击，使之在整个战争期间都无法恢复过来。"据法国人的记述，拉佩鲁斯·邦费斯的意见基本上也与此一致。对于细节方面一直保持沉默的希瓦利埃，曾经公平地说：联合舰队所进行的巡航战，不过是损害了法、西两国的声望罢了。这两个大国虽然声势浩大地炫耀了自己的实力，可结果却一无所成。"英国的海洋贸易也没有遭受到多大损失。基申伯爵曾在家信中如此写道："我从一场令人身心俱疲却毫不光荣的巡航战中回来了。"

（5）法军之所以遭受这种不幸，主要是基申伯爵这个老练且一向谨慎的海军司令指挥不当所造成的。凯姆本菲尔特与之遭遇的时候，所有的法国战舰都处于它们所护送的那一队商船的下风向，而英军则处于这支商船队的上风向。因此，法国战舰无法及时挡在英军和商船队之间；而唯一可以选择的补救措施，便是让那支商船队顺风驶向法国战舰的下风向，可商船数量实在太多，根本就做不到这一点。

（6）"1780年春，英国海军部在英吉利海峡沿岸诸港集结了45艘战舰。而布雷斯特的法国战舰，则减少到了12艘或15艘……为了满足西班牙的要求，法国派了20艘战舰，加入了加的斯的科尔多瓦上将麾下。由于此种部署，英国的海峡舰队便牢牢牵制住了我方在布雷斯特和加的斯两地的兵力。

In 1781 "the Cabinet of Versailles called the attention of Holland and Spain to the necessity of assembling at Brest a fleet strong enough to impose upon the ships which Great Britain kept in the Channel. The Dutch remained in the Texel, and the Spaniards did not leave Cadiz. From this state of things it resulted that the English, with forty ships-of-the-line, blocked seventy belonging to the allied powers." (p. 265.)

(7) "A question was very much agitated both in and out of Parliament; namely, Whether the intercepting of the French fleet under the Count de Grasse should not have been the first object of the British fleet under Vice-Admiral Darby, instead of losing time in going to Ireland, by which that opportunity was missed. The defeat of the French fleet would certainly totally have disconcerted the great plans which the enemies had formed in the East and West Indies. It would have insured the safety of the British West India islands; the Cape of Good Hope must have fallen into the hands of Britain; and the campaign in North America might have had a very different termination." (Beatson's Memoirs, vol. v. p. 341, where the contrary arguments are also stated.)

(8) This is one of the most common and flagrant violations of the principles of war, — stretching a thin line, everywhere inadequate, over an immense frontier. The clamors of trade and local interests make popular governments especially liable to it.

而敌人的巡逻舰，在利扎尔和直布罗陀海峡之间的海域却来去无阻。"(《希瓦利埃尔》，第202页)

1781年，"凡尔赛内阁要求荷兰和西班牙注意，必须在布雷斯特组建一支强大的舰队，使之足以压制英国部署在英吉利海峡的舰船才行。可荷兰舰队一直留在特塞尔，而西班牙舰队则没有离开加的斯。事态如此，所以英军便用40艘战舰，封锁了属于这三个盟国的70艘战舰。"(同上，第265页)

（7）"有一个问题，使得国会内外的人全都争执不休；那就是，达尔比中将所率英国舰队的第一目标，是否应当是截击德·格拉斯伯爵所率的法国舰队，而不是浪费时间赶往爱尔兰，从而错过了截击的大好机会。法国舰队战败，当然彻底违背了敌人在东、西印度群岛制定的伟大计划。倘若如此，就会确保英属西印度群岛的安全，好望角也必定早已落入了英国手中，而北美进行的战争也可能会有一个完全不同的结局了。"(参见比特森的《回忆录》，第五卷，第341页，该处还说明了一些与此相对的观点。)

（8）这是最常见和最明显的违背战争原则的行为之一，即沿着广袤的前线，将战线拉得过长，使得处处都兵力不足。民众进行贸易的诉求和地方利益，使得民选政府尤其易犯此种错误。

译者注：

［1］Algesiras：阿尔赫西拉斯。西班牙南部的一处港口，它与直布罗陀之间的海湾即称阿尔赫西拉斯湾。

［2］Yard：码。英制长度单位。1码等于3英尺或36英寸，相当于0.9144米。

CHAPTER XI
Critical Discussion of the Maritime War of 1778

The war of 1778, between Great Britain and the House of Bourbon, which is so inextricably associated with the American Revolution, stands by itself in one respect. It was purely a maritime war. Not only did the allied kingdoms carefully refrain from continental entanglements, which England in accordance with her former policy strove to excite, but there was between the two contestants an approach to equality on the sea which had not been realized since the days of Tourville. The points in dispute, the objects for which the war was undertaken or at which it aimed, were for the most part remote from Europe; and none of them was on the continent with the single exception of Gibraltar, the strife over which, being at the extreme point of a rugged and difficult salient, and separated from neutral nations by the whole of France and Spain, never threatened to drag in other parties than those immediately interested.

No such conditions existed in any war between the accession of Louis XIV. and the downfall of Napoleon. There was a period during the reign of the former in which the French navy was superior in number and equipment to the English and Dutch; but the policy and ambition of the sovereign was always directed to continental extension, and his naval power, resting on inadequate foundations, was ephemeral. During the first three-quarters of the eighteenth century there was practically no check to the sea power of England; great as were its effects upon the issues of the day, the absence of a capable rival made its operations barren of

第十一章[1] 批判性地讨论1778年海战

1778年大不列颠与波旁皇室之间进行的这场战争，虽说与美国革命战争紧密交织在一起，但也有其独立的一面。那就是，此次战争完全是一场海上战争。非但法、西等联合王国谨慎地避免陷入英国按照其原有政策努力想要激起的那种大陆战争，而且交战双方在海洋上的实力几近相等；这种情况，是自图维尔那个时代以来未曾有过的。双方争夺的地方，即引发此次战争或此次战争所指向的目标，大部分都远离欧洲，其中没有一处位于欧洲大陆上，只有直布罗陀例外；而由于此地处于一个崎岖不平、难以到达的凸出部分，且法国和西班牙将它与其他中立国完全隔开来了，所以除了那些与之有着直接利害关系的国家，决不会有让其他国家卷入进来的危险。

自路易十四登上王位到拿破仑垮台，其间没有哪一场战争存在过此种情况。在路易十四统治时期，法国海军曾一度在兵力和装备上都超过了英国和荷兰；不过，由于路易十四的政策和野心一向都是在欧洲大陆上进行扩张，所以他这种根基不牢的海军实力，不过是昙花一现罢了。在18世纪的前75年间，实际上英国的制海权丝毫都未受到遏制；尽管此种制海权对当时的争端影响巨大，但由于没有一个能够与之匹敌的对手，所以英国海军的作战行动并没有给我们留下军事上的什么经验教训。在法兰西共和国和法兰西帝国后期的历次战争中，双方舰船数量和火炮威力方面的平等只是表面上的一种错觉，

military lessons. In the later wars of the French Republic and Empire, the apparent equality in numbers of ships and weight of batteries was illusive, owing to the demoralization of the French officers and seamen by causes upon which it is not necessary here to enlarge. After some years of courageous but impotent effort, the tremendous disaster of Trafalgar proclaimed to the world the professional inefficiency of the French and Spanish navies, already detected by the keen eyes of Nelson and his brother officers, and upon which rested the contemptuous confidence that characterized his attitude, and to some extent his tactics, toward them. Thenceforward the emperor "turned his eyes from the only field of battle where fortune had been unfaithful to him, and deciding to pursue England elsewhere than upon the seas, undertook to restore his navy, but without reserving to it any share in a strife become more than ever furious. ... Up to the last day of the Empire he refused to offer to this restored navy, full of ardor and confidence, the opportunity to measure itself with the enemy." Great Britain resumed her old position as unquestioned mistress of the seas.

The student of naval war will therefore expect to find a particular interest in the plans and methods of the parties to this great contest, and especially where they concern the general conduct of the whole war, or of certain large and clearly defined portions of it; in the strategic purpose which gave, or should have given, continuity to their actions from first to last, and in the strategic movements which affected for good or ill the fortunes of the more limited periods, which may be called naval campaigns. For while it cannot be conceded that the particular battles are, even at this day, wholly devoid of tactical instruction, which it has been one of the aims of the preceding pages to elicit, it is undoubtedly true that, like all the tactical systems of history, they have had their day, and their present usefulness to the student is rather in the mental training, in the forming of correct tactical habits of thought, than in supplying models

因为法国海军官兵士气涣散，至于造成这种情况的原因，在此我们无需详述。经过数年勇敢却无效的努力之后，特拉法尔加海战这次巨大的惨败向世界宣告了法国和西班牙海军在职业上的无能，而纳尔逊及其军中同僚早已敏锐地洞察这一切，所以他在看待法国和西班牙海军时，便带有蔑视对手的信心，并且从某种程度上来说，他在采取对付两国海军的战术时，也是如此。从此以后，法国皇帝"便将注意力从命运唯一并未眷顾他的这个战场转移开去，决定不在海洋上而在别的地方与英国展开较量，并且开始重建海军，可他却并没有在一场空前激烈的战争中，为海军预留发挥作用的空间。……直到法兰西帝国的最后一刻，他都没有给这支已经得到重建、充满了热情和信心的海军提供与敌较量的机会。"于是，大不列颠便恢复了昔日的地位，再次成为了无可争议的海洋霸主。

因此，研究海军作战的学者，便会指望从此次大规模战争中各方所制定的计划和采取的方法中，尤其是在涉及到整个战争的总体部署或者某些重大而有着明确划分之阶段的总体部署中，找出自己特别感兴趣的方面来；还会希望在自始至终赋予或应当赋予各方作战行动以连续性的战略目标，以及对可称之为海军战役的那些范围更窄的阶段产生了有利或不利影响的战略运动中，找出自己特别感兴趣的方面来。因为，尽管我们不可能认为即便是在如今，具体的战斗也完全没有战术指导——这一点，正是我们在前面各个章节中想要得出的结论，但毫无疑问的是，跟历史上所有的战术体系一样，这些战术原则也有过辉煌的时候，而如今它们对于学者的价值，即在于它们能够锻炼意志，能够培养正确的战术思想习惯，而不是说它们提供了让人们进行准确模仿的典范。另一方面，在大规模战斗之前进行的机动和准备，或者说通过将这两方面熟练而有力地结合起

for close imitation. On the other hand, the movements which precede and prepare for great battles, or which, by their skilful and energetic combinations, attain great ends without the actual contact of arms, depend upon factors more permanent than the weapons of the age, and therefore furnish principles of more enduring value.

In a war undertaken for any object, even if that object be the possession of a particular territory or position, an attack directly upon the place coveted may not be, from the military point of view, the best means of obtaining it. The end upon which the military operations are directed may therefore be other than the object which the belligerent government wishes to obtain, and it has received a name of its own, — the objective. In the critical consideration of any war it is necessary, first, to put clearly before the student's eye the objects desired by each belligerent; then, to consider whether the objective chosen is the most likely, in case of success, to compass those objects; and finally, to study the merits or faults of the various movements by which the objective is approached. The minuteness with which such an examination is conducted will depend upon the extent of the work which the inquirer proposes to himself; but it will generally conduce to clearness if an outline, giving only the main features unencumbered by detail, should precede a more exhaustive discussion. When such principal lines are thoroughly grasped, details are easily referred to them, and fall into place. The effort here will be confined to presenting such an outline, as being alone fitted to the scope of this work.

The principal parties to the War of 1778 were, on the one hand, Great Britain; on the other, the House of Bourbon, controlling the two great kingdoms of France and Spain. The American colonies, being already engaged in an unequal struggle with the mother-country, gladly welcomed an event so important to them; while in 1780 Holland was deliberately forced by England into a war from which she had nothing to gain and all to lose. The object

来，从而能够不战而实现伟大的目标，由于它们依赖的不是当时的武器装备，而是更为恒久性的一些因素，所以能够提供具有更具永久性价值的作战原则。

无论战争的目标是什么，哪怕是以占领某一处具体的领土或位置为目标，从军事的角度来看，对觊觎已久的地方直接进击可能都并不是获取此处的最佳办法。因此，军事作战行动所针对的对象，就可以不是交战国政府希望得到的地方，从而使得这个对象有了自己的专属名称，即"作战目标"。在批判性地研究任何战争时，我们首先必须让学者看清各个交战国希望实现的目标，然后再来考虑各国所选取的作战目标，倘若进攻取胜的话，是否最有可能实现那些目标，最后再去研究用以接近作战目标的各种作战运动的优点和缺点。进行此种研究的精密程度，将取决于研究者为自己所设定的研究范围；但在进行更为详尽的讨论之前列出一份提纲，提纲中只标出主要特征，不涉及具体细节，通常都会让研究者了解得更加清晰。彻底理解了这些基本原则之后，细节情况就很容易归类，并且变得有条不紊了。我们在此也只是想列出这样的一个提纲来，因为只有这样的提纲，才适合于本书的论述范围。

1778年战争中主要的参战方，一边是大不列颠，另一边则是掌控着法国和西班牙这两个伟大王国的波旁皇室。业已在与母国进行一场力量悬殊之斗争的美洲殖民地，欣然欢迎这场对它们来说如此重要的战事；而在1780年，英国还刻意迫使荷兰加入了这场一无所获、只有损失的战争。美国人的目标很简单，那就是让自己的国家摆脱英国的控制。当时的美国很贫穷，又没有海军，只有为数不多的巡洋舰，用于破坏敌人的海上贸易，所以必定会使他们致力于陆上战争；虽说这一点事实上相当于一种有利于联军的强

of the Americans was perfectly simple, — to rid their country out of the hands of the English. Their poverty and their lack of military sea power, with the exception of a few cruisers that preyed upon the enemy's commerce, necessarily confined their efforts to land warfare, which constituted indeed a powerful diversion in favor of the allies and an exhausting drain upon the resources of Great Britain, but which it was in the power of the latter to stop at once by abandoning the contest. Holland, on the other hand, being safe from invasion by land, showed little desire for anything more than to escape with as little external loss as possible, through the assistance of the allied navies. The object of these two minor parties may therefore be said to have been the cessation of the war; whereas the principals hoped from its continuance certain changed conditions, which constituted their objects.

With Great Britain also the object of the war was very simple. Having been led into a lamentable altercation with her most promising colonies, the quarrel had gone on step by step till she was threatened with their loss. To maintain forcible control when willing adhesion had departed, she had taken up arms against them, and her object in so doing was to prevent a break in those foreign possessions with which, in the eyes of that generation, her greatness was indissolubly connected. The appearance of France and Spain as active supporters of the colonists' cause made no change in England's objects, whatever change of objective her military plans may, or should, have undergone. The danger of losing the continental colonies was vastly increased by these accessions to the ranks of her enemies, which brought with them also a threat of loss, soon to be realized in part, of other valuable foreign possessions. England, in short, as regards the objects of the war, was strictly on the defensive; she feared losing much, and at best only hoped to keep what she had. By forcing Holland into war, however, she obtained a military advantage; for, without increasing the strength of her opponents, several

大牵制，会极大地损耗大不列颠的资源，但是权力掌握在大不列颠手里，因为它可以马上放弃北美的这场争夺战。而另一方面，荷兰由于没有被别国从大陆入侵之虞，所以并无他求，只想在盟国海军的帮助之下，付出尽可能少的外部代价来摆脱这场战争。因此，美国和荷兰这两个小参战方的目标，便可以说是结束这场战争；然而，那3个主要参战方却希望继续进行并从中获益，自然使得形势发生了变化，这实际上就是它们的目标。

对于大不列颠来说，其目标也简单得很。英国连同那些前景广阔的殖民地都被拖入了这场可悲的纷争当中，而这场争夺战一步步地往下，发展到如今该国有失去这些殖民地的危险了。为了在美国人民不愿再依附于它的时候对这些殖民地维持强有力的控制，英国已经拿起武器，对这些殖民地兴师问罪；而它这样做的目的，则是阻止这些海外领地从英国分裂出去，因为在当时的那一代人看来，英国之伟大与这些殖民地是密不可分的。法国和西班牙积极支持殖民者独立的表象，无论英国所定作战计划中的作战目标可能或者应当发生何种改变，实际上都没有改变其战争目标。失去美洲大陆上这些殖民地的危险，还因这些殖民地加入英国的敌方阵列而大大增加了；而这一做法，又给英国带来了失去其他重要海外领地的危险，并且这种危险很快就部分地变成了现实。总而言之，从战争目标这个方面来看，英国完全处于被动防御的形势；该国因为担心失去太多，所以充其量也只是希望守住自己已经拥有的东西罢了。然而，通过迫使荷兰加入此次战争，英国却在军事上获得了一种优势；因为这样一来，既未增强对手的实力，而英国的兵力又可以毫不费力地进入荷兰那几个虽说重要、防御力量却很薄弱的军事和贸易据点。

important but ill-defined military and commercial positions were thereby laid open to her arms.

The views and objects of France and Spain were more complex. The moral incentives of hereditary enmity and desire of revenge for the recent past doubtless weighed strongly, as in France did also the sympathy of the salons and philosophers with the colonists' struggle for freedom; but powerfully as sentimental considerations affect the action of nations, only the tangible means by which it is expected to gratify them admit of statement and measurement. France might wish to regain her North American possessions; but the then living generation of colonists had too keen personal recollection of the old contests to acquiesce in any such wishes as to Canada. The strong inherited distrust of the French, which characterized the Americans of the revolutionary era, has been too much overlooked in the glow of gratitude which followed the effectual sympathy and assistance then given; but it was understood at the time, and France felt, that to renew those pretensions might promote, between people of the same race only recently alienated, a reconciliation by just concessions, which a strong and high-minded party of Englishmen had never ceased to advocate. She therefore did not avow, perhaps did not entertain, this object. On the contrary, she formally renounced all claim to any part of the continent which was then, or had recently been, under the power of the British crown, but stipulated for freedom of action in conquering and retaining any of the West India Islands, while all the other colonies of Great Britain were, of course, open to her attack. The principal objects at which France aimed were therefore the English West Indies and that control of India which had passed into English hands, and also to secure in due time the independence of the United States, after they had wrought a sufficient diversion in her favor. With the policy of exclusive trade which characterized that generation, the loss of these important possessions was expected

法、西两国的意图和目标则要复杂一些。道义、世世代代的敌意以及想一雪不久之前的耻辱，无疑都起到了重要的作用；而在法国国内，许多名流人士与思想家对于殖民者争取自由的斗争，也都感同身受。不过，尽管情感因素极大地影响到了两国的行动，但只是那些有望满足两国要求的切实办法，才值得我们来进行说明和权衡。法国有可能希望收复该国在北美洲的殖民地；不过，当时还活着的那一代殖民者全都对过去的那些战争记忆犹新，所以是不会容许法国重新占有加拿大的。对法国持有根深蒂固的不信任感，是革命年代美国人的普遍特征，可人们却因美国人在接受了法国有效的同情与援助之后所表现出来的感激之情，而极大地忽视了后者的这种不信任感；不过，当时的人都理解这一点，而法国也认为，重申那些领土要求，可能通过公平公正的让步，促使英、法这两个属于同一种族、关系最近才生疏起来的民族和解，因为一群强势而傲慢的英国人从未停止过这样的主张。因此，法国没有承认、或许甚至根本就并不怀有这样的一个目标。相反，该国还正式宣布，放弃对当时或最近才处于英国势力之下的所有北美大陆领土的主权声索，但前提条件是，法国能够自由攻取和保留西印度群岛中的任何岛屿，而英国的其他殖民地自然也应任由法国来进攻了。因此，法国的主要目标，便是英属西印度群岛和重新控制已经转入英国之手的印度，以及在充分而有利地分散了英国的注意力之后，确保合众国在适当的时候独立。由于当时各国普遍推行专有贸易政策，所以法国希望，失去这些重要的殖民地，会削弱英国那种伟大的贸易实力，因为此种实力正是英国繁荣兴旺起来的基础———也就是说，在削弱英国实力的同时，增强法国的实力。实际上，整个这场本该规模更大的冲突，可以说一直就是促使法国参战的原因；该国的所有目标，归

to lessen that commercial greatness upon which the prosperity of England depended, — to weaken her and to strengthen France. In fact, the strife which should be greater may be said to have been the animating motive of France; all objects were summed up in the one supreme end to which they contributed, — maritime and political superiority over England.

Preponderance over England, in combination with France, was also the aim of the equally humbled but less vigorous kingdom of Spain; but there was a definiteness in the injuries suffered and the objects specially sought by her which is less easily found in the broader views of her ally. Although no Spaniard then living could remember the Spanish flag flying over Minorca, Gibraltar, or Jamaica, the lapse of time had not reconciled the proud and tenacious nation to their loss; nor was there on the part of the Americans the same traditional objection to the renewal of Spanish sovereignty over the two Floridas that was felt with reference to Canada.

Such, then, were the objects sought by the two nations, whose interposition changed the whole character of the American Revolutionary War. It is needless to say that they did not all appear among the causes, or pretexts, avowed for engaging in hostility; but sagacious English opinion of the day rightly noted, as embodying in a few words the real ground of action of the united Bourbon Courts, the following phrase in the French manifesto: "To avenge their respective injuries, and to put an end to that tyrannical empire which England has usurped, and claims to maintain upon the ocean." In short, as regards the objects of the war the allies were on the offensive, as England was thrown upon the defensive.

The tyrannical empire which England was thus accused, and not unjustly, of exercising over the seas, rested upon her great sea power, actual or latent; upon her commerce and armed shipping, her commercial establishments, colonies, and naval stations in all parts of the world. Up to this time her scattered colonies had been bound to her by ties of affectionate sentiment,

结起来就是一个最高目标，即在海洋和政治两个方面都获得能够压制英国的优势。

与法国联起手来获得压制英国的优势，也是同样承受过耻辱但不那么强大的西班牙王国的目标；不过，该国所遭受的损失和所追求的目标都非常明确，而这一点，在其盟国那些更为广泛的意图当中，表现得却不那么明显了。尽管当时的西班牙人都不记得西班牙国旗曾经在米诺卡、直布罗陀和牙买加等地飘扬过，但时光的流逝，却并未让这个骄傲而顽强的民族甘心承受损失；而美国人这一边，对于西班牙重新统治牵涉到加拿大的东、西佛罗里达地区，也没有那种传统的反对态度。

所以，法、西两国的目标就是上述方面；这两个国家的干预，也改变了美国革命战争的整体性质。从两国与英国公开交战的种种原因或理由当中，并非全然能够看出这些目标来，这一点我们无需多说；不过，当时一些卓有远见的人士曾经正确地指出，法国政府的下述宣言，寥寥数语便体现出了这两个波旁王国联合起来参战的真正原因："为了一雪前耻，报复两国所遭受的损失，为了终结英格兰所篡取并在海洋之上保持的那个专制之帝国。"总而言之，从此次战争的目标来看，盟军处于主动进攻的态势，而英国则被迫采取了守势。

两国如此指责英国是一个残暴的帝国并非空穴来风，因为英国以其伟大的制海权为基础（不管是现实的还是潜在的），凭借商船、军舰、贸易机构、殖民地和遍及世界各地的海军基地，完全控制了各个海域。迄今为止，该国散布于各地的殖民地之所以一直都臣服于它，是因为有着殖民地对母国怀有深厚情感的这种纽带，是因为各殖民地仍然有着通过与母国保持密切的贸易联系而谋求自我利益的强大动机，是因为英国强大的海

and by the still stronger motive of self-interest through the close commercial connection with the mother-country and the protection afforded by the constant presence of her superior navy. Now a break was made in the girdle of strong ports upon which her naval power was based, by the revolt of the continental colonies; while the numerous trade interests between them and the West Indies, which were injured by the consequent hostilities, tended to divide the sympathies of the islands also. The struggle was not only for political possession and commercial use. It involved a military question of the first importance, — whether a chain of naval stations covering one of the shores of the Atlantic, linking Canada and Halifax with the West Indies, and backed by a thriving seafaring population, should remain in the hands of a nation which had so far used its unprecedented sea power with consistent, resolute aggressiveness, and with almost unbroken success.

While Great Britain was thus embarrassed by the difficulty of maintaining her hold upon her naval bases, which were the defensive element of her naval strength, her offensive naval power, her fleet, was threatened by the growth of the armed shipping of France and Spain, which now confronted her upon the field which she had claimed as her own, with an organized military force of equal or superior material strength. The moment was therefore favorable for attacking the great Power whose wealth, reaped from the sea, had been a decisive factor in the European wars of the past century. The next question was the selection of the points of attack — of the principal objectives upon which the main effort of the assailants should be steadily directed, and of the secondary objectives by which the defence should be distracted and its strength dissipated.

One of the wisest French statesmen of that day, Turgot, held that it was to the interest of France that the colonies should not achieve their independence. If subdued by exhaustion,

军常伴左右，能为诸殖民地提供保护。如今，美洲大陆上各个殖民地爆发的革命，在英国海军实力所倚赖的那一圈强大海港之链上打开了一个缺口；而这些殖民地与西印度群岛之间大量的贸易利益，也因随后的战争而受到了损害，从而分化了西印度群岛，使得各个岛屿的行动不一致了。此次战争，并非仅仅是为了政治占领和贸易利益。它还涉及到了一个最重要的军事问题——即覆盖了大西洋一侧海岸的那一连串的海军基地，非但将加拿大、哈利法克斯与西印度群岛联结起来，还有蓬勃增长的海上人口所支持，它们是否应当继续掌控在英国手里呢？因为迄今为止，英国已经利用其史无前例的那种制海权进行了一以贯之、坚定不移的侵略挑衅，并且几乎毫无例外地获得了胜利。

就在英国如此左支右绌，难以继续掌控它赖以保护其海军实力的那些海军基地之时，该国用于进攻的海军力量，即该国的舰队，也受到了法、西两国军舰实力日益增长的威胁；这两个国家的军舰，如今已经可以在英国曾经宣称是其领土的海域同英国舰队对阵，并且拥有了一支兵力与英军不相上下或者说甚至优于英军的有组织的军事力量。所以，此时正是进攻这个大国的有利时机；英国的财富都源自海上，且一直是上一个世纪欧洲历次战争中的决定性因素。接下来的问题，便是选择进攻地点——即进攻者始终都应当主攻的那些主要作战目标，以及选择可以分散英国的防御力量、削弱其实力的次要目标了。

当时属于法国最英明政治家之一的杜尔哥曾经认为，美洲诸殖民地不获得独立，符合法国的利益。如果这些殖民地因民穷财尽而屈服了，那么它们也不会给英国带来什么好处；倘若通过军事控制要害之地而攻克了这些殖民地，这些殖民地也没有民穷财尽的话，那么英国就必须不停地镇压它们的反抗，而这也会成为不断削弱英国实力的一个

their strength was lost to England; if reduced by a military tenure of controlling points, but not exhausted, the necessity of constant repression would be a continual weakness to the mother-country. Though this opinion did not prevail in the councils of the French government, which wished the ultimate independence of America, it contained elements of truth which effectually moulded the policy of the war. If benefit to the United States, by effecting their deliverance, were the principal object, the continent became the natural scene, and its decisive military points the chief objectives, of operations; but as the first object of France was not to benefit America, but to injure England, sound military judgment dictated that the continental strife, so far from being helped to a conclusion, should be kept in vigorous life. It was a diversion ready made to the hand of France and exhausting to Great Britain, requiring only so much support as would sustain a resistance to which the insurgents were bound by the most desperate alternatives. The territory of the thirteen colonies therefore should not be the principal objective of France; much less that of Spain.

The commercial value of the English West Indies made them tempting objects to the French, who adapted themselves with peculiar readiness to the social conditions of that region, in which their colonial possessions were already extensive. Besides the two finest of the Lesser Antilles, Guadeloupe and Martinique, which she still retains, France then held Sta. Lucia and the western half of Hayti. She might well hope by successful war to add most of the English Antilles, and thus to round off a truly imperial tropical dependency; while, though debarred from Jamaica by the susceptibilities of Spain, it might be possible to win back that magnificent island for an allied and weaker nation. But however desirable as possessions, and therefore as objects, the smaller Antilles might be, their military tenure depended too entirely upon control of the sea for them to be in themselves proper objectives. The French government, therefore, forbade

因素。尽管这种观点在当时希望美国最终独立的法国政府内阁中并不普遍，但其中还是含有一些真知灼见，从而有效地影响到了法国对于此次战争的政策。假如通过法国所提供的帮助，让合众国受益是法国的主要目标，那么美洲大陆就会变成一个自然而然的战场，而那些具有决定性意义的军事要地，便是主要的作战目标了；可是，法国的首要目标并非让美国受益，而是削弱英国，因此合理的军事判断，便决定了法国应当让这场大陆战争继续大张旗鼓地进行下去，而不是去帮助结束这场战争。这是法国手中现成的一种会消耗大不列颠实力的牵制手段，法国只需稍稍提供支持，让那些只能最孤注一掷的叛乱分子能够继续抵抗英国就行。因此，那13个殖民地的领土就不应当是法国的主要作战目标，而对于西班牙而言，就更是如此了。

英属西印度群岛的贸易价值，使得它们成为了让法国很感兴趣的目标；法国人已经带着罕有的敏捷，迅速适应了该地区的社会环境，而该国在这一地区的殖民地，范围本来也已经很广袤了。除了如今该国仍然拥有的、小安的列斯群岛中的瓜达鲁佩和马提尼克这两个最好的岛屿，法国当时还占领着圣卢西亚和海地岛的西半部分。法国有可能还想通过一场成功的战争，将安的列斯群岛中的大多数英属岛屿都纳入自己囊中，从而圆满地建立起一个真正辉煌的热带属国；尽管因为西班牙敏感多疑，法国的势力无法渗入牙买加，但重新获得这个伟大岛屿的支持，让实力较弱的牙买加成为法国的盟国，还是有可能做到的。不过，作为殖民地、并因此而成为法国的战争目标的小安的列斯群岛，无论是多么值得拥有，军事占领这些地方都太过完全依赖于制海权，因此它们本身都不是合适的作战目标。所以，就算可以夺取，法国政府也不允许其海军指挥官们去占

its naval commanders to occupy such as they might seize. They were to make the garrisons prisoners, destroy the defences, and so retire. In the excellent military port of Fort Royal, Martinique, in Cap Français, and in the strong allied harbor of Havana, a fleet of adequate size found good, secure, and well-distributed bases; while the early and serious loss of Sta. Lucia must be attributed to the mismanagement of the French fleet and the professional ability of the English admiral. On shore, in the West Indies, the rival powers therefore found themselves about equally provided with the necessary points of support; mere occupation of others could not add to their military strength, thenceforth dependent upon the numbers and quality of the fleets. To extend occupation further with safety, the first need was to obtain maritime supremacy, not only locally, but over the general field of war. Otherwise occupation was precarious, unless enforced by a body of troops so large as to entail expense beyond the worth of the object. The key of the situation in the West Indies being thus in the fleets, these became the true objectives of the military effort; and all the more so because the real military usefulness of the West Indian ports in this war was as an intermediate base, between Europe and the American continent, to which the fleets retired when the armies went into winter quarters. No sound strategic operation on shore was undertaken in the West Indies except the seizure of Sta. Lucia by the English, and the abortive plan against Jamaica in 1782; nor was any serious attempt against a military port, as Barbadoes or Fort Royal, possible, until naval preponderance was assured either by battle or by happy concentration of force. The key of the situation, it must be repeated, was in the fleet.

The influence of naval power, of an armed fleet, upon the war on the American continent has also been indicated in the opinions of Washington and Sir Henry Clinton; while the situation in the East Indies, regarded as a field by itself, has been so largely discussed under the head of Suffren's campaign, that it needs here only to repeat that everything there depended upon

领这样的地方。法国海军应当围困这些地方，俘虏其中的守军，毁掉这些地方的防御工事，然后就撤退。一支规模适中的舰队，可以将马提尼克岛上的皇家要塞这个优秀的军港、法兰西角以及哈瓦那这个实力强大的联合军港，当成是优良、安全而且布局合理的基地；而早前丢掉圣卢西亚这样的重大损失，既应归咎于法国舰队的指挥不当，也应归因于那位英国海军上将高超的职业才能。因此，在西印度群岛的陆地上，这两大交战国便发现，双方都拥有差不多势均力敌、提供支援所必需的据点；仅仅占领其他地方，并不能增强各自的军事实力，因为自此以后，双方的军事实力便都取决于舰队的数量和质量了。要想进一步安全地扩张占领范围，首先必须取得制海权，不仅要取得局部的制海权，还要取得整个战争领域的制海权。否则的话，这种占领就是不牢靠的，除非由一支兵力极其庞大的陆军来实施占领；可这样一来，所需代价就会超过目标地本身的价值了。由于西印度群岛形势的关键就在于舰队，所以这些舰队便变成了双方主攻的真正目标；而因为西印度群岛诸港在此次战争中真正的军事价值，在于它们是欧洲和美洲大陆之间的海军基地，使得陆军进入冬季营地进行休整时舰队可以撤回到这些港口，所以情况就更是如此了。除了英军夺取圣卢西亚，以及1782年计划进攻牙买加无果而终之外，在西印度群岛并未进行过什么战略上正确的陆上作战；而在通过战斗或者巧妙地集结起兵力，从而确保海军获得优势之前，也没有哪一方曾经正而八经地想去攻打像巴巴多斯或皇家要塞那样的军港。故我们必须重申，形势的关键就在于舰队。

海军力量与武装舰队对美洲大陆上进行的这场战争所产生的影响，在华盛顿和亨利·柯林顿两人的观点当中都体现出来了；而东印度群岛本身作为一处战场，其形势我

control of the sea by a superior naval force. The capture of Trincomalee, essential as it was to the French squadron which had no other base, was, like that of Sta. Lucia, a surprise, and could only have been effected by the defeat, or, as happened, by the absence of the enemy's fleet. In North America and India sound military policy pointed out, as the true objective, the enemy's fleet, upon which also depended the communications with the mother-countries. There remains Europe, which it is scarcely profitable to examine at length as a separate field of action, because its relations to the universal war are so much more important. It may simply be pointed out that the only two points in Europe whose political transfer was an object of the war were Gibraltar and Minorca; the former of which was throughout, by the urgency of Spain, made a principal objective of the allies. The tenure of both these depended, obviously, upon control of the sea.

In a sea war, as in all others, two things are from the first essential, — a suitable base upon the frontier, in this case the seaboard, from which the operations start, and an organized military force, in this case a fleet, of size and quality adequate to the proposed operations. If the war, as in the present instance, extends to distant parts of the globe, there will be needed in each of those distant regions secure ports for the shipping, to serve as secondary, or contingent, bases of the local war. Between these secondary and the principal, or home, bases there must be reasonably secure communication, which will depend upon military control of the intervening sea. This control must be exercised by the navy, which will enforce it either by clearing the sea in all directions of hostile cruisers, thus allowing the ships of its own nation to pass with reasonable security, or by accompanying in force (convoying) each train of supply-ships necessary for the support of the distant operations. The former method aims at a widely diffused effort of the national power, the other at a concentration of it upon that part of the sea where the convoy is at a given moment. Whichever be adopted, the communications will

们已经在关于苏弗朗的作战部分进行了充分的讨论，所以在这里只需再次强调下面这一点就行：此处的一切，皆取决于用一支兵力上占有优势的海军掌控住海洋。亭可马里对于并没有其他基地的法国舰队来说是不可或缺的，其陷落跟圣卢西亚的陷落一样令人震惊；而要攻取这个地方，只能是打败敌方舰队，或者像实际情况那样，只有在没有敌方舰队的情况下才能做到。在北美和印度地区，正确的军事政策都已表明，敌方舰队就是真正的作战目标，因为两地与母国的交通联系都是依赖舰队来进行的。剩下的就是欧洲了，但将其作为一个独立的战场来进行仔细研究并无好处，因为欧洲与全球战争的关系重要得多。我们可以简单指出，欧洲只有两个地方，即直布罗陀和米诺卡，它们的政治易手才是此次战争的目标；前者的政治易手过程贯穿战争始终，而在西班牙的敦促之下，直布罗陀也变成了盟军一个主要的作战目标。很显然，占领这两处倚赖的也是制海权。

在海战中，就像在其他所有的战争中一样，首先必须具备两个条件——边境上要有一个合适的基地，海战情况下就是在沿海地区拥有一个基地，作战行动即从此处开始；拥有一支有组织的军事力量，在海战情况下就是一支舰队，且其规模和质量都须胜任即将发起的作战行动。倘若像当前这个实例一样，战火蔓延到了世界上那些与本国相距遥远的地区，那么在每一个遥远的地区都应当拥有安全可靠的海港，将其当成局部战争的次级基地或者潜在基地才行。在这些次级基地与主要基地或国内大本营之间，必须有相当安全的交通联系，而此种安全的交通联系又取决于对中间海域的军事控制。这种控制，只能由海军来实施；或是全方位清除海上的敌方巡洋舰，从而让本国的舰船能够安全通过，或是对运送在这些遥远地区作战所需给养的每一支船队进行武装护送（即护

doubtless be strengthened by the military holding of good harbors, properly spaced yet not too numerous, along the routes, — as, for instance, the Cape of Good Hope and the Mauritius. Stations of this kind have always been necessary, but are doubly so now, as fuel needs renewing more frequently than did the provisions and supplies in former days. These combinations of strong points at home and abroad, and the condition of the communications between them, may be called the strategic features of the general military situation, by which, and by the relative strength of the opposing fleets, the nature of the operations must be determined. In each of the three divisions of the field, Europe, America, and India, under which for sake of clearness the narrative has been given, the control of the sea has been insisted upon as the determining factor, and the hostile fleet therefore indicated as the true objective. Let the foregoing considerations now be applied to the whole field of war, and see how far the same conclusion holds good of it, and if so, what should have been the nature of the operations on either side.

In Europe the home base of Great Britain was on the English Channel, with the two principal arsenals of Plymouth and Portsmouth. The base of the allied powers was on the Atlantic, the principal military ports being Brest, Ferrol, and Cadiz. Behind these, within the Mediterranean, were the dock-yards of Toulon and Cartagena, over against which stood the English station Port Mahon, in Minorca. The latter, however, may be left wholly out of account, being confined to a defensive part during the war, as the British fleet was not able to spare any squadron to the Mediterranean. Gibraltar, on the contrary, by its position, effectually watched over detachments or reinforcements from within the Straits, provided it were utilized as the station of a body of ships adequate to the duty. This was not done; the British European fleet being kept tied to the Channel, that is, to home defence, and making infrequent visits to the Rock to convoy supplies essential to the endurance of the garrison. There was, however,

航）。前一种方式旨在努力将国家实力分散部署，而后一种方式则旨在将国家实力集中在某个特定时间需要进行护航的那处海域。无论采取哪种方式，军事占领交通沿线某些优良的、间距合理但数量又不太多的海港，比如说好望角和毛里求斯，无疑都会让海上交通变得更加安全可靠。此种基地一向都是兵家必争之地，而如今则更是这样了，因为跟过去的装备补给相比，现在的汽船更需频繁地补充燃料。国内与海外这些强大据点的结合情况，以及它们之间的交通联络状况，可以称作一般军事形势的战略特征；而所有作战行动的性质，则由这些战略特征以及敌方舰队的相对实力所决定。在欧洲、美洲和印度这3大战区，制海权一直都是一个决定性因素，因而敌方舰队便都是双方真正的作战目标；为清晰起见，本书已经分别说明过上述每一战区的具体情况了。现在，我们不妨将前述思考所得应用于整个战场，来看一看同样的结论在多大程度上仍然有效，并且看一看在此种情况下双方的作战行动本应具有一种什么样的性质。

在欧洲，大不列颠的国内大本营，就是英吉利海峡边的普利茅斯和朴茨茅斯这两个重要的海军军舰修造所。而法、西联军的大本营则在大西洋沿岸，主要军港有布雷斯特、费罗尔和加的斯。在这些军港背面的地中海地区，则有土伦和卡塔赫纳两个海军造船厂，它们正对着米诺卡岛上的马翁港这个英国据点。然而，后者完全可以不予考虑，因为在此次战争期间，英国海军根本无法匀出舰队前往地中海地区，所以马翁港完全处于防守之中。相反，直布罗陀由于位置得天独厚，故只要将它用作一支能够胜任其任务的舰队的基地，就能够有效地监视从直布罗陀海峡出来的特遣舰队或援军的动向。但英国却没有这样做；英军的欧洲舰队被牵制在英吉利海峡中，也就是说，这支舰队需要防

a difference in the parts played by Port Mahon and Gibraltar. The former, being at the time wholly unimportant, received no attention from the allies until late in the war, when it fell after a six months' siege; whereas the latter, being considered of the first importance, absorbed from the beginning a very large part of the allied attack, and so made a valuable diversion in favor of Great Britain. To this view of the principal features of the natural strategic situation in Europe may properly be added the remark, that such aid as Holland might be inclined to send to the allied fleets had a very insecure line of communication, being forced to pass along the English base on the Channel. Such aid in fact was never given.

In North America the local bases of the war at its outbreak were New York, Narragansett Bay, and Boston. The two former were then held by the English, and were the most important stations on the continent, from their position, susceptibility of defence, and resources. Boston had passed into the hands of the Americans, and was therefore at the service of the allies. From the direction actually given to the war, by diverting the active English operations to the Southern States in 1779, Boston was thrown outside the principal theatre of operations, and became from its position militarily unimportant; but had the plan been adopted of isolating New England by holding the line of the Hudson and Lake Champlain, and concentrating military effort to the eastward, it will be seen that these three ports would all have been of decisive importance to the issue. South of New York, the Delaware and Chesapeake Bays undoubtedly offered tempting fields for maritime enterprise; but the width of the entrances, the want of suitable and easily defended points for naval stations near the sea, the wide dispersal of the land forces entailed by an attempt to hold so many points, and the sickliness of the locality during a great part of the year, should have excepted them from a principal part in the plan of the first campaigns. It is not necessary to include them among the local bases of the war. To the extreme south the

守本土，只是偶尔护送维持此处守军所必需的给养才会来到直布罗陀。然而，马翁港和直布罗陀两地所起的作用有所不同。前者由于处在一个完全无关痛痒的时期，所以直到战争后期才引起法、西联军的注意，于是联军在围困了6个月之后，便攻下了此地；但因为双方都认为后者即直布罗陀极其重要，所以它从一开始便遭到了联军多次进攻，从而形成了有利于大不列颠的一支重要的牵制力量。在如此看待欧洲自然战略形势的主要特征的同时，我们不妨还恰当地多说一句，即荷兰就算有意向联合舰队派遣援军，一路上的交通也是很不安全的，因为此种支援必须经由英吉利海峡上的英军基地才能到达。事实上，荷兰也从未给予过联军此种支援。

在北美地区，战争爆发之初有纽约、纳拉干塞特湾和波士顿等本地基地。前两地当时正由英军据守，因为位置得当、易于防守且资源丰富，所以它们是美洲大陆上最重要的据点。波士顿已经易手到了美国人的控制之下，故为联军所用。由于此次战争的实际走向，使得1779年英军的作战行动全都转移到了南部诸州，故波士顿不再属于主要战场，且因其位置而在军事上不再具有重要性了；不过，倘若采用了通过占领哈德逊河与尚普兰湖一线并将军事行动集中在其东面来孤立新英格兰地区的那个作战计划，那么我们就会看出，这3个港口对于战争结局都会产生至关重要的决定性作用。纽约南部的特拉华湾与切萨皮克湾，无疑都是海军大显身手的合适战场；不过，由于两个海湾的入口都太宽，附近海域又没有合适且易于防守的地方来建立海军基地，而陆军想要守住如此之多的地方便必须大量分散兵力，再加上那一年大部分时间里此地都疫病肆虐，所以在第一阶段的战役计划中，本来就不该让此地发挥主要作用。我们也没有必要将它们当成

English were drawn by the ignis fatuus of expected support among the people. They failed to consider that even if a majority there preferred quiet to freedom, that very quality would prevent them from rising against the revolutionary government by which, on the English theory, they were oppressed; yet upon such a rising the whole success of this distant and in its end most unfortunate enterprise was staked. The local base of this war apart was Charleston, which passed into the hands of the British in May, 1780, eighteen months after the first expedition had landed in Georgia.

The principal local bases of the war in the West Indies are already known through the previous narrative. They were for the English, Barbadoes, Sta. Lucia, and to a less degree Antigua. A thousand miles to leeward was the large island of Jamaica, with a dock-yard of great natural capabilities at Kingston. The allies held, in the first order of importance, Fort Royal in Martinique, and Havana; in the second order, Guadeloupe and Cap Français. A controlling feature of the strategic situation in that day, and one which will not be wholly without weight in our own, was the trade-wind, with its accompanying current. A passage to windward against these obstacles was a long and serious undertaking even for single ships, much more for larger bodies. It followed that fleets would go to the western islands only reluctantly, or when assured that the enemy had taken the same direction, as Rodney went to Jamaica after the Battle of the Saints, knowing the French fleet to have gone to Cap Français. This condition of the wind made the windward, or eastern, islands points on the natural lines of communication between Europe and America, as well as local bases of the naval war, and tied the fleets to them. Hence also it followed that between the two scenes of operations, between the continent and the Lesser Antilles, was interposed a wide central region into which the larger operations of war could not safely be carried except by a belligerent possessed of great naval superiority, or

此次战争中的本地基地。由于幻想着能够得到民众的支持，英军已经转战到最南部的诸州去了。他们没有想到，就算南方大部分民众更愿意和平地获取自由，这种品性也会让这些地区的民众不会起而反抗革命政府的，虽说在英国看来，这些民众是受到了革命政府的压迫；可英国还是将战胜这场遥不可及且结局极其不幸的战争的赌注，押在了南方民众的此种反抗之上。这次战争中还有一个与众不同的本地基地，那就是查尔斯顿；1780年5月，距第一支远征军在佐治亚登陆18个月之后，此地落入了英军手中。

通过前面的内容，我们已经了解到这场战争中西印度群岛地区那些主要的本地基地。英国这一方有巴巴多斯、圣卢西亚，以及作用较小的安提瓜。在其下风位置的1000英里之外，是牙买加这个大岛，而在该岛上的金斯敦，还有一个自然条件突出的造船厂。法、西联军一方所据基地，最重要的是马提尼克岛上的皇家要塞和哈瓦那，其次则是瓜达鲁佩和法兰西角。当时战略形势中的一个主导因素，便是信风以及随之而来的洋流；这一点，就算是在如今我们所处的这个时代，也并非全无重要性。要克服这些障碍迎风航行，即便是对单艘舰船来说，也是一件耗时甚久、危险重重的事情，故对于大型舰队而言就更是如此了。因此，双方舰队都只是在勉勉强强、确定敌方采用了相同航向的情况下，才会驶向西边的这些岛屿；就像罗德尼在桑特海峡之战后，因为知道法国舰队不得不前往法兰西角，所以他才率军前往牙买加那样。此种风向条件，使得向风或者说东边的那些岛屿，既是欧美之间自然航线上的要冲，也是进行海战的本地基地，从而将双方舰队都牵制在了此处。因此，我们也可以得出结论说，美洲大陆与安的列斯群岛这两个战场之间楔入了一个广袤的中心区域，除非交战一方在海军实力方面获得了重大

unless a decisive advantage had been gained upon one flank. In 1762, when England held all the Windward Islands, with undisputed superiority at sea, she safely attacked and subdued Havana; but in the years 1779-1782 the French sea power in America and the French tenure of the Windward Islands practically balanced her own, leaving the Spaniards at Havana free to prosecute their designs against Pensacola and the Bahamas, in the central region mentioned.[1]

Posts like Martinique and Sta. Lucia had therefore for the present war great strategic advantage over Jamaica, Havana, or others to leeward. They commanded the latter in virtue of their position, by which the passage westward could be made so much more quickly than the return; while the decisive points of the continental struggle were practically little farther from the one than from the other. This advantage was shared equally by most of those known as the Lesser Antilles; but the small island of Barbadoes, being well to windward of all, possessed peculiar advantages, not only for offensive action, but because it was defended by the difficulty with which a large fleet could approach it, even from so near a port as Fort Royal. It will be remembered that the expedition which finally sat down before St. Kitt's had been intended for Barbadoes, but could not reach it through the violence of the trade-wind. Thus Barbadoes, under the conditions of the time, was peculiarly fitted to be the local base and depot of the English war, as well as a wayside port of refuge on the line of communications to Jamaica, Florida, and even to North America; while Sta. Lucia, a hundred miles to leeward, was held in force as an advanced post for the fleet, watching closely the enemy at Fort Royal.

In India the political conditions of the peninsula necessarily indicated the eastern, or Coromandel, coast as the scene of operations. Trincomalee, in the adjacent island of Ceylon, though unhealthy, offered an excellent and defensible harbor, and thus acquired first-rate

优势，或者除非己方一翼获得了具有决定意义的优势，否则就不可能在此安全地进行规模较大的作战行动。1762年，英国就是在依赖其无可匹敌的海上优势占领了整个温德华群岛之后，才安全地进击并且征服了哈瓦那；但在1779年至1782年间，法国在美洲的海军实力以及法军对温德华群岛的占领，却抵消了英国本身的这种优势，使得哈瓦那的西班牙人能够任意实施他们攻取上述中心区域里的彭萨科拉和巴哈马群岛的计划了。[1]

因此，对于这场战争来说，像马提尼克和圣卢西亚这样的据点，就拥有了比牙买加、哈瓦那以及其他处于下风位置的据点更大的战略优势。它们凭借自身的位置优势而扼守着后面那些地方，因为它们的位置，使得舰队经由这些地方往西航行要比往东返回快捷得多；而在大陆战争中起决定性作用的一些要冲，与这些地方的距离实际上却都相差无几。小安的列斯群岛中的大多数岛屿，全都具有这一优势；不过，巴巴多斯这个小岛由于正处在安的列斯群岛的上风向，所以更具一些独特的优势：它非但有利于进攻，而且因为大型舰队即便是从皇家要塞这样近的港口出发也难以靠近该岛，故防守起来也很容易。我们应该还记得，那支最终在圣基茨岛驻扎下来的远征军，起初是准备攻打巴巴多斯的，可正是因为信风猛烈，而未能到达此处。因此，在当时的条件下，巴巴多斯便极适合于做英军在此次战争中的本地基地和补给站，同时它也是通往牙买加、佛罗里达甚至是通往北美地区这条交通线沿途的一个庇护所；而通过武力占领的、位于下风向100英里远的圣卢西亚，便成了英国舰队的一处前哨，可以严密监视皇家要塞内敌军的动向了。

在印度，半岛上的政治形势使得其东海岸即科罗曼德尔海岸必然地变成了战场。位于邻近的锡兰岛上的亭可马里，虽说不是一处良港，却是一处极佳的、适于防守的港

strategic importance, all the other anchorages on the coast being mere open roadsteads. From this circumstance the trade-winds, or monsoons, in this region also had strategic bearing. From the autumnal to the spring equinox the wind blows regularly from the northeast, at times with much violence, throwing a heavy surf upon the beach and making landing difficult; but during the summer months the prevailing wind is southwest, giving comparatively smooth seas and good weather. The "change of the monsoon," in September and October, is often marked by violent hurricanes. Active operations, or even remaining on the coast, were therefore unadvisable from this time until the close of the northeast monsoon. The question of a port to which to retire during this season was pressing. Trincomalee was the only one, and its unique strategic value was heightened by being to windward, during the fine season, of the principal scene of war. The English harbor of Bombay on the west coast was too distant to be considered a local base, and rather falls, like the French islands Mauritius and Bourbon, under the head of stations on the line of communications with the mother-country.

Such were the principal points of support, or bases, of the belligerent nations, at home and abroad. Of those abroad it must be said, speaking generally, that they were deficient in resources, — an important element of strategic value. Naval and military stores and equipments, and to a great extent provisions for sea use, had to be sent them from the mother-countries. Boston, surrounded by a thriving, friendly population, was perhaps an exception to this statement, as was also Havana, at that time an important naval arsenal, where much ship-building was done; but these were distant from the principal theatres of war. Upon New York and Narragansett Bay the Americans pressed too closely for the resources of the neighboring country to be largely available, while the distant ports of the East and West Indies depended wholly upon home. Hence the strategic question of communications assumed additional

口，因而具有了一流的战略重要性，而沿海其他各处港口，不过都是一些毫不设防的锚地罢了。从此种环境来看，该地区的信风或季风也具有战略意义。自秋分到春分，海上往往刮的是东北风，间或还刮得极其猛烈，掀起惊涛巨浪拍岸而起，因而难以登陆；但在夏季却盛行西南风，海面相对平静，而天气情况也相对较好。9、10月间"季风转换"期有个特点，那就是通常都会出现猛烈的飓风。因此，从此时起到冬北季风期结束，不用说实施积极的作战行动，即便是让舰队停留在沿海地区，也是很不明智的做法。在这个季节，紧迫的问题便是找到一个可以退守的港口。唯一的选择便是亭可马里，而此地因为处在向风位置，天气晴好的季节里可做主要战场，故又进一步提高了其独特的战略重要性。英国在印度半岛西海岸的孟买港距此地太远，无法将其当成本地基地，因此属于与母国之间交通联络线上的据点，就像法国的毛里求斯和波旁岛那样。

上述这些地方，便是交战双方国内外主要的支援点或者基地。关于那些海外基地，我们必须说，它们通常都是资源稀缺——可资源正是战略价值的一个重要因素。海陆两军的补给品和装备，以及海上航运所需的大部分给养物资，都必须从母国运往这些地方。周围都是蓬勃发展且态度友好之居民的波士顿，可能是一个例外，还有哈瓦那，它当时是一个重要的海军船坞，建造了大量舰船；不过，这两个地方离此次战争的主要战场都太远。美国人向纽约和纳拉干塞特湾逼近得太近，使得这两地的英军都无法获得附近地区大部分可以获取的资源，而东、西印度群岛那些相距遥远的港口，则完全依赖于国内运送的补给。因此，交通补给这个战略性的问题，便具有了更大的重要性。拦截一支运送给养的大型舰队，是仅次于击溃一支军舰舰队的作战行动；而用主力来护送这种给养舰队或者避开

importance. To intercept a large convoy of supply-ships was an operation only secondary to the destruction of a body of ships-of-war; while to protect such by main strength, or by evading the enemy's search, taxed the skill of the governments and naval commanders in distributing the ships-of-war and squadrons at their disposal, among the many objects which demanded attention. The address of Kempenfeldt and the bad management of Guichen in the North Atlantic, seconded by a heavy gale of wind, seriously embarrassed De Grasse in the West Indies. Similar injury, by cutting off small convoys in the Atlantic, was done to Suffren in the Indian seas: while the latter at once made good part of these losses, and worried his opponents by the success of his cruisers preying on the English supply-ships.

Thus the navies, by which alone these vital streams could be secured or endangered, bore the same relation to the maintenance of the general war that has already been observed of the separate parts. They were the links that bound the whole together, and were therefore indicated as the proper objective of both belligerents.

The distance from Europe to America was not such as to make intermediate ports of supply absolutely necessary; while if difficulty did arise from an unforeseen cause, it was always possible, barring meeting an enemy, either to return to Europe or to make a friendly port in the West Indies. The case was different with the long voyage to India by the Cape of Good Hope. Bickerton, leaving England with a convoy in February, was thought to have done well in reaching Bombay the following September; while the ardent Suffren, sailing in March, took an equal time to reach Mauritius, whence the passage to Madras consumed two months more. A voyage of such duration could rarely be made without a stop for water, for fresh provision, often for such refitting as called for the quiet of a harbor, even when the stores on board furnished the necessary material. A perfect line of communications required, as has been said, several

敌军的搜索，则会极大地考验政府和海军指挥官在众多需要注意的目标当中部署手下军舰和舰队的本领。在北大西洋海域，凯姆本菲尔特的老练与基申伯爵的指挥不当，加上一场猛烈的风暴，使德·格拉斯在西印度群岛陷入了严重的困境。而切断大西洋上一些小型的给养船队，也给位于印度海域的苏弗朗带来了类似的损失；但苏弗朗马上就通过派出己方的巡逻舰去劫掠英军的补给船只，而部分地弥补了这些损失，并给敌人造成了干扰。

因此，海军能够独自保护或危及此种至关重要的交通补给线这一点，同样关系到我们业已说明了各个部分的这场全面战争的持续进行。海军是将战争中各个部分联结成一个整体的中间环节，因而决定了交战双方都会将敌方海军当成己方恰当的作战目标。

欧洲与美洲之间的距离，并未远到绝对少不了居间补给港的程度；而倘若因为意料之外的原因而出现了补给困难，那么只要不遭遇到敌人，舰队也总是可以返回欧洲，或者在西印度群岛中找个友邦港口停靠的。可经由好望角前往印度时，由于航程遥远，所以情况并不一样。比克顿在2月份率领一支运输船队从英国起航，接下来的9月份便抵达了孟买，人们都认为他干得非常不错；可忠心耿耿的苏弗朗从3月起航，用了相同的时间才抵达毛里求斯，而接下来他从毛里求斯前往马德拉斯，又花了两个月的时间。进行如此旷日持久的一次航行，中途是不可能不停下来补充淡水和新鲜给养的，并且就算是船上储备有必要的物资，常常也因进行此种休整而需要港口风平浪静才行。前面我们已经说过，一条完美的交通补给线上，需要有数个这样的港口，它们之间须间距合适、防御力量充分并且有着丰富的补给品才行，就像如今英国主要贸易线路上的一些港口那样，它们都是该国在过去的战争中夺得的。在1778年战争中，交战各方在这条线路上都

such harbors, properly spaced, adequately defended, and with abundant supplies, such as England in the present day holds on some of her main commercial routes, acquisitions of her past wars. In the war of 1778 none of the belligerents had such ports on this route, until by the accession of Holland, the Cape of Good Hope was put at the disposal of the French and suitably strengthened by Suffren. With this and the Mauritius on the way, and Trincomalee at the far end of the road, the communications of the allies with France were reasonably guarded. England, though then holding St. Helena, depended, for the refreshment and refitting of her India-bound squadrons and convoys in the Atlantic, upon the benevolent neutrality of Portugal, extended in the islands of Madeira and Cape Verde and in the Brazilian ports. This neutrality was indeed a frail reliance for defence, as was shown by the encounter between Johnstone and Suffren at the Cape Verde; but there being several possible stopping-places, and the enemy unable to know which, if any, would be used, this ignorance itself conferred no small security, if the naval commander did not trust it to the neglect of proper disposition of his own force, as did Johnstone at Porto Praya. Indeed, with the delay and uncertainty which then characterized the transmission of intelligence from one point to another, doubt where to find the enemy was a greater bar to offensive enterprises than the often slight defences of a colonial port.

This combination of useful harbors and the conditions of the communications between them constitute, as has been said, the main strategic outlines of the situation. The navy, as the organized force linking the whole together, has been indicated as the principal objective of military effort. The method employed to reach the objective, the conduct of the war, is still to be considered.[2]

Before doing this a condition peculiar to the sea, and affecting the following discussion, must be briefly mentioned; that is, the difficulty of obtaining information. Armies pass through

没有此种港口；直到荷兰参战后，好望角才交由法国掌控，后来苏弗朗又适当地加强了此港的实力。由于这条交通补给线上有了好望角和毛里求斯，而航路的另一端则是亭可马里，因此联军与法国之间的交通补给便获得了一定的保障。尽管当时据有圣海伦那，但英国派往印度去的分舰队或运送给养的船队在大西洋上泊锚休整时，依赖的却是葡萄牙在马德拉群岛、佛得角和巴西诸港等地仁慈地实行的那种中立政策。此种中立，其实是一种脆弱的防御依赖心理，约翰斯顿与苏弗朗在佛得角的那场遭遇战，即表明了这一点；不过，由于一路上有着多个泊锚地，而敌人不可能知道我方将停靠哪一处，所以，只要海军指挥官不过分依赖停靠地，忽视了正确部署我方的兵力，就像约翰斯顿在波多普雷亚港的做法那样，那么敌方的这种不了解，本身就会给我方带来极大的安全。事实上，由于当时情报从一地传到另一地时经常会出现延误和不可靠的情况，所以不知道上哪儿去寻找敌人就是进击的一大障碍，难度甚至超过了去进攻防御力量通常都很脆弱的那些殖民地港口。

这些有用的海港与它们之间的交通补给条件结合起来，便组成了我们已经说过的、当时形势的主要战略性要点。作为将各个部分联结起来的有组织的军事力量，海军自然成了各方军事作战的主要目标。而为达成这一目标而采取的手段以及战争的指挥，则是一个仍需我们加以思考的问题。(2)

在此之前，我们还须简要说明一种属于海洋所特有、且会影响到后续讨论的情况；这就是，在海洋上获取情报非常困难。陆军经过之地，必定会是或多或少有着固定居民的那些地区，而在行进过程中，也必定会留下蛛丝马迹。而舰队却是在一望无边的水面航行，偶有船只掠过，可这些船只并不会在此久留；而且船只经过之后水面即行闭合，

countries more or less inhabited by a stationary population, and they leave behind them traces of their march. Fleets move through a desert over which wanderers flit, but where they do not remain; and as the waters close behind them, an occasional waif from the decks may indicate their passage, but tells nothing of their course. The sail spoken by the pursuer may know nothing of the pursued, which yet passed the point of parley but a few days or hours before. Of late, careful study of the winds and currents of the ocean has laid down certain advantageous routes, which will be habitually followed by a careful seaman, and afford some presumption as to his movements; but in 1778 the data for such precision were not collected, and even had they been, the quickest route must often have been abandoned for one of the many possible ones, in order to elude pursuit or lying-in-wait. In such a game of hide-and-seek the advantage is with the sought, and the great importance of watching the outlets of an enemy's country, of stopping the chase before it has got away into the silent desert, is at once evident. If for any reason such a watch there is impossible, the next best thing is, not attempting to watch routes which may not be taken, to get first to the enemy's destination and await him there; but this implies a knowledge of his intentions which may not always be obtainable. The action of Suffren, when pitted against Johnstone, was throughout strategically sound, both in his attack at Porto Praya and in the haste with which he made for their common destination; while the two failures of Rodney to intercept the convoys to Martinique in 1780 and 1782, though informed that they were coming, show the difficulty which attended lying-in-wait even when the point of arrival was known.

Of any maritime expedition two points only are fixed, — the point of departure and that of arrival. The latter may be unknown to the enemy; but up to the time of sailing, the presence of a certain force in a port, and the indications of a purpose soon to move, may be assumed to be

虽说船上偶尔掉落的漂浮物可以说明有船只经过此地，但这些漂浮物根本就无法表明船只的航向。尽管被追踪者数天前或数小时前才经过这个地方，但追踪者可能对被追踪者的动向还是一无所知。近来，在仔细研究风向和洋流的基础上，人们已经确定了一些便利的航线，一些谨慎的水手会习惯性地沿着这些航线航行，从而让别人可以推测其动向；但在1778年，人们还并未收集起如此准确的数据，而就算有了这些数据，人们也必定会经常在不久之后就放弃最快捷的那条航线，而改用其他许多可以走的水路之一，以躲避敌人的追踪或伏击。在这样一种捉迷藏式的游戏中，优势在于被追击者这一方，因此监视敌国的出海口，并在敌军进入茫茫大海之前停止追击，这样做的重要性马上就是显而易见的了。假如由于某种原因而无法监视敌国的出海口，那么最佳办法就是不要试图去监视那些敌军可能不会选择的路线，而是应当先于敌人到达其目的地，然后在那儿守株待兔；不过，这种方法意味着要知道敌人的意图，可敌方的意图并非总是能够获知的。在与约翰斯顿较量时，苏弗朗的行动从战略上来看是完全正确的，他进攻波多普雷亚并率军匆匆赶往约翰斯顿部通常的目的地，都是如此；而罗德尼在1780年和1782年两次截击前往马提尼克的法国给养船队时，尽管已经得知敌人正在前来，但截击都没有成功，这就说明，即便是在知道敌人目的地的情况下，守株待兔、等候敌人到来也并非易事。

对于任何海上远征队来说，只有两个地点是确定的，那就是远征队的出发地和到达地。敌方可能不知道我方的到达地；但一直到起航之前，港内有一支部队、有着种种很快会进行调遣的迹象，这些都是可以通过推测而得知的。对于交战双方来说，截击敌方的调遣可能都有着重大的意义；不过，防御方尤其更加且普遍地需要此种截击，因为防

known. It may be of moment to either belligerent to intercept such a movement; but it is more especially and universally necessary to the defence, because, of the many points at which he is open to attack, it may be impossible for him to know which is threatened; whereas the offence proceeds with full knowledge direct to his aim, if he can deceive his opponent. The importance of blocking such an expedition becomes yet more evident should it at any time be divided between two or more ports, — a condition which may easily arise when the facilities of a single dock-yard are insufficient to fit out so many ships in the time allowed, or when, as in the present war, allied powers furnish separate contingents. To prevent the junction of these contingents is a matter of prime necessity, and nowhere can this be done so certainly as off the ports whence one or both is to sail. The defence, from its very name, is presumably the less strong, and is therefore the more bound to take advantage of such a source of weakness as the division of the enemy's force. Rodney in 1782 at Sta. Lucia, watching the French contingent at Martinique to prevent its union with the Spaniards at Cap Français, is an instance of correct strategic position; and had the islands been so placed as to put him between the French and their destination, instead of in their rear, nothing better could have been devised. As it was, he did the best thing possible under the circumstances.

The defence, being the weaker, cannot attempt to block all the ports where divisions of the enemy lie, without defeating his aim by being in inferior force before each. This would be to neglect the fundamental principles of war. If he correctly decide not to do this, but to collect a superior force before one or two points, it becomes necessary to decide which shall be thus guarded and which neglected, — a question involving the whole policy of the war after a full understanding of the main conditions, military, moral, and economic, in every quarter.

The defensive was necessarily accepted by England in 1778. It had been a maxim with

御方有着众多的地点容易遭到敌方攻击，所以不可能确切知道哪一处有危险；而倘若能够骗过对手的话，进攻者对自己的攻击目标就会了如指掌。倘若进行此种远征的舰队分处两个或多个港口的话，对它们进行封锁堵截的重要性还会变得更加明显——当单个船坞的设备设施不足以在规定的时间内装备如此之多的舰船，或者像此次战争中的情形一样，盟国分别装备各自的分遣队时，就会很容易出现远征船队分处两个或数个港口的情况。阻止这些分遣队会合，是一件极其必要的事情，而在这些分遣队始发港口外的海域进行堵截，则是比在任何地方进行堵截都要更加稳妥的办法。防御方，顾名思义，就是想必势力没那么强大的一方，因此也就更有必要利用敌人分兵所带来的劣势。1782年罗德尼在圣卢西亚时，曾监视驻马提尼克岛的法国舰队，防止它与驻法兰西角的西班牙船队会合，就是一个扼守正确战略位置的例子；而倘若此处群岛的分布更佳，使得罗德尼处在法军及其目的地之间，而不是处在法军及其目的地后方的话，那么除了这样做，就没有别的什么更好的办法了。事实上，罗德尼在当时的形势下已经尽力而为了。

实力较弱的防御方，不能试图去封锁敌方分遣队所在的全部港口；因为这样做，会使防御方的实力在每支敌方分遣队面前都不如对方，从而让己方的目标落空。这样做，实际上是忽视了战争的基本原则。假如防御方正确地判断出不能这样做，而应当在一处或两处港口集中优势兵力，那么就必须决定哪些地方应当守卫、哪些地方应当忽略了——这可是一个涉及到在充分了解每个地区的军事、精神与经济等方面的主要情况之后，制定出整体的战争政策的问题。

在1778年战争中，英国必然会采取防御态势。前一个时代中那些最优秀的海军权

the best English naval authorities of the preceding era, with Hawke and his contemporaries, that the British navy should be kept equal in numbers to the combined fleets of the Bourbon kingdoms, — a condition which, with the better quality of the personnel and the larger maritime population upon which it could draw, would have given a real superiority of force. This precaution, however, had not been observed during recent years. It is of no consequence to this discussion whether the failure was due to the inefficiency of the ministry, as was charged by their opponents, or to the misplaced economy often practised by representative governments in time of peace. The fact remains that, notwithstanding the notorious probability of France and Spain joining in the war, the English navy was inferior in number to that of the allies. In what have been called the strategic features of the situation, the home bases, and the secondary bases abroad, the advantage upon the whole lay with her. Her positions, if not stronger in themselves, were at least better situated, geographically, for strategic effect; but in the second essential for war, the organized military force, or fleet, adequate to offensive operations, she had been allowed to become inferior. It only remained, therefore, to use this inferior force with such science and vigor as would frustrate the designs of the enemy, by getting first to sea, taking positions skilfully, anticipating their combinations by greater quickness of movement, harassing their communications with their objectives, and meeting the principal divisions of the enemy with superior forces.

It is sufficiently clear that the maintenance of this war, everywhere except on the American continent, depended upon the mother-countries in Europe and upon open communication with them. The ultimate crushing of the Americans, too, not by direct military effort but by exhaustion, was probable, if England were left unmolested to strangle their commerce and industries with her overwhelming naval strength. This strength she could put forth against them,

威人士、霍克及其同时代的人都有一条准则，那就是：英国海军应当维持能够与法、西这两个波旁王国的联合舰队相抗衡的兵力——因为英国海军人员素质更好、兵员也更充足，所以这种情况让英国具有了实实在在的优势。然而直到这些年，英国才注意到此种先见之明。这种失败究竟是像反对派所指责的那样，是因为英国内阁的无能，还是因为和平时期民选政府通常采用的节俭之法，对我们的研究来说并不重要。事实仍然是，尽管法、西两国很可能参战这一点人所共知，但英国海军此时的兵力却弱于法、西联军。从此种形势的所谓战略特征、国内大本营、海外次级基地来看，优势基本上都在英国一方。英国的各个战略要地，就算本身实力并不比敌方强大，至少在地理位置上都更具战略效应；但在战争的第二要素，即能够用于进攻作战的有组织的军事力量，或者说舰队方面，英国却任由自己的实力变得不如敌人了。因此，英国就只能凭借技术和气势来运用这支不如敌人的兵力，通过率先出海、巧妙抢占有利位置、凭借极为迅速的机动来抢占先机并防止敌军会合、干扰敌军与其作战目标之间的交通补给和集中优势兵力迎击敌方主要分遣队等方法，来挫败敌人的阴谋诡计了。

除了美洲大陆，此次战争能否在其他各地继续进行下去，取决于欧洲的那几个母国，取决于各地与这些母国之间的交通补给是否畅通，这一点是十分明显的。倘若让英国不受干扰地凭借其势不可挡的海军实力来扼制美国的贸易和工业，那么不用直接的军事行动，只需通过消耗战，最终将美国革命镇压下去也是很有可能的。假如摆脱盟国海军的压力，英国便可以用其海军来对付美国人；假如能够获得压制盟军的决定性优势——不仅仅是有形的优势，还有士气优势，就像20年后英军的士气那样，那么英国就

if relieved from the pressure of the allied navies; and relief would be obtained if she could gain over them a decided preponderance, not merely material but moral, such as she had twenty years later. In that case the allied courts, whose financial weakness was well known, must retire from a contest in which their main purpose of reducing England to an inferior position was already defeated. Such preponderance, however, could only be had by fighting; by showing that, despite inferiority in numbers, the skill of her seamen and the resources of her wealth enabled her government, by a wise use of these powers, to be actually superior at the decisive points of the war. It could never be had by distributing the ships-of-the-line all over the world, exposing them to be beaten in detail while endeavoring to protect all the exposed points of the scattered empire.

The key of the situation was in Europe, and in Europe in the hostile dock-yards. If England were unable, as she proved to be, to raise up a continental war against France, then her one hope was to find and strike down the enemy's navy. Nowhere was it so certainly to be found as in its home ports; nowhere so easily met as immediately after leaving them. This dictated her policy in the Napoleonic wars, when the moral superiority of her navy was so established that she dared to oppose inferior forces to the combined dangers of the sea and of the more numerous and well-equipped ships lying quietly at anchor inside. By facing this double risk she obtained the double advantage of keeping the enemy under her eyes, and of sapping his efficiency by the easy life of port, while her own officers and seamen were hardened by the rigorous cruising into a perfect readiness for every call upon their energies. "We have no reason," proclaimed Admiral Villeneuve in 1805, echoing the words of the emperor, "to fear the sight of an English squadron. Their seventy-fours have not five hundred men on board; they are worn out by a two years' cruise." A month later he wrote: "The Toulon squadron

能够摆脱联军的压力了。倘若那样的话，法、西两个盟国便会因为众所周知的财力不足，以及它们削弱英国实力的主要目标已经落空这两个原因而退出这场战争。然而，英国只有通过作战才能获得此种优势，只有通过向敌方表明，尽管兵力不如，但其海军的高超本领和丰富的财力资源，使得英国政府能够明智地运用这些实力，在此次战争中的关键时刻实实在在地胜敌一筹，才能获得这种优势。而将战舰分散部署在世界各地，使得它们在竭力保护这个散沙帝国中所有易受攻击之处时有被敌人逐一击溃的危险，这种做法却是绝不可能让英国获得此种优势的。

形势的关键在欧洲，而欧洲的关键则在于敌对双方的海军船坞。假如英国像事实业已证明的那样，无法发动一场大陆战争来对付法国，那么英国唯一的希望，便是找到并击溃敌人的海军。在敌方国内港口找到其海军最有把握，而待敌方海军离开这些港口后立即前去迎击也最为容易。正是这一点，决定了英国在拿破仑战争时期的政策；当时英国海军已经牢固地确立起了士气优势，所以敢于用不如敌方的兵力，去跟危险重重的海洋较量，去跟兵力和装备都精良得多、稳稳当当地泊在港内的敌方舰队进行较量。通过面对这种双重危险，该国也获得了双重的优势，既牢牢地监控着敌军，又让敌军在港内安逸的生活中逐渐消磨掉斗志，而英国自己的海军官兵却通过严峻的巡航锻炼，达到了一种准备好斗志昂扬地完成任何使命的完美状态。1805年，维尔纳夫上将附和法国皇帝的谕旨，宣布："我们没有任何理由一看到英国舰队便害怕得很。他们那些装有74门火炮的战舰上，兵力不足500人；而且，在历经了两年的巡航后，这些水兵都已经疲惫不堪了。"一个月后，他又写道："土伦舰队泊在港内时看上去好得很，官兵们着装整齐，操练得也不错；可暴风

appeared very fine in the harbor, the crews well clothed and drilling well; but as soon as a storm came, all was changed. They were not drilled in storms." "The emperor," said Nelson, "now finds, if emperors hear truth, that his fleet suffers more in a night than ours in one year. ... These gentlemen are not used to the hurricanes, which we have braved for twenty-one months without losing mast or yard." It must be admitted, however, that the strain was tremendous both on men and ships, and that many English officers found in the wear and tear an argument against keeping their fleets at sea off the enemy's coast. "Every one of the blasts we endure," wrote Collingwood, "lessens the security of the country. The last cruise disabled five large ships and two more lately; several of them must be docked." "I have hardly known what a night of rest is these two months," wrote he again; "this incessant cruising seems to me beyond the powers of human nature. Calder is worn to a shadow, quite broken down, and I am told Graves is not much better." The high professional opinion of Lord Howe was also adverse to the practice.

Besides the exhaustion of men and ships, it must also be admitted that no blockade could be relied on certainly to check the exit of an enemy's fleet. Villeneuve escaped from Toulon, Missiessy from Rochefort. "I am here watching the French squadron in Rochefort," wrote Collingwood, "but feel that it is not practicable to prevent their sailing; and yet, if they should get by me, I should be exceedingly mortified. ... The only thing that can prevent their sailing is the apprehension that they may get among us, as they cannot know exactly where we are."

Nevertheless, the strain then was endured. The English fleets girdled the shores of France and Spain; losses were made good; ships were repaired; as one officer fell, or was worn out at his post, another took his place. The strict guard over Brest broke up the emperor's combinations;

雨一来，一切都变了。他们没有在暴风雨里训练过。"纳尔逊则说："假如皇帝们听得到真话，那么法国皇帝此时就会发现，他的舰队在一夜之间所遭受的损失，比我方舰队一年遭受的损失还要大。……这些法国绅士不习惯在飓风中行动，而我们的舰队却已英勇地冒着飓风巡航了21个月，连一根桅杆和帆桁也没有损失过。"然而，必须承认的是，这种巡航给人员与船只都带来了巨大的压力，也有许多英国军官因舰船磨损、人员疲惫而反对继续让舰队在敌方沿海巡航。柯灵伍德就曾写道："我们每承受一次风暴，就是削弱了国家的安全一分。最后一次巡航让5艘大型战舰失去了作战能力，而不久前又有2艘无法作战了；其中有几艘，不得不拖回船厂去修理。"他还写道："这两个月来，我都不知道休息一个晚上是什么滋味了。在我看来，这种无休无止的巡航，似乎已经超出了人类承受能力之极限。卡尔德已经瘦得不成个样子，身体完全垮掉了，而手下还告诉我，格雷夫斯的状况也好不到哪里去。"就连豪勋爵这位高水平的专业人士，也是不赞同这种做法的。

除了人员和舰船的损耗，我们还必须承认，任何一种封锁，都是无法百分之百地确保不让敌方的舰队出港的。维尔纳夫曾率舰队从土伦港逃出，而米西埃斯也曾从罗什福尔逃走。柯林伍德曾写道："我正在此处监视罗什福尔的法国舰队，但我认为阻止法国舰队起航的做法是行不通的；不过，要是他们从我身边逃走的话，那我就一辈子都抬不起头了。……唯一能够阻止他们出海的，就是他们的担心；因为不可能知道我方的确切位置，所以他们会担心陷入我方的埋伏之中。"

尽管如此，当时的英国海军还是承受住了此种压力。英国舰队沿着法、西两国海岸巡航；损失得到了弥补，舰船也修好了；倘若某位军官阵亡，或者在岗位上累倒了，就

the watchfulness of Nelson, despite an unusual concurrence of difficulties, followed the Toulon fleet, from the moment of its starting, across the Atlantic and back to the shores of Europe. It was long before they came to blows, before strategy stepped aside and tactics completed the work at Trafalgar; but step by step and point by point the rugged but disciplined seamen, the rusty and battered but well-handled ships, blocked each move of their unpractised opponents. Disposed in force before each arsenal of the enemy, and linked together by chains of smaller vessels, they might fail now and again to check a raid, but they effectually stopped all grand combinations of the enemy's squadrons.

The ships of 1805 were essentially the same as those of 1780. There had doubtless been progress and improvement; but the changes were in degree, not in kind. Not only so, but the fleets of twenty years earlier, under Hawke and his fellows, had dared the winters of the Bay of Biscay. "There is not in Hawke's correspondence," says his biographer, "the slightest indication that he himself doubted for a moment that it was not only possible, but his duty, to keep the sea, even through the storms of winter, and that he should soon be able to 'make downright work of it.'" If it be urged that the condition of the French navy was better, the character and training of its officers higher, than in the days of Hawke and Nelson, the fact must be admitted; nevertheless, the admiralty could not long have been ignorant that the number of such officers was still so deficient as seriously to affect the quality of the deck service, and the lack of seamen so great as to necessitate filling up the complements with soldiers. As for the personnel of the Spanish navy, there is no reason to believe it better than fifteen years later, when Nelson, speaking of Spain giving certain ships to France, said, "I take it for granted not manned [by Spaniards], as that would be the readiest way to lose them again."

由另一名军官来取代。对布雷斯特的严密警戒，挫败了法国皇帝想将兵力联合起来的图谋；尽管遇到了种种异乎寻常的困难，但自土伦舰队动身的那一刻起，直到它越过大西洋并返回欧洲海岸，纳尔逊一直都在警惕地追踪着它的动向。很久以后双方才开始真正较量，而此时战略已经退居其次，结束特拉法尔加海战的是战术了；不过，英国却凭着那些粗犷而又纪律严明的水兵与那些锈迹斑斑、破旧不堪而又指挥有方的舰船，一步一步、一点一点地封锁着那些经验不足的对手的每一步行动。在敌方的每一个船坞前部署兵力，并通过大量的小型舰船将它们联结成一体，这种做法虽说偶尔会让英军在阻碍敌人袭击时失利，但还是有效地使得敌方的舰队没法声势浩大地联合起来。

1805年与1780年时的舰船，基本上并无多大差别。毫无疑问，舰船建造技术有了进步和改良；不过，这种改变是属于程度上的，而不是舰船种类上的变化。非但如此，就连20年前霍克及其同僚所指挥的舰队，也曾大胆地挑战过比斯开湾冬季的严寒天气。霍克的传记作者称："霍克的往来信件中并无一丝痕迹表明，对于即便是在冬季的暴风雪中巡航于海上非但能够做到、而且是他的义务这一点，他曾经心存疑虑；他也并不怀疑，不久自己就能'很快完成任务'了。"要是有人坚持说，与霍克和纳尔逊那个时代相比，此时法国海军的状况更好，法国海军官兵的品质和受训情况也更强，那么我们必须承认这是事实；但尽管如此，这些官兵在数量上仍然不足，从而严重地影响到了海军的服役质量，何况水兵也严重短缺，因而不得不用陆军士兵来补足，这种情况，法国海军部是不可能长期不知道的。至于西班牙海军，我们没有任何理由认为此时它的人员状况要好于15年之后的那种状况；当时，纳尔逊在谈到西班牙将某些舰船送给法国时，曾经这样说："我认为（西班牙人）并未

In truth, however, it is too evident to need much arguing, that the surest way for the weaker party to neutralize the enemy's ships was to watch them in their harbors and fight them if they started. The only serious objection to doing this, in Europe, was the violence of the weather off the coasts of France and Spain, especially during the long nights of winter. This brought with it not only risk of immediate disaster, which strong, well-managed ships would rarely undergo, but a continual strain which no skill could prevent, and which therefore called for a large reserve of ships to relieve those sent in for repairs, or to refresh the crews.

The problem would be greatly simplified if the blockading fleet could find a convenient anchorage on the flank of the route the enemy must take, as Nelson in 1804 and 1805 used Maddalena Bay in Sardinia when watching the Toulon fleet, — a step to which he was further forced by the exceptionally bad condition of many of his ships. So Sir James Saumarez in 1800 even used Douarnenez Bay, on the French coast, only five miles from Brest, to anchor the inshore squadron of the blockading force in heavy weather. The positions at Plymouth and Torbay cannot be considered perfectly satisfactory from this point of view; not being, like Maddalena Bay, on the flank of the enemy's route, but like Sta. Lucia, rather to its rear. Nevertheless, Hawke proved that diligence and well-managed ships could overcome this disadvantage, as Rodney also afterward showed on his less tempestuous station.

In the use of the ships at its disposal, taking the war of 1778 as a whole, the English ministry kept their foreign detachments in America, and in the West and East Indies, equal to those of the enemy. At particular times, indeed, this was not so; but speaking generally of the assignment of ships, the statement is correct. In Europe, on the contrary, and in necessary consequence of the policy mentioned, the British fleet was habitually much inferior to that in the French and Spanish ports. It therefore could be used offensively only by great care, and

给这些舰船配齐人员，因为那样做的话，就会再次轻而易举地损失掉这些舰船。"

不过，处于弱势的那一方压制敌方舰船最可靠的办法，就是当它们泊在港内时对它们进行监视，而倘若它们出动，便加以打击，这一点的确太过明显，因此无需多说。在欧洲，唯一严肃地反对此种做法的一个理由，便是法、西两国沿海天气恶劣，尤其是在冬季漫长的黑夜期里。这非但会让舰队有遭遇直接天灾的危险，连那些船体坚固、控制得当的舰船也难以承受，还会给船员带来一种任何本领都无法遏制的持久压力，故需要储备大量舰船，以替换那些送回港内维修的船只，并轮换船上的人员。

假如执行封锁任务的舰队，能够在敌方必经之路的两侧找到一处便利的锚地，就像纳尔逊在1804年和1805年间监视土伦舰队时利用撒丁岛上的马达莱纳湾那样，那么这个问题就变得极其简单了；当时，纳尔逊手下的许多舰船状况都异常糟糕，进一步迫使他采取了这一措施。詹姆士·索马勒兹爵士也是如此，他在1800年甚至利用了法国海岸上距布雷斯特仅仅5英里远的杜瓦尔纳内兹湾，在天气恶劣的时候让封锁部队中的近岸分队泊于此处。从这个角度来看，我们不能说普利茅斯和托贝的位置是尽善尽美的；因为它们不像马达莱纳湾那样处在敌方航线的一侧，而是像圣卢西亚那样，位于敌军航线的后面。尽管如此，霍克还是证明了勤勉和指挥舰船得当是能够克服此种不利因素的，而后来罗德尼也在他那个天气不那么恶劣的战位上证明了这一点。

在利用手下可调遣的舰船过程中，英国海军部纵览1778年这场战争的全局，使该国在美洲、西印度群岛和东印度群岛的海外分遣舰队在兵力上始终与敌人不相上下。实际上，在个别时候，情况也并非全然如此；不过，若只笼统地谈到舰船部署的情况，那

through good fortune in meeting the enemy in detail; and even so an expensive victory, unless very decisive, entailed considerable risk from the consequent temporary disability of the ships engaged. It followed that the English home (or Channel) fleet, upon which depended also the communications with Gibraltar and the Mediterranean, was used very economically both as to battle and weather, and was confined to the defence of the home coast, or to operations against the enemy's communications.

India was so far distant that no exception can be taken to the policy there. Ships sent there went to stay, and could be neither reinforced nor recalled with a view to sudden emergencies. The field stood by itself. But Europe, North America, and the West Indies should have been looked upon as one large theatre of war, throughout which events were mutually dependent, and whose different parts stood in close relations of greater or less importance, to which due attention should have been paid.

Assuming that the navies, as the guardians of the communications, were the controlling factors in the war, and that the source, both of the navies and of those streams of supplies which are called communications, was in the mother-countries, and there centralized in the chief arsenals, two things follow: First, the main effort of the Power standing on the defensive, of Great Britain, should have been concentrated before those arsenals; and secondly, in order to such concentration, the lines of communication abroad should not have been needlessly extended, so as to increase beyond the strictest necessity the detachments to guard them. Closely connected with the last consideration is the duty of strengthening, by fortification and otherwise, the vital points to which the communications led, so that these points should not depend in any way upon the fleet for protection, but only for supplies and reinforcements, and those at reasonable intervals. Gibraltar, for instance, quite fulfilled these conditions, being practically impregnable,

么这种说法就是正确的。在欧洲，情况则正好相反，且这也是前述政策的必然结果：英国舰队的兵力，经常大不如法、西两国港内舰队的兵力。因此，只有极其小心谨慎，并且有着逐一遭遇敌军的好运气，才能让英国舰队去进攻；即便如此，一场代价高昂的胜仗，除非具有重大的决定性意义，否则便会因为参战舰船暂时失去作战能力而带来巨大的风险。由此可知，英国的本土舰队（或英吉利海峡舰队）由于作战和天气两个原因而利用得并不多，并且只用于防卫本土沿海或破坏敌方交通补给的作战行动，而英国国内与直布罗陀和地中海地区的交通补给线，也是依赖于这支舰队来保护的。

印度与英国相距遥远，因此此处的政策不可能出现例外情况。舰队派去后，就会在此处留下来，而遇到突发的紧急情况时，既不可能得到增援，也不可能被召回国内。这完全就是一处孤立的战场。欧洲、北美和西印度群岛则应当看成是一个大战区，其间发生的战事都是相互依存的，其中不同地区也都紧密相关，有着或大或小的重要性，从而应当对这些地区加以相应的关注。

假定作为交通补给卫士的各国海军是此次战争中的决定性因素，而海军与此种称作"交通补给"的不间断给养都源自母国，并且全都集中在国内主要海军船坞的话，那么就可以得出如下两个结论：首先，处于防御态势的大不列颠，应当将主要兵力集中部署在这些海军船坞之前；其次，为了实现此种兵力集中，海外的交通补给线不应当毫无必要地扩张，以免需要超出最大必要性地增派船队前来保护它们。与最后一个方面紧密相关的，便是通过防御工事或者其他方式，来巩固这些交通补给线所通往的各个要塞，使之无需依赖舰队任何方式的护卫，只需舰队每隔适当的一段时间便为其运送给养与援兵。例如，直布

and storing supplies that lasted very long.

If this reasoning be correct, the English dispositions on the American continent were very faulty. Holding Canada, with Halifax, New York, and Narragansett Bay, and with the line of the Hudson within their grip, it was in their power to isolate a large, perhaps decisive, part of the insurgent territory. New York and Narragansett Bay could have been made unassailable by a French fleet of that day, thus assuring the safety of the garrisons against attacks from the sea and minimizing the task of the navy; while the latter would find in them a secure refuge, in case an enemy's force eluded the watch of the English fleet before a European arsenal and appeared on the coast. Instead of this, these two ports were left weak, and would have fallen before a Nelson or a Farragut, while the army in New York was twice divided, first to the Chesapeake and afterward to Georgia, neither part of the separated forces being strong enough for the work before it. The control of the sea was thus used in both cases to put the enemy between the divided portions of the English army, when the latter, undivided, had not been able to force its way over the ground thus interposed. As the communication between the two parts of the army depended wholly upon the sea, the duty of the navy was increased with the increased length of the lines of communication. The necessity of protecting the seaports and the lengthened lines of communication thus combined to augment the naval detachments in America, and to weaken proportionately the naval force at the decisive points in Europe. Thus also a direct consequence of the southern expedition was the hasty abandonment of Narragansett Bay, when D'Estaing appeared on the coast in 1779, because Clinton had not force enough to defend both it and New York.[3]

In the West Indies the problem before the English government was not to subdue revolted territory, but to preserve the use of a number of small, fruitful islands; to keep possession of

罗陀就完全满足了这些条件，非但固若金汤，还储备了可以长久坚持的给养。

如果这种推理正确的话，那么英国在美洲大陆的兵力部署就是相当不对的了。将加拿大、哈利法克斯、纽约、纳拉干塞特湾和哈德逊河一线掌控在手中，英国就有能力将叛乱殖民地中的一大部分（或许还是其中具有决定性的一部分）孤立起来。纽约和纳拉干塞特湾本来是可以做到让当时的法国海军无懈可击，从而确保守军安全，使之不会遭到来自海上的攻击，并且将海军的作战任务减到最低限度的；而万一敌方有哪支部队躲过欧洲某处海军船坞前英国舰队的监视而出现在此处沿海的话，英国海军也可以把这两个地方当成是一个安全的庇护所。可正好相反，他们却任由这两个港口防务空虚，使之有落入某个纳尔逊或者某个法拉格特之手的危险，而纽约的守军又曾两次分兵，先是前往切萨皮克，后来又被派往佐治亚，且这两部分兵力都不够强大，无法完成各自面临的任务。在这两种情况下，英国的制海权都被用于将敌人置于英国陆军的两支分队之间，而就算是在英国陆军不分兵的情况下，英军也一直无法从陆路强行穿过敌军交错的北美大陆。由于两支陆军分队之间的交通补给完全依赖于海路，所以，海军的任务便随着交通补给线变长而增加了。由于既要保护海港，又要保护延长了的交通补给线，部署在美洲的海军分舰队便越来越多，从而相应地削弱了欧洲那些关键之处的海军力量。所以，远征南方还有一个直接后果，那便是1779年德斯坦率军出现在纳拉干塞特湾海岸后，由于柯林顿勋爵的兵力并不足以同时保护此地和纽约，英军便只得迅速放弃了纳拉干塞特湾。[3]

在西印度群岛，英国政府所面临的问题不是镇压殖民地叛乱，而是守住并继续利用众多面积不大却很肥沃的岛屿，是独占这些岛屿并且挫败敌人的破坏，尽可能地维持本国与

them itself, and to maintain their trade as free as possible from the depredations of the enemy. It need not be repeated that this demanded predominance at sea over both the enemy's fleets and single cruisers, — "commerce-destroyers," as the latter are now styled. As no vigilance can confine all these to their ports, the West Indian waters must be patrolled by British frigates and lighter vessels; but it would surely be better, if possible, to keep the French fleet away altogether than to hold it in check by a British fleet on the spot, of only equal force at any time, and liable to fall, as it often did, below equality. England, being confined to the defensive, was always liable to loss when thus inferior. She actually did lose one by one, by sudden attack, most of her islands, and at different times had her fleet shut up under the batteries of a port; whereas the enemy, when he found himself inferior, was able to wait for reinforcements, knowing that he had nothing to fear while so waiting.[4]

Nor was this embarrassment confined to the West Indies. The nearness of the islands to the American continent made it always possible for the offence to combine his fleets in the two quarters before the defence could be sure of his purpose; and although such combinations were controlled in some measure by well-understood conditions of weather and the seasons, the events of 1780 and 1781 show the perplexity felt from this cause by the ablest English admiral, whose dispositions, though faulty, but reflected the uncertainties of his mind. When to this embarrassment, which is common to the defensive in all cases, is added the care of the great British trade upon which the prosperity of the empire mainly depended, it must be conceded that the task of the British admiral in the West Indies was neither light nor simple.

In Europe, the safety of England herself and of Gibraltar was gravely imperilled by the absence of these large detachments in the Western Hemisphere, to which may also be attributed

这些地方之间的自由贸易。这就要求英国在海上取得优势，从而既能压制住敌方的舰队，也能压制住敌方的单艘巡航舰，即如今所称的"贸易破坏舰"，这一点自然无需再说。由于任何警戒措施也无法做到将敌方的所有舰船都封锁在港内，所以西印度群岛海域必须有英国的护卫舰和小型舰船进行巡逻才行；不过，倘若能够将法国舰队完全拒于此处海域之外，无疑会比用一支英国舰队在此处对法军来加以遏制更可取，因为不论什么时候，此处英军的兵力都只能是与法军不相上下，并且结果经常是，一旦兵力不如法军，英军便会溃败。由于只能进行防御，所以一旦兵力上处于劣势，英军就总是会蒙受损失。事实上，由于敌军的突袭，该国的确一个接一个地丢掉了大多数岛屿，并且在不同的时期，英国舰队也曾因敌方港内火炮的压制而受阻；可在发觉己方兵力上处于劣势之后，敌军却可以静待增援，因为敌军明白，在等候援军的这段时间里，他们根本就用不着担心自己的安危。[4]

这种捉襟见肘的局面，并非只是西印度群岛地区才存在。西印度群岛距美洲大陆很近，使得进攻方总是能够在防御方确定其进攻意图之前，将分处两地的舰队集结起来；尽管此种集结因大家都很清楚的天气与季节变换情况而在一定程度上受到了限制，但1780年和1781年间的战事却表明，那位最杰出的英国海军司令也因这一原因而产生过纠结，他的部署虽说有缺陷，却反映出了他的心中也是拿捏不定的。而任何防御过程中通常都会出现的这种困局，再加上必须保护英国繁荣兴旺所依赖的大规模贸易，让我们不得不承认，驻守西印度群岛的这位英国海军司令肩上的担子既不轻，也不简单。

在欧洲，由于西半球没有了这些大型的分舰队，所以英国本土和直布罗陀的安全都受到了极大威胁，而英国丢掉了米诺卡岛，原因或许也在于此。当联军的66艘战舰对阵

the loss of Minorca. When sixty-six allied ships-of-the-line confronted the thirty-five which alone England could collect, and drove them into their harbors, there was realized that mastery of the Channel which Napoleon claimed would make him beyond all doubt master of England. For thirty days, the thirty ships which formed the French contingent had cruised in the Bay of Biscay, awaiting the arrival of the tardy Spaniards; but they were not disturbed by the English fleet. Gibraltar was more than once brought within sight of starvation, through the failure of communications with England; and its deliverance was due, not to the power of the English navy suitably disposed by its government, but to the skill of British officers and the inefficiency of the Spaniards. In the great final relief, Lord Howe's fleet numbered only thirty-four to the allied forty-nine.

Which, then, in the difficulties under which England labored, was the better course, — to allow the enemy free exit from his ports and endeavor to meet him by maintaining a sufficient naval force on each of the exposed stations, or to attempt to watch his arsenals at home, under all the difficulties of the situation, not with the vain hope of preventing every raid, or intercepting every convoy, but with the expectation of frustrating the greater combinations, and of following close at the heels of any large fleet that escaped? Such a watch must not be confounded with a blockade, a term frequently, but not quite accurately, applied to it. "I beg to inform your Lordship," wrote Nelson, "that the port of Toulon has never been blockaded by me; quite the reverse. Every opportunity has been offered the enemy to put to sea, for it is there we hope to realize the hopes and expectations of our country." "Nothing," he says again, "ever kept the French fleet in Toulon or Brest when they had a mind to come out;" and although the statement is somewhat exaggerated, it is true that the attempt to shut them up in port would have been hopeless. What Nelson expected by keeping near their ports, with

当时英国只能集结起来的那35艘战舰，并将后者赶回港内之后，拿破仑曾经说过的那句话，即控制了英吉利海峡必可让他成为英格兰的主人，就变成了现实。接连30天，组成法国分遣队的那30艘战舰都在比斯开湾巡弋，等候行动迟缓的西班牙舰队到来；而这支法国舰队，根本就没有受到英国舰队的袭扰。由于与英国之间的交通补给中断了，所以直布罗陀曾经不止一次地被逼到了弹尽粮绝的边缘；而此地最终得到解救的原因，并不在于英国政府部署海军兵力的正确，而是在于英军官兵的高超本领和西班牙军队的无能。在最后那次伟大的解围战中，豪勋爵麾下的舰队仅有34艘战舰，而联军的战舰却多达49艘。

那么，在英国所苦的种种困境中，下面哪种应对方针更好呢？是任由敌军出港，然后尽量通过在每处易受攻击的基地都部署足够的海军兵力去迎击敌军，还是克服当前局势的各种困难，试图警戒敌军本土的海军船坞，不抱阻止敌人的每一次进袭、截击敌军的每一支给养船队的无益幻想，而是期待着挫败敌军的大规模联合行动，并且对任何逃跑的大型敌方舰队进行穷追猛打呢？我们不能将此种警戒与封锁混为一谈，虽说"封锁"这个术语经常可以用于指警戒，但不是很准确。纳尔逊曾经写道："谨此告知阁下，我从来就没有封锁过土伦港；情况恰好与此相反。敌人完全拥有出港的机会，因为我们想在海上实现祖国的种种希望与期盼。"他还说："驻土伦或布雷斯特的法国舰队一心出港的时候，我们从未采取过任何措施来加以阻遏。"尽管这话有点儿言过其实，但不可能将法国舰队完全封锁在港内这一点，却是真的。纳尔逊之所以让舰队守在敌方港口附近，并且合理部署足够数量的警戒船只，是因为他想获知敌方舰队何时起航、去往何方等情报；这样做，用他自己的话来说，旨在"追击敌军至地球的另一边"。还有

enough lookout ships properly distributed, was to know when they sailed and what direction they took, intending, to use his own expression, to "follow them to the antipodes." "I am led to believe," he writes at another time, "that the Ferrol squadron of French ships will push for the Mediterranean. If it join that in Toulon, it will much outnumber us; but I shall never lose sight of them, and Pellew (commanding the English squadron off Ferrol) will soon be after them." So it happened often enough during that prolonged war that divisions of French ships escaped, through stress of weather, temporary absence of a blockading fleet, or misjudgment on the part of its commander; but the alarm was quickly given, some of the many frigates caught sight of them, followed to detect their probable destination, passed the word from point to point and from fleet to fleet, and soon a division of equal force was after them, "to the antipodes" if need were. As, according to the traditional use of the French navy by French governments, their expeditions went not to fight the hostile fleet, but with "ulterior objects," the angry buzz and hot pursuit that immediately followed was far from conducive to an undisturbed and methodical execution of the programme laid down, even by a single division; while to great combinations, dependent upon uniting the divisions from different ports, they were absolutely fatal. The adventurous cruise of Bruix, leaving Brest with twenty-five ships-of-the-line in 1799, the rapidity with which the news spread, the stirring action and individual mistakes of the English, the frustration of the French projects[5] and the closeness of the pursuit,[6] the escape of Missiessy from Rochefort in 1805, of the divisions of Willaumez and Leissegues from Brest in 1806, — all these may be named, along with the great Trafalgar campaign, as affording interesting studies of a naval strategy following the lines here suggested; while the campaign of 1798, despite its brilliant ending at the Nile, may be cited as a case where failure nearly ensued, owing to the English having no force before

一次，他如此写道："我曾经以为，由法国舰船组成的费罗尔分舰队会硬生生地闯入地中海。假如它与土伦舰队会师一处，那敌人的兵力就会大大超过我方了；但我决不能让这支舰队离开我军的视线，（指挥着费罗尔海域那支英国分舰队的）佩鲁很快便会追上它的。"因此，在这场旷日持久的战争中，法国的分舰队经常因为执行封锁任务的英国舰队在气候恶劣的时候暂时离开，或者因为英国舰队司令官的错误判断而脱逃出港；不过，在这种情况下，英军很快就会发出警报，众多护卫舰中的一些也会发现法国舰队的踪迹，并尾随侦察其可能的目的地，然后将情报从一地传到另一地，从一支舰队传递到另一支舰队，因此很快就会有一支兵力相当的分舰队去追击敌军，并且在形势需要的时候，还会"追至地球的另一边"去。因为从法国政府部署海军的一贯做法来看，其远征队出海，并不是要与敌方舰队作战，而是带有"隐秘的目标"；所以，当忙乱而狂热的追兵紧随其后时，即便是单支分舰队，也不可能不受干扰、有条不紊地去执行业已制定的计划了；而对于大规模联合行动来说，因为必须将各个分舰队从不同港口集结起来，这种追击便是绝对致命的因素了。1799年布吕克斯冒险率25艘战舰离开布雷斯特去巡航，这一消息传播得非常迅速，英军随后采取忙乱的行动，犯下了个别失误，法军的目标被挫败，[5]追兵紧紧咬住了敌人，[6]1805年米西埃斯率军逃出罗什福尔，1806年维罗梅兹和雷西盖斯率舰队从布雷斯特逃出——所有这些，连同伟大的特拉法尔加一役，都可以说是为研究一种遵循此处所提原则的海军战略提供了许多很有意思的资料；而1798年一役虽说在尼罗河河口取得了辉煌战果而告结束，也还是可以看作是一个由于法国远征队起航时英国在土伦港海域没有部署兵力，由于纳尔逊所率护卫舰兵力不足，因而使得英国随后差点儿就一败涂地的例

Toulon when the expedition sailed, and to Nelson being insufficiently provided with frigates. The nine weeks' cruise of Ganteaume in the Mediterranean, in 1808, also illustrates the difficulty of controlling a fleet which has been permitted to get out, unwatched by a strong force, even in such narrow waters.

No parallel instances can be cited from the war of 1778, although the old monarchy did not cover the movements of its fleets with the secrecy enforced by the stern military despotism of the Empire. In both epochs England stood on the defensive; but in the earlier war she gave up the first line of the defence, off the hostile ports, and tried to protect all parts of her scattered empire by dividing the fleet among them. It has been attempted to show the weakness of the one policy, while admitting the difficulties and dangers of the other. The latter aims at shortening and deciding the war by either shutting up or forcing battle upon the hostile navy, recognizing that this is the key of the situation, when the sea at once unites and separates the different parts of the theatre of war. It requires a navy equal in number and superior in efficiency, to which it assigns a limited field of action, narrowed to the conditions which admit of mutual support among the squadrons occupying it. Thus distributed, it relies upon skill and watchfulness to intercept or overtake any division of the enemy which gets to sea. It defends remote possessions and trade by offensive action against the fleet, in which it sees their real enemy and its own principal objective. Being near the home ports, the relief and renewal of ships needing repairs are accomplished with the least loss of time, while the demands upon the scantier resources of the bases abroad are lessened. The other policy, to be effective, calls for superior numbers, because the different divisions are too far apart for mutual support. Each must therefore be equal to any probable combination against it, which implies superiority everywhere to the force of the enemy actually opposed, as the

子。1808年冈托姆率军在地中海进行的那次为期9周的巡航也说明，即便是在如此狭窄的海域内，要控制一支出了海港且没有强大兵力对其加以监视的舰队，也是困难重重的。

尽管法国这个古老的君主国并未因为法兰西帝国那种严格的军事专制而用秘密手段隐藏其舰队的动向，但我们在1778年战争中却举不出类似的例子来。英国在这两个时期都处于防御态势；不过，在前一时期该国放弃了第一道防线，即敌方港口附近的海域，并且试图通过将英国舰队部署到各地来保护这个散沙帝国的每一个部分。我们已经尝试过，在说明一种政策的不足之处时，也承认另一种政策中存在难点与危险。后一种政策，是在认识到海洋同时可以将战场的各个部分或联结、或分隔开来，故海军就是形势的关键这一前提下，旨在通过封锁敌方海军或者迫使敌方海军交战，来缩短战争的时间和决定战争的结局。这就需要有一支兵力相当、作战效率却占有优势的海军，并且为其指定一个有限的作战区域，范围则应缩小到让这一区域内的分舰队能够相互支援。这样部署之后，拦截或者袭击敌方出海的任何分舰队所凭借的，便是技术和警戒了。此种政策，是通过进击敌方舰队来保护偏远地区的本国殖民地和贸易的，因为它将敌方舰队视作真正的敌人和己方主要的作战目标。由于地处本国港口很近的海域，因此就能用最短的时间将那些需要修理的舰船加以更换和补充，从而减轻对国外那些资源较稀缺的基地的需求。而另一种政策要想见效，就要求在兵力上占有优势，因为不同的分舰队之间相距太远，无法相互支援。因此，每一支分舰队的兵力，都必须与敌军可能联合起来向它发动进攻的兵力相当才行，而这意味着各处的兵力都得优于实际对抗的敌军兵力，因为敌人可能会出其不意地得到增援。尽管英国想方设法在各地都保持与敌人相当的兵力，但驻

latter may be unexpectedly reinforced. How impossible and dangerous such a defensive strategy is, when not superior in force, is shown by the frequent inferiority of the English abroad, as well as in Europe, despite the effort to be everywhere equal. Howe at New York in 1778, Byron at Grenada in 1779, Graves off the Chesapeake in 1781, Hood at Martinique in 1781 and at St. Kitt's in 1782, all were inferior, at the same time that the allied fleet in Europe overwhelmingly outnumbered the English. In consequence, unseaworthy ships were retained, to the danger of their crews and their own increasing injury, rather than diminish the force by sending them home; for the deficiencies of the colonial dock-yards did not allow extensive repairs without crossing the Atlantic. As regards the comparative expense of the two strategies, the question is not only which would cost the more in the same time, but which would most tend to shorten the war by the effectiveness of its action.

The military policy of the allies is open to severer condemnation than that of England, by so much as the party assuming the offensive has by that very fact an advantage over the defensive. When the initial difficulty of combining their forces was overcome, — and it has been seen that at no time did Great Britain seriously embarrass their junction, — the allies had the choice open to them where, when, and how to strike with their superior numbers. How did they avail themselves of this recognized enormous advantage? By nibbling at the outskirts of the British Empire, and knocking their heads against the Rock of Gibraltar. The most serious military effort made by France, in sending to the United States a squadron and division of troops intended to be double the number of those which actually reached their destination, resulted, in little over a year, in opening the eyes of England to the hopelessness of the contest with the colonies and thus put an end to a diversion of her strength which had been most beneficial to her opponents. In the West Indies one petty island after another was reduced, generally in the absence of

守海外的英军同驻守在欧洲的英军一样，兵力经常不如敌人；从这一事实就可以看出，当兵力不占优势时，这种防御战略是多么的不切实际，具有多么巨大的危险性。1778年豪勋爵在纽约、1779年拜伦在格林纳达、1781年格雷夫斯在切萨皮克湾海域、1781年胡德在马提尼克，以及1782年他在圣基茨岛时，所率兵力全都不如敌人，而与此同时，法、西联合舰队在欧洲的兵力，则压倒性地超过了英军。结果，英军连那些不适于航海的船只也留下来了，宁愿让船上的官兵身处危险之中，让舰船损伤日益增加，也不愿将这些船只打发回国内，以免削弱此处的兵力；因为殖民地的船坞不足，所以这些船舶只能横跨大西洋，否则就无法进行大修。至于这两种战略的相对代价，这个问题就不但涉及到哪种战略在相同的时间内付出的代价更大，还涉及到实施哪一种战略最有可能缩短战争的时间了。

由于采取攻势的一方较采取守势的一方具有优势是一种事实，因此法、西联军的军事政策比英国的军事政策更易遭到人们的严厉诟病。当盟军克服了起初难以将兵力联合起来的困难之后——而我们也已看到，大不列颠从未严重地阻遏过它们联合起来——联军就可以自由选择在什么地点、什么时间以及采取什么方式，利用己方的优势兵力来发动进攻了。可法、西两国又是怎样利用这种公认的巨大优势的呢？不过就是一点一点地蚕食大英帝国的边缘，把头往直布罗陀的岩石上撞罢了。法国最重大的一次军事行动，便是派遣了一支分舰队和一支陆军前往合众国，打算让业已抵达那里的兵力增加一倍。但一年多一点儿之后，结果却是让英国人看清了与殖民者较量毫无希望的形势，从而结束了北美对该国实力的牵制；可这种牵制对英国的敌人来说，其实却一直都是极其有利的。在西印度群岛，英国占领的那些小岛一个接一个地被敌军攻取，通常都是英国舰队

the English fleet, with an ease which showed how completely the whole question would have been solved by a decisive victory over that fleet; but the French, though favored with many opportunities, never sought to slip the knot by the simple method of attacking the force upon which all depended. Spain went her own way in the Floridas, and with an overwhelming force obtained successes of no military value. In Europe the plan adopted by the English government left its naval force hopelessly inferior in numbers year after year; yet the operations planned by the allies seem in no case seriously to have contemplated the destruction of that force. In the crucial instance, when Derby's squadron of thirty sail-of-the-line was hemmed in the open roadstead of Torbay by the allied forty-nine, the conclusion of the council of war not to fight only epitomized the character of the action of the combined navies. To further embarrass their exertions in Europe, Spain, during long periods, obstinately persisted in tying down her fleet to the neighborhood of Gibraltar; but there was at no time practical recognition of the fact that a severe blow to the English navy in the Straits, or in the English Channel, or on the open sea, was the surest road to reduce the fortress, brought more than once within measurable distance of starvation.

In the conduct of their offensive war the allied courts suffered from the divergent counsels and jealousies which have hampered the movements of most naval coalitions. The conduct of Spain appears to have been selfish almost to disloyalty, that of France more faithful, and therefore also militarily sounder; for hearty co-operation and concerted action against a common objective, wisely chosen, would have better forwarded the objects of both. It must be admitted, too, that the indications point to inefficient administration and preparation on the part of the allies, of Spain especially; and that the quality of the personnel[7] was inferior to that of England. Questions of preparation and administration, however, though of

不在场的时候轻而易举地攻下的；这表明，倘若对英国舰队取得一场决定性的胜利，就会让整个问题得到彻底解决。可法军尽管有着许多的大好机会，却从未想过用如此简单的办法，去进攻维系着英国的一切的那支舰队，来解决这一难题。西班牙则在佛罗里达一意孤行，虽然具有压倒性的优势兵力，却并未获得有什么军事价值的重大胜利。在欧洲，英国政府制定的计划，使得该国海军的兵力年复一年地处于毫无希望的劣势之中；而法、西联军所制定的作战计划，却似乎从未认真地考虑过，要去摧毁英国的这支武装力量。举个重大战例来说，当德比上将所率那支分舰队的30艘战舰，被联军的49艘战舰包围在托贝港那片空旷的锚地之后，联军作战会议不与之交战的决定，无非是集中体现出了联合海军作战行动的特点罢了。虽说为了进一步牵制英军在欧洲的行动，西班牙长期以来一直顽固地坚持将西班牙舰队限制在直布罗陀附近海域，但该国却从未真正认识到这样一个事实，那就是：在直布罗陀海峡、英吉利海峡或者公海上给予英国舰队以重击，是攻克直布罗陀这个多次被逼到弹尽粮绝边缘的要塞最可靠的一条途径。

在实施主动进攻作战的过程中，盟国政府都深受意见分歧和相互忌惮之苦，因为这些分歧与忌惮妨碍到了两国海军的绝大多数联合行动。西班牙政府的行为似乎一直都很自私，甚至差不多到了背信弃义的程度；法国政府的行为则更有信义一些，因而在军事上也更加正确——衷心合作、行动一致地来对抗一个精心挑选出来的共同目标，会更好地促进两国实现各自的目标。我们还必须承认，有迹象表明这两个盟国都管理无方，备战效率都很低下，西班牙则尤其如此；而联军的人员素质[7]也不如英军。然而，备战和管理虽说有着深远的军事意义和重要性，但这两个问题，与盟国政府在选取和进击作

deep military interest and importance, are very different from the strategic plan or method adopted by the allied courts in selecting and attacking their objectives, and so compassing the objects of the war; and their examination would not only extend this discussion unreasonably, but would also obscure the strategic question by heaping up unnecessary details foreign to its subject.

As regards the strategic question, it may be said pithily that the phrase "ulterior objects" embodies the cardinal fault of the naval policy. Ulterior objects brought to nought the hopes of the allies, because, by fastening their eyes upon them, they thoughtlessly passed the road which led to them. Desire eagerly directed upon the ends in view — or rather upon the partial, though great, advantages which they constituted their ends — blinded them to the means by which alone they could be surely attained; hence, as the result of the war, everywhere failure to attain them. To quote again the summary before given, their object was "to avenge their respective injuries, and to put an end to that tyrannical empire which England claims to maintain upon the ocean." The revenge they had obtained was barren of benefit to themselves. They had, so that generation thought, injured England by liberating America; but they had not righted their wrongs in Gibraltar and Jamaica, the English fleet had not received any such treatment as would lessen its haughty self-reliance, the armed neutrality of the northern powers had been allowed to pass fruitlessly away, and the English empire over the seas soon became as tyrannical and more absolute than before.

Barring questions of preparation and administration, of the fighting quality of the allied fleets as compared with the English, and looking only to the indisputable fact of largely superior numbers, it must be noted as the supreme factor in the military conduct of the war, that, while the allied powers were on the offensive and England on the defensive, the attitude of the allied

战目标、并因而实现战争目标的过程中所采取的战略计划或战略手段并不相同；而探究这两个问题，非但会不合理地扩大本书论述的范围，还会因为堆砌一些与本书主题无关的细节内容，而让那些具有战略性的问题变得模糊不清。

关于战略问题，我们可以简单地说，"隐秘目标"这种说法体现了海军政策中的根本性缺陷。所谓的隐秘目标，让法、西这两个盟国的希望落了空；因为只关注各自的隐秘目标，两国都轻率地错过了实现这些目标的途径。两国都一心盯着眼前的目标——或者更准确一点来说，就是盯着构成其目标的那些虽说重大却只属局部的利益，从而蒙蔽了两国的双眼，使之看不到仅凭这一点即可稳稳当当地实现这些目标的途径；因此，就像此次战争的结局那样，两国在哪儿都没有实现这些目标。我们不妨再次引述一下前面已经给出的总结性说法，即法、西两国的目标是"为了一雪前耻，报复两国所遭受的损失，为了终结英格兰所篡取并在海洋之上保持的那个专制之帝国。"但是两国如愿以偿地进行的这种报复，对两国本身却并无益处。当时的那一代人认为，两国通过解放美国而让英国遭受了重创；可是，两国却没有纠正各自对直布罗陀和牙买加两地的错误政策，英国舰队也并未受到足以削弱其傲慢自恃之势的任何打击，且两国还任由北方列强组成的武装中立同盟如昙花一现般地无果而终，从而使得大英帝国不久之后就在海洋上变得跟以前一样专横，并且比以前更加不受限制了。

倘若不去考虑备战和管理方面的问题，不考虑联军与英军相比而言的作战能力问题，只考虑联军兵力具有极大优势这个无可争辩的事实，那我们必定会注意到此次战争中军事行动上最重要的一个因素，那就是：虽说法、西两个盟国处于攻势而英国处于守

fleets in presence of the English navy was habitually defensive. Neither in the greater strategic combinations, nor upon the battlefield, does there appear any serious purpose of using superior numbers to crush fractions of the enemy's fleet, to make the disparity of numbers yet greater, to put an end to the empire of the seas by the destruction of the organized force which sustained it. With the single brilliant exception of Suffren, the allied navies avoided or accepted action; they never imposed it. Yet so long as the English navy was permitted thus with impunity to range the seas, not only was there no security that it would not frustrate the ulterior objects of the campaign, as it did again and again, but there was always the possibility that by some happy chance it would, by winning an important victory, restore the balance of strength. That it did not do so is to be imputed as a fault to the English ministry; but if England was wrong in permitting her European fleet to fall so far below that of the allies, the latter were yet more to blame for their failure to profit by the mistake. The stronger party, assuming the offensive, cannot plead the perplexities which account for, though they do not justify, the undue dispersal of forces by the defence anxious about many points.

The national bias of the French, which found expression in the line of action here again and for the last time criticised, appears to have been shared by both the government and the naval officers of the day. It is the key to the course of the French navy, and, in the opinion of the author, to its failure to achieve more substantial results to France from this war. It is instructive, as showing how strong a hold tradition has over the minds of men, that a body of highly accomplished and gallant seamen should have accepted, apparently without a murmur, so inferior a role for their noble profession. It carries also a warning, if these criticisms are correct, that current opinions and plausible impressions should always be thoroughly tested; for if erroneous they work sure failure, and perhaps disaster.

势，但在面对英国海军时，法、西联合船队却总是采取防御态势。无论是在较大规模的战略性联合行动中，还是在具体的某个战场之上，联合舰队似乎都没有认真考虑过用优势兵力去摧毁敌方舰队的一部分，让双方兵力上的差距变得更大，从而通过消灭英国赖以维持的有组织的军事力量，终结其海洋霸主的地位。除了苏弗朗那个唯一的精彩战例，法、西盟国海军要么是避免与英军交战，要么便是被动应战；它们从来都没有主动地向英军发动过战斗。然而，只要任由英国海军如此胆大妄为地横行海上，那么非但无法保证盟国在此次战争中的隐秘目标不会像以前那样一次又一次地落空，而且始终都存在这样一种可能性，那就是：英国可能通过某种机缘巧合，或者通过获得某次重大胜利，从而恢复该国与盟国之间的实力平衡。没有做到这一点，应该说是英国政府的一大失误；不过，英国任由其欧洲舰队的实力削弱到了远不如盟国舰队的地步，倘若这种做法不对的话，那么盟国舰队就更应该受到指责了，因为它们没能利用英国的这种错误获得好处。采取攻势、实力较强的一方，不能将防御一方因担心多地安危而过度分散兵力、从而造成了种种混乱局面当作借口，尽管这种混乱局面并不说明防御方的做法有道理。

法兰西民族所持有的那种成见，在此处的作战方针中再一次得到了体现，并且最后一次遭到了批评；当时的法国政府和海军将领，似乎都持有这种成见。这既是法国海军作战方针的关键，而在笔者看来，也是使得法国未能在此次战争中获得更多实质性成果的关键原因。此种成见表明，一种固有的传统可以力量强大地支配人们的心理，使得一批才能出众且英勇无畏的海军官兵虽说职业崇高，却甘愿毫无怨言地担当如此低劣的一种角色；这一点，是很令人深思的。假如这些批评意见中肯的话，那么这一现象也含有一种警

There was such an impression largely held by French officers of that day, and yet more widely spread in the United States now, of the efficacy of commerce-destroying as a main reliance in war, especially when directed against a commercial country like Great Britain. "The surest means in my opinion," wrote a distinguished officer, Lamotte-Picquet, "to conquer the English is to attack them in their commerce." The harassment and distress caused to a country by serious interference with its commerce will be conceded by all. It is doubtless a most important secondary operation of naval war, and is not likely to be abandoned till war itself shall cease; but regarded as a primary and fundamental measure, sufficient in itself to crush an enemy, it is probably a delusion, and a most dangerous delusion, when presented in the fascinating garb of cheapness to the representatives of a people. Especially is it misleading when the nation against whom it is to be directed possesses, as Great Britain did and does, the two requisites of a strong sea power, — a widespread healthy commerce and a powerful navy. Where the revenues and industries of a country can be concentrated into a few treasure-ships, like the flota of Spanish galleons, the sinew of war may perhaps be cut by a stroke; but when its wealth is scattered in thousands of going and coming ships, when the roots of the system spread wide and far, and strike deep, it can stand many a cruel shock and lose many a goodly bough without the life being touched. Only by military command of the sea, by prolonged control of the strategic centres of commerce, can such an attack be fatal;[8] and such control can be wrung from a powerful navy only by fighting and overcoming it. For two hundred years England has been the great commercial nation of the world. More than any other her wealth has been intrusted to the sea in war as in peace; yet of all nations she has ever been most reluctant to concede the immunities of commerce and the rights of neutrals. Regarded not as a matter of right, but

示,说明如今人们的观点和那些似是而非的印象,始终都应当得到全面检验才行;因为倘若这些观点和印象是错误的,那就必定会带来失败,或许还会带来灾难性的后果。

　　当时法国的军事将领们,大多持有这样一种印象——而在如今的合众国将领当中,此种印象则更为广泛——即认为战争主要依赖于贸易破坏战,尤其是在对像大不列颠这样以贸易为主的国家发动战争的时候。拉蒙特·皮凯这位杰出的将领曾经写道:"在我看来,征服英国最可靠的手段,便是进攻该国的贸易。"大家都会承认,对一个国家的贸易进行严重干扰,必定会给该国带来烦恼和危难。毫无疑问,贸易破坏战是海军战争中一种极其重要的辅助性作战行动,并且在战争本身结束之前,交战双方都不太可能放弃这种作战形式;不过,倘若将其看作是一种主要的、根本性的、本身足以击败敌人的手段,那么这种看法就很可能只是一种错觉罢了,并且当它披着"轻而易举"这种迷人的外衣呈现于一个民族的精英们眼前时,很可能还是一种极其危险的错觉。而当这个民族所对抗的那个国家,像大不列颠那样拥有一种强大制海权的两个必备条件——即一种分布广泛、兴旺发达的贸易和一支强大的海军——时,这种错觉则尤具误导性。假如一个国家的岁入与产业收入集中在为数不多的宝船上,像西班牙的大帆船舰队那样,或许一击便能斩断其维持战争所需的财源;不过,倘若一国的财富分散于成千上万来来往往的舰船之上,倘若其贸易体系像大树一样根脉广泛而深远的话,那么该国就能承受住多次猛击,可以失去众多枝干而不危及其生命。只有通过军事掌控海洋,通过长久控制那些具有战略意义的贸易中心,这样的攻击才具有致命性;[8]而只有通过作战并且打败一支强有力的海军,才能从其手中夺取此种控制权。200年来,英国一直都是世界上一个伟大的贸易之国。无论是在战争

of policy, history has justified the refusal; and if she maintain her navy in full strength, the future will doubtless repeat the lesson of the past.

The preliminaries of the peace between Great Britain and the allied courts, which brought to an end this great war, were signed at Versailles, January 20, 1783, an arrangement having been concluded between Great Britain and the American Commissioners two months before, by which the independence of the United States was conceded. This was the great outcome of the war. As between the European belligerents, Great Britain received back from France all the West India Islands she had lost, except Tobago, and gave up Sta. Lucia. The French stations in India were restored; and Trincomalee being in the possession of the enemy, England could not dispute its return to Holland, but she refused to cede Negapatam. To Spain, England surrendered the two Floridas and Minorca, the latter a serious loss had the naval power of Spain been sufficient to maintain possession of it; as it was, it again fell into the hands of Great Britain in the next war. Some unimportant redistribution of trading-posts on the west coast of Africa was also made.

Trivial in themselves, there is but one comment that need be made upon these arrangements. In any coming war their permanency would depend wholly upon the balance of sea power, upon that empire of the seas concerning which nothing conclusive had been established by the war.

The definitive treaties of peace were signed at Versailles, September 3, 1783.

时期还是在和平时期，该国的财富比其他各国都更加依赖于海洋；不过，该国一直也是世界上最不愿意承认贸易豁免权和中立国权利的一个国家。因为英国并未把这两个方面看成是权利问题，而把它们看成是政策问题，所以历史业已证明该国这种不愿意是有道理的；而假如英国维持其全部的海军力量，那么将来无疑还会重复过去的那种教训。

1783年1月20日，大不列颠与法、西等盟国政府在凡尔赛签署了和约草案，从而结束了这场大战；两个月之前，大不列颠已与美国派出的专员们缔结了一项协定，承认合众国独立了。这是此次战争的重大成果。至于欧洲的各个交战国，英国从法国手中收回了曾经失去的整个西印度群岛，只有多巴哥除外，同时还放弃了圣卢西亚。法国收复了印度的那些军事据点；由于亭可马里落到了敌人手中，所以英国无法阻止敌人将此地归还给荷兰，但它拒绝交出奈伽帕塔姆。英国还将东、西佛罗里达和米诺卡岛割让给了西班牙；假如西班牙的海军实力足够强大，能够一直占领该地的话，那么割让米诺卡岛就将是英国的重大损失了。可结果却是，在下一次战争中，米诺卡岛又落入了英国手中。此外，各国还对非洲西海岸的一些贸易站点进行了一些无关紧要的重新分配。

这些解决办法本身并不重要，但有一点，我们还是需要根据这些措施来加以说明才行。在日后的战争中，这些地方的归属是否会持久不变，将完全取决于各国的海权是否平衡，取决于英国这个没有通过此次战争确立下任何决定性问题的海洋帝国。

1783年9月3日，交战国在凡尔赛签署了正式的和约。

FOOTNOTES:

(1) It may be said here in passing, that the key to the English possessions in what was then called West Florida was at Pensacola and Mobile, which depended upon Jamaica for support; the conditions of the country, of navigation, and of the general continental war forbidding assistance from the Atlantic. The English force, military and naval, at Jamaica was only adequate to the defence of the island and of trade, and could not afford sufficient relief to Florida. The capture of the latter and of the Bahamas was effected with little difficulty by overwhelming Spanish forces, as many as fifteen ships-of-the-line and seven thousand troops having been employed against Pensacola. These events will receive no other mention. Their only bearing upon the general war was the diversion of this imposing force from joint operations with the French, Spain here, as at Gibraltar, pursuing her own aims instead of concentrating upon the common enemy, — a policy as shortsighted as it was selfish.

(2) In other words, having considered the objects for which the belligerents were at war and the proper objectives upon which their military efforts should have been directed to compass the objects, the discussion now considers how the military forces should have been handled; by what means and at what point the objective, being mobile, should have been assailed.

(3) Of this Rodney said: "The evacuating Rhode Island was the most fatal measure that could possibly be adopted. It gave up the best and noblest harbor in America, from whence squadrons, in forty-eight hours, could blockade the three capital cities of America, namely, Boston, New York, and Philadelphia." The whole letter, private to the First Lord of the Admiralty, is worth reading. (Life of Rodney, vol. ii. p. 429.)

(4) The loss of Sta. Lucia does not militate against this statement, being due to happy audacity and skill on the part of the English admiral, and the professional incapacity of the commander of the greatly superior French fleet.

(5) The plan of campaign traced by the Directory for Bruix became impossible of execution; the delay in

原注：

（1）此处我们可以顺便说一句，在时称西佛罗里达的那个地区，英属领地的门户是在彭萨科拉和莫比尔两处，全都依靠牙买加来提供支援；陆地条件、航运条件和进行全面陆上战争的条件，都不允许英国从大西洋上对此处进行支援。英国驻牙买加的海陆两军兵力，只够防卫该岛与保护贸易，并不足以救援佛罗里达。西班牙军队用压倒性的优势兵力，不费吹灰之力便攻下了佛罗里达和巴哈马群岛，还用多达15艘战舰、7000陆军的兵力进攻彭萨科拉。后面我们不会再提及这些战事了。它们对于这场战争的唯一意义，便是牵制了这支威武壮观得很的兵力，使之无法与法军联合行动；因为西班牙在此处也跟在直布罗陀那样，一心追逐该国自身的目标，而不是将注意力集中在两国共同的敌人身上——这是一种既目光短浅、又自私自利的政策。

（2）换言之就是，探究过交战各国的目标以及为了实现这些目标各国的军事行动应当针对哪些正确的作战目标之后，此时我们所讨论的，便是各国应当如何指挥其军事力量，应当采用什么样的手段，在什么地方对机动的作战目标发起进攻了。

（3）关于这一点，罗德尼曾说："撤离罗德岛，是可能采取的措施当中最具致命性的一种。这样做，就是放弃了美洲最优良、最出色的一个海港；从此处派出的舰队，48小时之后就可以封锁美国的3个主要城市，即波士顿、纽约和费城。"他写给英国海军大臣的这封私信，值得我们去读一读。（参见《罗德尼传记》第二卷，第429页）

（4）虽说失去了圣卢西亚，但由于这位英国海军上将有着乐观而勇敢的心态，而兵力上占极大优势的那支法国舰队的司令职业本领又很低劣，所以对这种说法并没有什么影响。

（5）督政府[2]给布吕克斯制定的那个作战计划是不可能实施的了；法、西两国分舰队耽搁了集结，使得英国在地中海地区集结了60艘舰船。

the junction of the French and Spanish squadrons having permitted England to concentrate sixty ships in the Mediterranean.

(6) The combined squadrons of France and Spain, under Bruix, reached Brest on their return only twenty-four hours before Lord Keith, who had followed them from the Mediterranean. (James: Naval History of Great Britain.)

(7) The high professional attainments of many of the French officers is not overlooked in this statement. The quality of the personnel was diluted by an inferior element, owing to the insufficient number of good men. "The personnel of our crews had been seriously affected by the events of the campaign of 1779. At the beginning of 1780 it was necessary either to disarm some ships, or to increase the proportion of soldiers entering into the composition of the crews. The minister adopted the latter alternative. New regiments, drawn from the land army, were put at the disposal of the navy. The corps of officers, far from numerous at the beginning of hostilities, had become completely inadequate. Rear-Admiral de Guichen met the greatest difficulty in forming the complements, both officers and crews, for his squadron. He took the sea, February 3, with ships 'badly manned,' as he wrote to the minister." (Chevalier: Hist. de la Marine Française, p. 184.) "During the last war [of 1778] we had met the greatest difficulty in supplying officers to our ships. If it had been easy to name admirals, commodores, and captains, it had been impossible to fill the vacancies caused by death, sickness, or promotion among officers of the rank of lieutenant and ensign." (Chevalier: Marine Française sous la République, p. 20.)

(8) The vital centre of English commerce is in the waters surrounding the British Islands; and as the United Kingdom now depends largely upon external sources of food-supply, it follows that France is the nation most favourably situated to harass it by commerce-destroying, on account of her nearness and her possession of ports both on the Atlantic and the North Sea. From these issued the privateers which in the past preyed upon English shipping. The position is stronger now than formerly, Cherbourg presenting a good Channel port which France

（6）法、西联合舰队在布吕克斯的率领下返回布雷斯特时，只比从地中海追击而至的凯思勋爵早了24个小时。（参见詹姆士的《大不列颠海军史》）

（7）此种说法，并未忽视许多法国将领具有高超职业素养的事实。由于优秀者不足，故军中还有许多素质较低的人员，从而降低了整体素质。"我国的船员素质，已经因1779年战役中的战事而受到了严重的影响。1780年初，我们要么必须裁撤掉一些战舰，要么必须提高船员编制中陆军士兵的比例。海军大臣采纳了后一种办法。从陆军中抽调人力组成了若干个新兵团，交由海军支配。在战争刚刚爆发的时候，各级军官的数量本来就不多，而后来则变得完全不足了。基申伯爵这位少将在为其所率舰队补充兵源时，在军官和船员两方面都遇到了最大的困难。他在写给海军大臣的信中说，他是2月3日率领舰队出海的，当时舰队'人员配备极其糟糕'。"（参见希瓦利埃的《法国海军史》，第184页）"在上一次战争（即1778年战争）期间，我们遇到了最大的困难，无法为我国的舰船配备足够多的军官。就算当时指定海军上将、准将和舰长并不难，但在上尉和少尉这一级中，因阵亡、疾病或升职而造成的空缺，却不可能得到补充。"（参见希瓦利埃的《法兰西共和国海军》，第20页）

（8）英国生死攸关的贸易中心，便是不列颠群岛周围的海域；由于英国如今主要依靠海外地区来为其提供粮食，故我们可以得出结论说，法国因为距英国很近，并且在大西洋和北海沿岸都拥有海港，所以其位置最适合于用贸易破坏战的形式来不断地袭扰英国。以前劫掠英国商船的那些私掠船，正是从这些港口出发的。如今此种情况比过去更加可靠了，因为法国在英吉利海峡上又有了瑟堡这样一个良港，而在过去的一场场战争中，该国在此地并无这样的优良海港。而另一方面，汽轮和铁路已让英国可以更为有效地利用北部沿海的那些港口，故英国商船无需再像过去那样以英吉利海峡为中心进行活动了。

lacked in the old wars. On the other hand steam and railroads have made the ports on the northern coasts of the United Kingdom more available, and British shipping need not, as formerly, focus about the Channel.

Much importance has been attached to the captures made during the late summer manoeuvres (1888) by cruisers in and near the English Channel. The United States must remember that such cruisers were near their home ports. Their line of coal-supply may have been two hundred miles; it would be a very different thing to maintain them in activity three thousand miles from home. The furnishing of coal, or of such facilities as cleaning the bottom or necessary repairs, in such a case, would be so unfriendly to Great Britain, that it may well be doubted if any neighboring neutral nation would allow them.

Commerce-destroying by independent cruisers depends upon wide dissemination of force. Commerce-destroying through control of a strategic centre by a great fleet depends upon concentration of force. Regarded as a primary, not as a secondary, operation, the former is condemned, the latter justified, by the experience of centuries.

不久前（1888年）在英吉利海峡及其附近地区由巡洋舰所进行的夏末演习，已经相当重视捕获私掠船只。合众国必定还记得，这种巡洋舰过去都是在本国港口附近海域活动的。虽说它们的燃煤补给线可以达到200英里，但要让它们在距本国3000英里远的地方维持活动，却是另外一回事了。在此种情形下，要获得燃煤以及清洗船底或进行必要的维修等所需的设备设施，对英国来说是很不方便的，因为我们完全有理由怀疑，附近地区的中立国究竟会不会向英国舰队提供这些东西。

由独立的巡洋舰所进行的贸易破坏战，倚赖的是广泛分布的兵力。由一支大型舰队通过控制一个战略中心而进行的贸易破坏战，倚赖的是将兵力集中起来。倘若将贸易破坏战看成是一种主要而非辅助性的作战行动，那么数个世纪的经验教训，业已表明前一种方式并不正确，而后一种方式却是很有道理的。

译者注：

[1] 原文第十二章、第十三章亦属于描述具体的海战经过，故略去未译。本章即原文第十四章。

[2] The Directory：督政府。指法兰西第一共和国时期，自1795年至1799年间掌握法国最高政权的政府，由元老院选出的5名督政官所组成。